D1216134

Narrative and Folk Psychology

Nyack College - Bailey Library
One South Blvd.
Nyack, NY 10960

Edited by

Daniel D. Hutto

imprint-academic.com

Copyright © Imprint Academic, 2009

No part of this publication may be reproduced in any form
without permission, except for the quotation of brief passages
in criticism and discussion.

Published in the UK by Imprint Academic
PO Box 200, Exeter EX5 5YX, UK

Published in the USA by Imprint Academic
Philosophy Documentation Center
PO Box 7147, Charlottesville, VA 22906-7147, USA

ISBN 9 781845 401658

A CIP catalogue record for this book is available from the
British Library and US Library of Congress

297148716

Contents

ABOUT AUTHORS

Kristin Andrews is an Associate Professor in the Department of Philosophy and Cognitive Science Program at York University, in Toronto, Canada. Her interests in animal and child social cognition and communication have always extended beyond the library, and she dirtied her hands with dolphins in Hawaii, children in Minnesota and, most recently, orangutans in Borneo.

Matthew Belmonte has studied computer science, neuroscience, and fiction writing — three complementary aspects of symbolic systems. His research in cognitive neurophysiology examines neural and narrative connectivity in the autistic brain and mind, and his literary scholarship addresses the tension between veridical and abstract representations in autistic narrative, with implications for the relationship between cognitive science and literature in general. Belmonte is currently an assistant professor in the Department of Human Development at Cornell University, and has worked with Simon Baron-Cohen at Cambridge, Deborah Yurgelun-Todd at McLean Hospital, and Eric Courchesne at the University of California San Diego.

Jeremy I.M. Carpendale is Professor of Developmental Psychology at Simon Fraser University. His areas of research include social cognitive and moral development. He is author with Charlie Lewis of *How Children Develop Social Understanding* (Blackwell 2006), co-editor of several books including the *Cambridge Companion to Piaget* and associate editor for *New Ideas in Psychology*.

Shaun Gallagher is Professor of Philosophy and Cognitive Sciences, and Senior Researcher at the Institute of Simulation and Training, at the University of Central Florida (USA); he also holds a position as Research Professor of Philosophy and Cognitive Science at the University of Hertfordshire (UK). He is currently a visiting researcher at Centre de Recherche en Epistémologie Appliquée (Paris), and has been Visiting Professor at the Ecole Normale Supériure, Lyon, and the University of Copenhagen, and Visiting Scientist at the Cognition and Brain Sciences Unit, Cambridge. His research is focused on embodied cognition and intersubjectivity. His recent books include *How the Body Shapes the Mind* (OUP 2005), *Brainstorming* (Imprint Academic 2008), and with Dan Zahavi, *The Phenomenological Mind* (Routledge 2007).

Jay Garfield is Doris Silbert Professor in the Humanities, Professor of Philosophy and Director of the Logic Program and of the Five College Tibetan Studies in India Program at Smith College, Professor in the graduate faculty of Philosophy at the University of Massachusetts, Professor of Philosophy at Melbourne University and Adjunct Professor of Philosophy at the Central Institute of Higher Tibetan Studies. He teaches and pursues research in the philosophy of mind, foundations of cognitive science, logic, philosophy of language, Buddhist philosophy, cross-cultural hermeneutics, theoretical and applied ethics and epistemology. Garfield's most recent books are his translation, with the ven Prof Geshe Ngawang Samten of the 14–15th Century Tibetan Philosopher Tsong Khapa's commentary on Nagarjuna's *Mulamadhyamakakarika (Ocean of Reasoning)* and *Empty Words: Buddhist Philosophy and Cross-Cultural Interpretation* (Oxford University Press 2002 and 2006, respectively). Garfield is also working on projects on the development of the theory of mind in children with particular attention to the role of pretence in that process; the acquisition of evidentials and its relation to the development of theory of mind (with Jill deVilliers, Thomas Roeper and Peggy Speas), the history of 20th-century Indian philosophy (with Nalini Bhushan) and the nature of conventional truth in Madhyamaka (with Graham Priest, Tom Tillemans, Georges Dreyfus, Sonam Thakchöe, Bronwyn Finnegan and Koji Tanaka).

David Herman, who co-founded the Project Narrative initiative at Ohio State University (http://projectnarrative.osu.edu) and served as its inaugural director, teaches in OSU's English Department. The author, editor, or co-editor of 10 books on various aspects of narrative, he has just finished editing a new volume titled *The Emergence of Mind: Representations of Consciousness in Narrative Discourse in English, 700 to the Present.* He serves as editor of the Frontiers of Narrative book series and the new journal *Storyworlds*, both published by the University of Nebraska Press, and he was recently awarded a research fellowship from the American Council of Learned Societies for his 2009 project on 'Storytelling and the Sciences of Mind'.

Jonathan Hill is Professor of Anthropology at Southern Illinois University, Carbondale, and is a specialist in South American ethnology with special interest in studies of indigenous verbal and musical artistry. He is author of *Keepers of the Sacred Chants: The Poetics of Ritual Power in an Amazonian Society* (1993) and *Made-from-Bone: Trickster Myths, Music, and History from the Amazon* (2009) and editor of various books including *Rethinking History and Myth* (1988), *History, Power, and Identity* (1996), and the journal *Identities: Global Studies in Culture and Power* (2002–2009, with Thomas Wilson).

Audio recordings made during his fieldwork with the Wakuénai (Curripaco) of Venezuela in the 1980s and 1990s are available as digitized sound files in the Curripaco (KPC) collection of the Archives of Indigenous Languages of Latin America (www.ailla.utexas.org).

Daniel D. Hutto was born and schooled in New York but finished his undergraduate degree as a study abroad student in St. Andrews, Scotland. He is currently the Research Leader for Philosophy at the University of Hertfordshire. He has published on wide range of philosophical topics in journals and is the author of *The Presence of Mind* (1999), *Beyond Physicalism* (2000), *Wittgenstein and the End of Philosophy* (2006) and *Folk Psychological Narratives* (2008). He is also the editor of *Narrative and Understanding Persons* (2007) and co-editor of *Folk Psychology Re-Assessed* (2007). A special yearbook issue of *Consciousness and Emotion*, entitled *Radical Enactivism*, which focuses on his philosophy of intentionality, phenomenology and narrative, was published in 2006.

David A. Leavens is a Senior Lecturer in the Department of Psychology at the University of Sussex, UK. He earned his PhD in 2001 from the University of Georgia. He has wide-ranging interests in non-verbal communication by humans, apes, and monkeys, with a particular focus on socio-ecological correlates of the development of joint attention in apes and humans. A long-term interest in communication ignited into an enduring intellectual passion when it became apparent to him, in 1994, that he had been subtly and skilfully trained to a high standard of performance by a chimpanzee named Clint.

Heidi Maibom is associate professor of philosophy at Carleton University. She gained her doctorate from University College London, and has held fellowships at Cambridge University and Princeton University. She works in the areas of folk psychology, emotion, moral psychology, and psychopathology. She is currently working on a book on moral emotions.

Katherine Nelson is Distinguished Professor of Psychology Emerita at the City University of New York Graduate School and University Center. She has published more than 200 articles and book chapters in Developmental Psychology and related fields, as well as eight books and monographs, the latest: *Young Minds in Social Worlds* (awarded the Eleanor Maccoby Book Award in Developmental Psychology from the American Psychological Association). Among honours are the G. Stanley Hall award for Distinguished Lifetime Contributions to Developmental Psychology from the American Psychological

Association and the Award for Distinguished Scientific Contributions to Child Development from the Society for Research in Child Development.

Timothy P. Racine is an Assistant Professor in the Department of Psychology at Simon Fraser University in Burnaby, BC, Canada. His research interests include the developmental and evolutionary origins of communication and social cognition and also the philosophy of psychology. Recently, he co-edited (with J. Zlatev, C. Sinha, and E. Itkonen) the volume *The Shared Mind: Perspectives on Intersubjectivity* (John Benjamins 2008) and a double special issue of *New Ideas in Psychology* (with U. Müller) entitled 'Mind, Meaning, and Language: Wittgenstein's Relevance for Psychology'.

Matthew Ratcliffe is Reader in Philosophy at Durham University, UK. Most of his recent work addresses issues in phenomenology, philosophy of psychology and philosophy of psychiatry. He is author of *Rethinking Commonsense Psychology: A Critique of Folk Psychology, Theory of Mind and Simulation* (Palgrave 2007) and *Feelings of Being: Phenomenology, Psychiatry and the Sense of Reality* (Oxford University Press 2008).

Chris Sinha is Professor of Psychology of Language at the University of Portsmouth. He gained his BA in Developmental Psychology at the University of Sussex and his doctorate at the University of Utrecht. Before moving to Portsmouth, Chris taught in Departments of Education, Psychology, and Language and Communication, in Britain, the Netherlands, Denmark and India. He has published over 100 articles in anthropology, linguistics, education, evolutionary biology and connection science, as well as developmental and cultural psychology. He is an experienced and sought-after plenary lecturer at international conferences. His books include *Language and Representation* (Harvester-Wheatsheaf 1988) and *Language, Culture and Mind* (Beijing: Foreign Language Teaching and Research Press 2009). He recently co-edited with Jordan Zlatev, Tim Racine and Esa Itkonen *The Shared Mind: Perspectives on Intersubjectivity* (John Benjamins 2008).

Corrado Sinigaglia (1966) is Associate Professor of Philosophy of Science at the University of Milan (Italy). His major research interest lies in the enactive and embodied roots of social cognition. He has recently published (with Giacomo Rizzolatti), *Mirrors in the Brain: How our Minds share Actions and Emotions* (2008).

Marc Slors is Professor of Philosophy of Mind at the Radboud University Nijmegen in The Netherlands. His publications include a book on personal identity and he metaphysics of mind, *The Diachronic Mind* (2001), and papers on psychological continuity, personal identity, mental causation, reduction and supervenience and social cognition in various books and in journals, including *The Philosophical Quarterly*, *The Journal of Philosophy* and *Erkenntnis*. His current research interest is in combining interpretationist theories of the mental with embodied cognition.

Michelle Scalise Sugiyama is a Research Associate at the University of Oregon Institute of Cognitive and Decision Sciences, an Affiliate of the University of Oregon Anthropology Department, and founder and Director of the Cognitive Cultural Studies Division at the Center for Evolutionary Psychology, UC Santa Barbara. Her research focuses on the cognitive foundations and evolutionary context of cultural transmission, with an emphasis on oral narrative. She has written numerous articles on the origins of storytelling, the role that folklore plays in foraging societies, and the psychological mechanisms involved in narrative production.

William Turnbull is Professor Emeritus at Simon Fraser University. His expertise is in the field of social interaction and conversation. He is author of *Language in Action: Psychological Models of Conversation* (Psychology Press 2003).

Jill de Villiers is the Sophia and Austin Smith Professor in Psychology and Professor of Philosophy at Smith College. She teaches courses in Linguistics, Language Acquisition and Cognitive Science, and her research is in the field of language acquisition. She has written widely on empirical and theoretical research on the acquisition of grammar for over thirty-five years, ranging from attention to grammatical morphemes to recursive embeddings in syntax. For the last fifteen years she has been immersed in understanding the relationship of language to Theory of Mind development, and hence the issue of the interface between language and thinking. Her joint work on Tibetan evidentials is an outgrowth of that work, as is a project with a software company on language intervention to teach 'language of the mind' to children at risk for failure in this domain. Currently she is also conducting research as part of a large preschool curriculum intervention project, on the course of development of language and Theory of Mind in children growing up in poverty. With Peter de Villiers, she is also designing and testing an assessment of pragmatic development, with a particular focus on children with autism.

Daniel D. Hutto

Folk Psychology as Narrative Practice

Abstract: *There has been a long-standing interest in the putative roles that various so-called 'theory of mind' abilities might play in enabling us to understand and enjoy narratives. Of late, as our understanding of the complexity and diversity of everyday psychological capacities has become more nuanced and variegated, new possibilities have been articulated: (i) that our capacity for a sophisticated, everyday understanding of actions in terms of reason (our folk psychology) may itself be best characterized as a kind of narrative practice and (ii) that acquiring the capacity for supplying and digesting reasons explanations might (at least normally) depend upon having a special training with narratives. This introductory paper to the volume situates the claims of those who support the narrative approach to folk psychology against the backdrop of some traditional and new thinking about intersubjectivity, social cognition and 'theory of mind' abilities. Special emphasis is laid on the different reasons for being interested in these claims about narrative practice and folk psychology in light of various empirical and philosophical agendas.*

I have thus endeavoured to preserve the truth of
the elementary principles of human nature,
while I have not scrupled to innovate upon their combinations.
The Iliad, the tragic poetry of Greece, Shakespeare
in *The Tempest* and *Midsummer's Night's Dream*,
and most especially Milton in *Paradise Lost*, conform to this rule;

— Percy Shelley, preface to *Frankenstein* 1817

1. Folk Psychology and Narrative

Folk psychology (or FP) is a moniker devised by philosophers which is meant to designate a specific sub-section of our everyday talk of, and thought about, the mental.[1] It has certain, somewhat unfortunate connotations but its wide currency makes it useful. I believe it picks out, univocally, a phenomenon that should be of special interest to all. When used in an appropriately restricted sense, FP denotes — *at a bare minimum* — our everyday practice of making sense of intentional actions (i.e. our own and those of others) in terms of reasons, where this implies having a capacity for the competent invocation of propositional attitude talk.[2] So construed, FP (or FP *stricto sensu* as I call it elsewhere) is a sophisticated, high level capacity; it involves being able to answer a particular sort of 'why'-question by skilfully deploying the idiom of mental predicates (beliefs, desires, hopes, fears, etc.).

Lots of folk — philosophically and scientifically minded folk, that is — are interested in FP and its related and supporting capacities — also known as 'Theory of Mind' (ToM) or 'Mindreading' abilities (as they are much better known in some circles). This volume brings together new work by some of these folk, who hail from a range of disciplines (anthropology, neuroscience, psychology, philosophy). The focus of this collective effort is to clarify, develop and challenge the claim that FP competence may be importantly, perhaps even constitutively, related to narrative practices. The *locus classicus* of this idea can be found in Bruner's (1990) seminal work, but it has been acknowledged approvingly by others too, who have explored it with varying degrees of commitment (Sterelny, 2003; Gallagher, 2006; Gallese, 2007; Herman, 2008b; Zahavi, 2007). My own variant, worked out most extensively in Hutto (2008a), incorporates two logically distinct but complementary claims.[3]

---

[1]   It travels under many other names too: common sense psychology; naïve psychology; *Homo sapiens* psychology; the person theory of humans; belief-desire psychology.

[2]   The FP label can be used to name a phenomenon of much greater complexity. Hornsby is right to note that 'Commonsense psychology ... is a pervasive subject matter, more easily gestured toward than precisely delimited: in practice it cannot be separated off from all the other subject matters that people engage with in everyday life. In the use of many philosophers, though, commonsense psychology is made to stand for something much more restricted than this' (Hornsby, 1997, p. 4). Moreover in stressing that FP, as I have defined it, minimally incorporates an understanding of beliefs and desires I do not deny that FP can include more, i.e. that it is pluralistic (see Andrews, 2008).

[3]   In fact, I had begun to toy with the idea that narratives might play this sort of role in an early paper of mine, long before I discovered and became inspired by Bruner's writings on the topic. In its first, embryonic formulation the NPH (then the 'narrative proposal')

The first is a familiar sort of philosophical equation. It aims to remind us that FP is essentially a narrative practice — its exercise, always and everywhere, invokes our capacity to construct or digest narratives of a special sort (I do not claim that the truth of this equation is obvious).[4] We do this when exercising our FP capacities in both second- and third-person contexts.

The second claim, which I call the Narrative Practice Hypothesis (NPH), is an empirical hypothesis. It conjectures that the normal route by which children acquire their FP competence is through exposure to narratives of a special sort — those with a particular subject matter. I call this class of narratives 'folk psychological narratives'. They are of the sort that make explicit mention of how mental states (most prominently, beliefs and desires) figure in the lives, history and larger projects of their owners, *inter alia*.

Just what are narratives and why might they be suited for this sort of work? As Scalise Sugiyama observes,

> The literary consensus is that stories consist of character, setting, actions and events — linked temporally and/or causally — and conflict and resolution ... in my own reading of the oral narratives of a wide range of foraging peoples, I have yet to encounter a culture whose stories do not exhibit the same structural features as Western narrative (Scalise Sugiyama, 2005, p. 180; see also Herman, 2008a).

Folk psychological narratives, as I have defined them, therefore (apparently) have the right sort of content and structure for enabling FP understanding.

Moreover, along with many others, I assume that 'Narrative is the vehicle of communicating representations of events between people by verbal means' (Nelson, 2003, p. 32). This is important since when

---

amounted to the idea that 'our ability to make psychological ascriptions and predictions is normally developed in the process of hearing, understanding and creating stories' (Hutto, 1997, p. 70). Admittedly, I was aware that 'At this stage the narrative proposal remains highly sketchy and speculative, but I maintain that it has peculiar advantages over its competitors in today's philosophy of psychology' (Hutto, 1997, p. 75).

[4] In a draft version of a recent paper Currie (2008) observed that reason explanations do not obviously appear to be narratives. Thus, saying that I went out 'to get milk' in response to a query does not seem to count as 'giving a narrative'. Here, I propose, appearances are deceiving. Because reason explanations function as normalizing, contrastive explanations, to give one's reason in response to a question is, for the well trained, only to tell the most relevant part of a potentially much longer story (see Hutto, 2004, pp. 563–4; 2008a, pp. 11–12). Thus, in line with the polite etiquette of conversational implicature reason explanations are generally extremely compressed, truncated and elliptical. It does not follow that our capacity to produce such truncated explanations is not an essentially narrative capacity.

it comes to engendering FP competence other non-verbal mediums apparently come up short:

> Imagine early *Homo sapiens* trying to tell the story of 'Little Red Riding Hood' through the medium of paint. Our artist immediately encounters difficulty in representing the thoughts, beliefs, and motives of the characters as well as the relationship between them .... A picture may be worth a thousand words, but sometimes a thousand pictures cannot match a few choice words (Scalise Sugiyama, 2005, p. 182).

As complex linguistic representations FP narratives can be objects of joint attention and thus the foci of conversational/narrative practices (in whatever particular verbal format they are conveyed). Still, it must be stressed that although folk psychological narratives will be the centre of attention in such engagements they do not engender FP competence on their own. According to the NPH, children develop this special ability by participating in narrative practices with the appropriate support and direction of others.

2. Rival Theories of the Basis of FP Competence

Over the years there have been only two notable proposals about the basis of our FP competence: Theory Theory (TT) and Simulation Theory (ST).[5] Defenders of TT hold that FP competence necessarily rests on a represented body of knowledge consisting of the laws or principles that comprise a core, naive theory of mind. When supported by auxiliary generalizations about what people typically do in a range of circumstances, this 'theory' is the putative engine of everyday interpersonal understanding, prediction and explanation. Simulation Theory (of which there are a plethora of versions) is TT's primary contender. Its supporters hold that as our minds are already populated with the relevant mental states and the means of systematically manipulating them, it is possible to explain FP competence by direct appeal to modelling or simulative capacities.

Accordingly, we make sense of others by manipulating our own cognitive resources in imaginative ways to get results – crudely by imagining ourselves in the other's situation and making relevant adjustments. This obviates the need for FP principles to be represented at all, at any level.

Construed as an empirical hypothesis about the basis of our FP competence proper, the NPH *directly* challenges those versions of TT and ST which posit dedicated mindreading mechanisms of various

---

[5] This is oversimplifying somewhat (especially as most theorists now promote hybrid TT–ST theories). But these niceties don't matter for the purposes of this exposition.

kinds or childhood scientific labour to do *the same* explanatory work.[6] As such, the NPH must be distinguished from the softer claim that narrative engagements merely add finishing touches and refinements to pre-existing mindreading capacities that are best explained by these familiar theories. That proposal is hardly controversial. As Currie notes, 'An advocate of ST is likely to agree enthusiastically that narratives build up our folk-psychological competence, because they scaffold our early attempts to simulate people's practical and theoretical reasoning' (Currie, 2008, p. 217). Supporters of TT are certain to agree that narratives could play *that* sort of role, so long as there is no threat to the idea that *their* favoured mechanism is the core engine of FP understanding (e.g. see Zunshine, 2006).

The NPH is interesting precisely because it makes a stronger claim than the one cited above. It says that appropriate engagement in narrative practices is what normally engenders FP competence. Consequently, we don't just refine our pre-existing FP understanding by means of narrative engagements — on the contrary, we don't begin to exhibit FP skills proper until we've had the right sorts of encounters with the right sorts of narratives. Children are not FP competent until they have mastered certain narrative skills. Engaging in narrative practice is the *source* of our FP understanding.

To see matters clearly it helps to bear in mind that 'being FP competent' requires more than merely the capacity to harbour 'beliefs about other people's mental states, in particular about their beliefs and desires' (Currie 2008, p. 211). Such capacities are necessary but not sufficient for being a skilled FP practitioner (as argued in Hutto, 2007; 2008a, ch. 2).[7] It is worth labouring this point because unless it is grasped one will not properly understand and situate the NPH's explanatory ambitions. The NPH does not, by itself, seek to explain the basis of all of our nonconceptual capacities for recognizing, tracking or responding to psychological attitudes. Indeed, it does not even seek to explain how we acquire our first grasp of explicit concepts of

---

[6] See Fodor (1987), Goldman (2006), Gopnik and Meltzoff (1997) and Nichols and Stich (2003) for some representative examples. See also Hutto (2008b) for a detailed analysis of the basis of this competition.

[7] There has been a great deal of empirical evidence collected, ostensibly to settle the debate between ST and TT. Such evidence does not however touch the question of what lies at the basis of our FP competence. As I argue in Hutto (2008b), even if the evidence marshalled could decide if simulation or theory-based heuristics play an ineliminable role in certain third-personal mind-guessing tasks this would do nothing, by itself, to provide insight into the basis, origin or acquisition of FP-competence *per se*. This is because the existing experimental data at best shows that simulative or theory-like generalizations (or both) might come into play, *as additional heuristics*, when making third-person speculations about another's reasons for acting in certain cases (or types of cases).

these attitudes. While these capacities are clearly important they do not add up to FP as traditionally understood — i.e. as 'networked' or structured ways of understanding actions in terms of reasons. It is *this* that the NPH seeks to explain (and it is this that TT and ST originally sought to explain before their interests travelled somewhat). So, again, the core claim of the NPH is that childhood engagement with narratives engender a new-order, *integrated, articulate and explicit* capacity to make sense of actions by systematically deploying propositional attitude (and other) concepts. Participating in narrative practices enable us to make sense of actions by giving and asking for reasons; i.e. this sort of activity makes us FP competent.

This might seem to afford a natural way to divide the labour between those who postulate mindreading mechanisms of *a certain kind* and the NPH. For this to be a viable partnership it would be crucial that the properties of any hypothesized mechanism did not merely replicate the kind of explicit understanding of FP that the NPH assumes our narrative practices engender (i.e. the two should not offer competing accounts of the *very* same explanandum). This amicable arrangement seems quite plausible given, as Maibom (2003) has persuasively argued, that we must *in any case* strongly distinguish the kind of subdoxastic, tacit knowledge that many suppose undergirds the exercise of our FP capacities and that ordinary sort of platitudinal knowledge which gets expressed when we explicitly reflect on what that practice involves. The former is understood as a kind of representational knowledge that is allegedly causally efficacious in the production of the relevant kinds of thought and behaviour — but its content is consciously inaccessible, inferentially encapsulated and nonconceptual. That is not surprising since it is thought to constitute a body of tacit knowledge that is used by modular systems not their owners. But, crucially, so understood, it need not — indeed, ought not — be thought to resemble or embed, in whole or part, the sort of knowledge of FP that the folk struggle to describe when they try to articulate FP's basic rules. We should no more expect this than we would expect everyday speakers to be conversant with the rules of transformational grammar that allegedly enable them to produce and detect well-formed sentences in their native tongue.

If we accept this it is at least possible to reconcile the NPH with the offerings of the traditional paradigm of mainstream cognitive science which has been pursued in a Chomskyan vein. Such an approach has emphasized the critical role played by internal, 'innate' knowledge-based mechanisms that call on represented bodies of information in enabling the performance of many tasks that are central to social life — including, at the high end, our distinctive FP abilities. The point is that as long as we are clear about our targets, the NPH is consistent with the possibility that ToM or mindreading abilities of some sort are sponsored by subpersonal, representational mechanisms of some kind or another (the precise number, forms, and features of such putative devices remains a matter of intense debate). With a better understanding of the putative content such devices might operate with it becomes clear that the NPH is compatible, in theory, with the claim that the best explanation of the essential kit needed for engaging in ToM or mindreading activities (or our capacity to develop such abilities) will be specialized mental machinery that forms part of our native cognitive endowment; a gift from our immediate evolutionary forebears.[8]

This sort of rapprochement is a live theoretical possibility. But the truth is that the NPH sits on an interesting fault-line and forging this alliance with orthodox cognitive science is not something I recommend. While I do not doubt that there are many mechanisms, specialized and otherwise, that underpin our FP abilities and even our narrative capacities, I am hugely suspicious of the idea that these are 'cognitive' mechanisms, 'mental' organs or modules where this implies that they are 'domain-specific systems of truth-evaluable mental representations that are innate and/or subject to informational restrictions' (Samuels, 2000, p. 18).

To be precise, while I don't doubt that there are many inherited mechanisms in the service of cognition (who would?), I do doubt that

---

[8]   There is, however, a direct conflict between Maibom's preferred account of the source of our knowledge of FP platitudes and that of the NPH. She casts such knowledge as theoretical (and hence subscribes to a version of TT) but also breaks with tradition by treating theories not as sets of law-like generalizations but as a collection of abstract models. As such FP knowledge only becomes representational when applied, by means of applying these models by forming hypotheses that apply to specific aspects of the world. Consequently, the true content of FP knowledge (and what the folk try to express when questioned about it) is really 'the composite knowledge of theoretical models and hypotheses, and not of counterfactual supporting generalizations ... [hence,] there is no reason to think that folk psychological knowledge is tacit because unenunciable' (Maibom, 2003, p. 313). Maibom provides one of the most plausible, sophisticated and attractive accounts of the nature of scientific theories I have yet to encounter. It treats them as 'abstract systems that are not, in and of themselves, true or false of anything. [For] only when combined with theoretical hypotheses ... does the model feature in a truth-evaluable way' (Maibom, 2003, p. 308). While that seems plausible enough, it is for this very reason that I would resist Maibom's picture of FP competence as grounded in theoretical knowledge per se. In my view the exercise of FP competence does not essentially involve making hypotheses, although sometimes it does — e.g. in some third-personal tasks, when we speculate about other minds. If so it does not look as if FP knowledge is in essence theoretical nor does it take the form of 'the content of a mentally represented body of information ... [that] functions in a subject's cognitive economy' (Maibom, 2003, p. 309).

such mechanisms perform their service by contentfully representing the domain-specific subject matter of their specialized concerns. Crucially, if we accept the argument that leads to recognition of Maibom's fork we are already close to reaching this conclusion. This is because, if she is right, the only kind of specialized knowledge that could putatively underpin FP abilities will not be of a sort that replicates or resembles the concepts and principles that we use when deploying such abilities. Even if we imagine that there are mindreading devices with representational contents the knowledge-base they depend upon will be nothing like that of the familiar FP sort.

More radically, it might be doubted that any such devices are genuinely 'knowledge-based' at all on the grounds that there is no adequate way to accommodate the idea that they contain any representational contents whatsoever (and it might be further doubted that there is any good reason to attempt such an accommodation). I have campaigned long and hard against representational theories for some time now, and I continue to develop and refine an alternative account — biosemiotics — which is a non-representational account of intentionality (Hutto, 1999; 2005; 2006; 2008a, ch. 3). Biosemiotics has a respectable pedigree as it is a theoretical adjustment of Millikan's biosemantics (regarded by many as the most promising naturalized theory of content available on today's market). Simply put, biosemiotics is biosemantics 'without the semantics'. It holds that basic intentional perceptual activity is a specific, evolutionarily-tailored way of interacting with the environment, but it is not, in any way, mediated by intensional 'contents' and so does not permit of a non-derivative analysis in semantic terms. Successful action requires informational sensitivity, i.e. a selective responsiveness to natural signs *in historically normal circumstances.*

Although organismic actions do not always succeed, the mere possibility of worldly misalignment does not necessarily imply (and hence need not be explained in terms of) the existence of semantic relations of truth and reference. In particular, no representations are involved/used in cases of basic perceptual responding (even though a competent observer of such activity can certainly talk of the mismatch in semantic terms). Biosemiotics provides a way of understanding the intentional aspects of on-line *perception* as exhibiting determinate 'directedness' without invoking representational contents.

This may smack of heresy or madness (or both). This is because, 'according to many, *any* functional architecture that is causally responsible for the system's performance can be characterized as encoding the system's knowledge-base, as implicitly representing the system's know-how. If we accept current attitudes about the nature of cognitive representation, a non-representational account is not simply implausible — it is virtually *inconceivable*' (Ramsey, 2007, pp. 3–4). Talk about being 'in the grip of a picture'! But like Ramsey, whose excellent book reveals the serious problems faced by those struggling to explicate a viable notion of mental 'representation', I take this to be a clear indicator that something has gone 'terribly wrong' (Ramsey 2007, pp. 3–4).[9]

The time is ripe to review, with an open mind, what comes before and below the development of our full-fledged FP competence. Empirical work has revealed that the heuristics used in our normal everyday engagements are more diverse and complex than traditionally supposed. It is now quite obvious to all that sophisticated belief/desire psychology is not the fundamental or ubiquitous foundation of all social cognition (as some were once wont to claim). This throws up puzzles about the nature of higher and lower capacities for intersubjective engagement and understanding and how they are related (see for example overviews by Ratcliffe and Hutto, 2007; Costall and Leudar, 2009; Slors and Macdonald, 2008; Zlatev *et al.*, 2008).

For example, recent evidence suggests that some sort of capacity to track false belief emerges in human children much earlier than originally supposed. Thus even 15 month-old infants are able to pass at least one type of false belief task (Onishi and Baillargeon, 2005; Onishi *et al.*, 2007). Some have concluded from this that children may have an 'implicit' mastery of the concept of belief much earlier than previously thought (a fact masked because their performance is marred by other factors such as, executive control, processing problems, etc.). If so, from this vantage point, this may make it look as if there is less of a gap between low-level and high-level capacities for understanding action. Yet this conclusion must be balanced by recognition that these highly contextual, on-line modes of engaging with other minds are quite distinct from, and limited in comparison with, those of the advanced sort in which older children invoke the standard network of mental concepts in a systematic way (see Herschbach, 2008; Hutto, 2009b, p. 230).

Or, to take another case, it is not unusual to hear that *some* kind of action 'understanding' is engendered in even the most rudimentary

---

[9] Many will insist that representationalism remains the *only possible* way forward for cognitive science. As such, we should continue to pour in time and resources in the hope of making it work. To my eyes this looks rather like having a strategy for staying in Iraq but not for success in Iraq. Change we need.

forms of social interaction and intersubjective engagement. Indeed, it has been claimed that this is the primary function of mirror neuron activity (Rizzolatti and Sinigaglia, 2006; Sinigaglia, 2008). Defenders of such views also stress that: 'this is a *pragmatic, pre-conceptual, and pre-linguistic* form of understanding' (Rizzolatti and Sinigaglia, 2006, p. xi, emphases added). But it remains unclear exactly how to ground such talk of 'understanding' (or precisely what it implies) if one is not also prepared to assume that contentful mental representations exist, and to provide a workable theory of content that can explain and delineate their properties.

A more cautious strategy, which I recommend, would be to reserve attributions of 'understanding' exclusively for those language-based (and more specifically narrative-based) forms of intersubjective engagement that have their own special properties and complexities. And the truth is that we have other, more perspicuous ways of making sense of primary forms of intersubjective interplay. Elsewhere I have defended the idea that these depend on an organism's having inten-tionally-directed *responsiveness* to the intentional attitudes of others, as perceived *in and through* their expressions (where the latter are understood as a special class of natural sign). Such encounters have distinctive phenomenal characters enjoyed by their participants, depending on the specifics of the particular engagement.

In all, there are strong reasons for not automatically construing primary intersubjective engagements as constituting or involving 'mindreading' (Zawidzki, 2008). Indeed, there are positive reasons to assume that they have features that preclude such a characterization. This is clearly seen, for example, in Gallagher's arguments that instances of neural resonance should not be understood as involving simulation because they do not allow for the sort of two-step percep-tion/attribution processes that certain versions of simulation require (i.e. there is no pretence/'as if' modelling stage, followed by subse-quent attribution of a mental state stage). If there is no such two-step process he argues that neural resonance is best understood as a kind of direct perception — *provided* we 'conceive of perception as an enactive sensory-motor phenomenon' (Gallagher, 2007, p. 358, Gallagher and Zahavi, 2008, pp. 178–9).[10]

---

[10] While this argument works against the idea that neural resonance could be a form of 'mind-reading simulation' it does not defeat the idea that it is any kind of 'mental simula-tion'. Goldman stresses this important distinction in his work, invoking notions such as 'mirroring' or 'mental matching': 'When mental matching occurs by means of a regular causal pathway I will consider it an instance of mirroring — an instance of mental simula-tion .... But it isn't yet ... an instance of simulation-based mindreading. What more is

Although this positive proposal is still very much up for discussion, what should not be overlooked is that there is an emerging consensus that the most basic forms of intersubjective engagement do not and could not constitute 'mindreading' activity — not even that of a low-level sort (see Gallese, 2007; Gallagher, 2007; Gallagher and Zahavi, 2007; Goldman, 2006; Gordon, 2008)![11] Crucially, such activity does not involve making attributions of contentful mental states to others.

It can no longer be 'taken for granted' that our capacity to engage with others successfully is predicated on a capacity to represent another's mental states (or their contents). More than this, there is a pressing need for new ways of interpreting and characterizing these various capacities. It is simply no longer obvious that the traditional theories, TT and ST, offer us the best tools for doing so. This helps the fortunes of the NPH, because once we see this, it is even clearer that we have no good reason to assume that TT and ST are the right tools for making sense of our more sophisticated capacities: it is left 'entirely open what form a full-blown system of intentional attribution might take' (Borg, 2007, p. 10).

While some basic capacities for social navigation and interaction are undoubtedly built-in, others — perhaps even the core aspects of FP — may be acquired or soft-assembled in ontogeny, where the drivers of this development will be socially scaffolded engagements and not active scientific theorizing (Carpendale and Lewis, 2004; Garfield *et al.*, 2001). My own view is that primary forms of social interaction are about shaping others, being 'transformed' by and 'transforming' others through unprincipled embodied engagements. The nature of intersubjective engagements become elaborated and extended in complex ways, especially in the human case, with the advent of capacities for non-linguistic joint attention and narrative practices. These enable sharing with and understanding others.

This fits with those approaches to intersubjectivity and social cognition that emphasise its shared, interactional basis and downplay the contributions of the individual and the specifics of their inherited

---

required for there to be mindreading? ... Mindreading involves the attribution to a target' (Goldman, 2006, p. 133). Gordon too has recently emphasized that 'there is no conflict between the simulation theory, *once it is freed from certain constraints carried over from theory theory*, and Gallagher's view that our primary and pervasive way of engaging with others rests on "direct", non-mentalizing perception of the "meanings" of others' facial expressions, gestures, and intentional actions' (Gordon, 2008, p. 219, emphasis added).

[11] Even those who still talk of understanding action at this level admit that this 'immediate understanding of the acts of others' is *not* based on mentalizing (Rizzolatti and Sinigaglia, 2006, p. 131). Indeed, they tell us that there is 'no neural mechanism that explains mindreading' (Rizzolatti and Sinigaglia, 2006, p. 130).

capacities and mechanisms (Reddy and Morris, 2004; Hobson, 2002; De Jeagher and Di Paolo, 2007). Approaches of this kind stress the importance of interaction-driven embodied engagements and the role of social institutions and practices in shaping, sharing with and understanding others. Although not yet mainstream, these alternatives, which revive and promote core phenomenological and Wittgensteinian insights, are gaining ground.[12] For the reasons stated above, their most interesting, and strategically viable versions ally themselves to revolutionary movements in cognitive science that also *directly* challenge its 'cognitivist' and 'representationalist' roots (Hutto, 2008c,d).

3. Empirical Implications and Standing

For those willing to assume that we — i.e. we, adult *humans* – make sense of actions by using folk psychology, the NPH offers fresh answers to the million dollar questions: How exactly do we do it? How are such capacities exercised? How did we first come to do it (What are FP's phylogenetic origins)?, How do we reliably come to be able to do it? (What is FP's developmental profile in ontogeny; What are FP's developmental precursors)?. And while, if true, it precludes the possibility that children and animals use FP proper, it raises important questions in comparative and developmental psychology about how other species and pre-verbal infants manage without it — e.g. whether they 'make sense' or 'understand' actions in everyday contexts by invoking or using anything that even approximates to FP (and if so, which species, and to what extent?).[13]

Ultimately, to take the NPH seriously requires putting it to the test. That would require looking again at the relevance of certain well-known empirical data and seeking novel varieties – perhaps even requiring new methods for collecting and assessing it. For example, ideally, comparative data on the parenting, schooling and general 'narrative' practices and explanatory tendencies of specific cultures is

---

[12] There has been, for example, a rapid growth in special issues and edited volumes dealing with and promoting these sorts of approaches Some recent titles include (to mention but a few): *Folk Psychology Re-Assessed* (2007), *The Shared Mind* (2008), *Alternatives to Theories of Mind* (2008), *Against Theory of Mind* (2009).

[13] There has been explosive interest in these sorts of questions of late. This has much to do with the development of new techniques and exciting findings, such as functional Magnetic Resonance Imaging (fMRI) and the much publicized discovery of mirror neurons. Both have helped to promote the development of new and fertile sub-fields, such as social neuroscience. But interest in the NPH and the narrative basis of FP is also fuelled from other sources, e.g. by the pressing practical and clinical demands of psychotherapy, such as investigations into the neuroscience, nature and treatment of autism and schizophrenia (see, e.g., Belmonte, 2007; Sparaci, 2008).

wanted. The need for new investigations is provoked by questions such as: When might the relevant narrative practices have emerged in our pre-history? What form did they take initially and subsequently? How do they relate to our more basic narrative competencies (and what do these look like)?; What is the nature and source of the latter? Are these competencies realized in our neurological hardware or are they more soft-wired (and, if so, how)?

Cross-disciplinary cooperation is a must if genuine progress is to be made in addressing such queries. Even though precise answers are a long way off, it is worth saying a word or two about the empirical plausibility of the NPH as things stand now. Apparently, its central claim that FP competence develops in stages, as children become more sophisticated in their narrative abilities, sits well with known developmental facts, especially since at critical points the developmental schedules overlap in important ways.

Human children exhibit a special responsiveness to the intentional attitudes of others early on. They selectively attend to goal-directed agency and animacy (circa 3 months); human actors as opposed to mechanical 'agents', goal-related actions as opposed to mere movements and the methods/paths taken to achieve these (circa 6–9 months); meaningful segments of complex behaviour streams (circa 10–15 months); intentional actions as opposed to incomplete/unintentional behaviour (circa 18 months) (Baldwin *et al.*, 2001; Baird *et al.*, 2000; Meltzoff, 1995). A major addition to this repertoire is development of the capacity for joint attention (Bard and Leavens, 2008). Basic forms of co-referential shared interactive activity (such as pointing, gaze following and social referencing) are strongly in play by 9 months, but full-blown, pre-linguistic joint attention is generally thought to start properly by the end of the first year and is normally well established by 18 months. These capacities, which are impressive in their own right, are transformed and extended in important ways after children become conversant with, and competent users of, language, which occurs during the course of the second year. At this point they are becoming budding conversationalists. This not only gives them new tools and opportunities for understanding the intentional attitudes of others in more sophisticated, linguistically-framed ways, it absolutely demands it of them.

Moreover, it is empirically well documented that this more sophisticated understanding of sententially-mediated propositional attitudes also unfolds in stages. For example, children have explicit command of the concept 'desire' roughly six months before that of 'belief' (Bartsch and Wellman, 1995; Harris, 1996). If we take false-belief tasks as a reliable indicator of (at least) a first pass explicit understanding of belief, then it is clear that such understanding can arrive as late as the fourth year of life. This is important, for if an understanding of belief is necessary but not sufficient for FP competence, it must be assumed that the latter emerges later still.

How does all of this compare with the development of narrative competence? Well, we know that:

> the ability to generate and process narrative is not limited to the exceptionally intelligent, nor is any formal instruction necessary for the acquisition of this faculty. Studies of Western children indicate that storytelling ability is reliably developing; the ability to tell stories emerges between the ages of 2 and 3 (Sutton-Smith, 1986, p. 69; see also Brown & Hurtig, 1983; Mancuso, 1986), and children as young as 30 months can distinguish between narrative and non-narrative uses of language (Scalise Sugiyama, 2001, p. 3; 2003, p. 392).

Encouragingly for the NPH, it seems that our FP competence comes on in stages that march in step with the growth of narrative ability. Although at the start of their story-telling careers (between the ages of 2 to 4 years) children borrow heavily from others, they become progressively better and more autonomous in the exercise of their narrative skills over time (Nelson, 2003, p. 31; 2007). The process is complex. Minimally, it requires developing such basic capacities as selecting a topic and seriating events, but ultimately it also involves keeping track of degrees of agency, multiple motives and perspectives, etc. (Bamberg, 1987, and in press). This requires active engagement on the part of the child and the support of others.

But over time, as children become more cognitively, communicatively and linguistically capable, they are better able to cope with and understand multiple perspectives; divergent points of view; the idea of stable persons with changing characteristics; what needs mentioning (and what can be taken for granted); descriptive language of the sort that enables ever more subtle distinctions in tense, complex use of names, and so on. New work in developmental psychology, which charts the ways in which children's more mature narrative productions depend upon, incorporate and extend pre-narrative competencies developed in earlier pretend play practices, helps us to better understand this process.

> pretend play, especially sociodramatic role play, highlights and fosters children's abilities to understand and coordinate multiple mental perspectives ... the plots of preschoolers stories are usually more complex and sophisticated than those of their pretend play narratives ... however at first these characters tend to remain generic types, described with

little detail or psychological depth ... In both their pretend play and their storytelling, young children *gradually master* the ability to construct a full narrative scenario (Nicolopolou, 2007, pp. 260–1, emphasis added; see also Sinha, 2005).

Importantly, it has been observed that 'the age of 5 years seems to mark a turning point in children's narrative skills, with further developments continuing to take place throughout the school years' (Tomasello, 2003, p. 276). This fits well with NPH's conjecture that the capacity for integrating more basic capacities to enable the ready deployment of mature FP skills only emerges relatively late-in-the-day, a good while after the explicit false belief tests are reliably being passed. It is interesting, in this context, that 'Proponents of the dominant theories have been notably quiet about what happens in development after the child's fifth birthday. However research that explores whether 5-year-olds can use simple false belief knowledge to make inferences about their own and other's perspectives finds that they singularly fail to do so' (Carpendale and Lewis, 2004, p. 91). To take but one example,

> children who understand false beliefs will, for example, realise that Little Red Riding Hood does not at first know that the wolf is dressed up as her grandmother. Some of these same young children, however, fail to correctly draw the emotional implications of this false belief and mistakenly state that Little Red Riding Hood would be afraid of her grandmother (Racine *et al.*, 2007, p. 481).

Moreover, it is natural to suppose that the development of FP competence and a growing narrative sophistication not only travel together but are mutually supporting. The process of producing and consuming more complex FP narratives feeds upon itself and thus extends FP competence in interesting ways, rendering it more nuanced and rich. Modifying a claim by Scalise Sugiyama, the basic idea is that there exists 'a feedback loop between storytelling and [FP competence]: storytelling may help build or strengthen [FP competence], which in turn enriches storytelling, which further enriches [FP competence], and so on' (Scalise Sugiyama 2005, p. 189).

The NPH is not only consistent with these ontogenetic facts, it holds up well in light of what we know of inherited capacities and pre-history. In Hutto (2008a) in an attempt to defend the NPH against a specially designed, FP-targeted variant of the 'Poverty of the Stimulus' argument I was forced to speculate about the origins of FP narratives and why they are so pervasive in human culture. Those were mere speculations but I have since discovered some fascinating work that helps to place them on firmer ground.

Calling on a wealth of anthropological and ethnographic evidence it has been proposed that narratives may function to impart vital information to listeners (Scalise Sugiyama, 1996; 2001; 2003; 2005). This is plausible given that humans have a voracious natural appetite and ability for telling and consuming stories.[14] Also it is arguable that 'recurrent themes in world literature are rooted in adaptive concerns' (Scalise Sugiyama, 2003, p. 391). For example, narratives the world over are replete with trickster stories, which emphasize and warn of the dangers of free-riders and the fact that taking what others say and do at face value can have heavy consequences (see Scalise Sugiyama, 2008; Hill, 2008).

Accepting the information-imparting thesis should not lead us to deny that engaging in narrative practices has other functions too. For example, it is easily partnered with the norm-imparting thesis according to which narratives help, through their content, to 'delimit behavioural boundaries by providing examples of appropriate and inappropriate behaviour and their consequences' (Scalise Sugiyama, 2005, p. 126). This connects with the plausible hypothesis that FP serves a primarily regulative function (McGeer, 2007; Zawidzki, 2008).

Importantly, in defending the view that stories impart crucial information in hunter-gatherer societies, Scalise Sugiyama notes that:

> The ethnographic record accords with the folklore record, providing evidence that foragers use narrative as a means of acquiring and storing fitness-related information ... Blurton-Jones and Konner (1976, p. 338) found that the !Kung often 'would begin to discuss some point among themselves and *recount observations* to each other' ... Finding little direct transmission of information between !Kung men Blurton-Jones and Konner concluded that 'Perhaps verbal transmission of information is indirect *through people telling the story of their day's excursion* as opposed to direct lecturing' (Scalise Sugiyama 2001, p. 10, emphases added)

By engaging in this sort of practice 'Men increase their hunting knowledge not only by observing other hunters but by listening to them "tell the hunt" (that is, recount their hunting experiences)' (Scalise Sugiyama, 2005, p. 190). If so, this dovetails beautifully with the core proposal of my modified version of Sellar's 'myth of Jones'. In chapter 12 of Hutto (2008a), I suggested that FP understanding is likely to have originally come into being along with practices in which

---

[14] Scalise Sugiyama reports 'stories are strikingly memorable. As Sperber (1985) notes that although the story "Little Red Riding Hood" is much more complex than a 20-digit number, the story is much easier to remember' (Scalise Sugiyama 2001, p. 8).

story-tellers learned to give *public expression* to their thoughts and, more specifically, their reasons for acting. This account of the genesis of FP competence looks a good bet if recounted narratives of our hunter-gather ancestors contain 'descriptions of problems and of character's plans for solving problems' (Scalise Sugiyama, 2001, p. 9).

In emphasizing these facts about human narratives and our capacities to produce/digest them, Scalise Sugiyama adopts an evolutionary psychology approach and assumes the unproblematic existence of ToM mechanisms. In this, like many others, she is inclined to follow Tooby and Cosmides in supposing that 'We are "mindreaders" by nature ... Humans evolved this ability because, as members of an intensively social, cooperative, and competitive species, our ancestors' lives depended on how well they could infer what was on one another's minds' (Tooby & Cosmides, 1995, p. xvii). I won't rehearse my reasons for doubting the existence of such devices yet again. I am more interested in assessing her claim that our narrative capacities may also have been 'selected for'. She writes:

> While it is impossible to pinpoint the birth of narrative, a number of lines of evidence indicate that it emerged in the Pleistocene, which would make [our capacity/appetite for] narrative a sufficiently ancient phenomenon to have developed through a process of natural selection (Scalise Sugiyama, 2001, p. 3).[15]

But, as far as I can see, the dates do not quite allow for this. For she notes:

> Given that modern humans have been in existence for approximately 100,000 years and are the only hominid species or subspecies known for certain to exhibit storytelling behaviour, we can safely say that oral narrative is a product of our hunting-and-gathering past, likely to have emerged between 30,000 and 100,000 years ago (Scalise Sugiyama 2001, p. 234).

That seems right. But if it is true, as Scalise Sugiyama maintains (and I concur), language is a necessary (but not sufficient) condition for the existence of narrative practices, then something does not add up here.[16] The trouble is that if narrative capacities were universally and

---

[15] The simple truth is that 'We have no information, of course, on how long humans have been storytellers. For all we know, this might be a very ancient use of language ... We have no way of assigning relative dates to, say, the emergence of our knowledge of the future, of other minds, and of full language' (Sterelny, 2006, p. 38).

[16] She writes 'the practice of story-telling is ancient ... Language, an obvious prerequisite for storytelling, is likely to have emerged by 50,000 and possibly 250,000 years ago... although the oldest known narrative (The Epic of Gilgamesh) dates back only 5,000 years ago' (Scalise Sugiyama 2001, p. 233).

uniformly selected for in our species then this must have occurred
sometime before 100,000 b.p. (or thereabouts). This entails that narrative practices will have had to have been well-established for a long,
long while. Put otherwise, if narrative practices (which are dependent
upon the use of complex language) only showed up late in the day
(after the designated deadline) then it isn't possible that mechanisms
fashioned specifically to support FP competence will have been
selected for (unless we are prepared to tolerate parallel biological evolution in our species over a very short timescale).

But what if the generally accepted dates on the emergence of complex language are wrong (i.e. out by a hundred thousand years or so)?
What if complex language emerged much, much earlier than many
suppose, early enough to have been in place and used in sophisticated
ways to support conversational narratives long enough before the
Diaspora out of Africa? Wouldn't that revive the prospects (or at least
the possibility) that sophisticated FP-supporting devices might have
evolved during our pre-history, as adaptations, and that they now form
an important part of our cognitive inheritance?

If we are prepared to make those adjustments, the answer is 'Yes'.[17]
Perhaps our natural proclivity for and skill with FP narratives just is
more ancient than generally supposed. Perhaps we inherited dedicated
and specialized mechanisms for producing and consuming narratives,
even if the mechanisms that enable this do not embed a 'theory of
mind' *per se*. The NPH tolerates this adjustment, as long as it remains
true that the normal development and function of these inherited FP
narrative capacities depends, in normal cases, on members of our species having the appropriate exposure to stories with the right content
and structure and where the FP narratives themselves are conceived of
as readily available features of the normal human environmental niche
— i.e. as staple sociocultural productions or items (in whatever particular format they are conveyed).

On this sort of model, a partnership is imagined to exist between
certain inherited capacities and certain normal, reliable features of
human environments, including, especially, cultural practices and
artifacts — features that critically shape our cognitive possibilities. To
think of narratives as playing this sort of role in engendering FP

[17] This might seem to lend believers in ToM mechanisms some hope. It would afford them
protection against one argument I advanced in Chapter 11 of Hutto (2008a). But this
would only make their proposals viable if they did not suffer in other, yet more fundamental ways too. As I argued in section 1, a fatal problem for those who take such conjectures
seriously is their inability to specify the content such mechanisms are meant to have or to
explain how their posited mechanisms get that content in the first place (see Hutto, 2008a,
ch. 3, 4, 5 and 8 where this problem is discussed at length).

competence fits snugly with the suggestion that 'the co-evolution of cognition with culture has built a mechanism that results in the cumulative change of human environments ... Humans are niche constructors: we rework our own environment: think of shelters and clothes; the domestication of animals; the use of tools' (Sterelny, 2006, p. 37). There is every reason to suppose that narratives are a distinctive and characteristic feature of human cultural niches, just as dams are for beavers.

What should be rejected if we abandon the idea that biologically-inherited mechanisms exist, which literally contain our 'theory of mind', is that 'the role of experience is merely to select from a menu of pre-specified alternatives by setting parameters to their appropriate settings' (Sterelny, 2006, p. 32, see also p. 26). Thus, even in speculatively entertaining the possibility of a more nativist-friendly version of the NPH, it is important that we do not become seduced into imagining that the role of local narrative productions in engendering our FP skills could be reduced to merely that of providing triggering 'inputs' in a pre-built ToM jukebox — one gifted to all members of our species. This familiar, Chomsky-inspired rendering of the modularist proposal is neither the only, nor the best, theoretical option on the market.

It must be remembered that, even if we put aside the very serious worries about the source and nature of the 'representations' that ToM devices putatively use, there are other objections to evolutionary psychology's basic paradigm that make its standard offerings suspect (Dupré, 2001; Buller, 2005; Richardson, 2007). In particular, we should not be persuaded of the need to accept some version of an adaptationist story about our narrative capacities simply because they appear to be culturally universal traits, for it is entirely possible that 'some cultural universals may have emerged without having been generated directly by evolved psychological mechanisms' (Buller, 2005, p. 467).

To demonstrate this, Buller convincingly shows that we can, for example, potentially explain universal human traits by appeal to an epidemiological spread from the original ancestral population (i.e. that from which we all descended). On these grounds he concludes that 'the existence of a cultural universal may signal only a common origin of all the world's cultures, rather than a common psychological adaption of all the world's peoples' (Buller, 2006, p. 468).[18] Richardson, who also promotes a wholly Darwin-friendly story about human

---

[18] Indeed, in arguing for the idea that minds are continually adapting (as opposed to having been pre-adapted) at both the population and individual levels, he claims 'the idea of a

evolution and defends the idea of common descent, also complains that 'evolutionary psychologists tend to assume that the *only* explanations will be in terms of adaptation' (Richardson, 2007, p. 11). He also supplies ample evidence that they are wrong to assume this. While this hardly settles matters, it reveals that there is more than one credible way of understanding how narratives might have originated and have come to play a critical role in the development of our mature FP competence.

4. Philosophical Considerations

Given their concerns, many analytic philosophers are likely to be unmoved if the familiar psychologistic theories about FP's basis, TT and ST, should go to the wall.[19] Their primary interest in FP only extends to constitutive questions about the content and status of mentalistic talk. As such, it matters little to them which mechanisms happen to make such talk possible. Thus it may not seem that it would affect their projects much (if at all) if FP competence should turn out to be fostered by narrative engagements or not. That is an empirical matter. Hence, as a developmental hypothesis and conjecture about the origins of such talk, the fate of the NPH (whether true or false) will have little impact on their philosophical agenda. All that matters is what we can know, *in advance*: that FP exists as a systematic and distinctive way of making sense of reasons for action. The existence of FP practice in no way depends on the success or failure of any particular theory about the mechanisms that underpin it.

I think we ought to be cautiously prepared to agree at least this much (though it has been challenged — see Ratcliffe, 2007; 2008; 2009 [this volume]). But what cannot be assumed without argument is that FP is essentially theoretical in nature, though this is precisely what many philosophers do assume. But that is a constitutive claim that can be challenged. It is important to distinguish this version of TT from those that advance empirical hypotheses about the basis of our FP competence. Thus Braddon-Mitchell and Jackson observe that accepting that knowledge of FP constitutes a form of implicit theory 'does not, of course, mean that we must have a theory ... explicitly worked out in our minds, but somehow hidden from view and guiding

---

universal nature is deeply antithetical to a truly evolutionary view of our species' (Buller, 2006, p. 419).

[19] I have only concerned myself with the 'inherited mechanism' versions of these theories here. I discuss other variants, such as the idea that our 'theory of mind' is forged by active childhood theorizing, in detail, in Hutto (2008a, see chapter 9).

our actions from its hiding place' (Braddon-Mitchell and Jackson, 2007, p. 63). Rather adopting such a view need only imply that 'there is *a theory to be had in principle* about what the regularities underlying [FP] judgements are' (Braddon-Mitchell and Jackson, 2007, p. 63, emphasis added). In adopting this line they endorse a position that trades under the name 'external theory theory' (or ETT). This is the view that FP is not 'an internally represented knowledge structure or body of information; it is not part of the mechanism that subserves [our everyday abilities]. On these readings, folk psychology "ain't in the head"' (Stich and Ravenscroft, 1996, p. 128).

This would entail that it is at least theoretically possible to describe or articulate the operative principles at work in FP practice, 'from the outside' as it were. It may seem obvious that it should be possible to identify, derive and articulate FP core principles, at least in principle. But it has proved notoriously difficult, even for professional philosophers to achieve more than a modicum of success in this enterprise (Maibom, 2003, p. 304). This may be because philosophers have misunderstood the structure of such knowledge. Certainly, those seeking to engage in this sort of Lewisian programme acknowledge that

> the collection of 'platitudes' is likely to be large and ungainly, [such that] we might reserve the label 'folk psychology' for a set of more abstract generalizations — a 'theory' if you will — that systematizes the platitudes in a perspicuous way and that (perhaps in conjunction with some other commonly known information) entails them (Stich and Ravenscroft, 1996, p. 127; see Lewis, 1972).

Leaving aside the question of whether what is proposed is *really* possible, what should not escape our notice is that this rendering of TT has extremely weak commitments – so weak in fact that it seems incapable of supporting the claim that FP is essentially theoretical in character. After all, is there *any* practice that would not admit of a similar treatment? Does the mere possibility of distilling such descriptions equally convert all other practices (e.g. angling, trading, etc.) into theoretical ones?[20] To fully grasp the central worry it is crucial that we understand the nature of this imagined product aright. For it cannot be

---

[20] A common thought is that FP has other, rather special features that make it theoretical in nature. Specifically, many characterize it as involving the positing of causally efficacious, internal mental states in order to yield third-person predictions and explanations of the behaviour of others. However, this would only make FP essentially theoretical if we assume that this is its primary or only function (as opposed to being something it might simply be used for in some contexts). I have argued elsewhere that the assumption that FP operates primarily to serve this sort of function (which requires endorsing what I call 'the spectatorial assumption') does not hold up under scrutiny (Hutto, 2004; 2008a, ch. 1).

assumed without further argument that what would be derived would be a FP 'theory' in any interesting or pertinent sense.

We might doubt this on several grounds. Firstly, the process of derivation hardly seems to constitute genuine theoretical activity. Although it would require reflecting on what we do and how we do it, the task seems to bear the hallmarks of being essentially descriptive rather than hypothetical in nature. A major part of divining and articulating the core operating principles of FP would seem to demand charting the constants and variables of FP. This would require attending to FP *as it is used in practice*. If successful, the result would be a description of an abstraction — i.e. a formal rendering of some general rules and features at work in that practice. There is room to question if that sort of product is really best described as 'a theory if you will'. Secondly, and pivotally, even if such an artifact could be successfully obtained it would *not* be a description of the tacit 'set of principles' *used by* FP practitioners in their daily affairs. Hence, even if it is possible that the basic 'operating principles' might be articulated in theory, this would hardly establish that FP practice itself (from which the relevant formalization would be derived) is essentially theoretical or that it embeds a theory as such.

If properly conducted this sort of project would be akin to an attempt to capture, in an appropriate meta-vocabulary, 'what one must *do* in order to *use* various vocabularies and so to count as *saying* or *thinking* various kinds of things' (Brandom, 2006, p. 3). As Brandom notes, this would be a significant pragmatist extension of the analytic project of understanding the semantic relations that hold between different vocabularies.[21] The result would be a description of what it is necessary for someone to do in order to make competent use of a certain vocabulary for a certain purpose. Hence, this way of understanding the project of codifying FP 'principles' (and the philosophical purpose of doing so) must be distinguished from another project, familiar to analytic philosophers — that of charting the patterns of assent and dissent associated with answering specific questions in order to reveal 'folk' patterns of judgment on specific topics.[22] This

---

[21] Brandom's own version of analytic pragmatism gets its inspiration from Sellars and takes seriously the important challenges facing programmatic versions of analytic philosophy, as laid down by Wittgenstein.

[22] There is a serious problem for the idea that philosophy, taking the form of conceptual analysis, could rely on the appeal to intuitions in order to adjudicate between philosophical theories concerning important topics (e.g. the nature of mental causation, consciousness, etc.). For the idea is that such arbitration will rest on 'appeal to what seems most obvious and central [about the concept in question], as revealed by our intuitions about possible

sort of product might be understood as a 'theory'. Dennett is right to suggest that:

> It is tempting to interpret the field of philosophy of mind as just this endeavour: an attempt at a rigorous unification and formalization of the fundamental intuitions the folk manifest in both their daily affairs and in reflective interaction with the questioning anthropologists. 'Consult your intuitions,' say the philosophers. 'Do they agree with the following proposition? ...' And if the task were done well, it would yield a valuable artefact for further study: the optimized 'theory' of late-twentieth-century-Anglophone folk psychology (Dennett, 2006, p. 33).[23]

But FP as I have been using the term does not amount to the sum total of what 'the folk' are inclined to say in response to certain probative questions. If we think of FP as naming a familiar practice then divining the principles of FP in action, when it is performing its usual office of making sense of intentional action, is not the same as determining what the folk collectively happen to think about FP-related topics (as we might elicit and reveal the content of their speculations about the behaviour of macroscopic items in order to discover their 'folk physics').[24]

For this reason not every 'folk psychological' claim commands the same degree of epistemic risk. Some are positively more flatfooted precisely while others will involve significant speculation. For example, compare A and B below:

A.   That there is something-it-is-like-to experience textures or colours (and this alters systematically with bodily/environmental changes in expected ways);

---

cases' (Jackson, 1998, p 31). But there is a serious and glaring problem with this proposed methodology since, if we follow those who endorse the existence of *only* an external TT then there is no separately existing shared, underlying folk 'theory' that could play the causal-explanatory role of justifying or making true our intuitive judgments. At best 'FP theory' is nothing more than a name for a distinctive set of intuitive patterns of assent and judgement about everyday psychological matters. This problem has not gone unnoticed. As Williamson observes: '"Intuition" plays a major role in contemporary analytic philosophy's self understanding. Yet there is no agreed or even popular account of how intuition works, no accepted explanation of the hoped-for correlation between our having an intuition that P and its being true that P. Since analytic philosophy prides itself on its rigor, this blank space in its foundations looks like a methodological scandal. Why should intuitions have any authority over the philosophical domain?' (Williamson, 2007, p. 215).

[23] Thus: 'My intuitions about possible cases reveal my theory ... Likewise, your intuitions reveal your theory. To the extent our intuitions coincide with those of the folk, they reveal the folk theory' (Jackson, 1998, p. 32).

[24] For a useful and illuminating discussion of this precise point see Sorell (1991, p. 140–50). Sorell makes an excellent case for believing that there is equivocation in the arguments about FP precisely because 'a number of different things can qualify as folk psychology' (Sorell, 1991, p. 144).

B.   That I can experience everything, in full detail, all the way out to the periphery of my visual field.

Claim A is not on a par with that of B. Observing this justifies pursuing a 'maximally minimalist' approach when seeking to characterize the implications of FP practice. Consider the utterance that could result from the exercise of our FP competence:

C.   Jack and Jill went up the hill because they *wanted* to fetch a pail of water and they *believed* that they would find water at the hilltop.

What is one committed to in saying this? Some hold that snippets of everyday mentalistic parlance like this imply a commitment on the speaker's behalf to the existence of complexly inter-related, causally efficacious, inner mental states — states with special representational properties that are hard to explain naturalistically. Famously, Fodor thinks this and many have followed his lead (Fodor, 1987). If this is right then the folk have rather hefty metaphysical commitments, which they are probably not aware of. This is made immensely more plausible by the fact that it is not claimed that the folk *know* that they are so committed, only that they are. Apparently in metaphysics, as in law, ignorance is no defense.

If ordinary FP claims, such as C, really entailed commitments of this kind then the truth of any particular FP utterance would depend on certain sophisticated 'theories' in the philosophy of mind (e.g. concerning representationalism; mental-property causation; Humeanism about mental states,[25] etc.) being true. Indeed, special excitement was injected into analytic philosophy of mind when worries were raised that ordinary FP talk about the mental may be systematically false. Proponents of eliminitivism predicted that developments in cognitive science would show (even if only over the course of geological time) that the seeming referents of mental state predicates are, as a matter of fact, empty. Accordingly, the labels 'beliefs' or 'desires' systematically fail to denote. More modestly, others have worried that C fails, for less radical reasons. In their view, even if citing one's 'beliefs' is not wholly empty, mental state talk might nevertheless be incapable of designating the relevant causal properties that could make C true, at least under its 'standard' interpretation (i.e. certain properties of the mental states of Jack and Jill were 'causally' responsible for their behaviour).

[25] For a recent challenge to Humeanism see Miller (2008).

The maximally minimalist approach I recommend brackets these worries in the first instance. All that follows if C is true is that Jack and Jill will have had to have acted on the basis of beliefs and desires with the relevant contents (i.e. and not, contrastively, because of a different set of beliefs or desires, or because of force of habit, the pull of magnetic forces, etc.). If so, the cited beliefs and desires will have made a difference in this case. We can (and should) insist on this without assuming that the truth of that simple utterance embeds or entails a commitment to other substantive and contentious philosophical 'theories' about the nature of mental states or their causal properties.

Depending on where one starts philosophically, it can be difficult even to make sense of this possibility. It is still *very popular* amongst philosophers to assume that our epistemic situation is bifurcated such that there are really only two ways of engaging with and knowing about the world. On the one hand, there is 'raw' unconceptualized sensory stimulation. At this level of encounter no claims are possible and concomitantly there is no risk of error. On the other hand, everything else, including the perceptions that feed cognition and action depend on making assumptions about 'what there is'. Such activity necessarily involves representation of some kind at the base level, with conceptualized thought, explicit judgment and linguistic claim-making coming in at later points. Unlike mere sensory stimulation this way of responding is an epistemically risky business. It follows that *any and all* representation or thinking is theorizing. The core idea and its motivations are epitomized in the following quotation from Churchland:

> The common opinion concerning scientific knowledge and theoretical understanding — of molecules, of stars, of nuclei and electro-magnetic waves — is that it is of a kind very different from our knowledge of apples, and tables, and kitchen pots and sand ... these specious contrasts are wholesale nonsense ... Upon close inspection the various contrasts thought to fund the distinctions are seen to disappear. If viewed warily, the network of principles and assumptions constitutive of our common-sense conceptual framework can be seen to be as speculative and artificial as any overtly theoretical system ... In short, it appears that all knowledge (even perceptual knowledge) is theoretical; that there is no such thing as *non*-theoretical understanding ... we are left with little more than a distinction between freshly minted theory and thoroughly thumb-worn theory whose cultural assimilation is complete (Churchland, 1979, p. 1–2).

Against what might be crudely, but usefully, identified as the 'Quinean first philosophy' stands the view that the epistemic foundations of our various discourses, including those of science are *pragmatically* and not theoretically grounded. Embedded in this thought is the recognition that although we ordinarily make claims about 'what there is' and that these can be true or false on occasion, our talk about everyday items is not rooted in forms of ancient *theorizing* about the familiar, (such as macroscopia, middle-sized dry goods) — an activity that is now allegedly long forgotten and hence hard to recognize as such. Rather, for the pragmatist, such talk has a wholly different origin, basis and status.

This is what Wittgenstein tried to get us to see by reminding us of the sorts of rock bottom certainties that are incorporated into and ground our everyday practices (see Moyal-Sharrock, 2007).

> Children do not learn that books exist, that armchairs exist, etc. etc., — they learn to fetch books, sit in armchairs, etc., etc. Later questions about the existence of things do of course arise. 'Is there such a thing as a unicorn?' and so on. But such a question is possible only because as a rule no corresponding question presents itself (Wittgenstein, 1974, *On Certainty*, §476,).

In the same vein, children do not learn that beliefs and desires exist they learn how to make sense of others using such terms. If so, our everyday mentalistic thought and talk (or at least an important sub-set of it) is not theoretical. Indeed, it is importantly insulated from the success or failure of the 'theories of mind' that are popular in certain branches of philosophy of mind and cognitive science.[26]

Doesn't this take us back to square one? Doesn't this mean that FP talk is somehow autonomous and that empirical findings are unimportant to a philosophical understanding of it? No. For the mere *fact* that the folk *can* readily and adeptly produce and consume the relevant utterances (at least when called upon to do so) entails that they have an interesting competency: FP-competence. Just how often or ubiquitously it is exercised is not important (at least not in the first instance); what matters is if that capacity exists it wants explaining.[27] And this is

---

[26] I am not suggesting that FP commitments are in some way purely instrumental because they are lighter than ordinarily supposed. For example, it is not as if FP practitioners are committed only to a kind of 'mild' realism about beliefs and desires (Dennett, 1987; 1991). It is rather that FP explanations do not compete with scientific proposals about the causes of human behaviour. Although these discourses are interested in the same subject matter (differently described) they are interested in it in different ways and for different purposes (Hutto, 2009a).

[27] Nor would adopting the sort of approach I recommend absolve us from dealing with other driving concerns of analytic philosophy; in particular, understanding how ordinary claims stand to scientific discourses and determining what would have to be the case for them to be true. Dealing with these issues raises crucial but tricky general questions about the relation between what the use of everyday vocabularies entails for theories of growing modern science (and *vice versa*). Settling such questions has been an, if not 'the', abiding

precisely where, if we are careful, the interests of philosophers and those in other disciplines can be fruitfully and mutually informative.

5. Worries and Objections

In all, equating FP practice with a kind of narrative practice and looking to our narrative practices to understand the basis of FP competence opens up new empirical possibilities and can help to re-orient our philosophical thinking in important ways. But even if the basic idea that FP and narrative practices are importantly related holds promise it must stand up to a range of serious challenges. For example, does the emphasis on narrative wrongly underplay, misconstrue, or overlook the critical epistemic role of empathy (or simulative imagination) in the way we make sense of others (Stueber, 2008)?[28] Is the focus on FP narratives a mistake because there is, in fact, no well-defined sub-section of our practices that can be properly identified with FP at all; have I contravened Wittgenstein's rule by not leaving 'ragged what is ragged' (Ratcliffe 2008)?

I leave the discussion of, and response to, these worries (and many others, including several new ones that surface in the chapters of this collection) for a future occasion. Exploring and dealing with such challenges is part and parcel of on-going engagement in philosophy and science. In staying the course, my FP-narrative equation and the NPH may get a bit battered, they may require patching, elaboration and refinement, or they may turn out to be miserably inadequate or just plain false in the end. Maybe, but we surely don't know yet. It will be fun finding out.

References

Andrews, K. (2008), 'It's in your Nature: A pluralistic folk psychology', *Synthese*, **165**, pp.13–29.

Baldwin, D.A., Baird, J.A., Saylor, M. and Clark, A. (2001), 'Infants Parse Dynamic Action', *Child Development*, **72**, pp. 708–17.

Bamberg, M. (1987), *The Acquisition of Narratives: Learning to Use Language* (Berlin: Mouton de Gruyter).

---

agenda item of analytic philosophy (whether in its empiricist or naturalist guise) in this century and the previous one.

[28]   Stueber makes this sort of objection to my approach in a footnote to a paper that argues, more generally, for the claim that making sense of reasons for acting centrally depends on empathically 'grasping another person's beliefs and desires as his or her own reason for acting' (Stueber, 2008, p. 34). Hence, he claims that my proposed understanding of folk psychology as essentially a kind of narrative practice 'insufficiently distinguishes among different epistemic aspects of our folk-psychological practice of understanding others that need to be held apart' (Stueber, 2008, p. 34).

Bamberg, M. (In press), 'Sequencing Events in Time or Sequencing Events in Story-Telling? From cognition to discourse — with frogs paving the way' in *Festschrift for Dan Slobin*, ed. J Guo, S Ervin-Tripp, N Budwig (New Jersey: Lawrence Erlbaum Associates).

Baird, J.A. and Baldwin, D.A. (2001), 'Making Sense of Human Behaviour: Action Parsing and Intentional Inference' In *Intentions and Intentionality: Foundations of Social Cognition* (ed. F. Malle, L.J. Moses, D.A. Baldwin) pp. 193–206 (Cambridge, MA: MIT Press).

Bard, K.A. and Leavens, D.A. (2008), 'Socio-emotional Factors in the Development of Joint Attention in Human and Ape Infants' in *Learning from Animals? Examining the Nature of Human Uniqueness*, ed. L Roska-Hardy, EM Neumann-Held), pp. 89–104 (London: Psychology Press).

Bartsch, K. and Wellman, H. (1995), *Children Talk about the Mind* (New York: Oxford University Press).

Belmonte, M. (2007), 'Human, but More So: What the autistic brain tells us about the process of narrative' in *Autism and Representation*, ed. M Osteen (London: Routledge).

Borg, E. (2007), 'If Mirror Neurons are the Answer, What was the Question?', *Journal of Consciousness Studies*, **14**, pp. 5–19.

Braddon-Mitchell, D. and Jackson, F. (2007), *Philosophy of Mind and Cognition* (Oxford: Blackwell).

Brandom, R.B. (2006), *Between Saying and Doing: Towards an Analytic Pragmatism* (Oxford: Oxford University Press).

Bruner, J. (1990), *Acts of Meaning* (Cambridge, MA: Harvard University Press).

Buller, D.J. (2005), *Adapting Minds: Evolutionary Psychology and the Persistent Quest for Human Nature* (Cambridge, MA: MIT Press).

Carpendale, J.L.M. and Lewis, C. (2004), 'Constructing an Understanding of the Mind: The development of children's social understanding within social interaction', *Behavioural and Brain Sciences*, **27**, pp. 79–151.

Churchland, P.M. (1979), *Scientific Realism and the Plasticity of Mind* (Cambridge: Cambridge University Press).

Costall, A. and Leudar, I. (ed. 2009), *Against Theory of Mind* (Basingstoke: Palgrave).

Currie, G. (2008), 'Some Ways of Understanding People', *Philosophical Explorations*, **11**, pp. 211–18.

De Jeagher, H. and Di Paolo, E. (2007), 'Participatory Sense-Making: An enactive approach to social cognition', *Phenomenology and the Cognitive Sciences*, **6**, pp. 485–507.

Dennett, D.C. (1987), *The Intentional Stance* (Cambridge, MA: MIT Press).

Dennett, D.C. (1991), 'Real Patterns', *Journal of Philosophy*, **88**, pp. 27–51.

Dennett, D.C. (2006), *Sweet Dreams: Philosophical Obstacles to a Science of Consciousness* (Cambridge, MA: MIT Press).

Dupré, J. (2001), *Human Nature and the Limits of Science* (Oxford: Oxford University Press).

Fodor, J.A. (1987), *Psychosemantics* (Cambridge, MA: MIT Press).

Gallagher, S. (2006), 'The Narrative Alternative to Theory of Mind' in *Radical Enactivism: Focus on the Philosophy of Daniel D. Hutto*, ed. R Menary, pp. 223–29 (Amsterdam: John Benjamins).

Gallagher, S. (2007), 'Simulation Trouble', *Social Neuroscience*, **2**, pp. 353–65.

Gallagher, S. and Zahavi, D. (2008), *The Phenomenological Mind: An Introduction to Philosophy of Mind and Cognitive Science* (London: Routledge).

Gallese, V. (2007), 'Before and below "theory of mind": Embodied simulation and the neural correlates of social cognition', *Philosophical Transactions of the Royal Society Biological Sciences,* **362**, pp. 659–69.

Garfield, J.L. Peterson, C.C. and Perry, T. (2001), 'Social Cognition, Language Acquisition and the Development of the Theory of Mind', *Mind and Language,* **16**, pp. 494–541.

Goldman, A.I. (2006), *Simulating Minds: The Philosophy, Psychology and Neuroscience of Mindreading* (New York: Oxford University Press).

Gopnik, A. and Meltzoff, A.N. (1997), *Words, Thoughts, and Theories* (Cambridge, MA: MIT Press).

Gordon, R.M. (2008), 'Beyond Mindreading', *Philosophical Explorations,* **11**, pp. 219–22.

Harris, P. (1996), 'Desires, Beliefs and Language' In *Theories of Theories of Mind,* ed. P Carruthers, P Smith, pp. 200–20 (Cambridge: Cambridge University Press).

Herman, D. (2008a), 'Description, Narrative, and Explanation: Text-Type Categories and the Cognitive Foundations of Discourse Competence', *Poetics Today,* **29**, pp. 437–72.

Herman, D. (2008b), 'Narrative Theory and the Intentional Stance', *Partial Answers,* **6**, pp. 233–60.

Herschbach, M. (2008), 'False-Belief Understanding and the Phenomenological Critics of Folk Psychology', *Journal of Consciousness Studies,* **15**, pp. 33–56.

Hill, J.D. (2008), *Made-from-Bone: Trickster Myths, Music, and History from the Amazon* (Champaign, IL: Illinois University Press).

Hobson, P. (2002), *The Cradle of Thought* (Basingstoke: Palgrave Macmillian).

Hornsby, J. (1997), *Simple Mindedness* (Cambridge, MA: Harvard University Press).

Hutto, D. and Ratcliffe, M. (ed. 2007), *Folk Psychology Re-Assessed* (Dordrecht: Springer).

Hutto, D.D. (1997), 'The Story of the Self: The Narrative Basis of Self-Development' in *Critical Studies: Ethics and the Subject,* ed. K Simms (Amsterdam: Rodopi).

Hutto, D.D. (1999), *The Presence of Mind* (Amsterdam: John Benjamins).

Hutto, D.D. (2000), *Beyond Physicalism* (Amsterdam: John Benjamins).

Hutto, D.D. (2004), 'The Limits of Spectatorial Folk Psychology' *Mind and Language,* **19**, pp. 54873.

Hutto, D.D. (2005), 'Knowing What? Radical versus conservative enactivism', *Phenomenology and the Cognitive Sciences,* **4**, pp. 389–405.

Hutto, D.D. (2006), 'Unprincipled Engagements: Emotional experience, expression and response' in *Radical Enactivism: Focus on the Philosophy of Daniel D. Hutto,* ed. R Menary, pp. 13–38 (Amsterdam/Philadelphia: Jon Benjamins).

Hutto, D.D. (2007), 'The Narrative Practice Hypothesis: Origins and applications of folk psychology', *Narrative and Understanding Persons: Royal Institute of Philosophy Supplement,* **82**, pp. 43–68.

Hutto, D.D. (2008a), *Folk Psychological Narratives: The Sociocultural Basis of Understanding Reasons* (Cambridge, MA: MIT Press).

Hutto, D.D. (2008b), 'The Narrative Practice Hypothesis: Clarifications and Consequences', *Philosophical Explorations,* **11**, pp. 175–92.

Hutto, D.D. (2008c), 'Limited Engagements and Narrative Extensions', *International Journal of Philosophical Studies,* **16**, pp. 419–44.

Hutto, D.D. (2008d), 'Articulating and Understanding the Phenomenological Manifesto', *Abstracta - Linguagem, Mente e Ação,* 10-9.

Hutto, D.D. (2009a), 'Lessons from Wittgenstein: Elucidating folk psychology', *New Ideas in Psychology. Special Issue: Mind, Meaning and Language: Wittgenstein's Relevance for Psychology*

Hutto, D.D. (2009b), 'ToM Rules, but it is not OK' in *Against Theory of Mind*, ed. A Costall, I Leudar (Basingstoke: Palgrave).

Jackson, F. (1998), *From Metaphysics to Ethics* (Oxford: Oxford University Press).

Lewis, D. (1972), 'Psychophysical and Theoretical Identifications', *Australasian Journal of Philosophy*, **50**, pp. 249–58.

Maibom, H.L. (2003), 'The Mindreader and the Scientist', *Mind and Language*, **18**, pp. 296–315.

McGeer, V. (2007), 'The Regulative Dimension of Folk Psychology' in *Folk Psychology Re-Assessed*, ed. DD Hutto, M Ratcliffe, pp. 137–56 (Dordrecht: Springer).

Meltzoff, A.N. (1995), 'Understanding the Intentions of Others: Re-enactment of Intended Acts by 18-Month-Old Children', *Developmental Psychology*, **24**, pp. 470–6.

Miller, C. (2008), 'Motivation in Agents', *Nous*, **42**, pp. 222–66.

Moyal-Sharrock, D. (2007), *Understanding Wittgenstein's On Certainty* (Basingstoke: Palgrave).

Nelson, K. (2003), 'Narrative and the Emergence of a Consciousness of Self' in *Narrative and Consciousness*, ed. GD Fireman, TEJ McVay, O Flanagan (Oxford: Oxford University Press).

Nelson, K. (2007), *Young Minds in Social Worlds* (Cambridge, MA: Harvard University Press).

Nichols, S. and Stich, S. (2003), *Mindreading: An Integrated Account of Pretence, Self-Awareness and Understanding of Other Minds* (Oxford: Oxford University Press).

Nicolopoulou, A. (2007), 'The Interplay of Play and Narrative in Children's Development: Theoretical reflections and concrete examples' in *Play and Development: Evolutionary, Sociocultural, and Functional Perspectives*, ed. A Göncü, S Gaskins (New York and London: Lawrence Erlbaum Associates).

Onishi, K.H. and Baillargeon, R. (2005), 'Do 15-Month-Old Infants Understand False Beliefs?', *Science*, **308**, pp. 255–58.

Onishi, K.H. Baillargeon, R. and Leslie, A.M. (2007), '15-month-old infants detect violations in pretend scenarios', *Acta Psychologica*, **124**, pp. 106–28.

Racine, T. Carpendale, J.I.M. and Turnbull, W. (2007), 'Parent-Child Talk and Children's Understanding of Beliefs and Emotions', *Cognition and Emotion*, **21**, pp. 480–94.

Ramsey, W.M. (2007), *Representation Reconsidered* (Cambridge: Cambridge University Press).

Ratcliffe, M. (2007), *Rethinking Commonsense Psychology: A Critique of Folk Psychology, Theory of Mind and Simulation* (Basingstoke: Palgrave Macmillan).

Ratcliffe, M. (2008), 'Farwell to Folk Psychology: A Response to Hutto', *International Journal of Philosophical Studies*, **16**, pp. 445–51.

Ratcliffe, M. (2009), 'There are no Folk Psychological Narratives', *Journal of Consciousness Studies*, **16**, No. 6–8, pp. 379–406.

Ratcliffe, M. and Hutto, D. (2007), 'Introduction' in Hutto and Ratcliffe (ed. 2007).

Reddy, V. and Morris, P. (2004), 'Participants Don't Need Theories: Knowing mind in engagement', *Theory and Psychology*, **14**, pp. 647–65.

Richardson, R. (2007), *Evolutionary Psychology as Maladapted Psychology* (Cambridge, MA: MIT Press).

Rizzolatti, G. and Sinigaglia, C. (2006), *Mirrors in the Brain: How Our Minds Share Actions and Emotions* (Oxford: Oxford University Press).

Samuels, R. (2000), 'Massively Modular Minds: Evolutionary Psychology and Cognitive Architectures' in *Evolution and the Human Mind: Modularity, Language and Meta-Cognition*, ed. P Carruthers, A Chamberlain (Cambridge: Cambridge University Press).

Scalise Sugiyama, M. (1996), 'On the Origins of Narrative: Storyteller Bias as a Fitness-Enhancing Strategy', *Human Nature,* **7**, pp. 403–25.

Scalise Sugiyama, M. (2001), 'Food, Foragers, and Folklore: The role of narrative in human subsistence', *Evolution and Human Behavior,* **22**, pp. 221–40.

Scalise Sugiyama, M. (2003), 'Cultural Variation is Part of Human Nature: Literary universals, context-sensitivity and "Shakespeare in the bush"', *Human Nature,* **14**, pp. 383–96.

Scalise Sugiyama, M. (2005), 'Reverse-engineering Narrative' in *The Literary Animal*, ed. J Gottschall, DSW Wilson (Evanston, Illinois: Northwestern University Press).

Scalise Sugiyama, M. (2008), 'Narrative as Social Mapping — Case Study: The trickster genre and the free rider problem', *Ometeca,* **12**, pp. 24–42.

Shelley, M. (2003/1817), *Frankenstein or the Modern Prometheus* (Ann Arbor: Border Classics).

Sinha, C. (2005), 'Blending out of the Background: Play, props and staging in the material world', *Journal of Pragmatics,* **37**, pp. 1537–54.

Sinigaglia, C. (2008), 'Mirror Neurons: This is the question', *Journal of Consciousness Studies,* **15**, pp. 70–92.

Slors, M. and MacDonald, C. (2008), 'Rethinking Folk Psychology: Alternatives to Theories of Mind', *Philosophical Explorations,* **11**, pp. 153–61.

Sorell, T. (1991), *Scientism: Philosophy and its Infatuation with Science* (London: Routledge).

Sparaci, L. (2008), 'Embodying Gestures: The social orienting model and the study of early gestures in autism', *Phenomenology and the Cognitive Sciences,* **7**, pp. 203–23.

Sterelny, K. (2003), *Thought in a Hostile World* (Oxford: Blackwell).

Sterelny, K. (2006), 'Language, Modularity and Evolution' in *Teleosemantics*, ed. G MacDonald, D Papineau (Oxford: Oxford University Press).

Stich, S. and Ravenscroft, I. (1996), 'What is Folk Psychology?' in *Deconstructing the Mind* (Oxford: Oxford University Press).

Stueber, K.R. (2008), 'Reasons, Generalizations, Empathy, and Narratives: The epistemic structure of action explanation', *History and Theory,* pp. 19–30.

Tomasello, M. (2003), *Constructing a Language: A Usage-Based Theory of Language Acquisition* (Cambridge, MA: Harvard University Press).

Tooby, J. and Cosmides, L. (1995), 'Foreword' in *Mindblindness: An Essay on Autism and Theory of Mind*, ed. S Baron-Cohen, pp. ix-xviii. (Cambridge, MA: MIT Press).

Williamson, T. (2007), *The Philosophy of Philosophy* (Oxford: Blackwell).

Wittgenstein, L. (1974), *On Certainty* (Oxford: Basil Blackwell).

Zahavi, D. (2007), 'Self and Other: The limits of narrative understanding' in *Narrative and Understanding Persons*, ed. DD Hutto. Royal Institute of Philosophy Supplement. (Cambridge: Cambridge University Press).

Zawidzki, T. (2008), 'The Function of Folk Psychology: Mind reading or mind shaping?', *Philosophical Explorations,* **11**, pp. 193–210.

Zlatev, J. Racine, T. Sinha, C. and Itkonen E. (ed. 2008), *The Shared Mind: Perspectives on Intersubjectivity* (Amsterdam/Philadelphia: John Benjamins).

Zunshine, L. (2006), *Theory of Mind and the Novel: Why We Read Fiction* (Columbus: Ohio State University Press).

David Herman

Storied Minds

Narrative Scaffolding for Folk Psychology

Abstract: Using Ian McEwan's 2007 novel On Chesil Beach as a case study, this paper seeks to enhance opportunities for dialogue between researchers in the cognitive sciences and scholars of story. More specifically, now that narrative alternatives to theories of mind have begun to shape debates about the nature and status of folk psychology, it is time to flesh out those alternatives by highlighting the action-modelling capacity built into the structure of stories. Narrative practices like McEwan's demonstrate how stories can be used to configure and reconfigure characters' behaviour from different temporal, spatial, and evaluative standpoints, in the way that a complex molecule or architectural structure can be displayed and manipulated in virtual space with the help of an advanced computer graphics program. In turn, interpreting narrative as a system for building models of action underscores the relevance of narratology for the philosophy of mind — and vice versa.

1. Interfaces Between Narrative and Mind

Scholars of narrative have recently begun drawing on developments in the cognitive sciences, including cognitive, evolutionary, and social psychology, Artificial-Intelligence research, language theory, neuroscience, and the philosophy of mind, to explore how frameworks for studying intelligent behaviour can throw light on storytelling practices as well as the narrative artifacts that emanate from them. Some of the research conducted in this domain — the domain of cognitive narratology, broadly speaking — has explored how interpreting stories depends on the same processes of folk-psychological reasoning that people deploy in everyday life to make sense of their own and others' conduct.[1] At issue is people's everyday understanding of how thinking works, the rough-and-ready heuristics to which they resort in thinking about thinking itself. We use these heuristics to impute motives or goals to others, to evaluate the bases of our own conduct, and to make predictions about future reactions to events. Daniel Dennett characterizes such folk-psychological rules of thumb in the following way: '[v]ery roughly, folk psychology has it that *beliefs* are information-bearing states of people that arise from perceptions and that, together with appropriately related *desires*, lead to intelligent *action*' (1987, p. 46).

For example, I will rely on broadly similar heuristics to make sense of the behaviour of the protagonists of two, ostensibly quite different movies, which evoke geographically and culturally disparate storyworlds that are also many centuries apart: Ridley Scott's *Gladiator* (2000) and Michael Winner's *Death Wish* (1974). In both narratives I can understand what is going on by assuming that the protagonists pursue courses of action motivated by the same underlying goal, namely, avenging the murder of loved ones. Indeed, interpreting both narratives as instantiations of the revenge-plot is tantamount to finding in these films the same basic interlocking structure of beliefs and desires — specifically, beliefs concerning the need to punish those who have committed offences against family members and desires converging on states of affairs in which the initiating offences have been met with equal and opposite inflictions of injury on the guilty parties. But I will also recognize the two narratives to be separable tokens of the revenge-plot type, since in one case the chief target of the revenge is a single, obviously evil individual and in the other the target is much more diffuse, with the movie thereby shading off into an apology for vigilantism.

Likewise, when I begin reading Ian McEwan's 2007 novel *On Chesil Beach*, which opens with two inexperienced and under informed newlyweds trying to navigate the complexities of their wedding night on the eve of the sexual revolution in England in 1963, I

---

[1] Cognitive narratology can be characterized as the study of mind-relevant aspects of story-telling practices, wherever — and by whatever means — those practices occur. Theorists working in this domain (e.g., Fludernik, 1996; Herman, 2002; 2003a; 2006; 2008; 2009; Jahn, 2005; Palmer, 2004; Zunshine, 2006) have sought to enrich earlier scholarship on stories with ideas about human intelligence either ignored by or inaccessible to previous narratologists, in an effort to build new foundations for the study of cognitive processes vis-à-vis various dimensions of narrative structure.

can make sense of this account by ascribing initially a range of beliefs, desires, emotions, intentions, and goals to the inhabitants of the storyworld. I will assume, for example, that though they live during a time in which for many people it was difficult if not impossible to communicate openly about such matters, each of the newlyweds believes (and believes that the other believes) that people typically have sexual intercourse on their wedding night. I will also assume that each desires (and believes that the other desires) to avoid being embarrassed or discomfited by events associated with their wedding-night encounter. Then, as I read further, in order to follow the unfolding plot I will need to fine-tune my interpretation of the newlyweds' understanding of and attitudes toward what is going on in the world of the narrative, focusing in particular on potentially conflict-generating asymmetries in their beliefs, desires, and intentions. If (as turns out to be the case) the two main characters believe quite different things about — and desire different things from — their wedding night and also the marriage for which it can be taken to be a kind of prelude or synecdoche, then I will look for the resulting mismatch of beliefs, attitudes, and goals to bring about a tragic finale or, alternatively, an eventual, more or less hard-fought dovetailing of the characters' purposes and values. Spoiler alert: true to form, McEwan opts for the less uplifting of these two possible storylines!

To account for the assumptions and inferences that readers make about the minds of characters in storyworlds such as these, theorists of narrative have adapted research by evolutionary and cognitive psychologists (among others) suggesting that human beings' mind-reading ability is a biological endowment, a capacity passed down as a phylogenetic inheritance that is acquired in ontogeny — except for people with developmental impairments such as autism. As noted by Slors and Macdonald (2008), one of the cornerstones of this research is Premack and Woodruff's 1978 article 'Does the chimpanzee have a theory of mind?', which argues on the basis of experimental evidence that chimps may be able to detect humans' intentions. As Slors and Macdonald put it:

> This paper shaped the [Theory of Mind] debate, on the one hand, by high-lighting two crucial presuppositions and, on the other, by engendering a discussion on the question of when an animal or person can be said to have a theory of mind. These presuppositions and discussion help to introduce the two main players in the debate, the theory-theory and the simulation theory. The first presupposition behind Premack and Woodruff's paper is that to detect intentionality in the behaviour of others is to have some knowledge of the other's mind [= presupposition 1]. The

second presupposition is that in order to acquire such knowledge one needs to have some sort of theory [= presupposition 2] (2008, p. 154).

The two accounts of folk psychology that have been dominant within the philosophy of mind and related fields over the last several decades, and that have also informed cognitive-narratological research, took shape against the backdrop of these presuppositions. According to one account, which accepts both presuppositions 1 and 2, folk psychology is a kind of low-level theory; it is based on a set of rules or explanatory principles similar in kind to those associated with scientific theories, but targeted specifically at propositional attitudes such as *believing X* and motivational attitudes such as *desiring Y*. This account is standardly called 'theory theory', with some variants emphasizing how the theory at issue is an innate endowment, bestowed upon us in the form of an inherited Theory of Mind module, and others stressing the way children use a trial-and-error procedure to build up and refine a theory of the minds of others — just as scientists (dis)confirm theories about the structure of the world on the basis of observational data. According to the second account, which denies presupposition 2 but at least on some versions accepts presupposition 1 (Slors and Macdonald, 2008, p. 156), folk psychology is a simulative ability, that is, an ability to project oneself imaginatively into a given scenario involving one's cohorts (or at least conspecifics). By running off-line a simulation of what one would do in similar circumstances, one can explain or predict what another has done or will do in the target scenario. This account is standardly called 'simulation theory'.[2]

Analysts of narrative have attempted to map aspects of theory theory (e.g., Zunshine, 2006) as well as simulation theory (e.g., Currie, 2004) onto the heuristics used by interpreters to make sense of characters' actions in storyworlds (for additional discussion, see Herman, 2006, pp. 371–4; and 2008, pp. 249–52; Palmer, 2004, pp. 143–7). But more recent developments in philosophy of mind, developmental psychology, and other fields have weakened support for both theory- and simulation-based models of folk psychology, pointing up the need for new approaches to studying the interfaces between narrative and mind. One such approach would involve factoring into the research on narrative understanding — that is, the interpretation of narratively organized texts or discourses — the alternatives to theories of mind alluded to in the title of Slors and Macdonald's special journal issue on that topic. These alternatives are united by their shared rejection of

[2] For more details about these two accounts, see e.g. Gallagher (2005), Hutto (2007a; 2007b; 2008), Nichols and Stich (2003), Slors and Macdonald (2008), and Zahavi (2007).

both presuppositions 1 and 2, as characterized above, and thereby raise questions about how parties to storytelling performances in face-to-face interaction, readers of novels, and viewers of films go about interpreting the beliefs, motivations, and goals of characters in narrative worlds.

For example, in Gallagher's interaction theory (2005, pp. 206–36), '[t]he understanding of the other person is primarily neither theoretical nor based on an internal stimulation. It is a form of embodied practice' (p. 208), and even 'in those cases where we do use theoretical and simulation strategies, these strategies are already shaped by a more primary embodied practice' (p. 208). Grounded in the phenomenological tradition as developed by Merleau-Ponty, interaction theory suggests that crucial aspects of understanding another are lodged in the process of interaction itself.[3] Hence the notion that in interacting with others we must 'theorize about an unseen belief, or "mind-read", is problematic' (p. 212) — as is the assumption that interaction with others is detached or 'spectatorial' (cf. Hutto, 2008, pp. 1–21), involving the formulation, from a third-person perspective, of explanations or predictions of others' behaviour. Rather, '[o]nly when second-person pragmatic interactions or our evaluative attempts to understand break down do we resort to the more specialized practices of third-person explanation and prediction' (Gallagher, 2005, p. 213).[4] Along the same lines, drawing on the work of phenomenologists like Max Scheler as well as Wittgenstein and other commentators, Zahavi (2007) argues that whereas both theory theory and simulation theory are based on the assumption that it is impossible to '*experience* other minded creatures', in this alternative philosophical tradition 'affective and emotional states are not simply qualities of subjective experience, rather they are given *in* expressive phenomena, i.e., they are expressed in bodily gestures and actions, and they thereby become visible to others' (p. 30). Hence, under 'normal circumstances, we understand each other well enough through our shared engagement in this common world, and it is only if this pragmatic understanding for some reason breaks down, for instance if the other behaves in an unexpected and puzzling way, that other options kick in and take over, be it inferential

---

[3]   Compare here Bruner's remark: 'Only by replacing [a] transactional model of mind with an isolating individualistic one have Anglo-American philosophers been able to make Other Minds seem so opaque and impenetrable' (1990, p. 33).

[4]   Similarly, Stawarska (2007) suggests that 'received thinking about folk psychology. ... privileges *a third-person approach* towards one's fellow beings, *about* whom one needs to theorize or whom one needs to model by means of simulational routines, [to] the exclusion of the *second-person* approach, where the interaction is a direct source of mutual understanding' (p. 79).

reasoning or some kind of simulation' (p. 38).[5] When I hear, read, or see a narrative representation, do I approach the characters in the world of the story using the same judgment heuristics, action routines, and embodied practices that orient my understanding of others in the everyday world, the world of the here and now? Do I engage with a written narrative told in the first person in the same way that I engage with a story told by an interlocutor in face-to-face interaction, despite the absence, in written texts, of gestural productions, prosodic cues, and other expressive resources regularly used in spoken discourse? And is the adoption of a third-person or spectatorial stance toward characters' minds in fact warranted in the case of, for example, graphic narratives using word-image combinations to represent characters (superheroes, say) acting and interacting in fictional worlds that are more or less dissimilar to the world of the here and now?

In the remainder of my discussion, I will largely bracket these and other questions about the folk-psychological competencies that might be required to make sense of actions represented in various kinds of narrative texts and instead focus on the converse issue: namely, how narrative itself provides scaffolding for folk psychology. This is a second way of (re)approaching the nexus of narrative and mind, this time in light of another recent alternative to theories of mind — namely, an alternative grounded in the practice of telling stories about what people have done and why they may have done that. Outlined initially by Bruner (1990; 1991), who argued that 'the organizing principle of folk psychology [is] narrative in nature rather than logical or categorical' (1990, p. 42), this alternative has been extended and refined by Hutto under the heading of the Narrative Practice Hypothesis (NPH) (Hutto, 2007a; 2008). Rather than focusing on ways in which narrative interpretation entails an attempt to make sense of characters' minds, both Bruner's work and Hutto's NPH suggest that storytelling practices are a basis for being able to make sense of minds in the first place — that is, for the ability to formulate appropriate, well-structured accounts of people's reasons for acting.

In what follows, after providing more details about this narrative alternative to theories of mind, I work to synthesize Bruner's and Hutto's insights with ideas developed by story analysts, in an effort further to substantiate the claim that narrative affords scaffolding for

---

[5] Although Hutto does not deny that heuristics of the sort discussed by theory theorists and simulation theorists come into play when people speculate about how others may have acted in the past or how they might act in the future, he argues that these are supplemental rather than primary methods for doing folk psychology — methods to which people resort when they 'lack direct and reliable access to the narratives of others' (2008, p. 5).

folk psychology. Returning to *On Chesil Beach* as a case study, I draw on this scholarship on stories to suggest how narrative as practiced by writers like McEwan furnishes a powerful technology for building models of action sequences. Such models enable storytellers and story-recipients to assess the motivations, structure, and consequences of actions by varying perspectival and attitudinal stances toward those actions and the situations in which they occur. Narrative can also be used to manipulate time-scales so as to compress or elongate event-chains, and to reorder events in ways that allow for targeted assessments of particularly salient links within those chains; to cluster together — or 'emplot' — discrete behaviours into goal-directed patterns of action, which both shape and are shaped by the material and sociocultural environments in which they unfold; and to generate and cross-compare counterfactual scenarios that allow the domain of the actual to be profiled against a larger universe of possibilities, such that what might have been can be used to take the measure of what has come to be. Although I will not have space here to explore in detail every aspect of this system for model construction, I do mean to suggest how stories embed a whole technology for action-modelling, perfected over millenia and distributed across the world's cultural (including literary) traditions. This technology makes narrative a unique resource for designing and testing folk-psychological accounts of people's actions based on their reasons for acting. My overarching argument is that, now that narrative alternatives to theories of mind have begun to shape debates about the nature and status of folk psychology, it is time to flesh out those alternatives by highlighting the action-modelling capacity built into the structure of stories — a capacity that can be illuminated via the large and growing body of research on narrative itself.[6]

In this respect the present discussion seeks to move a step beyond the pattern of argumentation that is typical in the domain of 'post-classical' narratology (Herman, 1999), or the ongoing attempt to develop frameworks for narrative study that build on classical, structuralist models but supplement that research with concepts and methods that were unavailable to earlier theorists such as Roland Barthes, Gérard Genette, A.J. Greimas, and Tzvetan Todorov. Whereas studies in this domain characteristically draw on work in other fields (linguistics, literary theory, social psychology, folklore, philosophy, etc.) to rethink core aspects of narrative structure and

---

[6]   See section 3.3 below for a discussion of how the account of story-based action models developed here relates to other recent characterizations of folk psychology as a species of 'model-based understanding' (Godfrey-Smith, 2005, p. 5).

narrative understanding, my own analysis suggests how the enriched accounts of narrative that result can be brought to bear, in turn, on problems in the disciplines from which story analysts have borrowed. Thus, whereas the strand of narrative scholarship mentioned earlier stresses the advantages of adapting ideas from the cognitive sciences to study how readers make sense of characters' actions and interactions, by contrast I mean to emphasize here the way traditions of narrative research can not only recruit from but also productively inform debates in the philosophy of mind, among other domains of cognitive science.[7] Indeed, the chief goal of my contribution is to enhance possibilities for genuine dialogue between theories of narrative, on the one hand, and research in the cognitive sciences, on the other.

2. Storytelling Practices and Folk Psychology: Narrative Alternatives to Theories of Mind

Bruner's suggestion that folk psychology is narrative in nature stems from his broader interest in building foundations for a cultural psychology, a psychology based on the idea that 'culture ... shapes human life and the human mind, [and] gives meaning to action by situating its underlying intentional states in an interpretive system' (1990, p. 34; cf. Cole, 1996). For Bruner, folk psychology is at the base of cultural psychology. It constitutes the interpretive system that allows actions to be dovetailed with intentional states, and narrative is, in turn, that system's organizing principle (p. 35). Hence the study of folk psychology requires analysing the 'elementary beliefs or premises that enter into the narratives about human plights of which folk psychology consists' (p. 39).[8] One such premise is that people have beliefs and desires, that they value some things more than others, and that their beliefs, desires, and values are more or less coherent — such that a person who intensely dislikes the colour yellow but then uses that same colour to paint the walls of his or her study would present something of a puzzle in folk-psychological terms. Indeed, it is

---

[7] In this way I seek to avoid the unidirectional borrowing — i.e., the importation of ideas from the cognitive sciences into traditions of narrative study but not vice versa — that Sternberg (2003) rightly characterizes as problematic.

[8] Bruner interestingly notes that the very term *folk psychology* was '[c]oined in derision by the new cognitive scientists for its hospitality toward such intentional states as beliefs, desires, and meanings' (1990, p. 36). Research on the subject began with studies of the structure of indigenous classification systems, and found support in the ethnomethodological work inspired by Harold Garfinkel, which sought to create 'a social science by reference to the social and political and human distinctions that people under study made in their everyday lives', as well as in Heider's studies of the native psychological theorizing that orients people's encounters with one another (pp. 37–8).

precisely when puzzles of this kind surface that the 'narratives of folk psychology' are needed: 'When anybody is seen to believe or desire or act in a way that fails to take the state of the world into account, to commit a truly gratuitous act, he is judged to be folk-psychologically insane unless he as an agent can be narratively reconstrued as being in the grip of a mitigating quandary or of crushing circumstances' (p. 40). The person with the yellow study may have honoured the wishes of a family member who loves yellow, for example, or may have been guided by a painfully thoroughgoing asceticism that requires doing the opposite of what one most desires. The more general point here is that 'while a culture must contain a set of norms, it must also contain a set of interpretive procedures for rendering departures from those norms meaningful in terms of established patterns of belief. It is narrative and narrative interpretation upon which folk psychology depends for achieving this kind of meaning. Stories achieve their meanings by explicating deviations from the ordinary in a comprehensible form' (p. 47).

Thus, for Bruner, the narrative organization of folk psychology can be traced to two key aspects of narrative: first, the way stories provide a means for explicating actions in terms of reasons for acting — reasons that concern how beliefs, desires, and values hang together for a particular agent or group of agents in a given set of circumstances; and second, the way narrative both emerges from and also provides a way of cognitively managing the dialectic of 'canonicity and breach', the interplay between expectations fulfilled and expectations violated, that characterizes everyday social experience (Bruner, 1991, pp. 11–3). Here in fact Bruner's account harmonizes with major traditions of narrative scholarship. Building on the work of Vladimir Propp (1928/1968), who characterized disruptive events (e.g., acts of villainy) as the motor of narrative, the narratologist Tzvetan Todorov (1968) sought to capture the intuition that stories prototypically involve a more or less marked disruption of what is expected or canonical. More specifically, Todorov argued that narratives characteristically follow a trajectory leading from an initial state of equilibrium, through a phase of disequilibrium, to an endpoint at which equilibrium is restored (on a different footing) because of intermediary events — though not every narrative will trace the entirety of this path (see also Bremond, 1980; Kafalenos, 2006). Indeed, for many story analysts, narrativity, or the set of properties that make a given text or discourse (more or less) amenable to being interpreted as a narrative, is inextricably interlinked with the way stories figure forth disruption in the order of a world, the violation of an established and therefore expected course of events (Herman, 2009, pp. 105–36). By the same token, the nexus between narrative and the non-canonical makes storytelling an ideal instrument for navigating the gap, in everyday experience, between what was expected and what actually takes place. When a generally timely person misses an appointment or a normally polite colleague makes a rude remark (or a yellow-hater paints his or her room yellow), stories frame such exceptional behaviours in a way that 'implicates both an intentional state in the protagonist (a belief or desire) and some canonical element in the culture. ... *The function of the story is to find an intentional state that mitigates or at least makes comprehensible a deviation from a canonical cultural pattern*' (Bruner, 1990, pp. 49–50). Narrative, then, provides scaffolding for formulating reasons about why, in the face of more or less entrenched expectations to the contrary, people engage in (or fail to engage in) the actions that they do.

Demonstrating the relevance of Bruner's insights for recent debates in the philosophy of mind, Hutto's Narrative Practice Hypothesis (2007a; 2008) likewise construes narrative as a primary resource for folk psychology. For Hutto, too, '[n]arratives are a potent means for establishing local standards about which actions are acceptable, which kinds of events are important and noteworthy, and even what constitutes having a good reason for acting' (2008, p. 38). But the NPH is framed explicitly as an alternative to theories of mind, in Slors and Macdonald's (2008) sense. Specifically, the NPH suggests that, rather than entailing mastery of a theory or a set of rules, and rather than requiring that people run off-line simulation routines that enable them to project themselves into the situation of others, folk psychology is a matter of practical know-how or skill. More specifically still, the NPH holds that interpreting and producing narratives is the means by which humans 'become skilled at the practice of predicting, explaining and explicating actions by appeal to reasons of the sort that minimally have belief/desire pairings at their core' (2007a, p. 44), a type of reasoning that Hutto characterizes as folk psychology in the strict sense. Accordingly, whenever a person's actions call for an explanation, it takes a 'folk psychological narrative' to construct an account based on that person's belief-set, contextual circumstances, and assumed desires given his or her beliefs and the circumstances in question.

Further, Hutto shares with Bruner an interest in how storytelling practices bear on the ontogeny of folk-psychological competence. Bruner argues that the early, culturally embedded and contextually triggered push to organize experience narratively regulates the process of language acquisition; he also suggests that learning the uses of narrative allows children to enter a culture in the first place, since, in everyday discourse, stories function not only to report but also to legitimize one's own actions vis-à-vis the beliefs, purposes, and values of members of one's family and broader community (1990, pp. 67–97). For his part, Hutto hypothesizes that it is through childhood engagement with narratives built around belief-desire schemata that humans learn the forms and norms of folk psychology, i.e., the forms folk-psychological reasoning needs to have as well as the norms for bringing such reasoning to bear. At the level of forms, the telling of stories about why characters were led to act in the way they did enables children to internalize narrative as a '*structural template* of means-end reasoning', into which particular beliefs and desires can be inserted, like arguments in place of variables (2007a, p. 57) and thus used to frame more or less complicated reasons for acting. At the level of norms, or protocols for the deployment of such folk-psychological accounts, the trigger for storytelling consists of just those violations of the expected or the canonical discussed by Bruner. Such violations require complex ascriptions of sets of propositional attitudes (goals, desires, thoughts, and beliefs) that the practice of narrative itself configures into well-formed reasons for the commission of non-canonical acts or the omission of canonical ones.

An important upshot of the NPH, and also of Bruner's work on storytelling as an entrée into folk psychology and hence into culture, is a new way of thinking about what Hutto calls the 'Universal Convergence Assumption' (2008, pp. 179–98) at work in debates within the philosophy of mind. According to some if not most researchers who hold this assumption (e.g., Botterill and Carruthers, 1999), the ability to make sense of intentional actions is instantiated in the same way across all (unimpaired) populations and thus best explained via an 'inherited mindreading device' (Hutto, 2008, p. 186). By contrast, Hutto suggests that the capacity to ascribe reasons for acting is 'acquired if and only if the right sociocultural practices exist and are exploited'. Although the NPH is not necessarily in tension with the Universal Convergence Assumption, since explaining actions in terms of reasons for acting could be a non-inherited but still pan-cultural phenomenon (like agriculture or, for that matter, storytelling), both the NPH and Bruner's precursor account stand in opposition to the view that folk-psychological abilities are a biological endowment, whether in the form of an inherited Theory of Mind module or any other phylogenetically transmitted mindreading device. Instead, given that in the narrative alternative to theories of mind folk-psychological competence emerges from storytelling practices, and given that such practices are socioculturally embedded, the narrative alternative can be affiliated with Lev Vygotsky's (1978) work on the social roots of human intelligence. If folk psychology in fact emerges through guided participation in storytelling practices, its origins would help bear out Vygotsky's broader sociocultural theory of ontogenetic development, according to which joint or intermental thinking precedes individual, intramental thinking.

Thus far, I have sketched out some of the motivations for and implications of the narrative alternative to theories of mind. Focusing on McEwan's *On Chesil Beach* as a test-case, my next section addresses more directly a key question to which proponents of the narrative alternative must be able to respond: namely, what is it about the structure of stories that makes them so well-suited to serve as scaffolding for folk psychology — scaffolding that has proven itself to be so durable, transportable, and serviceable, across both time and (cultural) space? Narrative's concern with the non-canonical is clearly only part of the answer, since lists, requests, commands and other non-narrative practices can likewise be used to represent departures from the normal or the expected. Answering more fully the question of what makes storytelling such a powerful instrument for folk psychology, I argue, requires a fuller engagement with recent frameworks for the study of stories — that is, a closer consideration of the relevance of narratology for the philosophy of mind.

3. Modelling Action Sequences through Story; or Why Narratology is Relevant for the Philosophy of Mind

Studying what makes stories especially suited for folk-psychological purposes is part of the broader enterprise of studying the 'tool' functions of narrative, and in particular its uses as a cognitive instrument or tool for thinking (Bruner, 1991; Herman, 2003; 2005; Scalise Sugiyama, 2005). Bruner (1991) describes narrative as a domain-specific 'symbolic system' that supports social cognition. For Bruner, the domain of social cognition is buttressed by principles and procedures that narrative provides as a 'cultural tool kit' (1991, p. 4). On the basis of this narrative toolkit social experience can be parsed into goal-directed actions that are embedded in and help define larger sequences of events, while also being refracted through some vantage-point or perspective on the world. These actions, highly particularised yet also linked to familiar genres (such as the revenge-plot described at the beginning of this essay), can also be construed as reinforcing a

community's sense of what is normal and normative even as they reg-
ister non-canonicality; and what is more, they can be cobbled together
to form more extended histories and entire cultural traditions (see
Bruner, 1990, p. 77; 1991, pp. 6–20). In my own earlier study (Herman,
2003, pp. 172–85), meanwhile, I characterized stories' functions as
domain-general and thus applicable for a broad variety of problem-
solving activities. I focused on five overlapping problem-solving
activities that extend beyond the domain of social experience and
argued that storytelling provides crucial support for all of those activities.[9] The five species of problem-solving include (1) 'chunking'
experience into workable segments; (2) imputing causal relations
between events; (3) managing problems with the typification of phenomena, i.e., the use of 'commonsense constructs of the reality of
daily life' (Schutz, 1962, p. 6); (4) sequencing behaviours, including
(4a) communicative behaviours bound up with the production and
interpretation of stories and (4b) the courses of action represented or
modelled in storyworlds; and (5) distributing intelligence. In connection with (5), storytelling can be used to promote the shared construction and revision of accounts of how the world is, embed non-current
scenarios within a current context of talk, and facilitate the methods of
reasoning about the actions of self and other that constitute the focus
of the narrative alternative to theories of mind.

In the present section, I use McEwan's novel to zoom in on just one
subcategory within this taxonomy of functions — namely, (4b) or the
employment of stories to model courses of action in more or less
richly detailed worlds. Recent frameworks for narrative research help
illuminate this action-modelling capacity of narrative, which in turn
helps account for the role of narrative in the distribution of intelligence, per category (5), and in particular its salience for reasoning
about the actions of self and other. I should note further that in characterizing narrative as a resource for constructing models of the structure, motivations, and consequences of actions in sociocultural as well
as material environments, I am drawing on the broad sense of *model*

---

[9] In a move that likewise extends beyond the realm of social experience the domain of phenomena for which narrative provides tools for thinking, Hutto associates stories with singular causal explanations. At issue are explanations of particular happenings, which
involve selecting relevant events, ordering them sequentially, and identifying the properties that will make the events intelligible within a particular explanatory context or idiom
(2008, pp. 10–11; cf. Herman 2003, pp. 175–8). For his part, however, Bruner seeks to dis-
sociate stories from causal accounts: 'The loose link between intentional states and subsequent action is the reason why narrative accounts cannot provide causal explanations.
What they supply instead is the basis for *interpreting* why a character acted as he or she
did. Interpretation is concerned with "reasons" for things happening, rather than strictly
with their "causes"' (1991, p. 7; cf. Malle, 2001).

explicated by Hodges (2005): 'you model a system or structure that you plan to build, by writing a description of it' (section 5, para. 44). Likewise, the *Oxford English Dictionary* defines model not only in the Tarskian sense of '[a] set of entities that satisfies all the formulae of a given formal or axiomatic system' (definition 8b; cf. Suppes 1960, p. 290), but also as '[a] simplified or idealized description or conception of a particular system, situation, or process, often in mathematical terms, that is put forward as a basis for theoretical or empirical understanding, or for calculations, predictions, etc.; a conceptual or mental representation of something' (definition 8a).[10] Yet what distinguishes the narrative modelling of actions from other species of model-construction is that here the model need not present simplified or idealized versions of the kinds of acting-situation being represented — to use von Wright's (1966) term for the environments in which particular courses of action are pursued in lieu of other possible courses (cf. Herman, 2002, pp. 53–84). Narrative models, rather, stand in a distinctive, perhaps sui generis relationship with the systems of action and interaction on which they are brought to bear, and from which they also emerge.

Admittedly, in folktales and (some) myths the lines between villainy and heroism may be starkly drawn; in these contexts narrative representations of action embody the simplifying and idealizing functions standardly attributed to models (see Godfrey-Smith, 2005, pp. 2–4; Hodges, 2005). But complex narratives like McEwan's purposely inhibit such ready value assignments, instead foregrounding the process by which reasons for acting come to be assessed. Stories of this kind are built in such a way as to compel consideration of characters' motives, means, and circumstances, through perspective-shifting, movements backward and forward along the time-line of events, and other representational strategies. Indeed, the potential isomorphism between the complexity of everyday acting-situations and the complexity of the acting-situations modelled in narrative practices like McEwan's may in itself help explain the special fitness of storytelling for folk-psychological purposes. In this case (perhaps uniquely?) the model *does* merge with the thing, the map with the territory. In turn,

---

[10] Hodges (2005, section 5, para. 45) observes that the English word *model* derives from late Latin *modellus*, which denotes a measuring device. Over time, this term generated three English words: *mould*, *module*, and *model*. Meanwhile, the *OED* lists definitions ranging from '[a] summary, epitome, abstract; the argument of a literary work', through '[a]n object or figure made in clay, wax, etc., as an aid to the execution of the final form of a sculpture or other work of art; a maquette', to '[a] person or thing eminently worthy of imitation; a perfect exemplar of some excellence'. See Herman (forthcoming) for a fuller discussion.

as I discuss in section 3.3, work by story analysts suggesting that narrative can be construed as a technology for building models of action needs to be brought into closer dialogue with recent attempts by philosophers to characterize folk-psychological reasoning itself as facility with a model (Andrews, 2009 [this issue]; Godfrey-Smith, 2005; Maibom, 2003; 2009 [this issue]).

3.1 On Chesil Beach: Some key actions and events

A somewhat fuller synopsis of McEwan's novel than that given in my first section will provide further context for the ensuing discussion, which explores dimensions of narrative structure — in particular, aspects of narrative temporality — that make stories optimal equipment for the modelling of (sequences of) actions. Opening *in medias res* with an account of the tense wedding-night situation described previously — 'They were young, educated, and both virgins on this, their wedding night, and they lived in a time when a conversation about sexual difficulties was impossible' (McEwan, 2007, p. 3) — the first chapter of the novel explores the characters' states of mind as they sit down to dinner in their honeymoon suite in a Georgian inn in Dorset, England. For Edward Mayhew, the groom, and the son of a father who is headmaster of a primary school and a mother who suffered brain-damage because of a freak accident on a railway platform, the idea of having sex with his new wife is at once tantalizing and a source of worry: 'For over a year, Edward had been mesmerized by the prospect that on the evening of a given date in July the most sensitive portion of himself would reside, however briefly, within a naturally formed cavity inside this cheerful, pretty, formidably intelligent woman. How this was to be achieved without absurdity, or disappointment, troubled him' (pp. 7–8). But for Florence Mayhew (née Ponting), a professional musician-in-the-making whose mother is a professor of philosophy and whose father owns an electronics company, the prospect of consummating her marriage with Edward is the cause of deep, paralyzing anxiety.[11] Thus, whereas Edward 'merely suffered conventional first-night nerves, she experienced a visceral dread, a helpless disgust as palpable as seasickness' (p. 8). What is more, '[h]er problem, she thought, was greater, deeper, than straightforward physical disgust; her whole being was in revolt against a

---

[11] Readers of *On Chesil Beach* familiar with Ford Madox Ford's 1915 novel *The Good Soldier* will recognize that the first names of McEwan's two main characters echo those of Edward Ashburnham and Florence Dowell, whose ill-fated, destructive affair is narrated *ex post facto* — and via a complex layering of time-frames — by Florence's perversely obtuse husband, John Dowell.

prospect of entanglement and flesh; her composure and essential happiness were about to be violated' (p. 10).

From this point until the final ten pages of McEwan's 203-page novel, the narrative alternates between, on the one hand, periodic shifts back in time that provide information about the main characters' family backgrounds, life stories, and courtship, and, on the other hand, a detailed, blow-by-blow recounting of the events of the present moment. The present-day events lead up to what proves to be a disastrous attempt at sexual intercourse by Edward and Florence and an angry, marriage-ending exchange on the beach — Chesil Beach — afterward. Then, in the final portion of the novel, the pace of narration speeds up drastically, covering some 40 years of story time in about 5% of the page space used previously to narrate events lasting just a few hours. Most of this final section is refracted through the vantage point of Edward, who eventually comes to the realization that though '[a]ll [Florence] needed was the certainty of his love, and his reassurance that there was no hurry when a lifetime lay ahead of them' (p. 202), on that night on Chesil Beach he had 'stood in cold and righteous silence in the summer's dusk, watching her hurry along the shore, the sound of her difficult progress lost to the breaking of small waves, until she was a blurred, receding point against the immense straight road of shingle gleaming in the pallid light' (p. 203).

Edward's and Florence's contrasting — indeed, clashing — stances toward their sexual encounter on their wedding night is one of the key interest-bearing features of the narrative. This complex, emotionally fraught acting-situation, momentous in its consequences for the characters' future life-courses, is also rooted in the characters' pasts and anchored in the cultural circumstances in which they find themselves. McEwan uses the powerful action-modelling resources of narrative to configure and reconfigure this situation from different temporal, spatial, and evaluative standpoints, in the way that a complex molecule or architectural structure can be displayed and manipulated in virtual space with the help of an advanced computer graphics program. Only in this case, the structure being modeled is itself a reason-driven process unfolding in time and space, its dynamic profile mirroring that of the apparatus — narrative — being used to construct a multidimensional model of action-sequences at issue. In my next subsection, I sketch how approaches to the study of time in narrative can illuminate aspects of this story-enabled construction procedure, narrative arguably being the action-modelling program *par excellence*.

3.2 Narrative structure for action modelling

Genette's (1972/1980) foundational work on narrative temporality, and subsequent refinements to his account proposed by later analysts (e.g. Herman, 2002, pp. 211–61; Sternberg, 1978), suggests how texts like McEwan's allow the motivations, structure, and consequences of actions to be examined from multiple positions in time. Stories, this research suggests, are a primary technology for making sense of how things unfold in time,[12] one that helps reveal how actions arise, how they are interrelated, and how much salience they should be assigned within a given environment for acting and interacting.

In the narratological tradition that Genette's work helped establish, narratives can be analysed into the dimensions or levels of *story* (= the basic sequence of states, actions, and events recounted); the *text* or *discourse* on the basis of which interpreters reconstruct that story; and the act of *narration* that produces the text. In this heuristic scheme, elements such as characters, their actions, and non-volitional events and happenings are aspects of story, whereas features of narrative time can be discussed in terms of all three dimensions. Flashforwards and flashbacks, for example, can be characterized as a non-correspondence between story order and discourse order. By contrast, the distinction between retrospective and simultaneous telling — a distinction discussed more fully below — turns on when the act of narration happens in relation to the events of the story (cf. Reichenbach, 1947, on *speech time* versus *event time*).

To capture the temporal relationships that obtain specifically between the story and text levels, Genette identified three sorts of relationship: duration, order, and frequency. Duration can be computed as a ratio between how long events take to unfold in the world of the story and how much text is devoted to their narration, with speeds ranging from descriptive pause to scene to summary to ellipsis. This aspect of the temporal system thus constitutes a metric of value or at least attentional prominence: in extended narratives the shift from rapidly surveyed backstory or expositional material to a slower, scenic mode of presentation can signal aspects of the storyworld valued (or at any rate noticed) by a narrator (cf. Sternberg, 1978). Meanwhile, order can be analysed by matching the sequence in which events are narrated against the sequence in which they can be assumed to have occurred, yielding chronological narration, analepses or flashbacks,

---

[12] Compare Abbott (2008): 'what does narrative do for us? ... if we had to choose one answer above all others, the likeliest is that *narrative is the principal way in which our species organizes its understanding of time*' (p. 3). See also Brockmeier (1995; 2009).

and prolepses or flashforwards, together with various sub-categories of these nonchronological modes. Finally, frequency can be calculated by measuring how many times an event is narrated against how many times it can be assumed to have occurred in the storyworld. Again, more than just a range of formal possibilities, frequency affords ways of allocating attention to and evaluating actions and events — with repetitive narration foregrounding some action or set of actions, iterative narration providing a summative gloss on multiple storyworld incidents, and singulative narration being the baseline metric in this context.

On Chesil Beach suggests the broad relevance of these categories for building models of action. As I discuss more fully below, McEwan manipulates narrative order in a way that frames the present moment within a longer life-course — a life-course stretching back into the past and extending forward into the future. By alternating between narration of what transpires on Florence's and Edward's wedding night, allusions to how their words and deeds will shape the future, and analeptic references to earlier actions and events that led them to this moment, the first 192 pages of the novel sketch out a constellation or network of behaviours that underscores how no action can be understood in isolation from the history of conduct from which it emerges, and on which it impinges in turn. In the final 10 pages, after the couple's angry exchange on the beach, McEwan shifts to a strictly chronological mode of narration but now resets the parameter of duration. Covering a relatively long period of time in a relatively short span of text, McEwan provides the narrative equivalent of time-lapse photography, enabling readers to witness the unfolding of the consequences of characters' actions over the longer term — especially for Edward.[13] And the parameter of frequency also comes into play. For reasons I explore below, the text repeatedly alludes to the sailing trips that Florence took with her father and also to actions associated with Florence's pursuit of a musical career, thereby highlighting the salience of these elements of the storyworld.

Likewise, when Genette distinguishes between simultaneous, retrospective, prospective, and 'intercalated' modes of narration (as in the epistolary novel, where the act of narration postdates some events

---

[13] Built into the narrative system, this capacity to vary duration so as to model long-term consequences of actions and events is not limited to fiction. Thus, in her memoir about the experience of being raped, *Lucky*, Alice Sebold devotes about 230 pages to the period immediately surrounding the rape (with many contextualizing flashbacks and flashforwards, as in McEwan's novel) and about 15 pages to an 'Aftermath' in which she covers decades — and thereby suggests just how long it took Sebold to start coming to terms with the traumatic experience.

but precedes others), he in effect identifies narrative modes that afford different kinds of structure for the modelling of characters' actions. In the case of simultaneous narration, like that used in sports broadcasts or on-site news reporting about events still underway, actions are presented in tandem with tellers' and interpreters' attempts to comprehend the contours and boundaries of the narrated domain; inferences about the impact of characters' doings on the larger history of the storyworld remain tentative, probabilistic, open-ended. By contrast, retrospective narration like McEwan's accommodates the full scope of a storyworld's history, allowing connections to be made between earlier and later actions and events. Narration of this sort allows for flashbacks to formative occasions as well as proleptic foreshadowings (anticipations-in-hindsight) of the eventual impact of a character's behaviour on his or her cohorts — and also of future events over which the characters have no control. For example, through the narrator's early evaluation of the food that Edward and Florence eat for their wedding-night dinner, McEwan's text signals a significant distance in time between the moment of narration and the events being recounted: 'This [i.e., the year 1963] was not a good moment in the history of English cuisine' (p. 5). Here the narrator's wry assessment implicitly suggests a larger temporal span within which this particular culinary moment can be located and judged to be deficient. In a manner that similarly positions events within a broader span of time, the narrator registers the enduring impact of what Florence and Edward do and say on their wedding night, noting how '[Florence] would torture herself with the memory of her part in [the angry exchange with Edward on the beach], but now she added, "It was absolutely revolting"' (p. 175) — referring with this utterance to events associated with her and Edward's unsuccessful attempt at sexual intercourse.

An extended instance of this strategy for temporal modelling, whereby actions and events are profiled against a longer time-span so that their implications can be evaluated more holistically, occurs late in the novel. Just after Florence turns away from Edward on the beach and walks back to the hotel, having said, 'I am sorry, Edward. I am most terribly sorry', the narrative continues:

> Her words, their particular archaic construction would haunt him for a long time to come. He would wake in the night and hear them, or something like their echo, and their yearning, regretful tone, and he would groan at the memory of that moment, of his silence and of the way he angrily turned from her, of how he then stayed out on the beach another hour, savouring the full deliciousness of the injury and wrong and insult

she had inflicted on him, elevated by a mawkish sense of himself as being wholesomely and tragically in the right (p. 192).

As in the passage concerning Florence's own tortured memories, McEwan uses the subjunctive verbal mood (*would torture herself with the memory, he would wake in the night*, etc.) to provide a kind of thumbnail sketch of actions that, rooted in the episode on the beach, take place repeatedly in the future.[14] Telescoping forward in time, the passage also compresses into a reportable sequence a ramified, temporally diffuse network of actions — thereby bringing into relation Edward's angry spurning of Florence's final gesture of conciliation and the years and indeed decades over the course of which that action bears the fruit of regret, self-analysis, and ultimately self-contempt. In this way narrative provides equipment for modelling how one action entails others over time, how an action performed at one temporal location can generate reasons for acting that are distributed across time.

Accordingly, stories not only require for their understanding but also provide a basis for building what Giora and Shen (1994) characterize as an *action structure*, i.e., 'a higher-order organization which hierarchically connects not only adjacent events ... but also events which are remote from one another on the temporal axis of a given discourse. Thus a story ... is more than pairwise relationships among events[; it is] a string of events combined into a psychological whole' (1994, p. 450). Thus far, I have been discussing how McEwan's text facilitates the construction of forward-pointing action structures, i.e., sequences of actions extending forward in time from the critical episode on which the narrative focuses; in such contexts narrative can be used to trace out the cascade of consequences flowing from any given action, i.e., the future behaviours for which it in turn constitutes reasons for acting.[15] But stories help us build action structures that extend backward in time, too. When narrative is used in this way, to turn

---

[14] In Genettean terms, this technique can be characterized as iterative narration, a mode of frequency in which what happens more than once is narrated only once.

[15] Along the dimension of modality rather than temporality, narrative also facilitates the construction of counterfactual scenarios that in turn support action-modelling through the cross-comparison of actual and non-actual occurrences. McEwan uses counterfactuals to suggest a larger background of event possibilities that define the acting-situations in which the characters find themselves, and that thus provide a context in which the consequentiality of their chosen actions can be profiled (cf. the concept of 'comparators' developed by Labov 1972, p. 381). Hence the heart wrenching counterfactual scenario included at the very end of the novel, as Edward looks back on events from his decades-later perspective: 'On Chesil Beach he could have called out to Florence, he could have gone after her. He did not know, or would not have cared to know, that as she ran away from him, certain in her distress that she was about to lose him, she had never

time's arrow back toward the past, it enables present actions to be explained in terms of a broader pattern of behaviours leading up to the moment at hand. Action structures of this sort are at the heart of Bruner's work as well as Hutto's account of the NPH, and McEwan's text places special emphasis on how past actions quite widely separated in time can be chained together into storylines trending toward — and helping account for — what is being done in the present moment (cf. Bruner, 1990, pp. 99–138). The historian Hayden White (2005) coined the term *emplotment* to describe this event-connecting dimension of narrative, and *On Chesil Beach* emphasizes the extent to which making sense of the minds of self and other entails emplotting actions as elements of a storyline terminating at some temporal point in the past. What is more, the novel also deploys third-person or heterodiegetic narration — narration produced by someone not involved in the events being reported — to stage what happens when the characters are unable to link past events to emergent storylines on which those events bear. This technique affords a two-layered environment for modelling actions, in which narration that moves backward and forward in time to situate and explicate actions recounts how the characters are also attempting, with more or less success, to construct storylines as a means for interpreting their own and others' actions.[16]

The narrative features a number of episodes in which the characters work to construct storylines of this sort — or at least sense the need for some kind of account that would bridge between the actions and events of the past and situations encountered in the present. For example, after the couple's ill-fated wedding-night encounter but before their angry conversation on the beach, Edward remembers an earlier episode in which Florence took him to see the performance space in Wigmore Hall. The text reads: 'The green room, the tiny changing room, even the auditorium and the cupola could hardly account, he thought, for her reverence for the place' (p. 152). Though Edward is unable to perform it here, the narrator's framing story suggests that some further work of narrative construction, by means of which Florence's reverential response could be integrated into a larger storyline and thus made sense of, is needed in this connection. Along similar lines, again in the time between Florence's sudden departure from the

---

loved him more, or more hopelessly, and that the sound of his voice would have been a deliverance, and she would have turned back' (p. 203).

[16] As explored in Herman (2006), the same basic structure can be found in framed narratives, i.e., narratives in which characters in the storyworld engage in the construction of other, embedded storyworlds by telling narratives in their own right.

hotel room and Edward's confrontation with her on the beach, the text signals a gappiness or 'penumbra of oblivion' (p. 160) in Edward's own memories that suggests some kind of active repression on his part — possibly (and here the larger framing narrative induces readers to engage in their own acts of narrative construction) repression stemming from Edward's anxieties concerning how his family's humble living situation might appear to Florence: 'They must have arrived at the cottage to find his mother alone — his father and the girls would have still been at school. ... Edward retained no impression of introducing Florence, or of how she responded to the crammed and squalid rooms, and the stench of drains. ... He had only snatches of memories of the afternoon, certain views, like old postcards' (pp. 160–1).

Most crucially, the text points to the need for narrative construction to make sense of the central conflict in the novel, namely, that between Edward's and Florence's attitudes toward the wedding night and all that it entails. What accounts for Florence's deep-seated revulsion at the prospect of sex with Edward? And by the same token, why is it that Edward reacts so angrily and impatiently to Florence's unorthodox but well-meant suggestion that they remain married but that Edward sleep with other women? For their part, Edward's actions are elements of a storyline stretching back through a history of violent outbursts. Edward, as the narrative reveals while the couple is still attempting to negotiate their difficult sexual encounter, did not trust himself: 'He was known to his university friends as one of those quiet types, prone to the occasional violent eruption. According to his father, his very early childhood had been marked by spectacular tantrums ... [and] he was drawn now and then by the wild freedom of a fistfight', in which he found 'a thrilling unpredictability, and discovered a spontaneous, decisive self that eluded him in the rest of his tranquil existence' (pp. 112–3). This passage points to a storyline whose explanatory power is sufficient to encompass both Edward's actions on his and Florence's wedding night and his decades-later realization that 'Love and patience — if only he had had them both at once — would surely have seen them both through' (pp. 202–3).

Meanwhile, Florence's attitudes toward and actions during her wedding night are rooted in a more diffuse — and difficult-to-build — action structure or storyline. Nodes of this narrative network surface at intervals in the text, beginning with Edward's reflection, while he and Florence are still dining, that she 'seemed able to get her rather frightening father to do what she wanted' (p. 20). Later, as part of the extended flashback that opens chapter 2, which begins 'How did they meet, and why were these lovers in a modern age so timid and innocent?' (p. 45), the narrative reveals that Florence's father used to take her out on his sailboat when she was twelve and thirteen (p. 62) and that he now 'aroused in her conflicting emotions' (p. 61). Sometimes Florence finds her father 'physically repellent and … could hardly bear the sight of him' (p. 62), but at other times 'in a surge of protective feeling and guilty love, she would come up behind where he sat and entwine her arms around his neck and kiss the top of his head and nuzzle him, liking his clean scent. She would do all this, then loathe herself for it later' (p. 62). And later still, as Edward undresses just before they attempt sexual intercourse in earnest, the smell of the sea summons up the past for Florence:

> She was twelve years old, lying still like this, waiting, shivering in the narrow bunk [on her father's sailboat] with polished mahogany sides. Her mind was a blank, she felt she was in disgrace [...] It was late in the evening and her father was moving about the dim cramped cabin, undressing, like Edward now. She remembered the rustle of clothes, the clink of a belt unfastened or of keys or loose change. Her only task was to keep her eyes closed and think of a tune she liked. Or any tune [...] She was usually sick many times on the crossing, and of no use to her father as a sailor, and that surely was the source of her shame (p. 123).

This passage, coupled with a later episode in which the couple's attempt at sex 'dragged with it the stench of a shameful secret locked in musty confinement' (p. 131), as well as Edward's intuition that father and daughter 'were intensely aware of each other' (p. 140) and that when Edward announced his intention to marry Florence Geoffrey Ponting was 'rather too keen to give his daughter away' (p. 141), allows for the construction of a storyline in which past sexual abuse by her father constitutes the reason for Florence's behaviour on her wedding night and also for her compensatory immersion in the world of music. Recall that early in the novel, while the couple is still dining in their hotel room, the narrator characterizes Florence's visceral dread of sexual intercourse as 'a helpless disgust as palpable as seasickness' (p. 8). Recall, too, Edward's earlier surmise that Florence showed disproportionate reverence for the space in which she hoped one day to perform with her quartet.

Yet even as it suggests the possibility of finding reasons for Florence's actions by integrating them into a tragic storyline of this sort, the novel signals the limits as well as the explanatory power of narrative constructions as such. Specifically, McEwan indicates the dangers associated with what might be called narrative overgeneration, or the construction of over-inclusive storylines under which any and all actions and events can be subsumed, and for which there is thus no criterion for falsification. This is the structure manifested in conspiracy narratives, for example, and it is also evident in the practices of confabulation in which Edward's brain-damaged mother engages: 'When Marjorie [Mayhew] announced that she was making a shopping list for Watlington market, or that she had more sheets to iron than she could begin to count, a parallel world of bright normality appeared within reach of the whole family. But the fantasy could be sustained only if it were not discussed' (pp. 84–5). In a similar manner, as he steels himself for his confrontation with Florence on the beach, Edward constructs a narrative in which Florence, a fraud through and through, has tricked him into marrying her: 'He [...] thought it through all over again, smoothing out the rough edges and difficult transitions, the bridging passages that lifted free of his own uncertainties, and so perfected his case, and felt as he did his anger surge again' (pp. 164–5). As the parallel between Edward's and his mother's narrative practices here suggests, efforts to make the story — any story — too neat jeopardizes the integrity and reliability of the action models that story is used to construct. The challenge is to strike a balance between narrative over-generation and narrative under-generation, confabulatory practices in which no action or event could give the lie to an account-under-construction, and the gappiness or incoherency characterizing models of action that are insufficiently supported by the scaffolding of story.

3.3 Narrative modelling vis-à-vis model theory

I will conclude this section by contrasting the account sketched here with previous attempts to characterize folk-psychological reasoning as facility with a model of human conduct. Notably, the story-enabled modelling procedure that I have used McEwan's narrative to illustrate can be distinguished from both theory- and simulation-based approaches to folk psychology, to which previous model-based accounts remain (more or less firmly) committed.

In her contribution to this special issue, Maibom draws on work in the philosophy of science to argue that folk psychology can be described as a process of explaining actions via models brought to bear on people's conduct. She holds that these models may or may not be instantiated in narrative form (see also Andrews, this issue), and that the models in fact lose their explanatory power in proportion with the degree to which they are embedded in particular circumstances, in the manner characteristic of stories. For Maibom, the role of models in theoretical explanations, coupled with their suitability for describing what goes on when people reason folk-psychologically, provides support for theory-based accounts: facility with a folk-psychological model translates into a capacity to deploy a theory of mind. For his part, Godfrey-Smith (2005) suggests that elements of theory theory and simulation theory can be blended if folk psychology is redescribed in terms of model-based understanding (p. 5). At issue is facility with more or less agreed-upon models of why people act in the way they do, which can in turn be construed in different ways in various kinds of situations (contrast using a given model of folk psychology to predict drivers' behaviour on the freeway with using it to reason about a defendant's state of mind in a court case [p. 10]). For Godfrey-Smith, theory-based approaches to folk psychology correspond to top-down methods for constructing model systems, where one 'begins with a general principle or pattern and then generates specific cases from it' (p. 8). By contrast, simulation-based approaches correspond to bottom-up modelling methods, in which the modeller seeks to work from local elements of the system being modelled to an understanding of how those elements interact in the target system. Here 'the interpreter uses his or her own reasoning mechanisms as a physical simulator of how a particular set of hypothetical beliefs and desires might interact', such that 'the role for prior general knowledge is very minimal indeed' (p. 8).

But story-based procedures for action modelling, as characterized above, can be distinguished from folk-psychological models as they are described by both Maibom and Godfrey-Smith. On the one hand, using such narrative procedures does not presuppose or entail having a theory of one's own or another's mind. Rather, it involves building a model of how *actions* are situated in time and (social) space, and of how they emerge from and impinge upon the larger pattern of actions that constitutes all or part of a person's life-course. Ascriptions of mental states to self and other are predicated on situated action models of this sort; that is, the mind is a function of emplotment — mental states derive from storylines — not the other way around. To put the same point yet another way, it is not that a model-based theory of mind enables the construction of a story of self or other; instead, the construction of the story facilitates reasoning about one's own and others' mental states by allowing them to be modelled as intermeshed with broader contexts for acting and interacting. This same approach undercuts Maibom's argument that, in folk-psychological as well as other forms of reasoning, explanatory power trades off with particularity. If links between behaviours and mental states always take shape in — are predicated on — particular contexts for acting, and if stories function as a technology for modelling those contexts, then narrative particularity is directly rather than inversely proportional with explanatory power.[17]

On the other hand, the narrative construction of action models should not be conflated with the process of running bottom-up, off-line simulations, by means of which one uses one's mind as a model to construe how elements of a target system interact — and thereby explain or predict what another has done or will do in a given scenario. Granted, narratives can in some contexts serve simulative functions, as when children (and adults!) identify themselves with superheroes or stories support simulation routines used for training purposes (the floor of your office building has caught fire and several coworkers have been injured; what will you do now?). Yet story-based action-modeling lends itself to non-simulative as well as simulative uses. Modelling actions through narrative is not tantamount to projecting oneself 'vertically' into a target scenario in order to impute to another the mental states one would likely have in that same situation, *mutatis mutandis*. Rather narrative-enabled modelling procedures can also be used 'horizontally', to locate behaviours, their motivations, and their consequences within an emergent storyline and a broader environment for action. Again, ascriptions of beliefs, desires, goals, and other mental states emerge from these horizontally constructed storylines, rather than providing the basis for them.

4. Extending this Pilot-Study: Directions for Further Inquiry

In this paper, I have used just one (literary) narrative to examine only one of the ways in which stories provide an optimal environment for coming to terms with the nature, sources, and implications of human conduct: namely, by allowing for the manipulation of the variable of time. Going forward, the approach sketched in this pilot-study needs to be developed in two main ways. On the one hand, the analysis needs to be extended to explore how the action-modelling system I have begun to describe via McEwan's narrative practices is harnessed in other kinds of situations. How exactly do interlocutors in contexts of face-to-face interaction, for example, recruit from this system to make sense of expectation-violating actions of another? For that matter, how do different kinds of communicative or situational exigencies — the norm-transgressing actions of a stranger or acquaintance versus a

---

[17] For a discussion of the more general issue of how narratives relate to explanations, see Herman (2009, pp. 100–4).

friend or family member — necessitate reliance on different aspects of the system in question? And do storytelling practices across different media anchor themselves differently in the system for modelling actions that narrative affords, such that it is easier to model certain kinds of actions in some narrative media than in others? If so, what specific constraints and affordances shape the action-modelling power of different forms of narrative practice?

On the other hand, more research is needed to clarify the nature of narrative models of action — that is, how various aspects of narrative structure contribute to the action-modelling capacity of stories. Shifts in narrative viewpoint, for example, afford multidimensional spatial models that complement those based on juxtapositions of different time-frames. In addition, narratives can be used to stage and comment on the deployment, by the characters in storyworlds, of standard folk-psychological categories — categories such as those associated with the operations of memory and emotion, for example. Along the same lines, stories can hold up for inspection folk understandings of the relation between the mental and physical domains, as when McEwan portrays Edward as feeling 'mentally cramped by unresolved desire' (p. 28; cf. pp. 147–8) or has him misconstrue Florence's behaviour as grounded in wholly transparent reasons for acting: 'How could he fail to love someone so strangely and warmly particular, so painfully honest and self-aware, whose every thought and emotion appeared naked to view, streaming like charged particles through her changing expressions and gestures?' (p. 19). Over the longer term, study of a range of narrative corpora associated with different cultures and epochs would facilitate research on the emergence, distribution, and transformation of such folk-psychological categories and understandings across time and space. But more genuine dialogue between narrative studies and the cognitive sciences will be needed to reconstruct this genealogy of concepts of mind.[18]

References

Abbott, H.P. (2008), *The Cambridge Introduction to Narrative* (Cambridge: Cambridge University Press).

Andrews, K. (2009), 'Telling Stories Without Words', *Journal of Consciousness Studies*, **16** (6–8), pp. 268–88. [This issue]

Botterill, G. & Carruthers P. (1999), *The Philosophy of Psychology* (Cambridge: Cambridge University Press).

[18] My work on this essay was supported by a research fellowship from the American Council of Learned Societies and a supplemental external fellowship subsidy awarded by the College of the Arts and Humanities at Ohio State University.

Bremond, C. (1980), 'The Logic of Narrative Possibilities', trans. E.D. Cancalon, *New Literary History*, **11**, pp. 387–411.

Brockmeier, J. (1995), 'The language of Human Temporality: Narrative Schemes and Cultural Meanings of Time', *Mind, Culture, and Activity*, **2**, pp. 102–18.

Brockmeier, J. (2009), 'Stories to Remember: Narrative and the Time of Memory', *Storyworlds: A Journal of Narrative Studies*, **1**, pp.115–32.

Bruner, J. (1990), *Acts of Meaning* (Cambridge, MA: Harvard University Press).

Bruner, J. (1991), 'The Narrative Construction of Reality', *Critical Inquiry*, **18**, pp. 1–21.

Cole, M. (1996), *Cultural Psychology: A Once and Future Discipline* (Cambridge, MA: Harvard University Press).

Currie, G. (2004), *Arts and Minds* (Oxford: Oxford University Press).

Dennett, D.C. (1987), *The Intentional Stance* (Cambridge, MA: MIT Press).

Fludernik, M. (1996), *Towards a 'Natural' Narratology* (London: Routledge).

Gallagher, S. (2005), *How the Body Shapes the Mind* (Oxford: Oxford University Press).

Genette, G. (1972/1980), *Narrative Discourse: An Essay in Method*, trans. J.E. Lewin (Ithaca: Cornell University Press).

Giora, R. & Shen Y. (1994), 'Degrees of Narrativity and Strategies of Semantic Reduction', *Poetics*, **22**, pp. 447–58.

Godfrey-Smith, P. (2005), 'Folk Psychology as a Model', *Philosophers Imprint*, **5** (6), pp. 1–16.

Herman, D. (1999), 'Introduction', in D. Herman (ed.) *Narratologies: New Perspectives on Narrative Analysis* (Columbus: Ohio State University Press), pp. 1–30.

Herman, D. (2002), *Story Logic: Problems and Possibilities of Narrative* (Lincoln: University of Nebraska Press).

Herman, D. (2003), 'Stories as a Tool for Thinking', in *Narrative Theory and the Cognitive Sciences* (Stanford, CA: CSLI Publications) pp. 163–92.

Herman, D. (2005), 'Narrative as Cognitive Instrument', in D. Herman, M. Jahn & M.L. Ryan (ed.), *Routledge Encyclopedia of Narrative Theory* (London: Routledge), pp. 349–50.

Herman, D. (2006), 'Genette meets Vygotsky: Narrative Embedding and Distributed Intelligence', *Language and Literature*, **15** (4), pp. 375–98.

Herman, D. (2008), 'Narrative Theory and the Intentional Stance', *Partial Answers*, **6** (2), pp. 233–60.

Herman, D. (2009), *Basic Elements of Narrative* (Oxford: Wiley-Blackwell).

Herman, D. (forthcoming), 'Formal Models in Narrative Analysis', in A. Doxiadis & B. Mazur (ed.), *Mathematics and Narrative*.

Hodges, W. (2005), 'Model theory', in E.N. Zalta (ed.), *The Stanford Encyclopedia of Philosophy* (Winter 2005 Edition), <http://plato.stanford.edu/archives/win2005/entries/model-theory/>.

Hutto, D.D. (2007a), 'The Narrative Practice Hypothesis: Origins and Applications of Folk Psychology', in Hutto, 2007b, pp. 43–68.

Hutto, D.D. (ed, 2007b), *Narrative and Understanding Persons*, Royal Institute of Philosophy Supplement, **60**.

Hutto, D.D. (2008), *Folk Psychological Narratives: The Sociocultural Basis of Understanding Reasons* (Cambridge, MA: MIT Press).

Jahn, M. (2005), 'Cognitive Narratology', in D. Herman, M. Jahn & M.-L. Ryan (ed.), *Routledge Encyclopedia of Narrative Theory* (London: Routledge), pp. 67–71.

Kafalenos, E. (2006), *Narrative Causalities* (Columbus: Ohio State University Press).

Labov, W. (1972), 'The Transformation of Experience in Narrative Syntax', in *Language in the Inner City* (Philadelphia: University of Pennsylvania Press), pp. 354–96.

Maibom, H. (2003), 'The Mindreader and the Scientist', *Mind and Language*, **18** (3), pp. 296–315.

Maibom, H. (2009), 'In Defence of Model Theory', *Journal of Consciousness Studies*, **16** (6–8), pp. 360–78. [This issue]

Malle, B.F. (2001), 'Folk Explanations of Intentional Action', in B.F. Malle, L.J. Moses & D.A. Baldwin (ed.), *Intentions and Intentionality: Foundations of Social Cognition* (Cambridge, MA: MIT Press), pp. 265–86.

McEwan, I. (2007), *On Chesil Beach* (New York: Anchor Books).

Nicols, S & Stich S.P. (2003), *Mindreading: An Integrated Account of Pretence, Self-Awareness and Understanding of Other Minds* (Oxford: Oxford University Press).

Palmer, A. (2004), *Fictional Minds* (Lincoln: University of Nebraska Press).

Premack, D. & Woodruff G. (1978), 'Does the Chimpanzee Have a Theory of Mind?', *The Behavioral and Brain Sciences*, **1**, pp. 515–26.

Propp, Vladimir (1928/1968), *Morphology of the Folktale*, trans. L. Scott; revised by L.A. Wagner (Austin: University of Texas Press).

Reichenbach, H. (1947), *Elements of Symbolic Logic* (New York: Macmillan).

Scalise Sugiyama, M. (2005), 'Reverse-engineering Narrative: Evidence of Special Design', in J. Gottschall & D.S. Wilson (ed.), *The Literary Animal* (Evanston, IL: Northwestern University Press), pp. 177–96.

Schutz, A. (1962), 'Common-sense and the Scientific Interpretation of Human Action', in M. Natanson (ed.) *Collected Papers*, vol. 1 (The Hague: Martinus Nijhoff), pp. 3–47.

Slors, M. & Macdonald C. (2008), 'Rethinking Folk-psychology: Alternatives to Theories of Mind', *Philosophical Explorations*, **11** (3), pp. 153–61.

Stawarska, B. (2007), 'Persons, Pronouns, and Perspectives', in D.D. Hutto & M. Ratcliffe (ed.), *Folk Psychology Re-Assessed* (Berlin: Springer), pp. 79–99.

Sternberg, M. (1978), *Expositional Modes and Temporal Ordering in Fiction* (Baltimore: Johns Hopkins University Press).

Sternberg, M. (2003), 'Universals of Narrative and their Cognitivist Fortunes (I)', *Poetics Today*, **24**, pp. 297–395.

Suppes, P. (1960), 'A Comparison of the Meaning and Uses of Models in Mathematics and the Empirical Sciences', *Synthese*, **12** (2/3), pp. 287–301.

Todorov, T. (1968), 'La Grammaire du récit', *Langages*, **12**, pp. 94–102.

von Wright, G.H. (1966), 'The Logic of Action — a Sketch', in N. Rescher (ed.), *The Logic of Decision and Action* (Pittsburgh: University of Pittsburgh Press), pp. 121–36.

Vygotsky, L.S. (1978), *Mind in Society: The Development of Higher Psychological Processes*, (ed.) M. Cole, V. John-Steiner, S. Scribner & E. Souberman (Cambridge, MA: Harvard University Press).

White, H. (2005), 'Emplotment', in D. Herman, M. Jahn & M.-L. Ryan (ed.), *Routledge Encyclopedia of Narrative Theory* (London: Routledge), p. 137.

Zahavi, D. (2007), 'Expression and Empathy', in D.D. Hutto & M. Ratcliffe (ed.), *Folk Psychology Re-Assessed* (Berlin: Springer), pp. 25–40

Zunshine, L. (2006), *Why We Read Fiction: Theory of Mind and the Novel* (Columbus: Ohio State University Press).

Katherine Nelson

Narrative Practices and Folk Psychology

A Perspective from Developmental Psychology

Abstract: *Herein developmental psychological research complementary to Hutto's narrative practices hypothesis is considered. Specifically, I discuss experiential development from the perspective of first, second and third person in the acquisition of knowledge and the construction and comprehension of narratives, with relevance for theories of 'theory of mind' and in particular tests of the child's understanding of false belief. I propose that the development of distinct third person belief states requires significant developmental work, which is advanced through social sharing of memory and knowledge, by means of linguistic representations especially through narrative practices of different kinds, personal narratives and story telling. The final sections summarize the view that these developments are part of a broader expansion of consciousness that is evident in many aspects of cognitive change during the later preschool years (Nelson, 2007).*

The Narrative Practices Hypothesis advanced by Hutto (2008; 2009 [this issue]) assumes the existence of social and cultural engagements with narratives in early childhood of a kind that leads the child eventually into synchrony with cultural models of Folk Psychology. This hypothesis is secondary to Hutto's assumption that in the great majority of situations in everyday life neither the child nor the adult engage in complex reasoning about other minds. Rather, others' actions are readily interpreted in situational context fulfilling expectations based on social routines and cultural roles and rules. Only puzzling third person actions that violate social/cultural expectations might challenge these intuitive interpretations and require reasoning about the states of mind of other agents. Therefore, in this view the child does not construct a theory of other minds, nor is it necessary for either child or adult to simulate other minds in order to take part knowingly in everyday social interactions. Hutto proposes that by engaging in common social practices of narrative interpretation the child gains experience in *reasoning* about the mental states (beliefs, goals, motivations, emotions) underlying puzzling third person actions of others, and acquiring thereby some of the skills needed for solving problems of Folk Psychology, as well as for interpreting the strange and unexpected behaviours that are used to test the child's understanding of false belief (FB).

Hutto's hypothesis diverges from those currently most favoured in developmental psychology (as well as philosophy) that are based on the philosophical abstractions of theory theory or the mental imagining of simulation theory together with the assumption of either early-developing theories of mind or innate mechanisms of social cognition. In my view the NPH fills the social practices gap in social cognitive theory and is highly compatible with a social/cultural reading of relevant evidence from developmental psychology. The experiential basis for understanding the social world of childhood proposed in Nelson (2007) provides a complementary developmental perspective. This proposal also assumes that understanding narrative has a special role to play in children's developing understanding of self and other and interpreting others' actions. Thus my view is roughly in line with Hutto's, although my central concern is with the developmental process that takes place over the early childhood years as language becomes a significant representational mode in communicative and cognitive transactions. In that perspective the younger child's failure and later success in solving false belief (FB) tasks and the eventual mature understanding of other folks' subtle motives, emotions, beliefs and goals is of considerable interest. Children's narrative experience is expected to be relevant to these achievements (Nelson *et al.*, 1998; Plesa, 2001).

In this essay I discuss children's experiential development from the perspective of first, second and third person in the acquisition of knowledge, the construction and comprehension of narratives, and understanding of the actions of others. I begin by considering the limitations of a first person perspective for many learning or knowledge gathering activities and of the second person interpretation of others' knowledge, noting that both the first and second person perspectives are held for a longer period and to a far greater extent than the early 'theory of mind' claim presumes to be the case. I propose that the development of distinct third person belief states requires significant developmental work, which is advanced through social sharing of memory and knowledge, by means of linguistic representations especially through narrative practices of different kinds, personal narratives, and story telling. In the last section I summarize the view that these developments are part of a broader expansion of consciousness that is evident in many aspects of cognitive change during the later preschool years (Nelson, 2007).

First, Second and Third Person Perspective in Interpreting Experience

The first person perspective of the young is often referred to as egocentricity, traditionally thought to be typical of the young child (e.g., Piaget, 1929). Against this assumption, recent theorists have emphasized that even during the second year of life infants are able to interpret others' actions from a second-person perspective (e.g., Tomasello, 1999), attributing to the other a different view of the scene they are sharing, different tastes or desires, and different goals and intentions from the child's own. Although theorists differ as to whether such attributions are part of a 'built-in' human capacity (e.g., Reddy, 2008) or are based on early social experience (Nelson, 2007), it is widely accepted that even very young children are not restricted to a strict egocentric view of the world. In direct interaction with others, whether with mother/father/caregiver in infancy or nonfamilial interactors such as teachers or family friends in early childhood, the child understands the others' actions and interactions, both verbal and nonverbal, in terms supported by context, familiarity, routines, and everyday expectations of reasonable actions, on the basis of cumulated social experience. Thus the child can be seen to understand others' goals, desires, intentions and emotions as different from his or her own (first person) mental states and as the basis for the others' actions.

It is important to bear in mind, however, that this second person perspective does not necessarily imply that the child has a concept of mental state or of individual states of desire, belief or intention, or in fact a conscious awareness of differences between self and other. These interpretations may not only begin on a very concrete and intuitive perception-action basis, but continue to exist on that basis for years.[1] Reasoning about actions from a *third person* perspective is only required in restricted kinds of social situations that seem to violate expectations of reasonable action in context.

Third person FB task

The short and simple narrative in the standard false belief (FB) task of the unobserved moving of a desired object, specifically the Sally/ Anne version serves here as an example that requires third person interpretation. In this display a doll/puppet/picture of a girl named Sally enters the arena or stage from the left and places a marble in a small basket, then leaves the stage. The Anne doll/puppet then enters from the right and goes to the basket, picks up the marble and moves it to a box on the other side of the stage and leaves. Next, Sally returns to the scene of the action and the observing test child (OC) is asked 'where will Sally look for her marble?'.

This commonly used scenario to test for the attainment of false belief is a stripped down version of a third-person narrative drama. Typically 3-year-olds fail the test (pointing to the box where the marble now resides) while 4-year-olds pass it (identifying the box where Sally left it). The narrative involves two characters previously unknown to the observing child (OC), who have apparently different (or conflicting) desires for the same object, different goals and intentions, and different beliefs about the location of the desirable object, the marble. The scene is bare, revealing no specific situational context or pre-existing relation between the characters. The OC is not given any information about what is in the mind of either of these characters that might explain their actions — no emotion, no reaction, no motivation. In Bruner's (1986) terms it is a story with a landscape of action and *no* landscape of consciousness. The central puzzle (where will Sally look?) should be easily solveable from the action alone, given that OC remembers the original action (which additional questioning almost always establishes to be the case). When the OC gives the wrong answer to the question of where Sally will look for her marble — that she will look in the box where Anne put it — it indicates that the OC has a false belief about Sally's belief (which has not changed but is no longer true to reality).

Unlike second person situations and stories where familiar contexts and cultural activities and routines make actions reasonable and interpretable in context, in this story the actions are unreasonable and there

---

[1]   Language terms for these abstractions are presumed to aid in their becoming more accessible to consciousness. See later discussion.

are no clues offered for why they might have occurred as they did. It might be argued that Sally's looking for her marble in the second basket is hardly more unreasonable than Anne's moving it there in the first place. Neither has an obvious motivation. This is then a good example of a third person story about which reasons involving hidden mental states must come into play in order to interpret the action, rightly or wrongly. Of course, adults ignore the mystery of Anne's action and find the required answer obvious: Sally remembers where she put the marble, thus she believes it is there, she wants it, and thus that is where she will look. Why don't 3-year-old children routinely give the same 'obvious' answer?

Knowing in First and Second Person Perspective

In considering this question and the general notion of false belief from a psychological perspective I find it convenient — even necessary — to substitute the term *know* for the critical concept of *believe,* used by philosophers and psychologists in this context. What is most perplexing about the FB tasks to the developmental psychologist is not the child's lack of a concept of *belief* but the observing child's (OB) concept of *knowing*. Both concepts rely on the psychological constructs of memory, forgetting, learning and knowing. Belief is another way of talking about all of these, with the caveat that a person may remember, learn or know something (from the first person phenomenal perspective) that is objectively (from the third person perspective) false. Insofar as we consider FB as a psychological problem (as opposed to an abstract logical puzzle) it is important to recognize that most people feel strongly about many of their beliefs, namely that these are matters of knowledge, of facts. This is doubly true, I believe, for the infant and young child for whom all learning and memory is derived from direct personal experience rather than being indirectly mediated by language or other symbolic means. A person may think she knows something that turns out to be false (e.g., Sally in the FB story). But there is no difference in the state of mind of that person before and after the fact was proved to be wrong; it is the state of the world that has changed, not her mind. The state of the mind of the observer, however, has undergone change; she has *updated* her knowledge of where the item is, and, with little interest in the source of knowledge (see later discussion) she expects Sally to update as well.

To track the transition in early childhood from first person perspective to the complexity of Folk Psychology (or FB) then, the concept of *knowing* is a critical starting point. It seems very clear that the young preschool child of 2 or 3 years of age does not have an abstract concept of belief, true or false. Three-year-old children, however, do often have beginning ideas about *knowing* and *remembering*. For an example, consider the following excerpt from a conversation that took place at lunch between a 3 ½ -year-old, K (42 mo.) and her mother M (from Nelson & Kessler-Shaw, 2002, relevant terms italicized; some utterances omitted for conciseness).

> K: You *know* something?
> M: What?
> K: Let me *think*.
> K: What's her name again?
> K: Don't you *remember* her?
> K: You've *seen* her before.
> -
> K: Somebody has a rocket. I don't *know* her.
> M: Where'd you meet her?
> K: At our house!
> M: Was I home for this?
> K: (shakes head).
> M: No.
> M: So how would I *know* who this is?
> M: How do you *know* she had a rocket?
> K: Cause she *told* us.
> M: Oh, okay.

In this excerpt K displays command of several uses of mental terms, specifically *know*, together with the idea of evidence for knowing: seeing and telling. Yet to the dismay of her mother, the child does not restrict knowledge of an event (the girl's telling about a rocket) to those who were there, but rather expects M(other) to fill in the elusive name of the child (which she eventually does after more probing), on the basis of *shared knowledge*. The difference between shared and unshared knowledge appears to be obscure for this child. From a first person perspective, what is learned — derived from — experience is spoken of as *remembered* or *known*. In the quoted conversation, K does not distinguish her own knowing from that of another — her mother — much like the 3-year-old observing child (OC) in the FB task.

The relevant question for both K and the OC, I would claim, is not 'why does the observing child in the FB task (or K in the rocket example) credit the deceived character (Sally; or Mother) with *knowledge* that by our lights they *most likely*[2] do not have?'. If we assume that the OC is treating the FB situation from a second person perspective, the

---

[2] The deceived character in the TOM narrative might have been told about the movement of the desired object by the mover or by someone else.

conversation between K and her Mother is instructive: K is assuming that other people share her own knowledge and when her knowledge is updated to include new facts, such as a girl's possession of a rocket, so is that of others with whom knowledge is shared. This is a peculiarity of the young child's notion of *knowing*, not just of her understanding of the term 'know'. It suggests that second person understanding of others during the early childhood years is limited in significant ways, such that generalizing from adult second person understanding to young children is not valid.

Limits on Second Person Perspective in Early Childhood

The prevalent view in developmental psychology is that the infant may begin with a limited first person perspective on the world, but that quite early in life this expands to incorporate a second person perspective applicable to social others. Even a very young infant views the caregiver as a separate person acting a role in their routines (e.g., feeding, diapering) different from her own, and predictable in its own right. A different perspective is attributed to the other late in the second year with respect to such things as different tastes and desires. The situation is more obscure with respect to different knowledge or belief, as illustrated above. There is substantial evidence in the cognitive development literature that children (like K) below the age of five or even six years are indifferent to the distinctions of knowing — who has it, who doesn't, when, why and how, and are thus easily confused by questions asked about it. It is not that the child is unaware personally of knowing and not knowing. 'I don't know' is often the child's first use of the term 'know' (Kessler Shaw, 1999). She accepts that adults (and older siblings) know things that she does not, but she may believe implicitly that they also know everything that she does, and more (see conversation quoted above).

This belief is not apparently conscious or accessible to reflection, but reflects characteristics of the basic primate (and general mammalian) memory or knowing system, which is *nonverbal* and thus *non-shareable* (see Terrace & Metcalfe, 2005; Nelson, 2005a). For this reason, a preverbal child cannot check what she remembers, or knows, against the knowledge of others. The conversation between K and her mother shows how necessary such checking may be in advancing the child's understanding. In the initial state of the infant's knowledge/memory system all information about the world is gained from direct experience through perception and action. There is no compelling reason for making distinctions as to when some piece of knowledge appeared or how it was obtained (Nelson, 1993; 2005a). The brain, operating on its own without specific directions from the conscious mind, presumably takes facts as facts, to be held for future reference and to be discarded when superceded or no longer relevant.

From the young child's perspective then, facts of the world of experience are simply known; some are known by older people; all relevant facts about the world are presumably accessible to everyone through personal exploration. Further, when facts change, the child's knowledge system is readily updated, and the old 'known' is discarded (Nelson, 1993; 1996; 2005a). At 3 years of age, and to some extent as late as 5 years, the child's knowing system is undifferentiated as to either source or timing, a product of the ancient design of organismic memory systems. Tracking knowledge as to its *source* — whether acquired in experience or told by someone, or just 'thought' — and *when* and *where* it was acquired are not part of the basic system. That they are part of the adult's personal memory system — in fact are essential to autobiographical memory, as well as to social negotiations in everyday life — may mislead adults, including researchers, to expect children to track these aspects.

Source monitoring

The difficulties encountered in relation to this perspective on knowing have been studied extensively in terms of *source monitoring* (Roberts & Blades, 2000). The term 'source monitoring' derives from Marcia Johnson's theory of reality monitoring in relation to memory for real or imagined events.[3] It is not only a problem for children, but was originally revealed and studied in adults by Johnson and her colleagues (see review by Johnson *et al.*, 1993). Adults frequently engage in reality monitoring in situations of uncertainty, asking themselves questions such as 'Did I really turn the oven off or did I just intend to do it?' or 'Did we go to that restaurant last year or did we just talk about going?'. (Note that these questionable actions become false beliefs if they occur in the mind and not in reality). The fact that adults must often expend effort to distinguish real events from 'mind events' strongly implies that the human cognitive system lacks automatic (inborn) safeguards of this kind and that they must be constructed in development.

False belief tasks incorporate two monitoring problems: tracking temporal relations (when was the item stored and when was it

---

[3]   Roberts (2000) provides an overview of both reality and source monitoring in adults and children.

moved?); and source of knowing (inferring, seeing, hearing about, being told, etc.). Gopnik and Graf (1988) tested memory in 3- to 5-year-olds, where small items were placed in one of three small drawers, and after a brief delay children were asked where an item was and how they knew — whether they saw it being put there, or were told about it, or just knew (inferred the answer from the information available). Even the three-year-olds were able to remember the placements above chance level, but they were not able to tell *how* they knew; they were especially poor (at chance) at recalling that they had been told the information. A number of studies since have replicated and extended these findings.

Indifference to tracking the *time* of the acquisition of knowledge suggests that for the child knowing is strictly cumulative; it is not marked as having been experienced at a particular time in the past. This is dramatically apparent in research revealing that even some 5-year-olds are indifferent to when or how they have learned a bit of knowledge even after a very brief delay. Taylor and her colleagues (Taylor *et al.*, 1994) told preschoolers facts about animals that were previously unknown to them. Later they questioned the children about the same facts, and when a child provided the newly learned information they were asked *when* they had learned the fact. Most children under the age of 5 years reported that they had *always known* what they had just recently been told. Many similar findings related to the problem of source monitoring confirm that for young children neither the *source* nor the *time* of knowledge acquisition is significant. In some ways the situation seems even more dire: young children seem to assume that facts appear from nowhere. This conclusion is consistent with the results of FB tests, as others have pointed out (Perner, 1991; Robinson, 2000; Welch-Ross, 2000).

What children do not know and need to learn about the mind and its beliefs, true and false has been the focus of many developmental studies. For example, research on children's understanding of mental terms such as *think, know,* and *guess* reveal that the concepts underlying these are not well understood until the school years, in spite of their everyday uses by children of 3 and 4 years of age (e.g., Moore *et al.*, 1989). Rather than assuming that because children are using these terms at an early age they have the adult concepts signified by them, we find that meanings change with experience in the world and with language. For example, for the young child *knowing* is not equivalent to justified belief; moreover, it is not something that must be identified with an origin; it may arrive in the head unheralded and unmarked.

Children then must learn differently: that knowing is not in the air, is not magical, but that it has distinctive sources.

The relevance of this state of knowing to the special question of false belief consists in the lack of difference that the child attributes to self and other knowledge as a result of neglect of source. The source monitoring work implies that the intuitive sense of intentionality ascribed to the 2-year-old actually must be quite limited. Children do have to be very smart to get along in a world that they understand on so limited a level as that of a 2- or 3- or even 4-year-old. But they are smart in a limited way, and the more expansive ways open to the consciousness of a language user in a complicated symbolic culture involve a radical mind change in relation to the limited powers of the basically nonverbal young child's mind (Nelson, 2007). The preschooler appears to view life from a first person perspective on many levels and for much longer than might be concluded on the basis of recent claims about early theory of mind. This perspective is broadened through linguistic discourse, including everyday conversations about the child's experience as well as other narrative practices, launching the child into the cultural world, with its shared understandings of minds and other mysteries (Nelson, 2005b; 2007).

The first, second and third person understanding discussed in this section and attributed to the developing child from birth to about five years of age can be summarized as follows. The first person perspective is the basis for knowledge gathering from birth through direct action and perception supported by social scaffolding and enriched through processes of generalization, differentiation and integration into schemas, scripts, concepts and categories. Second person perspective enables interpreting the actions, interactions and reactions of other persons in direct contact providing *interactive understanding* of intentions, goals, emotions and motivations based on experiential knowledge of familiar others and situations. Other sources of knowledge only become available gradually, first through mimesis and then through complex language (Nelson, 1996). Third person perspective as a basis for interpreting unexpected actions by familiar or strange persons in unfamiliar contexts must be acquired with the help of adult models, the topic of the next section.

Narrative and Narrative Practices

Narratives play a prominent role in the lives of most young children. Every culture and subculture tells stories for and with children, richly packed with cultural expectations and rules (Miller, 1994). In the contemporary American culture, parents are urged to read stories to their young ones — even to infants; and the commercial world has responded with an overload of story books, in addition to narrative videos and television, all designed to be suitable for the young. It is appropriate to ask what these stories offer that might be relevant to false belief issues, but little or no research has been directed toward that question. In addition to stories, personal narratives based on life events are the natural stuff of everyday conversations between adults as well as with parents and their very young children, usually beginning at about 18 months of age (Engel, 1986; Reese, 2002). Such parent-child conversations about shared and unshared past events have been studied extensively in relation to the beginnings of children's autobiographical memory (Nelson & Fivush, 2004). Both sources of narrative experience — personal memories and fictional stories — and the accompanying parent-child interaction are relevant to the present FB-oriented inquiry.

What's in a Narrative?

The skeleton framework of narrative is the simple action sequence, implicating the intentions and goals of the actors, and there is ample evidence of children's engagement with such sequences in everyday life. Infants and toddlers are expert at learning action routines and scripts (Bauer & Mandler, 1989; Nelson, 1986) and are attentive to the intentions and goals of self and others (Carpendale & Lewis, 2004; Tomasello, 2003). Narrative play also emerges early in primitive forms, as toddler and adult take on pretend roles (e.g., 'meow I'm a kitty-cat') and action games ('rrr goes the train down the tracks'). Over the course of the preschool years such games become more elaborate and framed in more complex language. Young children also become story constructors and tellers with or without action props (Nicolopoulou & Weintraub, 1998; Comay, 2008).

Evidence of narrative in action (as in dramatic play) might suggest that narrative is a natural 'built-in' mode of human thought (Bruner, 1986). Yet there is much more to narrative than an action sequence; as Bruner proposed, narrative consists of both a landscape of action and a landscape of consciousness, the when, why and how of the story. In their own story telling young children are quite inattentive to the landscape of consciousness; when children of 3 or 4 years of age tell real or imaginary stories they typically report only the action, omitting any mention of mental states or emotions (Applebee, 1978; Bruner & Lucariello, 1989; Comay, 2008; Nelson, 1996). This omission suggests that the active and interactive components of intentionality noted in 2- and 3-year-olds are not salient in the child's consciousness. Even when the child is engaged in reporting on her own experience in a prior event, the account tends to be focused on activity, lacking the expression of motivations, attitudes, emotions or evaluations (Fivush, 1993; Nelson, 1989; Nelson & Fivush, 2004). Reference to mental states is rare even in the stories and memory recounts of 5- and 6-year-olds (Comay, 2008; Henseler, 2000; Nelson, 2005b).

The absence of mind components cannot be attributed to lack of vocabulary for expressing these matters, as perceptual, emotional and cognitive terms appear in children's everyday talk between two and four years of age (Bartsch & Wellman, 1995; Bretherton & Beeghly, 1982; Nelson & Kessler Shaw, 2002). Moreover, expression of emotion, motivation and cognition are typically a focus in stories for children and in adults' reminiscing with children, especially in discussions about the actions of characters. Differences among different people's knowledge, motivations and actions are often highlighted in both fictional and personal stories, together with explanations provided by the story or story teller/reader.

Young children's omission of the landscape of consciousness raises an important question: are children not aware, not conscious, of these elements; do they not have the relevant concepts? Does children's sensitivity to second person perspective exist only on an action level that is not conceived in mental terms? Or are these matters considered irrelevant or unnecessary to the stories they are listening to and telling? As Hutto has noted, much of human action is readily interpretable in terms of social and cultural expectations in everyday situations or in terms of everyday routines (Nelson, 1986). On this basis the absence of expression of reasons for action (mental, emotional, motivational) in children's own stories and recounts might be expected. Moreover, children may simply take any action — no matter how unexpected — for granted. That adult activities must often seem (and remain) mysterious to young children makes this possibility seem especially plausible. Unfortunately the present state of research does not allow us to provide definitive answers to these questions. In the remainder of this section I suggest how the child's encounter with fictional narratives may be seen from the point of view of first, second and third person perspective.

The Child's First Experience of Stories

Many of the stories designed for the youngest children (1 to 2 ½ years) tend to be organized around a single character, or one obvious protag- onist whose actions may be repeated with variations throughout. The popular 'Are You My Mother?' tale of the baby bird who relentlessly asks a series of other animals whether they might be his lost mother fits this pattern. These may be called 'first person stories'. Often the same story is repeatedly read at the child's request, until the child is able to repeat a surprising amount of the story text (Miller *et al.*, 1993). One- to two-year-old children often appear to *project* them- selves into these stories, taking over the role of the protagonist and often acting it out (Miller *et al.*, 1993; Wolf & Heath, 1992). Miller *et al.* provided a case study of a 2-year-old child's projection into the persona of Peter Rabbit in the classic tale of that name. The little boy took on Peter's name as he acted out disobediently stepping into his own grandmother's garden. Wolf & Heath (1992) described a girl who, beginning at the age of one year, 'became' a succession of story characters for extended periods of weeks or even months, announc- ing, for example, 'I'm Raphunzel' as she lay in her bath, or engaged in some other prosaic activity. Projection of this kind is far from the detached simulation proposed in some accounts of theory of mind. Rather, in first person perspective the child projectively *becomes* the character in the story, more identification than empathetic simulation (Nelson, 1991), and very different from 'figuring out' what a character might do; using projection a child 'just knows'.

Second Person Stories and Beyond

Second-person perspective in story interpretion is a step removed from the total immersion of first person projection. Second-person perspective is presumed by Hutto (2008) and others to be the natural mode for adults in responding to others in everyday interactions and young children apparently engage this mode in their routine social interactions with intimate others (e.g., siblings, parents, caregivers). By three years (perhaps earlier) children appear to bring this predispo- sition to the interpretation of the main character in a story. In effect, children in this mode apply to the main characters of the story the same interpretive skills that are based in the intimate intersubjectivity of the family. Rather than the child taking on the protagonist's per- sona, the story character is viewed as a different but knowable person. This is usually possible because most stories draw on the routines, situations, settings and objects with which the child is familiar in everyday life.

Story interpretation by children through the preschool years appears to be largely based in the child's real-life experience, and indeed, children typically assert that story characters and the activities they engage in are 'real' (Applebee, 1978; Fontaine, 2002). Experiencing the stories of other lives draws the child into contact with other selves, applying second-person intersubjectivity to third-person unknown characters, thus widening the set to which children's intuitions apply. In this period also some children create imaginary companions who share their lives (Taylor, 1999). The imaginary friend is not a simulated but imagined person; that is, imaginary friends are different from the child. They are claimed by the child as 'real', just as the child thinks of fictional stories as reports of real events and people.

Between three and five years of age children may encounter more complex stories and are likely to be engaged in question and answer sessions involving such queries as 'why do you think he's doing that?' or 'how does the boy feel now?'. These stories and the accompanying expectations of the adult interlocutor may lead the child toward a more third-person approach to interpretation, especially when the unfamiliarity of character and action are involved. Children may continue to believe that stories are about something 'real' that happened and are not imaginary, although they may also recognize the unreality of fantasy worlds. For example, children in Fontaine's (2002) study claimed that a character was not 'real' because real people cannot take off their heads, as the witch in the story does. More complex stories, with multiple characters and action lines, whether fantasy or not, widen the range of goals and interests that children might consider, as well as the set of rules and strategies that people might follow, and the range of conflicts that might arise. Sameness and difference in knowledge state, motivations and expectations are also often emphasized in stories so that particularities of situations and conflicts of interest become salient. Similarly, 'weird' stories such as those of Dr. Seuss, or the antics of Sesame Street characters Bert and Ernie, all contribute, over time, to the challenge to the child's understanding of how to interpret and reason about the actions of third person, unfamiliar actors.

Stories that involve fantasy and alien settings, such as classical fairy tales and fables, often present puzzling actions that require the hearer to reason about motivations, emotions, even mystery and magic. These more complex and distanced stories require holding in mind the mental motivations, thoughts, goals and desires of more than one character, and they may require third person reasoning about hidden beliefs and desires that are not made clear in the text of the story. *Aesop's Fables* are examples of this kind, as are the classic folk tales such as 'Little Red Riding Hood' and 'Jack and the Bean Stalk'. Such tales present many opportunities for adults to illustrate concepts of mind. The lack of scholarly research on the question of children's experience of stories means that we have little evidence about the frequency with which children experience the kinds of stories that make these good examples, or how children comprehend them. The inclination of adults to decide more or less arbitrarily what is a good story for children (such as Bible stories; see Heath, 1983) and what is too scary (such as 'Hansel and Gretel') further complicates this picture. In summary, there is a dearth of research on precisely the questions raised in the Narrative Practices Hypothesis with respect to how children may come to take a third person perspective on stories and to reason about the actions that others engage in, in contrast to the expectations based on culturally familiar everyday events.

One thing that is eminently clear from even this brief overview of children's stories, is that a command of language is essential to the child's narrative experience. It is not irrelevant that the stories discussed here are presented to the child orally, either through telling or reading aloud from a book.

Personal Narratives

In addition to fictional stories that children are presented with, narratives of self and other in past experiences, shared and unshared, are highly pertinent to the development of consciousness of the mental and emotional, as they may highlight for the child the difference between her own experience of an event and that of someone else (Nelson & Fivush, 2004). Fivush (1993) has found that in adult-child reminiscing of past events it is the adult who supplies the 'landscape of consciousness' — the mental and emotional content that makes sense of the action. There is a considerable literature now on this topic (Bauer, 2007; Nelson & Fivush, 2004; Fivush & Nelson, 2006), but it has not yet been integrated with the work in social cognition.

That children may work at understanding their own past experiences became evident in the study of the night time monologues of the 2-year-old child Emily, which were tape-recorded by her parents (Nelson, 1989). A brief excerpt of an early monologue provides a sample:

> When my slep and, and, Mormor[4] came. Then Mommy coming then get
> up, time to go ho-o-ome. Time to go home. Drink p-water [Perrier]. Yes-
> terday did that. Now Emmy sleeping in regular bed.

This excerpt represents about 1/6 of the total content devoted that
night to this 'narrative' of Mommy waking her and taking her home
for her nap earlier that day. Several versions of the same event were
constructed, as though she were trying to 'get it right'. It is not based
on any 'telling' from Father or Mother, but on her own experience of
this variation on a familiar event. Many of her monologues followed
and partially reproduced her father's account of what would happen
the next day. Emily spent considerable effort — indeed, struggle — to
follow these future-looking accounts and to reconstruct them for herself. It is notable that these musings appear in the form of public
speech, not that is, in silent thought. The eminent Russian psychologist Vygotsky (1934/1986) theorized that the child's private speech
went underground in the later preschool years to become 'inner
speech', the adult mode of thought. Seen from this perspective,
Emily's monologues could be viewed as preparing the ground for a
new mode of mental functioning, preparatory for the radical mind
change from preverbal to verbal.

Hearing stories, telling stories and recounting personal experiences
all involve complex language skills, skills that are also strongly and
positively related to performance on false belief tasks (such as the
Sally/Anne task) in typically-developing young children (Milligan *et
al.*, 2007). Children without language and those with limited language
and thus limited exposure to conversation (e.g., children with autism
or the profoundly deaf) usually fail false belief (FB) tasks at the standard ages (Tager-Flusberg & Joseph, 2005; deVilliers, 2005).
Although it has not been shown that any *specific* linguistic or cognitive mechanism makes false belief success possible (Astington &
Baird, 2005; Lohmann *et al.*, 2005), narrative practices involve third
person social understanding and engaging in these practices both
requires and further supports advanced language skill. Practice with
using and interpreting complex language constructions is essential to
the understanding and constructing of narratives and other complex
discursive genres. These are reciprocal activities: the more complex
language the child is exposed to, the more easily he or she will be able
to understand a story. And the more practice that children have listening to stories, the better will be their understanding of complex language. It is not the *form* of language that is critical to the developments

---

[4]   Mormor = grandmother

of interest here — narrative and the understanding of minds — but rather language *use* or function. Language use is of critical importance to social, cognitive, emotional and personal growth. An experiential perspective on psychological development indicates that it is the expansion of meaning and consciousness through language use that is critical (Nelson, 2007).

Language, Narrative and Consciousness

Learning from language requires the ability to interpret *representations in language* communicated by other persons, and then to re-represent these representations in one's own memory/knowledge scheme for future reference. The representation function of language is not just referential; it does not simply point, but describes. A speaker's description requires that the listener interpret what is heard in terms of a reciprocal representation about the matter referred to, dislocated in time or space. When the description is a narrative of an event, a grasp of the basic if not the fine points of grammar and meanings of words in use are inevitably required, together with adequate working memory to follow the steps of the account, and appropriate experiential memory for interpreting the situations reported on. Finally, this process requires using language interpretation to fuel imagination and conceptual thought. This intricate process both calls on and constructs shared knowledge involving temporal and causal connections among events and the people who participate in them, as well as detailed experiential knowledge of situations and places where actions occur. In sum, using representational language not only may construct new knowledge by a speaker, but calls on old knowledge for its comprehension.

The claim here is that learning to engage with others in verbal activities such as listening to and telling stories and conversing about the causes of actions and events, the emotions and goals of the actors and the like, enables a child to enter into a radically new relation in the social-cultural world. Central to this relation is the ability to learn from language how others see and think about the world. Tracking what one knows, who knows it, what and when it was learned are critically involved in these activities. As we have seen, younger children are indifferent to these aspects of stories or of real life; more specifically, they are unconscious of the importance or even existence of these matters. From this point of view, what is needed to understand the complexities of stories, and of one's own life, is an expansion of consciousness.

Expansion of Consciousness

Consciousness is viewed here in terms of transactions between mind and world. Most basically it relates the mind to conditions in the world that elicit or require attention or monitoring, including conditions that demand sustained attention and interpretation of the unexpected or novel (e.g., Damasio, 1999). The experiential theory (Nelson, 2007) assumes that what a person is conscious of at any time is determined by what is or may become personally *meaningful* in that experiential situation, which in turn is under the influence of specific personal and social conditions that exist at that time and place. These conditions can be conceptualized as forces variably and simultaneously imping-ing on experience. These include the biological (general species char-acteristics plus the specific characteristics and developmental states of the brain and body), ecological, social and cultural conditions (including language use); and, crucially, prior meaningful experience in the form of memory, conscious and unconscious (Nelson, 2007). All of these conditions are present during any experience, but they continually change over time at different scales — momentarily to very slowly in development. What *may be* in consciousness in any sit-uation thus varies among persons and over time for the same person. Specifically, for the young child an important aspect of development is the expansion of consciousness that emerges in response to experi-ence, social guidance and interaction, and biological change, as these each affect what is *meaningful* for the individual.

We can think of the child as moving progressively through six lev-els of expanding consciousness over the years from birth to school age (Nelson, 2007; see Figure 1). Consciousness level roughly determines the extent of inclusion and integration of potentially meaningful ele-ments of experience. Moving to a higher level depends on the emer-gence of a new perspective opened usually via social and symbolic interactions highlighting previously unattended dimensions of poten-tial experience. In terms of the previous discussion, it may be noted that the first two levels support the child's participation in the world and appreciation of stories from a first person perspective. The third level supports the emergence of a second-person perspective that persists through the critical levels of reflective and narrative consciousness.

The level of reflective consciousness emerges from social-sym-bolic transactions that involve public and shared representations of real or pretend states of the world or mind, present, past or imagined. Some level of reflection appears during the second year as the child

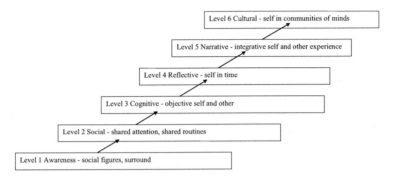

Figure 1
Levels of Consciousness
From Nelson, 2007, Figure 1–2

puzzles about a move in social play or in meeting new people or situations.[5] Language is the prime vehicle for shared public representations, but mimetic means such as play, art, music, and dance may also invoke a level of reflection on meaning. As the child gains experience with language in use, complex discourse in conversations and stories makes new demands on the child?s comprehension of rapidly fading speech. Interpreting the meaning then requires reflection on another's linguistic representations of the not-here-and-now: on states of mind, past and future situations, and other possible worlds. Acquisition of a knowledge base *shared* with others through linguistic representation has its beginnings in this level. The reflective level is then a critical transition move toward mind change where language serves not only as an accompaniment to shared action in the present but as a representational system that brings other possible realities, including the not-experienced, into the child's mental and experiential focus for reflection, transformation and further use.

Sharing memories of experiences, past, present and future, with others, and listening to stories, eventually leads the child to a level of *narrative consciousness* that includes temporality, that is, an awareness of the specificity of past and future, as well as to a recognition of the motivations of characters for engaging in actions. These are critical features of the third person interpretations of false belief. Narrative consciousness is a critical level for many reasons, prepared for by reflective consciousness — the ability to think about what has been

---

[5] I am not aware of any standardized investigation of this attitude at this time.

said — and integrative of prior levels, preparative for the more mature level of cultural consciousness. It is the level that, by hypothesis, is most closely aligned with success on standard FB tasks at four years of age[6] (Nelson, 2007). This level builds on the experiences with language representations at the reflective level and further expands consciousness in two ways. First, the child is able to integrate extended complex discourse, including narrative and ongoing episodes temporally, causally and psychologically to re-construct the meaning of the whole, taking into account the goals and beliefs (knowledge states) of different characters in a story. Second, the child recognizes past and future as temporal periods distinct from the present and conceives of herself in a specific past and possible future, distinct from those of other people in the real or fictional world. Further, the child's awareness of who has knowledge and where it comes from is a product of expanded consciousness at the narrative level. Children become open to differences in knowledge sources, recognizing that not all 'knowledge' is equally reliable; some is experientially-based, while some is gained through knowledge sharing in language or in other media; and some emerges from cognitive and imaginative processes.

A further level beyond the narrative, where language becomes an entrée into unknown worlds and knowledge sources available in the common culture, brings the child into formal education and to more complex reasoning about matters of mind and action. By the end of the preschool period then the child is on the verge of moving into a level of sharing the *awareness of consciousness* with others, establishing a sense of identity and making distinctions among groups and their members that may lead to new understandings of others and other minds. This expansion is termed 'cultural consciousness' or 'community of minds' (Nelson, 2005b; Nelson *et al.*, 2003), indicating that this is where states of mind are taken into account readily and openly, and where contents — specifically knowledge — are widely shared. At this more advanced level the child's own cognitive categories are stretched by exposure to cultural concepts and categories, from the 'right ways' to do things at home and in school, to the study of other languages and cultures.

---

[6] Several studies have indicated a relation between narrative understanding and success on ToM tasks (Henseler, 2000; Plesa, 2002) but more work is needed to establish the direction of the relation.

Narrative Consciousness and 'Theory of Mind'

Some of the many interrelated aspects of the child's developing understanding of self and social relations, in real life and in narratives, personal tales and stories, have been considered here as they may affect what has come to be known as 'theory of mind'. I have stressed here the notion of coherence in development in the sense that competences that emerge at the end of the preschool years depend on a suite of experiential preparations in the preceding years. The frame of experience at any given point is related to its entire bio-social-cultural preparation. Thus no emergent competence — such as passing False Belief tests — can be understood on its own but only in the context of how the child's past has prepared for the present success. In the case of FB tests the child requires competence at interpreting linguistic representations as well as interpreting problematic narratives with unusual actions suggesting strange goals and motivations. The child cannot simply transfer intuitive knowledge of everyday second-person interactions to this situation. Narrative practice is absolutely essential. Practice with linguistic representations of reality and irreality is necessary for interpreting many aspects of the adult world. Individuals without such practice (e.g., autistic persons) are at a loss in this context, as are very young children. The simplistic idea that a mechanism exists in the child's head that is simply turned on at some point and is then applied to direct interactive relations and to manipulate representations of unknown peoples and situations is clearly false.

As sketched here, the expansion of consciousness over the early years of life depends on all of the elements of the biological and social/cultural contributions to development. One does not need much in the way of observation to indicate that a child of one year sees and hears a more restricted and different set of visual and auditory sources in the environment than the adult does. Most notably, what she hears of language is babble, not meaning. What she sees is seen from a different angle, and a different knowledge perspective. This cannot avoid being a first person perspective, a perspective very different from the adult's.

We do not know how widespread or universal experience with narratives of different kinds (personal stories, fiction, folk tales, myths) may be for children in different groups, societies or cultures. The processes referred to in this paper are based on children from European-American 21st century mostly middle class families. The conjecture that in every child's life interactions around narratives are sufficient to educate social understanding within each social-cultural setting may be very wide of the mark. But contemporary Westerners are not alone in assuming that narrative is the means through which cultures impose their beliefs and values on the young. The anthropologist Carrithers (1991) argued that narrativity 'allows humans to grasp a longer past and a more intricately conceived future, as well as a more variegated social environment' (p. 306). The strongest claim in this line is that humans and human societies could not have evolved without the shared constructions of narratives that enable viewing personal and societal relationships through time and over shifting complexities. Like many others (e.g., Bruner, 1990) Carrither's position suggests a kind of inborn cognitive disposition toward narrative thinking. Yet other writers emphasize the differences, large and small, among narrative products found in different cultures and sub-cultures (e.g., Bartlett, 1932; Heath, 1983), implying that narratives are social products to which people become enculturated from childhood. From this perspective, 'we learn to tell the stories that our social world values, and our storied thoughts come to conform to the models of our society' (Nelson, 1996, pp. 184–5). There is no necessity that all of the models need be alike, any more than that all of our languages are cut from the same template.

The important point is that a society's narratives encapsulate the valued ways of viewing human actions, goals, beliefs, and intentions through stories in which these are displayed and, often violated, with consequences. Narratives model behaviour and, importantly, different perspectives from different positions in society. As many have emphasized, it is also through narratives that children come to an understanding of the self in relation to others, thereby taking a place in the societal web; the self cannot be defined except in relation to other selves. That problem is embedded in other equally compelling problems of mind and world that the child must come to grips with. Fortunately, cultures are ideally designed to overcome childhood ignorance and naivete in the domains of both practice and thought. They do it with stories.

References

Applebee, A.N. (1978), *The Child's Concept of Story* (Chicago: University of Chicago Press).

Astington, J.W. & Baird, J. (ed, 2005), *Why language matters to theory of mind* (New York: Oxford University Press).

Bartlett, F.C. (1932), *Remembering: A Study in experimental and social psychology* (Cambridge: Cambridge University Press).

Bartsch, K. & Wellman, H.M. (1995), *Children talk about the mind* (New York: Oxford University Press).

Bauer, P. (2007), *Remembering the times of our lives: Memory in infancy and beyond* (Mahwah NJ: Erlbaum/Psychology Press).

Bauer, P.J. & Mandler, J.M. (1989), 'One Thing Follows Another: Effects of temporal structure on one- to two-year-olds' recall of events', *Developmental Psychology*, **25**, pp. 197–206.

Bretherton, I. & Beeghly, M. (1982), 'Talking about Internal States: The acquisition of an explicit theory of mind', *Developmental Psychology*, **18**, pp. 906–21.

Bruner, J.S. (1986), *Actual minds, possible worlds* (Cambridge MA: Harvard University Press).

Bruner, J.S. (1990), *Acts of meaning* (Cambridge MA: Harvard University Press).

Bruner, J.S. & Lucariello, J. (1989), 'Monologue as Narrative Recreation of the World', in K. Nelson (ed.), *Narratives from the Crib* (Cambridge MA: Harvard University Press), pp. 73–97.

Carpendale, J.I.M. & Lewis, C. (2004), 'Constructing an Understanding of Mind: The development of children's social understanding and social interaction', *Behavioral and Brain Sciences*, **27**, pp. 79–15.

Carrithers, M. (1991), 'Narrativity: Mindreading and Making Societies', in A. Whiten (ed.), *Natural theories of Mind: Evolution, Development and Simulation of Everyday Mindreading* (Oxford: Basil Blackwell), pp. 305–18.

Comay, J. (2008), *Individual Differences in Narrative Perspective-taking and Theory of Mind* (Unpublished Ph.D. Dissertation, University of Toronto, Toronto, Canada).

Damasio, A. (1999), *The feeling of what happens: Body and emotion in the making of consciousness* (New York: Harcourt, Inc).

de Villiers, P.A. (2005), 'The Role of Language in Theory-of-Mind Development: What Deaf Children Tell Us', in J.W. Astington & J. Baird (ed.), *Why Language Matters to Theory of Mind* (New York: Oxford University Press), pp. 266–98.

Engel, S. (1986), *Learning to reminisce: A developmental study of how young children talk about the past* (Unpublished Ph.D. Dissertation, City University of New York Graduate Center).

Fivush, R. (1993), 'Emotional Content of Parent-child Conversations about the Past', in C.A. Nelson (ed.), *Memory and affect in development,* Vol. 26 (Hillsdale, N.J.: Lawrence Erlbaum Assoc), pp. 39–77.

Fivush, R. & Nelson, K. (2006), 'Parent-child Reminiscing Locates the Self in the Past', *British Journal of Developmental Psychology*, **24**, pp. 235–51.

Fontaine, R.G. (2002) *Preschoolers' understanding of story books: The influence of story genre, affect, and language* (Unpublished Ph.D. Dissertation, City University of New York Graduate School, New York.15).

Gopnik, A. & Graf, P. (1988), 'Knowing How you Know: Young children's ability to identify and remember the sources of their beliefs', *Child Development*, **59**, pp. 1366–71.

Heath, S.B. (1983), *Ways with words* (Cambridge: Cambridge University Press).

Henseler, S. (2000), *Young children's developing theory of mind: Person reference, psychological understanding and narrative skill* (Unpublished Ph.D. dissertation, City University of New York Graduate Center, New York).

Hutto, D.D. (2008), *Folk Psychological Narratives: The Sociocultural Basis of Understanding Reasons* (Cambridge MA: MIT Press).

Hutto, D.D. (2009), 'Folk Psychology As Narrative', *Journal of Consciousness Studies*, **16** (6–7), pp. 9–39.

Johnson, M.K., Hashtroudi, S. & Lindsay, D.S. (1993), 'Source Monitoring', *Psychological Bulletin*, **114**, pp. 3–18.

Kessler Shaw, L. (1999), *The development of the meanings of 'think' and 'know' through conversation* (Unpublished Ph.D. Dissertation, City University of New York Graduate Center, New York).

Lohmann, H., Tomasello, M. & Meyer, S. (2005), 'Linguistic Communication and Social Understanding', in J.W. Astington & J.A. Baird (ed.), *Why Language Matters to Theory of Mind* (Oxford: Oxford University Press), pp. 245–65.

Miller, P.J. (1994), 'Narrative Practices: Their role in socialization and self construction', in U. Neisser & R. Fivush (ed.), *The Remembered Self: Construction and accuracy in the self-narrative* (New York: Cambridge University Press).

Miller, P.J., Hoogstra, L., Mintz, J., Fung, H. & Williams, K. (1993), Troubles in the garden and how they get resolved: A young child's transformation of his favorite story', in C.A. Nelson (ed.), *Memory and Affect in Development,* Vol. 26 (Hillsdale, NJ: Lawrence Erlbaum Assoc), pp. 87–114.

Milligan, K., Astington, J.W. & Dack, L.A. (2007), 'Language and Theory of Mind: Meta-analysis of the relation between language ability and false-belief understanding', *Child Development,* **78**, pp. 642–6.

Moore, C., Bryant, D. & Furrow, D. (1989), 'Mental Terms and the Development of Certainty', *Child Development,* **60**, pp. 167–71.

Nelson, K. (1986), *Event knowledge: Structure and Function in Development* (Hillsdale NJ: Lawrence Erlbaum Assoc).

Nelson, K. (ed, 1989), *Narratives from the crib* (Cambridge MA: Harvard University Press).

Nelson, K. (1991), 'Remembering and Telling: A Developmental Story', *Journal of Narrative and Life History,* **1**, pp. 109–27.

Nelson, K. (1993), 'The Psychological and Social Origins of Autobiographical Memory', *Psychological Science,* **4**, pp. 1–8.

Nelson, K. (1996), *Language in cognitive development: The emergence of the mediated mind* (New York: Cambridge University Press).

Nelson, K. (2005a), 'Evolution and Development of Human Memory Systems', in B. Ellis & D. Bjorklund (ed.), *Origins of the Social Mind: Evolutionary Psychology and Child Development* (New York: Guilford Publications, Inc.), pp. 319–45.

Nelson, K. (2005b), 'Language Pathways to the Community of Minds', in J.W. Astington & J. Baird (ed.), *Why language matters to theory of mind* (New York: Oxford University Press), pp. 26–49.

Nelson, K. (2007), *Young Minds in Social Worlds: Experience, Meaning, and Memory* (Cambridge, MA: Harvard University Press).

Nelson, K. & Fivush, R. (2004), 'The Emergence of Autobiographical Memory: A Social Cultural Developmental Theory', *Psychological Review,* **111**, pp. 486–511.

Nelson, K., Plesa, D. & Henseler, S. (1998), 'Children's Theory of Mind: An experiential interpretation', *Human Development,* **41**, pp. 7–29.

Nelson, K. & Kessler Shaw, L (2002), 'Developing a Socially Shared Symbolic System', in E. Amsel & J. Byrnes (ed.), *Language, literacy and cognitive development* (Mahwah NJ: Erlbaum), pp. 27–58.

Nelson, K., Plesa, D. *et al.* (2003), 'Entering a Community of Minds: An Experiential Approach to Theory of Minds', *Human Development,* **46**, pp. 24–46.

Nicolopoulou, A. and Weintraub, J. (1998), 'Individual and Collective Representations in Social Context: A Modest Contribution to Resuming the Interrupted Project of a Sociocultural Developmental Psychology', *Human Development,* **41**, pp. 215–35.

Perner, J. (1991), *Understanding the representational mind* (Cambridge, MA: MIT Press).

Piaget, J. (1929), *The child's conception of the world*, Trans. J.A. Tomlinson (New York: Harcourt Brace & World).

Plesa, D. (2001), 'Children's Early Construals of Subjectivity: Understanding the Interpretive Mind'. Unpublished PhD Dissertation, Psychology, City University of New York Graduate School.

Reddy, V. (2008), *How Infants Know Minds* (Cambridge, MA: Harvard University Press).

Reese, E. (2002), 'Social Factors in the Development of Autobiographical Memory: The state of the art', *Social Development*, **11**, pp. 124–42.

Roberts, K.P. (2000), 'An Overview of Theory and Research on Children's Source Monitoring', in K. Roberts & M. Blades (ed.), *Children's Source Monitoring* (Mahwah, NJ: Erlbaum Assoc), pp. 11–59.

Roberts, K.P. & Blades, M. (ed, 2000), *Children's Source Monitoring* (Mahwah, NJ: ERlbaum Assoc).

Robinson, E.J. (2000), 'Belief and Disbelief: Children's Assessments of the Reliability of Sources of Knowledge about the World', in K. Roberts & M. Blades (ed.), *Children's Source Monitoring* (Mahwah, NJ: Erlbaum), pp. 59–83.

Tager-Flusberg, H. & Joseph, R.M. (2005), How Language Facilitates the Acquisition of False-Belief Understanding in Children with Autism', in J. Astington & J. Baird (ed.), *Why language matters for theory of mind* (New York: Oxford University Press), pp. 298–318.

Taylor, M. (1999), *Imaginary companions and the children who create them* (New York: Oxford University Press).

Taylor, M., Esbensen, B.M. & Bennett, R.T. (1994), 'Children's Understanding of Knowledge Acuisition: The tendency for children to report that they have always known what they have just learned', *Child Development*, **65**, pp. 1581–604.

Terrace, H.S. & Metcalfe, J. (ed, 2005), *The Missing Link in Cognition: Origins of Self-Reflective Consciousness* (New York: Oxford University Press).

Tomasello, M. (1999), 'Having Intentions, Understanding Intentions, and Understanding Communicative Intentions', in P.D. Zelazo, J.W. Astington & D.R. Olson (ed.), *Developing theories of intention: Social understanding and self-control* (Mahwah NJ: Erlbaum Associates), pp. 63–76.

Tomasello, M. (2003), 'The Key is Social Cognition', in D. Gentner & S. Goldin-Meadow (ed.), *Language in Mind: Advances in the Study of Language and Thought* (Cambridge MA: MIT Press), pp. 47–57.

Vygotsky, L. (1934/1986), *Thought and Language*, translation revised and edited by A. Kozulin (Cambridge MA: MIT Press).

Welch-Ross, M.K. (2000), 'A Mental-State Reasoning Model of Suggestibility and Memory Source Monitoring', in K.P. Roberts & M. Blades (ed.), *Children's Source Monitoring* (Mahwah NJ: Erlbaum), pp. 227–56.

Wolf, S.A. & Heath, S.B. (1992), *The Braid of Literature: Children's Worlds of Reading* (Cambridge, MA: Harvard University Press).

Michelle Scalise Sugiyama

The Plot Thickens

What Children's Stories tell us about Mindreading

Abstract: *Because a major selection pressure on humans has been humans themselves, ancestral humans needed to construct a map of their social world. The ability to attribute mental states to others is necessary for this map, but not sufficient: a social map must show the intentions, emotions and beliefs of individuals relative to one another. This task, which I call goal mapping, can be divided into four subcomponents: (1) noting and remembering the actions performed by a specific individual; (2) determining which of the individual's actions subserve which of the individual's goals; (3) integrating this representation with representations of the goals and actions of the other individuals in one's social world; and (4) identifying points of conflict between the goals of these individuals. Stories told by children point to the existence of capacities dedicated to this task. Children's stories initially lack plot, which consists of three key components that appear to emerge independently and correspond to the tasks of goal mapping: character constancy, goal-directed action and conflict. This study traces the development of these capacities in two existing samples of children's narratives.*

> The principles readers use to explain and understand the actions of storybook characters are much the same as those they use to understand people's actions in everyday life.
>
> Bower and Morrow (1990, p. 48).

Introduction

In this article, I propose that stories told by young children point to the existence of a heretofore unidentified set of mindreading mechanisms, which can be characterized as a goal-mapping system. This proposition stems from a view of the mind and mindreading that is very different from that of several other contributors to this volume (see, e.g., Herman, Hutto, Nelson, Turnbull *et al.*, this volume). My research is founded on the following premises: (1) the mind consists of hundreds — perhaps thousands — of modules, each dedicated to solving a different task; (2) many of these modules are themselves modular, consisting of a set of integrated mechanisms, each of which performs a specific subgoal of the overarching task; and (3) many of these modules are vertically and/or hierarchically integrated with one or more other modules, enabling 'communication' between various information-processing and decision-making structures. I will take advantage of the fact that these points have been extensively argued elsewhere (e.g., Cosmides & Tooby, 1992; 1994; Tooby & Cosmides, 1992; Pinker, 1997; Barrett & Kurzban, 2006; for a critical take, see Hutto, 2008, chs. 3, 8, 11 and 12), and focus instead on explaining how these premises inform my view of the relationship between narrative and goal mapping.

A wealth of evidence indicates that mindreading involves several different capacities, and that these capacities have different developmental trajectories. For example, at around 9 months, infants begin developing the ability to follow another's gaze, direct another's attention by pointing to or holding up objects, and check to see whether the self and another agent are looking at the same thing (Scaife & Bruner, 1975; Butterworth & Cochran, 1980; Tomasello, 1995; 1999; Carpenter *et al.*, 1998). By 15 months, infants appear to understand that 'seeing leads to knowing' — that conspecifics acquire knowledge of the world through their sense of sight. For example, Onishi and Baillarageon (2005) found that 15-month-old infants looked longer when the place in which an actor searched for a toy was inconsistent with the actor's belief about the toy's location (see also O'Neill, 1996; Onishi *et al.*, 2007). This study also indicates that, by 15 months, toddlers are able to attribute agency (i.e., volition) to conspecifics: subjects' expectations regarding where the actor will look for the toy imply an understanding that the actor has the goal of finding the toy. Further evidence of this capacity comes from language learning studies. Baldwin *et al.* (1996) showed toddlers (19–20 months) a novel object while an actor simultaneously produced a novel label (e.g., 'A *dawnoo*!'). In the first condition, the actor was seated next to the infant and looking at the novel object when the novel label was vocalized; in the second condition, the actor was seated out of sight of the infant. When later asked to find the *dawnoo*, infants in the first condition readily chose the correct object over an equally salient distractor object, but infants in the second condition were just as likely to choose the distractor object as the correct object. These results suggest that toddlers are capable of understanding that speakers intend to talk about objects and of using this information to learn new object-word associations (see also Baldwin, 1991; 1993). Other studies suggest that children can detect certain emotional states in others, and use these cues to learn about properties of the environment. For example, when 12- and 18-month-old children heard an actor utter an exclamation of disgust ('Iiuu! Yecch!'), they immediately checked the actor's face; subsequently, subjects remained wary of the object the actor had been looking at, but untroubled by a distractor object they had been looking at, when the exclamation occurred (Moses *et al.*, 2001). Studies also show that children as young as 18 months use emotional cues to infer speakers' intended references (e.g., Tomasello & Barton, 1994; Tomasello *et al.*, 1996).

Research on mental-state term (MST) acquisition provides further evidence that mindreading may be modular, and that these modules have different developmental trajectories. These studies indicate that internal-state language begins to emerge late in the 2nd year (Limber, 1973; Shatz *et al.*, 1983; Bartsch & Wellman, 1995). For example, in a sample of 30 20-month-old children, Bretherton *et al.* (1981) found that 30% used words for fatigue, pain, disgust, distress, affection and moral conformity, while a subsequent study of 30 28-month-old children found that 90% used terms for fatigue, pain, disgust, distress, affection and moral conformity (Bretherton & Beeghly, 1982). The latter study divided MSTs into six categories: perception (including hearing, taste, touch); physiology (e.g., hunger, thirst, states of consciousness); positive/negative affect; volition/ability (e.g., desire, need, know-how); cognition (e.g., knowledge, memory, uncertainty, dreaming, pretending); and moral judgment (e.g., permission, transgression, obligation). Results suggest that children do not acquire all categories of MSTs at the same time: a greater percentage of subjects used terms for volition (m = 69.3%), physiology (m = 69.0%), and perception (m = 64.1%) than for affect (m = 46.2%), moral judgment (m = 44.3%), and cognition (m = 28.6%, with the exception of terms for *knowing*, which were used by 66% of subjects). This pattern is echoed in Wolf *et al.*'s (1984) longitudinal study of pretend play with action figures, which scored instances of play for levels of representation of human behaviour. At Level I, the child treats the figure as a representation of a human being but does not make it act as independent agent; at Level II, the child ascribes speech and action to the figure, but no internal states; at Level III, the child ascribes sensations, perceptions and physiological states to the figure; at Level IV, the child ascribes emotions, obligations, simple moral judgments and elective social relations to the figure; and at Level V, the child ascribes 'cognitive' abilities such as thinking, planning, knowing and wondering to the figure. Wolf *et al.* (1984) found that the children (n = 9) began to attribute speech and agency to figures between 98–124 weeks (m = 113 weeks/26 months); perception and sensation between 111–37 weeks (m = 120 weeks/28 months); emotion and obligation between 112–50 weeks (m = 132 weeks/31 months); and cognition between 132–210 weeks (m = 176 weeks/41 months). These levels of representation emerge in the same order as the different MST categories in Bretherton and Beeghly's (1982) study and, with the exception of cognition, at comparable ages. This suggests that different mind-reading capacities — e.g., agency detection, understanding that seeing-leads-to-knowing, detecting affective states, attributing beliefs to others — have different developmental onsets.

These findings accord with Baron-Cohen's (1995; 2005) model of the empathizing system, which subdivides the task of mindreading into six components (for a slightly different but highly compatible model, see Leslie, 1994). The Intentionality Detector (ID), which interprets agents' self-propelled movements as goal-directed, emerges in early infancy. The Eye Direction Detector (EDD), which embodies the understanding that an entity with eyes can see, identifies eye-like stimuli, and determines whether the eye-like stimuli are trained on its bearer or something else, also emerges in early infancy. These modules are the building blocks of the Shared Attention Mechanism (SAM) — the ability to follow and direct another's gaze and, by implication, to understand that seeing leads to knowing — which emerges between 9–15 months (Scaife & Bruner, 1975; Butterworth & Cochran, 1980; Tomasello, 1995; 1999; Carpenter *et al.*, 1998). The function of the Emotion Detector (TED), which emerges at around 3 months, is to represent affective states, and the function of the Empathizing System (TESS), which begins emerging at around 14 months, is to enable empathetic responses to the affective states of others. Finally, the Theory-of-Mind Mechanism (ToMM), which represents the mental states of others and embodies the understanding that behaviour is caused by these mental states, begins to emerge around

18 months, as children come to understand the epistemic state 'pre-tend' (Leslie, 1987). False-belief tests suggest that ToMM develop-ment is not complete until approximately age four (Wimmer & Perner, 1983; Baron-Cohen *et al.*, 1985; Wellman & Bartsch, 1988; Moses & Flavell, 1990; Wellman *et al.*, 2001); however, as discussed below, these findings are controversial.

In this essay, I argue that mindreading development does not end with the ability to understand the behaviour of others in terms of men-tal states. Stories told by children point to the existence of a set of competencies that can be characterized as a goal mapping system. Based on a survey of over 1,000 stories told by children ranging in age from 2 to 11 years, Sutton-Smith (1986) argues that, in its initial stages, children's narrative is marked by the absence of plot. Plot, of course, is the plan of a story: a set of causally linked actions and reac-tions related to the pursuit of a central character's goal. According to Sutton-Smith, the stories of very young children are characterized not by a plan but by a central theme. After age three or four, children begin to organize their stories around a central character, but their stories still lack conflict — that is, a central goal and opposition to that goal. Moreover, children 'can state a conflict before they can develop and resolve it. We are able to perceive the child's beginning acquisition of plotting when there is a clear central character who has a clear conflict of some sort. Generally this is not with us until somewhere between five and seven years' (1986, p. 82), and mastery of plot structure may not be attained until as late as age ten. Sutton-Smith's observations raise the question, do children's stories lack plot because young chil-dren are unable to track (a) people's plans for attaining their goals and (b) the conflicts and countermoves that ensue as the plans of multiple individuals collide with one another?

Tracking the plans and conflicts of the people around us is just as important as understanding their beliefs, feelings and desires. This is because humans are a highly social species, characterized by food sharing (Rassmussen, 1931; Isaac, 1978; Tonkinson, 1978; Wiessner, 1982; Lee, 1984; Cashdan, 1985); high parental investment and allo-parenting (Hrdy, 1999; 2009); and coalitional and exchange behaviours (Harcourt & de Waal, 1992; Cosmides & Tooby, 1992), all of which involve cooperation and planning. Thus, over the course of their evolution, a major selection pressure on humans has been humans themselves (Holloway, 1967; 1975; Humphrey, 1976; Byrne & Whiten, 1988; Alexander, 1989; Dunbar, 2003; Flinn & Ward, 2005; Flinn *et al.*, 2005; Geary, 2005). In order to navigate their com-plex social environment, our ancestors 'needed to construct ... a social map of the persons, relationships, motives, interactions, emotions, and intentions that made up their social world' (Cosmides & Tooby, 1992, p. 163). The ability to attribute specific motives, emotions and intentions to others provides the scaffolding for this map. However, this ability alone is not sufficient to generate a map of the social world. Maps chart the relative positions of things: a spatial map shows the location of specific points in relation to one another, and a social map shows the motives, emotions and intentions of individuals in relation to one another. In order to make such a map, a person must be able to (1) note and remember the actions performed by a specific individual; (2) determine which of the individual's actions subserve which of the individual's goals (i.e., infer the individual's plans for attaining his/her goals); (3) integrate this representation with representations of the goals and actions of the other individuals in his/her social world; and (4) identify points of conflict between the goals of these individuals. In short, mapping one's social world requires the ability to track interactions between multiple lines of goal-directed action.

On this view, the absence of plot — sustained, focussed, goal-directed action — in early children's narratives is striking. Equally striking is the fact that plot structure can be broken down into at least three components, which appear to emerge in stages and which roughly correspond to the task demands of goal mapping. These components are what I refer to as *character constancy, goal-directed action* and *conflict*. This study defines these components and the cognitive tasks that underlie them, and traces the course of their emergence in two samples of children's narratives, one collected by Pitcher and Prelinger (1963) and one collected by Sutton-Smith (1981).

A caveat: I am not arguing that the emergence of plot structure in children's stories coincides with the developmental onset of goal mapping competencies. As with verbal false-belief tests and children's conversation, using narrative to study mindreading is potentially problematic in that being able to attribute mental states to others and being able to talk about the mental states of others are distinct capabilities (e.g., Bretherton & Beeghly, 1982; Chandler *et al.*, 1989). Indeed, several researchers have argued that younger children may fail standard false-belief tests not because they lack ToMM but because of linguistic, computational and/or other demands associated with the test (e.g., Leslie, 1987; Chandler *et al.*, 1989; Lewis & Osborne, 1990; Siegal & Beattie, 1991; Call & Tomasello, 1999; Bloom & German, 2000; Garnham & Ruffman, 2001; Pratt & Bryant, 1990). This problem is avoided, however, if one views narrative as providing evidence of the *presence* rather than the onset of goal mapping capacities.   Narrative is a logical place to look for such evidence: stories are fundamentally about characters, and characters are representations of human agents — that is, of human thoughts, feelings, and intentions. As Bruner puts it, narrative constructs 'the landscape of consciousness: what those involved in the action know, think, or feel, or do not know, think, or feel' (1986, p. 14). Moreover, there is widespread agreement in both cognitive psychology and literary theory that stories are representations of human goals in conflict — specifically, that narrative simulates the pursuit of a specific goal by a target agent with a human psyche (*protagonist*), using a specific set of strategies within a specific set of constraints (for a review, see Scalise Sugiyama, 2005). Narrative processing, then, is an exercise in mindreading: monitoring the reputations and relationships, behaviour and beliefs of characters in narrative worlds requires the same cognitive mechanisms that are used to monitor the reputations and relationships, behaviour and beliefs of people in the real world. On this point, it is telling that story comprehension is difficult for people with autism: Temple Grandin, the well-known author and professor of animal science, claims that she never understood *Romeo and Juliet* because, in her words, 'I never knew what they were up to' (2006, p. xvi). Knowing what people are up to is precisely what goal mapping entails.

Components of Plot Structure and the
Cognitive Mechanisms they Imply

A salient property of our environment is that it contains a plethora of human goals and plans that frequently come into conflict. Because this feature of our environment impacts fitness, it would be highly advantageous to be able to track it. This requires a set of mechanisms dedicated to charting individuals' plans for achieving their goals, and the revisions made to these plans as they come into conflict with the plans of others: a goal-mapping system. As noted above, this task can be divided into at least four subcomponents: (1) noting and remembering the actions performed by a specific individual; (2) determining which of the individual's actions subserve which of the individual's goals (i.e., inferring the individual's plans for attaining his/her goals); (3) integrating this representation with representations of the goals and actions of the other individuals in one's social world; and (4) identifying points of conflict between the goals of these individuals. These abilities are highly useful for predicting and manipulating behaviour, serving in effect as a Marauder's Map (of *Harry Potter* fame;

Rowling, 1999) of the intentional world. The Marauder's Map continually updates the spatial positions of others, enabling the viewer to see where people currently are in relation to one another and, when applicable, the direction in which they are moving. Similarly, an effective social map must continually update the goal-positions of individuals, enabling the viewer to see individuals' goals in relation to one another, as well as any changes that have occurred in their respective goal directions.

The construction of plot is, in essence, the construction of a Marauder's Map of intentionality in a given narrative world. Plot involves tracking a series of actions performed by a central character in pursuit of a goal, the goals and actions of others as they relate to and conflict with the goal of the main character, and the outcome of this conflict. As noted above, plot structure consists of several components, which children appear to acquire in stages: organization around a central character (*character constancy*), organization around a central character with a clear goal (*goal-directed action*), and organization around a central character with a clear goal and obstacles to the attainment of that goal (*conflict*). In this section, I will present examples of children's narratives that illustrate these components and the cognitive tasks that underlie them, and trace the course of their emergence. As we will see, these tasks are distinct from ToMM as traditionally understood in that they solve a different set of cognitive problems. Moreover, the subcomponents of goal mapping are distinct from one another, performing different cognitive tasks and exhibiting what appear to be distinct developmental trajectories.

The stories used for this study come from two different samples, neither of which claims to be representative. The first was assembled by Pitcher and Prelinger (1963), who collected a total of 360 stories from 70 girls and 67 boys between the ages of 2;2 and 5;11. These children all attended private preschools in or near New Haven, Connecticut, and are described by the authors as being 'socioeconomically rather privileged children' (p. 26) and of above-average intelligence. With the exception of the 5-year-old cohort, two stories were collected from each child at least one month apart. For the 2-year-old cohort, stories were collected from 30 children (15 male, 15 female), and for the remaining cohorts, stories were collected from 60 children (30 male, 30 female). Only one story was collected from each child in the 5-year-old cohort. Stories were collected from 1955–1958; as a result, 49 of the 137 children contributed stories at more than one age level.

The second sample is the work of Sutton-Smith (1981) and his associates, who collected 1000 stories from 141 New York preschool and grade school children ranging from 2 to 11 years of age. Stories were collected at a preschool for children age 2 through 5 and a public school for children age 5 through 11 in Greenwich Village. These children are described as the 'offspring of highly intelligent parents (working in the arts, advertising, and the professions)' (Sutton-Smith, 1981, p. 34), with IQ scores in the 115–30 range. Sutton-Smith acknowledges that this 'bright' sample is not representative: 'we know from some of our own work elsewhere that the stories told in other middle-socioeconomic-range schools are typically two years below the present sample in structural level' (p. 34). Due to space limitations, Sutton-Smith could not include all 1000 stories in the published collection, so he chose the children who had contributed the most stories and who had volunteered stories throughout the course of the study. Consequently, stories in the collection tend to be from the most verbal children. Additionally, more stories were collected from some children than others; thus, those children most inclined to tell stories are over-represented. The published collection contains approximately 500 stories from 52 children.

Character constancy

It is one thing to understand that another person has a goal, but quite another to understand a person's plan for, and track their progress toward, achieving that goal. The first step in goal mapping, then, is to stay focussed on a given individual long enough to acquire this information. Tellingly, one of the first plot constituents that appears in children's narratives is character constancy — organization around a central character. Prior to this, when they exhibit any sort of organizing principle at all, children's early narratives are characterized by a central theme and variations on that theme. This pattern is illustrated by the following story told by Bill (2;5), who improvises on the theme of falling down:

> The monkeys
> They went up sky
> They fall down
> Choo choo train in the sky
> The train fell down in the sky
> I fell down in the sky in the water
> I got on my boat and my legs hurt
> Daddy fall down in the sky. (Sutton-Smith, 1981, pp. 53–4).

In this story, consistent attention to a single agent is lacking: the story presents four different characters, but does not focus on any one of them. Similarly, a story told by Beatrice (3;4) does not focus on any of its four characters. Rather, it is organized around the theme of going out and coming back:

> The mother went out
> then the father went out
> then the mother went out again
> and then the father went out
> then policeman came
> the mother came back from the meeting
> then the father came back from the meeting
> then a Cookie Monster came
> and the policeman came again
> then the Cookie Monster went away. (Sutton-Smith, 1981, p. 53).

This pattern is evident in the Pitcher and Prelinger sample as well. Dulcy (3;6) told a story loosely organized around the theme of shooting babies:

> Once there was a baby and he got killed. The big hunter got the baby. He put on the stove and cooked and ate him up. It was happened. The little girl ran a hundred miles. She fell down. Then she called her mommy. And her mommy put a Band-aid on it. They got another baby, and he got shot, too. And another baby, and he got shot. (Pitcher & Prelinger, 1963, p. 60).

The agent to which the actions and events in these stories refer is not constant throughout the narrative: some actions are performed by one character, some by another, and some by yet another. To put it another way, these stories are not organized around a series of actions committed by or events that happen to a single agent. Instead, they are organized around an action or event that happens repeatedly (e.g., babies getting shot) or to multiple individuals (e.g., falling down, going out/coming back). Alternatively, children's early narratives may be organized around a series of temporally related events, as in the following story, told by Upton (3;4):

> Then the train came to pick the paper up. Then the people threw the paper out of the train. Then Mr. Knife came up to get on the train. Then somebody came and got dead. Then a policeman came and put him in heaven and he got dead. Then the mother Knife came out and saw the other Knife has gone. (Pitcher & Prelinger, 1963, p. 52).

Central characters begin to make their appearance in the Sutton-Smith sample after age three, as seen in the following stories. The first was told by Cathy (3;0), and the second by David (3;11):

Batman
Batman crashed in a car
Batman walked home
he see his mommy
Batman had toys. (Sutton-Smith, 1981, pp. 57–8).

My cat went to the doctor
the doctor was on vacation
my cat jumped onto a big airplane
and after that the airplane went to the airport
and after that the cat came out of the airport and went home.
(Sutton-Smith, 1981, p. 76).

In the Pitcher and Prelinger sample, central characters begin to emerge in the second half of the third year, as seen in the next two stories, the first told by Tobias (2;7) and the second by Dorothy (2;9):

Froggie goes crash in the water, bumps his head. And he fell in dirt. Then he bumped his head off. (Pitcher & Prelinger, 1963, p. 34).

Little girl played in her back yard. She had a big mouth. She played 'Woof, woof' with that little boy. (Pitcher & Prelinger, 1963, p. 37).

All the actions and events in these stories revolve around a single character, which implies an ability to follow a series of actions committed by a single individual. As noted above, the ability to track this information may emerge prior to the ability to represent this information in narrative form. Children's narratives point not necessarily to the onset of this ability but simply to its existence: the lack of character constancy in children's early narratives and its emergence late in the third year suggests that at some point children lack the ability to track a series of actions committed by a single individual, and that at some point they acquire it.

Although character constancy appears somewhat earlier in the Pitcher and Prelinger sample than in the Sutton-Smith sample, it is not universal at this age, as evinced in the following stories, the first told by Eliot (2;9) and the second by Lucy (2;11):

David makes a pipe in his mouth and Woody and Daddy. They go to the bank. And Mommy, she eats breakfast. Lisa, he picks snow up. He throw it away, like this. (Pitcher & Prelinger, 1963, p. 31).

A little baby and a big girl is her sister. My baby goes to sleep — my baby didn't sleep yesterday. She just went to rest. The doggie ran away, and the little girl told her mommy. He ran away on the street. She gonna buy a new dog. (Pitcher & Prelinger, 1963, p. 38).

Character constancy marks a shift from stories consisting of sets of causally unrelated actions committed by multiple characters to sets of causally unrelated actions committed by a single character. That is, the lines of action initially represented by children are episodic: the actions exhibit temporal relationships, but their causal relationships are obscure. In the cat story, for example, we can tell that the cat first went to the doctor, then on an airplane, then to the airport, and then home, but we don't know why the cat went to the doctor, or why the cat jumped on an airplane afterwards. We know that Batman got in a car crash, then walked home, and then saw his mommy, and we can infer that he walked home because driving was no longer an option; however, we don't know whether he went home because he wanted to see his mommy or for some other reason. We can tell that Froggie fell in the water before he fell in the dirt, but we have no sense whatsoever of what is causing Froggie to fall in the first place.

When reading these stories, it becomes evident that children attribute mental states to story characters independently of their ability to organize a story around the actions of a single character. For example, the shooting babies story features the mental state term *called*, and the Mr. Knife story features the term *saw*, but both lack a central character. The following example, told by a girl age 3;6, contains multiple mental state terms but no central character:

> Animals went in the woods. Then Indians came and took animals away. The animals died in the water. Then they walked and walked. A girl came to the boat and *saw* the animals. The Indians died too. The horses came in the boat; the boat took the horses away. The girl *wanted* to go on the boat, so the boat came back. Then the boat went in the water, and the *real* clown *wanted* to go on the boat. (Pitcher & Prelinger, 1963, p. 67, emphasis added).

Similarly, Garrett, who at age 4 was using the terms *said, know, found* and *thought* in his narratives, told the following story at age 5;10:

> Once there was a tiger
> and there were two cats
> they were friends
> and there was a mouse too
> and the mouse went over to a leaf
> and he got on the leaf
> and then a bird came and picked the mouse up and flew away with him
> and he was for supper
> the end. (Sutton-Smith, 1981, pp. 104–5).

When Garrett finished telling the story, the collector asked him, 'Who's the story about?' Garrett replied, 'I don't know' (Sutton-Smith, 1981, p. 105). Conversely, a child may tell a story that features a central character but lacks mental state terms, as in the cat, Froggie, and little girl stories cited above. This pattern suggests that attributing mental states to others and following the actions of an agent are different tasks. Although the ability to track a series of actions committed by a particular person might seem trivial, it is prerequisite to tracking a series of causally linked actions related to the pursuit of a goal.

Goal-directed action

Being able to follow the actions of an agent is integral to understanding who did what, and when. However, in order to understand *why* an agent did what she did when she did, one must be able to link specific actions with a specific goal. That is, one must be able to follow goal-directed action. This entails sifting through all the actions one sees an agent perform, and determining which of those actions subserve which goals. Without this ability, it would be virtually impossible for us to determine, in Grandin's words, what others were up to.

Like goal mapping, story structure is rooted in tracking the actions performed by an individual in pursuit of a given goal. According to Sutton-Smith (1986), children's stories are not consistently organized around goal-directed action until somewhere between 5 and 7 years. An appreciation of this accomplishment can best be gained by viewing its absence, as illustrated in the following story, told by Frank (4;10):

> One day there was a boy
> boy found the cat
> the cat round around and the boy too
> and a dog came and chased the cat away
> and the boy was sad
> another dog came and a cat came and chased the dog away
> and the boy went home
> and he went to the store and buy some bread and buy some cookies
> the end. (Sutton-Smith, 1981, pp. 96–7).

The actions and events in this story are all organized around the boy, but they are episodic: the boy simply does things, or things happen to him. Similarly, a story told by Gina (3;5) is filled with action, but there is no sense that the actions are taken deliberately, as steps toward a specific end:

> The girl went out
> the girl went away
> and she went on the boat
> she came back home
> she drew herself
> then the girl went down the thing
> yeah

the thing you go down on a boat
the girl jump on the ceiling and she went on a car
she fell down
then she went out the boat
then she went out in a car so she could make up her mind.
(Sutton-Smith, 1981, pp. 97–8).

Although there is a central character in this story, the closest we get to goal-directed action is 'she went out in a car so she could make up her mind'. This sentence is organized around a goal, but the story itself is not. The same is true of the following story, from Brenda (3;11), which contains two sentences (indicated by italics) in which an agent's goal and an action taken to achieve it are stated. However, these goals are unrelated to one another, and do not subserve a larger, overarching goal:

Once upon a time there was a big horsie. Once upon a time there was a little horsie. And once upon a time there was a middle-sized horsie. And one got lost. *Then he went to a cupboard to put his shirt there. And he went to another barber to cut his baby's hair.* Then they went home. (Pitcher & Prelinger, 1963, p. 56).

When compared with these episodic narratives, stories with goal-oriented action are quite striking. The following story, told by Deidre (5;6), is noteworthy in that all of the action advances or is related to the kitten's goal of being a Christmas present:

Once upon a time there was a little pussy cat that wanted to be a Christmas present. He went to Mr. Rabbit's house and said 'I want to be a Christmas present'. And he said, 'Let's go ask Mr. Squirrel'. And then he said, 'We shall go to the bear's house; they probably will know'. The bear said, 'Today's not Christmas — tomorrow will be Christmas'. In a minute Santa Claus came dashing through the sky and the kitty called up. 'I want to be a Christmas present'. And then Santa said, 'I think I know where to put you'. So the next morning he wasn't in Santa's sleigh any more, he was in a little girl's house. And then the little girl said when she saw him, 'I guess Santa knew what I wanted for Christmas'. (Pitcher & Prelinger, 1963, p. 135).

Unfortunately, precise ages of the elementary school children in the Sutton-Smith sample were not available, because birth dates for the 5-to-10-year-old cohort were not given, and stories were collected over a 2-year period. Thus, a given story from the 5-year-old cohort may have been told when the child was 5, 6, or even 7 years old. However, the movement from episodic action to goal-directed action that is seen in the Pitcher and Prelinger sample is evident in the Sutton-Smith stories as well. For example, in the following story, told by a boy from the 5-year-old cohort, all of the action subserves the dinosaur's goal of satisfying his hunger:

> Once upon a time there was a great big dinosaur. He wanted a giant rabbit dinner. He found a tree. He never saw a tree before. He thought it was a rabbit. He tried to eat it but it was too hard. He looked and he found a real rabbit. He took it home, then he ate it. Someone knocked on the door and he opened it. He was still hungry. He saw an ant at the door and he ate it up. Then he ate a cow up. Then he found an elephant and he ate it up. Then when he was so fat he went to bed then he blew up. The end. (Sutton-Smith, 1981, p. 120).

The same is true of the following story, told by a girl from the 8-year-old cohort:

> Once there was a fox. He was very lonely. One day he went on a walk and he met a tiger. He asked the tiger, 'Can you help me find my home?' 'Sure, where do you live?' said the tiger. 'That's it. I don't know where I live'. 'Okay. Why don't we go on a walk and if you think you live there, you tell me'. So the fox got on the tiger's back and they walked and walked until it got dark. 'Oh', said the fox. 'It's getting light'. 'We can sleep and go on in the morning', said the tiger. And so they started off in the morning. And they walked and they walked again. One week later the tiger said, 'Well, we can't find your home. What will we do?' 'Let's sit down and think', said the fox. 'Okay', said the tiger. Then the tiger said, 'You can come home and live with me'. So the fox went to live with the tiger and he was never lonely again. (Sutton-Smith, 1981, p. 255).

Although the ability to attribute mental states to others is essential to tracking goal-directed action, the use of mental state terms in children's early narrative is not necessarily accompanied by goal-directed action. This suggests that the ability to attribute intentionality to others and the ability to link a specific goal with a set of actions taken to attain that goal are distinct capacities. The following story, told by Rose (4;0), is a case in point:

> About a clown who was making a funny face. And then he went bumping on the ball. He went in a house and knocked all the dishes out. Then the people came home and they were sad and didn't know what to do. And they took him out of the house and then he went to a building and knocked some more dishes over. And then he went to bed and tipped it over. He said, 'I'll go back to the circus and make some more tricks'. And then he went out to the circus and knocked some more dishes and threw them up in the air and it cracked up. (Pitcher & Prelinger, 1963, p. 109).

Although the informant attributes a variety of mental states and capacities to the characters (e.g., *funny*, *sad*, *know*, *said*), the action in the story is episodic rather than goal-oriented. The Sutton-Smith sample exhibits the same pattern, as seen in the following story told by 6-year-old Dierdre:

> Once upon a time there was a bear. The bear was unhappy because he was jumping on rocks. And once he was not very happy because he couldn't find a rock to jump on. He found something he was hunting for. He tried to get away. He got stung. So he found some honey in a can. He saw a man who set the trap with it. But he didn't go near. He jumped with it and stuck his head in. He tried to get away from the bees. The man did not help him; he was scared of bears. (Sutton-Smith, 1981, p. 161).

Dierdre's use of the mental state terms *unhappy, find/found, hunting, tried, saw* and *scared* suggests that ToMM is present, but the story is not organized around a central goal and actions taken to attain it. This suggests that the abilities to attribute intentionality (ID) and epistemic states (ToMM) to others are not sufficient for tracking a series of actions committed by a particular person to achieve a particular goal.

Conflict

Following the goal-directed actions of a single individual is equivalent to charting one path in a given space. In order to construct a map of our social world, we need to chart all of its paths of goal-directed action in relation to one another, and identify the points at which they cross one another. At the simplest level, this involves tracking the interaction between the competing, goal-directed actions of two individuals.

On this point, there is widespread agreement that a key ingredient of narrative is conflict (e.g., Cassil, 1981; Kermode, 1981; Oates, 1992). As Clayton observes, having a central character in pursuit of a goal is not enough: 'Imagine this as a story: George wants someone to love. He walks into a room and meets Eloise. He loves her and is happy. Clearly that's not a story. There's desire but no obstacle, and without an obstacle, there's no conflict' (1984, p. 13). In narrative, as in life, conflict may arise from the physical environment, the self, from animal agents, or from human agents. When the source of conflict is the physical environment or the self, only one agent is involved — the main character — and it is not necessary to track two lines of goal-directed action. However, when the source of conflict is another agent, two competing lines of goal-directed action are at play. In this case, the audience must track the moves and counter-moves of the agents whose goals are in conflict with one another. It is in the representation of the actions and reactions of agents that plot structure and goal mapping overlap.

Tracking these actions and reactions is simpler when one or more of the agents are animals. Tellingly, many of children's early representations of conflict involve animal characters, as seen in the following, told by Wayne (3;7):

> Little tiny bear saw a little squirrel. The little squirrel jumped on the bear and he got killed. The bear jumped in a hole and closed the door up. The squirrel jumped in the hole, and he says, 'Why do you get in my hole?'. The squirrel jumped out of the window. Then the bear jumped out of the window. He was trying to kill the squirrel. The daddy bear came and said, 'Jump to the hole again'. Then the squirrel jumped in his own hole. And that's the end. (Pitcher & Prelinger, 1963, pp. 54–5).

The depiction of human moves and countermoves appears at around age 5. As with goal-directed action, the depiction of two competing lines of action is perhaps best recognized when it is absent. In the following story, told by Alan at approximately age 6, there is a clear conflict between the boy and his parents; however, only one line of goal-directed action is developed:

> Once upon a time there was a little house, and people lived inside it. They were friendly. There was a little kid and he wanted a pet, but his mother and father didn't want to have a pet. The next morning he woke up. He was crying and he wanted a kitten so bad that he went to this mother and father's room to tell them that he wanted a kitten. He was begging so much for a kitten, so his mother and father got a kitten. Anywhere he goes, anything he does, he takes the kitten with him. (Sutton-Smith, 1981, p. 127).

We see the steps that the boy takes to attain his goal of acquiring a kitten: he cries, he goes to his parents' room, he tells them he wants a kitten, he begs for a kitten. The fact that the boy takes all these measures indicates that his parents are resisting his request, but we don't see the steps they take to effect this resistance. In contrast, 8-year-old Fred tells a story in which we see evidence of two competing lines of action. Although this story is about a cheetah and a deer, the animals are highly anthropomorphized:

> Once there was a cheetah. The cheetah was his name and he lived in the forest. He was a very smart cheetah. Once in the middle of the night he heard footsteps. He thought it was a hunter he ran up a tree. He said, 'yum' because he saw a big deer walking along the path in which he came. So since he was so hungry, he crept down to the top of the trunk of the tree and he waited until the deer got near him. When the deer got very near him, he jumped on him. Then the deer looked around and saw Speedy so he ran like any deer would. Speedy scrambled down the tree and chased him like a bullet and everybody knows that the cheetah is the fastest animal in the world. He came nearer and nearer to the deer. And

the deer leaped away like a bullet but Speedy just kept on going on and on and finally he got so near to the dear [sic] that he leaped at him and the deer fell dead. And I would say that everybody has to die sometime. Well he did not know what to do with the deer so he went home and his family and told them about it and they went to the place where Speedy left the deer. It wasn't there so they searched for the deer. They found another deer but it wasn't the same one so they brought it home. After all that work Speedy ate it all with his family. (Sutton-Smith, 1981, pp. 216–7).

Although the story focuses mostly on the steps taken by the cheetah to catch the deer, in the brief descriptions of the deer's attempts to out-maneuver the cheetah we see the rudiments of a second line of goal-directed action. Full development of two competing lines of action can be seen in a story told by Colin (5;3), which also features highly anthropomorphized animal characters:

Once upon a time there was a little duck and a fox and this little duck and fox were friends. One day they didn't have any food to eat and then they both went into people's houses and got their favorite food. And then the children said, 'Hey, Mommy, there's someone been in our food!'. Then the children made a little trap for them, and then they came and said, 'Oh, there's a trap'. They got a stick from their home and then they just put it in the little mouse trap and let it snap and then they made a little wooden thing like themselves and then they put it in the trap and then the children said, 'Hey, Mommy, we caught them'. Then they ate the wood up. (Pitcher & Prelinger, 1963, pp. 116–7).

By age 5 or so, some children are also capable of depicting conflict between two lines of human goal-directed action, as seen in the following story, told by 5-year-old Agatha:

Once upon a time there lived a beautiful movie star. She lived in the old western days, but not far from her cabin where she lived there was these bandits and they had a plan; first to rob the stage coach and then get her. Then they began their plan. The girl not knowing about the robbery she sat and she just felt the warm fire in her log cabin fireplace. Not long after that the bandits soon finished robbing the stage coach and then they began to go to her house. They snuck in the window of the log cabin. They grabbed her inside a bag after they had snuck up on her. They brought her to their leader. Then they showed what they had got in the bag. Then they tied her up to a chair. There was a big fair for all the bandits and the movie star was all tied up in the chair with the fair. Not long after the cops heard about it. They came scrambling to the fair as fast as they could. They saved the movie star and they arrested the ban-dits. And the chief of the cops had a wedding with the movie star and they lived happily ever after. (Sutton-Smith, 1981, p. 122).

The same ability is evinced in the Pitcher and Prelinger sample, as seen in a story told by Calvin (5;10):

> The boy was playing with a girl and the girl started to get tough. And the boy didn't like it; then he started to get tough, too. Their mother said, 'What are you doing?'. And the brother said, 'Nothing, Mother, we're just playing around the yard'. The boy had a gun in his pocket. He drawed it and he shot the girl. Then the mother knew what he was doing and she called up the police. The police came and said, 'Why did you kill that girl?'. The boy said, 'I just wanted to do that because she got tough'. Then the police said, 'There is no reason to shoot a girl that is tough because she still is nice when she isn't tough'. (Pitcher & Prelinger, 1963, p. 115).

In this story, there are essentially three lines of action: the girl's, the boy's, and the mother's. The girl initiates the conflict by getting 'tough', and the boy responds by shooting her. The mother responds to the boy's action by calling the police in to discipline him. At this point the 'police' becomes a proxy for the mother, and interrogates the boy. The boy responds to the interrogation by justifying his action, and the 'police' responds by chastising the boy.

As we can see in the examples presented here, the ability to represent conflict — that is, competing lines of action — entails more than attributing agency or other mental states to others. Whereas ID and ToMM enable us to understand that Rick wants Ilsa and that Victor wants Ilsa, goal mapping enables us to understand that Rick and Victor's goals conflict with one another, and to track their actions in relation to their respective goals and in response to this conflict. These abilities underlie the negotiation of adult social relations and politics. Given the large quantity of information that must be integrated to perform this task, it is not surprising that humans do not master plot structure until late childhood.

General Remarks

What children's narratives tell us about mindreading development is that, while young children appear to understand that others have intentions, thoughts and feelings, they don't appear to have a firm grasp on the relationships between intentions, thoughts and feelings on the one hand, and the accomplishment of goals on the other. Things just happen to characters, and characters react. In the stories of older children, the characters make things happen: they act deliberately in order to achieve a goal that is articulated at the outset. And in the stories of even older children, the central character pursues her goal in opposition to the goals of other characters.

This long developmental trajectory is instructive. Full-blown folk psychological abilities, whereby individuals are able not only to attribute mental states to others but to chart others' goals and strategies in relation to one another, may require sequential assembly of the cognitive subroutines involved coupled with a lengthy learning period, during which feedback from correct and incorrect interpretations of mental states and exposure to a variety of complex goal conflicts fine-tunes the system. This, in turn, has implications for the evolution of human life history: prolonged juvenility in humans may be necessary — in part — for the building and calibration of mind-reading competencies (Flinn & Ward, 2005). Like other cognitive faculties, such as language (Pinker, 1994) and incest avoidance (Wolf, 1970; Shepher, 1971; Wolf & Huang, 1980; Lieberman, 2009), mindreading development and implementation are likely to be dependent upon specific inputs from the social environment. By simulating that environment (Scalise Sugiyama, 2005) — that is, by simulating human behaviour and the mental processes that underlie it — narrative provides another venue for these inputs. In ancestral environments, on-demand nursing would have exposed infants to storytelling from birth, whenever their mother heard or told a story. Thus, from the time it emerged, storytelling presented a source of social inputs relevant to mindreading development.

Specifically, storytelling enables us to create a hypothetical situation and cast of players, and observe as those players — each with different goals, personalities, attributes and life histories — react to the situation and to each other. Narrative thus enables us to see a given situation from a variety of interested positions — e.g., parent, child, sibling, in-law, friend, lover, ally, enemy. In so doing, narrative may help assemble our encyclopedia of mental state knowledge and exercise our mindreading faculties, making them more penetrating, farsighted and swift. Storytelling is a fitness bargain, providing an energy-efficient means of enhancing our ability to predict and manipulate the behaviour of others (Scalise Sugiyama, 1996; 2005; 2008).

Admittedly, the findings presented here are tentative. Further study using a representative sample is needed, as is a quantitative study of the developmental trajectory of character constancy, goal-directed action and conflict in children's narratives. Also needed is experimental research aimed at teasing out the quantity and design of the hypothesized mechanisms: obviously, we should not rely exclusively on children's narratives to identify mindreading capacities. These caveats notwithstanding, children's narrative merits further attention. Storytelling is an evolutionarily relevant context in which to study mindreading development: oral narrative is a universal, reliably developing behaviour, and converging lines of evidence indicate that it emerged tens of thousands of years ago (Scalise Sugiyama, 2001; 2005) — that is, under social and ecological conditions similar to those under which mindreading capacities evolved. Moreover, as I have shown here, narrative points to the existence of a set of mind-reading capacities — a goal mapping system — that other approaches have missed. It may lead us to others as well.

Acknowledgements

The author thanks Larry Sugiyama, Dan Hutto, and two anonymous reviewers for their helpful comments on an earlier draft.

References

Alexander, R. (1989), 'The Evolution of the Human Psyche', in P. Mellars & C. Stringer (ed.), *The Human Revolution: Behavioral and Biological Perspectives on the Origins of Modern Humans* (Princeton: Princeton University Press).

Baldwin, D. (1991), 'Infants' Contribution to the Achievement of Joint Reference', *Child Development*, **62**, pp. 875–90.

Baldwin, D. (1993), 'Infants' Ability to Consult the Speaker for Clues to Word Reference', *Journal of Child Language*, **20**, pp. 395–418.

Baldwin, D., Markman, E., Bill, B., Desjardins, R., Irwin, J. & Tidball, G. (1996), 'Infants' Reliance on a Social Criterion for Establishing Word-object Relations', *Child Development*, **67**, pp. 3135–53.

Baron-Cohen, S. (1995), *Mindblindness* (Cambridge, MA: MIT Press).

Baron-Cohen, S. (2005), 'The Empathizing System: A revision of the 1994 model of the mindreading system', in B. Ellis & D. Bjorklund (ed.), *Origins of the Social Mind* (New York: The Guilford Press).

Baron-Cohen, S., Leslie, A.M. & Frith, U. (1985), 'Does the Autistic Child have a "Theory of Mind"?', *Cognition*, **21**, pp. 37–46.

Barrett, H.C. & Kurzban, R. (2006), 'Modularity in Cognition: Framing the debate', *Psychological Review*, **113**, pp. 628–47.

Bartsch, K. & Wellman, H.M. (1995), *Children Talk About the Mind* (New York: Oxford University Press).

Bloom, P. & German, T.P. (2000), 'Two Reasons to Abandon the False Belief Task as a Test of Theory of Mind', *Cognition*, **77**, pp. B25–31.

Bower, G. & Morrow, D. (1990), 'Mental Models in Narrative Comprehension', *Science*, **247**, pp. 44–8.

Bretherton, I. & Beeghly, M. (1982), 'Talking about Internal States', *Developmental Psychology*, **18**, pp. 906–21.

Bretherton, I., McNew, S. & Beeghly-Smith, M. (1981), 'Early Person Knowledge as Expressed in Gestural and Verbal Communication: When do infants acquire a "theory of mind"?', in M.E. Lamb & L.R. Sherrod (ed.), *Infant Social Cognition* (Hillsdale, NJ: Ehrlbaum).

Bruner, J. (1986), *Actual Minds, Possible Worlds* (Cambridge, MA: Harvard University Press).

Butterworth, G.E. & Cochran, E.C. (1980), 'Towards a Mechanism of Joint Attention in Human Infancy', *International Journal of Behavioural Development*, **3**, pp. 253–72.

Byrne, R. & Whiten, A. (ed, 1988), *Machiavellian Intelligence* (Oxford: Clarendon).

Call, J. & Tomasello, M. (1999), 'A Non-verbal False Belief Task: The performance of children and great apes', *Child Development*, **70**, pp. 381–95.

Carpenter, M., Nagell, K. & Tomasello, M. (1998), 'Social Cognition, Joint Attention, and Communicative Competence from 9 to 15 Months of Age', *Monographs of the Society for Research in Child Development 63*.

Cashdan, E. (1985), 'Coping with Risk: Reciprocity among the Basarwa of Northern Botswana', *Man*, **20**, pp. 454–74.

Cassill, R.V. (1981), 'Talking about Fiction', in R.V. Cassill (ed.), *The Norton Anthology of Short Fiction* (New York: Norton).

Chandler, M., Fritz, A.S. & Hala, S. (1989), 'Small-scale Deceit: Deception as a marker of 2-, 3- and 4-year-olds' early theories of mind', *Child Development*, **60**, pp. 1263–77.

Clayton, J. (ed, 1984), Preface to *The Heath Introduction to Fiction* (Lexington, MA: D.C. Heath).

Cosmides, L. & Tooby, J. (1992), 'Cognitive Adaptations for Social Exchange', in J. Barkow, L. Cosmides & J. Tooby (ed.), *The Adapted Mind* (New York: Oxford University Press).

Cosmides, L. & Tooby, J. (1994), 'Origins of Domain Specificity: The evolution of functional specialization', in L. Hirschfeld & S. Gelman (ed.), *Mapping the Mind: Domain Specificity in Cognition and Culture* (Cambridge: Cambridge University Press).

Dunbar, R. (2003), 'Evolution of the Social Brain', *Science*, **302**, pp. 1160–1.

Flinn, M. & Ward, C. (2005), 'Ontogeny and Evolution of the Social Child', in B. Ellis & D. Bjorklund (ed.), *Origins of the Social Mind* (New York: The Guildford Press).

Flinn, M., Geary, D. & Ward, C. (2005), 'Ecological Dominance, Social Competition, and Coalitionary Arms Races: Why humans evolved extraordinary intelligence', *Evolution and Human Behavior*, **26**, pp. 10–46.

Garnham, W. & Ruffman, T. (2001), 'Doesn't See, Doesn't Know: Is anticipatory looking really related to understanding of belief?', *Developmental Science*, **4**, pp. 94–100.

Geary, D. (2005), *The Origin of Mind: Evolution of Brain, Cognition, and General Intelligence* (Washington, DC: American Psychological Association).

Grandin, T. (2006), *Thinking in Pictures* (New York: Random House).

Harcourt, A.H. & de Waal, F.B.M. (ed, 1992), *Coalitions and Alliances in Humans and Other Animals* (Oxford: Oxford University Press).

Holloway, R. (1967), 'The Evolution of the Human Brain: Some notes toward a synthesis between neural structure and the evolution of complex behavior', General Systems, **12**, pp. 3–19.

Holloway, R. (1975), *The role of human social behavior in the evolution of the brain. The 43rd James Arthur Lecture on the evolution of the human brain at the American Museum of Natural History, 1973* (New York: American Museum of Natural History).

Humphrey, N. (1976), 'The Social Function of Intellect', in P.P.G. Bateson & R.A. Hinde (ed.), *Growing Points in Ethology* (New York: Cambridge University Press).

Hutto, D. (2008), *Folk Psychological Narratives* (Cambridge, MA: MIT Press).

Hrdy, S. (1999), *Mother Nature: A History of Mothers, Infants, and Natural Selection* (New York: Pantheon).

Hrdy, S. (2009), *Mothers and Others: The Evolutionary Origins of Mutual Understanding* (Belknap Press).

Isaac, G. (1978), 'The Food-Sharing Behaviour of Proto-Human Hominids', *Scientific American*, **238**, pp. 90–108.

Kermode, F. (1981), 'Secrets and Narrative Sequence', in W.J.T. Mitchell (ed.), *On Narrative* (Chicago: University of Chicago Press).

Lee, R.B. (1984), *The Dobe !Kung* (New York: Holt, Rinehart & Winston).

Leslie, A.M. (1987), 'Pretense and Representation: The origins of "theory of mind"', *Psychological Review*, **94**, pp. 412–26.

Leslie, A.M. (1994), 'ToMM, ToBy, and Agency: Core architecture and domain specificity', in L. Hirschfeld & S. Gelman (ed.), *Mapping the Mind: Domain Specificity in Cognition and Culture* (Cambridge: Cambridge University Press).

Lewis, C. & Osborne, A. (1990), 'Three-year-olds' Problems with False Belief: Conceptual deficit or linguistic artifact?', *Child Development*, **61**, pp. 1514–9.

Lieberman, D. (2009), 'Rethinking Taiwanese Minor Marriage Data: Evidence the mind uses multiple kinship cues to regulate inbreeding avoidance', *Evolution and Human Behavior,* **30**, pp. 153–60.

Limber, J. (1973), 'The Genesis of Complex Sentences', in T. Moore (ed.), *Cognitive Development and the Acquisition of Language* (New York: Academic Press).

Moses, L. & Flavell, J.H. (1990), 'Inferring False Beliefs from Actions and Reactions', *Child Development*, **61**, pp. 929–45.

Moses, L., Baldwin, D., Rosicky, J. & Tidball, G. (2001), 'Evidence for Referential Understanding in the Emotions Domain at 12 and 18 months', *Child Development,* **72**, pp. 718–35.

Oates, J.C. (1992), 'Introduction', in J.C. Oates (ed.), *The Oxford Book of American Short Stories* (Oxford: Oxford University Press).

O'Neill, D.K. (1996), 'Two-year-old Children's Sensitivity to a Parent's Knowledge State when Making Requests', *Child Development*, **67**, pp. 659– 77.

Onishi, K. & Baillargeon, R. (2005), 'Do 15-month-old Infants Understand False Beliefs?', *Science*, **8**, pp. 255–8.

Onishi, K., Baillargeon, R. & Leslie, A. (2007), '15-month-old Infants Detect Violations in Pretend Scenarios', *Acta Psychologica,* **124**, pp. 106–28.

Pinker, S. (1994), *The Language Instinct* (New York: William Morrow).

Pinker, S. (1997), *How the Mind Works* (New York: Norton).

Pitcher, E. & Prelinger, E. (1963), *Children Tell Stories* (New York: International Universities Press).

Pratt, C. & Bryant, P. (1990), 'Young Children Understand that Looking Leads to Knowing (so long as they are looking into a single barrel)', *Child Development*, **61**, pp. 973–82.

Rassmussen, K. (1931), *The Netsilik Eskimos: Social Life and Spiritual Culture. Report of the 5th Thule Expedition 1921–24, vol. VIII, no. 1–2* (Copenhagen: Gyldendalske Boghandel, Nordisk Forlag).

Rowling, J.K. (1999), *Harry Potter and the Prisoner of Azkaban* (New York: Scholastic).

Scaife, M. & Bruner, J. (1975), 'The Capacity for Joint Visual Attention in the Infant', *Nature*, **253**, pp. 265–6.

Scalise Sugiyama, Michelle (1996), 'On the Origins of Narrative: Storyteller bias as a fitness-enhancing strategy', *Human Nature*, **7**, pp. 403–25.

Scalise Sugiyama, M. (2001), 'Food, Foragers, and Folklore: The role of narrative in human subsistence', *Evolution and Human Behavior,* **22**, pp. 221–40.

Scalise Sugiyama, M. (2005), 'Reverse-engineering Narrative', in J. Gottschall & D.S. Wilson (ed.), *The Literary Animal* (Evanston, IL: Northwestern University Press).

Scalise Sugiyama, M. (2008), 'Narrative as Social Mapping — Case Study: The trickster genre and the free rider problem', *Ometeca*, **12**, pp. 24–42.

Shatz, M., Wellman, H.M. & Silber, S. (1983), 'The Acquisition of Mental Verbs: A systematic investigation of the first reference to mental state', *Cognition*, **14**, pp. 301–21.

Shepher, J. (1971), 'Mate Selection among Second Generation Kibbutz Adolescents and Adults: Incest avoidance and negative imprinting', *Archives of Sexual Behavior*, **1**, pp. 293–307.

Siegal, M. & Beattie, K. (1991), 'Where to Look First for Children's Knowledge of False Beliefs', *Cognition*, **38**, pp. 1–12.

Sutton-Smith, B. (1981), *The Folkstories of Children* (Philadelphia: University of Pennsylvania Press).

Sutton-Smith, B. (1986), 'Children's Fiction Making', in T. Sarbin (ed.), *Narrative Psychology: The Storied Nature of Human Conduct* (New York: Praeger), pp. 67–90.

Tomasello, M. (1995), 'Joint Attention as Social Cognition', in C. Moore & P. Dunham (ed.), *Joint Attention: Its Origins and Role in Development* (Hillsdale, NJ: Erlbaum).

Tomasello, M. (1999), *Cultural Origins of Human Cognition* (Harvard: Harvard University Press).

Tomasello, M. & Barton, M. (1994), 'Learning Words in Non-Ostensive Contexts', *Developmental Psychology*, **30**, pp. 639–50.

Tomasello, M., Strosberg, R. & Akhtar, N. (1996), 'Eighteen-month-old Children Learn Words in Non-Ostensive Contexts', *Journal of Child Language*, **23**, pp. 157–76.

Tonkinson, R. (1978), *The Mardudjara Aborigines: Living the Dream in Australia's Desert* (New York: Holt, Rinehart & Winston).

Tooby, J. & Cosmides, L. (1992), 'The Psychological Foundations of Culture', in J. Barkow, L. Cosmides & J. Tooby (ed.), *The Adapted Mind* (New York: Oxford University Press).

Wellman, H.M. & Bartsch, K. (1988), 'Young Children's Reasoning about Beliefs', *Cognition*, **30**, pp. 239–77.

Wellman, H.M., Cross, D. & Watson, J. (2001), 'Meta-analysis of Theory-of-Mind Development: The truth about false belief', *Child Development*, **72**, pp. 655–84.

Wiessner, P. (1982), 'Risk, Reciprocity and Social Influences on !Kung San Economics', in E. Leacock & R.B. Lee (ed.), *Politics and History in Band Societies* (Cambridge: Cambridge University Press).

Wimmer, H. & Perner, J. (1983), 'Beliefs about Beliefs: Representation and constraining function of wrong beliefs in young children's understanding of deception', *Cognition*, **13**, pp. 103–28.

Wolf, A. (1970), 'Childhood Association and Sexual Attraction: A further test of the the Westermarck hypothesis', *American Anthropologist*, **72**, pp. 503–15.

Wolf, A. & Huang, C. (1980), *Marriage and Adoption in China, 1845–1945* (Stanford: Stanford University Press).

Wolf, D., Rygh, J. & Altshuler, J. (1984), 'Agency and Experience: Actions and states in play narratives', in I. Bertherton (ed.), *Symbolic Play: The Development of Social Understanding* (New York: Academic Press).

Matthew K. Belmonte

What's the Story behind 'Theory of Mind' and Autism?

*Abstract: Complex, mature cognition is the endpoint of a develop-
mental process in which elementary capacities interact with the environment and with each other in predictable ways that depend on
appropriate inputs. 'Theory of mind', the capacity to attribute
thoughts and beliefs to other persons, is characterised by the Narrative Practice Hypothesis as emerging from the interactive experience
of stories about people acting for reasons. The case of autism has
been cited in support of the contrary view, that 'theory of mind' is an
innately specified cognitive module, because the surface characteristics of autistic behaviour seem explicable as a circumscribed failure
of such a module. So if one accepts the Narrative Practice Hypothesis,
is one then robbed of an explanation for autism? The answer is an
emphatic no: 'theory of mind' dysfunction is not universal in autism,
and is developmentally preceded and predicted by abnormalities of
attention, executive function and language consonant with the
Narrative Practice Hypothesis.*

Modules, Myths and Mechanisms

Human beings operate by attaching semantics to physical objects. Our
very desperation for a meaningful, tractable and ordered world leads
us to overload objects with significance, to mediate a universe of
physical objects with a universe of signs. Scientists in general, and
neuroscientists in particular, are no different from the rest of us in this
mode of cognition. In instances in which biological reality conforms

to this predilection of ours to attach meaning to single, physically delimited objects, we've done very well: neuroscience is full of success stories in understanding clinical disorders that involve damage to single pieces of brain tissue (left inferior frontal cortex and Broca's aphasia, right parietal cortex and spatial neglect, striate cortex and homonymous hemianopia) or mutations of single genes (e.g., sodium channels and familial epilepsy). Indeed, these successes have rather led us to expect, tacitly, that nature somehow will have arranged its own experiments for us, in which one independent variable (the lesioned brain area, the mutated gene) is manipulated whilst all others are held constant. Hardly a day passes in which some biological result is not framed as the discovery of the brain area for this or that capacity, or the gene for this or that trait. In anthropological terms, single brain structures and single genes have become neuroscience's fetish symbols. To confirm the existence of a delimited genetic, anatomical, or cognitive module subserving a particular function, it seems, all that we need do is to seek and find the clinical disorder that results when that module is taken out of service by injury or disease.

This state of affairs is rather like that of the hapless fool who searches under the streetlamp for his lost keys only because that's where the light is. There is a vast world out there, unilluminated by one-to-one, iconic mappings between symbol (a gene or a brain region) and referent (a clinical disorder and its neural and cognitive effects). We should not expect every neurological disorder, or even most neurological disorders, to correspond neatly to the failure of a delimited module. This is particularly true in the case of developmental disorders, where the perturbation of one neural component or system can evoke knock-on effects on many other brain structures and cognitive capacities that include or depend on that component. Thus the neuroscience of developmental disorders is essentially a multivariate science rather than a univariate one, and an understanding of developmental disorders depends on — and is in large part identical with — an understanding of the complicated and multifactorial processes of interactive specialisation (Karmiloff-Smith, 2007) from which a fully developed brain emerges. Brains do not spring fully armed as Athena from the forehead of Zeus; their capabilities emerge, gradually, through prenatal life and on into infancy and childhood, from deterministic interactions of cognitive and neural systems with each other and with properly formed inputs. Thus the mature, adult brain with which one ends up might function like a collection of modules, might even malfunction like a collection of modules when lesioned, but this doesn't mean that all these apparently modular capacities arrive in the world completely specified and independent of all the others.

The Narrative Practice Hypothesis, as framed by Hutto (this volume), takes on this challenge of explaining developmental endpoints in terms of temporally extended processes of interactive specialisation. Specifically, the Narrative Practice Hypothesis denies the existence of a specialised, innately modular 'theory of mind' mechanism, and in its place sketches a cognitive developmental process (albeit not a biological implementation) by which the capacity to attribute conceptual ('he/she/it knows/thinks/believes') states to other minds emerges from the interaction of a capacity for imputing lower-level, volitional ('he/she/it wants or wants to') states with a capacity for understanding narratives about people who act for reasons. Key to this process is Vygotsky's notion of scaffolding, in which social support from teachers or caregivers facilitates the development of a rudimentary, foundational capacity into a refined, specialised capacity – and key to understanding its development is the distinction between the large class of problems of social attribution that *admit* solution via a 'theory of mind' and the proper subset of those problems that *require* solution via a 'theory of mind'.

Many of the everyday problems of social attribution faced by mature, adult, narratively competent humans are represented by invoking what is conventionally described as a 'theory of mind' — a capacity for maintaining propositional knowledge about other minds which in the mature mind and brain has become so overlearnt and automatic that it demands hardly any cognitive effort. The situation bears analogy to that of handwriting: the adult has only to think of a word and out it comes onto the paper, whereas the young child must devote effort to each stroke of the pen within each letter of each word. In an adult, the specialised capacity of handwriting is so finely developed that it seems easier than making individual strokes or glyphs — as users of palmtop computers can attest — even though the latter is the computationally simpler activity. A small child who is unable to produce fluid and effortless handwriting can nevertheless interact with a palmtop computer, by producing individual characters as glyphs. Thus the palmtop computer *admits* handwritten interaction, but does not *require* the skill of handwriting for interaction. An adult witnessing the child's performance on the palmtop might be stunned by how quickly and precociously the child has mastered handwriting — except, of course, that is not what the child has done.

Similarly, when we see an infant returning a social smile, we may be amazed at how effortlessly that infant knows, even without words, that its caregiver thinks that something good has happened — except, of course, the infant does not necessarily know anything of the sort, and its behaviour can just as well be implemented by social perceptual mechanisms that allow mirroring of a social partner's affective state without explicit, narrative representation of the partner's conceptual state. The observation that we adults annotate everyday social interactions with mentalistic attributions of belief doesn't imply that mentalising is *required* in order to navigate the social world, or that this is how young children do it.

Autism is often held up as the clinical evidence — or perhaps the clinical 'justification' is a more apt term — of the notion of a 'theory of mind' module. To see a person with autism, we are told, is to see what happens to a human being when the ability to mentalise — to attribute distinct beliefs to other people — is switched off as though it had been excised. On the surface this claim seems neatly specific: it's clear that people with autism have severe difficulties in interacting with the social world, and severe social difficulties are exactly what one might expect from a failed 'theory of mind' module. The 'theory of mind' explanation seems to fit the facts. If we accept the Narrative Practice Hypotheses and so deny the existence of modular 'theory of mind', then, are we robbed of an explanation for autism? The answer is no, because on close inspection the 'theory of mind' explanation reveals itself never to have been a sufficient one in the first place. First, far from being an all-or-none trait that is either present or absent, 'theory of mind', like autism itself, is a matter of degrees. Second, social impairment attributable to a lack of 'theory of mind' is neither the only nor the earliest manifesting abnormality in autism. Third, it isn't even clear that 'theory of mind' is a well defined, anatomically or functionally localised capacity in adults, not to mention developing children.

'Theory of Mind' and the Autism Spectrum

The meaning of the term 'theory of mind', like that of the term 'autism', has been a slippery one (Belmonte, 2008b). At its introduction (Premack & Woodruff, 1978), the term 'theory of mind' was equated expansively with the ability to impute mental states in general, yet the instances used to exemplify it relied on verbs such as 'believes', 'thinks', 'guesses' and 'doubts' — verbs specific to conceptual states rather than the simpler perceptual ('sees') or volitional ('wants') attributions via which so much social inference proceeds. As a matter of practice if not outright definition, most studies of 'theory of mind' adopt its narrow sense, that of attribution of conceptual states. As even a chimpanzee can pass tests of perceptual or volitional perspective-taking, it is this narrower, conceptual sense that seems to distinguish humans. Whereas normal children pass such tests around the age of four years, many children with autism do not (Baron-Cohen *et al.*, 1985). This is not to say, though, that failure at false-belief tests is universal to autism. In fact, many autistic children pass the false-belief test (Frith & Happé, 1994). Those who do fail tend eventually to pass at later ages. So by this measure, failure at the false-belief test is not an essential trait of autism, nor is it a constant trait throughout autistic development. Although many of those children who pass the first-order ('X believes that P') false-belief test fail the second-order ('X believes that Y believes that P') form, in this case again the failure is not universal and not always sustained with age.

Even if the autistic variation in false-belief test performance were not by itself to sow doubt about the equation of autism with failed 'theory of mind', the conventional false-belief test paradigm leaves much ground unexplored because it is such a blunt instrument: a subject views a social scenario, a question requiring attribution of belief is asked, and the answer is either correct or incorrect, with no middle ground. A child may handily pass such a test, in which the social relevance is rendered explicit by the act of questioning, yet remain quite impaired at more everyday, ecologically valid instances of mentalising, instances in which socially relevant details are more difficult to sort out from irrelevant ones, and in which the the child must decide the relevant social questions rather than having them asked explicitly. Even in non-autistic children, a great deal of 'theory of mind' development takes place after the point at which false-belief tests are passed (Carpendale & Lewis, 2004). There is no reason to suspect that autistic children differ in this regard, and quite a lot of evidence indicating that impairments of social attribution more subtle than those detected by the standard false-belief test paradigm remain even when false-belief tests are passed (Brent *et al.*, 2004; Peterson *et al.*, 2007). Thus in its practical instantiation no less than in its theoretical conceptualisation, 'theory of mind' is a term difficult to pin down.

If 'theory of mind' is a slippery concept, 'autism' is even more so. Narrowly defined 'autism' lies at the extreme end of a continuum of cognitive variation known as the 'autism spectrum'. At its most severe, autism's symptoms can include not just an inability to use speech for social communication, but an inability to speak at all. In milder cases of autism, speech may be intact but not applied pragmatically to flexible social communication. In Asperger syndrome, a still milder variant distinct from 'autism' but part of the 'autism spectrum', communicative skills are intact but social function remains impaired. People with Asperger syndrome easily pass false-belief tests, yet remain subtly impaired at more everyday, ecologically valid applications of mentalising. Beyond Asperger syndrome, the autism spectrum begins to shade into normal cognitive variation with no exact boundary between the clinical condition and the extreme of normality, as demonstrated by a continuous distribution in the general population's scores on the Social Responsiveness Scale, a measure of autistic social traits (Constantino & Todd, 2003). Many first-degree relatives of people with autism, though not diagnosable with any clinical condition, manifest subtle social abnormalities in a phenomenon known as the 'Broader Autism Phenotype' (Piven *et al.*, 1997; Dawson *et al.*, 2002), and here again, these deficits can be quantified by psychometric tests, such as the Broader Phenotype Autism Symptom Scale (Dawson *et al.*, 2007) and the Social Responsiveness Scale (Constantino *et al.*, 2006). Again, all these people have no trouble at all with the false-belief paradigm; where they run into difficulties is in tasks of everyday social attribution. Indeed, the social impairments in Asperger syndrome and in the Broader Autism Phenotype are in a way all the more insidious because they are not straightforwardly detectable: many people with Asperger syndrome are initially quite successful at scientific, engineering or legal occupations but seize up when they reach a level of seniority at which they become expected to manage people. For this same reason of a lack of flexible social abilities, some people with Asperger syndrome are more successful socially at university than they are after leaving university: once the ready-made social structure of undergraduate life drops away, one finds oneself expected to define a social life of one's own instead of being enveloped and supported by college life — and without this scaffold, social insufficiencies that were always present can become much more manifest. Because such people with Asperger syndrome might not seem overtly to have a disability, they are not offered accommodation and acceptance. Does the deficit that they have qualify as a 'theory of mind' deficit? The answer seems to depend in part on whether one construes 'theory of mind' as a modular, all-or-none capacity in line with what is being tested by the false-belief paradigm, or whether one construes it as a continuum in line with what is being measured by the Social Responsiveness Scale and the Broader Phenotype Autism Symptom Scale. If 'theory of mind' ability does vary continuously throughout the normal and autism-spectrum populations, then the concept of a categorical dysfunction of 'theory of mind' as a distinguishing feature of autism is in line for some revision.

The reason behind this discontinuity between concepts of 'theory of mind' as it relates to autism in particular, to autism spectrum conditions in general, or to normal population variance perhaps stems from a corresponding discontinuity between the understanding of belief and the understanding of agents acting for reasons (Hutto, 2003). The latter understanding is a broader one, because it entails connecting beliefs to affective motivations and actions — a more applied and practical form of mentalising than that which is assayed by the false-belief test. Significantly, it's exactly this affectively laden connection between motivation and action that has been proposed as an area of fundamental dysfunction in the development of autistic behaviour (Greenspan, 2001). Changes in motor activity are closely linked with changes in attention from infancy (Robertson *et al.*, 2001), and autistic deficits in coordination of motor activity (Teitelbaum *et al.*, 1998; Landa & Garret-Mayer, 2006) seem to share computational structure with autistic deficits in coordination of attention (Haas *et al.*, 1996). In addition to this deficit at connecting affect to action in their own minds, people with autism may be at least as impaired at connecting affect to action in their representations of social partners (Greenspan, 2001). There is some neurophysiological evidence to back up this connection between affect diathesis and impaired mentalising: a network of brain structures involved in monitoring of one's own internal states is abnormally modulated in autism (Kennedy *et al.*, 2006), both in conditions that require monitoring of one's own state and in conditions that require monitoring of another's (Kennedy & Courchesne, 2008).

If 'theory of mind' were a reliably modular capacity not only in the adult brain but from the earliest stages of development, it ought to be measurable independently of general cognitive factors such as IQ and executive function. In fact, it is not. 'Theory of mind' ability as measured by false-belief tests is predicted by language ability (Astington & Jenkins, 1999; Dunn & Brophy, 2005); even when the test is administered in pictures instead of words, it covaries with measures of executive function (Russell *et al.*, 1999) — although executive function is not the only determinant of 'theory of mind' (Pellicano, 2007). On reflection these results are unsurprising, as making sense of people's actions involves the executive skills of selecting events of importance, suppressing insignificant events, and ordering or re-ordering all these observations into a coherent narrative that can explain what happened (Belmonte, 2008a).

What is Autism, if not Absent 'Theory of Mind'?

If people with autism cannot be said absolutely or universally to lack a 'theory of mind', what is it, then, that they do lack? Or is the autistic difference most accurately conceived as a lack at all, or as a surfeit of something that pre-empts and interferes with social processes? A decade and a half ago, the link between perspective-taking and 'theory of mind' was vividly described to me by a person with autism: 'It's just that putting myself in someone else's shoes means that I first have to force that person out of their own shoes.' In other words, difficulty in adopting another person's frame of belief may stem fundamentally not from any broken 'theory of mind' mechanism, but from the very salience of that person within one's own frame, and the attendant difficulty of taking the counterfactual perspective in which one would replace — and displace — the social partner. This realisation has the potential to link autistic social and communicative deficits with autism's non-social features.

Clinical diagnosis of autism rests on behavioural symptoms in three domains: social impairment, communicative impairment and restricted and repetitive interests and behaviours. This latter category is not an essentially social one, and encompasses a range of behavioural complexities from very concrete motor stereotypies such as hand-flapping and finger-flicking to elaborately sequenced rituals or verbalisations. This domain of repetitive behaviours is most identified with an autistic cognitive style that has been described as 'weak central coherence' (Happé & Frith, 2006) in which the drive to represent objects as complex wholes is weakened or, in a complementary view, as 'enhanced perceptual function' (Mottron et al., 2006) in which the veridical representations of objects as individual pieces are so salient that they may prevent the automatic construction of higher-order, abstract, centrally coherent representations. Repetitive behaviours may arise as an adaptive cognitive strategy (Belmonte et al., 2004b; Belmonte, 2008a), an attempt to render a cacophony of sensory stimuli tractable by forcing one's sensory experience to conform to a rigidly predictable script. This relationship between repetitive behaviours and sensory perception may also prove important for understanding autism's social deficits.

Supporting these notions of enhanced perceptual salience and correspondingly weak central coherence is a host of generalisable results on autism that have nothing directly to do with social function. People with autism perform superiorly at the Embedded Figures Test (Shah & Frith, 1983), a test of the ability to pick out local detail from geometric figures without succumbing to distractions posed by irrelevant, more complex geometric forms in which the target figures are embedded. Likewise, people with autism excel at the Block Design portion of the standard Wechsler IQ test, in which they are asked to replicate a target pattern by building it from physical blocks, and unlike non-autistic people they are not aided by segmentation of the target figure into block-sized pieces (Shah & Frith, 1993); they seem already to have perceptually implemented their own segmentation. For this same reason, children with autism frequently excel at jigsaw puzzles and other games and tasks that demand attention to matching up local details. When children with autism learn to read, they often manifest a phenomenon known as 'hyperlexia' in which phonetic decoding outpaces comprehension — the former depends only on the local combinations of letters within words, whereas the latter depends on embedding the meanings of words within the context established by the surrounding sentences, paragraphs and other elements of discourse. When people with autism learn skills, these skills often are not generalised to other contexts: for instance, a savant calculator of calendar dates might show no interest in other applications of arithmetic calculation.

The acts of abstraction that produce 'central coherence' confer formidable power to see the forest instead of the trees — that is, to represent and to transform entire classes of objects using the same single cognitive operations as otherwise might be applied to represent only single objects. The absence of such abstractions thus can easily be viewed as a deficit. At the same time, though, as has been made clear by literary criticism (Lacan, 1966), the substitution of an abstract class or category for a specific and unique exemplar, though it preserves the properties essential to category membership, entails the falsification of that exemplar's accidental properties: each instance within the category is projected onto the dimensions present within the category, whilst its dimensions not represented within the category are collapsed. The act of abstraction thereby unavoidably loses information — and that loss is anathema to an autistic cognitive style in which veridical detail is sacrosanct (Belmonte, 2008a). Return now to the problem of taking the perspective of the social partner: the difficulty might not rest actually in adopting the other's perspective but rather in turfing the other out of their own perspective, adopting a counterfactual point of view that is at odds with the veridical percept. In this regard (pardon the pun), the autistic deficit in 'theory of mind' reduces to a deficit in shifting from egocentric to allocentric perspective (Frith & de Vignemont, 2005), and autism's social dysfunction becomes unified with its abnormalities in non-social perception. As with so many capacities presumed to be absent in autism, autistic social perceptual and social cognitive capacities might be fundamentally intact — as demonstrated by cases of success on the false-belief test — but simply not engaged automatically and rapidly during flexible social interaction, because an overly salient egocentric perspective gets in the way.

We've seen, then, that a straightforward and exclusive identification of autism with a deficit in 'theory of mind' is something of a myth. The absence of any selective dysfunction in 'theory of mind', though, still leaves open the possibility that autism might involve fundamentally a more general dysfunction in social cognition. It's commonly said that people with autism lack empathy or social motivation. Indeed, conventional, timed tests or evaluations do seem to demonstrate a profound lack of awareness or concern for the feelings of social partners. As with so many autistic capabilities, though, the answer may be all in the timing: the capacity to feel what others feel, and to respond in kind, may be fully intact, but its expression during real-time social interactions may be flummoxed by an inability to connect affect with action (Greenspan, 2001). As caregivers can attest, people with autism may manifest entirely appropriate emotional responses to events or to news — it's just that these responses may be separated from the evoking experiences by minutes, hours or even days. Thus autistic social expression may fall victim to the same disconnection between motivation and action cited above in the context of autistic social perception. Although this disconnection between social motivation and social expression may be news to basic scientists and philosophers, any therapist, teacher or parent of someone with autism is quite familiar with the phenomenon of 'parallel play', in which a child with autism stands at the edge of a social group, wanting to join the group and perhaps imitating the actions of members of the group, but unable to discern how and when to jump onto the rapidly moving train of social interaction around the activity. (Though it has been claimed that people with autism are impaired at imitation of bodily expressions, under appropriately controlled conditions of testing they are perfectly capable of such imitation [Bird *et al.*, 2007; Hamilton *et al.*, 2007] — again, it's all in the timing.) It seems significant in this regard that if social interactions are slowed and confined to a single perceptual channel — as implemented, for instance, in interaction by textual messages — autistic social deficits can become much less severe (Forsey *et al.*, 1996). Again, the issue seems more one of the brief time allowed to bring social cognition to bear on rapidly evolving social interactions, rather than an absolute absence of capacity for social cognition. The fundamentals of social cognition are there; it's just with so few opportunities to sync up with social partners, these fundamentals aren't elaborated into social narratives.

Even at the very concrete level of brain scans, it has been demonstrated repeatedly that 'social brain' regions and social cognitive subsystems thought to be non-functional in autism do in fact activate if only a sufficient amount of time is allowed for the person with autism to bring them online (Hadjikhani *et al.*, 2004; Pierce *et al.*, 2004). In this regard, social brain deficits in autism share structure with autism's non-social deficits (Belmonte *et al.*, 2009): in both cases, intact functions can be brought out when an appropriate amount of time is allowed to prepare a response, when instructions, cognitive strategies, and problems to be focused on are stated explicitly rather than left implicit. Social and communicative impairments, though they are some of the most obvious, most diagnostic, and most debilitating characteristics of autism, are not necessarily the most ætiologically primary. What seems most impaired in autism is not the neural systems associated with basic social functions but rather the efficiency with which these regions are connected with each other (Belmonte *et al.*, 2004a), and with medial frontal cortex involved in constructing explicit, narrative representations of 'theory of mind'. What is important, in neural terms just as in behaviour, is the link between 'theory' of mind and *practice* of mind. It seems no coincidence that this link between 'theory of mind' and practical, second-person engagement with social narratives lies at the core of the Narrative Practice Hypothesis.

This insight as to the crucial role of timing and engagement of autistic social cognitive processes comes from basic science, but a corollary for the applied science of therapeutics is that if ways can be found for teachers and caregivers to guide people with autism through the experience of social narratives, to match the pace and focus of the narrative to the pace and focus of autistic cognition, then people with autism ought to be able to engage with those narratives and to develop folk psychological skills in the same manner that people without autism do. Again, second-person engagement is crucial (Hutto, 2004). Human learning of language — even of phonetics! — is strongly facilitated by interactive social partners (Kuhl *et al.*, 2003) with whom one can participate in second-person, affectively labelled interactions. It is such interactions that permit learning that is guided by social intention, without which the developing child would have to fall back on mere statistical association. Both in the case of language acquisition and in the case of 'theory of mind', the argument from the 'poverty of the stimulus' — that is, the lack of sufficient exemplars within the linguistic or social environment to which the developing child is exposed — makes an excellent case for the insufficiency of statistical association as a mechanism of learning. The answer to this argument, in part, is not to deny the possibility that both language and social cognition may be learnt rather than innately modular, but rather to deny that they are learnt by statistical association alone, and to affirm that the acquisition of language and the acquisition of social cognition require the affective labelling that is conferred by second-person interaction (Kuhl, 2007). As we have seen, this combination of affect with action is difficult for people with autism to implement — and from this difficulty may flow a host of developmental ills — but given time and appropriately accommodative and scaffolded interactions, people with autism can succeed.

We have pointed out the central role of timing and coordination of cognitive capacities in a range of complex skills in autism, and we have pointed out some insufficiencies of an explanation of autism in terms of a selective dysfunction in 'theory of mind'. What evidence exists for autism as a dysfunction of timing and coordination of complex cognitive processes? In a word: plenty. One of the earliest signs of autism in infancy is a 'sticky' style of attention with a long latency to disengage from a focus once that focus is established (Zwaigenbaum et al., 2005). This long latency to shift attention from one perceptual channel to another persists into adolescence and adulthood (Akshoomoff & Courchesne, 1992), and holds whether it's a question of shifts between two sensory modalities such as vision and hearing (Courchesne et al., 1994), between two spatial locations within the visual field (Wainwright-Sharp & Bryson, 1993; 1996; Townsend et al., 1996; 1999; Harris et al., 1999; Belmonte, 2000), or between two object features such as colour and form (Courchesne et al., 1994; Rinehart et al., 2001). The spatial distribution of attention around a locus of attentive focus also is abnormal (Townsend & Courchesne, 1994). As in the domain of social cognition, the fault in attentional processing seems one of anticipation or prediction of likely inputs, and preparation and coordination of appropriate responses (Allen & Courchesne, 2001); people with autism do have the capacity to shift attention; they just don't implement it rapidly in response to sudden cues. In fact, where a non-autistic person may take two to three tenths of a second to shift attention from one place to another, or from one feature to another, or from one sense to another, a person with autism takes two to three seconds. This profound difficulty in shifting and integrating attention to multiple competing sources of information begins to explain the difficulty with social exchanges. In particular,

joint attention — the rapid shifting of attention between a social partner and an object or event of mutual interest — is closely associated
with language development, and with social and communicative outcomes in autism (Charman, 2003; Yoder *et al.*, 2009).

  This long latency to shift attention can be seen not only in autistic
behaviour, but also imaged directly in autistic brain physiology. The
neural circuits comprising the visual system will, like any physical
system that takes time to respond to changes in its input, resonate
more or less well with certain frequencies of input. For the visual system, flashing a stimulus about ten times a second evokes a particularly
strong electrical resonance which can be detected as a ten hertz alternating voltage on the scalp. Attention to the flashing stimulus
increases this voltage. Changes in attention then can be detected by
measuring how long it takes the voltage to rise or to fall as attention
shifts towards or away from the flashing stimulus. This method
reveals that when people with autism are asked to shift attention faster
than they're able to do, their immediate response is to rely on general
arousal (Belmonte, 2000) — turning up the volume, as it were, on
every stimulus arriving in every perceptual channel, rather than
attending selectively to just one channel. In effect, when the sources
of relevant stimuli shift and change too quickly for their attention to
keep pace, they are reduced to either letting in everything or letting in
nothing. When they let in everything, they then are left with more
work to do to sort out the relevant from the irrelevant stimuli, and this
is reflected in abnormally intense activations in sensory brain regions
(Belmonte & Yurgelun-Todd, 2003). These sensory systems activate
first, and only after two to three more seconds have passed by does
attention-related brain activation in the frontal lobe reach its maximum (Belmonte *et al.*, 2009) — a concrete, physiological result that
mirrors the two to three second delay in behavioural responding.
Again, this physiological limitation seems crucial in the abnormal
development of intersubjective experience: social interaction is a syn-
chronous activity, and those two to three seconds following an utterance or an expression can be critical. By the time the person with
autism becomes able to respond to a rapid social stimulus, the train has
left the station.

  When considered in this context of slowed attentional and executive processes, the integration of egocentric and allocentric perspectives that underlies 'theory of mind' processing becomes not a
domain-specific deficit but rather one feature of a domain-general
impairment in complex, integrated cognitive processing. Autism, in
all of its aspects social and non-social, seems most completely

described as a superiority at maintaining veridical detail in single pieces or streams of information, with a corresponding deficit at integrating multiple pieces or sources of information. This domain-general deficit in complex information processing (Minshew *et al.*, 1997) is a description in psychological terms that meshes well with autism's description in neurobiological terms as an abnormality in neural connectivity (Belmonte *et al.*, 2004a). Within families affected by autism, impaired neural connectivity strongly differentiates autistic from non-autistic family members (Belmonte *et al.*, 2009). Impaired neural connectivity produces impaired narrative connectivity (Belmonte, 2008a), and a corresponding deficit in developing a 'theory of mind' because the basics of social cognition, though intact, cannot be efficiently exercised in combination with folk psychological narratives. An apparent impairment in 'theory of mind' thus is a symptom and a developmental endpoint, not a developmental foundation of autism.

On the severe end of the autism spectrum, social behaviours can be especially difficult to discern given all the communicative impairments and all the time given over to repetitive behaviours. It's the milder, Asperger end of the spectrum, and also the Broader Autism Phenotype, that suggest that the development of 'theory of mind' may not be completely explicable as a process of scientific discovery involving social experiment and refinement of social hypotheses. Children with Asperger syndrome actually are superior at purely scientific thinking (Baron-Cohen, 2008) — a cognitive style marked by statistical association and causal inference. In instances when they do succeed at 'theory of mind' tasks, they tend to rely on explicit, rule-based learning, and indeed remediation strategies aimed at teaching social skills to this population focus on reducing such skills to tractable sets of rules (Golan & Baron-Cohen, 2006) — in this sense, people with autism spectrum conditions are the only ones who really do have access to a 'theory' of mind, as distinct from a less explicit *practice* of mind. So, people with autism are superior at scientific modelling, but nevertheless impaired at mentalising. If a third-person, detached stance sufficed for the development and elaboration of mentalising, people with Asperger syndrome or the Broader Autism Phenotype would be superior at mentalising. What they lack is second-person engagement.

Folk psychological narratives take over when scripts fail (Hutto, 2004). People with autism excel at following scripts, as evidenced by their propensity for repetitive behaviours. What they lack, physiologically, is the ability to reconfigure cognitive resources so as to respond rapidly to unpredictable, unscripted stimuli. Especially when subjected to great cognitive loads or other sources of stress, they tend to fall back on strategies that treat people as inflexibly as objects. Similarly, language often is not treated as something with communicative content but rather as a set of physical stimuli. Autistic attention is most drawn not by stimuli signalling social relevance but rather by physical covariance within stimuli (Klin *et al.*, 2009). All these traits are consistent with a style of learning that is driven by statistical covariance rather than by shared intentions. Although much can be learnt by statistical association, this autistic learning style draws attention away from precisely those unpredictable social stimuli that have the richest information content, causing people with autism to hew to reinforcement of what is known and familiar rather than to seek socially guided and scaffolded experience of what remains novel. In the absence of flexible narratives to describe how and why things are, children with autism rely on scripts to determine how things ought to be. It's no great surprise, therefore, that language deficits and repetitive behaviours in autism are correlated (Paul *et al.*, 2008).

Where to Place Belief?

As a final point, it ought not to escape discussion that the putative 'theory of mind' module has long been in search of a home within some or other particular patch of cerebral cortex, and it isn't entirely clear whether that home has been found. The locus has hopped about, and seems in many cases to depend on how a 'theory of mind' task is framed. The first physiological studies of 'theory of mind' used verbal stories, and compared story comprehension tasks that demanded mental-state attribution to those that demanded only knowledge of physical relationships (Fletcher *et al.*, 1995). Within this paradigm, mental-state attribution seemed to associate with activation of medial frontal cortex. A similar result was obtained in the case of stories told in pictures (Gallagher *et al.*, 2000). Defining a control condition for the mental-state case's great demand on contextual embedding, though, seems difficult; questions about physical relationships might not do it, and thus the observed activation in medial frontal cortex might be more associated with social interaction, joint attention, or contextual problem-solving in general than with 'theory of mind' in particular. Indeed, the very difficulty of defining an experimental paradigm that could factor out 'theory of mind' from more domain-general executive capacities raises the question of whether 'theory of mind' is a well defined capacity. More recent studies, in which social stories about beliefs were contrasted with a tighter control condition

involving social stories about personal appearance or bodily sensations, have placed 'theory of mind' not in medial frontal cortex but at
the junction of the parietal and temporal lobes (Saxe & Kanwwisher,
2003; Saxe & Wexler, 2005; Saxe & Powell, 2006).

If indeed there exists any single, exclusive anatomical locus for
'theory of mind', then these results make an excellent case for pinning
it on the temporo-parietal junction. One has to consider, though,
whether the question of localisation of such a complex function is well
posed. Complex capacities activate not just single brain regions, but
networks of brain regions that come together in flexible combinations
to solve a wide range of problems. Brain imaging with current analyti-
cal methods can contrast activations within individual brain regions,
but it has a more difficult time identifying causal activity in widespread networks of brain regions — and, to come full circle to the
point with which we began, scientists as human beings have a more
difficult time interpreting such non-localised information. Any network of brain regions will contain one or more nodes onto which
information converges from many source regions, and from which
information is widely distributed to many target regions. These nodes
of convergence therefore are likely to be more strongly activated in
association with the task than are the other regions of the network —
yet the cognitive capacity remains a function of the network as a
whole, rather than exclusively proper to one key node within the network. In the case of 'theory of mind' in particular, although the
response of medial prefrontal cortex to mental-state attribution is not
as pronounced as that of temporo-parietal junction, this fact alone
does not mean that temporo-parietal junction is the only brain region
involved in mentalising. In fact, medial prefrontal cortex does activate
more strongly for mental-state attribution than for attribution of character traits or other social background (Saxe & Wexler, 2005); just not
as strongly and selectively as temporo-parietal junction does. Furthermore, 'theory of mind' is not the only function that activates this same
temporo-parietal region; it or a very nearby region also is activated by
demands to translate from egocentric to allocentric perspective
(Aichhorn et al., 2006); this involvement lends further support for a
relationship between 'theory of mind' and more concrete forms of
shifting attention and perspective. At some point, the question of
where in the brain a capacity is localised ceases to be useful. Whether
we have reached that point with the question of 'theory of mind' is yet
to be determined, but we ought at least to keep the question in mind.

An important initial study of 'theory of mind' in autism examined
the attribution of mental states to animated geometric shapes (Castelli

et al., 2002), showing hypoactivation of medial prefrontal cortex. However, the mental states in these animations were perceptual ('sees'), intentional ('wants'), and affective ('feels'), but not proposi- tional ('believes'), and subjects were not explicitly instructed to attribute mental states. Reinforcing the association between more nar- rowly defined 'theory of mind' and right temporo-parietal junction, a behavioural assay of 'theory of mind' skills correlates with activation in this region (Kana *et al.*, 2009) — however, data from the same experiment reveal that functional connectivity between frontal and posterior regions involved in 'theory of mind' is abnormally low in autism, suggesting that this latter measure, reflecting network abnor- malities, may be the more revealing. Also not to be ignored is the role of preparation time and explicit instruction in bringing out latent abili- ties in autism. People with autism might not engage 'theory of mind' skills when viewing interactions of animated geometric shapes because there is simply no reason to do so: why engage in some fanci- ful and clearly counterfactual attribution of feelings and desires to a triangle, when the visible evidence calls for a mechanistic rather than a mentalistic explanation?

Conclusion

In a false interpretation that heaped wrongful blame and misplaced guilt on tragedy, autistic behaviour once was viewed as a response to a mother's rejection of her child. In light of a combination of neuro- physiological and psychological evidence, we now can understand that autism is in a way a response to rejection — but rather than a par- ent or any social partner, it is the autistic person's own perceptual and cognitive environment that separates them from the broader social world. This physiologically based rejection deprives the developing mind of the normal, interactive, second-person experience of social narratives, and substitutes a scientific, third-person experience in which the perceived connections between events are directed by sta- tistical association, rather than by affectively laden intentions shared with social partners. Without the scaffolding of this social helping hand, and with a deficit in neural connectivity producing a corre- sponding deficit in the connectivity of narrative representation, the problem of organising perceptual experience in general, and social experience in particular, becomes all the more immediate and effortful. In this regard, people with autism are 'human, but more so'; their experience has much to tell us about the interaction between neu- ral representations, narrative representations, and the development of complex social cognition from fundamental perceptual antecedents. 'Theory of mind' and the brain regions that have been associated with it are part of the explanation, but we ought not to mistake them for all of it. A complete explanation demands that we take time to tell the whole story.

Acknowledgement

The author is indebted to Dan Hutto for organising the July 2007 'Narrative Alternatives to Theories of Mind' meeting at Hertfordshire, and also for several pints at his local, without either of which this paper would never have been conceived, and for his many months of patience and forbearance with deadlines.

References

Aichhorn, M., Perner, J., Kronbichler, M., Staffen, W. & Ladurner G. (2006), 'Do Visual Perspective Tasks need Theory of Mind?', *NeuroImage*, **30**, pp. 1059–68.

Akshoomoff, N.A. & Courchesne E. (1992), 'A New Role for the Cerebellum in Cognitive Operations', *Behavioral Neuroscience*, **106**, pp. 731–8.

Allen, G. & Courchesne, E. (2001), 'Attention Function and Dysfunction in Autism', *Frontiers in Biosciences*, **6**, pp. D105–19.

Astington, J.W. and Jenkins, J.M. (1999), 'A Longitudial Study of the Relation between Language and Theory-of-Mind Development', *Developmental Psychology*, **35**, pp. 1311–20.

Baron-Cohen, S. (2008), 'Autism, Hypersystemizing, and Truth', *Quarterly Journal of Experimental Psychology*, **61**, pp. 64–75.

Baron-Cohen, S., Leslie, A.M. & Frith, U. (1985), 'Does the Autistic Child have a "Theory of Mind"?', *Cognition*, **21**, pp. 37–46.

Belmonte, M.K. (2000), 'Abnormal Attention in Autism shown by Steady-state Visual Evoked Potentials', *Autism*, **4**, pp. 269–85.

Belmonte, M.K. (2008a), 'Human, but More So: What the autistic brain tells us about the process of narrative', in M. Osteen (ed.), *Autism and Representation* (New York: Routledge), pp. 166–79.

Belmonte M.K. (2008b), 'Does the Experimental Scientist have a "Theory of Mind"?', *Review of General Psychology*, **12**, pp. 192–204.

Belmonte, M.K., Allen, G., Beckel-Mitchener, A., Boulanger, L.M., Carper, R.A. & Webb, S.J. (2004a), 'Autism and Abnormal Development of Brain Connectivity', *Journal of Neuroscience*, **24**, pp. 9228–31.

Belmonte, M.K., Cook, E.H. Jr., Anderson, G.M., Rubenstein, J.L., Greenough, W.T., Beckel-Mitchener, A., Courchesne, E., Boulanger, L.M., Powell, S.B., Levitt, P.R., Perry, E.K., Jiang, Y., DeLorey, T.M. & Tierney, E. (2004b), 'Autism as a Disorder of Neural Information Processing: Directions for research and targets for therapy', *Molecular Psychiatry*, **9**, pp. 646–63. Unabridged edition at http://www.cureautismnow.org/conferences/summitmeetings/.

Belmonte, M.K., Gomot, M. & Baron-Cohen, S. (2009), 'Visual Attention in Autism Families: "Unaffected" sibs share atypical frontal activation', under review.

Belmonte, M.K. & Yurgelun-Todd, D.A. (2003), 'Functional Anatomy of Impaired Selective Attention and Compensatory Processing in Autism', *Cognitive Brain Research*, **17**, pp. 651–64.

Bird, G., Leighton, J., Press, C. & Heyes, C. (2007), 'Intact Automatic Imitation of Human and Robot Actions in Autism Spectrum Disorders', *Proceedings of the Royal Society B*, **274**, pp. 3027–31.

Brent, E., Rios, P., Happé, F. & Charman, T. (2004), 'Performance of Children with Autism Spectrum Disorder on Advanced Theory of Mind Tasks', *Autism*, **8**, pp. 283–99.

Carpendale, J.I. & Lewis, C. (2004), 'Constructing an Understanding of Mind: The development of children's social understanding within social interaction', *Behavioral and Brain Sciences*, **27**, pp. 79–96.

Castelli, F., Frith, C., Happé, F. & Frith, U. (2002), 'Autism, Asperger Syndrome and Brain Mechanisms for the Attribution of Mental States to Animated Shapes', *Brain*, **125**, pp. 1839–49.

Charman, T. (2003), 'Why is Joint Attention a Pivotal Skill in Autism?', *Philosophical Transactions of the Royal Society B*, **358**, pp. 315–24.

Constantino, J.N., Lajonchere, C., Lutz, M., Gray, T., Abbacchi, A., McKenna, K., Singh, D. & Todd, R.D. (2006), 'Autistic Social Impairment in the Siblings of Children with Pervasive Developmental Disorders', *American Journal of Psychiatry*, **163**, pp. 294–6.

Constantino J.N. & Todd, R.D. (2003), 'Autistic Traits in the General Population: A twin study', *Archives of General Psychiatry*, **60**, pp. 524–30.

Courchesne, E., Townsend, J., Akshoomoff, N.A., Saitoh, O., Yeung-Courchesne, R., Lincoln, A.J., James, H.E., Haas, R.H., Schreibman, L. & Lau, L. (1994), 'Impairment in Shifting Attention in Autistic and Cerebellar Patients', *Behavioral Neuroscience*, **108**, pp. 848–65.

Dawson, G., Estes, A., Munson, J., Schellenberg, G., Bernier, R. & Abbott, R. (2007), 'Quantitative Assessment of Autism Symptom-related Traits in Probands and Parents: Broader Phenotype Autism Symptom Scale', *Journal of Autism and Developmental Disorders*, **37**, pp. 523–36.

Dawson, G., Webb, S.J., Schellenberg, G.D., Dager, S.R., Friedman S.D., Aylward E.H. & Richards T.L. (2002), 'Defining the Broader Phenotype of Autism: Genetic, brain, and behavioral perspectives', *Development and Psychopathology*, **14**, pp. 581–611.

Dunn, J. & Brophy, M. (2005), 'Communication, Relationships, and Individual Differences in Children's Understanding of Mind', in J.W. Astington & J.A. Baird (ed.), *Why Language Matters for Theory of Mind* (New York: Oxford University Press), pp. 50–69.

Fletcher, P.C., Happé, F., Frith, U., Baker, S.C., Dolan, R.J., Frackowiak, R.S. & Frith, C.D. (1995), 'Other Minds in the Brain: A functional imaging study of "theory of mind" in story comprehension', *Cognition*, **57**, pp. 109–28.

Forsey, J., Kay-Raining Bird, E. & Bedrosian, J. (1996), 'Brief Report: The effects of typed and spoken modality combinations on the language performance of adults with autism', *Journal of Autism and Developmental Disorders*, **26**, pp. 643–9.

Frith, U. & de Vignemont, F. (2005), 'Egocentrism, Allocentrism, and Asperger Syndrome', *Conscious and Cognition*, **14**, pp. 719–38.

Frith, U. & Happé, F. (1994), 'Autism: Beyond "theory of mind"', *Cognition*, **50**, pp. 115–32.

Gallagher, H.L., Happé, F., Brunswick, N., Fletcher, P.C., Frith, U. & Frith, C.D. (2000), 'Reading the Mind in Cartoons and Stories: An fMRI study of "theory of mind" in verbal and nonverbal tasks', *Neuropsychologia*, **38**, pp. 11–21.

Golan, O. & Baron-Cohen, S. (2006), 'Systemizing Empathy: Teaching adults with Asperger syndrome or high-functioning autism to recognize complex emotions using interactive multimedia', *Development and Psychopathology*, **18**, pp. 591–617.

Greenspan, S.I. (2001), 'The Affect Diathesis Hypothesis: The role of emotions in the core deficit in autism and the development of intelligence and social skills', *Journal of Developmental and Learning Disorders*, **5**, pp. 1–45.

Haas, R.H., Townsend, J., Courchesne, E., Lincoln, A.J., Schreibman, L. & Yeung-Courchesne, R. (1996), 'Neurologic Abnormalities in Infantile Autism', *Journal of Child Neurology*, **11**, pp. 84–92.

Hadjikhani, N., Joseph, R.M., Snyder, J., Chabris, C.F., Clark, J., Steele, S., McGrath, L., Vangel, M., Aharon, I., Feczko, E., Harris, G.J. & Tager-Flusberg, H. (2004), 'Activation of the Fusiform Gyrus when Individuals with Autism Spectrum Disorder View Faces', *NeuroImage*, **22**, pp. 1141–50.

Hamilton, A.F., Brindley, R.M. & Frith, U. (2007), 'Imitation and Action Understanding in Autistic Spectrum Disorders: How valid is the hypothesis of a deficit in the mirror neuron system?', *Neuropsychologia*, **45**, pp. 1859–68.

Happé F. & Frith, U. (2006), 'The Weak Coherence Account: Detail-focused cognitive style in autism spectrum disorders', *Journal of Autism and Developmental Disorders*, **36**, pp. 5–25.

Harris, N.S., Courchesne, E., Townsend, J., Carper, R.A. & Lord, C. (1999), 'Neuroanatomic Contributions to Slowed Orienting of Attention in Children with Autism', *Cognitive Brain Research*, **8**, pp. 61–71.

Hutto, D.D. (2003). 'Folk Psychological Explanations: Narratives and the case of autism', *Philosophical Papers*, **32**, pp. 345–61.

Hutto, D.D. (2004), 'The Limits of Spectatorial Folk Psychology', *Mind and Language*, **19**, pp. 548–73.

Kana, R.K., Keller, T.A., Cherkassky, V.L., Minshew, N.J. & Just, M.A. (2009), 'Atypical Frontal-posterior Synchronization of Theory of Mind Regions in Autism during Mental State Attribution', *Social Neuroscience*, **4**, pp. 135–52.

Karmiloff-Smith A. (2007), 'Atypical Epigenesis', *Developmental Science*, **10**, pp. 84–8.

Kennedy, D.P. & Courchesne, E. (2008), 'Functional Abnormalities of the Default Network During Self- and Other-reflection in Autism', *Social Cognitive and Affective Neuroscience*, **3**, pp. 177–90.

Kennedy, D.P., Redcay, E. & Courchesne, E. (2006), 'Failing to Deactivate: Resting functional abnormalities in autism', *Proceedings of the National Academy of Sciences of the United States of America*, **103**, pp. 8275–80.

Klin, A., Lin, D.J., Gorrindo, P., Ramsay, G. & Jones, W. (2009), 'Two-year-olds with Autism Orient to Non-social Contingencies rather than Biological Motion', *Nature*, **14**, pp. 257–61.

Kuhl, P.K. (2007), 'Is Speech Learning "Gated" by the Social Brain?', *Developmental Science*, **10**, pp. 110–20.

Kuhl, P.K., Tsao, F.M. & Liu, H.M. (2003), 'Foreign-language Experience in Infancy: Effects of short-term exposure and social interaction on phonetic learning', *Proceedings of the National Academy of Sciences of the United States of America*, **100**, pp. 9096–101.

Landa, R. & Garrett-Mayer, E. (2006), 'Development in Infants with Autism Spectrum Disorders: A prospective study', *Journal of Child Psychology and Psychiatry*, **47**, pp. 629–38.

Lacan, J. (1966). 'Fonction et Champ de la Parole et du Langage en Psychanalyse', *Écrits* (Paris: Éditions du Seuil), pp. 237–322.

Minshew, N.J., Goldstein, G. & Siegel, D.J. (1997), 'Neuropsychologic Functioning in Autism: Profile of a complex information processing disorder', *Journal of the International Neuropsychological Society*, **3**, pp. 303–16.

Paul, R., Chawarska, K., Cicchetti, D. & Volkmar, F. (2008), 'Language Outcomes of Toddlers with Autism Spectrum Disorders: A two year follow-up', *Autism Research*, **1**, pp. 97–107.

Mottron, L., Dawson, M., Soulières, I., Hubert, B. & Burack, J.A. (2006), 'Enhanced Perceptual Functioning in Autism: An update, and eight principles of autistic perception', *Journal of Autism and Developmental Disorders*, **36**, pp. 27–43.

Pellicano E. (2007), 'Links Between Theory of Mind and Executive Function in Young Children with Autism: Clues to developmental primacy', *Developmental Psychology*, **43**, pp. 974–90.

Peterson, C.C., Slaughter, V.P. & Paynter, J. (2007), 'Social Maturity and Theory of Mind in Typically Developing Children and those on the Autism Spectrum', *Journal of Child Psychology and Psychiatry*, **48**, pp. 1243–50.

Pierce, K., Müller, R.A., Ambrose, J., Allen, G. & Courchesne, E. (2004)'Face Processing Occurs Outside the Fusiform "face Area" in Autism: Evidence from functional MRI', *Brain*, **124**, pp. 2059–73.

Piven, J., Palmer, P., Jacobi, D., Childress, D. & Arndt, S. (1997), 'Broader Autism Phenotype: Evidence from a family history study of multiple-incidence autism families', *American Journal of Psychiatry*, **154**, pp. 185–90.

Premack, D. & Woodruff, G. (1978). 'Does the Chimpanzee have a Theory of Mind?', *Behavioral and Brain Sciences,* **1**, pp. 515–26.

Rinehart, N.J., Bradshaw, J.L., Moss, S.A., Brereton, A.V. & Tonge, B.J. (2001), 'A Deficit in Shifting Attention Present in High-functioning Autism but not Asperger's Disorder', *Autism*, **5**, pp. 67–80.

Robertson, S.S., Bacher, L.F. & Huntington, N.L. (2001), 'The Integration of Body Movement and Attention in Young Infants', *Psychological Science*, **12**, pp. 523–6.

Russell, J., Saltmarsh, R. & Hill, E. (1999), 'What do Executive Factors Contribute to the Failure on False Belief Tasks by Children with Autism?', *Journal of Child Psychology and Psychiatry*, **40**, pp. 859–68.

Saxe, R. & Powell, L.J. (2006), 'It's the Thought that Counts: Specific brain regions for one component of theory of mind', Psychological Science, **17**, pp. 692–9.

Saxe, R. & Wexler, A. (2005), 'Making Sense of Another Mind: The role of the right temporo-parietal junction', *Neuropsychologia*, **43**, pp. 1391–9.

Saxe, R. & Kanwisher, N. (2003), 'People Thinking about Thinking People. The role of the temporo-parietal junction in "theory of mind"', *NeuroImage*, **19**, pp. 1835–42.

Shah, A. & Frith, U. (1983), 'An Islet of Ability in Autistic Children: A research note', *Journal of Child Psychology and Psychiatry*, **24**, pp. 613–20.

Shah, A. & Frith, U. (1993), 'Why do Autistic Individuals show Superior Performance on the Block Design Task?', *Journal of Child Psychology and Psychiatry*, **34**, pp. 1351–64.

Teitelbaum, P., Teitelbaum, O., Nye, J., Fryman, J. & Maurer, R.G. (1998), 'Movement Analysis in Infancy may be Useful for Early Diagnosis of Autism', *Proceedings of the National Academy of Sciences of the United States of America*, **95**, pp. 13982–7.

Townsend, J. & Courchesne, E. (1994), 'Parietal Damage and Narrow "spotlight" Spatial Attention', *Journal of Cognitive Neuroscience*, **6**, pp. 220–32.

Townsend, J., Courchesne, E., Covington, J., Westerfield, M., Harris, N.S., Lyden, P., Lowry, T.P. & Press, G.A. (1999), 'Spatial Attention Deficits in Patients with Acquired or Developmental Cerebellar Abnormality', *Journal of Neuroscience*, **19**, pp. 5632–43.

Townsend, J., Harris, N.S. & Courchesne, E. (1996), 'Visual Attention Abnormalities in Autism: Delayed orienting to location', *Journal of the International Neuropsychological Society*, **2**, pp. 541–50.

Wainwright-Sharp, J.A. & Bryson, S.E. (1993), 'Visual Orienting Deficits in High-functioning People with Autism', *Journal of Autism and Developmental Disorders*, **23**, pp. 1–13.

Wainwright-Sharp, J.A. & Bryson, S.E. (1996), 'Visual-spatial Orienting in Autism', *Journal of Autism and Developmental Disorders*, **26**, pp. 423–38.

Yoder, P., Stone, W.L., Walden, T. & Malesa, E. (2009), 'Predicting Social Impairment and ASD Diagnosis in Younger Siblings of Children with Autism Spectrum Disorder', *Journal of Autism and Developmental Disorders*, in press.

Zwaigenbaum, L., Bryson, S., Rogers, T., Roberts, W., Brian, J. & Szatmari, P. (2005), 'Behavioral Manifestations of Autism in the First Year of Life', *International Journal of Developmental Neuroscience*, **23**, pp. 143–52.

William Turnbull, Jeremy I.M. Carpendale
& Timothy P. Racine

Talk and Children's Understanding of Mind

Abstract: Research has demonstrated that language is important for the development of an everyday understanding of mind. The Theory of Mind (ToM) framework is the dominant conception of what and how children develop in coming to understand mind. As such, much current thinking in developmental psychology about the way language makes a difference to the development of mentalistic understanding is tainted by certain deeply entrenched philosophical assumptions. Following an examination of views of language and mind that continue to frame, if only tacitly, the ToM tradition, we offer an alternative conception of the nature of mental state concepts and how language-based engagements between children and care-givers introduce an understanding of such concepts. Based on that alternative conception of language and mind we propose that parent-child discussion about situations involving minds facilitate the child's development of an understanding of mind. We attempt to demonstrate that the development of the foundational skills necessary for understanding the meaning of psychological terms through such conversation make the construction and appreciation of narratives possible, deepening and extending the child's mentalistic understanding. We then review three studies of parent-child talk about situations involving mind that offer empirical support for the claim that such talk is an important context for developing an understanding of aspects of human activity that involve reasons for action, emotion and belief. We conclude by describing the situated and sequential nature of meaning that our view of language and mind entails.

The issue of how people explain and understand actions (their own and others) in their everyday affairs is a central and continuing concern of both developmental and social psychology. Philosophers refer to this activity as 'folk psychology'. Understanding persons in psychological terms, using mentalistic terms, is an essential part of being a competent person. How children come to develop this ability is, thus, an important issue. Broadly, the research literature demonstrates that most developmental scientists assume that mental states, when appropriately combined, cause action, and therefore explaining or understanding a particular action amounts to saying which mental states and processes gave rise to it. In the present article we present an alternative to the Cartesian-inspired view of minds and what it required for making sense of them, i.e. Theory of Mind (ToM) approaches, that have become predominant in developmental psychology. In doing so we explore the role of the content and nature of parent-child talk in the development of the child's understanding of mind.

We begin with a brief summary of the developmental literature documenting a relationship between language and children's understanding of mind. We then turn to an examination of conceptions of 'mind' and 'language' that pervade the contemporary psychological literature, the critical terms in that relationship. After briefly summarizing the Cartesian-inspired view of mental states, as inner causes, and related views of what the learning of public language labels for mental state concepts involves, we cast doubt on the core assumptions and central tenets behind such views.[1] This, in turn, leads to the claim that the development of children's understanding of mind is facilitated by engaging in conversations consisting of demonstrations of appropriate ways to talk about such things as reasons for beliefs, knowledge, action and consequences, plus the connections, causal and otherwise, that might hold between these aspects of mind (see also e.g., Budwig, 2002; Canfield, 1993; Montgomery, 2002; Nelson, 2005; Wootton, 1997). Coming to understand what it is to act for a reason is a necessary skill for the construction and consumption of more complex narratives. Thus, Hutto's Narrative Practice Hypothesis (NPH, see Hutto, this issue) is consistent with our claims.

This special issue is devoted to exploring links between narrative and social cognitive development. Exactly how best to understand

---

[1] Wittgenstein (1958) already did this critical spadework but it needs re-doing since that Cartesian thinking about the mind and Augustinian views about the nature of language are alive and well. For contemporary authors who whole-heartedly endorse such views see for example (Carruthers, 2008; Fodor, 2008).

what constitutes a narrative and their role in this process is an open question. Our contribution to this special issue concerns the development of the foundational skills necessary for understanding the meaning of psychological terms that make the construction and appreciation of narratives possible, however they are conceived. Furthermore, our methodology involves mothers constructing narratives with their children on the basis of a series of pictures depicting a sequence of interrelated actions.

Over the last ten years, we have conducted a program of research exploring the influence of the content and structure of mother-child talk on the development of 3- to 8-year-old children's understanding of mind. We describe the methodology and major results of several studies from that research. In considering the nature of mother-child talk, we propose that although many studies convincingly document the importance of language for the development of an understanding of mind, there has been a failure to examine the details of the content of parent-child talk and of the nature of the parent-child interactional relationship (see Fivush & Nelson, 2006, for a similar emphasis on the relevance of the details of parent-child reminiscing for the child's developing understanding of self). We explore those aspects of parent-child talk about mind and their implications for the development of the child's understanding of mind.

Language and the Development of Social Understanding

Children's linguistic ability is strongly correlated with their social cognitive development (e.g., see chapters in Astington & Baird, 2005). One reason for the interest in children's use of language is that the words that they use can act as a window that reveals their level of social understanding (Bartsch & Wellman, 1995). Crucially, children's linguistic ability tends to be associated with their understanding that beliefs can be false (for a meta-analysis see Milligan et al., 2007). However, as Nelson (e.g., 1996; 2005) reminds us, children's language is likely to be only an imperfect reflection of social understanding because children tend to begin using words with only partial understandings of their full adult meaning. A number of aspects of language have been proposed to play a causal role in social cognitive development. De Villiers and de Villiers (2000) argue for the importance of the syntactic structure of complementation, claiming that it provides a linguistic structure for thinking about false beliefs. Harris (2005) has argued that language is related to social cognitive development because in conversation children are exposed to different perspectives. Consistent with these claims, support for the effect of training in complementation as well as conversation was found in a study by Lohmann and Tomasello (2003), although the greatest improvement in children's false belief understanding was in a training condition involving both syntax and discourse.

The language that children are exposed to has also been shown to be an important factor in their social cognitive development (Carpendale & Lewis, 2006), beginning with Dunn's pioneering studies on the influence of family interaction on social cognitive development (e.g., Dunn et al., 1991). In much of the recent research the focus has been on mental state terms. Typically, a positive relationship is found between parents' use of mental state terms and children's social cognitive development, and Ruffman, Slade and Crowe (2002) reported evidence suggesting that mothers' use of mental state terms plays a causal role in the development of an understanding of false belief and emotions (see also Adrián et al., 2007; Taumoepeau & Ruffman, 2006; 2008). A common assumption in the developmental literature as to why mental state terms and social cognitive development are positively related is that exposure to such terms 'provides children with an opportunity to integrate their own behavior with an external comment that makes reference to the mental states underlying that behavior. Such comments thus offer a scaffolding context within which infants can begin to make sense of their own behavior in terms of its underlying mental states' (Meins et al., 2002, p. 1724). How such a process might actually occur is trickier than it might appear.

Claims about the special status of exposure to mental state terms for developing an understanding of mind are difficult to evaluate. Merely mentioning psychological terms may not be as important as elaboration and explanation (Ontai & Thompson, 2008; Peterson & Slaughter, 2003; Racine et al., 2006; Slaughter et al., 2007). Parents and children of different ages may differ in the social acts they perform with the same mental state terms (Budwig, 2002). Researchers are aware of this and are careful to code the various uses of mental state terms (e.g., Bartsch & Wellman, 1995; Shatz et al., 1983). For example, in the research literature, mental state terms used for pragmatic or conversational functions (e.g., modal uses of 'think' that display uncertainty, as in 'It's raining, I think') are typically considered separately from cases of 'genuine' mental reference (e.g.,' think' referring to the action of thinking).

It is also difficult to evaluate the relations between the use of mental state terms and social cognitive development given that it is not clear what should count as a mental state term. Words that appear on lists of mental state terms include 'believe', 'intend', and 'know', each of which is interpreted as referring to a specific cognitive state. However, 'hide' and 'trick' are actions that involve the intention to prevent another from knowing about some state of affairs, but they would not be on the typical list of mental state terms (Russell, 1992; Turnbull & Carpendale, 1999). Perhaps the list should be expanded to include them. That, however, would raise the issue of where to stop.

The underlying issue here is that the meaning of mental state terms are tied up with a particular context of use (Carpendale & Lewis, 2004; 2006; Nelson, 2009; Racine & Carpendale, 2008; Turnbull, 2003; Turnbull & Carpendale, 1999; 2001) and it is not possible to specify a priori what should count as a 'genuine' mental state reference. To put this differently, there is no essential defining feature to a given mental state term, but rather its uses are many and complex. As Wittgenstein (1958, §66) remarked, 'Don't think, but look!', and his advocacy for a varied diet of examples is meant to break the essentialist vision that developmental scientists tend to have of the meaning of such concepts.

Another difficulty with claims about the special status of mental state terms and social development is that one can talk about mind without using mental state terms. Consider, for example, the situation in which a man, Rick, thought he had lost his car keys but then was relieved to see them lying on the kitchen table. Whereas 'see' is not a mental state term, when used in the above situation, 'seeing' provides a reason for, and is more or less equivalent to, holding a certain belief and having certain knowledge (i.e., Rick was incorrect in believing he had lost his keys; he now knows that he has not lost his keys). In sum, if the relevant issue is what aspects of talk facilitate the child's developing understanding of mind, then research should focus on what is said about a specific situation involving mind and how what is said helps the child understand that specific situation.

The claim that children's exposure to mental state terms facilitates their psychological development may appear to be a strictly empirical claim. In fact, as illustrated in the quote from Meins *et al.* (2002), the claim is based on specific conceptions of what a mental state is, of the relation between a mental state and a mental state term, and of the nature of communication. Empirical investigations of the development of mind are necessarily and unavoidably based on conceptions of language and mind. Accordingly, we next describe the conceptions of mind, language and communication that seem to underlie developmental research concerning ToM, followed by an alternative and, we would argue, more defensible view.

Conceptions of Mind, Language and Communication

The dominant view of mind in developmental psychology seems to be that each person has special private and accurate access to his/her own mind but that the minds of other persons are not accessible (e.g., German & Leslie, 2000). From this point of view, learning about ones own mind requires only introspection. However, in developing an understanding of mind children must also learn to recognize and attribute mental states of various kinds to others. It is claimed that the main difficulty in accomplishing this is the assumption that the mental states of others are not open to view (e.g., German & Leslie, 2000). Although the major theories of the development of an understanding of mind agree that this is the problem children face, they each take different views of how it is solved; specifically, it is proposed that learning about other minds can occur through analogy with one's own mind, by inference from another's observable behaviour, or by innate mechanisms and modules that have evolved for dealing with this problem (see Hutto, 2004).

The Cartesian-inspired view of mental states is typically partnered with a familiar view of what it is to learn public language labels for mental state concepts. That view is based on thinking of mental state concepts in terms of word-referent relations; that is, words point to, and thus refer to, objects in the world. Many developmental psychologists seem to assume that we and young children can refer to mental states unproblematically. In the case of mental state terms the referents are taken to be mental entities (e.g., beliefs, desires or intentions) that are causally connected to behaviour (Carpendale & Lewis, 2004; 2006; Racine & Carpendale, 2008). The issue of how 'exposure' to mental state terms can facilitate the development of an understanding of mind seems to introduce, for those who accept this model, a code or conduit model of communication (see Turnbull, 2003; and Reddy, 1979, for critiques of such models). Applied to mental state terms, the essence of the code model is that a mother, for example, encodes her private mental state into a public mental state term, she speaks to her child using that term, and her child tries to find the referent for the term in the private, unseen mental state that is being referred to. In effect, something that the child cannot observe directly, the mother's mental state, is encoded into a form that is perceptible, the mental state term. Once the child has learned that mental state term T stands for mental states of that type Ts, the child can correctly encode mental states into and decode mental states from mental state terms and can now enter into successful communication about mind with others.

Wittgenstein (1958) already cast serious doubt on these pictures of mind and language and provided us with a valuable alternative (for in-depth discussions of the relevance of his arguments for research on social cognitive development, see Carpendale & Lewis 2004; 2006; Chapman, 1987; Montgomery, 2002; Racine, 2004; Racine & Carpendale, 2007; 2008). Briefly, the argument is that learning about mind cannot be a naming game involving mapping a word to a private inner mental entity. Rather, to learn about mind, to understand situations involving mind, involves learning the appropriate, quite public, ways to talk about mind. There is a reflexivity to the relation between language and social cognitive development such that mental state language is often based on and replaces early natural reactions and responses exhibited in patterns of intersubjective engagement (Carpendale & Lewis, 2004; 2006; Racine, 2004; Racine & Carpendale, 2008). Such language then affords children the ability to learn distinctions that they otherwise would not have been able to and to acquire concepts, such as belief, that are far removed from early patterns of engagement. An important implication is that parent-child conversations that help children learn the appropriate ways to talk about mind will help children more fully understand aspects of human activity and should, therefore, be beneficial for social cognitive development.

What has not been specified, however, is precisely which aspects of talk about the mind facilitate such understanding. The problem is explaining how children come to understand and talk about people in psychological terms. Much of the research in the 'theory of mind' tradition assumes a particular way of setting up the problem that children allegedly have to solve, thus promoting a limited range of possible solutions. However, if, as we argue, there is a misconception about the problem children must solve, then the situation looks entirely different. We now outline a possible alternative conception of how children learn to talk about human activity in psychological terms.

Children begin to use psychological words while engaging with their caregivers in routine patterns of interaction in which they have developed expectations about some sequence of interpersonal events. This claim follows from a view of language as an extension of human activity — a part of, and a refinement of, human action. Thus, psychological talk refers to human action. Words are learned in the context of routine situations in which a child has learned what typically happens. These patterns of activity are rooted in natural reactions and words come to be used in the context of these human forms of life. For example, a child's fear of an approaching dog or happiness when receiving a gift are clearly manifest to adults; there is nothing hidden or private about such reactions. Typically, adults will talk about children's emotions in such situations, and children can learn the use of emotion words through these experiences. If a child is interested in something her directedness toward the object is clearly manifest, and a parent may respond by giving the desired object or commenting on it. A parent may use a word like 'want' in such as situation to inquire about and clarify a child's desires, and the child may begin using 'want' to make a request, if they cannot get the object themselves, or later in development when they can achieve their goal, to ask for permission (Budwig, 2002).

For an example of how a more complex cognitive term such as 'forgot' is learned consider the anecdote of a mother bringing her 3-year-old daughter a piece of toast that had no jam on it. The daughter had asked for jam, and said to her mother, 'you forgot'. The child could not explain what the word 'forgot' means, but she used it correctly in the appropriate situation. Most likely she had previously heard the word used when something similar had happened and her mother had said, 'Oh, I forgot…'. In order to begin using the cognitive term 'forgot' the child would not need to have made use of a representational theory of minds. No simulation and introspection of beliefs underlying behaviour and inferences to read others' minds would be required. Instead, all that would be needed is that the child has come to understand that in situations where something agreed upon has not been done, the word 'forgot' may be appropriately used. Further, the reasons for failure can differ as a function of differences in context. Thus, initial and partial understanding may lead to uses that are not completely or strictly speaking correct (cf. Nelson, 1996; 2005).

Cognitive terms such as 'think' and 'know', often focused on in the developmental research literature, can be used for many different functions and can be linked to earlier uses of simpler terms such as 'see' and 'look'. The routines in which children begin to use 'see' and 'look' are the forms of interaction referred to as joint or shared attention. For example, when a child has learned how to direct another's attention with a pointing gesture or has learned how to follow another person's pointing gesture she could begin to use the word 'look' along with the gesture, and, later in development, in place of the gesture. This is a form of interaction in which 'look' could be used. Within such situations children also learn what happens when attention is not coordinated, when the other person does not see the object or event indicated. This is the sort of experience that is later transformed into false belief understanding (Carpendale & Lewis, 2004; 2006).

We have conducted a program of research that is consistent with the above view of language and mind over the past ten years. Next, we review three recent studies from this body of work.

Mother-child Talk and the Child's Understanding of Mind

The studies reported in this section of the paper are based on a data set generated from a procedure in which mothers were asked to make up a story with their child (age range 36 to 70 months) based on a picture book involving false beliefs and emotional reactions. This procedure encouraged mother-child dyads to talk about a sequence of actions, their causes and consequences in terms of beliefs, desires, intentions, reasons and emotions. Mother-child talk, as they constructed the narrative, was videotaped and subsequently transcribed and coded for information relevant to an understanding of the events, and for which of mother or child elicited and produced relevant items of information. Given their emphasis in the literature, all standard mental state terms in the transcripts were identified. Children's understanding of mind was assessed using standard tests. This was a longitudinal study in which these mothers and their children returned to the lab 30 months later for further testing (Time 2). Data analyses explored the relation of the child's understanding of mind and various aspects of dyads' talk, which aspects depending on the details of the study.

Two points should be stressed for readers who are not developmental psychologists. The first concerns the age range of the children in this research. Children below the age of 4 years typically fail tests of false belief, whereas 4- to 5-year-old children typically pass such tests. Thus, we expected, and found, children in our sample with no understanding of false belief, others with a partial understanding and still others with a solid understanding. That variability allows for a statistical examination of a possible relationship between aspects of parent-child talk and the child's level of false belief understanding. The second point is that there is a heavy emphasis in the developmental literature on false belief understanding as *the* marker or ability that is most crucial for an understanding of mind. By contrast, our own view is that false belief understanding is only one of a number of abilities that are important for a mature understanding of mind. In spite of that, in order to relate our research findings to the literature, we felt it necessary to focus on false belief understanding.

The picture book of 17 coloured drawings had no text other than the names of the principal characters; namely, two children, Sarah, her brother Billy, and their mother. The pictures depict Sarah and Billy getting chocolate bars from their mother. Sarah immediately eats her chocolate bar, making a mess in the process. Billy saves his chocolate to eat later by hiding it under a sleeping dog. Sarah sees Billy hide his chocolate, but Billy is not aware of this. While he is outside playing Sarah takes Billy's chocolate and puts it in her pocket. Billy returns to look for his chocolate, but it is not under the dog. Sarah laughs at this. Billy gets angry, pushes Sarah, and the chocolate bar falls out of her pocket. Mother intervenes and the conflict between Sarah and Billy is resolved. Using the picture book without text provides structure so that all the parent-child dyads talked about the same sequence of events depicted in the book of drawings. This allows for comparison between dyads and ages. At the same time, what participants said and how they said it was not constrained by the procedure, thereby providing a representative sample of how these family dyads might naturally talk about events involving beliefs and emotions.

A major goal of the research program was to examine how the content of mother-child talk is related to the child's understanding of mind. The story of Billy and Sarah is constituted by a temporal, and sometimes causal, sequence of specific items of information. To understand the narrative is to understand those items and their connections. In the first study reported (Turnbull *et al.*, 2008) we examined transcripts for the presence of items of information (elements) that vary in the extent to which they are important for understanding the story. The story hinges on Billy's false belief about the location of his chocolate bar. The false belief component of the story consists of Billy's concern about leaving his chocolate bar; his decision to hide his chocolate under the family dog; his lack of awareness that Sarah sees him hide the chocolate; his going outside to play and, thus, his lack of awareness that Sarah takes the chocolate bar and puts it in her pocket; his hunger that leads him to think about his chocolate bar hidden under the dog; his going back into the house and looking under the dog; his failure to find his chocolate bar where he hid it; and his reaction of sadness and anger, and his wonder about where it is. Whereas understanding other aspects (e.g., the resolution of Sarah and Billy's conflict) contributes to a fuller understanding of the story, a child who fails to understand the false belief component fails to understand the essence of the story. Accordingly, it was hypothesized that the presence in mother-child talk of elements that constitute the false belief component of the story, False Belief Elements, should be predictive of the child's understanding of mind. Frequency counts of mental state terms were made for overall maternal mental state talk and for maternal mental state talk present in False Belief and Non-False Belief

Elements. Children's false belief understanding was assessed using the unexpected transfer and unexpected contents tasks (Gopnik & Astington, 1988; Wimmer & Perner, 1983). In the unexpected transfer task, children see a puppet (Maxi) put a toy in one location, leave the room, and while out of the room another puppet moves the toy to another location. When Maxi returns to look for the toy, the children are asked, 'Where do you think Maxi will look for the toy', and 'why do you think Maxi will look there?'. Children who predicted incorrectly where Maxi would look were then told where he would look for the chocolate bar and then asked the explanation question. In the unexpected contents task, each child was shown a Smarties box (a candy very familiar to Canadian children), and asked 'What do you think is inside this box?'. After they had answered 'Smarties' or 'candies' they were shown that the box actually contained crayons. Children were then told that a puppet, Mary, had not seen inside the box, and they were asked 'What would Mary think is inside the box?'.

We found that all mother-child dyads produced a coherent narrative that revolved around Billy's false belief, its causes and consequences, but there was considerable variability in the nature of those stories. Relative to the maximum possible for each type of element, dyads' talk contained a higher proportion of False Belief than Non-False Belief Elements. Perhaps this is an indicator of the importance of the False Belief Elements for understanding the story. However, the data did not provide support for the importance of mothers' use of mental state terms. Although mental state term use was positively associated with children's performance on measures of false belief understanding, it did not predict false belief scores when discussion of the false belief component of the story was taken into account. Further, the number of actual mental state terms used in the false belief component of the story was less than what would be expected by chance. This demonstrated another sense in which the frequency of mothers' use of mental state terms is not to be equated with the characteristic of mother-child talk that facilitates an understanding of mind. In sum, frequency of talk about the false belief component of the story was related to the child's false belief understanding, but talk about other sections of the story and mothers' use of mental state terms was not. Presumably, talk about false beliefs directed children's attention to these important features of this episode of human activity, whereas other types of talk did not (Carpendale & Lewis, 2004; Turnbull & Carpendale, 1999; 2001).

Understanding Beliefs and Emotions

Understanding beliefs and emotions is necessary for a fuller under-standing of persons and their actions. Researchers often stress the importance of emotion understanding in the development of children's understanding of mind (e.g., Hobson, 2004). Accordingly, we next describe a study that examined the relations between parent-child talk about emotions of varying levels of complexity and children's under-standing of beliefs and emotions of varying levels of complexity.

An understanding of basic emotions, such as happy or angry might be expected to be unrelated to an understanding of belief (other than related due to a third variable, age). Consistent with that view, Den-ham (1998) reports that young children understand basic emotions at an age when most of them would not pass a false belief task. However, in considering the complexity of emotion, we note that people experi-ence or recognize specific instances of an emotion (i.e., a situated emotion), not the category to which the instance belongs (e.g., one recognizes a specific instance of anger, not anger in the abstract). What makes a situated emotion simple or not is mainly the complexity of the situation in which the emotion is felt or displayed. Consider, for example, a situation in which a youngster, Joe, who likes toy trucks, is nevertheless angry when he gets a toy truck for his birthday. Imagine also that Joe's mother promised him a puppy as a birthday gift. Clearly, Joe's anger is due to the broken promise, and to the contrast between what he received and what he believed he had a right to expect. Anger is one of the basic and universal emotions and, thus, it is a 'simple' emotion, one that children should understand early in development. However, to understand why Joe is angry requires an understanding of beliefs, expectations, conceptions of fairness/morality, etc. For example, one needs to understand what his mother has done by promising; what beliefs and expectations Joe will have given the promise; that violating the promise is a moral offence; and that how Joe feels depends on the contrast between what he expected and what he received. And given an understanding of the bases of Joe's anger, there are potential implications regarding how Joe will feel about his mother (perhaps he will no longer totally trust her) and how he might feel about promises (don't trust them). As a conse-quence, to understand 'anger' in this situation requires the under-standing of many other aspects of mind, including an understanding of how human activity is embedded in a normative context. It is, thus, not likely that young children will be able to understand that situated emotion. A parent who wanted to help a child understand Joe's anger should talk to the child in a way that focuses the child's attention on beliefs etcetera that are relevant to emotions and describe the ways those beliefs are consequential for emotions.

Understanding some emotions requires understanding false beliefs; for example, understanding that Little Red Riding Hood will be happy to see the Wolf depends on understanding her false belief. Bradmetz and Schneider (1999) found that children who understand false beliefs realise Little Red Riding Hood does not know the Wolf is dressed up as her grandmother. Some of these same children, however, mistakenly state that Little Red Riding Hood will be afraid of her grandmother. Thus, it appears that some aspects of an understanding of belief are required to understand particular emotions situated in complex social situations. Accordingly, we predicted that parents' talk about emotions that are dependent on beliefs would be correlated with children's understanding of false beliefs, whereas talk about emotions that do not depend on beliefs would be associated with children's understanding of basic emotions in simple situations.

To test that prediction, we used the data from the parent-child stories described above (Racine *et al.*, 2007). Children's understanding of emotions was assessed with emotion labelling tasks and affective perspective-taking tasks. We first explored the relation between performance on the false belief tasks and the tests of emotion understanding. We then examined the relationship between talk about emotions that were (i.e., belief-dependent) or were not (i.e., not belief-dependent) based on characters' beliefs and the child's false belief understanding. Eight of the Storybook Elements are related specifically to emotions. Of these, four involve Sarah's emotions that are dependent on her having deceived Billy (i.e., belief-dependent emotions). For example, Sarah's laughing in 'Sarah is laughing/finds it funny when Billy cannot find his chocolate' is based on Sarah's understanding that Billy is acting on a false belief. The other four elements involve Billy's emotions of being sad or angry when he cannot find his chocolate bar and being angry with Sarah because she is laughing. Those emotions could be understood by relying on the situation without an understanding of the false belief involved (i.e., non-belief-dependent emotions).

We hypothesized that talk about belief-dependent emotions in the context of the storybook would be positively related to false belief understanding, and that talk about non-belief-dependent emotions would be positively related to emotion understanding. In our analysis, we controlled for shared variance between emotion and false belief understanding and found that child age and amount of non-belief-dependent emotion talk about the storybook were associated with emotion understanding, whereas child age and amount of belief-dependent emotion talk were associated with false belief understanding. Why was talk about Sarah's emotions related to children's understanding of false beliefs? Parents who talked about Sarah's happy emotions on tricking Billy made salient the fact that at that point in the story Sarah believed that Billy had a false belief. By contrast, talking about Billy's emotions or how both Billy and Sarah felt *after* the events does not explicitly make Sarah's beliefs about Billy's beliefs salient. This pattern of results would obtain if parents talked about emotions contingent on beliefs about beliefs only if they believed their child could already understand such talk or was capable of learning to understand such talk. The fact that both age and the different forms of talk were associated with emotion and false belief understanding is consistent with our general emphasis on the importance of particular kinds of parent-child conversation.

Understanding Conflict and Understanding Mind

In addition to false belief and emotion components, the storybook also presents a situation of conflict, its causes and its resolution; specifically, Billy is angry when Sarah laughs at his failure to find his chocolate, he pushes her off a chair, Sarah cries, the two of them accuse one another, Mother intervenes and the conflict is resolved. Disciplinary situations that arise when there is a conflict between children constitute an important opportunity for parents to facilitate their children's social understanding. For example, Ruffman, Perner and Parkin (1999) asked parents what they had or would do in five different disciplinary situations. Parents who reported they would ask their child to reflect on the feelings of others had children who were more advanced in false belief understanding than their age-mates. Dunn and her colleagues (1991) have suggested that disciplinary situations expose children to conflicting perspectives that might facilitate their understanding of false beliefs and emotions. When dyads make up their story, they can talk about the conflict in different ways. Consistent with our general view, we suggest that talk that draws the child's attention to and ties together into a sequence the intentions, motivations and consequences of the protagonists' actions that generated the conflict (i.e., *explanatory talk*; e.g., 'It is not good/funny that Sarah took Billy's chocolate bar because she shouldn't take other peoples things') should facilitate an understanding of mind (see also Hutto, 2008). By contrast, talk that consists of simply telling the child what should be done without explaining why the conflict has arisen (i.e., *non-explanatory talk*; e.g., 'Sarah and Billy tell their sides') is unlikely to help the child understand the situation and, thus, is unlikely to facilitate the development of the child's understanding of mind. We hypothesized that explanatory talk would predict children's understanding of mind, whereas non-explanatory talk would not.

Unlike the two previous studies discussed, the conflict study (Racine *et al.*, 2006) involved an examination of talk and understanding in both a cross-sectional (i.e., measures taken at the same point in time) and a longitudinal design (comparing measures taken at Time 1 to measures taken 30 months later, Time 2). In particular, we examined the relation between type of talk at Time 1 and concurrent measures of the child's understanding of false belief and emotion. Those measures are the same as used in the two studies previously discussed. We also examined the relation between type of talk at Time 1 and children's understanding of beliefs and emotions at Time 2 with tasks appropriate for the age of this sample; namely, a test of interpretative understanding (Carpendale & Chandler, 1996) and a test of the understanding of mixed emotions (Dunn, 1995). As in the other studies in this research program, we identified 10 Storybook Elements that specifically addressed the conflict between Billy and Sarah and the manner in which mother dealt with it. Talk about the conflict was coded as either explanatory or non-explanatory.

Our analyses revealed that explanatory talk about the conflict (Time 1) predicted 3- to 5-year-old children's concurrent understanding of emotions and false beliefs. We also found that explanatory talk at Time 1 predicted children's understanding of interpretation and mixed emotions at Time 2, thirty months later. The latter effect provides evidence for a causal influence of parent-child talk on the child's developing understanding of mind.

Limitations of these Studies

One objection to our interpretation of the results of the above studies is that a child might understand false belief but be unable to pass a false belief task because of limits in her ability to express her understanding. If that were true then the observed relation between talk and the measures of an understanding of mind is an artifact of children's language understanding. Various statistical techniques can be used to assess whether it is attributes of talk or the child's level of linguistic ability that is related to the child's understanding of mind. However, instead of this either/or sort of approach, although the influence of talk and linguistic ability *can* be teased apart, whether it makes sense to always do so is another matter. If children were being tested in a second language they had not fully mastered, their ability to pass tests of an understanding of belief and emotion would depend not only on their understanding of the relevant concepts, but also on the extent to which they had mastered the second language. In this case, children's understanding of beliefs and emotions would be confounded with their ability to understand and respond in the second language, and it would make sense to separate the effects of understanding mind from facility in the second language. However, if, as we have argued, coming to understand the mental world is intertwined with learning to talk about that world, then social understanding and language are naturally confounded.[2]

We have presented evidence suggestive of an important role for talk; specifically, parent-child explanatory talk about conflict predicts the child's understanding of interpretation and of mixed emotion 30 months later. Most of the supportive data, however, come from correlational designs, and correlation is not causality. It may be that parents fit the way they talk to the level of their child's understanding of mind, and this may facilitate the child's understanding of mind. Further, parents talking with their children *is* social interaction which, by definition, has bidirectional influences. Talk is necessarily co-constructed and, thus, each participant influences and is influenced by the other.

Language Versus Talk-as-Social Interaction

This article is structured around the claim that children's understanding of mind is facilitated by explanatory talk/conversation about particular social situations that directs their attention to important features of human activity (Carpendale & Lewis, 2004; 2006; Turnbull & Carpendale, 1999; 2001). Talking with others in this way is an important activity because it is the major way in which children are exposed to and learn the use of psychological terms. Since in most situations, such explanatory talk will constitute provision of a narrative, the results of our research are consistent with the NPH. Given that engaging in episodes of talk with others is crucial for the child's development of an understanding of mind, we next turn to an

---

[2] By claiming this we do not assume they are completely the same thing, and we acknowledge that it is possible for 3- to 5-year-olds to misunderstand the language in tests. But we are arguing that it is not possible to completely separate social understanding and language, as would be required in order for it to be sensible to partial out statistically the effects of language.

examination of the structure of talk and its importance for social development.

People interact to advance courses of action; for example, they interact to buy a cup of coffee, to get a mortgage or divorce, to claim certain images of self, and to express their commitment or opposition to cultural, esthetic, intellectual, legal, political or spiritual standards. Whereas many requirements must be satisfied to buy a cup of coffee or secure a divorce (e.g., specific aspects of the economic and legal systems of a culture), it is normally the case that talking both accompanies and is partially constitutive of those activities. Talking is, thus, a form of social interaction; indeed, talking is the universal and most frequent form of social interaction.

Talking is an orderly activity that participants create together by employing certain practices or methods (Sacks, 1992; Turnbull, 2003, ch. 6). These methods mainly involve sequential relations. In particular, talk proceeds over time, turn by turn with a sequential alternation of speakers/participants. In a turn at talk a speaker/participant orients to the prior turn of another participant and makes relevant potential actions by another participant in the next turn. Because participants orient the present turn to the prior and next turn, because turns are conditionally relevant, connections are established between adjacent turns. Given that turns are conditionally relevant, participants' turns at talk must be recipient-designed. In particular, a speaker, S, must construct her turn to fit that specific point in their interaction for that specific addressee, A (i.e., depending on what identities are relevant for that interaction at that moment, for S's image of A, of A's relationship to S, of A's culture, etc.). Likewise, A must recognize what action(s) S performed in her turn on the assumption that S's turn was designed by S to fit that specific point in the interaction for A specifically. One implication of the recipient-designed nature of talk is that every turn at talk, by its very nature, displays both self-identity and the self's view of the other and of the self-other relationship. Thus, in advancing courses of action in talk, participants also negotiate identity (Bamberg, 2008; Malone, 1997; Rawls, 1989; 1990). Another implication is that talk is necessarily co-constructed, constructed by participants acting together according to certain practices.

Observation of episodes of talk reveals that participants use linguistic resources to co-construct their talk, but they also use non-linguistic resources such as gaze, gesture, facial expression, written records, pictures, and other aspects of the environment in which the talk occurs (e.g., puppets, dolls and costumes [especially, but not only, when children are participants]; instruments and technologies of various kinds, such as signs and computer monitors). Consider an example of an interaction that took place in a hospital recovery room holding patients who had just undergone a medical procedure to test for cancer. The participants, identified as S and A, seemed to be married couple. Material in double parentheses describes what action was performed. Material in single parentheses describes how an action was performed.

Example 1

1   S: we:::ll? (drawn out 'well' with rising or questioning intonation)

2   A: ((simultaneous right thumb up gesture, head nod, and smile; followed by waving a computer printout of test results))

3   S: phe:::w (drawn out sigh, big outbreath, falling intonation; head drops to chest)

4   A: yeah ((nod, outbreath)) what a relief

The interaction consists of a sequence initiated by S asking if A has cancer (i.e., asking what the test results are), to which A responds he does not have cancer (i.e., test results are negative), followed by S displaying her relief at this good news, and ending with A acknowledging and confirming the relief that both experience. Clearly, S and A produce and recognize a sequence of actions even though many of those actions are constituted by non-linguistic resources, as for example A's first turn in which no verbal action of any sort occurs. Further, the production of action involves the coordination of various resources, as when a linguistic 'yeah' occurs simultaneously with a non-linguistic head nod and an outbreath.

It is evident from the above that talk is not just to be equated with linguistic performance. Neither is talk a deficient reflection of inner processes. Rather, talk is a co-ordinated activity of participants who together, using a range of linguistic and non-linguistic resources, produce and recognize action in pursuit of practical and interpersonal ends. Talk is, thus, a skilled performance that is constitutive of social life. In order to engage in talk, participants must have certain linguistic, cognitive-perceptual, and physical skills, including the ability to coordinate such skills, but it is also the case that engaging in episodes of talk is where persons can practice those skills. We next explore the relation of talk and the development of an understanding of mind.

Talk and the Development of an Understanding of Mind

Social interaction is required for social development. As children engage in talk, they are learning how to perform and recognize actions. Consider the following example of mother (M)-child (C; 2 year 2 month old daughter) talk that appears in Susswein and Racine (2008, p. 154). '[ ]' indicates overlapping talk; '[' indicates where overlap begins and ']' where it ends. Line 3 indicates a one-half second pause occurred before M took her turn.

Example 2

    1   M: the [skin is really soft on those kind]
    2   C: [too sour mommy] I han havva drink
    3   (.5)
    4   M: [you're going to have a drink?]
    5   C: [((C drinks from cup))]

C's intention utterance 'I han havva drink' does not describe a hidden, mental event but rather licenses expectations about a projected course of action, that action to occur soon/next in the immediate sequence. The projected action occurs (C drinks from cup) in overlap with M's ratification of C's intention ('you're going to have a drink?'). The example illustrates how sequential structures of talk license expectations about what should occur in the next slot of an ongoing sequence. Thus, as children engage in talk, they are also developing expectations about the sequential unfolding of actions. Engaging in talk, however, requires the child to already possess certain skills, such as being able to remember, at minimum, three-turn sequences, who produced each turn and each turn's content. Engaging in talk gives the child practice in improving those skills. To further illustrate the reflexive relation between talk and various social/cognitive skills, consider perspective-taking, a requirement for a mature understanding of mind.

    Recall that participants in talk must produce and recognize recipient-designed contributions. That, in turn, requires the child to be perspectival, to respond to that specific turn of that specific other at that specific moment in their interaction. As noted earlier, conflict has been claimed to be a good context for the child to understand that persons can adopt different perspectives. But cooperation and positive alignment between participants also requires tailoring ones contributions for the specific other. Once the child can engage in interaction, she must therefore be able to take perspectives in action. Talk-in-interaction is an important context where perspective-taking occurs, where it is practiced and learned, and this is the case whether or not narratives per se are involved. When discussion of narratives do feature, it can be expected that the more recipient-designed the discussions of the narrative are, the more effective they should be for developing an understanding of mind.

Persons interact to advance courses of action. In Example 2, M offers C a potato, and C rejects that offer by exclaiming 'too sour mommy'. Following that, C attempts to display to M that she intends to have a drink; that is, the sequence consists of the action pairs of offer-reject and statement of intention-act on intention. That is what the interaction was for the participants. As developmentalists, however, we focussed on talk about reasons for acting. The point here is that although some interactions may have a person's reasons as their primary topic, in most cases it will be in the course of doing everyday actions with ones child, such as buying groceries, discussing the pre/school day, preparing and eating food, playing games, dressing and undressing, bathing and getting ready for bed, that reasons will be invoked. In sum, our claim is that talk about mental states and reasons will typically occur in the course of carrying out and discussing everyday activities.

The structure of talk also allows participants to monitor on a turn-by-turn basis whether or not shared understanding is occurring. Because of the responsiveness of a next turn to the prior, when A responds to S's prior turn, A displays how he understood S's turn. That understanding is manifestly available to S who in her next turn can accept that understanding (e.g., by explicitly ratifying A's response, or by moving on with her talk) or object to A's (mis)understanding. In the latter case, S initiates a repair of A's problematic turn or turn-component. Typically, repair-initiation leads to a sequence by which speaker and addressee re-establish shared understanding. Talk, thus, contains its own self-righting procedures.

If a child is to develop a mature understanding of mind, it is important that failures to understand are made salient to the child and are corrected. But there is no need for participants to 'read minds' in order to monitor whether or not shared understanding is being maintained. Rather, on the basis of what a child hearably and seeably *does*, parents or other 'experts' can correct and scaffold the child's understanding of mind. We suggest that repair sequences are a useful environment for examining the influence of narrative on the development of an understanding of mind. In particular, there are many ways to initiate a repair and many ways to make a repair. Thus, repair sequences can be expected to vary in the extent to which narratives are involved, and the extent to which certain narratives facilitate understanding more than others. In the next section we turn to an examination of the ways in which the nature of the mother-child relationship might influence narratives and the extent to which such narratives facilitate social cognitive development.

The Role of Relationships in Achieving Understanding

A focus on talk and interaction highlights the different ways in which interactions can be co-constructed within different relationships and the effects of those differences on cognitive development. Although a turn sets limits on the possible next turn (i.e., it must be conditionally relevant), there is a range of options as to how a turn can be constructed. Consider two examples from the storybook data, both of which occurred as dyads were looking at the picture of Billy hiding his chocolate under the sleeping dog, a critically important event in the storybook. [Note: a number in parentheses indicates a pause of specified duration].

Example 3

    1   M: what's he doing
    2   C: I don't know
    3   M: he's hiding the chocolate. then he goes outside to play

Example 4

    1   M: what's Billy doing?
    2   (2.0)
    3   C: putting up
    4   M: putting what?
    5   C: that ((simultaneously pointing to the picture of the candy))
    6   M: what is it?
    7   C: candy
    8   M: putting the candy where?
    9   C: eh under dere
    10 M: what's this? ((simultaneously pointing to the picture of the dog))
    11   (1.0)
    12 C: a dog
    13 M: so he's putting the candy under the dog (.) why do you think he's doing that

In Example 3, mother immediately corrects her child but does so without providing any rationale for why that is the correct answer. Further, mother fails to explain why Billy's action is relevant for the events that are unfolding. In contrast, when the mother in Example 4 asks the same question (line 1) and her child cannot answer, rather than providing the answer mother instead breaks the question down into smaller questions each of which the child can answer. In this way, mother enables the child him/herself to eventually provide the complete and correct answer to mother's initial question. After twelve turns, mother then summarizes the child's understanding (i.e., what the child has conveyed over those turns), in that way crediting the child as the source of the correct information. She also emphasizes and confirms that answer. And, finally, she then begins to explore with the child why the answer to her initial question is of relevance to an understanding of the story. We suggest that the way the mother in Example 4 talks with her child is likely to be more effective in getting the child to understand that critical aspect of the story than is the way the mother in Example 3 talks to her child.

But how can we characterize the relevant differences in the interactions of Examples 3 and 4? Relationships, and, we would add, forms of talk, can be seen as varying on a continuum from constraint to cooperation, according to Piaget (1932/1965). In relations of constraint, characterized by one-sided control, the more powerful person (e.g., mother) feels no obligation to explain why her position is correct and, instead, imposes her view on the child (Example 3). In cooperative relations, characterized by mutual respect, a mother builds on her child's understanding and provides a rationale for her position (Example 4).[3] Piaget suggested that cooperative relations facilitate the development of knowledge. In a similar vein, Mercer (2000) suggests that classroom talk can take one of three forms; namely, exploratory talk, the joint negotiation of ideas; disputational talk, the competitive negotiation of knowledge claims; and cumulative talk, the uncritical addition of knowledge claims. Mercer argues that only exploratory talk creates the active engagement required for joint reasoning. In particular, exploratory talk invites students to build on to, extend, and question others' contributions. Exploratory talk is, thus, cooperative interaction. Mercer (2008; Mercer & Littleton, 2007) provides data to support the claim that compared to other forms of talk, exploratory talk in classrooms leads to the best level of student understanding.

What we conclude from the above is that co-operative interaction facilitates understanding. The education literature leads us to believe

[3] Clearly mothers and children are not equal in their social and linguistic competence, but this does not entail that mothers necessarily assume that they do not have to explain themselves to their children. It is equality in the goal of reaching mutual understanding rather then imposing views, not equality in level of skill that is important here.

that this is true for all kinds of understanding, not just an understanding of mind. And it is true, also, across the lifespan, not just for young children. Thus, our claim is a claim about learning, not simply a claim about how children learn about mind. In the context of the child's developing an understanding of mind, it is the child's understanding of the attitudes of the agents and how they relate to the unfolding of a given sequence of events, as can be captured in a narrative, that is essential, and some relationships are better suited to achieve mutual understanding of such narratives. Thus, how narratives are told or, in some cases, co-constructed (i.e., the nature of the interaction) should be an important factor in how effective a narrative is in facilitating children's understanding of human activity in psychological terms. We suggest that the nature of the interactions in which the child is involved is a fruitful issue for further research on talk and the development of an understanding of mind.

Conclusion

In considering the role of talk in social cognitive development we began by reviewing evidence of correlations between children's social cognitive development and aspects of the language they are exposed to, as well as their own linguistic ability. We then critiqued the conceptions of mind and language underlying the developmental ToM research tradition. As an alternative we proposed that children's understanding of psychological terms is based on their experience within routine human forms of interaction. It is within these patterns of activity rooted in natural reactions that children gradually learn how to talk about human activity in psychological terms. We then reviewed research consistent with the view that what is essential is not simply the mention of mental state terms, but rather children's understanding of the routines of human action that are being referred to. Thus, it is the quantity and quality of the talk and the forms of interaction rather than simply mentioning mental state words that is important. We concluded that children's understanding of mind is based on their emerging ability to talk about human activity in psychological terms. The development of this ability is facilitated by appropriate forms of talk, which is a form of social interaction. The practices necessary to participate in such interactions require social and cognitive skills, and those skills are practiced by engaging in episodes of talk. Some of the required skills, such as perspective-taking, have special relevance for the development of an understanding of mind. We then described how talk can vary on a continuum from cooperative to constraining interaction. We proposed that cooperative interaction based on mutual respect is best suited for reaching mutual understanding. Accordingly, coming to understand human activity and learning how to talk about and to think about human action in psychological terms should be facilitated by cooperative interaction.

Social cognitive development begins in infancy with forms of understanding that could only be linked to the most minimal definition of narrative (see also Leavens & Racine, this issue). More complex narratives would be associated with children's understanding of psychological terms, although their development of such understanding would likely occur bi-directionally as they engage in talk and also become more socially competent in this process. Narratives provide support to the child in coming to a shared understanding of the social world. Finally, we have highlighted the important role of cooperative parent-child relationships in the process of reaching mutual understanding.

Acknowledgements

The research described in this article was supported by grants from the Social Sciences and Humanities Council of Canada. We thank the anonymous reviewers and Daniel D. Hutto for comments on earlier versions of this paper.

References

Adrián, J.E., Clemente, R.A. & Villanueva, L. (2007), 'Mothers' use of Cognitive State Verbs in Picture-book Reading and the Development of Children's Understanding of Mind: A longitudinal study', *Child Development*, **78**, pp. 1052–67.

Astington, J.W. & Baird, J.A. (ed, 2005), *Why Language Matters for Theory of Mind* (New York: Oxford University Press).

Bamberg, M. (2008), 'Selves and Identities in the Making: The study of microgenetic processes in interactive practices', in J.I.M. Carpendale, U. Müller, N. Budwig, B. Sokol (ed.), *Social life and social knowledge: Toward a process account of development* (New York: Erlbaum), pp. 205–24.

Bartsch, K. & Wellman, H.M. (1995), *Children talk about the mind* (Oxford: Oxford University Press).

Bradmetz, J. & Schneider, R. (1999), 'Is Little Red Riding Hood afraid of her grandmother? Cognitive vs. emotional response to a false belief', *British Journal of Developmental Psychology*, **17**, pp. 501–14.

Budwig, N. (2002), 'A Developmental-Functionalist Approach to Mental State Talk', in E. Amsel & J.P. Byrnes (ed.), *Language, literacy, and cognitive development: The development and consequences of symbolic communication* (Mahwah, NJ: Erlbaum), pp. 59–86.

Canfield, J.V. (1993), 'The Living Language: Wittgenstein and the empirical study of communication', *Language Sciences*, **15**, pp. 165–93.

Carpendale, J.I.M. & Chandler, M.J. (1996), 'On the Distinction Between False Belief Understanding and Subscribing to an Interpretive Theory of Mind', *Child Development*, **67**, pp. 1686–706.
Carpendale, J.I.M. & Lewis, C. (2004), 'Constructing an Understanding of Mind: The development of children's social understanding within social interaction', *Behavioral and Brain Sciences*, **27**, pp. 79–96.
Carpendale, J.I.M. & Lewis, C. (2006), *How children develop social understanding* (Oxford: Blackwell).
Carruthers, P. (2008), 'Cartesian Epistemology: Is the theory of self-transparent mind innate?', *Journal of Consciousness Studies*, **15**, pp. 28–53.
Chapman, M. (1987), 'Inner Processes and Outward Criteria: Wittgenstein's importance for psychology', in M. Chapman & R.A. Dixon (ed.), *Meaning and the growth of understanding: Wittgenstein's significance for developmental psychology* (Berlin: Springer-Verlag), pp. 103–27.
Denham, S.A. (1998), *Emotional development in young children* (New York: The Guilford Press).
de Villiers J.G. & de Villiers, P.A. (2000), 'Linguistic Determinism and the Understanding of False Beliefs', in P. Mitchell & K.J. Riggs (ed.), *Children's reasoning and the mind* (Hove, UK: Psychology Press), pp. 191–228.
Dunn, J. (1995), 'Children as Psychologists: The later correlates of individual differences in understanding of emotions and other minds', *Cognition and Emotion*, **9**, pp. 187–201.
Dunn, J., Brown, J., Slomkowski, C., Tesla, C. & Youngblade, L. (1991), 'Young Children's Understanding of Other People's Feelings and Beliefs: Individual differences and their antecedents', *Child Development*, **62**, pp. 1352–66.
Fivush, R. & Nelson, K. (2006), 'Parent-child Reminiscing Locates the Self in the Past', *British Journal of Developmental Psychology*, **24**, pp. 235–51.
Fodor, J.A. (2008), *LOT 2: The language of thought revisited* (Oxford: Oxford University Press).
German, T.P. & Leslie, A.M. (2000), 'Attending to and Learning About Mental States', in P. Mitchell & K.J. Riggs (ed.), *Children's reasoning and the mind* (Hove, UK: Psychology Press), pp. 229–52.
Gopnik, A. & Astington, J.W. (1988), 'Children's Understanding of Representational Change and its Relation to the Understanding of False Belief and the Appearance-Reality Distinction', *Child Development*, **59**, pp. 26–37.
Harris, P.L. (2005), 'Conversation, Pretense, and Theory of Mind', in J.W. Astington & J.A. Baird (ed.), *Why language matters for theory of mind* (New York: Oxford University Press), pp. 70–83.
Hobson, R.P. (2002/2004), *The cradle of thought* (London: Macmillan/Oxford University Press).
Hutto, D.D. (2004), 'The Limits of Spectatorial Folk Psychology', *Mind & Language*, **19**, pp. 548–73.
Hutto, D.D. (2008), *Folk psychological narratives: The sociocultural basis of understanding reasons* (Cambridge, MA: MIT press).
Lohmann, H. & Tomasello, M. (2003), 'The Role of Language in the Development of False Belief Understanding: A training study', *Child Development*, **74**, pp. 1130–44.
Malone, M.J. (1997), *Worlds of talk: The presentation of self in everyday conversation* (Cambridge: Polity Press).
Meins, E., Fernyhough, C., Wainwright, R., Das Gupta, M., Fradley, E. & Tuckey, M. (2002), 'Maternal Mind-Mindedness and Attachment Security as Predictors of Theory of Mind Understanding', *Child Development*, **73**, pp. 1715–26.
Mercer, N. (2000), *Words and minds* (New York: Routledge).

Mercer, N. (2008), 'Talk and the Development of Reasoning and Understanding', *Human Development*, **51**, pp. 90–100.

Mercer, N. & Littleton, K. (2007), *Dialogue and the development of children's thinking: A sociocultural approach* (London: Routledge).

Milligan, K., Astington, J.W. & Dack, L.A. (2007), 'Language and Theory of Mind: Meta-analysis of the relations between language ability and false-belief understanding', *Child Development*, **78**, pp. 622–46.

Montgomery, D.E. (2002), 'Mental Verbs and Semantic Development', *Journal of Cognition and Development*, **3**, pp. 357–84.

Nelson, K. (1996), *Language in cognitive development: The emergence of mediated mind* (New York: Cambridge University Press).

Nelson, K. (2005), 'Language Pathways to the Community of Minds', in J.W. Astington & J. Baird (ed.), *Why language matters for theory of mind* (New York: Oxford University Press), pp. 26–49.

Nelson, K. (2009), 'Wittgenstein and Contemporary Theories of Word Learning', *New Ideas in Psychology*, **27**, pp. 275–87.

Ontai, L.L. & Thompson, R.A. (2008), 'Attachment, Parent-Child Discourse and Theory-of-Mind Development', *Social Development*, **17**, pp. 47–60.

Peterson, C. & Slaughter, V. (2003), 'Opening Windows into the Mind: Mothers' preferences for mental state explanations and children's theory of mind', *Cognitive Development*, **18**, pp. 399–429.

Piaget, J. (1932/1965), *The moral judgment of the child* (New York: The Free Press).

Racine, T.P. (2004), 'Wittgenstein's Internalistic Logic and Children's Theories of Mind', in J.I.M. Carpendale & U. Müller (ed.), *Social interaction and the development of knowledge* (Mahwah, NJ: Erlbaum), pp. 275–6.

Racine, T.P. & Carpendale, J.I.M. (2007), 'The Role of Shared Practice in Joint Attention', *British Journal of Developmental Psychology*, **25**, pp. 3–25.

Racine, T.P. & Carpendale, J.I.M. (2008), 'The Embodiment of Mental States', in W.F. Overton, U. Müller & J. Newman (ed.), *Developmental perspectives on embodiment and consciousness* (Mahwah, NJ: Erlbaum), pp. 159–90.

Racine, T.P., Carpendale, J.I.M. & Turnbull, W. (2006), 'Cross-sectional and Longitudinal Relations between Mother-Child Talk about Conflict and Children's Social Understanding', *British Journal of Psychology*, **97**, pp. 521–36.

Racine, T.P., Carpendale, J.I.M. & Turnbull, W. (2007), 'Parent-child talk and children's understanding of beliefs and emotions', *Cognition & Emotion*, **21**, pp. 480–94.

Rawls, A. (1989), 'Language, self, and social order: a reformulation of Goffman and Sacks', *Human Studies*, **12**, pp. 147–92.

Rawls, A. (1990), 'Emergent sociality: A dialectic of commitment and order', *Symbolic Interaction*, **13**, pp. 63–82.

Reddy, M.J. (1979), 'The conduit metaphor — a case of frame conflict in our language about language', in A. Ortony (ed.), *Metaphor and thought* (New York: Cambridge University Press), pp. 284–324.

Ruffman, T., Perner, J. & Parkin, L. (1999), 'How parenting style affects false belief understanding', *Social Development*, **8**, pp. 395–411.

Ruffman, T., Slade, L. & Crowe, E. (2002), 'The relation between children's and mothers' mental state language and theory-of-mind understanding', *Child Development*, **73**, pp. 734–51.

Russell, J. (1992), 'The theory theory: So good they named it twice?', *Cognitive Development*, **7**, pp. 485–519.

Sacks, H. (1992), *Lectures on conversation, Vols 1–2* (Oxford: Basil Blackwell).

Shatz, M., Wellman, H.M. & Silber, S. (1983), 'The acquisition of mental verbs: A systematic investigation of the first reference to mental state', *Cognition*, **14**, pp. 301–21.

Slaughter, V., Peterson, C.C. & Mackintosh, E. (2007), 'Mind what mother says: Narrative input and theory of mind in typical children and those on the autism spectrum', *Child Development*, **78**, pp. 839–58.

Susswein, N. & Racine, T.P. (2008), 'Causal and definitional issues in intersubjectivity', in J. Zlatev, T.P. Racine, C. Sinha & E. Itkonen (ed.), *The shared mind: Perspectives on intersubjectivity* (Amsterdam: John Benjamins), pp. 141–63.

Taumoepeau, M. & Ruffman, T. (2006), 'Mother and infant talk about mental states relates to desire language and emotion understanding', *Child Development*, **77**, pp. 465–81.

Taumoepeau, M. & Ruffman, T. (2008), 'Stepping stones to others' minds: Maternal talk relates to child mental state language and emotion understanding at 15, 24, and 33 months', *Child Development*, **79**, pp. 284–302.

Turnbull, W. (2003), *Language in action: Psychological models of conversation* (Hove, UK: Psychology Press).

Turnbull, W. & Carpendale, J.I.M. (1999), 'A social pragmatic model of talk: Implications for research on the development of children's social understanding', *Human Development*, **42**, pp. 328–55.

Turnbull, W. & Carpendale, J.I.M. (2001), 'Talk and social understanding', *Early Education and Development*, **12**, pp. 455–77.

Turnbull, W., Carpendale, J.I.M. & Racine, T.P. (2008), 'Relations between mother-child talk and 3- to 5-year-old children's understanding of belief: Beyond mental state terms to talk about the mind', *Merrill-Palmer Quarterly*, **54**, pp. 367–85.

Wimmer, H. & Perner, J. (1983), 'Beliefs about beliefs: Representation and constraining function of wrong beliefs in young children's understanding of deception', *Cognition*, **13**, pp. 103–28.

Wittgenstein, L. (1958), *Philosophical investigations* (Oxford: Basil Blackwell).

Wootton, A.J. (1997), *Interaction and the development of mind* (Cambridge: Cambridge University Press).

Chris Sinha

Objects in a Storied World
Materiality, Normativity, Narrativity

Abstract: There exists broad agreement that participatory, intersubjective engagements in infancy and early childhood, particularly triadic engagements, pave the way for the folk psychological capacities that emerge in middle childhood. There is little agreement, however, about the extent to which early participatory engagements are cognitively prerequisite to the later capacities; and there remain serious questions about exactly how narrative and other language practices can be shown to bridge the gap between early engagements and later abilities, without presupposing the very abilities that they are supposed to account for. A key issue here is the normativity inherent in requesting, proferring and inferring reasons. I point out that normativity is not a property only of linguistic interactions. Normativity and conventionality are also materially instantiated in the artefactual objects that are most frequently implicated in early triadic engagements. The conventional, canonical functions of artefacts may, however, be overlaid in symbolic play by significations rooted in children's experience of blended actual and virtual worlds. Artefactual objects are amplifiers, as well as objects of consciousness. Interwoven with the symbolic forms of language, they co-constitute a specifically human biocultural niche, within and in virtue of which developing human beings become competent folk psychologists.

1. Introduction

It is a strange, but often unremarked, characteristic of many discussions of human folk psychological capacities and practices that the world in which they are exercised is frequently entirely absent, at least insofar as that world is external to the mental processes of the subjects who are engaged in folk psychological reasoning. One reason for this absence of 'the world', in all its tangible materiality and evident sociality, is not hard to find. Folk psychology is the term of art for dealings between people in which the objects dealt in are subjective. These subjective mental objects are beliefs, desires and, in their most developmentally advanced level, conjunctions of beliefs and desires organized in what Hutto (2008, p. 29) calls 'the folk psychological schema': an integrated 'belief/desire pair with interlocking contents' (*ibid.* p. 26). For example, I might attribute the reason for my friend running past me on the station platform without stopping to greet me, or suggesting sharing a cup of coffee, to his desire to catch the next train coupled with his belief that the next train is about to depart.

Folk psychology, then, concerns reasoning to, or about, reasons, and reasons are commonly understood to be mental entities. It is this common understanding that motivates usages such as 'mentalizing' and 'understanding other minds' as labels for folk psychological capacities. Such usages are not neutral: they betray a central theoretical presupposition, that the explanation of the capacities involved in folk psychological practices must appeal solely to individual mental representational processes and their neurological foundations. This is the fundamental guiding principle of cognitivism. Before I go on to subject the cognitivist view to critique, and suggest an alternative, let me avoid possible misunderstanding by declaring that my anti-cognitivism should not be confused with behaviourist assaults on 'mentalism'. I do not challenge the general assumption that reasons are attributes of mind, attributable to individual subjects. My critical take on the dominant cognitivist understanding of mind and folk psychological practice is directed to the deeper theoretical commitments of cognitivist accounts, that lead them to not only background, but effectively erase, both the material world and the social dimension of mind from their story of how developing human beings become practitioners of folk psychology.

Mind, I shall argue, has an often-neglected material aspect *in the world and not just in the brain*, as well as a mental aspect; and while it is individuals that entertain (singly or jointly) propositional attitudes such as beliefs and desires, the intersubjective negotiation and establishment of their shared mental universe depends upon its prior normative structuring in communities of practice. These two key theses of my argument, that can be summed up as (i) the *materiality* of representation (Sinha, 1988) and (ii) the *social* nature of representation (and mind), find both a theoretical and practical intersection in the *artefactual object*.

The adoption of a non-cognitivist, social-material approach to cognition and representation makes it possible to advance an ontogenetic account of the emergence and growth of symbolization that is consistent with, and indeed blends into, Hutto's sociocultural Narrative Practice Hypothesis of the origins of folk psychology. In brief, I will propose that it is in large part through their guided engagements with artefactual objects that young children become participants in a normatively structured, storied world. Later, children spontaneously extend this initial ability by imaginatively transforming the status of objects as bearers of meaning within a shared universe of discourse. Children's imaginative sociodramatic play, I will suggest, is a natural laboratory both for the exercise and for the study of the narrative practices that are the enabling matrix for practical, folk psychological reasoning.

2. Materiality, Sociality, Normativity

The Cartesian dualist split between mind and matter, that which immaterially represents and that which has bodily extension, is commonly discussed in the context of the relation between mind and brain, a context in which Descartes' theories no longer have significant support. Only relatively recently[1] have critical discussions focussed on mind-matter dualism as manifested in the supposed representational relation between *mind and world*. This dualism underlies the ubiquitous, but often unexamined, concept of *mental representation*, in which representation — and its subject — occupy a theoretical space that is over-and-outside that which represented.[2] Radical mind-world dualism can and does persist even when mind-brain dualism is rejected; nowadays, the Cartesian *res cogitans* is substituted by a fictive blend of logical space and neuroanatomy commonly called 'the mind/brain', in which two mysteries — how can matter represent and in what does representation consist? — are typographically conjoined in the optimistic — but I think futile — belief that we can thereby bootstrap our way to an explanation of both.

The archetype of mind-world dualism is the representational mind as a 'mirror of nature' (Rorty, 1979), but varieties of it are discernible everywhere in the landscape of cognitive science. They occupy a spectrum extending from the apotheosis of rules-and-symbols cognitivism (Fodor, 1975; 2008); to embodied-enactivist approaches that reject the notion of mental representation, yet struggle to escape

---

[1] At least in cognitive science, although as Göran Sonesson (pc) has pointed out, it is exactly this that was at stake in Brentano's and Husserl's understanding of intentionality.

[2] This is the philosophical picture that was the starting point for Wittgenstein's *Tractatus Logico-Philosophicus* (1961 [1922]).

its fatal embrace (Lakoff and Johnson, 1999). According to the standard cognitivist view, Representation is primarily, indeed foundationally, a relationship between mind and reality. Externally embodied representations such as pictures, signs and symbols (including the symbols of natural language) derive or inherit their representational properties from *mental* representations, which may vary in form from analog images, to schemas, to linguaform symbols. Language, and other public representations, represent the world at one remove: by representing mental representations.

This view has a long history. Aristotle wrote[3] that 'spoken words are the signs of affections of the soul, and written words are the signs of spoken words'. The Aristotelian theory of representation and meaning is expressed in slightly different terms by John Locke[4]: 'That then which Words are the Marks of, are the *Ideas* of the Speaker: Nor can anyone apply them, as Marks, immediately to anything else, but the *Ideas*, that he himself hath.' Ferdinand de Saussure, widely viewed as the founder of modern linguistics, repeats, in almost as many words, Locke's formulation: 'The linguistic sign unites, not a thing and a name, but a concept and a sound-image' (Saussure, 1966, p. 66).

There are several problems that this view brings in its train, not the least of which is the problem sometimes referred to as Hume's problem, or the problem of Other Minds. If words stand for, or express, 'ideas', how can I (as speaker) be, in fact, sure that you (as hearer), actually share the same "ideas" of things as I do? How, in other words, can I know that the mental content that I ascribe to you is the mental content that you actually have, even excluding cases of mistaken or false ascriptions? This problem is of particular consequence for folk psychological reasoning, and in general for the ascription to other subjects of propositional attitudes. If, for example, I (correctly) think that my neighbour believes that fairies live at the bottom of his garden, how do I know that whatever it is that my neighbour believes is what I think they believe? To know *that*, I have to be sure that what my neighbour's mental content is about is *the same* as what my neighbour's mental content *under my representation* is about.

The Other Minds problem is closely related to, perhaps at some level of abstraction identical to, or the other side of the coin of, the *Grounding Problem*: how do linguistic terms, and the concepts expressed in language, get to fit with the world? A common (and essentially Aristotelian) solution to the Other Minds and Grounding

---

[3] W.D. Ross (ed.) *Works of Aristotle,* Vol. 1, tr. E.M. Edghill, Oxford: Clarendon, 1928, 16a.

[4] *An Essay concerning Human Understanding* (1690), Book III, Ch. 2, section 2.

problems, largely shared by both empiricist and rationalist philoso-phies, is *category realism*: our ideas (categories of the mind) are either reflections of objective reality, or innate. On the nativist account, we all inherit the same categories of mind. The nativist account, in its strongest form, posits a universal Language of Thought (Fodor, 1975) of which natural language categories and corresponding expressions are local translations. On the empiricist account, we all live in the same (objective) world, and have the same experiences of that world, and this means that our concepts of the things that cause these experi-ences (affections of the soul) are also the same.

Language, for both sides of the empiricist-rationalist debate, is a reflection, or print-out, of these universal categories. A third solution is at least hinted at by Saussure, namely that our concepts are supplied by language itself, as a socially shared sign system. However, not only is it far from clear what Saussure intended in this matter, it also cannot be said that such a 'linguistic turn' provides a ready solution, since it brings in its train a commitment to the linguistic relativity of all con-cepts. In relocating the Grounding Problem from 'concepts-and-lan-guage' to 'language-as-concepts' (Sinha, 1999), linguistic relativism of this deterministic kind also relocates the Other Minds problem from being one applying at the level of individuals to being one applying at the level of linguistic communities. For the strong linguistic relativist, the puzzle is how any two linguistic communities can have sufficient similarity in their concepts as to be able to communicate at all.

The nativist account attributes no role to linguistic communities other than the minimalist one of triggering the locally applicable set of concepts from amongst the innate universal inventory—much as, in nativist approaches to the acquisition of grammar, linguistic input is held to trigger parameter setting (Chomsky, 1981). The empiricist account, dependent as it is, in a simplistic version, on the vagaries of individual experience, is usually supplemented by an acknowledge-ment of the importance of tuition by the community on the correct meanings of terms and the right categories of things. Although Hutto's Narrative Practice hypothesis is not a simplistic empiricism, I think it can rightly be said to propose just such an account of how the linguistic experience of the developing child, in a community of dis-cursive practices, can provide the necessary and sufficient conditions for 'solving' the Other Minds and Grounding problems.[5]

---

[5] Of course the Grounding and Other Minds problems are not empirical problems encoun-tered by the child; rather they are theoretical problems encountered by explanatory

Hutto's Narrative Practice Hypothesis thus meshes with a cluster of developmental accounts, that has emerged over the last three decades, that challenge the cognitivist consensus from a position that elevates the importance of community to a position superior to a mere supplement to empiricism, seeing social agreement as the fundamental means by which shared categories of mind are established. These accounts are based upon the grounding of shared linguistic and conceptual categories in *intersubjective engagements* with both world and 'other minds'; involving the establishment and growth of joint attention, joint reference and joint action between infants and caretakers (Bruner, 1975; Lock, 1978; Tomasello, 1999; Tomasello *et al.*, 2005; Trevarthen, 1979; 1998). These approaches to the development of the 'shared, social mind', encapsulated in the increasing frequency of use in a variety of disciplines of the term *intersubjectivity* (Zlatev *et al.*, 2008), are sufficiently well known that it is unnecessary to revisit them in detail here.

That the structure of early infant intersubjectivity, and particularly triadic subject-object-subject engagements in joint action and joint attention, is a key precursor to 'Theory of Mind' is now widely accepted, even if its developmentally causal status is disputed. However, even granted a strong interpretation of early intersubjectivity as a developmental prerequisite for, not merely precursor of, folk psychologiocal capacities, the appeal to intersubjective engagement *per se* does not of itself solve another crucial aspect of the 'Other Minds' problem: namely, that in order to ascribe some kind of mental content, or intention, to a co-acting or co-communicating other, it would seem necessary to be able to entertain the notion that this other is a minded being — a subject capable of entertaining propositional attitudes, and having reasons for the way they behave.

Empiricism, in its traditional form, seems to have little to offer to our understanding of how this kind of understanding might emerge, since abstraction and association can only result in, at best, the categorization of behaviours. The mental states (intentional or propositional: Hutto, 2008) of which the behaviours are manifestations, and which render the behaviours intersubjectively intelligible, remain 'beyond the information given' (Bruner, 1974). How do we get from manifest behaviour to intentions and, ultimately, the ascription of reasons? It would seem that a version of Chomsky's Argument from the Poverty of the Stimulus must compel us to accept that human understanding of

---

accounts. The assumption that the Other Minds problem is an *empirical* one is, I would suggest, one of the fundamental errors of Theory of Mind Theories.

the intentionality of others is innate, either in the form of a Theory of Mind module, or as a capacity for simulation, perhaps based in an evolutionary elaboration of the primate mirror neuron system.

It would be foolish to deny the uniqueness (in complementarity with the phylogenetic continuity) of the human neurocognitive system; or to rule out the likelihood that this uniqueness underpins the equally unique human understanding of, and reasoning about, other minds. It is, however, over-optimistic to assume that biology, unaided, can do all the heavy lifting in explaining the ontogenesis and phylogenesis of human folk psychological capacities and practices. Hutto (2008) makes the case against the adequacy of the encapsulated neurocognitive mechanisms proposed by Theory and Simulation theories with verve; and there is one particular aspect of this case that I wish to take up and expand, namely the centrality of *normativity* in the development of folk psychological capacities.

Currently, most accounts of folk psychological competence regard this as consisting of an encapsulated mechanism operating on representations with the form of propositional attitudes. However, any putative encapsulated mechanism for attributing reasons for other people's actions suffers from an exactly analogous problem to that which would afflict an unconstrained natural language grammar acquisition device; that is that the space of viable hypotheses is, in principle, infinite, and in the absence of 'negative evidence' serving to eliminate inappropriate hypotheses, some system of innate constraints must be built into the mechanism.

In the case of the innate Language Acquisition Device postulated by generativist linguistic theories, these constraints are built into Universal Grammar as universally valid principles whose parametric variation is set by input (Chomsky, 1981). Whether or not this theory is correct (and I would be the last to endorse it), it has the advantage of being (at least in principle) testable against data: the theory will be at least plausible if it can be shown empirically that the Principles and Parameters are sufficient to account for both universals and variation in the grammars of the languages of the world.[6] The same cannot be said for any analogous set of constraints hypothesized to operate in the domain of folk psychology, for the simple reason that the attribution of reasons for actions is extremely variable and contextually dependent. Homing in on a reason for someone's actions is many orders of magnitude more complex, as a problem in pure logical space, than homing in on a grammar.

[6]   In practice, because the Principles and Parameters are always subject to revision the theory is effectively insulated against empirical test.

Consider the example I used earlier, in which a subject attributes a friend running past them on a station platform to the friend's desire to catch the next train coupled with the friend's belief that the next train is about to depart. How could it be possible, given the richly textured and culturally specific background knowledge necessary to entertain this attribution, to view the attribution as simply an exemplification or instantiation of a universal 'grammar of reasons', similarly to the way in which an utterance exemplifies a natural language grammar? To make this problem manageable, it would be necessary to establish a universal inventory of types of desires (including, for example, the desire to move to a goal location) and types of beliefs (such as that enabling conditions for satisfying desires are temporally limited). It would be necessary to specify a mechanism by means of which the specific occasion for mobilizing the relevant belief/desire pair serves to trigger the correct 'grammatical' reading, into which the constituent items making up the occasion slot, supplying the necessary information enabling the appropriate folk psychological attribution.

I suggest that such a hyper-theoretical account is both unprovable and superfluous. A more plausible and parsimonious account will appeal to the *normativity* of intersubjectively shared understanding of beliefs and desires, rooted in participation in shared practices regulated by the norms in question. This is the essence of Hutto's Narrative Practice Hypothesis, which he fleshes out by proposing that folk tales are the prototypic shared practice by means of which both the process of attributing reasons, and the norms regulating such attributions, are exemplified for the developing child. In the light of my critical discussion above of the problems afflicting any nativist, encapsulated mechanism account of folk psychological capacities, a further discussion of the nature of norms and normativity is called for.

Norms, though they belong to the realm of the mental, are quintessentially *shared*. There can no more be a private norm than there can be a private language — indeed, Wittgenstein's argument against the possibility of a private language is built around the understanding that language is a normative system (Itkonen, 1978; 2008; Winch, 1958; Wittgenstein, 1953). Norms are intersubjective or *intermental* entities (Vygotsky, 1978). Being shared is not a merely accidental property of the norms that are oriented to by individuals in the process by which behaviour and cognition are regulated. Although norms cannot exist without being known and oriented to by individual participants, the norm (as well as the community that shares the norm) is logically, and indeed ontogenetically, prior to this individual knowledge. Again, although a norm may be proposed by an individual, it is only through its adoption by the community (which may be as minimal as a dyad) that the proposal is lodged *as a norm*; and the same is true for the negotiation of norms (negotiability and conventionality also being fundamental properties of norms). In virtue of this property of the *priority* of the intersubjectivity of normative knowledge over individual internalization of the knowledge, norms are the basic form of the *social fact* and social institution (Durkheim, 1895; Searle, 1995).

Intersubjectivity, then, is an essential property of norms. Reasons, by contrast, although they may appeal to norms, should properly be understood as *primarily* individual mental entities. Although my reason for doing something may be simply because that's what I understood should be done, nonetheless it is the *understanding and following of,* and *orientation to* the norm that is the reason for the behaviour, not the norm itself. Norms regulate behaviour, they do not cause it. Reasons may also be shared, when dyads or groups act collectively on the basis of the same reason, but this kind of sharing is *secondary to* and *derived from* the reasons entertained by the individual participants in the collective action.[7]

As I pointed out above, reasons cannot be observed. Reasons can be inferred on the basis of behaviour, but such inferences presuppose a folk psychological competence that (I argued) is unlearnable if viewed as an encapsulated mechanism. Norms, as intermental entities, are also unobservable; they can, however, be learned, on the basis of *participation* and *observation*. There is no mystery about this. Imagine a small child joining, as a complete novice, in a game (say, football) whose rules are known by the other players. The child's observations will enable him or her to imitate the actions of the other players; and as a result of this participation the child will be provided with feedback about whether they are following the rules, and sometimes receive explicit instruction in the rules. Having acquired the rule, the child can both orient to the rule in following it, and use knowledge of the rule to decide whether others are following it. As Itkonen (2008, p. 291) puts it: 'Norms are learned on the basis of observation, but once they are known, they can no longer be just a matter of observation because they are made use of to judge whether an observed (or imagined) action is correct or not.' In other words, I cannot

---

[7] An interesting issue, that I do not have space to pursue in detail, is that of shared systems of beliefs or ideologies. Ideologies are social, normative facts inasmuch as they serve as the objects (or mediators) of beliefs. Ideologies, then, are not themselves reasons for actions, but ground the reasons for actions, and when we say someone acted out of ideological reasons, we mean that the person's actions are comprehensible on the basis of reasons motivated and grounded by ideological beliefs. Ideologies supply reasons.

observe whether another person knows a norm, I can only observe and
decide (on the basis of my own knowledge of the norm in question)
whether or not the person is acting in accordance with the norm.

As pointed out above, most accounts of folk psychological competence regard this as consisting of an encapsulated mechanism operating on representations with the form of propositional attitudes. Many
of the problems that beset the problem of learning to be a folk psychological practitioner dissolve when we abandon this model, and instead
view the child as a novice participant in practices that are normatively
regulated, such that ascriptions of reasons for the behaviours of others
are in many (prototypic) cases simultaneously judgements of the normative validity and intelligibility of the actions in question — as, for
example, 'she is running that way because she wants to score a goal'.
It is this conflation of (individual) reason with (social) normativity
that both constrains (without any appeal to implausible representational or computational mechanisms) the space of possible reasons;
and affords the child a first, practical grasp of what it means to be a
user of folk psychology.

Clearly, this argument is compatible with, if not identical to, the
arguments that Hutto (2008) uses to advocate the Narrative Practice
Hypothesis, in that Folk Psychological Narratives are the linguistic
vehicles and speech genres *par excellence* in which socio-cultural
norms and individual reasons are co-articulated in a canonical (normative) format. Engagement with this format, and with the perspectives and predicaments of its protagonists, is a privileged mode of
apprenticeship in folk psychology. As I shall now argue, such apprenticeship builds on a long developmental history of engagement with a
world imbued with normativity, not just in its interactional and symbolic forms, but also in the material objects that are such a salient part
of the cultural ecology of child development.

3. Object, Sign and the Materiality of (Normative) Representation

I cited Saussure (1966, p. 66) above to the effect that 'The linguistic
sign unites, not a thing and a name, but a concept and a sound-image.'
Saussure's move here, calculated to establish a theoretical object for
linguistic science independent of age-old philosophical debates
between nominalism and realism, relegated the world of 'things' to a
place *outside* meaning and meaning-making. 'Things' not only do not
signify, but they are not even, in any direct way, signified. Semiotic
value exists only in the realm of signs, semantic 'substance' is

immaterial and conceptual, and the material world is only a necessary condition for the organization of that immaterial substance as Signified. For Saussurean structuralism, the material world, in short, does not *have* meaning, it is merely an a-semiotic (or pre-semiotic) *condition for* meaning.

Meaning has had equally short shrift in developmental psychology's treatment of the role of objects in cognitive development. Objects play a crucial role in Piaget's account of sensori-motor development (Piaget, 1953), with the achievement of the concept of the permanence of the object occupying centre stage in the transition to representational and symbolic thought. But the object that the infant and young child encounters in Piaget's world is a curiously abstract thing, lacking semiotic and functional value, any object being substitutable for any other object. Whether it is a cup or a dolly that the infant bangs on a table, a ball or a brick that it searches for under a cover, is quite literally *immaterial* to the theory. In a curious complementarity with Piaget's abstract epistemic Subject, the object in Piagetian theory becomes an Object with a capital O, a ground for, but not a vehicle of, meaning and value.

Objects, however, and in particular artefactual objects, are not just abstract Newtonian particles, nor even just topological or mereological structures, existing in a merely physical or logico-mathematical space. Artefactual objects in particular, in order to be categorizable as such, are required to have certain *functional* properties: cups are for containing, tables are for supporting. As Searle (1995, p. 28) points out: 'in order that something be a chair, it has to function as a chair; and hence, it has to be thought of or used as a chair.'

Let us now examine more carefully the social semiotics of material artefacts. In fact, *anything* can be *used* as a chair, provided it naturally or contingently has the affordances, in the sense of Gibson (1979), which permit it to be sat in or on. Such affordances would, for Searle, be part of what he calls the 'brute' or 'natural' facts, as opposed to institutional or social facts; although in a Gibsonian relational epistemology the affordances have no existence independently of the behavioural repertoire of the organism.

Is there any sense in which something can be said to properly 'count as' a chair, in the sense in which Searle (1995) defines 'counting as' as proper to institutional facts? The answer is yes: an object *counts as* a chair if it is an artefact *intended and designed* to be used as a chair, having the *canonical function* of a chair. Such designed functions are *canonical* for the category of objects, and to know into which category an artefactual object falls necessitates knowing what its canonical function is (Sinha, 1988).

Canonical function is a normative phenomenon. The physical properties of an artefact are not merely physical: they are socially constructed and normatively regulated cultural affordances (Sonesson, in press), which make possible the canonical function of the artefact. The canonical functions of artefacts are therefore social facts, and the material world of artefactual objects is one of materiality not only in its physical aspect, but also in its social semiotic aspect of normative meaning.[8] In analogous fashion to the way that a twenty dollar bill signifies its normative identity as a token of monetary exchange value, the artefactual object (such as a cup, a chair, or a computer) signifies its normative canonical function as a token of a category with a particular use value. Not only, then, can objects be *signs* for something else (as when, for example, a pair of scales is a conventional sign representing justice); more frequently, when they are artefacts, as most objects we encounter in our everyday lives are, objects are also *signifiers* of their proper, socially standard, canonical functions in a context of social practices (Sinha, 1988; Sinha and Rodríguez, 2008).

Of course, a condition for this social semiotic status of material artefacts, as with any semiotic status, is that human subjects are capable of cognitively grasping that status. As Searle says, for a chair to function as a chair, it has to be not only used, but also thought of — or at least recognized — as a chair. When do human infants begin to display such a cognitive grasp, and where does it come from? In a series of experiments Walkerdine and Sinha (1978), Freeman *et al.* (1980), Lloyd *et al.* (1981), Freeman *et al.* (1981), and Sinha (1982; 1983) investigated infants' and young children's understanding of object function, using infant search, action imitation and acting-out language comprehension paradigms.

In an age range from 9 months to 3 years and 6 months, we found error patterns which were characterized by 'canonicality effects'. Infants at the end of the first year of life were more successful in A-not-B search tasks (otherwise known as object permanence tasks) when the object was hidden in an upright rather than in an inverted cup. It seems that these infants understood that a cup is a 'better' container when in an upright orientation than when inverted. Slightly older infants were generally unable to imitate the placement of a small block on the bottom of an inverted cup, preferring to turn the cup back

---

[8] Expressed in an older philosophical lexicon, canonicality of object function is a normative phenomenon existing at the interface between 'Erste Natur' and 'Zweite Natur'.

into an upright orientation and place the block inside the cup. In this response strategy, the infants showed that they were 'locked' into a normative apprehension of the cup as a canonical container, which over-rode the 'brute' affordance of the flat surface of the bottom of the inverted cup. Even after this response strategy disappeared in action imitation tasks, it re-appeared in language comprehension tasks: for example two year olds, when asked to place a block 'on' an inverted cup, turned it to the upright position and placed the block inside it.

These experiments can be interpreted as showing that, in the first place, objects are cognitively apprehended by infants, from an early age, in terms of their socially-imposed, normative and canonical function (the object 'counts as' a container). In the second place, the emerging conceptualization of spatial relations *between* objects is also derived as much from the canonical functional relations which objects contract with each other as from purely perceptual-geometric information (for a discussion of the functional basis of spatial relational meaning, see Vandeloise, 1991).

Where does this understanding, on the part of the infant, of the canonical function of objects come from? This question is important, because of the intimate relationship between the physical properties of the artefact, and its socially 'baptized' canonical function. In contrast with, for example, the monetary token (in which the relationship between the material from which the token is made, and its exchange value, has historically become increasingly attenuated, arbitrary and even virtual, as money assumes the mantle of pure informational form), the physical structure of 'traditional' artefacts such as cups is not only non-arbitrary, but essential to its fulfilment of its canonical function.

Infants' motivation to explore the physical world is well known, and it might be hypothesized that their apprehension of object properties in terms of function derives from an untutored, spontaneous sensori-motor engagement with the object as a purely physical entity (for example, the exploration of the cavity of a container giving rise to the dominance of this cavity in the early pre-conceptual representation of the object). There are several sources of evidence that this is not so. First, while there is evidence of understanding of containment as a physical relationship at 6 months (Hespos and Baillargeon, 2001), Freeman *et al.* (1980) were unable to detect canonicality effects in search tasks below the age of 9 months. Since Hespos and Baillargeon used a preferential looking task, however, this difference may be a consequence of a motor-involving against a violation-of-expectancies experimental methodology. Second, and more convincingly, when the perceptual-cognitive link between canonical *orientation* and canonical containment *function* of cups was broken, by painting schematic faces either upright or upside down on the cups, the canonicality effect in infant search was abolished (Lloyd *et al.*, 1981). This finding reinforces the conclusion that the canonicality effect is dependent upon socially cued expectations about the normative use of the object.

Even more decisive experimental evidence for the role of joint action in establishing canonical object concepts comes from the experimental design used in Freeman *et al.* (1981), where the object was functionally 'ambiguous', consisting of a set of stacking / nesting cubes. The child was invited by the experimenter to play with the entire set of cubes, and the experimenter set up this pre-test game as *either* a nesting *or* a stacking activity. After successfully completing, as joint action, an activity of constructing either a nest of cubes, or a tower of stacked cubes, the experimenter extracted a medium-size cube and a small cube, and conducted either an action imitation task involving the placement of the smaller cube on top of/ inside/under the larger cube, or an acting-out language comprehension task with instructions to place the smaller cube 'in', 'on' or 'under' the larger cube. The results were dramatic. After playing a nesting game, the children's error patterns showed a response bias similar to the 'canonicality effect' manifested in the same task using cups. In other words, there was a response preference for placing the small cube inside the larger cube. However, this effect was abolished in the stacking condition, in which there was a tendency to preferentially place the smaller cube *on top of* the larger cube (see also Sinha, 1988).

To conclude this review of experimental evidence, I emphasize that canonical function and orientation, though they are in some sense 'intrinsic' to the object as a material entity with determinate structure and affordances for human action, are not *essential* object properties in the same way as object substance. The stacking / nesting cubes experiment showed that the framing of the object in terms of its normatively appropriate function and orientation can be 'locally' taught and negotiated. There can also, however, be inter-cultural variation in the canonical orientation and function assigned to classes of objects which may be materially identical between the cultures. For example, in the indigenous agrarian Zapotec culture of Southern Mexico, woven baskets are commonly stacked in what we would regard as 'inverted' orientation: that is, with their opening downwards. They are also frequently used in that same orientation as covers for foodstuffs and in children's games of catching chickens. For Zapotec culture, then, the canonical orientation of a basket is less unequivocally cavity-upwards than is the case in 'Western' cultures.

As well as these differences between Zapotec and Euro-American cultural practices, the Zapotec language lexicalizes the different spatial relations that are lexically distinguished by English 'in' and 'under' using a single body-part term, translatable as the English word 'stomach'. Young Zapotec children differed from their Danish counterparts not only in their response patterns in language comprehension tasks using baskets, but also in non-linguistic action imitation tasks. The Zapotec children clearly did not regard the relationship of what *we* consider to be canonical containment, and the orientation that *we* would regard as 'upright', as being canonical (Sinha and Jensen de Lopez, 2000; Jensen de Lopez, 2003; Jensen de Lopez *et al.*, 2005). Hence, variation in normative cultural practice and in linguistic marking of spatial relations can, it seems, have the same effect as variation in its 'locally' negotiated framing (as in the nesting/stacking cubes experiment) by joint action.[9]

The experimental evidence resulting from my and my colleagues' work supports the view, then, that it is the culturally guided, intersubjective structuration of the child's participation in joint action, as much as (and indeed more so) than the 'brute' affordances of the object 'in itself', that enables the child, in a process of 'guided reinvention' (Lock 1980), to appropriate the norms governing object use, and to achieve a cognitive representation of the object in terms of canonical function. This process has a long developmental history, and the episodes of joint action are accompanied and mediated at every stage by the use of communicative signs by the adult participant, as is attested by observations reported in an extensive research programme by Cintia Rodríguez and Christiane Moro (Moro and Rodríguez, 2005; Rodríguez and Moro, 1999; 2002; 2008). Throughout this developmental process, 'objects are invested with significance. They become, for the child, material representations and signifiers of the rules, norms, values, rituals, needs and goals of the entire ... matrix within which they are embedded. In short, they become part of a meaningful system of signs' (Sinha, 1988, p. 204).

The conclusion of this research is clear, and challenges many assumptions of both developmental psychology and the philosophy of

---

[9] This crosscultural difference in children's response patterns may be directly due to crosslinguistic differences, although the early age at which it manifests itself tells against such a Whorfian interpretation. It may alternatively be due to non-linguistic cultural practices. More likely it is due to a combination of non-linguistic practices entrenched in crosslinguistic differences.

cognition. The physical world, in its artefactual presence, is a social-material world. Normative meaning and normative cognition do not pertain to a special domain of 'mentalizing', separate from cognition of the material world; rather, normativity inheres in the materiality of the made, human world. Normativity, as cultural affordance within the ensemble of cultural practices, is made available to the infant as a developing participant in activities grounded in shared meanings and shared objects, long before he or she becomes a practitioner of discursively based folk psychology. Objects, as bearers of canonical function, are at hand to the developing infant as 'ready-mades' concretizing conventional and norm-governed intentional action, and canalizing the child's interpretation of the behaviours of other people in terms of the norms of which they are the bearers. It is through participation in joint actions normatively structured around the use of artefactual objects, not by way of an encapsulated mind-reading device, that the child finds an entry into the intersubjective realm of reasons for actions.

4. Play, Props and Staging:
Objects as Signs in Narrative Play

In this section I highlight the role, also often neglected, of artefactual objects and their complex significations in the child's development from first apprenticeship in reason attribution to mastery of the construction of narrative scenarios and fictive narrative identities. The elaboration of narrative skill and narrative structure from early to middle childhood — that is, at the developmental phase when children first become able to pass false belief tasks — implicates not only story-telling but also socio-dramatic play, one of the forms of play that Piaget (1962) called 'symbolic play' (Sinha, 2005; Nicolopolou, 2007).

Characteristic of all symbolic play is pretence: the child pretends that an object is other than what it really is, or that he or she is a different person than he or she really is. Symbolic or pretend play involves the projection of imaginary cognitive and symbolic values onto entities and relationships in the child's immediate environment. The entities may be objects, as for example when a child pretends that a stick is a gun, or animates a doll through making it speak, act or interact. They may be social roles, such as when children play school or play mothers and fathers, adopting roles and perspectives of imagined others. And they may be entire settings, such as when children construct a play house or play in a play corner, allocating roles, functions and identities to both human participants and the things to hand which serve as the props to the staging of the symbolic play.

Symbolic play, like narrative, is thus an instance of 'virtual cognition', in which the imaginary and the real fuse or blend in an experiential arena in which the 'mental' and the 'physical' are, as it were, dissociated from their customary, conventional or canonical correlations, and re-assembled in a new, blended mental space (Fauconnier and Turner, 2002). Play is also *mimetic*. Mimesis is hypothesized to be fundamentally implicated in the evolution of human capacities for intersubjective engagement (Donald, 1991; Zlatev, 2008). Feldman (2005, p. 503) has proposed that narrative and play have in common that 'they share an important pattern or structure in the way they work as mental instruments, *mimesis*'.

The characteristics of the play space are thus primarily governed by the mimetic and enactive understanding of the player(s) of the mimetic and narrative 'play domain'. This knowledge overlays their understanding of the canonical functions of artefacts making up the physical setting. In this respect, symbolic play represents a crucial step in the actualization of the symbolic power of language as a vehicle for the construction of imaginary and counterfactual mental spaces. However, this step is not achieved through a 'retreat from' or 'replacement of' the actual material world of the setting. Rather, the actual setting is backgrounded, and then re-integrated into the symbolic play space. This process, in shared symbolic play, often involves social negotiation of the symbolic values to be accorded to the elements of the setting (including, but not only, the human participants). In the microgenetic process of symbolic play, a central role is played by the material world, as a world saturated by socially shared meaning and value.

The transcribed play episode below is reproduced with permission from Smolka *et al.* (1997). It is translated (by these authors) from Portuguese into English, and is a segment from a transcribed observation of spontaneously occurring socio-dramatic play in a Brazilian primary school classroom. To understand the play episode, the reader should know that there is a popular Brazilian theme park called Beto Carrero World. Beto Carrero is the proprietor, but also the eponymous cowboy hero protagonist, of Beto Carrero World. Beto Carrero 'himself' sometimes appears in Beto Carrero World, mounted on his white horse and wearing his white cowboy hat and gear. The white hat is both an attribute of the character, and (conventionally enough) a signifier of his being a cowboy and a 'good guy'.

The play is staged in the house corner of a primary school classroom, where there are props including a cowboy hat. The participants in the socio-dramatic play episode are three 5–6 year old girls: Alcione, Thaís, Camila. At the beginning of the transcribed segment, Alcione is in the role of Thaís's daughter, Tháis is in the role of Alcione's mother, and Camila has no role yet assigned. Suddenly, the cowboy hat falls off a shelf and Alcione picks it up and puts it on. This is the beginning of the transcribed episode.

Transcript (translated from Portuguese by Smolka et al. 1997)

1. Alc: (to Tha.) You were, you were ... Do you want to play with this hat?

    (puts hat on Thaís' head, who takes it off again and puts it aside)

2. Alc: Then give it to me, give it to me, Thaís!

(picks up the hat)

3. Tha: (to Alc.) Honey, mom doesn't like hats

    (Alc. puts the hat on again and looks at Tha.)

4. Tha: You look pretty!

    (Alc. laughs. Camila takes the hat from Alc. Tha. is writing)

5. Tha: (to herself and/or the group) Veronica

(writing down the name she has given herself)

6. Tha: (to Alc.) What's your name?

7. Alc: My name is ... mine is Bete, Bete Carrera

8. Cam: (to Tha.) Mine is Bete Carrera too.

9. Tha: (to Cam.) Ahn... it can't be. Then I'm called ... Bete.

10. Alc: (to others) I'm called ... I'm called ...

11. Tha: (to others) I'm called Bete Carrera!

Analytic Gloss of the transcript

In turns 1–4, Alcione and Thaís are engaged in a dialogue whose setting is 'house', and whose universe of discourse is the fictive mother-daughter relationship between them. They are enacting familiar roles, exchanging comments about the hat and their appearance when wearing it. The hat, in this universe of discourse, is a feminine attribute, evaluated according to whether it is comely for the wearer. The hat is exchanged between them. At the end of turn 4, the hat is taken by Camila, who has not yet engaged, and has no role assigned in, this universe of discourse. At this point, Thaís decides it is time to assign names to the characters, starting with herself, in turn 5, in which she claims (in the role of 'mother') the name 'Veronica'. In turn 6, she asks Alcione to assign a name to her role as 'daughter'.

Turn 7 constitutes a break, involving the introduction of a new dimension in the universe of discourse. Alcione claims the name 'Bete Carrera', suggested by the hat. Notice, now, that 'Bete Carrera' is a grammatically regular *feminization* (in Portuguese) of the name 'Beto Carrero'. Alcione displays here her knowledge of grammatical gender in her native language, as well as employing this knowledge to signify her gendered identity. The *form* 'Bete Carrera' can properly be viewed as a lexico-grammatical constructional blend, but this form is motivated by a blend at the conceptual level (Fauconnier and Turner, 2002). Alcione does not say (as we might suppose a boy might say) that she is the cowboy Beto Carrero. Rather, she adopts a name signifying a feminine equivalent of that identity in the fictive world of enactment. Whether this involves a transformation of this fictive world to incorporate other aspects of the Beto Carrero World is unclear from the transcript, since possession of the name "Bete Carrera" is immediately contested, first by Camila, who is now in possession of the hat. Camila says in turn 8 that she too is Bete Carrera. Thaís, who has been in charge of name assignment, first tries in turn 9 to prohibit this appropriation by Camila, then changes her mind and appropriates the name Bete Carrera herself. The transcript ends with the girls all claiming competitively to be called (that is, to *be*, in the play world of enactment), Bete Carrera.

As Smolka, Góes and Pino point out in their article analysing this episode of symbolic play, the cowboy hat, *qua* artefact, remains a hat, and it is never used by the children as anything other than a hat. At the same time, the cowboy hat 'became' — or, rather, came to signify — *more than* the canonical rules of object-usage that it embodies *qua* artefact.

> Through language, the children created Bete Carrera (Turn 7), the feminine of Beto Carrero ... Language allows for this specific appropriation, for such a construction and transformation; it allows for a 'performance' that synthesizes old and new modes and models of acting. Through language, it is possible to become another, to become *homo duplex* ... or, in fact, *multiplex*. In this consists the dramatic character of human experience (Smolka *et al.*, 1997, p. 161).

The hat, in this interaction, is simultaneously situated at two levels of meaning and construal. At the first level, its canonical function is appropriated enactively by the participants (by putting it on and taking it off). Although its canonical function remains unchanged , the e significations carried by the hat as a constituent of discourse change over time: it is 'differently imagined' at different stages of the play. First, it is imagined by Thaís (Turns 1–4) as being an ornamentation, or fashion accessory. At this first level, the construal of the hat is intersubjectively shared, non-contested and constant: the hat remains 'just' a hat. Next, it is 're-imagined' by Alcione (Turn 7) as a *particular cowboy hat*, indexing a specific and imagined *identity* (that of the imaginary Bete Carrera).

As Smolka *et al.* point out, both the new meaning of the hat, and the gendered identity which it signifies, are brought into being *by means of language and discourse*. These meanings are constructed in socially shared cognition: specifically, by the blending of the conceptual space of 'Beto Carrero World' into the discourse frame of 'playing house', from which emerges the new 'cowboy girl' identity signified by 'Bete Carrera'. At this second level, the hat is invested with a 'surplus meaning' which goes beyond its construal as an artefact: it comes also to signify the subjective positionings and perspectives of the individual participants within a more comprehensive, discursively constituted frame, which has the form of a *narrative-in-becoming*.

Oliveira (1998, p. 110), reporting another study of children's interactions and the development of gender concepts and gendered identity, adopts a Vygotskian perspective (Vygotsky, 1978; 1986; Wertsch, 1985) in arguing that the development of social interactions is best understood as 'a dynamic process of expanding or constructing shared semiotically organized fields of conduct'. This characterization applies also to the 'Bete Carrera' episode discussed above. In the course of the developmental process, roles, identities and conventions are contested and re-negotiated, against the background of *relatively* stable, socially shared, narratively organized norms. What I have tried to emphasize is that the semiotic bearers of these norms are not *only* linguistic: they are to be found also in the material setting.

5. Conclusions

The brief analysis I offer of the episode of socio-dramatic play in the foregoing section is highly condensed, and does not elaborate on the cognitive processes that permit children to appropriate, elaborate and transform the semiotic potential that is to hand in the setting (see Sinha, 2005, for a fuller account). However, I hope that it serves to highlight the differences between the approach that I am advocating, and standard cognitivist accounts of the development of 'mind-reading'. In such cognitivist accounts, narratives and other semiotic vehicles are viewed as the inputs and outputs of a Theory of Mind module whose operations are indifferent to the particular meanings that they convey.

I have stressed, on the contrary, that narratives and play exemplify the normative network of meanings by which we make sense of other people's actions, agency and identities. They are given life, created and re-created by children's *participation* in meaning-making as imaginative activity. To be sure, this participation requires a high degree of cognitive sophistication: in the mimetic enactment of narrative episodes; in entertaining and coordinating different perspectives; in projecting and blending mental spaces; and in using the semiotic resources supplied by language and by material artefacts. We are far from a full understanding of the cognitive developmental processes involved. Still, I would submit that the ultimate explanation for the development of folk psychological reasoning will call upon such non-domain specific, semiotically grounded processes, rather than upon modular mechanisms dedicated to understanding 'Other Minds'.

The theoretical splitting of human cognitive processes into separate mechanisms for understanding the physical world and the social, intersubjective world is a specific manifestation of the more general prevalent dualism of mental *vs* material that I discussed in Section 2. It stems from the same source as the failure to recognize the social and semiotic status of artefactual objects, the *meaningfulness of materiality.*

Artefacts, like language and other semiotic vehicles, function to extend the horizons of the landscape of consciousness. Artefacts are 'ready-mades' for the elaboration of the child's developing understanding of the workings of both world and mind; they are *amplifiers*, not merely *objects* of consciousness. Artetefacts are interwoven with the symbolic forms of language, co-constituting the specifically human biocultural niche (Sinha, 2009), and inter-articulating actual and virtual in what the semiotician Yuri Lotman (1990) called the 'semiosphere'. It is within this niche, and as a function of their appropriation of its semiotic and socio-cultural affordances, that developing human beings become competent folk psychologists.

The emphasis I have placed on the material and semiotic context of the developmental process should not be understood as downplaying children's own agency in this process. Piaget rightly emphasized the centrality of action, including imitative action, in cognitive development, but his genetic epistemology defined and theorized the cognitive operations of a transpersonal epistemic subject. Agency, however, is an attribute neither of subpersonal cognitive modules nor of transpersonal cognitive operations. The development of folk psychological abilities, in short, is not a 'process without a subject', but a process in which subjectivity is co-emergent with cognitive and linguistic competences. Becoming a 'folk psychologist' involves, to be sure, learning *what it is* to be a person; but this is itself part of the process of *becoming* a person, in a meaning-bearing world.

Acknowledgements

I am very grateful for the critical and constructive comments of Jill de Villiers and Göran Sonesson, which have helped me greatly in clarifying the main points I wish to convey in this article. The remaining gaps and puzzles are partly due to the still evolving nature of our field; partly to restrictions of space; and partly to my own very real uncertainties about how it all fits together.

References

Bruner, J.S. (1974), *Beyond the Information Given. Studies in the psychology of knowing* (London: Allen & Unwin).

Bruner, J.S. (1975), 'From communication to language: a psychological perspective', *Cognition,* **3**, pp. 225–87.

Chomsky, N. (1981), *Lectures on Government and Binding* (Dordrecht: Foris).

Donald, M. (1991), *Origins of the Modern Mind. Three stages in the evolution of culture and cognition* (Harvard: Harvard University Press).

Durkheim, E. (1895), *Les Règles de la méthode sociologique* (Paris: Alcan). 1894a, with slight modifications, and a preface. Tr. 1982 as 'The Rules of Sociological Method', in *The Rules of Sociological Method and Selected Texts on Sociology and its Method,* S. Lukes (ed.), 29–163. (London and Basingstoke: Macmillan).

Fauconnier, G. and Turner, M. (2002), *The Way We Think. Conceptual blending and the mind's hidden complexities* (New York: Basic Books).

Feldman, C.F. (2005), 'Mimesis: where play and narrative meet', *Cognitive Development,* 20, pp. 503–13.

Fodor, J. (1975), *The Language of Thought* (Cambridge, MA: Harvard University Press).

Fodor, J. (2008), *LOT 2: The language of thought revisited* (Oxford: Oxford University Press).

Freeman, N. Lloyd, S. and Sinha, C. (1980), 'Infant search tasks reveal early concepts of containment and canonical usage of objects', *Cognition,* **8**, pp. 243–62.

Freeman, N., Sinha, C. and Condliff, S. (1981), 'Confrontation and collaboration with young children in language comprehension tasks' In W.P. Robinson (ed.) *Communication in Development,* pp. 63–88 (London: Academic Press).

Gibson, J.J. (1979), *The Ecological Approach to Visual Perception* (Boston, MA: Houghton Mifflin).

Hespos, S. and Baillargeon R. (2001), 'Knowledge about containment events in very young infants', *Cognition,* **78**, pp. 204–45.

Hutto, D.D. (2008), *Folk Psychological Narratives: The sociocultural basis of understanding reasons* (Cambridge, MA: Bradford Books/MIT Press).

Itkonen, E. (1978), *Grammatical Theory and Metascience* (Amsterdam: John Benjamins).

Itkonen, E. (2008), 'Normativity in language and linguistics' In Zlatev, J., Racine, T., Sinha, C. and Itkonen, E. (2008), *The Shared Mind: Perspectives on intersubjectivity*, pp. 279–305 (Amsterdam, John Benjamins).

Jensen de López, K. (2003), 'Baskets and Body-Parts: a cross-cultural and cross-linguistic investigation of children's development of spatial cognition and language' (PhD dissertation, University of Aarhus).

Jensen de López, K., Hayashi, M. and Sinha, C. (2005), 'Early shaping of spatial meanings in three languages and cultures: linguistic or cultural relativity?' In A. Makkai, W. J. Sullivan, and A.R. Lommel (eds.) *Selected Papers from the LACUS Forum XXXI 2003: Interconnections*, pp. 377–86 (Houston, Texas: Linguistic Association of Canada and the Unites States).

Lakoff, G. and Johnson, M. (1999), *Philosophy in the Flesh. The embodied mind and its challenge to Western thought* (New York: Basic Books).

Lloyd, S., Sinha, C. and Freeman, N. (1981), 'Spatial reference systems and the canonicality effect in infant search', *Journal of Experimental Child Psychology*, **32**, pp. 1–10.

Lock, A. (ed. 1978), *Action, Gesture and Symbol: The emergence of language* (London: Academic Press).

Lock, A. (1980), *The Guided Reinvention of Language* (London: Academic Press).

Lotman, Y. (1990), *Universe of the Mind: A semiotic theory of culture*, transl. Ann Shukman (New York: I.B. Tauris and Co. Ltd).

Moro, C. and Rodríguez, C. (2005), *L'objet et la construction de son usage chez le bébé. Une approche sémiotique du développement préverbal* (Berne & New York: Peter Lang).

Nicolopolou, A. (2007), 'The interplay of play and narrative in children's development: theoretical reflections and concrete examples' In A. Göncü and S. Gaskins (eds.) *Play and Development. Evolutionary, sociocultural and functional perspectives* (London: Taylor and Francis).

Oliveira, Zilma de (1998), 'Peer interactions and the appropriation of gender representations by young children' In M. Lyra and J. Valsiner (Eds.) *Construction of Psychological Processes in Interpersonal Communications* (London: Ablex).

Piaget, J. (1953), *The Origins of Intelligence in the Child* (London: Routledge & Kegan Paul).

Piaget, J. (1962), *Play, Dreams and Imitation* (London: Routledge & Kegan Paul).

Rodríguez, C. and Moro, C. (1999), *El mágico número tres. Cuando los niños aún no hablan* (Barcelona: Paidós).

Rodríguez, C. and Moro C. (2002), 'Objeto, comunicación y símbolo. Una mirada a los primeros usos simbólicos de los objetos', *Estudios de Psicología*, **23** (3), pp. 323–33.

Rodríguez, C. and Moro C. (2008), 'Coming to agreement: object use by infants and adults' In Zlatev, J., Racine, T., Sinha, C. and Itkonen, E. *The Shared Mind: Perspectives on intersubjectivity*, pp. 89-114 (Amsterdam, John Benjamins).

Rorty, R. (1979), *Philosophy and the Mirror of Nature* (Princeton, N.J.: Princeton University Press).

Saussure, Ferdinand de (1966), *Cours de Linguistique Générale* (New York: McGraw-Hill).

Searle, J. (1995), *The Construction of Social Reality* (London: Allen Lane).

Sinha, C. (1982), 'Representational development and the structure of action' In G. Butterworth and P. Light (eds.) *Social Cognition: Studies in the Development of Understanding*, pp. 137–62 (Brighton: Harvester).

Sinha, C. (1983), 'Background knowledge, presupposition and canonicality' In T. Seiler and W. Wannenmacher (eds.) *Concept Development and the Development of Word Meaning*, pp. 269–96 (Berlin: Springer-Verlag).

Sinha, C. (1988), *Language and Representation: A socionaturalistic approach to human development* (Hemel Hempstead: Harvester-Wheatsheaf).

Sinha, C. (1999), 'Grounding, mapping and acts of meaning' In T. Janssen and G. Redeker (eds.) *Cognitive Linguistics: Foundations, Scope and Methodology*, pp. 223–55 (Berlin, Mouton de Gruyter).

Sinha, C. (2005), 'Blending out of the Background: Play, props and staging in the material world', *Journal of Pragmatics*, **37**, pp. 1537–54.

Sinha, C. (2009), 'Language as a biocultural niche and social institution' In V. Evans and S. Pourcel (eds.) *New Directions in Cognitive Linguistics*, pp. 289–309 (Amsterdam: John Benjamins).

Sinha, C. and Jensen de López, K. (2000), 'Language, culture and the embodiment of spatial cognition', *Cognitive Linguistics*, **11**, pp. 17–41.

Sinha, C. and Rodríguez, C. (2008), 'Language and the signifying object: from convention to imagination' In Zlatev, J., Racine, T., Sinha, C. and Itkonen, E. *The Shared Mind: Perspectives on intersubjectivity*, pp. 358–78 (Amsterdam: John Benjamins).

Smolka, Ana-Luisa, Góes, Maria de and Pino, Angel, (1997), '(In)Determinacy and the semiotic constitution of subjectivity' In A. Fogel, M. Lyra and J. Valsiner (eds.) *Dynamics and Indeterminism in Developmental and Social Processes*, pp. 153–64 (Mahwah, NJ: Lawrence Earlbaum Associates).

Sonesson, G. (in press), 'New considerations on the proper study of man – and, marginally, some other animals', *Cognitive Semiotics*.

Tomasello, M. (1999), *The Cultural Origins of Human Cognition* (Cambridge, MA: Harvard University Press).

Tomasello, M., Carpenter, M., Call, J. Behne, T. and Moll, H. (2005), 'Understanding and sharing intentions: The origins of cultural cognition', *Behavioral and Brain Sciences*, **28**, pp. 675–735.

Trevarthen, C. (1979), 'Communication and cooperation in early infancy : a description of primary intersubjectivity' In *Before Speech: The Beginning of Interpersonal Communication*, M. Bullowa (ed.), pp. 321–47 (Cambridge: Cambridge University Press).

Trevarthen, C. (1998), 'The concept and foundations of infant intersubjectivity' In *Intersubjective Communication and Emotion in Early Ontogeny*, S. Bråten (ed.), pp. 15–46 (Cambridge: Cambridge University Press).

Vandeloise, C. (1991), *Spatial Prepositions: A Case Study from French* (Chicago: Chicago University Press).

Vygotsky, L.S. (1978), *Mind in Society: The Development of Higher Psychological Processes* (Cambridge, MA: Harvard University Press).

Vygotsky, L.S. (1986), *Thought and Language* (Cambridge, MA: MIT Press).

Wertsch, J. (1985), *Vygotsky and the Social Formation of Mind* (Cambridge, MA: Harvard University Press).

Walkerdine, V. and Sinha, C. (1978), 'The internal triangle: Language, reasoning and the social context' In I. Markova (ed.) *The Social Context of* Language, pp. 151–76 (London: Wiley).

Winch, P. (1958), *The Idea of a Social Science* (London: Routledge).

Wittgenstein, L. (1953), *Philosophical Investigations* (Oxford: Blackwell).

Wittgenstein, L. (1961), *Tractatus Logico-Philosophocus* (London: Routledge).

Zlatev, J. (2008), 'The co-evolution of intersubjectivity and bodily mimesis' In Zlatev, J., Racine, T., Sinha, C. and Itkonen, E. *The Shared Mind: Perspectives on intersubjectivity*, pp. 215–44 (Amsterdam, John Benjamins).

Zlatev, J., Racine, T., Sinha, C. and Itkonen, E. (2008), *The Shared Mind: Perspectives on intersubjectivity* (Amsterdam: John Benjamins).

Jill de Villiers and Jay Garfield

Evidentiality and Narrative

Abstract: *In this paper we argue that the phenomenon of evidentiality, the grammatical marking in some languages of the source of one's knowledge, gives us a revealing window into the developmental processes in middle childhood that subserve the achievement of narrative competence. First, we argue that the mastery of evidentiality is connected to the development of an understanding of inference, and of the ability to mobilize this understanding in the construction of human narratives. Second, we examine the role that parent-child discourse plays in clarifying the contrastive uses of sources of knowledge. Finally, we discuss the difference between first person and third person narratives, and suggest that evidentials might reveal something of the sources of evidence for persistence of self as the protagonist in one's own life story.*

Introduction

Human cognitive development emerges from a complex interaction between biologically structured maturation and social interaction. In this paper, we explore the parallels and possible interactions among the developmental tracks of three distinct but related intellectual capacities. The first of these is specifically *linguistic*. As we will discuss in detail below, many of the world's languages contain grammatical devices for marking the source of evidence a speaker has for his/her assertions, a feature called 'evidentiality'. We are interested in the surprisingly difficult question: How do children who speak these languages master this system? The second question is specifically *cognitive*: How do children develop the capacities to draw inferences and to represent the structure of the inferences that they and others draw? The third is *cultural*. How do children develop the ability to tell narratives, whether third or first person? Despite the fact that these three capacities appear to fall into such different developmental domains, it turns out that they are mutually entangled, and the study of the development of language may yield insight into the development of narrative self-understanding.

1. Narrative and Development

There is a growing consensus that our self-understanding and many of our most important complex cognitive skills rest on our ability to construct narratives about ourselves and others. We know ourselves first and foremost as characters in an ongoing autobiography. We make sense of our own actions and mental states as well as those of our fellows by situating them in the context of stories in which they make sense. The inability to tell a good story is hence not just a minor social failing; it is a serious cognitive disability potentially issuing in dramatic self-alienation.

There is also a growing consensus that narrative competence is an acquired skill, and that it has an extended developmental track. It is significant that narrative is one of the principal forms of discourse in which the young child first has an extended turn at speaking. Narrative is not topically bound to a current discourse situation, and it both allows and requires children to refer in a coherent way to past events and to absent people and objects. In addition, narration requires the child to express connections between different utterances and involves particular 'text-making' linguistic devices that are important to later literacy and communicative skills (Perera, 1986; Engen, 1994; Snow, 1991; Snow *et al.*, 1995).

It is useful to distinguish between a narrative's *coherence* and its *cohesion*. A narrative is *coherent* to the extent that the story hangs together, has a central storyline, has characters with relatively stable dispositions, and a plot structure. The plot structure has been used as a framework for describing and analysing children's growth in narrative coherence. For example, Labov's influential scheme (Labov, 1972; Labov & Waletsky, 1967) defines the minimal characteristics of a well-formed, coherent story. It begins with an *onset* that introduces the characters and establishes an orientation or setting for the story and can also provide a preview of what the story is to be about. The central nucleus is an *unfolding* of one or more complicating actions or events, leading to a *high point* or climax and finally a *resolution* of the story.

These are broad, open-textured qualities, and may be subject to cultural variation and to literary style. (On this dimension, William Faulkner may be faulted, and four year olds may look pretty good, depending on one's standards). A narrative is also *cohesive* to the extent that it is represented in language that cues the listener and reader to the relationships between fragments of the narrative, using such devices as appropriate pronominal reference, appropriate tense markers, conjunctions, relative clauses, and adverbial phrases. Cohesion is more regular, and more stable across cultures, and covaries more directly with age and cognitive development than does coherence. Indeed, cohesion is used as an assessment criterion in some language development instruments (de Villiers, 2004).

Until approximately the age of four, normally developing children, contrary to their grandparents' reports, do not produce discourses that qualify as narratives. Their discourse lacks both coherence and cohesion; this is not just a matter of degree, but of fundamental structure. Their discourse is either punctate or associative, and such coherence or cohesion as is represented is supplied by the listener, not by the child. This is why young children are so strikingly incompetent at talking with someone who does not share their knowledge of the topic under discussion. While children at this age are developing increasingly sophisticated skills at pretence, these skills are primarily enactive, and while they almost certainly scaffold the development of narrative skills, they precede them. It is one thing to be a character in a story; it is another to tell a story about that character.

Between approximately age four and age six, children's narrative competence develops dramatically. First, children shift from mere descriptions of observable actions to the attribution of conative states and the representations of goals and purposes. At about this time, they also begin to respect discourse representation conventions such as the introduction of nominal antecedents for pronouns, and restrictions on indefinite and definite articles. A bit later, doxastic, epistemic and indirect speech verbs enter narratives, enabling reference to participants' mental states, and inferences. Finally, devices for indicating temporal relations appear, allowing clear sequencing of multiple events, and the use of tense to distinguish figure from ground, e.g. the difference between, 'while he was eating, the train was stolen', vs. 'while the train was stolen, he was eating', each of which is much richer than 'the train was stolen and he was eating' (de Villiers, 2004).

An important distinction can be drawn between the external plot structure, consisting of action sequences and events, and the subjective evaluative component of the plot, involving the internal responses of the characters (Labov, 1972). Bruner (1986) refers to this as the distinction between the 'landscape of action' and the 'landscape of consciousness' in stories. The landscape of action refers to the sequence of events that took place — who did what to whom, and when they did it. Rich narratives have in addition, a landscape of consciousness that expresses the characters' motivations and goals for actions, their emotional reactions to events, and their interpretations of events in the light of their beliefs and knowledge or ignorance. Children's ability to handle the landscape of consciousness of stories depends on their growing 'theory of mind' in the late preschool years (Astington, 1993; Wellman, 1990).

There is a reciprocal connection between the development of Theory of Mind and the development of narrative competence. Theory of Mind, of course, is not a single, monolithic capacity that emerges in an instant. Component Theory of Mind skills emerge quite early both ontogenetically and phylogenetically. For instance, infants as young as one year demonstrate the ability to track gaze (Tomasello & Rakoczy, 2003; Onishi & Baillargeon, 2005; Southgate et al., 2007), as do adult chimpanzees (Tomasello & Rakoczy, 2003). On the other hand, these basic skills hardly suffice even to solve simple false belief puzzles, though they may enable simple deception. An understanding of desire clearly precedes an understanding of belief (Perner et al., 2003); understandings of the conditions of perception may precede both of these, but the connection to belief fixation is a later attainment (de Villiers, 2007).

Many have urged that Theory of Mind is fully in place when, and only when, a child can attribute a false belief to another. But even this capacity, while it postdates the simplest capacities comprised by Theory of Mind, is far from the pinnacle of this cognitive development (Hutto, 2007). Consider that the standard tasks of Theory of Mind require the child to deploy a distinction between who saw something and who did not, and therefore what that character knows or not. We describe in a later section just how limited a condition that is compared to the subtle inferences we can draw as adults about someone's state of knowledge, based in turn on the inferences that another person must have drawn.

Second order belief attribution lags about a year behind first order belief attribution (Sullivan et al., 1994; Hollebrandse et al., in press). Moreover, second order attribution is a crucial cognitive skill for beings like us. For the ability to deploy this knowledge in inference and in the development of an explanatory narrative about another's behaviour develops even later, and it is not until a child can deploy this knowledge in sophisticated reasoning and narration that it makes sense to say that she understands the role of the mind in human life. So, while the *emergence* of early Theory of Mind enables narrative, narrative in turn enables the *maturation* of Theory of Mind.

Adults play a crucial role in teaching the narrative skills that enable the transition from primitive to mature Theory of Mind. In many cultures, children are surrounded by tales: fairy tales, folk tales, pretence scenarios, retellings of family dramas, all of which entail bringing together motives, reasons, misunderstanding and their resolution, and differing perspectives from different characters. These practices provide examples of the use of cognitive state attributions in the prediction, explanation and rich description of behaviour (Dunn & Brophy, 2005; Harris, 2005). But we must not overlook another crucial function that they serve: They also demonstrate the range of *linguistic* devices that enable both the attribution of these states and the narrative cohesion necessary for them to play their role in narration. While adult-child interactions clearly serve this pedagogical role, insufficient attention has been paid to cross-linguistic or cross-cultural study of the variation in such interaction, and to the range of devices that might subserve this function.

Narration serves many cognitive functions. It not only facilitates the development of important Theory of Mind skills; it also contributes to our *self*-understanding, and hence to the achievement of agency in the full sense. We know that, just as four year olds are not simply tiny adults with self-understandings comparable to our own, even adolescents do not have a mature autobiographical narrative or a complete sense of reflective agency. The fact that this skill is mastered so late in life, coupled with the complexity that often confronts adolescents can often have tragic results (Chandler & Ball, 1990).

While we are developing an increasingly rich picture of the beginnings and the end of the development of narrative competence and so of self-understanding, there is much still to be learned about the middle years of childhood. In this period, between the ages of six and ten years old, children's ability to reason about others' states of mind expands dramatically as their linguistic, narrative and inferential competence increases. With the basic ability to represent beliefs in place by four or five, and most of the syntactic devices mastered for extended discourse, it is in this period that knowledge of Theory of

Mind is expanded and consolidated through rich experience (Hutto, 2007).

Exploration of the cognitive and linguistic development during this crucial period may be facilitated by the fact that some of the world's languages incorporate an important grammatical device, the development of competence with which extends significantly into middle childhood. Moreover, that device may have important roles in the narrative self-understanding of children. These languages are those with evidential systems. By studying the acquisition of evidentials we may gain important insights into several aspects of the development of narratives in childhood. The current paper discusses three such aspects: the role of inference in explanations of action, the role of discourse in assisting reasoning about the mind, and the relation between third person and first person narrativity. First we provide some background on evidentiality. We will then turn to an examination of the Tibetan evidential system and of what we can learn about cognitive development from investigating its acquisition pattern.

2. All about Evidentiality

Evidential morphemes are grammatical devices that express the nature of the speaker's evidence for a statement. In all languages there are ways to express the source of one's evidence, but in languages with evidentials there is a specialized grammatical system for encoding what type of evidence the speaker has for her statement, and about a quarter of the world's languages (including many central Asian and indigenous languages of the Americas) have such specialized markings (Aikhenvald, 2004).

It is helpful to compare evidentials with the other linguistic devices used to convey related meanings. In many languages, attitude predicates (I saw that … ; I infer that …) are used to convey information about the speaker's epistemic grounds for a statement, but evidentials differ from attitude predicates in four important ways. The evidential always takes the perspective of the speaker, expressing what kind of evidence the speaker has for the statement. Second, evidentials do not have their own grammatical subjects. In contrast, attitude predicates have a subject that need not be the speaker (*I* heard that; *She* heard that; *John* heard that).

Third, evidentials convey information about *how* the speaker's epistemic state was achieved rather than the *nature* of the epistemic state itself. In particular, they do not encode the degree of certainty, for even hearsay evidentials do not necessarily qualify the speaker's commitment to the truth of the assertion.

Fourth, as a general rule evidentials occur only in main clauses, and do not introduce a subordinate clause. Though evidentials convey the same type of information as 'I infer that', 'I saw that' or 'They say that', the possibilities of recursive embedded structures that occur with attitude verbs do not occur with evidentials.

Epistemic modals also convey information about mental states; but the kind of meaning conveyed by an evidential is also different from that conveyed by epistemic modals. Whereas epistemic modals express *how likely* the information is to be true, or how *certain* the speaker is, evidentials convey the *nature of the evidence* that the speaker has for the statement (Oswalt, 1986; de Haan, 1999; Hardman, 1986; DeLancey, 1986; Lazard, 2001; Plungian, 2001; Aikhenvald, 2004). Evidentials are used to make unqualified assertions, whereas even the stronger epistemic modals (e.g. 'must') weaken the assertoric force of utterances (Davis *et al.*, 2007).

Note that as listeners we can often *infer* the degree of certainty of a claim from the type of evidence the speaker invokes. If someone makes it clear that a claim is made based on her having witnessed the actual event, we can infer that she is quite certain that the claim is true. If someone claims that something 'must' be the case, we can infer that he or she has reasonably reliable evidence for it, less so in the case of e.g. 'might'. So epistemic modals express a speaker's *judgment* about probability or necessity, which in turn is based on the type of evidence she has for her assertion. But evidentials express the type of evidence the *speaker* has for her claim and leave the *hearer* to make estimates about the probability of the assertion being true. Evidentials hence differ markedly from the linguistic devices of attitude predicates and modal auxiliaries, despite overlap in the semantic and pragmatic roles they play.

Evidentials are *egophoric,* meaning always from the point of view of the speaker. The egophoricity of evidentials gives them a special role in autobiographical narrative construction. In a language (such as Tibetan, which we consider below) in which evidentials are mandatory in most sentences, representing one's own source of evidence for the claims one makes is a central aspect of any assertion. Inasmuch as the development of competence with evidentials reflects the development of one's own reflective knowledge of one's epistemic states, it also reflects competence in autobiographic narrative. It follows that understanding the information conveyed by others when they use evidentials hence requires projecting an epistemic biography that makes sense of their evidential use. Thus it is impossible to understand evidentials without representing at least the skeleton of a narrative in which one's interlocutor acquires evidence of some type for the claim he has just made.

All of this gives rise to an important and fascinating acquisition puzzle. Since the felicity conditions of the use of an evidential consist in the evidence (generally in the past) that the speaker has for an assertion, those felicity conditions (or their failure for that matter) are in general not available in the conversational context in which evidentials are used. It is therefore somewhat mysterious how children project not only the correct meaning on evidential expressions, but even that those expressions are evidentials. Solving this problem will provide an interesting window into cognitive development.

3. A bit about Tibetan

Tibetan evidentials are distinctive forms of the copula or the verb of existence, which occur at the end of virtually every sentence in Tibetan, a head-final language. Therefore evidentiality is a feature of virtually every Tibetan assertion or question.

Published descriptions of the Tibetan evidential system generally distinguish three categories of evidentials — direct, ego and indirect (Garrett, 2001; Denwood, 1999). However there is also a fourth category — neutral — which is used when a speaker is noncommittal about the kind of evidence for the assertion. *Direct* evidentials are reserved for cases in which the speaker has directly witnessed a situation with her own eyes, but also to report internal states. The most common direct evidential in Tibetan is *'dug*, with a form *song* used as a direct evidential for past tense. A speaker who says *Tsi tsi pha gir 'dug* (there is a mouse over there) is *asserting* that there is a mouse over there, and indicating by the use of *'dug* that she *saw* it.

Indirect evidentials are used in situations where the speaker did not witness the event but has some kind of indirect evidence for the assertion. The indirect evidentials are *yod sa red* and *yod kyi red*. *Yod sa red* is used when the speaker directly experiences specific evidence that points to the truth of the utterance, but does not directly witness the situation described. For instance, a speaker could say *Tsi tsi pha gir yod sa red* (there is a mouse over there) when she directly sees mouse footprints in the dust, but not the mouse itself. The statement is an unqualified assertion that there is a mouse over there, but it reveals that her evidence is, though perceptual, indirect.

Yod kyi red is an indirect evidential used when the evidence for the assertion is non-perceptible, for instance hearsay, general knowledge, or inference from general facts. A speaker uttering *Tsi tsi pha gir yod kyi red,* asserts that there is a mouse over there, but indicates that she knows it by inference of a more general sort. It could be that the mouse is always there at this time every day, or that this is the place where mice are always to be seen, or some reliable source may have told her that there is a mouse there.

Ego evidentials are used for reporting a state of the speaker's own mind or body to which she has privileged access, for example, to talk about emotional states or hunger or pain. The ego evidential morphemes in Tibetan are *yin* and *yod* but also *'dug,* the latter being a kind of 'inner eye'. Note that in English, we often use perception verbs such as 'see' to mean something concluded with inner certainty, 'I see, I see'.

Finally, Tibetan has a neutral evidential category (*red, yod red*). These verb forms give no information about the kind of evidence on which the speaker is relying, but are generally infelicitous where the direct or ego evidential would be felicitous. In this way the neutral form resembles the indirect evidentials, but does not commit to the nature of that indirect evidence. Tibetan also has a range of epistemic modals and propositional attitude verbs, like those of English, but evidentials differ from these in the ways noted above.

One final point is worth noting. In asking a question in Tibetan, the speaker anticipates the kind of evidence the respondent will use in her reply, and uses the evidential that matches that anticipated source of evidence. In the context of a question, therefore, a point of view shift occurs, and, evidentials are anchored not to the perspective of the questioner, but to that of the respondent. From the point of view of Theory of Mind, this property of Tibetan evidentials opens up a very interesting opportunity for developmental research.

4. The Developmental Track of Evidentiality in Tibetan

Tibetan children use the evidential *'dug* early (by age 2), and well before they use any other evidentials, even the neutral evidentials which appear soon after initial uses of *'dug.* However, it appears both from the distribution of expressive uses and from the inability to make effective use of the use of *'dug* by others that these early uses do not reflect a representation of the evidential force of this particle. Instead, children appear to take *'dug* to be simply a generic form of the copula.

By age 3–4, Tibetan children discriminate *'dug* from the class of indirect evidentials. At this age, they are able to determine that a speaker using *'dug* is a more reliable informant than one using an indirect evidential (de Villiers *et al.*, 2005; de Villiers *et al.*, in press). However, at this age it is not clear whether children are representing these particles as evidentials or as epistemic modals. That is, they may be taking *'dug* to mean *must be* and *yod kyi red/yod sa red* to mean something like *could be*.

However, by age 5–6, Tibetan children treat these particles grammatically as evidentials, as opposed to modals. For instance, they always take denial of a sentence containing an evidential to be a denial of the content of the matrix sentence, as opposed to the denial of the felicity of the evidential (Gernet-Girard, 2008; de Villiers *et al.*, in press). This contrasts with modals, whose felicity can be denied independent of the judgment regarding the truth value of the matrix sentence they govern. At this age children also begin to respect the point of view shift in questions, using evidentials in questions in a way that appropriately anticipates the felicity of the evidential to be used by their respondent (de Villiers *et al.*, 2008).

Mastery of the distinction between the two indirect evidentials in Tibetan, however, is not achieved until much later, around age 9–10 (de Villiers *et al.*, submitted). Until this time, while *yod kyi red* appears in children's speech as a contrast to *'dug,* the form *yod sa red* never appears, and *yod kyi red* is often used when *yod sa red* would be felicitous. Indeed, when this distinction is important, and at earlier ages when even distinctions between direct and indirect evidentials are important, we find that children often avoid commitment either by using elliptical (such as one word) utterances that avoid the evidential (something permitted in casual spoken Tibetan, just as it is in English) or by retreating to neutral evidentials.

Until approximately age 9–10, Tibetan children appear to be insensitive to the distinction between the two indirect evidentials. That is, they fail to mark, or to exploit, the distinction, represented by all adult Tibetan speakers, between specific inference and general inference, between knowing that you are home because I see your bicycle on the porch and knowing that you are home because you usually get home by 6pm, and it is 6.30. Our evidence suggests that only at about age 9–10 do they come to mark reliably and to exploit this distinction.

We might ask what cognitive skills enable them to master this distinction. First, we note that this transition is developmentally much too late to depend simply on basic Theory of Mind skills, even the representation and use of false belief, as these are well in place in normally developing children by age 4 or 5. Even higher-order false belief skills are in place by age 6 or 7 (Hollebrandse *et al.*, in press). On the other hand, we have discovered that children's ability to draw inferences based upon available signs develops more slowly. Although this kind of inference might seem to be the most elementary, it is actually very challenging. As we have learned from Tversky & Kahneman (1981), Wason (1960), and a host of their successors, even those with tenure in Philosophy departments, or who teach classes in statistics fail what appear to be elementary inferential tasks. It turns out that the ability to engage in inference from observable signs does not emerge until well into middle childhood.

5. Inference

Everyday inference is itself a complex and rich phenomenon. Indeed 'inference' denotes a broad and ill-defined range of phenomena. There is little consensus on just what constitutes inference. Many would not describe an infant watching a toy train pass behind a screen as *inferring* that it will emerge from the other side, as simple expectation based on habit does not qualify. Marr (1968) argued that even ordinary perception is inferential, since we need to reconstruct the distal layout based upon data consisting only in sensory stimulation. Other theorists, such as Recanati (2002), argue that perception is a paradigm of *immediate, non-inferential knowledge.* Even ordinary classical conditioning could be construed as a kind of inference to the unknown, but we do not generally say that Pavlov's dogs drew an inference that food would follow the bell.

For purposes relevant to the distinctions reflected in an evidential system such as Tibetan, and for purposes relevant to the development of the cognitive competences we have been investigating, we find it useful to reserve the term 'inference' for cognitive tasks requiring more explicit, deliberate, introspectable reasoning from consciously entertained premises. Recanati uses Reid (1970) for a definition of reasoning: the process by which we pass from one *judgement* to another which is the consequence of it. But even to exploit obvious, readily available information in direct, simple logical inference construed in this sense requires a host of skills whose structure and developmental trajectory is little-understood. Consider the kind of inferences drawn by a detective investigating a crime. One needs to *notice* the relevant information (the footprint in the snow), and moreover, notice *that* it is relevant to the task at hand (finding the thief who came after the snowstorm). One needs to know *that* an inference is called for (the thief won't turn himself in), and moreover, to know what *kind* of inference is necessary (inductive, based on shoe size and criminal record) and *how* to draw inferences of that kind (the logical form of a Bayesian inference). So we see that elementary reasoning requires us to draw on a host of skills and information including metacognitive knowledge.

There is a deeper question: might the computation of the meanings and use of inferential evidentials proceed by some process internal to the linguistic system, or is it parasitic on inference skills developed more broadly outside of language proper? Such questions are central to recent debates in the pragmatics of language, for example, in Relevance Theory (Sperber & Wilson, 1986; Sperber, 1995). Recanati (2002) draws a distinction between Inferentialism and Anti-Inferentialism in the area of language comprehension. According to Inferentialists, semantic interpretation is crucially dependent on pragmatic interpretation, so that the content of the speech act provides only part of the evidence used. Inferentialists argue that the meaning has to be inferred from premises concerning what the speaker could intend by the utterance in this context. Anti-inferentialists on the other hand, argue that semantic interpretation by itself usually gives us the content of the speech act. On this view, the speaker in ordinary circumstances means what he says: to interpret an utterance one has only to figure out what the sentence says. In some circumstances (jokes, sarcasm, irony, metaphor), the interpretation involves a secondary inference process from pragmatics, which requires evidence concerning the speaker's beliefs and intentions to work out what he means on the basis of what he says.

Recanati recognizes that many more ordinary acts of semantic interpretation are bedevilled by under-determination, such as the use of indexicals (I/you) or deixis (here/there). Recanati argues that these cases are not easily constrained by limited contextual considerations, but also take into account speaker's intents, beliefs and so forth.

> either semantic interpretation delivers something gappy, and pragmatic interpretation must fill the gaps until we reach a complete proposition, or we run semantic interpretation only after we have used pragmatic interpretation to pre-determine the values of semantically underdetermined expressions, which values we artificially feed into the narrow context. Either way, semantic interpretation by itself is powerless to determine what is said, when the sentence contains a semantically underdetermined expression (p. 112).

Having acknowledged the influence of context in the interpretation of semantically undetermined forms, Recanati allows that both inferentialism and anti-inferentialism are consistent with the process. In particular he argues that the use of the contextual information could be an automatic process, like seeing, in which the contents of the inferences made are not available at the personal level, but at the subpersonal, especially if there is a relatively circumscribed set of factors to be consulted, as in resolving deixis:

> The determination of what is said takes place at a sub-personal level, much as the determination of what we see. But the determination of what the speaker implies takes place at the personal level, much like the determination of the consequences of what we see. (Seeing John's car, I infer that he did not leave). The crucial fact is that pragmatic, background-dependent processes may well take place at a sub-personal level in an automatic and non-reflective manner. Such processes are not 'inferential' in the strong sense in which secondary pragmatic processes are inferential (p. 114).

What, then, do we make of evidentials? If we construe them as semantically analogous to deictic terms and indexicals, their resolution may well be sub-personal, in some automatic processes unavailable to the general cognitive apparatus of inferences and reflective consideration. It might therefore turn out that however 'inferential' the figuring out of evidential meaning is, the process is beneath awareness and hence not connected to ordinary inferential skill in non-linguistic domains, like detective work. On the other hand, given the analysis that Recanati gives to the case of 'seeing John's car, I infer that he did not leave', we might surmise that at least indirect evidentials could involve the apparatus of ordinary inference, and hence await its full development.

Tibetan raises a further complexity: the correct use of the two indirect evidentials in Tibetan represent two distinct kinds of inference, and distinguishing them requires that children master and represent this distinction. In particular, to master the distinction between *yod sa red* and *yod kyi red* in Tibetan, the child must attend to the evidential base for the speaker's claim and to the kind of inference that evidence would warrant. Imagine the case of a bicycle left outside on a porch, which is a reliable sign that the bicycle's owner is at home. The child hears an evidential used in this context in a sentence asserting that the owner is at home. (*Sonam-lags nang la yod sa red*. Sonam is at home). In order to understand this sentence the child must:

a) know the contingency between the bicycle and the presence of the owner, and be capable of drawing the deduction himself (or he cannot understand that the evidential marks this contingency);

b)   know that the speaker knows the same contingency (or he cannot represent the egophoricity of the evidential); and

c)   recognize that the speaker has used that information, and not other information, to draw the inference (or else he cannot distinguish *yod sa red* from *yod kyi red,* or even *'dug*).

It follows that the child must also represent the difference between *seeing* and *seeing that.* Many narratives, including not only murder mysteries but other more mundane human dramas revolve around such differences: did his lover spot the second used wineglass by the sink? Did my mother spot the roach in the ashtray? Will the customs official see the price tag on the computer? The person who is intensely aware of the significance of the cue is often amazed that it could be overlooked by the other. The objects of perception do not always trigger inferences, and we are not always aware of what others notice, or what they infer on the basis of what they notice. It is hence hard, in a community speaking a language such as English, to tell when children are aware of this distinction. But the Tibetan evidential system requires that children draw this distinction in order to master their language. This gives us a valuable window into this developmental process so central to the achievement of narrative competence.

We have found that the development of both receptive and expressive competence in the use of Tibetan evidentials correlates not with the development of Theory of Mind skills, but with the development of inferential competence (de Villiers *et al.*, 2005). In particular, children do not master the distinction between general and specific inference evidentials until they are very good at tasks that require them to infer unseen events from visible signs even when these tasks do not require the use of any evidentials (de Villiers *et al.*, in press). This suggests that the mastery of this portion of Tibetan grammar demands not simply linguistic maturation, but the development of a broad range of non-linguistic cognitive skills. It also suggests that the kind of reflective awareness of one's own epistemic activity (and the representation of that kind of epistemic activity in one's interlocutors) that is necessary for the distinction between these evidentials matures quite late in middle childhood.

In exploring the relationship between evidential use and inference, we have been inventing or adapting inferential tasks that might parallel the demands placed on children by the comprehension and production of *indirect* evidentials. We have uncovered a range of skills that require further study, and have made some interesting errors in method along the way, and our mistakes in methodology reveal that the kinds of inference marked by indirect evidentials are not as simple as we might have thought.

In our very first attempts to study the development of inferential ability, we asked when children could answer questions based on the use of a general rule, coupled with a specific clue. For instance, we told the children that two people shared a house, and only one could be home at one time. One of them liked to cook, and always lit a fire to cook. The other character always liked to dance, so whenever she was home, she played music. Then we showed the house, either with music blaring out, or smoke coming from the chimney. We then asked, 'who is home?'. While it is true that with four year olds we sometimes needed to point out the music or the smoke before they would respond, most children of this age could answer, if they could remember who did what! This is an inference from sign, and it goes beyond simple conditioned expectation, but we found that success in this kind of inference was insufficient to enable children to understand indirect evidentials.

In a slightly more demanding scenario, we told children a brief story about a school, and then explained that when the children went into class, they hung their coats up outside, but took their notebooks with them. We then showed them a picture with four coats hanging up, and asked them how many children were in the classroom. Note that to answer, the child has to use the coats as an indirect clue, because the children themselves are not visible (adapted from Sophian, 1988; Sophian et al., 1995). We also showed a single notebook left outside, and asked them how many notebooks were in the classroom. To get this right involves inferring that one of the (inferred) children in the classroom left his or her notebook behind, and so also involves a very elementary arithmetic computation. By age four, the children we tested could count the coats and draw the inference about the number of children, but children could not reliably answer the question about notebooks until age seven. The inference here involved additional skills concerning arithmetic with hidden objects, but this skill again was insufficient to underpin successful use of indirect evidentials. Although we had discovered a more difficult inference, we had not discovered what kind of inferential ability or knowledge is necessary to enable successful use of the Tibetan evidential system.

Our most recent attempt is more revealing. The task involved a book written for children to expose them to inferential logic, by Nozaki & Anno (1993). It introduces the child to a hatter, who has a predetermined number of red or white hats. From this set, he then places a hat of unknown colour on the reader's head and visibly, on the heads of one or two other children pictured on the page. The child reader is asked to imagine that a shadow pictured on the page is his/her own shadow, and of course therefore s/he cannot tell the colour of his/her own hat directly. Instead, the reader must use clues from what the other characters say, and as the book proceeds, also from what the characters can infer about the colours of their own hats, which of course the reader can see but they cannot. An illustration is provided in Figure 1.

The book is a *tour de force* of inferential reasoning, and the final puzzle challenges even advanced logic students. The language is very simple and direct, and does not depend on particular epistemic language. The child is asked in each case, 'what colour is your hat?'. The book explains each answer as it proceeds, so that the reader can see the reasoning in the examples after the question has been asked. We used the book by slightly shortening the explanations provided, and it was translated by our research assistants into Tibetan, using parallel language and neutral evidentials.

Figure 1

Sample item from Shadowchild task. The hatter shows the hats he has available on that turn. You, the reader, project the shadow. Tom, your friend, says he can see your hat, and so he knows that his hat is red. What colour is your hat?

We continued through the book excluding the most difficult item, and we counted the number of questions that the children got correct. The 23 Tibetan children were tested at a Tibetan refugee community in Mungod, India, and the 17 English speakers were volunteers from a local school in a Western Massachusetts city that draws on a primarily working class, racially mixed community (Gernet-Girard, 2008). There is of course no way to ensure that the groups were equivalent in other measures of intellect, but we tried to ensure they were both from relatively low-income environments, without professional or highly educated parents. Despite this, the material wealth, environmental and educational resources of the Tibetan children was judged to be considerably lower than the American children. In addition, the Tibetan children had no experience of being 'tested', i.e. subject to questioning by a relative stranger, although a native Tibetan speaker, outside of their classrooms.

For all these reasons, we were surprised by the strong inferential ability of the Tibetan speaking children relative to the English-speaking sample. An analysis of variance comparing the two groups on the Shadowchild task reveals a highly significant effect of language $(F(1,32)=23.7, p<.001)$. The mean score was 7.9 out of 11 for the Tibetan children, and only 4.2 for the English speakers. Furthermore, while competence steadily increased with age for the Tibetans, it remained stagnant for the English speakers.

It appears to be the case that Tibetan children are significantly advantaged at this task, but it is too early to tell whether it is because of the parallel to the demands of evidential use in their linguistic experience, or some other factor in their culture or education that promotes such reasoning more than for this sample of American children.

This result at least raises the possibility that because Tibetan evidentiality demands attention to the direct and indirect sources of knowledge to which others have access, mastering this language might not only depend on but also *promote* inferential reasoning. We are pursuing the idea that success on the Shadowchild task is predictive of success on indirect evidentials, as these tasks were used with different subjects to date. If we do find a significant correlation, not attributable to age or intelligence per se, then it would provide evidence that at least indirect evidentials may involve the secondary pragmatic processes of which Recanati writes, suggesting that the semantic processing of evidentials is carried out at a personal, rather than a sub-personal, level.

This led us to ask how young children get exposed to inferential reasoning in ordinary discourse, a topic that has been neglected to date. Like Hutto (2007), Harris (2005), Dunn & Brophy (2005) and others have argued, language provides important information to the child acquiring Theory of Mind that goes beyond the learning of linguistic devices for representing belief, such as the semantics and syntax of propositional attitude verbs. So, we now ask: what role can discourse play in making the felicity conditions for their use more transparent to the language learning child?

6. Teaching Evidentials

Reflection on the task confronting a young native speaker of Tibetan as she masters the evidential system of her native language suggests some significant obstacles. Reflection on these obstacles in turn suggests the broad role of narratives and of didactic parent-child discourse in language learning. The principal obstacle is this: the information encoded by evidentials is almost never present in the conversational context in which Tibetan evidentials are used. That is because the felicity conditions for evidentials comprise states of affairs in the past of the speaker that are not explicitly represented in typical discourses. For instance, consider two speakers in the living room each reporting the presence of yaks in the kitchen (in an outhouse). Dolma says, *gyag thab tshang nang la 'dug* (there is [direct] a yak in the kitchen); Tashi says, *gyag than tshang nang la yod sa red* (there is [specific inference] a yak in the kitchen). Dolma conveys, but does not state, that she saw the yak. Tashi conveys, but does not state, that he saw something (perhaps a trail of yak footprints going into the kitchen) that warrants his confident assertion.

Now, consider poor little Yangzom's task, as she tries to figure out what the difference in meaning is between *'dug* and *yod sa red* given data like this. *Nothing* in the discourse situation as it stands provides information regarding the difference in meaning. Although evidentials are egophoric, to learn their meaning requires attending to others' sources of knowledge. The distinction between who saw and who did not see is elementary compared to the inferences required of the indirect evidential contrast.

Evidentials present a classic problem of negative evidence in language learning: since the morphemes cannot themselves be denied, there is no way that caregivers can subject the evidentials to correction. Recall that evidentials and epistemic modals differ in a crucial respect: if I utter a sentence containing an evidential, and you deny the truth of the sentence, that denial *cannot* be taken as a denial of the felicity of the evidential, but only as a denial of the truth of the sentence. If you say, 'Rogers *must be* the thief', and I say 'No!' I could either be denying that Rogers is the thief *or* leaving open the possibility that she is, but denying that current evidence supports the *must be* locution. If, on the other hand, you say in Tibetan, using a direct evidential, that Rogers is the thief, and I deny that sentence in Tibetan, I can *only* be denying that Rogers is a thief, not challenging the felicity of the evidential. To do the latter requires a great deal of circumlocution and metalinguistic discourse.

So, without fairly explicit conversational intervention by adults or access to an oracle, Yangzom is doomed. This is more than normal stimulus poverty — it is abject stimulus destitution! But Tibetan children do eventually master the system. How? The answer seems to be that adults come to the rescue, and that they do so using extended, contrastive elucidations of the distinct felicity conditions of the evidentials.

A further property of Tibetan helps here; the demonstrative *'dug ga*, used almost always with a demonstrative gesture to elicit shared attention on a focal object (like the English *look!*). This draws a child's attention over time not only to the object of shared attention, but to the fact that *'dug* is being used to reflect the fact that something can be seen by the speaker. This demonstrative construction probably plays a crucial role in scaffolding the direct evidential meaning. When the time comes to master the distinction between *yod sa red* and *yod kyi red,* the fact that *'dug* is in hand is a real facilitator. For when *yod sa red* is felicitous, there is always some *other* state of affairs — the relevant evidence — for which a *'dug* statement is felicitous, unlike in the case of *yod kyi red*:

> *gyag gi rjes pha gir 'dug!*
> yak (possessive) footprints over there (direct evidential)
> 'There are yak footprints over there!'.

Consider now the spontaneous dialogues between Tibetan mothers and their children that we have recently collected (see Table 1 for illustrations). These dialogues contain cases of indirect evidentials used in statements in close conjunction with direct evidentials to justify the inference being drawn. That is, the mother uses a specific inferential evidential for a broad claim, and backs it up with a statement about visible 'signs' justifying the inference, this being marked by the direct evidential, just as in the fanciful example of the yak and the footprints. Hearing conjunctions of claims like these provides good

Table 1
Examples of Tibetan mother's use of indirect (inferential)
evidentials in natural samples

Example 1:

kyod rang gyi cho cho coolie rgyugs ga phyin *yod sa red* gzugs po la nag po god *'dug*

you <genitive> brother labourer became is (*specific inference evidential*) body <locative> black dirt is *(direct evidential)*

'Your brother looks like a coolie; he has black dirt on his body'.

Example 2:

phun tsok yang so rus *'dug* co yang so rus *'dug* Youngling slob gra la cong tso mngar mo kyang kyang bza' sdad kyi *yod sa red*

Phuntsok <possessive> tooth rotten is *(direct evidential)* he <possessive> tooth rotten is *(direct evidential)*. Youngling school <locative> kid <plural> sweet over and over eat <present continuous> is (*specific inference evidential)*

'Phuntsok's teeth are rotten and his teeth are also rotten. Youngling school kids are always eating sweets'.

---

information for the child about the warrants for inferences, as well as helping to fix the meaning of the different indirect evidentials. These dialogues thus draw attention to the particular felicity conditions for specific indirect evidentials versus direct evidentials.

Attention to these pedagogical strategies and to the role of this kind of conversation, in which the contrast in use is apparent, provides further evidence that adults not only understand the felicity conditions of these evidentials but may also be sensitive to the need for justification/ clarification of their use with small children. This suggests that the use of these evidentials is not determined purely by processes internal to the language module, but is sensitive to explicitly represented information and skills, information and skills that parents transmit to their children through discourse. It may even be that this kind of explicit transmission in natural discourse facilitates the development of inferential ability and understanding in children who speak languages incorporating these evidentials. It will be informative to compare these conversations with uses of say, epistemic modals in English mother-child conversations, though we stress that these are not the same category. Does the use of say, epistemic 'must' occasion similar statements about the grounds for using a strong assertion marker?

7. Development of Narrative Competence in Tibetan and English

Slobin (1991) drew attention to the influence of different linguistic resources in story telling, a process he calls 'learning to think for speaking'. We have some preliminary evidence about narrative competence in young Tibetan speakers, collected from 20 children aged four to nine years. Our interest was motivated by the comparative properties of the two languages with respect to epistemic language. English speaking children have available propositional attitude verbs to describe the epistemic states of characters in a story, as do Tibetan speaking children. But Tibetan speaking children also have a rich evidential system: how does this influence the stories they tell?

The stories we have collected from young speakers of Tibetan and English reveal some parallel developments. Both groups begin with behavioural, event descriptions and gradually with age, incorporate descriptions of the characters' motives, desires, beliefs and knowledge. That is, both groups move from a landscape of action to a landscape of consciousness (Bruner, 1986), and at a similar age. Both groups were tested on picture sequences depicting wordless narratives from the field testing of the DELV language assessment instrument (Seymour et al., 2003). Children are told to look at the sequence of pictures in turn, then to start at the beginning and tell the examiner the story. The stories are depictions of unseen displacement Theory of Mind stories, complete with a final picture in which the deceived protagonist looks in the wrong place for an object that has been moved. After that, the examiner points to the penultimate picture and asks the child to describe what is happening in the picture, which shows a character with a thought balloon entering a room to retrieve an object.

If the child fails to mention the mental state at all, no points are given. One point is given if the characters' motive or desire is mentioned, and two if a thought or cognitive state is attributed. The last question is about why a character is looking in the wrong place for an object. Zero points are given if there is no appropriate explanation, one point is given for a motivational explanation (e.g. for why the character is looking), and two points for a Theory of Mind explanation for why the character is looking in the wrong place (e.g. 'because that's where he left it' or 'he doesn't know it was moved').

If we consider only those answers, the developmental paths look quite similar despite a massive difference between the Tibetan and American English speakers in language, education and culture. Figure 2 shows the composite graph, and there are no statistical differences between the Tibetans and a very large normative sample of American English speakers (719 children aged 4 to 9 years).

There is nothing in these data so far that would suggest that the obligatory attention to knowledge states required by evidentials has an impact on third party narrative description. Papafragou et al.

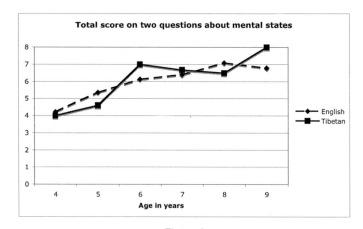

Figure 2

Competence with mental state descriptions in English
and Tibetan in third person narratives

(2007) and Aksu-Koç *et al.* (2005) studying evidentials in Korean and Turkish, and our data on Tibetan (de Villiers *et al.*, 2005), show similarly negative results about the impact of speaking an evidential language on passing elementary Theory of Mind tasks.

8. Third party vs First person Narrative and the Significance of the Narrative Self

Consider, however, the potential impact of evidentiality on first person narrative. If a personal narrative is the basis for a coherent self, what might be the implications of speaking a language that demands attention to sources of knowledge?

Chandler and Lalonde have done pioneering research on how children and adolescents understand their self-continuity, that is, that there is something constant over time in their personhood (Chandler *et al.*, 2003). This is a central aspect of self-knowledge, the recognition that the self has a passage through time, a past, a present and a future. Chandler has asked children and adolescents, 'How do you know that you are the same (boy/girl) that you were when you were 5?'. American children begin by answering this question in terms of physical continuity: 'See this scar? I got it when fell off my bike', or 'I have this birthmark'. But older children, and adolescents, reject physical evidence and adopt one of two general strategies for dealing with the conflicting facts of persistence and change in one's self.

One strategy is 'Essentialist', of varying degrees of sophistication, locating some enduring property of self that is present despite apparent change, for example of character, or values, or attitudes. A second strategy is 'Narrative', which varies in sophistication from a recounting of the time line of simple life events, to a coherent story that makes a causally sensible and believable autobiography. Interestingly these two strategies are quite differently represented in the white mainstream youth that they interview compared with Inuit youth in Canada. Mainstream youth prefer Essentialist accounts of persistence, while Inuit youth prefer Narrative accounts (Chandler *et al.*, 2004).

Chandler and Ball (1990) have a powerful story to tell about those Inuit youth who are in mental health clinics as suicide risks. Inuit youth have the highest suicide rate in the world, and the causes are most likely the centuries of neglect and destruction of their land, their culture and their hopes. In interviews with these youth the researchers find evidence of a disproportionate disintegration of the idea of a persistent self, a lack of a sense of a past mental continuity, a lack of self-coherence. The research suggests that there is a developmental process of working through transitional stages in maturing ideas of self-continuity, and the risks are high when a youth is stranded between rejecting old conceptions and not yet able to mobilize new warrants for self-continuity. The consequences of this are disturbing: a youth with no coherent past, has no coherent future. As they put it,

> ... for most of us, most of the time, there is a 'rub' — some future possibility that death would put an end to, or some future prospect that we are not prepared to forego. For these reasons, then, adolescents, for whom transformations of identity often come thick and fast, are, we propose, at special risk of at least temporarily losing the continuity preserving thread that guarantees them a sufficient personal stake in the future, a stake capable of insulating them against self-harm (p. 32).

Chandler and Lalonde attribute the staggeringly high suicide rate among Inuit youth to this breakdown. Many historical, political and social factors have created the disastrous climate for Inuit young people, as for aboriginal people around the world in varying ways, but the proximate cause of suicide is argued to be the disintegration of the personal narrative of self-continuity.

In this paper we have pointed to the linguistic demands of Tibetan for attention to the sources of our knowledge. A speaker must attend to whether she saw or inferred, whether the information was private or public, and whether the basis of the inference was specific sensory clues or more general knowledge. These demands do not imply that third person narratives should be different, but what of first person narration? What are the consequences for the inner story of the self? If narrative consciousness is couched in terms of language, that is, it is construed as personal story told, updated, rehearsed and revised that takes place under conscious reflection, then it should reflect at least partially the linguistic sophistication in oral narrative that people can tell. It may be less linguistically sophisticated, in that the audience is the self, so skills such as reference specification, care with pronoun use and so forth become irrelevant. It may be more conceptually sophisticated, given that the release from these audience demands may allow complexity elsewhere, perhaps in the chains of reasoning or recursion. To the extent that it is expressed orally, it should reflect the style, vocabulary and grammar of any other narrative from the individual.

However, in a language like Tibetan with evidentials, a story of the self would have to contain different varieties of evidentials than a story about other persons. The child learning Tibetan has enhanced opportunities to hear adults justify their expressed knowledge by marking its source, richly extending the kinds of data available for a complex self-narrative. A comparative exploration of the self-narratives of Tibetan and English children may be very revealing about the different paths to a continuous and persistent self, made possible by different cultural and linguistic experiences. To date, relation between the structure and development of first-person narratives and the acquisition of evidentiality in languages containing evidentials has not been studied. There is evidence that at least some Inuit languages represent evidentiality (Bybee *et al.*, 1994) and the detailed study of the acquisition of this aspect of the grammar of these languages might generate interesting insights into the development of narrative self-consciousness in these cultures.

9. Conclusion

The grammatical marking of evidentiality hence gives us a revealing window into the developmental processes in middle childhood that subserve the achievement of narrative competence. First, evidentiality enables us to study the development of an understanding of inference, and of the ability to mobilize this understanding in the construction of human narratives. Second, it allows us to examine the role that parent-child discourse plays in clarifying the contrastive uses of sources of knowledge. Finally, it permits us to investigate the difference between first person and third person narratives, and so potentially allows the investigation of the development of a distinctive sense of oneself as the protagonist in one's own life story. We concur with the importance of the development of narrative skills to the development of a coherent sense of self, and to mental health. There is a dearth of understanding of the processes that enable this development in middle childhood, the very point at which evidentiality is mastered. Further attention to the mastery of evidentiality promises to be revealing for understanding human maturation.

References

Aikhenvald, A. (2004), *Evidentiality* (Oxford: Oxford University Press).

Aksu-Koç, A., Avci, G., Aydin, C., Sefer, N. & Yasa, Y. (2005), *The Relation Between Mental Verbs and ToM Performance: Evidence from Turkish children* (Paper presented at IASCL, Berlin, July).

Astington, J.W. (1993), *The Child's Discovery of Mind* (Cambridge, MA: Harvard University Press).

Bruner, J. (1986), *Actual Minds, Possible Worlds* (Cambridge, MA: Harvard University Press).

Bybee, J.L., Perkins. R.D. & Pagliuca, W. (1994), *Evolution of Grammar: Tense, aspect and modality in the language of the world* (Chicago: University of Chicago Press).

Chandler, M.J. & Ball, L. (1990), 'Continuity and Commitment: A developmental analysis of the identity formation process in suicidal and non-suicidal youth', in H. Bosma & S. Jackson, *Coping and Self-concept in Adolescence* (New York: Springer-Verlag), pp. 149–66.

Chandler, M.J., Lalonde, C.E. & Teucher, U. (2004), 'Culture, Continuity, and the Limits of Narrativity: A comparison of the self-narratives of Native and Non-Native youth', in C. Daiute & C. Lightfoot (ed.), *Narrative Analysis: Studying the development of individuals in society* (Mahwah, NJ: Erlbaum), pp. 245–65.

Chandler, M.J., Lalonde, C.E., Sokol, B.W. & Hallett, D. (2003), 'Personal Persistence, Identity Development, and Suicide: A study of Native and non-Native North American adolescents', *Monographs of the Society for Research in Child Development*, **68** (2), Serial No. 273.

Davis, C., Potts, C. & Speas, M. (2007), 'The Pragmatic Values of Evidential Sentences', to appear in M. Gibson & T. Friedman (ed.), *Proceedings of SALT 17* (Ithaca, NY: CLC Publications).

De Haan, F. (1999), 'Evidentiality and Epistemic Modality: Setting boundaries', *Southwest Journal of Linguistics*, **18**, pp. 83–101.

DeLancey, S. (1986), 'Evidentiality and Volitionality in Tibetan', in W. Chafe & J. Nichols (ed.), *Evidentiality: The Linguistic Encoding of Epistemology* (Norwood NJ: Ablex Publishing Corporation), pp. 203–13.

Denwood, P. (1999), *Tibetan* (London: John Benjamins).

de Villiers, J.G. (2007), 'The Interface of Language and Theory of Mind', *Lingua*, **117**, pp. 1858–78.

de Villiers, J.G., Garfield, J., Speas, P. & Roeper, T. (2005), *Preliminary Studies of the Acquisition of Tibetan Evidentials* (Paper presented at SRCD, Boston, April).

de Villiers, J.G., Garfield, J., Gernet-Girard, H., Roeper, T. & Speas, P. (in press), 'Evidentials in Tibetan: Acquisition, semantics and cognitive development', in T. Matsui & S. Fitneva (ed.), Special Issue.

de Villiers, J.G., Garfield, J. & Topgyal, T. (2008), *The Acquisition of Evidentials in Questions in Tibetan* (Paper presented at UUSLAW, workshop in language acquisition, Smith College, December).

de Villiers, J.G., Garfield, J., Kravitz, M., Norbu, N., Sluyter, C., Speas, M & Topgyal, T. (submitted), *Who Knows What and How? New evidence about the acquisition of evidentials in Tibetan*.

de Villiers, P.A. (2004), 'Assessing Pragmatic Skills in Elicited Production', *Seminars in Speech and Language*, **25**, pp. 57–72.

Dunn, J. & Brophy, M. (2005), 'Communication, Relationships and Individual Differences in Children's Understanding of Mind', in J.W. Astington & J.A. Baird (ed.), *Why Language Matters for Theory of Mind* (Oxford: Oxford University Press).

Engen, E. (1994), 'English Language Acquisition in Deaf Children in Programs using Manually-coded English', in A. Vonen, K. Arnesen, R. Enerstvedt & A. Nafstad (ed.), *Bilingualism and Literacy: Proceedings of an international workshop* (Oslo, Norway: Skadalan Publications).

Gernet-Girard, H. (2008), *Evidentials and Inference in Tibetan* (Undergraduate thesis, Northampton, Massachusetts: Smith College).

Garrett, E. (2001), *Evidentiality and Assertion in Tibetan* (PhD dissertation, UCLA).

Hardman, M.J. (1986), 'Data-source Marking in the Jaqi Languages', in W. Chafe & J. Nichols (ed.), *Evidentiality: The linguistic encoding of epistemology* (Norwood NJ: Ablex Publishing Corporation), pp. 113–36.

Harris, P. (2005), 'Conversation, Pretense, and Theory of Mind', in J.W. Astington & J.A. Baird (ed.) *Why Language Matters for Theory of Mind* (Oxford: Oxford University Press).

Hollebrandse, B., Hobbs, K., de Villiers, J.G. & Roeper, T. (in press), 'Second Order Embedding and Second Order False Belief', in *Proceedings of GALA, Barcelona 2007*.

Hutto, D.D. (2007), *Folk Psychological Narratives: The social basis of understanding reasons* (Cambridge, MA: MIT Press).

Labov, W. (1972), *Language in the Inner City: Studies of Black English vernacular* (Philadelphia, PA: University of Pennsylvania Press).

Labov, W. & Waletsky, J. (1967), 'Narrative Analysis: Oral versions of personal experience', in J. Helms (ed.), *Essays on the verbal and visual arts* (Seattle, WA: University of Washington Press).

Lazard, G. (2001), 'On the Grammaticalization of Evidentiality', *Journal of Pragmatics*, **33**, pp. 359–67.

Marr, D. (1968), *Vision: A Computational Investigation into the Human Representation and Processing of Visual Information* (San Francisco: W.H. Freeman and Co.).

Nozaki, A. & Anno, M. (1993), *Anno's Hat Tricks* (New York: Philomel books).

Onishi, K.H. & Baillargeon, R. (2005), 'Do 15-month-old Infants Understand False Beliefs?', *Science*, **308**, pp. 255–8.

Oswalt, R. (1986), 'The Evidential System of Kashaya', in W. Chafe & J. Nichols (ed.), *Evidentiality: The linguistic encoding of epistemology* (Norwood, NJ: Ablex Publishing Corporation), pp. 29–45.

Papafragou, A., Li, P., Choi, Y. & Han, C-H. (2007), 'Evidentiality in Language and Cognition', *Cognition*, **13**, pp 253–99.

Perera, K. (1986), 'Language Acquisition and Writing', in P. Fletcher & M. Garman (ed.), *Language Acquisition* (Second edition) (Cambridge, UK: Cambridge University Press).

Perner, J., Sprung, M., Zauner, P. & Haider, H. (2003), 'Want that is Understood well before Say That, Think That, and False Belief: A test of de Villiers' linguistic determinism on German-speaking children', *Child Development*, **74**, pp. 179–88.

Plungian, V.A. (2001), 'The Place of Evidentiality within the Universal Grammatical Space', *Journal of Pragmatics*, **33**, pp. 349–57.

Recanati, F. (2002), 'Does Linguistic Communication Rest on Inference?', *Mind & Language*, **17** (1/2), pp. 105–26.

Reid, T. (1970), *An Inquiry into the Human Mind* (Chicago: University of Chicago Press).

Seymour, H.N., Roeper, T. & de Villiers, J.G. (2003), DELV-CR (Diagnostic Evaluation of Language Variation-Criterion Referenced), (San Antonio TX: The Psychological Corporation).

Slobin, D.I. (1991), 'Learning to Think for Speaking: Native language, cognition, and rhetorical style', *Pragmatics*, **1**, pp. 7–26.

Snow, C. (1991), 'The Theoretical Basis for Relationships between Language and Literacy Development', *Journal of Research in Childhood Education*, **11**, pp. 443–65.

Snow, C., Tabors, P., Nicholson, P. & Kurland, B. (1995), 'SHELL: Oral language and early literacy skills in kindergarten and first grade', *Journal of Research in Childhood Education*, **10**, pp. 37–48.

Sophian, C. (1988), 'Early Developments in Children's Understanding of Number: Inferences about numerosity and one-to-one correspondence', *Child Development*, **59**, pp. 1397–414.

Sophian, C., Wood, A.M. & Vong, K.I. (1995), 'Making Numbers Count: The early development of numerical inferences', *Developmental Psychology*, **31** (2), pp. 263–73.

Southgate, V., Senju, A. & Csibra, G. (2007), 'Action Anticipation though Attribution of False Belief by 2-Year-Olds', *Psychological Science*, **18**, pp. 587–92.

Sperber, D. (1995), 'How do we Communicate?', in J. Brockman & K. Matson (ed.), *How Things Are: A science toolkit for the mind* (New York: Morrow).

Sperber, D. & Wilson, D. (1986), *Relevance: Communication and cognition* (Oxford: Blackwell).

Sullivan, K., Zaitchik, D. & Tager-Flusberg, H. (1994), 'Preschoolers can Attribute Second-order Beliefs', *Developmental Psychology*, **30**, pp. 395–402.

Tomasello, M. & Rakoczy, H. (2003), 'What makes Human Cognition Unique? From individual to shared to collective intentionality', *Mind and Language*, **18**, pp. 121–47.

Tversky, A. & Kahneman, D. (1981), 'The Framing of Decisions and the Psychology of Choice', *Science*, **211**, pp. 453–8.

Wason, P.C. (1960), 'On the Failure to Eliminate Hypotheses in a Conceptual Task', *Quarterly Journal of Experimental Psychology*, **12**, pp. 129–40.

Wellman, H.M. (1990), *The Child's Theory of Mind* (Cambridge, MA: MIT Press).

Jonathan D. Hill

'Hearing is Believing'

Amazonian Trickster Myths as
Folk Psychological Narratives

Abstract: This essay explores cultural and psychological dynamics in indigenous Amazonian narratives about a powerful trickster figure named Made-from-Bone. Particular attention is given to the ways in which speaking verbs, quoted speeches, and dialogical interactions are used as psychological tools for understanding and explaining others' inner thoughts and emotions. Comparative analysis of two narratives set in the distant mythical past demonstrates how intentionality is a semiotic ideology that emerges through dialogical interaction. These narrative practices are deeply rooted in shamanic healing practices, especially the use of musical and other symbolic sound elements as a privileged sense modality for expressing and experiencing psychological processes of making dreams, emotions, and inner thoughts into objects of conscious thought and discourse.

> Signifyin(g) turns on the play and chain of signifiers, and not on some supposedly transcendent signified. As anthropologists demonstrate, the Signifying Monkey is often called the Signifier, he who wreaks havoc upon the Signified. One is signified upon by the signifier (Henry Louis Gates, Jr., 1988, pp. 52–3).

Introduction

This essay will focus on narratives about a mythic trickster figure as expressions of a non-Western, indigenous Amazonian folk psychology (FP), or 'everyday practices of making sense of intentional actions (i.e., our own and those of others) in terms of reasons' (Hutto, 2009). Building upon my ongoing ethnographic research with the Arawak-speaking Wakuénai (or Curripaco) of southernmost Venezuela (Hill, 1993; 2009), I will provide an in-depth analysis of culturally specific dimensions of narrative FP practices and show how these are related to shamanic ritual performances. At the same time, I will be equally concerned with revealing the trans-cultural significance of the central character of Wakuénai mythic narratives, a trickster-creator known locally as 'Made-from-Bone'. In particular, I will explore the narratives about this mythic character as a semiotic process of creating reflexive, interpretive distancing through opening up and playing upon the gap between literal-semantic and critical-semiotic levels of interpretation (Eco, 1990, p. 54).[1] As stories about an omniscient character who always knows others' thoughts in advance, narratives about Made-from-Bone give us rich insight into indigenous Amazonian notions of psychological depth at the same time as they provide indigenous people with conceptual tools for making sense of beliefs, desires, hopes, and intentions.[2]

Mythic tricksters such as Made-from-Bone are intrinsically interesting figures for psychologists (see Jung, 1956/1972 on Winnebago trickster myths) as well as for cognitive scientists interested in broadening the cultural reach of Folk Psychology studies (Scalise Sugiyama, 2003; Lillard, 1997). The particular ways in which desire, fear, reason, belief, doubt, premeditation, and other mental states are verbally depicted in mythic narratives about Made-from-Bone shed light on how language — especially speaking verbs, dialogical interaction, and quoted speech — are used as conceptual tools for understanding and explaining the thoughts and emotions of the self and other sentient beings. One of the most prominent features of these narratives is their reliance on quoted speech, dialogues, and conversations as vehicles for storytelling. To a certain extent, the narratives are built around the verb 'to say' or other speaking verbs: 'she asked them', 'they told her', 'he said to her', 'tell them', 'she said to them', 'they said', 'I will say to her', and so forth.[3] The prevalence of speaking verbs as building blocks for mythic narratives is found elsewhere

---

[1]   In a previous essay (Hill, 2002), I argued that Amazonian and West African mythic tricksters illustrate Eco's concept of general semiosic competence, 'which permits one to interpret verbal and visual signs, and to draw inferences from them, by merging the information they give with background knowledge' (1990, p. 204).

[2]   See Hutto (2008) for a more complete theoretical account of the role of public narrations and the origins of folk psychological abilities.

[3]   It is clear that the use of speaking verbs and quoted speech in Wakuénai narratives is related to the more general issues of evidentiality and inferential reasoning (see de Villiers

in the Americas (see, e.g., Navajo coyote stories in Webster, 2004), and in some of the Quechua-speaking oral cultures of the Andean highlands the verb 'say' acts as a root for mental state terms. 'For example, they [Junín Quechua] use phrases that roughly translate as *What would he say?* For *What would he think?* and *Say no* for *deny*' (Vinden, 1996, p. 1708).[4] The narratives about Made-from-Bone are called 'Words from the primordial times' (*yákuti úupi pérri*), and narrators mark them as different from everyday speech by opening with a phrase that means 'They say that' or 'It is said that'.[5]

Dialogues, quoted speech, and doubly quoted speech peppered with verbs of speaking are the stuff making up roughly half of Wakuénai narrative discourse. Although I have not made a precise quantitative study of the exact percentages of dialogues and quoted speech in the entire corpus of Wakuénai mythic narratives, the numerical figures for the two narratives given detailed treatment in this essay are 50 per cent for 'The Origin of Made-from-Bone' and 47 per cent for 'Made-from-Bone Creates Evil Omens'. Researchers working in other regions of Amazonia have discovered comparable or even higher figures. In an essay on 'Quoted Dialogues in Kalapalo Narrative Discourse', for example, Ellen Basso found that quoted speech 'constitutes as much as eighty percent or even more of a text' and that it 'is clearly the most important way of developing characters and of giving meaning to their activities, because quoted speech constructs socially dynamic differences in the characters' attitudes towards one another's action' (1986, p. 122).

In the following pages, I will explore some of the ways in which such quoted speeches serve as 'reflectors', or 'centers of consciousness through whom [or which] situations and events told about by a heterodiegetic or third-person narrator are refracted' (Herman, 2007, p. 245). The analysis of mythic narratives will follow Duranti's early call for 'a theory of mind that systematically links intrapsychological processes to interpsychological ones' (1988, p. 30) and for the relevance of Vygotsky's socio-historical approach to cognition in which language is defined as 'a *psychological tool*, that is, an object that

---

and Garfield, 2009). However, Wakuénai (or Curripaco) and other Northern Arawakan languages do not have grammatical evidentials like the neighbouring Eastern Tukanoan languages of the Vaupés basin (Aikhenvald & Dixon, 2003; Barnes, 1984; Malone, 1988; Miller, 1999; Morse & Maxwell, 1999).

[4] Itzaj, a Lowland Mayan language spoken in the Lake Peten region of Guatemala, also allows a speech verb (*t'an*) to refer to thought (Andrew Hofling, personal communication).

[5] Reportative markers, or enclitics, are common throughout the Americas as a way of establishing that a narrative discourse belongs to a special genre.

mediates either interpsychologically (between actors) or intra-psychologically (within the same person)' (1988, p. 31). As a general rule, the extensive use of quoted speech serves as the vehicle for expressing thoughts and emotions, usually in the context of second-person dialogues, or direct discourse, within narratives.[6] In one exceptional case, the thinking of Made-from-Bone's nemesis is revealed through first-person thinking aloud, or 'thoughts' (statements) about future 'thoughts' (statements).[7] All these quoted speeches, dialogues, and thoughts stand in sharp contrast with other critically important passages that contain third-person descriptions of situations and events. Exploring the dynamic tensions between these third-person episodes in which quoted speeches and speaking verbs are either entirely absent or at most minimally present and the lengthy passages of quoted speeches and dialogues will serve as a key method for understanding these mythic discourses as Folk Psychological narratives.

Sociocultural, Historical and Mythic Contexts

Before going into a detailed study of Made-from-Bone's exploits in two mythic narratives, it is important to establish the broader contexts in which this mythic trickster has flourished. The Wakuénai of south-ernmost Venezuela (also known as 'Curripaco' in Venezuela and Colombia and 'Baniwa' in Brazil) are the largest remaining speech community of the Northern, or Maipuran, branch of the Arawak language family (Hill & Santos-Granero, 2002). The Wakuénai organize themselves into internally ranked phratries occupying a set of riverine territories at the headwaters of the Negro, Isana, and Guainía rivers in Venezuela, Colombia, and Brazil (see Figure 1). They subsist mainly on fishing and swidden cultivation of bitter manioc and other crops. Hunting game animals and gathering edible wild plants in the region's

[6] Linguistic anthropologists (Duranti, 1984; 1988; 1993; 2008; Keane, 2008; Schiefflin, 2008) have used ethnographic studies of speaking to critique speech act theory (SAT) for its rationalist, ethnocentric assumption that speaker's intentions, or 'meanings', are logi-cally prior to interaction and context. 'It is often implied that meaning is already fully defined BEFORE the act of speaking' (Duranti, 1984, p. 1). My analysis of Amazonian mythic narratives diverges from the SAT model of intentionality and embraces instead a more interactivist and intersubjectivist approach to intentionality as a semiotic ideology that emerges in the process of dialogical interaction.

[7] This case is truly exceptional, as it is the only place in the entire corpus of mythic narra-tives where first-person thinking aloud occurs. There are numerous places in the narra-tives where characters reveal their thoughts and feelings in first-person dialogues with other characters, but this episode in 'The Origin of Made-from-Bone' is the only occasion in which a person speaks in first-person to himself (rather than to another character) about what he is planning to say in an imagined future context.

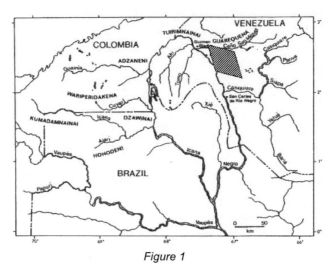

Figure 1

Area of Field Research indicated by hatched region

forests provide important supplementary sources of food. The Upper
Rio Negro region is an acidic, blackwater tropical rain forest ecosys-
tem with very low animal biomass and sandy, nutrient-poor soils
(Herrera *et al.*, 1978). Levels of fishing and hunting productivity are
modest even during the relative abundance of the so-called 'dry' sea-
son months (December through March), but these levels fall almost to
zero during long wet seasons (April through August) when rivers rise
7 metres and 65% of surrounding forests become flooded, allowing
fish and aquatic animals to disperse over an immense area.[8]

The Wakuénai living in the Upper Rio Negro region today are sur-
vivors of a long history of predatory political-economic expansions
across Lowland South America, first by competing European colonial
powers in search of indigenous slave labourers and religious converts,
and more recently by indebted national states during the forced labour
campaigns of the Rubber Boom (ca. 1860–1920) (Taussig, 1987;
Stanfield, 1998; Hill, 1999). The omniscience and omnipotence of

---

[8]   From an adaptationist perspective, Made-from-Bone signifies an original state of undif-
      ferentiated animal-humanness, or a 'natural-social' mode of ecological orientation (Hill,
      1984). Made-from-Bone is strongly associated with ceremonial exchanges of surplus
      foods between communities in times of relative abundance, egalitarian social relations
      between men and women and kin and affines, and the expansion of intercommunal or
      interethnic ties of trade, intermarriage, and alliance (Hill, 1989).

Made-from-Bone continue to play an important role in local ways of interpreting and engaging with the contemporary world (Hill, 2009, Ch. 7). From the beginning of primordial mythic times, Made-from-Bone has embodied the shamanic human ability to escape from death and loss, and to return to life and abundance. Perhaps not surprisingly, Made-from-Bone has become a ready-made cultural tool for navigating centuries of historical struggle by allowing the Wakuénai to create new interpretive and political spaces in contexts of traumatic changes driven by macro-scale forces.[9]

The mythic figure of Trickster-Creator in Wakuénai society bears striking resemblance to the West African-derived myths about *Esu*, or the 'signifying monkey' (Gates, 1988). 'Monkey speaks figuratively, while the Lion reads his discourse literally. For his act of misinterpretation, he suffers grave consequences. This valorization of the figurative is perhaps the most important moral of these poems, although the Monkey's mastery of figuration has made him one of the canonical heroes in the Afro-American mythic tradition' (Gates, 1988, p. 85). Gates' pathbreaking study demonstrates how Trickster's privileging of the tropes forms the cornerstone of an African-American theory of language use that informs not only a variety of overtly literary oral and written genres but also many varieties of speech in everyday social life. 'Signifyin(g) ... is the figurative difference between the literal and the metaphorical, between surface and latent meaning' (Gates, 1988, p. 82).

Defined as a general process of creating reflexive, interpretive distancing through opening up and playing upon the gap between literal-semantic and critical-semiotic levels of interpretation, mythic tricksters encompass a nearly incomprehensible diversity of specific qualities and manifestations. In Gates's words,

> A partial list of these qualities might include individuality, satire, parody, irony, magic, indeterminacy, open-endedness, ambiguity, sexuality, chance, uncertainty, disruption and reconciliation, betrayal and loyalty, closure and disclosure, encasement and rupture. But it is a mistake to focus on one of these qualities as predominant. Esu possesses all

---

[9] For extensive examples of this indigenous process of historical interpretation, creativity, and resilience in Northwestern Amazonia as well as other regions of South America, see Guss (1986), Hill & Wright (1988), Basso (1995), Staats (1996), Santos-Granero (1998), Whitten (1976; 1985), Whitten & Whitten (1988; 2008) and Hill (2009, ch. 4). Comparative examples of mythic histories from Andean and Amazonian societies across South America are explored in *Rethinking History and Myth* (Hill, ed., 1988). Studies of powerful African-derived trickster figures in the Afro-Atlantic diaspora include Henry Louis Gates Jr.'s *The Signifying Monkey* (1988), Richard and Sally Price's *Two Evenings in Saramaka* (1991), and John Roberts's *From Trickster to Badman* (1989).

of these characteristics, plus a plethora of others which, taken together, only begin to present an idea of the complexity of this classic figure of mediation and of the unity of opposed forces (1988, p. 6).

In keeping with Gates's warning, I do not attempt to pin down the Wakuénai mythic trickster, or Made-from-Bone, to any single quality but instead explore several key dimensions of trickster's abilities to interpret, manipulate, and create meanings as a practical activity of strategic social interaction.

Mythic tricksters are found in other regions of Amazonia, such as the Upper Xingu, where there are strong parallels between the Kalapalo trickster figures in whom 'deception and language go together' (Basso, 1987, p. 9) and Made-from-Bone's uses of verbal and other misrepresentations to deceive others. What sets Made-from-Bone apart from other Amazonian trickster figures is the extent to which these powers of deception are integrated into a single, omniscient, and omnipotent character whose presence continues across the entire span of the three periods of mythic space-time.

These three periods can be summarized as follows. In 'The Primordial Times' (*úupi pérri*), Made-from-Bone struggles against a series of adversaries who attempt without success to kill him by various means (burning, drowning, poisoning, hanging, shooting, etc.). The primordial times are the period of Made-from-Bone *par excellence*, since almost everything that happens revolves around Made-from-Bone and his interactions with a series of potentially lethal enemies. This is also an undifferentiated space-time when there are still no clear boundaries between humans and animals, men and women, day and night, here and there. The period begins with Made-from-Bone's demonstrations that he is always able to escape his enemies' plots ('Nobody can kill us') and ends with a complete, triumphant victory over his enemies ('I have finished off all of them').

A second period is called 'The World Begins' (*Hekuápi Ikéeñu-akawa*) and explains how Made-from-Bone created night, cooking fire, ceremonial dance-music, and other important features of the natural and social worlds by obtaining them from various mythic owners. These narratives are less about life-and-death struggles between mortal enemies than the solving of riddles or puzzles in which Made-from-Bone must outsmart his interlocutors in order to take away their goods.

The third and final period of mythic space-time is called 'The World Opens Up' (*Hekuápi* [h]*liméetakawa*) and describes the complex creations of the world set in motion by the powerful musical sounds of the primordial human being and his later transformation into a set of

sacred flutes and trumpets. Although not as central to the sequence of
events in these creation myths, Made-from-Bone continues to display
the same powers of omniscience and invincibility that he had wielded
since his creation in primordial times and that had become the basis of
his fame in the period of 'The World Begins'.

The two narratives that I have selected for detailed treatment in this
essay come from the first period of mythic space-time, or The Primordial Times. By focussing on the first and last narratives in this period,
the analysis will show how Made-from-Bone journeys from an initial
situation in which he had to struggle just to survive, to a final one in
which he has defeated all enemies. This transformation from being a
target of others' actions to a master-signifier in complete control of his
own and others' thoughts, emotions, and actions is crucial to understanding the dynamics of the narratives set in The Primordial Times.
Made-from-Bone's transition from 'intelligent responder' to 'omniscient initiator' provides the narrative embodiment of shamanic
empowerment, which is enacted in healing rituals through music,
dance, actions and objects.[10] From being the target of lethal plots and
schemes against him and his family, Made-from-Bone emerges as a
master of semiotic warfare who is able to terrorize and destroy his
opponents. Those who set out to trap, hunt, or kill Made-from-Bone
become the hunted who must perish, traitors 'hoisted by their own
petards'.

'Nobody can Kill us'
The Origin of Made-from-Bone

The primordial times are explored in a cycle of narratives that focuses
on the invincibility of Made-from-Bone (*Iñápirríkuli*). Although
these narratives are set in the distant past before there are culturally
differentiated kinds of beings, what *is* present from the very beginning
of primordial times is an irreducible principle of violence, deceit, and
hostility between kin and affines. The story of how Made-From-Bone
originally came into being starts with an act of violence in which a
woman's husband kills her brother. Specifically, an evil animal-
person whose name means 'Great Sickness' (*Kunáhwerrim*), murders
his wife's brother. The woman saves the bones of her slain brother's

[10] The present essay is primarily focussed on mythic narratives about Made-from-Bone
rather than ritual enactments of shamanic power through music, dance, and related activities. I will provide a brief overview of shamanic ritual practices near the end of this essay
as part of the analysis of the narratives. For more complete ethnographic documentation
and analysis of shamanic healing rituals, see Hill (1992; and forthcoming).

outer fingers, which then transform into two Cricket-Brothers (the older of whom is Made-from-Bone).

> *Great Sickness had a wife. That woman had a brother. Great Sickness killed his wife's brother. They gathered the bones. The wife of Great Sickness gathered the bones of her dead brother. She kept them in a hollow gourd and tied the top shut. She never left the gourd. Great Sickness said, 'Why is it that she never leaves this gourd? Some day in the future she will leave it'.*
>
> *One day the woman left for her manioc garden. Great Sickness went to look for her, but he could see no sign of the gourd. They say that one day the woman said, 'I am going for a few minutes to my manioc garden', and she left her house in a hurry. They say that she forgot her gourd. She left, arrived at her garden, and immediately began searching for her gourd. Then she said, 'Now I am in trouble, for I have left my gourd behind. Now it is certain that they will kill the bones of my family'.*
>
> *Then Great Sickness said, 'I'm going to see if she has left her gourd'. When he went to look, there was the gourd. 'Yes, now it is so. I am going to find out what it is that she has been hiding inside the gourd'.*
>
> *When Great Sickness opened the gourd to look inside, he saw two Cricket-Brothers. 'Tse', he said, 'Now I will kill them'. He took them out of the gourd and threw them violently against the ground. He stepped on them and broke their stomachs, broke their stomachs until their guts came outside them. He picked them up and threw them on the trash heap.*

In his earliest form as a cricket, Made-from-Bone already possesses the invincibility for which he was to become famous through a prolonged series of struggles against his arch adversary, Great Sickness, and a variety of other dangerous animal-spirits: a poison-bearing Owl-Monkey, a lecherous Anaconda-Person, bloodthirsty Bat-People, dangerous Fish-Spirits, and carrion-eating Vulture-People. In the opening story, Made-from-Bone and his brother sew up each other's bodies and decide to tell their aunt that they are alive so that she will stop crying.

> *Then one of the boys said, 'Let's go to warn our aunt that we are fine and that she does not need to continue crying'.*
>
> *'Okay', said his brother, and he went and climbed on his aunt's shoulder and pinched her. The woman stopped crying and turned to see the boy. 'You don't need to cry any longer; we are alive and well', he told her. The woman did not cry any longer; she was happy and resumed her work. On the next day, the two Cricket-Brothers already began to turn into people.*

The narrative continues with a series of episodes in which Great Sickness tries in vain to kill the Cricket-Brothers. Made-From-Bone always knows in advance what Great Sickness is planning and manages to escape by transforming into different species of forest animals, insects, or birds. In one short episode, Great Sickness takes Made-from-Bone and his brother fishing and transforms himself into a jaguar-person who comes to kill and eat the boys. However, Made-from-Bone and his brother have already turned themselves into hummingbirds that can catch fish from the safety of a high tree, and they call upon jaguar-ants to protect them from Great Sickness.

The next episode reinforces the theme of trickster's invincibility through self-transformation but adds an important new dimension. Made-from-Bone and his brother not only manage to escape from the trap that Great Sickness has set for them but they also leave behind a sign that is intended to convince Great Sickness that he has truly succeeded in killing them.

> 'How did it go?' the boys' aunt asked. They told her about everything that had happened. Great Sickness had cleared a large area of forest for a new manioc garden. 'Tell them that they must accompany me while I burn the clearing', he said to the woman.

> 'Okay', she replied. Later she told her nephews, 'Go with him to burn the new garden, but be careful not to let him burn you'.

> 'No', they said to her, 'don't even think about him killing us'.

> 'Okay', she said, 'Go with him'.

This episode, in which Great Sickness tries to murder Made-from-Bone and his brother by burning them alive in a newly felled manioc garden, thus begins as a series of second-person dialogues between the boys' aunt and Great Sickness and between her and the boys. Only a single sentence (Great Sickness had cleared a large area of forest for a new manioc garden) is narrated in the third person to establish the situation. The rest of the passage consists entirely of quoted speeches (question, answer, command, affirmation, warning, denial and agreement) that are connected by speaking verbs: 'asked', 'told', 'said', and 'replied'.

However, in the continuation of the story of the origin of Made-From-Bone, the next paragraph contains only two short quotations – a command by Great Sickness to the boys and their affirmative response — followed by a lengthy third-person description of how the boys transform themselves into leaf-cutter ants and escape from the burning garden by going underground. Before leaving the garden, the boys also spit into their wooden whistles and throw them on the ground so that Great Sickness will be tricked into believing that their bodies have exploded when the fire consumes the two whistles.

Already they went and arrived there at the new garden. Great Sickness made whistles out of yagrumo (Cecropia Sp.) for the boys and said, 'You two are going to dance for me in the middle of the clearing'.

'Okay', the boys replied, 'Light the fire while the two of us are dancing'. Great Sickness lit the fire and went rapidly around the edge of the garden until he had made a complete circle of fire. He looked at the two boys and saw that there was no way for them to escape. The boys remained in the middle of the garden and danced: 'Hee, hee, hee [sound of their whistles]'. The fire came close to where they were dancing. 'Let's go', they said, before spitting into their whistles and throwing them on the ground. Already they left. They went under the ground and came up in the forest outside the garden. And that is the origin of leaf-cutter ants that we see today.

At the end of this largely descriptive paragraph, the narrator returns to a complex set of quotations as Great Sickness thinks out loud and rehearses how he will explain the boys' deaths to their aunt.

Great Sickness saw the fire arriving at the place where the boys were dancing. 'Now it is certain that they are burning up. I will return home and tell their aunt, "I warned them, but they did not listen to me". That's what I'll tell her. "That is how they burned", I will say to her'. Great Sickness stood up so that he could see the fire. 'They are burning up. Now their guts are going to explode'. Just then one of them broke open, and he heard 'Too!' 'Now it is certain. His guts already broke open; one more to go'. After a minute he heard again, 'Too'. That was all. 'Now I will return'.

What is interesting in this paragraph is the way quoted speech itself is made into an object of reflection through embedding quotations within quotations. The effect of this doubly quoted speaking is to take us more deeply into the consciousness of Great Sickness and to give us a vicarious perspective on his innermost thoughts and feelings.[11] When we read 'That's what I'll tell her', we can understand just how badly Great Sickness wants to kill the two Cricket-Brothers. Their deaths are already a *fait accompli* in his mind, and it is only a matter of putting a good spin on events so that his wife, or the boys' aunt, will quit asking him all those annoying questions. The sound of the whistles popping open in the fire only strengthens his belief that the boys have indeed perished in the flames. But the sounds — 'Too', 'Too' —

---

[11] Writing about avoidances of statements about other people's inner thoughts (called the 'opacity claim', or the claim that it is impossible to know what is in the minds of other people) in Melanesia, Keane identifies an '"inner theatre", in which the self is divided into a speaker and an addressee' (2008, p. 475) as an important local trope for the 'hidden interior'. 'Thus my own thoughts in this inner theatre are portrayed as so many words in an introjected social interaction in which I play two parts' (Keane, 2008, p. 475).

also heighten the ironic humour of the story, since we already know that the two boys have escaped to safety outside the burning garden.

Through first-person quoted and doubly quoted speech-thoughts in this episode, Great Sickness becomes a reflector whose consciousness refracts — or openly contradicts — the situation and events that had been related in the previous passage. It is interesting that speaking verbs are used not only in the quoted speech-thoughts but even in the doubly quoted speech-thoughts in which Great Sickness is contemplating what he will say to the boys' aunt: 'I will return home and *tell* their aunt, "I *warned* them, but they did *not listen* to me". That's what I'll *tell* her'. These first-person speech-thoughts demonstrate how speaking verbs are used in local Folk Psychology as cognitive tools for expressing and understanding desire, reason, belief, and premeditation.

'I have Finished Off all of them'
Made-From-Bone Creates Evil Omens

The narrative about evil omens (*hinimái*) forms the last part of a cycle of stories set in the distant, undifferentiated mythic past about Made-from-Bone and his ongoing, violent struggles against a group of animal-affines. As usual, the trickster-creator's brothers-in-law are eager to kill him, but this time they are especially angry because in the penultimate story of the cycle Made-from-Bone had finally succeeded in killing their father, Great Sickness. The brothers send their sister[12] with Made-from-Bone into the forest with instructions to seduce him at night so that they could come and kill him by throwing poison down from the treetops. As always, Made-from-Bone knows in advance exactly what his enemies are saying and thinking about him.

> One day she said, 'Now I want you to take me to see my family'.
>
> 'Okay', he said, 'Let's go'. They left and arrived in her family's village. Made-From-Bone was staying with them.
>
> 'Now we are going to kill him, in revenge of our father', they said. Made-From-Bone knew that they wanted to kill him.
>
> Later Made-From-Bone said: 'Let's return home again'.
>
> 'Okay, let's go', said the woman. Then she said to her family, 'Now we are going away from here'. Made-From-Bone was there, some distance away.

---

[12] This woman is also identified as the wife of Made-from-Bone.

> *'Go with him and sleep at the halfway point of the trail. We are going to kill him', they said to her.*

> *'Okay', she said. And Made-From-Bone and the woman left.*

This short set of quoted dialogues establishes an initial situation in which the brother-in-laws' intention to murder Made-from-Bone is reinforced by their sister's complicity. Against this doubly malicious, incest-tinged plot of seduction and betrayal, Made-from-Bone knows about their scheme and will proceed to turn it against his brothers-in-law and their sister by creating a series of signs, or 'evil omens', that progressively terrify the woman. In this narrative, it is the woman's character, mainly in second-person dialogical interlocutions with Made-from-Bone, who becomes a reflector whose consciousness refracts the situation and events, which consist largely of Made-from-Bone's killing and beheading of the two brothers-in-law.

The first indication of how Made-from-Bone is going to reverse the plot to kill him comes in a relatively lengthy descriptive paragraph that is narrated in third-person, except for one second-person dialogue at the very beginning.

> *'It's already afternoon. Let's sleep here. Tomorrow we can start again', she said.*

> *Made-From-Bone cut down a log and implanted it. 'Hang your hammock', he told her. Made-From-Bone had a blowgun. He cut a plantain leaf and lied down on it. He gathered some kindling that made white ashes. He had many poisoned darts, and his quiver was very full. The woman picked up one of the darts and started to weave with the pointed end. Made-From-Bone stole two of the darts from the quiver; it was still early. The woman did not know that he stole the two darts. He put them inside the blowgun. He lit a fire and lay down next to the flame. His wife lay down in her hammock.*

This passage sets the scene for the middle portion of the narrative, which takes place out in the middle of the forest at night. We learn that Made-from-Bone has hidden two poisoned darts inside the barrel of his blowgun and that the woman is unaware of this important information. A gap has thus begun to open between the woman's consciousness, which is still set squarely upon the knowledge of her brothers' intentions to kill Made-from-Bone during the night as he sleeps, and the actions and events that are beginning to unfold between Made-from-Bone and his two brothers-in-law.

The woman then tries to tempt Made-from-Bone to have sex and sleep with her in her hammock, but Made-from-Bone resists her invitations and puts her into a deep sleep by blowing tobacco smoke over her.

Then she said, 'Made-From-Bone, come here to lie down with me'.

'No, I cannot lie down with you. I am a person who does not lie down in a hammock with a woman', said Made-From-Bone.

'It's alright, lie down. Come and lie down with me', she said, 'come and hold me'.

'No, I am a person who does not like to do this'. Made-From-Bone blew tobacco smoke; he blew smoke over her. She slept like a dead person, like a drunkard.

In this episode we see how the woman's consciousness, or unconsciousness, is becoming increasingly central to the narrative's development. Made-from-Bone uses tobacco smoke like a switch that turns off the woman's consciousness, setting the stage for the events leading to her brothers' deaths, deep in the forest and late at night.[13]

Later Made-From-Bone blew over the fire, and white ashes fell over him. It was getting very close to dawn. He heard them coming, 'to-ro!' 'Here they come, those bastards', he said. Made-From-Bone jumped up and grabbed his blowgun. He went to wait for them, 'to-ro!'.

They arrived above him and took out their poison. 'Here comes blood, Made-From-Bone', they said. He jumped to one side. They began to throw poison again. 'Here comes blood, Made-From-Bone', they said. He leapt to one side.

Made-From-Bone looked and saw dark shapes against the moon. 'For you the blood is coming', he said. Made-From-Bone shot one of them with a dart, 'tsa!'. Again he loaded a dart, 'tsa!'. He shot the other one with a dart. And he went back.

He returned and lit a cigar. He blew smoke over the woman to wake her up. Then Made-From-Bone jumped and lay down next to the fire. He blew over the fire, and white ashes fell on top of him. His wife woke up. Her two brothers fell from the trees to the ground. She heard: 'Ti!', then the other one, 'Ti!'. She tried to wake up Made-From-Bone. 'Made-From-Bone! Made-From-Bone!' He was sound asleep, snoring. 'Made-From-Bone! Made-From-Bone!'.

At this point, the initial gap between the woman's consciousness and the series of events that took place while she was asleep has erupted into a full-blown contradiction. Now Made-from-Bone uses the power of tobacco to return the woman to consciousness even as he pretends to have been sleeping soundly through the night. The loud

---

[13] Tobacco smoke is the most central material symbol of shamanic power in all major rituals. The imagery of the narrative evokes witchcraft, which is believed to happen to people while they are sleeping at night when their dream-souls are attacked by enemy witches.

sounds[14] made by her dead brothers' bodies crashing to the ground frighten the woman, and in the ensuing dialogue with Made-from-Bone we get a first glimpse of the woman's inner emotions and thoughts.

'He, hee', said Made-From-Bone, 'What happened to you?'

'I was frightened by what I heard', she said.

'Paa', said Made-From-Bone, 'I was sleeping like a man dying of old age. Just now I woke up because you woke me. What did you hear?'

'What I heard was frightening. Right here I heard something fall close to us. What I heard falling was heavy. Ti!'[15]

Then she said, 'Made-From-Bone, you didn't kill my two brothers?'

'Not at all. Why would I kill your brothers?' he said.

'Okay. I am going to look at the darts', she said.

'Go ahead and look at them', he said.

The woman counted all the darts. They were all there.

'What you heard was nothing important; let's go to sleep', said Made-From-Bone. She went and lay down again in her hammock. Already she was asleep again. Made-From-Bone lit a cigar and blew tobacco smoke over her.

The middle portion of the narrative concludes with a third-person description of how Made-from-Bone finished off the two monkey-brother witches while their sister slept 'like a dead person'.

She slept like a dead person. Already Made-From-Bone was standing up. He lit up a torch so that he could see his way. He saw a cuchicuchi monkey lying on the ground and lifted up its arm. He plucked and bent in

---

[14] The repetition of this sound — 'Ti' — is very similar to the repeated 'Too!' sounds in the mythic narrative about the origin of Made-from-Bone. In both cases, the repetition of sound elements acts to symbolically mark narrative peaks. These high points are accompanied by other important symbolic sound elements, such as 'to-ro' (the sound of nocturnal monkeys) and 'tsa!' (the sound of Made-from-Bone blowing a dart through his blowgun). These lesser sound elements are also repeated and reinforce the higher valencing of auditory over visual and other sense modes.

[15] The loud sound 'Ti!' is reproduced here in first-person ('What *I* heard ... Ti!'), transposing it from the third person ('*She heard: "Ti!"'*) of the previous episode. This pronominal shift from 'she' to 'I' is accompanied by heightened emotional tension: 'What I heard was *frightening*'. There has been a shift from narrative to meta-narrative, or narrative about narrative, in which the woman is narrating her personal version of the narrator's story. If readers detect some slippage between 'speech' and 'sound' or 'hearing' in the (meta)narrative, it is because the sounds are both non-verbal sounds and verbal representations of those sounds. The sounds and their production in third and first-person narrative episodes are trans-semiotic elements that bridge the divide between speech and sounds, since they are verbally produced representations of non-verbal sounds.

half the hairs from the monkey's armpit. That is how it would be for the
new people in the future world.[16] This was the beginning of poison in the
world of people. He cut off the monkey's head and stomped on it until it
entered the ground. He went and found the other monkey, cut off its
head, and stepped on it until it went under the ground. This would
become food for the new people in the future world. It is a tree called
dzapúra. Made-From-Bone went back. He lit a cigar again and blew
tobacco smoke over the woman.

In the third and final portion of the narrative, the woman decides to
return to her village with Made-from-Bone following close behind
her. A rapid series of events narrated in third-person are interspersed
with quoted dialogues between Made-from-Bone and the woman.

*She woke up early in the morning. They were conversing when
Made-From-Bone said, 'Paa, I had a terrible dream. I think that your
family has fallen ill'.*

'Is it possible that this happened?' she asked.

'Yes, it is so', he said.

*'Okay. Wait for me while I go back and find out', she said. 'Okay', 'let's
go'. And they went off on the path, back towards the village of the family
of Great Sickness.*

*She had an evil omen. She went ahead of Made-From-Bone, who car-
ried the blowgun in his hand. He placed the blowgun in front of her at a
curve in the path. Her foot tripped over the blowgun, and she nearly fell
down. 'Paa, Made-From-Bone. Just now I stubbed my foot. What does
this mean?' she asked.*

*'Hmm. You are having an evil omen. To stub one's foot, this is an evil
omen', he said. 'This is not a good sign for your family. You, you have an
evil omen. Let's go and see what's happening with your family'. And
they set off again.*

*He found some guambé (palúwaa) vine. He took the knots off the
guambé vine and threw them in front of the woman. She found the knots
as she went along the path.*[17] *They spoke, 'Tse, tse, tse'.*

[16] I have translated this phrase from the original (*Walimanai isru watsa páwali hekwápi
mepidaliaku*) as 'Thus it will be for the new people living in the future world'. This phrase
is almost a refrain that comes up at or near the very end of many mythic narratives, especially in the period known as 'The World Begins'. *Pawali hekwápi* literally means 'next
world' and refers to the world of living human beings (the 'new people', or Walimanai)
who came later in time (i.e., in the future) than the three periods of Made-from-Bones
mythic creation. See Wright (1998) for a detailed discussion of the concept of
'Walimanai' among the Baniwa-Coripaco of Brazil.

[17] The sequence of sensory stimuli — first auditory, then tactile, and finally visual — is the
same as that found in a Clackamas myth, called 'The "Wife" Who "Goes Out" Like a
Man'. 'The third strand of imagery focuses on the girl. She HEARS the urination. She then

'What could this be, Made-From-Bone?' she asked.

'It's a little bird, called hádzee. These are hádzee, and they are an evil omen; very bad for your family. You, you have an evil omen', he said. And they set off again. They were getting close to where they had started.

He ran across some worm shit, which he took and put under his loin-cloth along the side of his torso. 'Yaa!' he shouted in pain.

'What happened to you?' she asked.

'Something bad just happened; my glands are swollen', he said. 'Ayaa, I cannot go on. Go and see your family'.

'Okay, you stay here. I will go to see my family'. And she left. When she was still close by, Made-From-Bone stood up. He took the worm shit from his body and threw it away. Thus it was to be [this inflamation of the glands] for the new people in the future world.

The woman arrived at their place. 'Hoh, it is serious', they told her.

'What happened to you?' she asked.

'We are sick', they said. 'Made-From-Bone, where is Made-From-Bone?'

'Made-From-Bone is right over there. He fell ill, too', she said. 'I think he already died there'.

Made-From-Bone had already returned to his house. 'I have killed them. I have finished off all of them, the revenge for my younger brother', he said.[18]

Cultural and Psychological Dynamics
in the Myth of Evil Omens

I have presented the myth of evil omens in its entirety because the structure of the narrative is inseparable from its cultural and psycho-logical meanings. The myth consists of three basic movements, each having its own spatial and temporal dimensions. The narrative starts out as a movement by Made-from-Bone and his wife from her broth-ers' village out into the extrasocial, or natural, space of the forest. The

---

hears, but first FEELS, what drips down (on her face). At the climax she SEES blood' (Hymes, 1981, p. 295).

[18] This entire sequence of narrative events, beginning with the woman's act of counting the darts to erroneously conclude that none have been removed for nefarious purposes and continuing with Made-from-Bone's dream narrative and his production of tactile and visual signs, are clear examples of what Gates and others have defined as 'signifyin(g)' in African American vernacular language rituals. 'In this sense, one does not signify *something;* rather one signifies in *some way* (1988, p. 54), or one signifies *on* someone else, who is in turn signified *upon* by the signifier.

second movement begins when Made-from-Bone and his wife make camp in the forest in the late afternoon and continues until very late at night, or just before dawn. The final movement reverses the initial pattern and consists of a return from forest to village during the day. This relatively simple, tripartite pattern of movement away from the human social world, transformative events in an extrasocial setting, and return to the human social world is the basic template for a complex variety of shamanic ritual activities.

Shamanic singing (*malirríkairi*) is a musical and choreographic process of journeying from the world of living people to the houses of the dead located in a dark netherworld and retrieving the lost souls of sick or dying persons. This process of journeying away from the living and returning with the patient's soul is enacted in a number of ways. Movement, or breaking through to the houses of the dead, is musically performed through the use of sacred rattles made with powerful quartz stones. The accelerating and decelerating percussive sounds of the shaman's rattle serve as sensible markers charting the course of his spiritual travel. In their singing, shamans repeat each verse in a soft, almost ventriloquistic, echoing that musically embodies a return to the world of the living. In addition, the shamanic activity of bringing back the patient's lost soul is acted out in dramatic gestures and bodily actions between songs, which are always performed while seated on a low bench and facing the eastern horizon. The shaman stands up, takes several steps away from his bench, and begins pulling spirits into his rattle by sucking in air and tobacco smoke. He returns to the patient and his or her family, blows tobacco smoke over their heads, sucks on the patient's body, and vomits up splinters or other disease-causing agents. Shamanic ritual mobilizes a combination of musical sounds and bodily actions to transform subjective relations — fear of death, illness and misfortune, conflict and anger — into sensuous, audible, visible, tangible materialities.

In cultural terms, the myth of evil omens is a narrative exploration of these shamanic ritual activities. In shamanic rituals, especially in cases where life-threatening illness or injury is attributed to an evil omen, shamans require the patient and all close relatives to reveal their dreams, feelings, and knowledge of any unusual events. Failure to openly share these personal emotions and experiences undermines the shamanic process of bringing the patient's soul back from the houses of the dead by reversing the harmful or lethal effects of witchcraft and sorcery.

The myth of evil omens is about these same psychodynamic processes of bringing dreams, emotions, and unusual events into the open realm of conscious thought and speech as part of a broader social process of reversing the lethal effects of witchcraft and sorcery. By the second part of the myth, the woman's consciousness has taken centre stage, and Made-from-Bone's actions of killing and beheading her two brothers have become merely the background against which the more complex psychodrama of discovery and self-revelation unfolds. Just as shamans take control of their patients' emotions and consciousness in healing rituals, so too does Made-from-Bone take over his wife's consciousness by waking her up just in time to hear the loud sounds of her dead brothers' bodies hitting the ground. And just as musical and other sounds are the privileged sense mode for expressions and experiences of shamanic power, so too it is through *sounds* that Made-from-Bone takes control over his wife's consciousness and gets her to explicitly reveal the source of her fear: 'Made-From-Bone, you didn't kill my two brothers?'. The woman then temporarily alleviates her fear by counting the darts in Made-from-Bone's quiver and finding that they were all still there. One might interpret the act of counting as a merely neutral process of ascertaining the facts, but the woman's facts are inaccurate because she does not know that Made-from-Bone had previously hidden two poisoned darts inside his blowgun.[19]

Concluding Thoughts

As Folk Psychological narratives, Amazonian trickster myths demonstrate sophisticated ways of making sense of intentional actions in terms of reasons. In these narratives, Made-from-Bone's adversaries become centres of consciousness in whom desire, fear, belief, skepticism, intention and other mental states are explained dialogically through first- and second-person quoted speeches and dialogues that diverge from, or openly contradict, situations and actions that are described through third-person narration. In both of the two narratives selected for analysis in this essay, sound and hearing are privileged over other sense modes in Made-from-Bone's acts of signifyin(g) on his enemies. However, the trickster's use of sounds as signifiers works in opposing directions in the two narratives. In the myth of the origin of Made-from-Bone, the trickster and his brother make loud popping sounds by spitting into their wooden whistles before escaping from the burning garden in order to fool Great Sickness into falsely believing that they have been killed. In the myth of evil omens, the trickster

---

[19] Elsewhere I have shown that the activity of counting and expressions of quantity are anything but neutral or value-free for the Wakuénai (Hill, 1988; forthcoming).

uses the loud sounds of the two brothers-in-law's deaths in order to frighten his wife into revealing her fear of learning that her brothers really have been killed. In both narratives, hearing is believing.

Acknowledgements

Fieldwork with the Wakuénai of Venezuela in 1980, 1981, 1984, 1985 and 1998 was supported by grants from Fulbright-Hays Dissertation Research Abroad, Social Science Research Council and the American Council of Learned Societies, Fulbright-Hays Faculty Research Abroad, National Endowment for the Humanities Summer Research Stipend, the Wenner-Gren Foundation for Anthropological Research, and the Office of Research and Development at SIUC. I am grateful to the Editor, Dan Hutto, and an anonymous reviewer for the *Journal of Consciousness Studies*; Ellen Basso at the University of Arizona and Michael Cepek at University of Texas San Antonio; and to Juan Luis Rodriguez, Andrew Hofling, Aimee Hosemann, Anthony Webster, Janet Fuller, and other members of the newly formed working group on 'Discourse, Culture, and Power' at SIUC for their constructive comments on an earlier version of this essay.

References

Aikhenvald, A. & Dixon, R.M.W. (2003), *Studies in Evidentiality, Typological Studies in Language*, volume 54, (Amsterdam: John Benjamins Publications).

Barnes, J. (1984), 'Evidentials in the Tuyuca verb', *International Journal of American Linguistics,* **50** (3), pp. 255–71.

Basso, E. (1986), 'Quoted Dialogues in Kalapalo Narrative Discourse', in J. Sherzer & G. Urban (ed.), *Native South American Discourse* (Amsterdam: Mouton de Gruyter), pp. 119–68.

Basso, E. (1987), *In Favor of Deceit: A study of tricksters in an Amazonian society* (Tucson: University of Arizona Press).

Basso, E. (1995), *The Last Cannibals: A South American oral history* (Austin: University of Texas Press).

Duranti, A. (1984), *Intentions, Self, and Local Theories of Meaning: Words and social action in a Samoan context* (La Jolla, CA: Centre for Human Information Processing, University of California, San Diego).

Duranti, A. (1988), 'Intentions, Language, and Social Action in a Samoan Context', *Journal of Pragmatics,* **12**, pp. 13–33.

Duranti, A. (1993), 'Truth and Intentionality: An ethnographic critique', *Cultural Anthropology,* **8** (2), pp. 214–45.

Duranti, A. (2008), 'Further Reflections on Reading Other Minds', Social Thought and Commentary special section: *Anthropology and the Opacity of Other Minds, Anthropological Quarterly,* **81** (2), pp. 483–94.

Eco, U. (1990), *The Limits of Interpretation* (Bloomington: Indiana University Press).

Gates, H.L. Jr. (1988), *The Signifying Monkey: A theory of African-American literary criticism* (New York: Oxford University Press).

Guss, D. (1986), 'Keeping It Oral: A Yekuana ethnology', *American Ethnologist,* **13**, pp. 413–29.

Herman, D. (2007), 'Cognition, Emotion and Consciousness', in D. Herman (ed.), *The Cambridge Companion to Narrative,* pp. 245–59 (Cambridge: Cambridge University Press).

Herrera, R., Jordan, C. & Medina, E. (1978), 'Amazonian Ecosystems: Structure and function with particular emphasis on nutrients', *Interciencia,* **3**, pp. 223–31.

Hill, J.D. (1984), 'Social Equality and Ritual Hierarchy: The Arawakan Wakuenai of Venezuela', *American Ethnologist,* **11** (3), pp. 528–44.

Hill, J.D. (1988), 'The Soft and the Stiff: Ritual power and mythic meaning in a Northern Arawakan classifier system', *Antropologica,* **69**, pp. 3–25.

Hill, J.D. (ed, 1988), *Rethinking History and Myth: Indigenous South American Perspectives on the Past* (Urbana: University of Illinois Press).

Hill, J.D. (1989), 'Ritual Production of Environmental History among the Arawakan Wakuenai of Venezuela', *Human Ecology,* **17** (1), pp. 1–25.

Hill, J.D. (1992), 'A Musical Aesthetic of Ritual Curing in the Northwest Amazon', in E. Jean Langdon (ed.), *Portals of Power,* pp. 175–210 (Albuquerque: University of New Mexico Press).

Hill, J.D. (1993), *Keepers of the Sacred Chants: The poetics of ritual power in an Amazonian society* (Tucson: University of Arizona Press).

Hill, J.D. (1999), 'Indigenous Peoples and the Rise of Independent Nation-States in Lowland South America', in F. Salomon & S. Schwartz (ed.), *The Cambridge History of Native Peoples of the Americas: South America,* Volume III, Part 2, pp. 704–64.

Hill, J.D. (2002), '"Made from Bone": Trickster myths, musicality, and social constructions of history in the Venezuelan Amazon', in G. Schrempp & W. Hansen (ed.), *Myth: A New Symposium,* pp. 72–88 (Bloomington, IN: Indiana University Press).

Hill, J.D. (2009), *Made-from-Bone: Trickster Myths, Music, and History from the Amazon* (Urbana: University of Illinois Press).

Hill, J.D. (forthcoming), 'Materializing the Occult: An approach to understanding the nature of materiality in Wakuénai ontology', in F. Santos-Granero (ed.), *The Occult Life of Things: Native Amazonian Theories of Materiality and Personhood* (Tucson: University of Arizona Press).

Hill, J.D. & Santos-Granero, F. (ed, 2002), *Comparative Arawakan Histories: Rethinking Language Family and Culture Area in Amazonia* (Urbana: University of Illinois Press).

Hill, J.D. & Wright, R.M. (1988), 'Time, Narrative, and Ritual: Historical interpretations from an Amazonian society', in J. Hill (ed.), *Rethinking History and Myth,* pp. 78–106 (Urbana: University of Illinois Press).

Hutto, D.D. (2008), *Folk Psychological Narratives: The Sociocultural Basis of Understanding Reasons* (Cambridge, MA: MIT Press).

Hutto, D.D. (2009), 'Folk Psychology as Narrative Practice', *Journal of Consciousness Studies,* **16** (6–8), pp. 9–39. [This issue]

Hymes, D. (1981), *'In Vain I Tried To Tell You': Essays in Native American Ethnopoetics* (Philadelphia: University of Pennsylvania Press).

Jung, C.G. (1956/1972), 'On the Psychology of the Trickster Figure', in P. Radin (trans. R.F.C. Hull), *The Trickster: A Study in American Indian Mythology* (New York: Schocken Books), pp. 195–211.

Keane, W. (2008), 'Others, Other Minds, and Others' Theories of Other Minds: An afterword on the psychology and politics of opacity claims', Social Thought and Commentary special section: *Anthropology and the Opacity of Other Minds,* *Anthropological Quarterly,* **81** (2), pp. 473–82.

Lillard, A. (1997), 'Other Folk's Theories of Mind and Behaviour', *Psychological Science,* **8**, pp. 268–74.

Malone, T. (1988), 'The Origin and Development of Tuyuca Evidentials', *International Journal of American Linguistics,* **54**, pp. 119–40.

Miller, M. (1999), *Desano Grammar,* Summer Institute of Linguistics and the University of Texas at Arlington publications in linguistics, publication 132 (Dallas, TX: Summer Institute of Linguistics).

Morse, N. & Maxwell, M. (1999), *Cubeo Grammar,* Summer Institute of Linguistics and University of Texas at Arlington, Publications in Linguistics, publication 130 (Dallas, TX: Summer Institute of Linguistics).

Price, R. & Price, S. (1991), *Two Evenings in Saramaka* (Chicago: University of Chicago Press).

Roberts, J. (1989), *From Trickster to Badman: The black folk hero in slavery and freedom* (Philadelphia: University of Pennsylvania Press).

Santos-Granero, F. (1998), 'Writing History into the Landscape: Space, myth, and ritual in contemporary Amazonia', *American Ethnologist,* **25** (2), pp. 128–48.

Scalise Sugiyama, M. (2003), 'Cultural Variation is Part of Human Nature: Literary universals, context-sensitivity and "Shakespeare in the Bush"', *Human Nature,* **14**, pp. 383–96.

Schiefflin, B. (2008), 'Speaking Only your Own Mind: Reflections on talk, gossip and intentionality in Bosavi (PNG)', Social Thought and Commentary special section: *Anthropology and the Opacity of Other Minds. Anthropological Quarterly,* **81** (2), pp. 431–41.

Staats, S. (1996), 'Fighting in a Different Way: Indigenous resistance through the Alleluia religion of Guyana', in J. Hill (ed.), *History, Power, and Identity: Ethnogenesis in the Americas, 1492–1992* (Iowa City: University of Iowa Press), pp. 161–79 .

Stanfield, M.E. (1998), *Red Rubber, Bleeding Trees: Violence, Slavery, and Empire in Northwest Amazonia, 1850–1933* (Albuquerque: University of New Mexico Press).

Taussig, M. (1987), *Shamanism, Colonialism, and the Wild Man* (Chicago: University of Chicago Press).

de Villiers, J. & Garfield, J. (2009), 'Evidentiality and Narrative', *Journal of Consciousness Studies,* **16** (6–8), pp. 191–217. [This issue]

Vinden, P. (1996), 'Junin Quechua Children's Understanding of Mind', *Child Development,* **67**, pp. 1707–16.

Webster, A. (2004), 'Coyote Poems: Navajo Poetry, Intertextuality and Language Choice', *American Indian Culture and Research Journal,* **28** (4), pp. 69–91.

Whitten, D. & Whitten, N. Jr. (1988), *From Myth to Creation* (Urbana: University of Illinois Press).

Whitten, N. (1976), *Sacha Runa: Ethnicity and Adaptation of Ecuadorian Jungle Quichua* (Urbana: University of Illinois Press).

Whitten, N. (1985), *Sicuanga Runa: The other Side of Development in Amazonian Ecuador* (Urbana: University of Illinois Press).

Whitten, N. & Whitten, D. (2008), *Puyo Runa: Imagery and Power in Modern Amazonia* (Urbana: University of Illinois Press).

Wright, R.M. (1998), *Cosmos, Self and History in Baniwa Religion. For Those Unborn.* (Austin, TX: University of Texas Press).

David A. Leavens & Timothy P. Racine

Joint Attention in Apes and Humans

Are Humans Unique?

Abstract: *Joint attention is the ability to intentionally co-orient towards a common focus. This ability develops in a protracted, mosaic fashion in humans. We review evidence of joint attention in humans and great apes, finding that great apes display every phenomenon described as joint attention in humans, although there is considerable variation among apes of different rearing histories. We conclude that there is little evidence for human species-unique cognitive adaptations in the non-verbal communication of humans in the first 18 months of life. This conclusion is consistent with the Narrative Practice Hypothesis (NPH) because the NPH posits training in folk psychological narratives as a basis for folk psychological competence.*

Humans communicate before they can speak. As far as we know, all other animals communicate without speech or any communicative system analogous to speech. There are points of comparison between language and non-human animal systems of communication (e.g., Burling, 1993; Hauser *et al.*, 2002), but there is no evidence that any other organism tells stories, with or without language. Even in humans, storytelling is an advanced communicative skill, which takes years to develop. Yet, as Hutto (2009 [this issue]) points out, mainstream theory in cognitive developmental psychology interprets the pre-speech communicative behaviour of human infants as evidence for the early acquisition, in our species, of a complex, if tacit,

story-like understanding of mental processes in others. This is especially apparent in discussions of joint attention, which, in humans, is
widely taken as evidence for a nascent theory of mind (ToM). Joint
attention is the intentional co-orientation of two or more organisms to
the same locus. By 'intentional' we mean that at least one of the organisms displays a pattern of behaviour that defines a sequence as goal-
directed: the signaller might point to a distant locus, alternate his or
her gaze between that locus and an interlocutor, and, in the face of
miscommunication, attempt to repair that communication by persist-
ing in its signalling or elaborating upon the initial signal (Bard, 1992;
Bates *et al.*, 1975; Leavens, 2004; Leavens *et al.*, 2005a). Thus, joint
attention is a class of distinctively patterned sequences of behaviour
defined by objective, publicly available behavioural measures of
visual orienting, and the deployment of visual, auditory, and tactile
signals (Leavens, 2004; Leavens *et al.*, 2005a).

According to a variety of theoretical perspectives on human cognitive development, joint attention is diagnostic of the acquisition of
complex representations that mediate young infants' social interactions (reviewed by, e.g., Hutto, 2008a; Racine & Carpendale, 2007;
Reddy, 1996; Reddy & Morris, 2004). According to these kinds of
theoretical perspectives, later linguistic competence simply gives
symbolic expression to pre-existing, but previously unspoken, representations of what are taken to be the invisible causes of the behaviour
of babies' social partners. Even when granting that epistemic concepts, such as beliefs and knowledge, might be co-constituted by linguistic input, it is nevertheless widely argued that infants as young as
12 months of age, who manifestly lack the linguistic competence to
verbally express pre-epistemic mental states pertaining to intentionality, somehow construe others as psychological agents with mental
stances vis-à-vis events in the world (e.g., Tomasello, 1995; among
many others).

In making his case, Hutto focuses on a form of narrative practice
that makes use of certain kind of narrative, which he calls a folk
psychological (FP) narrative:

> FP narratives are a specific sub-type of narrative; distinguished by their
> content — they are about people (or their analogues) who act for rea-
> sons of the kind that minimally implicates beliefs and desires (Hutto,
> 2008b, p. 178).

These narratives assist children in integrating their initial, practical
capacities to attribute intentions, desires and beliefs so that they
become able to produce and understand accounts of why we and

others act for reasons. Importantly, Hutto does not claim that engaging in such practices is the origin of children's first understanding of desires and beliefs. The Narrative Practice Hypothesis (NPH) is an account of the human development of 'FP-competence', which situates this competence in the narrative experiences of human children. According to this view, organisms that lack exposure to these FP narratives will not develop FP-competence (see, esp., Hutto, 2008a, ch. 6–8). Thus, by extension, non-linguistic or pre-linguistic organisms could not display FP-competence, even in an incipient form. This is the proposal examined, here. In this article, we review joint attentional skills in human primates and consider whether species-unique kinds of social cognition are required in order for such behaviours to emerge. We then turn to a consideration of these skills in non-human primates and conclude that on empirical and logical grounds there is little evidence for qualitatively different cognitive capacities operating in humans and their nearest living relatives, the great apes.

If this is the case, it favours Hutto's proposal (that it is only through engaging in narrative practices that one comes by full FP-competence) because we also deny that the social cognitive abilities shared by humans and other primates rest on their possessing bona fide 'Theory of Mind' abilities. As such, our findings may lend some much needed ammunition to Hutto's cause since a standard complaint against the NPH is that it depends on children already having a theory of mind if they are to engage in the kind of narrative practice that Hutto describes.

Joint Attention in Humans

According to a widely used descriptive scheme by Mundy and his colleagues (e.g., Mundy & Gomes, 1998), the development of joint attention in humans can be charted by measuring their increasing skills in *initiating behaviour regulation* (IBR), *initiating joint attention* (IJA), and *responding to joint attention* (RJA). Examples of these developmental milestones include reaching out the hand in the apparent request for delivery of an object (IBR), pointing to a distant dog (IJA), and following a caregiver's head turn so that the child is looking in the same direction as the caregiver (RJA). Some researchers restrict the term 'joint attention' to RJA, or to IJA plus RJA, but we use the term, here, in a more inclusive sense, including IBR, RJA, IJA and related triadic phenomena such as social referencing (use of emotional information about novel objects to regulate one's own reaction to those objects) and imitation (Bard & Leavens, 2008; Leavens *et al.*, 2008; Striano & Bertin, 2005).

As IBR skills develop, infants become increasingly competent at manipulating adults into acting on the world for them, for example, by raising their arms to be picked up and cuddled or, later, pointing to dropped toys or out-of reach bottles, until an adult retrieves them. IBR is conceptually the same sort of thing as *protoimperative* signalling, a term introduced by Bates and her colleagues (Bates *et al.*, 1975). Considered in many theoretical perspectives to be an important developmental milestone, IBR describes the onset of intentional use of ritualized or conventionalized gestures in our species. Again, by 'intentional' we simply mean that babies exhibiting IBR are working toward a contextually appropriate end. For example, Blake, O'Rourke, and Borzellino (1994) reported that 'reaching out' gestures displayed in the context of out-of-reach items were displayed by 8-month-old infants with accompanying vocalizations, but the same gestures by 4-month-old infants in the same eliciting contexts were not accompanied by vocalizations; they interpreted this bimodal elaboration at 8 months as evidence for the onset of intentional, gestural communication. Similarly, Bates and her colleagues (1975) noted that only in the latter part of the first year of life do babies begin to visually monitor adult caregivers during goal-directed sequences, as though they are beginning to perceive the relevance of the adults for achieving their aims. Pointing with the index finger in apparent requests for object delivery (protoimperative pointing) appears at about 12 months of age, although reaching out with all fingers extended occurs several months earlier (Blake *et al.*, 1992; 1994; Leung & Rheingold, 1981; Lock *et al.*, 1994).

For many years developmental psychologists thought that pointing (for any reason) was a uniquely human activity (see, e.g., Butterworth & Grover, 1988; Povinelli *et al.*, 2003), and therefore even IBR was widely taken to signify human species-unique psychological processes. However, as we will see, great apes and other animals that depend upon humans or conspecifics for provisioning also develop signalling strategies that meet the same objective criteria for IBR, so IBR is a widespread mammalian phenomenon (Arbib *et al.*, 2008; Bard, 1992; Leavens, 2004; Leavens & Hopkins, 1999; Leavens *et al.*, 2008; 2009). Although IBR is subject to a variety of theoretical interpretations, few would dispute that, empirically, sometime near the end of the first year of life, human children, in Western and some other cultures, begin to point and otherwise use manual gestures in apparent attempts to manipulate others to act on the world for them. Few researchers have assessed the degree to which babies respond to requests (RBR — but see, e.g., Mundy & Gomes, 1998); rather surprisingly, the comprehension of protoimperative pointing, *per se*, has not been well-studied in experimental and naturalistic contexts (see Colonnesi *et al.*, 2008, for a recent corrective).

Psychologists do traditionally distinguish IJA from RJA. Developmentally, these skills seem to be distinct, in so far as they are only rarely found to be significantly correlated competencies either at the same age or longitudinally (e.g., Desrochers *et al.*, 1995; Mundy & Gomes, 1998; Striano & Bertin, 2005). At some risk of over-simplification, RJA seems to have an earlier onset than IJA and is more frequently associated with later language skills (e.g., Baldwin, 1993; 1995; Morales *et al.*, 1998; Mundy & Gomez, 1998; but see Carpenter *et al.*, 1998, for the opposite pattern; and Flom *et al.*, 2007, for a review of the development of RJA). RJA has a complex developmental profile, which has been studied in human infancy with two primary eliciting contexts: either an experimenter turns his or her gaze (with or without head turns) or the experimenter points (to near and far targets).

The development of RJA has been reviewed by Adamson (Adamson, 1996; Adamson & Bakeman, 1991), Butterworth (e.g., Butterworth, 2001; Butterworth & Grover, 1988), Doherty (2006), and Reddy (2003), among many others. Although even 6-month-old human infants will turn their heads in the same direction as an adult's head turn, it is not until about 10 months of age that babies turn their heads to the correct side more than the opposite side (e.g., Corkum & Moore, 1995; 1998). Not until about 18 months of age will babies follow an adult's gaze to a specific target behind themselves (e.g., Butterworth & Grover, 1988). Beginning at about 10 months of age, babies in cultures that use manual pointing will follow pointing gestures to close objects, and then, as with gaze-following, to ever more distant targets (e.g., Adamson, 1996).

In terms of IJA, babies in most cultures studied, to date, evince a developmental sequence from exhibition of self at about 10 months of age, followed by exhibition of objects, giving objects to others and, finally, at about a year of age, pointing to objects and events (e.g., Adamson, 1996; Miles, 1990). This kind of pointing is referred to as *protodeclarative* pointing (e.g., Baron-Cohen, 1995; Bates *et al.*, 1975). Bates and her colleagues (1975) originally portrayed protoimperative and protodeclarative signalling as types of non-verbal requests: protoimperatives were requests to deliver objects, to pick up a child, or to convey the child somewhere (use of adults to obtain objects or objectives), whereas protodeclaratives were requests to engage with the child (use of objects to obtain adult attention). Although many contemporary writers construe protodeclarative pointing as springing from a different motivational or conceptual structure than protoimperative pointing (e.g., Baron-Cohen, 1989; 1995; Franco & Butterworth, 1996; Tomasello, 2006; Tomasello *et al.*, 2007), numerous others have noted that there is no empirical evidence that forces the interpretation that protodeclarative pointing is anything other than the use of objects to obtain the attention or an affective response from a caregiver (Leavens, 2004; Leavens *et al.*, 2005a; Moore & Corkum, 1994); indeed, Bates and her colleagues (1975), in introducing these terms, were explicit in defining protodeclaratives as a subset of imperative signals — these points were described as the use of objects to elicit some kind of adult behavioural response (reviewed by Leavens *et al.*, 2009), and it is in this sense of the term that we will evaluate evidence for protodeclarative behaviour in nonhumans (we take as an example of protodeclarative pointing, the 'informative' pointing described by Liszkowski *et al.*, 2006).

Joint Attention and the Mind

Infants as young as 12 months of age are widely believed to appreciate the invisible mental causes of the behaviour of their caregivers (e.g., Baron-Cohen, 1989; 1995; Meltzoff, 1995; Tomasello, 1995; 1999; 2006; see reviews in Colonnesi *et al.*, 2008; Racine & Carpendale, 2007; among others). In particular, protodeclarative pointing, which emerges early in the second year of life (in Western populations), is taken to be the quintessential sign of mental state awareness in humans: why would one point to change the knowledge state of an observer, the argument goes, if one does not appreciate that there are minds with mental contents? Thus, when babies point to events or objects in their environments, in apparent attempts to share attention to these objects with their social partners, this is taken as evidence that infants are attempting to influence the state of mind of their interlocutors, which entails that they have at least a tacit understanding of others as mental beings (e.g., Baron-Cohen, 1995; Camaioni *et al.*, 2004; Legerstee & Barillas, 2003; Liszkowski *et al.*, 2004; Tomasello, 1995). Developmental psychologists rely on a number of mental process models in which mental states (a) exist; (b) reside entirely within the cranium; (c) are available to introspection; (d) cause behaviour; and therefore can be (e) indexed by overt behaviour.

Although a full review is beyond the scope of this paper, in recent years these kinds of mentalistic interpretations of infant behaviour have been increasingly criticized on epistemological and empirical grounds by numerous researchers, including ourselves (e.g., Leavens, 1998; 2002; 2004; 2006; Leavens *et al.*, 2005a; 2008; 2009; Racine & Carpendale, 2007; 2008; Racine *et al.*, 2008; Susswein & Racine, 2008; 2009) and many others (e.g., Boesch, 2007; Doherty, 2006; Hutto, 2008a; 2008b; 2008c; Leudar & Costall, 2004; Moore & Corkum, 1994; Reddy, 1996; Reddy & Morris, 2004). For example, Moore and Corkum (1994) pointed out that there is no compelling evidence that young babies cannot learn, through experience, the typical consequences of their own signalling behaviour — so that babies with mothers who respond with positive and intense emotional displays to the babies' points, could learn the socially embedded, contingent structure of communication in the absence of any mental state representation. Indeed, Corkum and Moore (1998) demonstrated that babies could be trained to follow gaze two months earlier than is typical, simply by exposing babies to a training regimen; hence, this aspect of RJA can be learned through relevant experience. Because we are unaware of any set of empirical findings that unambiguously rules out learning from experience as a route into the development of joint attention, a brief digression on principles of learning is warranted.

A training regimen is nothing more nor less than life experience that is intentionally manipulated; if a behaviour is acquired, yet not explicitly trained, this does not imply that the behaviour was not learned. *A fortiori*, this would not imply that the capacity was innate (see Bateson & Mameli, 2007). Examples are legion in which human babies display some behavioural competency at joint attention, and researchers conclude that there is a 'poverty' of environmental stimuli to account for this novel skill (see Leudar & Costall, 2004, for a critique of this argument). This cannot follow from the present state of knowledge in which we do not know nearly enough, in terms of natural history, about how parents respond to babies' communicative signals to conclude that babies have not been differentially reinforced to display such joint attentional skills as gaze-following and pointing. If, for example, positive affective displays are reliable consequences of children's pointing, then pointing to elicit positive emotion can be both untrained and learned (e.g., Leavens, 2004; Leavens *et al.*, 2005a). There are few empirical data on parents' responses to infant pointing behaviour, but what few studies have been performed are consistent with a learning model. For example, Masataka (1995; 2003) reported that parents respond more positively to speech-like infant vocalizations; because index-finger extensions more frequently accompany speech-like vocalizations than non-speech-like vocalizations, index-finger extensions are, thus, subject to what he terms 'inadvertent conditioning of index-finger extension' (2003, p. 74). There is no aspect of human joint attention in infancy (IBR, RJA & IJA) that simply could not have been acquired through experience (i.e., learned). An astonishingly large number of contemporary researchers seem to believe, incorrectly, that any behaviour acquired as a result of reinforcement must be cognitively uninteresting, or, as Reddy and Morris (2004) concisely observed in a related context, 'that anything learned from reinforcement cannot constitute genuine knowledge' (p. 650). What is acquired through learning, trained or incidental, is knowledge — real knowledge, in real organisms, operating in the real world. Thus, to suggest that humans might learn to exhibit joint attention skills through experience is to simply assert that we have no *a priori* basis to promulgate a theoretical perspective that human infants, alone among vertebrates, are so appallingly obtuse that evolution had to come up with human species-specific cognitive modules to do the same things that, as we shall see, other animals manage to do without such modules.

Others have noted that social engagement is suffused with intense subjective awareness that can only be experienced in participation, and is only weakly caricatured in any objective, third-party analysis; without the rapport that characterizes the experience of self-other engagement (e.g., Reddy, 2003). As Reddy and Morris poignantly put it,

> Such definitions [of intentional communication] presume the existence
> of a prior script, the isolation of the communicator from the receiver,
> and a separation of the act of communication from its content, and make
> the loneliness of the subject almost insurmountable (2004, p. 653).

Leudar and Costall (2004) discussed how the use of an information-theoretic model of communication — in which previously existing messages are encoded, transmitted through some channel, received in some sensory modality, then decoded, appraised, and finally responded to — force a *telementational* view of even early human communication: individuals must infer the meaning of communicative acts. In the telementational perspective, the possibility of directly perceiving meaning in the shared sensory space of interactants, outside their crania, is not permissible (see also, e.g., Johnson, 2001; King, 2004; Leavens *et al.*, 2008; 2009; Racine & Carpendale, 2007; 2008; Savage-Rumbaugh *et al.*, 1998; Susswein & Racine, 2009).

Thus, the reliance of psychology on telementational models to interpret human infant communication creates the illusion of a chasm between babies and their caregivers that can only be bridged through a computational process involving either inference or simulation. Such a perspective is belied by the experience of any parent who has held their young babies in their arms, played peek-a-boo, tickled their young child, etc.; in these contexts we do not doubt that we are directly engaged with our children, long before the ages at which they might start to point to distant objects or reliably follow our gaze to distant events. Communication in early infancy is emotionally intense, vibrantly dynamic, and, as far as we can tell, non-inferential. The earliest communication of human infants is not a meeting of minds across an epistemological abyss, but a direct interdigitation of feeling in which it is often difficult to point out an ownership of separate feelings at specific times. If we can engage so directly with our children before they achieve joint attentional skills, then telementational accounts of joint attention impose a wholly unnecessary psychical cleavage upon infancy at approximately one year of age. There is developmental change in communicative abilities at approximately this age, but there is no empirical evidence that this involves the kind of psychological re-birth into a state of extreme solipsism required by telementational perspectives, which can only be bridged through computational processes; rather, the common ground simply expands, with novel opportunities to apply the emotional routines of early infancy to increasingly disparate elements in a common sphere of experience (e.g., Adamson & Bakeman, 1991; Bard, 1998; Bard & Leavens, 2008; Reddy, 2003; Striano & Bertin, 2005).[1]

As Gregory Bateson pointed out years ago, mentality is a distributed phenomenon, reaching out across the transductive envelope of the neuromuscular and neurosensory junctions:

> … we may say that 'mind' is immanent in those circuits of the brain which are complete within the brain. Or that mind is immanent in circuits that are complete within the system, brain *plus* body. Or, finally, that mind is immanent in the larger system — man *plus* environment (1972, p. 317, emphasis in original).

---

[1] One of the greatest intellectual tragedies of the present age is that scientists often assess the communicative behaviour of animals that have never experienced these kinds of early communion and conclude that these animals lack basic joint attention skills because of their evolutionary histories, rather than their specific, impoverished or very different species-typical developmental histories (Bard & Leavens, 2008; Leavens, 1998; 2004; Leavens *et al.*, 2008; Racine *et al.*, 2008).

Recently, numerous researchers from different traditions have independently converged upon a view of cognition as 'embodied' (e.g., Clark, 1997; De Jaegher & Di Paolo, 2007; Gallagher, 2001; 2008; Griffiths & Stotz, 2000; Johnson, 2001; Lakoff & Johnson, 1999; Leavens et al., 2008; Lickliter, 2008; Leudar & Costall, 2004; King, 2004; Racine & Carpendale, 2008; Reddy & Morris, 2004). The central significance of these emerging perspectives on cognition, at least for the purposes of the present article, is that increasing numbers of researchers are taking seriously the notion that minds, meanings and even evolutionary adaptations are properties of systems, with specific histories, embedded in particular sociocultural contexts. If communication between caregiver and child (of any species) crucially involves parameters outside the participating neural systems, then a full scientific understanding of the development of joint attention (in any species) must take into account the specific learning histories of the interactants, the emotional tones of the engagements, the quality of the relationships between the interactants; everything, in short, that influences what babies and their caregivers might come to expect in the specific unfolding of their interactions (Bard & Leavens, 2008; Boesch, 2007; Leavens et al., 2008). These expectations form the warp through which the weft of creative performance is drawn — surprise, a key essential of rudimentary humour, can only exist against the less variant properties of the familiar (e.g., King, 2004; Savage-Rumbaugh, 1991). This kind of dynamic engagement is referred to as intersubjectivity (Trevarthen, 1977; 1998; Trevarthen & Hubley, 1978).

Earlier dyadic engagement is referred to as *primary* intersubjectivity, and the suite of triadic skills comprising joint attentional competence is known as *secondary* intersubjectivity. Thus, while Hutto and many others argue that FP-competence is 'socioculturally grounded' (Hutto, 2008a, p. x) — with Hutto making the specific case that this is because FP-competence is acquired through narrative practice — it is nevertheless widely believed that the much earlier human capacity for secondary intersubjectivity involves species-unique competencies for engagement with others (e.g., Hutto, 2008a, ch. 6; Tomasello, 1999; Tomasello et al., 2007; Zlatev, 2008).[2] If this is true,

---

[2] Arguments are also made for human-unique aspects of primary intersubjectivity, but there is little empirical support for this idea; however, this lies beyond the scope of the present article (see, e.g., Bard, 1998; 2007; Bard et al., 2005; Susswein & Racine, 2008; reviewed by Tomonaga, 2007). Generally speaking, human infants stand out from the other ape infants in their slower development of locomotor competence and their unusual vocal behaviour, including babbling and the development of phonation over the first year of life.

then we might expect to find fundamental behavioural discontinuities between humans and the other apes in their joint attentional competencies; we now briefly review the empirical data to determine whether this is indeed the case (see Gómez, 1998, for an earlier review of joint attention in apes).

Intersubjective Primates

Gallagher and Hutto (2008) explored a triad of competencies to account for developmental precursors to FP-competencies. These were (a) intersubjective perception; (b) pragmatically contextualized (i.e., secondary) intersubjectivity; and (c) narrative competency (Gallagher & Hutto, 2008, p. 20). Here we briefly examine the evidence for the second of these competencies, pragmatically contextualized joint attention, in nonhuman primates and other animals in each of the three domains reviewed above.

Initiating behavioural regulation

There are many examples of manual gestures used by both wild and captive great apes in which they manipulate the behaviour of others. Here we list a few illustrative examples.

Begging gestures. Chimpanzees and orangutans exhibit apparent 'request' gestures in dyadic contexts, both in the wild and in captivity. Systematic studies have demonstrated that ape infants initiate nursing and play bouts and, later, both infants and adults display begging gestures, in which the palm is supinated, oriented towards their mothers or other social partners, and often with outstretched arm, typically beginning between 9 and 12 months of age (e.g., Bard, 1990; 1992; Goodall, 1986; Leavens & Hopkins, 1998; Leavens *et al.*, 2004a; Plooij, 1978; Teleki, 1973; see Figure 1).

Directed scratching (touching). Chimpanzees in the Kibale National Park, Uganda, have been recently reported to scratch parts of their own bodies in apparent requests for their grooming partners to groom that area (Pika & Mitani, 2006). Other systematic studies have shown that apes often touch parts of their own bodies in apparent requests for another ape or a human to direct tickles or other activities at the location indicated (e.g., Plooij, 1978; Tanner *et al.*, 2006;

Otherwise, at least in the domains studied to date, early competencies of human and ape infants are remarkably similar: early in infancy, representatives of both species display neonatal imitation (Bard, 2007; Myowa-Yamakoshi *et al.*, 2004), face-recognition (Myowa-Yamakoshi *et al.*, 2005), and recognition of direct gaze (Bard *et al.*, 1992; Myowa-Yamakoshi *et al.*, 2003).

Figure 1
A juvenile chimpanzee displays a typical begging gesture through cage mesh. Palm is supinated (facing up), hand held in a slightly 'cupped' posture, and the arm is outstretched towards the experimenter.
Photograph by David A. Leavens.

Tomasello *et al.*, 1985). Included in this category might be points to oneself, in apparent requests to elicit action directed at a particular place on the signaller's body. For example, Yerkes (1943) described an episode in which a caregiver had examined the oral cavity of a chimpanzee named Booey, who had gone off his food. After a fruitless search for dental problems, Booey pointed to one of its own teeth, where the caretaker then found an abscess, upon further scrutiny.

Pointing to request.[3] There are hundreds of published examples of apes pointing in apparent requests for food or other object delivery

[3]   There has been a debate over the structural aspects of pointing, with some researchers limiting the category of pointing to 'canonical' pointing with an outstretched arm and index finger only (e.g., Butterworth, 2003; Povinelli & Davis, 1994; Povinelli *et al.*, 2003). We simply note, here, that (a) not all humans always point with their index fingers (e.g., Enfield, 2001; Wilkins, 2003); (b) researchers who study infant communication have generally failed to find significant differences between 'reaching-to-request' and '[index-finger] pointing-to-request' in terms of accompanying visual checking towards caregivers or vocalizations, and therefore it is often quite ambiguous whether children are iconically reaching or indexically pointing with their whole hands (e.g., Leung & Rheingold, 1981; Masur, 1983; reviewed by Leavens & Hopkins, 1999); and (c) some infancy researchers now include pointing with the whole hand as part of their coding scheme for pointing (e.g., O'Neill, 1996; Brooks and Meltzoff, 2002). See Leavens (2004) for extended discussion of this point.

Figure 2
Merv, a young adult chimpanzee, points with his index finger to a juice
bottle, located on the ground, just out of camera view.
Photograph by David A. Leavens, used with permission from the
American Psychological Association (from Leavens & Hopkins, 1998).

(reviewed by Leavens, 2004; Leavens & Hopkins, 1999; Leavens *et al.*, 2009; see Figure 2). Although other forms of gesturing may be frequent in wild populations (Pika, 2008), pointing of any form seems almost nonexistent. Nevertheless, pointing is very frequently displayed by captive apes, and occasionally displayed by more distantly related monkeys (e.g., Hess *et al.*, 1993; Mitchell & Anderson, 1997).[4] Apes point in apparent requests for food delivery, but also to request other objects, such as shoes (e.g., Leavens *et al.*, 1996), tools required to open containers containing desirable food (e.g., Call & Tomasello, 1994; Russell *et al.*, 2005; Whiten, 2000), and to manipulate sexual partners to assume different positions for copulation (Savage-Rumbaugh *et al.*, 1977). There are also reports of pointing by dolphins (through orientation of their bodies, Xitco *et al.*, 2001) and, of course, many hunting dogs ('pointers') are routinely trained to orient towards fallen prey, by capitalizing upon some breeds' propensities to freeze in the presence of prey. Very occasionally, researchers report training apes to point (e.g., Call & Tomasello, 1994; Woodruff

---

[4] Intriguing claims to the effect that explicitly training monkeys to point results in generalized facilitation in other domains of social cognition have been reported by Blaschke and Ettlinger (1987) and Kumashiro and his colleagues (Kumashiro *et al.*, 2002; 2003).

& Premack, 1979), but the vast majority of pointing by captive apes emerges 'spontaneously' (that is to say, in the absence of any explicit training).

Numerous researchers have remarked on the apparent paucity of manual pointing in wild populations of apes (e.g., Butterworth, 2003; Povinelli *et al.*, 2003; Tomasello *et al.*, 2007). We have argued that the reason wild apes do not point manually is that they simply have no need (cf. Menzel, 1973): unlike human children and captive apes, wild apes virtually never experience a 'Referential Problem Space' in which they are dependent upon others to act on the world for them (e.g., Leavens *et al.*, 2008; 2009). This is because wild apes achieve locomotor independence at approximately 5 months of age, and there-fore can directly locomote to and manipulate any object that takes their interest. In contrast, both human children, by virtue of the large proportion of time they spend in restraints (car seats, feeding chairs, cots, papooses, etc.), and captive apes in cages, very frequently encounter desirable, but out-of-reach objects; in this Referential Prob-lem Space, pointing to request delivery of these objects develops in both humans and captive apes (see Leavens, 2004; Leavens *et al.*, 1996; 2005b; 2008; Leavens *et al.*, 2009, for elaboration). Although apes frequently gesture between themselves (Pika, 2008), it is some-times stated that apes do not point between themselves (e.g., Povinelli *et al.*, 2003; Tomasello, 2006); in fact, this is rather far from the truth. Although infrequent, pointing between apes has been reported in the wild (Inoue-Nakamura & Matsuzawa, 1997; Veà & Sabater-Pi, 1998), among captive apes in zoo environments (de Waal, 1982), and among language-trained apes (Savage-Rumbaugh, 1986). For example, Sav-age-Rumbaugh (1986) described 37 instances of pointing between two chimpanzees, Sherman and Austin, who were working on a food-sharing task. In this task, the first chimpanzee selected a lexigram (an arbitrary visual symbol, representing a type of food), from a panel of lexigrams. The second chimpanzee was charged with retrieving the food from a tray, delivering half to the first chimpanzee, and then consuming the second half of that food item. The first chim-panzee frequently augmented his selection of the lexigram with a point to the food in the tray. According to the Referential Problem Space hypothesis, it is to be expected that this behaviour will be rare between apes, because, they usually do not depend upon other apes to act on the world for them (e.g., Leavens, 2004); in the example involv-ing Sherman and Austin, they were explicitly trained to take turns and to share food, and ape-ape pointing emerged in this specific context. In terms of joint attention, successful pointing to request delivery of objects requires the capture and re-direction of a caregiver's attention to a specific locus, and the further conveyance of the expectancy that the caregiver will deliver that object to the signaller.

Responding to joint attention

There are also numerous demonstrations of RJA among the great apes, and other animals. Here we selectively concentrate on a few illustrative examples.

Gaze- and point-following. Following the gaze of social partners, both ape and human, is well-demonstrated in great apes (reviewed by Leavens *et al.*, 2008). It is well-demonstrated by systematic studies that apes follow humans' gaze shifts (e.g., Itakura, 1996; Itakura & Tanaka, 1998; Povinelli & Eddy, 1996; Tomasello *et al.*, 1999) and gaze-shifting of conspecifics (e.g., Tomasello *et al.*, 1998) and that some great apes will also follow pointing and other deictic gestures (e.g., Call & Tomasello, 1994; Peignot & Anderson, 1999; Povinelli *et al.*, 1990; Warneken & Tomasello, 2006), although, as with humans, this takes some time and experience to develop. Some apes that have experienced less day-to-day interaction with humans, such as those raised in institutional settings such as zoos and biomedical research centres, or animals raised in the wild and taken into institutional settings as juveniles, have displayed either a reluctance or an incapacity to follow human points (e.g., Hermann *et al.*, 2007; Povinelli *et al.*, 1997). However, we are unaware of any language-trained or home-raised ape who does not follow pointing; this pattern, taken together with the observations of ape-ape pointing, clearly demonstrates that, empirically, many great apes do easily follow pointing gestures. There is, thus, no evidence for a species-level incapacity for RJA.[5]

---

[5] There are numerous recent demonstrations of apes failing to follow pointing on initial presentation of experimental conditions (e.g., Hermann *et al.*, 2007; Povinelli *et al.*, 1997). Tomasello and his colleagues (e.g., 2007) interpret these kinds of findings as evidence to the effect that apes cannot recognize altruistic intentions in others; however, we note that it takes humans at least 9 to 12 months to acquire point-following, and some perfectly normal humans, evidently, make it to adulthood without understanding the referential significance of the pointing gesture (see Wilkins, 2003). One of us (Leavens) recalls a strange pursing of the lips displayed by his then fiancée towards food at a dinner — he failed utterly to follow what is the canonical pointing gesture for millions of people, worldwide: pointing with the lips (Enfield, 2001; Wilkins, 2003). We submit that his failure does not implicate a profound cognitive deficit in Leavens's (much less the human species') ability to recognize communicative intentions of one sort or another, but simply a lack of familiarity with this particular gesture. (A reviewer confused this logical argument with an anecdote: to be clear, Leavens really did fail to comprehend the canonical lip-pointing gesture — that is an empirical fact; logically, the incomprehension cannot be attributed to Leavens's evolutionary history). Because so many apes (and other animals, including

Tactical communication. Great apes also alter the modality of their signalling, depending upon whether an observer is looking at them (i.e., they spontaneously discriminate visual attention; it was not explicitly trained). Thus, apes will display visual signals if an observer is looking at them, but switch to auditory or tactile signalling if the observer is facing away. This has been demonstrated in ape-ape communication (e.g., Liebal *et al.*, 2006; Pika *et al.*, 2003; 2005; Tomasello *et al.*, 1994), as well as in communication with humans (Cartmill & Byrne, 2007; Hostetter *et al.*, 2001; Leavens *et al.*, 2004b; in press).

Initiating joint attention

Exhibition of self. This behaviour is commonplace in both wild and captive populations of great apes, and would include the kinds of self-directed gestures described above, as examples of initiating behavioural regulation (Pika & Mitani, 2006). In addition, apes and many other primates present their hindquarters in sexual solicitation and to signal submission (e.g., Goodall, 1986, for chimpanzees). Plooij (1978) describes infant chimpanzees presenting their backs to their mothers, accompanied by arms raised above their heads, in an exhibition of self that initiates tickling.

Showing and giving objects. Systematic studies have demonstrated showing of objects in a variety of environmental and rearing contexts. For example, Plooij (1978) described the use of objects to elicit attention in wild chimpanzees, for example, grabbing an object and running away with it, while looking back at another ape. These kinds of behaviours are commonplace in apes, particularly juvenile apes. Russell, Bard and Adamson (1997) reported showing of a novel object to a favourite caregiver. Savage-Rumbaugh (1986) noted that while showing objects is a common part of both captive and wild ape repertoires, giving these objects to another is very atypical in captive populations. However, both showing and giving objects was reported for a sign-language-trained orangutan by Miles (1990) and language-trained chimpanzees by Savage-Rumbaugh (1986), and Carpenter, Tomasello, and Savage-Rumbaugh (1995), among others. Moreover, bartering, the offering of low-quality food (e.g., peanut shells) for more desirable food (e.g., grapes) has been reported by Hyatt and Hopkins (1998) in laboratory chimpanzees at a biomedical research

---

humans) clearly do follow pointing gestures, *given adequate experience*, failures to follow pointing are not diagnostic of any cognitive implication beyond a lack of either motivation or sufficient task-relevant experience to use the gesture.

facility; these apes differ from language-trained apes in having very reduced frequencies and durations of communicative engagement with humans.

Protodeclarative pointing. Pointing with no apparent motivation to manipulate the observer to act on the indicated locus is a relatively rare behaviour among both wild and captive apes, but such acts are far from non-existent. The only well-described example of pointing that we have been able to find by a wild ape involved a bonobo pointing to hidden human observers, and looking back towards his troop — a quintessentially protodeclarative point (Veà & Sabater-Pi, 1998). Among captive apes, Witmer (1909) reported that Peter, a circus chimpanzee, would point to himself when asked where Peter was, and point to the indicated person (for example, one of his trainers) when asked where they were. In a systematic study of language comprehension spanning many months, Gua, a home-raised chimpanzee, pointed to her nose when asked where her nose was (Kellogg & Kellogg, 1933, see Figure 3). Systematic studies have demonstrated that virtually all great apes who have undergone language training can easily point informatively when asked to indicate the location of somebody or something and, also, to point to a picture of a named object (e.g., Gardner *et al.*, 1989; Kellogg & Kellogg, 1933; Miles, 1990; Savage-Rumbaugh *et al.*, 1998). Carpenter *et al.* (1995) reported a single instance of possible declarative pointing by a language-trained chimpanzee. It is important to emphasize that these examples are relatively rare and limited, for the most part, to language-trained apes operating in particular task environments. Even in these rare populations of language-trained apes, protodeclarative pointing is not nearly as frequent as in typical Western human infants, after about a year of age. However, as noted by Leavens and his colleagues (Leavens, 2004; Leavens *et al.*, 2008; 2009), these apes, who have unusually rich exposure to language-using human communities, do sometimes point protodeclaratively. Leavens and his colleagues (Leavens, 2004; Leavens *et al.*, 2005a; 2008; 2009) have speculated that protodeclarative pointing requires a social environment in which such acts reliably receive positive emotional responses — very few apes experience these kinds of social contingencies. As noted above, pointing to request the delivery of an object and pointing to request positive affect or attention are both instrumental acts (e.g., Leavens *et al.*, 2005a; 2009); if this view is correct, then it can be only the rarest of circumstance in which human smiles, laughter and attention gain reinforcing properties for great apes. Because humans who develop protodeclarative pointing also have emotionally rich exposures to language-using

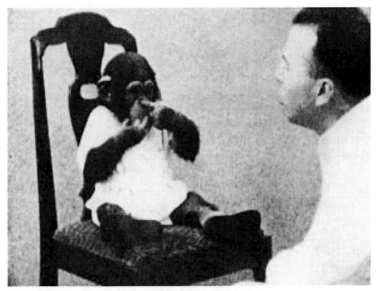

Figure 3
Gua pointed to her nose in response to the query 'Where is your nose?'
(informative point) and also in response to the command, 'Show me your
nose' (declarative point). Photograph from Kellogg and Kellogg (1933),
courtesy of Jeff Kellogg.

human communities, it is not logically possible to determine whether
human protodeclarative pointing is best viewed as (a) an interaction of
mammalian, primate, ape or human psychological adaptations with
particular human sociocultural contexts or (b) an interaction of
uniquely human psychological adaptations with particular human
sociocultural contexts, the latter of which is the dominant perspective
in psychology, today. However, the empirical data clearly show that it
is not impossible for great apes to display protodeclarative pointing;
thus, what we do not know is which experiences foster protodeclarative pointing in apes (or humans).

Conclusion

This brief review demonstrates that no element of joint attention in
humans is beyond the reach of our nearest living relatives, the great
apes. Some of these aspects, such as exhibition of self, use of objects
to elicit attention, and requesting behaviours through manual gestures, are characteristic of apes in all environments, whereas some elements, such as pointing with the fingers, are largely (although not

exclusively) restricted to captive environments, and other elements, such as apparently declarative behaviours, are primarily restricted to apes that have had, like human children, intensive exposure to human sociocultural environments. If representatives of closely related species display similar behavioural repertoires, and if these behavioural repertoires are even more similar after cross-fostering of one or both species, then this implicates epigenetic processes in behavioural acquisition (Leavens, 2004; Leavens et al., 2005b). In other words, apes display every major category of joint attention, including IBR, IJA and RJA; differences that exist between groups of apes with radically different rearing histories result in only minor differences in sub-categories of these major motivations. Great apes are ontogenetically flexible in their accommodation to different communicative environments (e.g., Bard, 1998; Bard & Leavens, 2008). Thus, wild apes, in contrast to captive apes, only rarely point with their hands, but they routinely display IBR (e.g., begging) and IJA (e.g., using objects to gain attention); RJA has been less systematically studied in wild populations, perhaps because of the difficulty in imposing the kinds of controls that characterize captive ape studies, but it would be very surprising, indeed, if captive apes but not wild apes displayed RJA. RJA has been well-documented in both ape-ape and ape-human communication by apes of large variety of different rearing histories. For another example, apes of virtually every background (barring isolation-reared animals) display IJA, although only a few display protodeclarative pointing.

With respect to the NPH, the fact that apes display joint attention with and without exposure to humans does not either challenge or directly support the hypothesis. It does receive indirect support from the necessary entailments of our claim that great apes acquire most types of joint attention with no special training, presumably because, like humans, they learn from experience what are the usual consequences of their signals. People who study human children do not need to invoke qualitatively different modes of explanation to account for human communicative development; indeed, to the degree that apes display joint attention, the exercise is fraught with logical pitfalls and potential mythmongering (endless creation of causative entities that cannot be empirically verified, in principle). A particularly egregious example of this seems to be the claim by Povinelli and his colleagues that similar behaviour displayed by individuals of different species does not implicate similar mental processes in humans and non-humans (e.g., Povinelli & Giambrone, 2001; Povinelli et al., 2003). Yet, ironically, they support this claim by purporting to show that apes and human children, in fact, behave *dissimilarly*, which — even if it were true — obviously cannot speak to the premise.

The weaknesses of telementational approaches (summarized above) apply equally to the understanding of human infant and great ape cognition. What we have tried to show in the present review is that (a) either FP-competence is a necessary foundation for joint attention, and therefore it is a shared cognitive trait of humans and apes or (b) FP-competence is not a necessary foundation for joint attention in apes or humans. If the former is implausible, then the latter is a far stronger starting point for theory-building than the currently fashionable idea that humans require FP-competence to display joint attention, whereas other animals achieve joint attention through old-fashioned learning or, to put this another way, that joint attention in humans indexes FP-competence, but joint attention in animals indexes mere learning. The similarities between humans and apes in joint attention behaviours that we have reviewed, here, argue for psychological continuity between humans and their nearest living relatives, the great apes. Importantly for the NPH, it is by no means necessary to attribute a 'Theory of Mind' of any kind to great apes in accounting for their joint attentional skills, and it would be, besides, impossible to confirm this through experiment, even if we made such an attribution, because, like human infants, great apes cannot tell us about their mental functioning (e.g., Leavens *et al.*, 2004a; 2004b). Thus, that great apes readily display every major category of joint attention described for human infants can be interpreted as being fully consistent with the NPH, which also denies to preverbal or nonverbal organisms the capacity to account for the behaviour of others in terms of folk psychological concepts such as intention and belief.

Acknowledgements

We thank our collaborators, especially Kim A. Bard, Jeremy I.M. Carpendale, William D. Hopkins, Jamie L. Russell, Noah Susswein, Brenda K. Todd, and the many colleagues with whom we have discussed joint attention in human and nonhuman primates, especially George Butterworth, Mark A. Krause, Simone Pika and Vasudevi Reddy. We thank Daniel D. Hutto and two anonymous reviewers for their helpful comments.

References

Adamson, L.R. (1996), *Communication Development during Infancy* (Boulder, CO: Westview).

Adamson, L.B. & Bakeman, R. (1991), 'The Development of Shared Attention During Infancy', *Annals of Child Development*, **8**, pp. 1–41.

Arbib, M.A., Liebal, K. & Pika, S. (2008), 'Primate Vocalization, Gesture, and the Evolution of Human Language', *Current Anthropology*, **49**, pp. 1053–76.

Baldwin, D.A. (1993), 'Early Referential Understanding: Infants' ability to recognize referential acts for what they are', *Developmental Psychology*, **29**, pp. 832–43.

Baldwin, D.A. (1995), 'Understanding the Link Between Joint Attention and Language', in C. Moore & P.J. Dunham (ed.), *Joint Attention: Its Origins and Role in Development* (Hillsdale, NJ: Lawrence Erlbaum).

Bard, K.A. (1990), '"Social tool use" by Free-ranging Orangutans: A Piagetian and developmental perspective on the manipulation of an animate object', in S.T. Parker & K.R. Gibson (ed.), *'Language' and Intelligence in Monkeys and Apes: Comparative Developmental Perspectives* (Cambridge: Cambridge University Press).

Bard, K.A. (1992), 'Intentional Behavior and Intentional Communication in Young Free-Ranging Orangutans', *Child Development*, **62**, pp. 1186–97.

Bard, K.A. (1998), 'Social-experiential Contributions to Imitation and Emotion in Chimpanzees', in S. Bråten (ed.), *Intersubjective Communication and Emotion in Early Ontogeny* (Cambridge: Cambridge University Press).

Bard, K.A. (2007), 'Neonatal Imitation in Chimpanzees (*Pan troglodytes*) Tested with Two Paradigms', *Animal Cognition*, **10**, pp. 233–42.

Bard, K.A. & Leavens, D.A. (2008), 'Socio-emotional Factors in the Development of Joint Attention in Human and Ape Infants', in L. Roska-Hardy & E.M. Neumann-Held (ed.), *Learning from Animals? Examining the Nature of Human Uniqueness* (London: Psychology Press).

Bard, K.A., Myowa-Yamakoshi, M., Tomonaga, M., Tanaka, M., Costall, A. & Matsuzawa, T. (2005), 'Group Differences in the Mutual Gaze of Chimpanzees (*Pan troglodytes*)', *Developmental Psychology*, **41**, pp. 616–24.

Bard, K.A., Platzman, K.A., Lester, B.M. & Suomi, S.J. (1992), 'Orientation to Social and Nonsocial Stimuli in Neonatal Chimpanzees and Humans', *Infant Behavior and Development*, **15**, pp. 43–56.

Baron-Cohen, S. (1989), 'Perceptual Role Taking and Protodeclarative Pointing in Autism', *British Journal of Developmental Psychology*, **7**, pp. 113–27.

Baron-Cohen, S. (1995), *Mindblindness: An Essay on Autism and Theory of Mind* (Cambridge, MA: MIT Press).

Bates, E., Camaioni, L. & Volterra, V. (1975), 'Performatives Prior to Speech', *Merrill-Palmer Quarterly*, **21**, pp. 205–26.

Bateson, G. (1972), 'The cybernetics of "self": A theory of alcoholism', in G. Bateson (ed.), *Steps to an Ecology of Mind* (New York: Ballantine Books). (Original article published 1971 in *Psychiatry*, **34**, pp. 1–18.)

Bateson, P. & Mameli, M. (2007), 'The Innate and the Acquired: Useful clusters or a residual distinction from folk biology?', *Developmental Psychobiology*, **49**, pp. 818–31.

Blake, J., McConnell, S., Horton, G. & Benson, N. (1992), 'The Gestural Repertoire and its Evolution over the Second Year', *Early Development and Parenting*, **1**, pp. 127–36.

Blake, J., O'Rourke, P. & Borzellino, G. (1994), 'Form and Function in the Development of Pointing and Reaching Gestures', *Infant Behavior and Development*, **17**, pp. 195–203.

Blaschke, M. & Ettlinger, G. (1987), 'Pointing as an Act of Social Communication by Monkeys', *Animal Behaviour*, **35**, pp. 1520–3.

Boesch, C. (2007), 'What Makes us Human (*Homo sapiens*)? The challenge of cognitive cross-species comparison', *Journal of Comparative Psychology*, **121**, pp. 227–40.

Brooks, R. & Meltzoff, A.N. (2002), 'The Importance of Eyes: How infants interpret adult looking behavior', *Developmental Psychology*, **38**, pp. 958–66.

Burling, R. (1993), 'Primate Calls, Human Language, and Nonverbal Communication', *Current Anthropology*, **34**, pp. 25–53.

Butterworth, G. (2001), 'Joint Visual Attention in Infancy', in J.G. Bremner & A. Fogel (ed.), *Blackwell Handbook of Infant Development* (Hove: Blackwell).

Butterworth, G. (2003), 'Pointing is the Royal Road to Language for Babies', in S. Kita (ed.), *Pointing: Where Language, Culture, and Cognition Meet* (Mahwah, NJ: Erlbaum).

Butterworth, G. & Grover, L. (1988), 'The Origins of Referential Communication in Human Infancy', in L. Weiskrantz (ed.), *Thought without Language* (Oxford: Clarendon Press).

Call, J. & Tomasello, M. (1994), 'Production and Comprehension of Referential Pointing by Orangutans (*Pongo pygmaeus*)', *Journal of Comparative Psychology*, **108**, pp. 307–17.

Camaioni, L., Perucchini, P., Bellagamba, F. & Colonnesi, C. (2004), 'The Role of Declarative Pointing in Developing a Theory of Mind', *Infancy*, **5**, pp. 291–308.

Carpenter, M., Nagell, K. & Tomasello, M. (1998), 'Social Cognition, Joint Attention, and Communicative Competence from 9 to 15 Months of Age', *Monographs of the Society for Research in Child Development*, **65** (4), Serial No. 255.

Carpenter, M., Tomasello, M. & Savage-Rumbaugh, S. (1995), 'Joint Attention and Imitative Learning in Children, Chimpanzees, and Enculturated Chimpanzees', *Social Development*, **4**, pp. 217–37.

Cartmill, E.A. & Byrne, R.W. (2007), 'Orangutans Modify their Gestural Signaling According to their Audience's Comprehension', *Current Biology*, **17**, pp. 1345–8.

Clark, A. (1997), *Being There: Putting Brain, Body and World Together Again* (Cambridge MA: MIT Press).

Colonnesi, C., Rieffe, C., Koops, W. & Perucchini, P. (2008), 'Precursors of a Theory of Mind: A longitudinal study', *British Journal of Developmental Psychology*, **26**, pp. 561–77.

Corkum, V. & Moore, C. (1995), 'Development of Joint Visual Attention in Infants', in C. Moore & P.J. Dunham (ed.), *Joint Attention: Its Origins and Role in Development* (Hillsdale, NJ: Lawrence Erlbaum Associates).

Corkum, V. & Moore, C. (1998), 'The Origins of Joint Visual Attention in Infants', *Developmental Psychology*, **34**, pp. 28–38.

De Jaegher, H. & Di Paolo, E. (2007), 'Participatory Sense-making: An enactive approach to social cognition', *Phenomenology and Cognitive Science*, **6**, pp. 485–507.

Desrochers, S., Morissette, P. & Ricard, M. (1995), 'Two Perspectives on Pointing in Infancy', in C. Moore & P.J. Dunham (ed.), *Joint Attention: Its Origins and Role in Development* (Hillsdale, N.J.: Lawrence Erlbaum Associates).

Doherty, M. (2006), 'The Development of Mentalistic Gaze Understanding', *Infant and Child Development*, **15**, pp. 179–86.

Enfield, N.J. (2001), '"Lip-pointing": A discussion of form and function with reference to data from Laos', *Gesture*, **1**, pp. 185–212.

Flom, R., Lee, K. & Muir, D. (2007), *Gaze-following: Its Development and Significance* (Malwah, NJ: Lawrence Erlbaum Associates).

Franco, F. & Butterworth, G. (1996), 'Pointing and Social Awareness: Declaring and requesting in the second year', *Journal of Child Language*, **23**, pp. 307–36.

Gallagher, S. (2001), 'The Practice of Mind: Theory, simulation or primary interaction?', *Journal of Consciousness Studies*, **8**, pp. 83–108.
Gallagher, S. (2008), 'Direct Perception in the Intersubjective Context', *Con-
sciousness and Cognition*, **17**, pp. 535–43.
Gallagher, S. & Hutto, D.D. (2008), 'Understanding Others through Primary Inter-
action and Narrative Practice', in J. Zlatev, T.P. Racine, C. Sinha & E. Itkonen
(ed.), *The Shared Mind: Perspectives on Intersubjectivity* (Amsterdam: John
Benjamins).
Gardner, R.A., Gardner, B.T. & van Cantfort, T.E. (ed, 1989), *Teaching Sign
Language to Chimpanzees* (Albany, NY: State University of New York Press).
Gómez, J-.C. (1998), in S. Bråten (ed.), *Intersubjective Communication and Emo-
tion in Early Ontogeny* (Cambridge: Cambridge University Press).
Goodall, J. (1986), *The Chimpanzees of Gombe: Patterns of Behavior* (Cam-
bridge, Massachusetts: Belknap Press).
Griffiths, P.E. & Stotz, K. (2000), 'How the Mind Grows: A developmental per-
spective on the biology of cognition', *Synthese*, **122**, pp. 29–51.
Hauser, M.D., Chomsky, N. & Fitch, W.D. (2002), 'The Faculty of Language:
What is it, who has it, and how did it evolve?', *Science*, **298**, pp. 1569–79.
Hermann, E., Call, J., Hernandez-Lloreda, M.V., Hare, B., & Tomasello, M.
(2007), 'Humans have evolved specialized skills of social cognition: The cul-
tural intelligence hypothesis', *Science*, **317**, September 7, pp. 1360–66.
Hess, J., Novak, M.A. & Povinelli, D.J. (1993), '"Natural Pointing" in a Rhesus
Monkey, but no Evidence of Empathy', *Animal Behaviour*, **46**, pp. 1023–5.
Hostetter, A.B., Cantero, M. & Hopkins, W.D. (2001), 'Differential use of Vocal
and Gestural Communication in Response to the Attentional Status of a
Human', *Journal of Comparative Psychology*, **115**, pp. 337–43.
Hutto, D.D. (2008a), *Folk Psychological Narratives: The Sociocultural Basis of
Understanding Reasons* (Cambridge, MA: The MIT Press).
Hutto, D.D. (2008b), 'The Narrative Practice Hypothesis: Origins and applica-
tions of folk psychology', in D.D. Hutto (ed.), *Narrative and Understanding
Persons*, *Royal Institute of Philosophy Supplement*, **60** (Cambridge: Cambridge
University Press).
Hutto, D.D. (2008c), 'The Narrative Practice Hypothesis: Clarifications and
implications', *Philosophical Explorations*, **11**, pp. 175–92.
Hutto, D.D. (2009), 'Folk Psychology as Narrative Practice', *Journal of Con-
sciousness Studies*, **16** (6–8), pp. 9–39. [This issue]
Hyatt, C.W. & Hopkins, W.D. (1998), 'Interspecies object exchange: Bartering in
apes?', *Behavioural Processes*, **42**, pp. 177–87.
Inoue-Nakamura, N. & Matsuzawa, T. (1997), 'Development of Stone Tool Use by
Wild Chimpanzees (*Pan troglodytes*)', *Journal of Comparative Psychology*,
111, pp. 159–73.
Itakura, S. (1996), 'An Exploratory Study of Gaze Monitoring in Nonhuman Pri-
mates', *Japanese Psychological Research*, **38**, pp. 174–80.
Itakura, S. & Tanaka, M. (1998), 'Use of Experimenter-given cues During
Object-choice Tasks by Chimpanzees (*Pan troglodytes*), an Orangutan (*Pongo
pygmaeus*), and Human Infants (*Homo sapiens*)', *Journal of Comparative Psy-
chology*, **112**, pp. 119–26.
Johnson, C.M. (2001), 'Distributed Primate Cognition: A review', *Animal Cogni-
tion, **4**, pp.167–83.
Kellogg, W.N. & Kellogg, L.A. (1933), *The Ape and the Child: A Study of Early
Environmental Influence upon Early Behavior* (New York: McGraw-Hill).
King, B.J. (2004), *The Dynamic Dance: Nonvocal Communication in African
Great Apes* (Cambridge, MA.: Harvard University Press).

Kumashiro, M., Ishibashi, H., Itakura, S. & Iriki, A. (2002), 'Bidirectional Communication Between a Japanese Monkey and a Human through Eye Gaze and Pointing', *Cahiers de Psychologie/Current Psychology of Cognition*, **21**, pp. 2–32.

Kumashiro, M., Ishibashi, H., Uchiyama, Y., Itakura, S., Murata, A. & Iriki, A. (2003), 'Natural Imitation Induced by Joint Attention in Japanese monkeys', *International Journal of Psychophysiology*, **50**, pp. 81–99.

Lakoff, G. & Johnson, M. (1999), *Philosophy in the Flesh: The Embodied Mind and its Challenge to Western Thought* (New York: Basic Books).

Leavens, D.A. (1998), 'Having a Concept 'see' does not Imply Attribution of Knowledge: Some general considerations in measuring "theory of mind"', *Behavioral and Brain Sciences*, **21**, pp. 123–4.

Leavens, D.A. (2002), 'On the Public Nature of Communication', *Behavioral and Brain Sciences*, **25**, pp. 630–1.

Leavens, D.A. (2004), 'Manual Deixis in Apes and Humans', *Interaction Studies*, **5**, pp. 387–408.

Leavens, D.A. (2006), 'It Takes Time and Experience to Learn how to Interpret Gaze in Mentalistic Terms', *Infant and Child Development*, **9**, pp. 187–90.

Leavens, D.A. & Hopkins, W.D. (1998), 'Intentional Communication by Chimpanzees: A cross-sectional study of the use of referential gestures', *Developmental Psychology*, **34**, pp. 813–22.

Leavens, D.A. & Hopkins, W.D. (1999), 'The Whole Hand Point: The structure and function of pointing from a comparative perspective', *Journal of Comparative Psychology*, **113**, pp. 417–25.

Leavens, D.A., Hopkins, W.D. & Bard, K.A. (1996), 'Indexical and Referential Pointing in Chimpanzees (*Pan troglodytes*)', *Journal of Comparative Psychology*, **110**, pp. 346–53.

Leavens, D.A., Hopkins, W.D. & Bard, K.A. (2005b), 'Understanding the Point of Chimpanzee Pointing: Epigenesis and ecological validity', *Current Directions in Psychological Science*, **14**, pp. 185–9.

Leavens, D.A., Hopkins, W.D. & Bard, K.A. (2008), 'The Heterochronic Origins of Explicit Reference', in J. Zlatev, T.P. Racine, C. Sinha & E. Itkonen (ed.), *The Shared Mind: Perspectives on Intersubjectivity* (Amsterdam: John Benjamins).

Leavens, D.A., Hopkins, W.D. & Thomas, R.K. (2004a), 'Referential Communication by Chimpanzees (*Pan troglodytes*)', *Journal of Comparative Psychology*, **118**, pp. 48–57.

Leavens, D.A., Hostetter, A.B., Wesley, M.J. & Hopkins, W.D. (2004b), 'Tactical use of Unimodal and Bimodal Communication by Chimpanzees, *Pan troglodytes*, *Animal Behaviour*, **67**, pp. 467–76.

Leavens, D.A., Racine, T.P. & Hopkins, W.D. (2009), 'The Ontogeny and Phylogeny of Non-verbal Deixis', in R. Botha & C. Knight (ed.), *The Prehistory of Language* (Oxford: Oxford University Press).

Leavens, D.A., Russell, J.L. & Hopkins, W.D. (2005a), 'Intentionality as Measured in the Persistence and Elaboration of Communication by Chimpanzees (*Pan troglodytes*)', *Child Development*, **76**, pp. 291–306.

Leavens, D.A., Russell, J.L. & Hopkins, W.D. (In press), 'Multimodal communication in captive chimpanzees (Pan troglodytes)', *Animal Cognition*.

Legerstee, M. & Barillas, Y. (2003), 'Sharing Attention and Pointing to Objects at 12 months: Is the intentional stance implied?', *Cognitive Development*, **18**, pp. 91–110.

Leudar, I. & Costall, A. (2004), 'On the Persistence of the "Problem of Other Minds" in Psychology: Chomsky, Grice and theory of mind', *Theory & Psychology*, **14**, pp. 601–24.
Leung, E.H.L. & Rheingold, H.L. (1981), 'Development of Pointing as a Social Gesture', *Developmental Psychology*, **17**, pp. 215–20.
Lickliter, R. (2008), 'The Growth of Developmental Thought: Implications for a new evolutionary psychology', *New Ideas in Psychology*, **26**, pp. 353–69.
Liebal, K., Pika, S. & Tomasello, M. (2006), 'Gestural Communication of Orang-utans (*Pongo pygmaeus*)', *Gesture*, **6**, pp. 1–38.
Liszkowski, U., Carpenter, M., Henning, A., Striano, T. & Tomasello, M. (2004). 'Twelve-month-olds Point to Share Attention and Interest', *Developmental Science*, **7**, pp. 297–307.
Liszkowski, U., Carpenter, M., Striano, T. & Tomasello, M. (2006), '12- and 18-month-olds Point to Provide Information for Others', *Journal of Cognition and Development*, **7**, pp. 173–87.
Lock, A., Young, A., Service, V. & Chandler, P. (1994), 'Some Observations on the Origins of the Pointing Gesture', in V. Volterra & C.J. Erting (ed.), *From Gesture to Language in Hearing and Deaf Children* (Washington, DC: Gallaudet University Press). Originally published in 1990, by Springer-Verlag.
Masataka, N. (1995), 'The Relation Between Index-finger Extension and the Acoustic Quality of Cooing in three-month-old Infants', *Journal of Child Language*, **22**, pp. 247–57.
Masataka, N. (2003), 'From Index-finger Extension to Index-finger Pointing: Ontogenesis of pointing in preverbal infants', in C. Moore & P.J. Dunham (ed.), *Joint Attention: Its Origins and Role in Development* (Hillsdale, NJ: Lawrence Erlbaum Associates).
Masur, E.F. (1983), 'Gestural Development, Dual-directional Signaling, and the Transition to Words', *Journal of Psycholinguistic Research*, **12**, pp. 93–109.
Meltzoff, A.N. (1995), 'Understanding the Intention of Others: Re-enactment of intended acts by 18-month-olds', *Developmental Psychology,* **31**, pp. 838–50.
Menzel, E.W., Jr. (1973), 'Leadership and Communication in Young Chimpanzees', in E.W. Menzel, Jr. (ed.), *Symposia of the IVth International Congress of Primatology: Vol. 1. Precultural Primate Behavior* (Basel: Karger).
Miles, H.L. (1990), 'The Cognitive Foundations for Reference in a Signing Orang-utan', in S.T. Parker & K.R. Gibson (ed.), *'Language' and Intelligence in Monkeys and Apes: Comparative Developmental Perspectives* (Cambridge: Cambridge University Press).
Mitchell, R.W. & Anderson, J.R. (1997), 'Pointing, Withholding Information, and Deception in Capuchin Monkeys (*Cebus apella*)', *Journal of Comparative Psychology*, **111**, pp. 351–61.
Moore, C. & Corkum, V. (1994), 'Social Understanding at the End of the First Year of Life', *Developmental Review*, **14**, pp. 349–72.
Morales, M., Mundy, P. & Rojas, J. (1998), 'Following the Direction of Gaze and Language Development in 6-month-olds', *Infant Behavior & Development*, **21**, pp. 373–7.
Mundy, P. & Gomes, A. (1998), 'Individual Differences in Joint Attention Skill Development in the Second Year', *Infant Behavior & Development*, **21**, pp. 469–82.
Myowa-Yamakoshi, M., Tomonaga, M., Tanaka, M. & Matsuzawa, T. (2003), 'Preference for Human Direct Gaze in Infant Chimpanzees (*Pan troglodytes*)', *Cognition*, **89**, pp. B53–64.

Myowa-Yamakoshi, M., Tomonaga, M., Tanaka, M. & Matsuzawa, T. (2004), 'Imitation in Neonatal Chimpanzees (*Pan troglodytes*)', *Developmental Science,* 7, pp. 437–42.

Myowa-Yamakoshi, M., Yamaguchi, M.K., Tomonaga, M., Tanaka, M. & Matsuzawa, T. (2005), 'Development of Face Recognition in Infant Chimpanzees (*Pan troglodytes*)', *Cognitive Development,* 20, pp. 49–63.

O'Neill, D.K. (1996), 'Two-year-old Children's Sensitivity to a Parent's Knowledge State when Making Requests', *Child Development,* 67, pp. 659–77.

Peignot, P. & Anderson, J.R. (1999), 'Use of Experimenter-Given Manual and Facial Cues by Gorillas (*Gorilla gorilla*) in an Object-Choice Task', *Journal of Comparative Psychology,* 113, pp. 253–60.

Pika, S. (2008), 'Gestures of Apes and Pre-linguistic Human Children: Similar or different?' *First Language,* 28, pp. 116–40.

Pika, S. & Mitani, J. (2006), 'Referential Gestural Communication in Wild Chimpanzees (*Pan troglodytes*)', *Current Biology,* 16, pp. R191–2.

Pika, S., Liebal, K. & Tomasello, M. (2003), 'Gestural Communication in Young Gorillas (*Gorilla gorilla*): Gestural repertoire, learning, and use', *American Journal of Primatology,* 60, pp. 95–111.

Pika, S., Liebal, K. & Tomasello, M. (2005), 'The Gestural Repertoire of Bonobos (*Pan paniscus*): Flexibility and use', *American Journal of Primatology,* 65, pp. 39–61.

Plooij, F.X. (1978), 'Some Basic Traits of Language in Wild Chimpanzees?', in A. Lock (ed.), *Action, Gesture & Symbol: The Emergence of Language* (New York: Academic Press).

Povinelli, D.J. & Davis, D.R. (1994), 'Differences Between Chimpanzees (*Pan troglodytes*) and Humans (*Homo sapiens*) in the Resting State of the Index Finger: Implications for pointing', *Journal of Comparative Psychology,* 108, pp. 134–9.

Povinelli, D.J. & Eddy, T.J. (1996), 'Chimpanzees: Joint visual attention', *Psychological Science,* 7, pp. 129–35.

Povinelli, D.J. & Giambrone, S. (2001), 'Reasoning about Beliefs: A human specialization?', *Child Development,* 72, pp. 691–5.

Povinelli, D.J., Bering, J.M. & Giambrone, S. (2003), 'Chimpanzee "pointing": Another error of the argument by analogy?', in S. Kita (ed.), *Pointing: Where Language, Culture, and Cognition Meet* (Mahwah, NJ: Lawrence Erlbaum Associates).

Povinelli, D.J., Nelson, K.E. & Boysen, S.T. (1990), 'Inferences about Guessing and Knowing by Chimpanzees (*Pan troglodytes*)', *Journal of Comparative Psychology,* 104, pp. 203–10.

Povinelli, D.J., Reaux, J.E., Bierschwale, D.T., Allain, A.D. & Simon, B.B. (1997), 'Exploitation of Pointing as a Referential Gesture in Young Children, but not Adolescent Chimpanzees', *Cognitive Development,* 12, pp. 423–61.

Racine, T.P. & Carpendale, J.I.M. (2007), 'The Role of Shared Practice in joint Attention', *British Journal of Developmental Psychology,* 15, pp. 3–25.

Racine, T.P. & Carpendale, J.I.M. (2008), 'The Embodiment of Mental States', in W.F. Overton, U. Mueller & J. Newman (ed.), *Body in Mind, Mind in Body: Developmental Perspectives on Embodiment and Consciousness* (Mahwah, NJ: Erlbaum).

Racine, T.P., Leavens, D.A., Susswein, N. & Wereha, T. (2008), 'Conceptual and Methodological Issues in the Investigation of Primate Intersubjectivity', in F. Morganti, A. Carassa & G. Riva (ed.), *Enacting Intersubjectivity: A Cognitive and Social Perspective to the Study of Interactions* (IOS Press: Amsterdam).

Reddy, V. (1996), '"Psychologists" Problems with Infant Communication', *First Language*, **16**, pp. 115–28.

Reddy, V. (2003), 'On Being the Object of Attention: Implication for self-other consciousness', *Trends in Cognitive Science*, **7**, pp. 397–402.

Reddy, V. & Morris, P. (2004), 'Participants don't Need Theories: Knowing minds in engagements', *Theory & Psychology*, **14**, pp. 647–65.

Russell, C.L., Bard, K.A. & Adamson, L.B. (1997), 'Social Referencing by Young Chimpanzees, *Journal of Comparative Psychology*, **111**, pp. 185–93.

Russell, J.L., Braccini, S., Buehler, N., Kachin, M.J., Schapiro, S.J. & Hopkins, W.D. (2005), 'Chimpanzee (*Pan troglodytes*) Intentional Communication is not Contingent upon Food', *Animal Cognition*, **8**, pp. 263–74.

Savage-Rumbaugh, E.S. (1986), *Ape Language: From Conditioned Response to Symbol* (New York: Columbia University Press).

Savage-Rumbaugh, E.S. (1991), 'Language Learning in the Bonobo: How and why they learn', in N.A. Krasnegor, D.M. Rumbaugh, R.L. Scheifelbusch & M. Studdert-Kennedy (ed.), *Biological and Behavioral Determinants of Language Development* (Hillsdale, N.J.: Lawrence Erlbaum Associates).

Savage-Rumbaugh, E.S., Shanker, S.G. & Taylor, T.J. (1998), *Apes, Language, and the Human Mind* (Oxford: Oxford University Press).

Savage-Rumbaugh, E.S., Wilkerson, B. & Bakeman, R. (1977), 'Spontaneous Gestural Communication among Conspecifics in the Pygmy Chimpanzee (*Pan paniscus*)', in G. Bourne (ed.), *Progress in Ape Research* (New York: Academic Press).

Striano, T. & Bertin, E. (2005), 'Social-cognitive Skills between 5 and 10 Months of Age', *British Journal of Developmental Psychology*, **23**, pp. 559–68.

Susswein, N. & Racine, T.P. (2008), 'Sharing Mental States: Causal and definitional issues in intersubjectivity', in J. Zlatev, T.P. Racine, C. Sinha & E. Itkonen (ed.), *The Shared Mind: Perspectives on Intersubjectivity* (Amsterdam: John Benjamins).

Susswein, N. & Racine, T.P. (2009), 'Wittgenstein and not-just-in-the-head cognition', *New Ideas in Psychology*, **27**, pp. 184–96.

Tanner, J.E., Patterson, F.G. & Byrne, R.W. (2006), 'The Development of Spontaneous Gestures in Zoo-living Gorillas and Sign-taught Gorillas: From action and location to object representation', *Journal of Developmental Processes*, **1**, pp. 69–102.

Teleki, G. (1973), *The Predatory Behavior of Wild Chimpanzees* (Lewisburg, PA.: Bucknell University Press).

Tomasello, M. (1995), 'Joint Attention as Social Cognition', in C. Moore & P.J. Dunham (ed.), *Joint Attention: Its Origins and Role in Development* (Hillsdale, NJ: Lawrence Erlbaum Associates).

Tomasello, M. (1999), *The Cultural Origins of Human Cognition* (Cambridge, MA: Harvard University Press).

Tomasello, M. (2006), 'Why don't Apes Point?', in N. Enfield & S.C. Levinson (ed.), *Roots of Human Sociality: Culture, Cognition and Interaction* (Oxford: Berg).

Tomasello, M., Call, J. & Hare, B. (1998), 'Five Primate Species Follow the Gaze of Conspecifics', *Animal Behaviour*, **55**, pp. 1063–9.

Tomasello, M., Call, J., Nagell, K., Olguin, K. & Carpenter, M. (1994), 'The Learning and Use of Gestural Signals by Young Chimpanzees: A trans-generational study', *Primates*, **35**, pp. 137–54.

Tomasello, M., Carpenter, M. & Liszkowski, U. (2007), 'A New Look at Infant Pointing', *Child Development*, **78**, pp. 705–22.

Tomasello, M., George, B.L., Kruger, A.C., Farrar, M.J. & Evans, A. (1985), 'The Development of Gestural Communication in Young Chimpanzees', *Journal of Human Evolution,* **14**, pp. 175–86.

Tomasello, M., Hare, B. & Agnetta, B. (1999), 'Chimpanzees, *Pan troglodytes*, Follow Gaze Direction Geometrically', *Animal Behaviour,* **58**, pp. 769–77.

Tomonaga, M. (2007), 'Development of Chimpanzee Social Cognition in the first Two Years of Life', in T. Matsuzawa, M. Tomonaga & M. Tanaka (ed.), *Cognitive Development in Chimpanzees* (Tokyo: Springer-Verlag).

Trevarthen, C. (1977), 'Descriptive Analyses of Infant Communicative Behavior', in H.R. Schaffer (ed.), *Studies in Mother-infant Interaction* (London: Academic Press).

Trevarthen, C. (1998), 'The Concept and Foundations of Infant Intersubjectivity', in S. Bråten (ed.), *Intersubjective Communication and Emotion in Early Ontogeny* (Cambridge: Cambridge University Press).

Trevarthen, C. & Hubley, P. (1978), 'Secondary Intersubjectivity: Confidence, confiding and acts of meaning in the first year', in A. Lock (ed.), *Action, Gesture and Symbol* (New York: Academic Press).

Veà, J.J. & Sabater-Pi, J. (1998), 'Spontaneous Pointing Behaviour in the Wild Pygmy Chimpanzee (*Pan paniscus*)', *Folia Primatologica,* **69**, pp. 289–90.

de Waal, F.B.M. (1982), *Chimpanzee Politics: Power and Sex among Apes* (New York: Harper and Row).

Warneken, F. & Tomasello, M (2006), 'Altruistic Helping in Human Infants and Young Chimpanzees', *Science,* **311**, pp. 1301–3.

Whiten, A. (2000), 'Chimpanzee Cognition and the Question of Mental Re-representation', in D. Sperber (ed.), *Metarepresentation: A Multidisciplinary Perspective* (Oxford: Oxford University Press).

Wilkins, D. (2003), 'Why Pointing with the Index Finger is not a Universal (in Sociocultural and Semiotic Terms)', in S. Kita (ed.), *Pointing: Where Language, Culture, and Cognition Meet* (Hillsdale, NJ: Erlbaum).

Witmer, L. (1909), 'A Monkey with a Mind', *The Psychological Clinic,* **III**, pp. 179–205.

Woodruff, G. & Premack, D. (1979), 'Intentional Communication in the Chimpanzee: The development of deception', *Cognition,* **7**, pp. 333–62.

Xitco, M.J., Gory, J.D. & Kuczaq, S.A. (2001), 'Spontaneous Pointing by Bottlenose Dolphins (*Tursiops truncatus*)', *Animal Cognition,* **4**, pp. 115–23.

Yerkes, R.M. (1943), *Chimpanzees: A Laboratory Colony* (New Haven: Yale University Press).

Zlatev, J. (2008), 'The Co-evolution of Intersubjectivity and Bodily Mimesis', in J. Zlatev, T.P. Racine, C. Sinha & E. Itkonen (ed.), *The Shared Mind: Perspectives on Intersubjectivity* (Amsterdam: John Benjamins).

Kristin Andrews

Telling Stories without Words

Grown-ups never understand anything by themselves, and it is tiresome
for children to have to explain things to them always and forever

Antoine de Saint-Exupéry in *The Little Prince.*

1. Introduction

Folk psychology (FP) can be understood functionally or structurally.
The functional approach to FP is to identify it with a set of practices.
Those who take this approach generally focus on the prediction and
explanation of intentional action (with an emphasis on prediction,
Andrews, 2003). Recent critiques have suggested that FP can be more
profitably studied if we consider its other functions (Andrews, 2008a;
Zawidzki, 2008). Both the standard approach and these critiques
assume a functional take on FP.

More common is a structural approach to FP. Rather than beginning
with the social cognitive practices, and asking about the cognitive
mechanisms that are involved in those practices, those who take a
structural approach to FP offer a fuller definition, and begin with a
more robust commitment to the cognitive mechanisms involved in our
FP practices. Most commonly, this approach takes FP to involve
manipulation and attribution of the propositional attitudes. Daniel
Hutto's recent claim that FP is essentially a narrative practice is
grounded in this approach; this claim involves identifying FP as the
use and comprehension of the propositional attitudes (Hutto, 2008).
Hutto's view implies that having language is necessary for one to be a
folk psychologist, and that those who lack language cannot engage in
the FP practices. I think that Hutto's theory also implies a rejection of
the familiar claim that FP is primarily used to predict behaviour
(Andrews, 2009b).

One of the central projects of those who take a functional approach to FP is to determine its structural properties. For example, when one regards FP as the practice of explaining behaviour, the behaviour is the object of investigation, and the mechanisms that underlie the behaviour have to be determined. Whether those mechanisms include having concepts of belief or desire, or whether they take the form of narrative practice, is an open question for those who take a functional approach. On the other hand, for those who take a structural approach to FP, there are certain concepts that are analytically identified with FP, and the primary research questions are: Under what conditions, and for what purposes, do we utilize those concepts? On Hutto's narrative approach, it turns out that the function of FP is not for prediction, but rather for explanation and social cohesion.

While I think Hutto is right to see FP as involving explanation more than prediction, and while I am sympathetic to the view that FP explanation is closely connected to narrative practice, I think that these commitments are consistent with an account that does not rely on a commitment to FP as manipulation and attribution of the propositional attitudes. I will argue here that we can take a functional approach to FP that identifies it with the practice of explaining behaviour without being led to all of Hutto's structural commitments. That is, we can understand folk psychology as having the purpose of explaining behaviour and promoting social cohesion by making others' behaviour comprehensible, without thinking that this ability must be limited to those with linguistic abilities. One reason for thinking that language must be implicated in FP explanations arises from the history of theorizing about the nature of scientific explanation. I will show that there are other models of explanation that are free from the metaphysical linguistic baggage of the traditional models, and argue that such models can be profitably used to make sense of an explanation-centred FP that need not involve the attribution of propositional attitudes or a functioning linguistic competence. Further, I will argue that there is evidence that pre-linguistic human children engage in explanatory practices, and that some of these explanations may be seen as narrative explanations in an important sense.

2. Explaining Intentional Action

At first, it may seem obvious that in order to even try to explain intentional behaviour, one must at least be able to engage in a linguistic act. After all, when we give examples of explanations, they take the form of propositions, such as: *because she was happy,* or *I think he wanted her to win the race.*

In addition, one might expect that psychological explanations are propositional in form due to accounts of scientific explanation that portray explanation propositionally. If scientific explanations are propositional, and FP explanations are a variety of scientific explanation, then we should expect that FP explanations are propositional as well.

However, this conclusion can be challenged by examining the two assumptions on which it relies. To begin with, even if FP explanation is a type of scientific explanation, it does not follow that it relies on a linguistic model since not all accounts of scientific explanation do. One can also question whether FP explanation is a variety of scientific explanation at all. I will first expand on both of these challenges, and then sketch out an account of FP explanation that does not presuppose that explanation requires linguistic competence.

2a. Varieties of scientific explanation

The 20th century saw an explosion of interest in the nature of scientific explanation, beginning with the deductive-nomological (D-N) account (Hempel & Oppenheim, 1948). On this model, an explanation of an event takes the form of a valid deductive argument that consists of a general covering law and initial conditions, the explanans, which deductively entails the phenomenon to be explained, the explandum. The scheme of the argument is presented as follows:

$$C_1, C_2, ..., C_k$$
$$\underline{L_1, L_2, ..., L_r}$$
$$E$$

where the Cs represent the initial conditions or facts implicated, the Ls represent the relevant general laws, and E describes the explanandum. On this account of a scientific explanation, an explanation is propositional in form, and thus competence with propositional thought is necessary for an explanation to be entertained. Subsequent variations of the D-N model retained the commitment to explanations as arguments, including the inductive-statistical approach (I-S) (Hempel, 1965). Even as criticisms of the D-N and I-S models of explanation ultimately undermined such models, many of the accounts that replaced them continued to assume that the structure of scientific explanations is propositional.[1] It wasn't until Cartwright explicitly challenged the propositional structure of explanation that non-

---

[1]   Importantly, some theories of FP explicitly deny the D-N model of explanation, and can be seen as beneficiaries of Salmon's critique that the covering law model of explanation

propositional explications of scientific explanation as models were proposed (Cartwright, 1983).

Despite the existence of many different accounts of scientific theories, the influence of the D-N model of explanation dominates the FP literature (Andrews, 2003). For example, the theory-theory version of FP explanation can be extracted from David Lewis's account of mental states in terms of psychophysical identifications (Lewis, 1972) and Paul Churchland's formalization of FP as a theory (Churchland, 1981). Both accounts accept that FP explanation consists of a general covering law connecting mental content and behaviour, and an attribution of mental content to the individual whose behaviour is to be explained. Since the behaviour can be inferred from the general law and the individual's mental state, the result is an explanation of the actor's behaviour that fits the D-N model of explanation. Such a move — from a disputed account of scientific explanation to FP explanation — is rarely, if ever defended. If D-N explanations were the only available model, this lack might be forgiven. However, there exist other accounts of scientific explanation that do not treat explanations as arguments, and many that do not take explanation to be propositional in structure.

An example is Cartwright's simulacrum account of explanation as model manipulation (Cartwright, 1983). A model is a simplified fiction that captures the form of the state of affairs to be explained, while leaving aside the substance details. Explanations of the same phenomenon will differ depending on the amount of detail contained in the model, and while more detail can help to provide a better explanation, the model must be simplified enough to be usefully manipulated. A good model provides greater understanding to the model-builder, and thus helps to explain the modelled phenomenon.

While accounts of scientific *theories* as models have been taken by some as a useful way at looking at the cognitive architecture of FP (Giere, 1996; Maibom, 2003; Godfrey-Smith, 2005), so far as I know no one has developed a detailed account of what FP explanation might look like given a model account of explanation. Applying the model approach to explanation in folk psychology, we might say that a folk psychological explanation requires developing a model of the target that will provide a simplified version of the causal relations that are of interest to the model-builder. On this account, explanations are causal,

---

neglects causation (see e.g. Glennan, 2005; Godfrey-Smith, 2005; Gopnik & Schulz, 2007; Maibom, 2003). In more recent philosophy of science, varieties of causal models of explanation (see e.g. Cartwright, 1979; Glennan, 2002; Salmon, 1984; 1994; Spirtes *et al.*, 1983; Woodward, 2003) vie for dominance with unification models.

given the assumption of closeness of fit between model and world and the assumption that the world is causally structured. This account captures the intuition that explanations cite some causal factor without assuming that the structure of explanation is propositional. Model explanations are not linguistic entities; an explanation is the ability to manipulate the model successfully, to call forth the target behaviour. Thus, a model account of FP explanation seems consistent with a rejection of explanation as a linguistic entity, and allows for the possibility that one could engage in FP explanatory behaviour while lacking linguistic competence.

2b. *Differences between scientific explanation & FP explanation*

While a model theory of FP explanation might give some *prima facie* reason for rejecting the notion that linguistic competence is necessary for seeking or providing explanations, to be compelling this argument must include an answer to the many questions that surround model accounts of explanation more generally — questions having to do with the role of model interpretation and construal, and the relationship between the model and the world. Such questions must be satisfactorily answered before we can accept a model account of scientific explanation. But must the same questions be answered in the case of FP explanation? Only if FP explanation is a variety of scientific explanation, and it seems clear that we ought not think of FP in this way.

Scientific explanation has as its primary goal an accurate description of the world. If that description is a linguistic entity, the requirement is for that proposition to be true of the state of affairs it describes. If it is not a linguistic entity, it must somehow correspond to the relevant state of affairs, even if it is a simplified version of the state of affairs. Truth or some kind of correspondence is a necessary condition for an adequate scientific explanation.

However, the goals of FP explanation are rather different from those of scientific explanation. First off, when we explain people's behaviour we do so because they have done something odd; normal behaviour does not require explaining. But the oddness of the behaviour is relativised to an observer; it is only odd if you don't have some understanding of the behaviour. And we develop FP explanations in a social context, so explanations often come about through conversations with others, or with the target herself. If Klara is a stalwart member of the book club, and she doesn't show up for the weekly meeting, then you might ask for an explanation for her nonappearance. That explanation may be supplied by a third party who had a private inter-action with Klara, and who has information that makes sense of Klara's absence. For example, the third party may have talked to Klara about a doctor appointment scheduled during book club, or she might have seen that Klara was experiencing depression, and she may explain Klara's absence in reference to such facts.

Note too that FP explanations are what people actually construct when engaged in non-scientific inquiry about people's intentional actions, not about what caused the behaviour. After all, we are talking about *folk* psychology, rather than scientific psychology. Thus, identi-fying something as a FP explanation is more of a descriptive act, and not so much an evaluative one. While the explainer accepts the explanation as true, an explanation need not be in fact accurate to count as an ade-quate FP explanation. When psychologists study FP explanations, the truth of an individual's FP explanations is irrelevant; as Heider puts it, regardless of whether a person's explanations are true, they are *her* explanations, and 'must be taken into account in explaining certain of his or her expectations and actions' (Heider, 1958, p. 5).

Finally, there is a normative component to the practice of explain-ing behaviour. People provide explanations for their own and others' behaviours for a variety of purposes, such as impressing one's audi-ence, condemning individuals and actions, as well as for simply reducing one's own cognitive dissonance (Malle, 2004).

Since FP explanations are offered for behaviours that are not already understood, we might say that FP explanation is, minimally, something that fulfills an individual's drive to understand a person, and the goal of FP explanation is to somehow make sense of the target behaviour in the social context. Knowing the biological or chemical facts that played a causal role in the person's behaviour may not gen-erate a feeling of understanding in the explanation-seeker, and in such cases those facts do not serve as a FP explanation, even if they do serve as a scientific explanation. For example, we may seek an expla-nation for a person's suicide attempt even if we were to have a full neurological description of her just before she pulled the trigger.

This minimal definition of FP might concern those who think that explanations should be true, but this concern is based on a misunder-standing of the differences between scientific and folk practices. The goals of science are truth and manipulability, and scientists have developed epistemic criteria with an eye towards those aims. FP explanation is a folk practice, and has as its goals whatever the goals of the explainers are. One goal may be truth, but there are many other goals of FP explanation, so truth or accuracy is not necessarily implicated in FP explanations. FP explanation is a natural practice, so our account of FP explanation will be a descriptive one; it is an answer to the question, 'How do people actually go about explaining behaviour?'. Since people explain those behaviours that are not understood, FP explanation will be something that fulfills one's drive to understand a person (including one's self), where that 'understanding' may rely on false or epistemically unjustified beliefs.

The minimal account might also worry those who see it as uncomfortably subjective, since it is defined in terms of satisfying someone's psychological state. However, FP explanation shares this feature with some pragmatic accounts of scientific explanation. Following van Fraassen, since a good explanation only exists in relation to a why-question (van Fraassen, 1980), a good FP explanation will resolve some tension on behalf of the explanation-seeker. What this means is that a FP explanation is initiated due to an affective state that will drive a person to engage in some explanation-seeking behaviour.

I propose the following features for a satisfactory FP explanation:

1. FP explanations are constructed by individuals as a response to an affective tension, such as a state of curiosity, puzzlement, disbelief, etc. about a person or behaviour. The affective tension drives explanation-seeking behaviour.
2. FP explanations reduce cognitive dissonance and resolve the tension that drives the explanation-seeking behaviour; generating an explanation promotes a feeling of satisfaction.
3. FP explanations are believed by the explanation-seeker, and are not believed to be incoherent given the individual's other beliefs, regardless of whether the belief is in fact true or consistent with those beliefs.
4. FP explanations can be given for one's own behaviour or the behaviour of another, and can either be communicated to others or remain private (Andrews, in preparation).

This account of FP explanation emphasizes the phenomenal aspect of explanations by identifying an explanation with the quality of our feeling toward the explanandum. Such a view goes at least back to Hobbes, who wrote: 'There is a lust of the mind, that, by a perseverance of delight in the continual and indefatigable generation of knowledge, exceedeth the short vehemence of carnal pleasure' (quoted in Gopnik, 2000, p. 299).

Some have argued that the feeling of needing an explanation is an essential part of explanations more generally, and that it is a biological drive that leads us to construct and accept theories (Schwitzgebel,

1999). Others have argued that although a feeling of understanding is not an essential aspect of explanatory behaviour, humans evolved to experience such satisfaction with the development of explanations (Gopnik, 2000). Gopnik suggests that we receive intense satisfaction from generating explanations for the same reason we receive intense satisfaction from having sex; it is nature's way of encouraging us to engage in that behaviour. And like having sex, generating explanations often, but not always, provides beneficial consequences for the species. The more often individuals have sex, the more likely it is that they will successfully reproduce, and the more often individuals generate explanations, the more likely it is that they will come upon an accurate account of the world, says Gopnik. Or, to modify Gopnik's view slightly, the more likely it is that they will come upon a useful account of the world, including useful explanations of behaviour, regardless of whether those explanations are true or not. After all, truth is not always aligned with survival.

Either way, paradigmatically, explanations have a phenomenal aspect to them that involves what Velleman calls the initiation and resolution of an 'emotional cadence' (Velleman, 2003).[2] Following Velleman, the paradigm of FP explanation will involve the coming to be and resolution of an affective tension. I won't take a position on whether this pattern of affective experience is a necessary condition for a FP explanation, but do accept that it is the paradigmatic form of FP explanation, and by examining the paradigm we can gain a greater understanding of FP explanation.

The tensions that lead one to seek an explanation may include curiosity, fear, wonderment, and other affective states. For convenience's sake, I call these states *curiosity states*. When an individual is in a curiosity state, it leads her to search for an explanation, and explanation-seeking can take a number of forms. It might involve observable behaviours such as manipulation of the physical world (such as exploratory behaviour) or verbal behaviour (such as thinking out loud), or it might take the form of unobservable contemplative activity (such as building and manipulating a mental model). These explanation-seeking behaviours typically lead an individual to generate an explanation (or explanations), and often later lead to accepting an explanation. Once an explanation is generated that meets

---

[2]   While Velleman was describing narrative explanation more specifically, much of what he says about the nature of stories can be said of FP explanation without prejudicing the issue with regard to the necessity of explanations as propositional. The job of a good story, according to Velleman, is to lead the reader to gain a greater understanding of the events by first initiating and later resolving a pattern of emotional experience.

the very limited rationality constraints described above, namely, the belief that the explanation is true and the belief that it doesn't conflict with any of one's other beliefs, the affective state that led the seeking behaviour is replaced with a different affective state of satisfaction, such as relief, or happiness.

Each of the three steps of FP explanation — the arising of a curiosity state, the explanation-seeking, and the explanation-generating — can be experienced without going on to the next step. One might experience curiosity and have a drive to seek an explanation, but have other reasons for avoiding a search. For example, one's society may prohibit curiosity on the matter, and the prohibition may be sufficient to curtail explanation-seeking behaviour. One might also land in a curiosity state, and seek for an explanation, but fail to generate one, perhaps because one becomes bored or distracted, or because one lacks the cognitive capacity to do so.

Let me add something about the fourth aspect of FP explanation. I do not think that all FP explanations need to be communicated to another in order to count as an explanation. For example, if I see a person walking erratically down the street talking to himself, I might wonder what's wrong with him. Looking more closely, I notice a device attached to his ear, and the affective tension is resolved. I need not articulate to myself or to anyone else that the individual is talking to another using a hands-free cell phone; just noticing the phone places the behaviour in a familiar context, one that does not need further elucidation.

Given this account of FP explanation, it becomes clear how FP explanation and scientific explanation differ. The difference here is like the difference between knowledge and belief. Knowledge, like scientific explanation, is necessarily veristic. On the other hand, FP explanation is like belief, and while it might be aimed at truth, it can still be had even if it is false. For FP explanation, a lack of truth does not entail a lack of explanation.

FP explanation is a folk activity, and when we examine what people do when they explain, we see that truth is only one of the pragmatic goals. Sometimes, we seek explanations in the face of a truth we don't want to accept, like the mother who posted the following to Yahoo! Answers:

> My 17 year old son has been very secretive with me lately, recently he has started to refuse to go to church with the family and tonight when I was going through his room I found a magazine with naked men in it. He obviously has a girlfriend that he is hiding from me that brought that

magazine into my home and I am afraid they are having intercourse and I am greatly concerned that he is going to get her pregnant.[3]

The truth can be too painful to accept, and in the social domain there may be pragmatic advantages to denying what is evident.

The prima facie reasons for thinking that FP explanation must be propositional in form came from thinking that scientific explanation is propositional, and that FP explanation is a form of scientific explanation. I have argued that both those assumptions are false, and thus the prima facie motivation for thinking that FP explanation is propositional falls by the wayside. In the next section I will offer evidence for a contrasting conclusion, namely that practices of FP explanation do not rely on linguistic competence.

3. Explanation Without Language

In the account of FP explanation I sketched in the previous section, I suggested that we should understand FP explanation as consisting of both explanation-seeking and explanation-accepting. A young child may be able to seek an explanation — insofar as there is a tension between her beliefs that she strives to resolve — yet be incapable, due to cognitive limitations, of resolving the tension by postulating hypotheses. For example, if an explanation in terms of the actor's belief is the only satisfactory explanation, and the child is unable to engage in reasoning about beliefs, she would fail to satisfy her need. However, if an explanation in terms of the individual's emotional state would suffice to resolve the tension, then the same child might be successful in devising an explanation, since an understanding of emotional states develops before a child is proficient at attributing propositional attitudes.

Thus, I propose that we consider any practice that falls within the first three steps involved in offering an FP explanation (the arising of a curiosity state, the explanation-seeking, and the explanation-generating) as part of FP explanation. This move might strike some as extremely minimal — so much so that I may be charged with inappropriately extending the application of the word 'explanation'. However, recall that I have defined a curiosity state as some affective state that motivates people to engage in exploratory behaviour. From the seminal work on exploratory play by Berlyne (1954) and Piaget (1951), developmental psychologists have suggested that the following behaviours can be associated with exploration in children (Chak, 2007):

---

[3] Thanks to Fail Blog for bringing this to my attention. Retrieved 02/02/2009, http://answers.yahoo.com/question/index?qid=20081226174833AA5LmiA.

- Touching objects
- Manipulating objects
- Observing attentively
- Detailed observation
- Listening attentively
- Asking questions
- Searching for answers
- Using different methods to search for answers.

The exploratory behaviour, when successful, will provide additional information about the world that will resolve the tension that led to the curiosity state to begin with. Piaget suggested that human infants have an innate drive to explore the world, and that such behaviour is associated with the intelligence that allows children to make sense of the world (Piaget, 1936/1952). Thus, it makes some sense to see the curiosity state as part of the practice of FP explanation.

In addition, since the exploratory behaviour of children that arises from a curiosity state helps them to make sense of the world, exploratory behaviour can be seen as explanation-seeking behaviour. These two aspects of FP explanation, curiosity and explanation-seeking, can be observed and do not necessarily involve verbal behaviour. Facial expressions, behaviour, gestures, and non-verbal vocalizations can indicate that one is in a curiosity state, and the non-verbal exploratory behaviours can indicate explanation-seeking. Explanation accepting is a more difficult behaviour to observe when it is not accompanied by a verbal act. There are many reasons why someone might stop seeking an explanation — the explanation-seeker might get bored or distracted — so we cannot identify the cessation of exploratory behaviour with explanation accepting. Obviously, if one asserts some FP explanation, we can infer from that behaviour that the explanation has been accepted. But if we are to avoid prejudicing the question against the possibility of nonverbal FP explanation behaviour, then we must not require that an explainer offer what we take to be a paradigmatic explanation. Instead, we must look for evidence in the other behaviours associated with FP explanation. Thus, if we examine explanation functionally rather than structurally, and focus on curiosity, explanation-seeking behaviour, and behaviour that suggests the formulation of an explanation, the claim that explanation requires language should be seen as a hypothesis open to empirical examination, rather than as an initial premise.

3a. The early development of FP explanation in humans

Explaining behaviour is perhaps one of the primary activities humans engage in. From gossip magazines that speculate on the odd behaviours of celebrities, to idle chatter about our friends and neighbours, humans have a special interest in understanding others' intentional actions. An analysis of adult human communication confirms this; Robin Dunbar claims that our conversations are dominated by discussion of what others are doing and why they are doing it (Dunbar, 1996). Even young children show an overwhelming interest in the actions of others, including the causes of those actions and the reasons for their performance. When children's conversations are analysed, the content is predominantly comprised of people and actions (Hood *et al.*, 1979), and even young infants ask more questions about people's behaviour than any other topic (Dunn, 1988; Callanan & Oakes, 1992). And while children are not able to ask why-questions until they are about 3 years old (Clancy, 1989), they demonstrate interest in the causes of people's behaviour long before, and are thought to understand explanations for behaviours and use other verbal means to ask for explanations of behaviour by at least 2 years old (Bloom *et al.*, 1980).

Others think that verbal requests for an explanation arise even earlier. In a series of studies, Chouinard found that children start verbally asking for explanations of intentional action using truncated why-questions around 1 ½ years-old (Chouinard, 2007). For example, a child who asks 'daddy break?' in the right context is interpreted as asking for an explanation for her father's breaking some object. This seems to constitute a plausible understanding of the child's verbal behaviour, given her inability to formulate 'why?' questions. Though there is an early verbal interest in seeking explanations for people's behaviour, the requests for information rarely cite others' beliefs, desires, knowledge, or other mental states before the child is 2 ½–3 years old (Chouinard, 2007). While this might suggest that children do not ask for FP explanations until just before they are able to pass false belief tasks, some of children's earliest questions are about people and their actions. At a year and a half, children are wondering why people and animals do what they do, and before asking questions directly about mental states, children ask questions that fall within the domain of social cognition, such as 'What is he doing?' (p. 19) or 'Why is he sleeping?' (p. 64). While these questions differ from the questions that children ask a year later insofar as they don't refer to unobservable mental states, the answers to these questions about people's behaviour will often cite mental states. Indeed, we know that children talk about goals and desires before they pass the false belief task (Wellman & Phillips, 2001; Bartch & Wellman, 1995; Bretherton & Beeghly, 1982), and we might expect that children ask questions about others' behaviour that are answered by reference to goal, emotion, desire, etc. by 18 months.

At 2 years, children are already offering explanations for a variety of things, and there is evidence from children's naturalistic language that 2- and 3-year-olds are very interested in psychological explanations that focus on people, their behaviour, and their mental experiences (Hood *et al.*, 1979; Dunn & Brown, 1993; McCabe & Peterson, 1988; Hickling & Wellman, 2001). However, it isn't until much later that children offer explanations of people's actions that fit the standard belief/desire propositional attitude structure. Children's early explanations often cite emotional states and desires, or are descriptions of the world. For example, to answer a why-question, young children will often cite their own desire (Child: 'Open it', Adult: 'Why?', Child: 'Because I want you to open it') (Hood *et al.*, 1979, p. 6), or will cite an emotion 'I not gon go up … because I'm afraid of her' (Hickling & Wellman, 2001, p. 671), or will describe the situation (Adult: 'Why are you taking off your socks?', Child: 'Because it's not cold outside') (Hood *et al.*, 1979, p. 6).

For humans, the early development of language is quickly put to use seeking explanations and, soon after, for offering explanations of behaviour. But is the development of language necessary for seeking and generating explanations, and does the interest in explanations appear as part of the linguistic competence? There is some reason to think that children's interest in explanations, and in particular explanations of human and animal behaviour, precedes their ability to articulate that interest verbally.

3b. FP explanation in preverbal humans

If we divide FP explanation into curiosity states, explanation-seeking behaviour, and explanation generating, we can see how preverbal children engage in FP explanatory behaviours. Let's take curiosity states first. Among developmental psychologists, early childhood educators, and parents, it is widely accepted that preverbal children experience curiosity. Parents are instructed to be sensitive to the objects of their child's curiosity, and to encourage exploration as part of cognitive development. Facial expressions, behaviour, gestures, and vocalizations are all taken as indicators that an infant is in a curiosity state. Like adults, infants express curiosity with a pursed mouth or furrowed brow (Gopnik, 2000).

What are children curious about? If preverbal children are involved in FP explanatory behaviour, some of the objects of their curiosity must involve the behaviour of people and other intentional agents. While infants are interested in many things in their world, people and animals appear to be the most interesting. When children begin to ask questions, the objects of those questions reflect these early interests (Chouinard, 2007).

While infant curiosity is an accepted starting point in developmental psychology, the question of whether infants take action in order to resolve their curiosity states remains largely unexplored. Very little research has been done on whether pre-linguistic infants act to seek explanations, whether of behaviour or of other events. Still, given the limited research, there is sufficient evidence to conclude that infants are seeking explanations.

Explanation-seeking behaviours in infants, like in older humans, can include both trying to determine the explanation for oneself and requesting information from another. Since pre-linguistic infants cannot verbally ask questions of their caregivers, any request for information must be in nonverbal form. Some developmental psychologists conclude that the best interpretation of some infant behaviour is that the child is seeking information from a caregiver (Chouinard, 2007). Nonverbal 'questions', as described by parents and coded by research assistants, involve some combination of gesture, facial expression, and vocalizations (Chouinard, personal communication). A nonverbal question might take the form of a child's pointing toward an object and vocalizing with a rising cadence (e.g. 'uh?').

In addition to asking nonverbal 'questions', infants can seek information from adults by looking toward them to see how they are responding to an event. Infants engage in this social referencing as early as 10 months, looking toward their caregiver's face when confronted with a novel event, and modulating their response based on the emotion expressed on the caregiver's face (Walden & Ogan, 1988). Such infants might try to make sense of an unknown adult, or an unusual behaviour such as a wink or a silly face, by engaging in social referencing and looking toward the caregiver to determine whether the behaviour is a threat.

Infants' exploratory behaviour also indicates that they seek to uncover an explanation for themselves. From an early age, humans engage in exploratory behaviours such as touching and manipulating novel objects in systematic ways or turning to look for the source of an unfamiliar noise. As they get older, preverbal infants can seek to uncover causes of events through manipulation and re-enaction. For example, a child who hurts herself when falling or bumping her head might return to the scene of the injury and re-enact the events leading up to the event in order to determine the cause of her accident. Or a child who figures out how to open a puzzle box may be seen as looking for an explanation of how the box works.

In the social domain, infants seek explanations when they intently attend to novel human behaviour, move to look from the perspective of another person, or when they re-enact others' behaviours. Even at 12 months old, children will move their bodies in order to see what an adult is looking at (Moll & Tomasello, 2004). For an infant to engage in such behaviour, she must be motivated to uncover the object of the adult's gaze, and must also have some understanding of how to do so. Such an act neatly fits the first two stages of FP explanation behaviour: the infant is curious about the adult's behaviour, and acts to resolve that curiosity by engaging in explanation-seeking behaviour.

Though such behaviours are a far cry from the sophisticated explanations we can generate as adults, in which we talk about motivations for action in terms of mental states, these very simple cases of FP explanation should be taken as part of the FP explanatory repertoire for humans. The fact that the behaviour to be explained is not very interesting to you, as an adult with much experience in the domain of human interaction, does not mean that it cannot be the target of an infant's explanation-seeking behaviour. This may be very simple FP explanatory behaviour, but we should not deny that it counts as explanation-seeking merely because the action is not of interest to us, or simply because the infant cannot verbally articulate her interest in this act.

The third aspect of explanation-seeking behaviour, generating the explanation, is much more difficult to observe. The behaviour we usually associate with constructing an explanation is verbal in structure, and of course we do not see that behaviour in the pre-linguistic infant. Behaviours that we might associate with explanation generating, such as a cessation of exploratory behaviour, could alternatively be due to boredom or a shift in attention due to a new stimulus. On the other hand, a child who successfully solves a problem after engaging in exploratory behaviour may be said to have generated an explanation. For example, we might want to say that the child who successfully opens the puzzle box, and then closes and opens it a few additional times, has successfully generated an explanation. In the same spirit, a child who moves to follow the gaze of a caregiver, and then retrieves the object of the adult's gaze and gives it to the adult, may be said to have formulated an explanation of the adult's behaviour. The child who engages in such behaviour is certainly acting as if she understands why the adult was gazing where she was. A natural interpretation of this behaviour is to say that the child successfully found out why the adult was behaving as she was.

The facial expressions associated with curiosity, and the searching or 'asking' behaviours associated with explanation-seeking, while not definitive proof that infants engage in the first two aspects of explanation-seeking, offer strong evidence. Indeed, even without a prior theoretical commitment to a view that associates explanation-seeking with language, such behaviours would be seen as displays of a child's wondering why, and are often described as such by the layman. A parent responds to her child's behaviour by saying, 'She's wondering why we're out in the middle of the night' or 'He wants to know why you are making those noises'. If such responses are natural interpretations of the behaviour, then without theoretical argument against such interpretation, we ought to take seriously the lay expertise of the adult caregiver, and treat it as some evidence for the attribution (Andrews, 2009a). In addition, if such behaviours are not examples of the first two aspects of explanation-seeking behaviour, then some plausible alternative interpretation of them would be required.

One might worry that nonverbal explanations of the sort I am suggesting are impossible, because the content of such explanations requires language. In response to this worry, let me say only that the same kinds of arguments for attributing beliefs or concepts to animals can be used to defend preverbal infant belief (e.g. Allen, 1999; Dennett, 1995; Smith, 1982).[4] There is no special worry about attributing explanatory beliefs to non-linguistic agents; if nonverbal creatures can have beliefs, there is no reason to think they cannot have explanatory beliefs. Explanatory beliefs, as we saw in the first section, need not rely on having some knowledge of propositional structure, since they need not take the form of arguments. Explanatory beliefs are not like grammatical beliefs, which require the thinker to have some knowledge of language. If thought without language is possible, then explanations without language are possible. Explanations, even FP explanations, are not intrinsically tied to any linguistic concept.

---

[4]   Allen (1999) offers criteria for ascribing concepts to nonhuman animals. Dennett (1995) suggests that we can use the intentional stance to ascribe to animals the beliefs and desires they should have given their evolutionary fitness to their environment. Smith (1982), following Armstrong (1973), argues that we can ascribe de re content to animals. See Andrews (2008b) for a discussion of the issues associated with ascribing content to animals.

One might also object that FP explanations must include reference to the target's belief or desire, and that these concepts, like grammatical concepts, require proficiency with language. Since children do not gain proficiency with the concept of belief until, at the earliest, after they pass the false belief task at around 4 years old, critics may argue that younger children cannot possibly explain intentional action.

But recall that I am taking a functional approach to FP, and not assuming the content of such explanations pre-empirically. Not all explanations of behaviour cite the target's reasons, nor do they all imply anything about the target's beliefs (see Andrews, 2008a, for an elaboration of this point). I might explain my neighbour's rude behaviour by saying, 'They have a new baby and I'll bet he didn't get much sleep'. This could satisfy as an explanation without giving reasons for the neighbour's rudeness. Or I might come to believe that my otherwise progressive coworker votes Republican because her family is deeply involved in the party. Such things are given as explanations of behaviour, yet they do not imply anything about the actor's reasons. My coworker might not realize that her family influences her to vote as she does, and the neighbour might not even know that he was being rude. Explanations of behaviour, then, are more than just ascriptions of beliefs and desires to others.

The fact that children ask questions about human behaviour as soon as they are capable of formulating such questions offers additional evidence that children are wondering about people's actions, and seeking explanations, before they are able to speak. Without good reason to reject this interpretation of infant behaviour, we ought to accept that such children are folk psychological explainers.

4. Conclusion

If I am right and we can conceive of non-linguistic explanations, then the class of folk psychological explainers is potentially much larger than we might have thought. Not only might pre-linguistic children be explaining intentional action, nonhuman animals might be engaged in this FP practice as well. If we want to know whether any nonhuman animals do what humans do in the domain of FP, such as predicting and explaining behaviour, we shouldn't make the mistake of asking whether the animal has a theory of mind, for I have suggested that one can be a FP explainer without having the ability to attribute mental states. Rather, we should look to see whether other species experience curiosity states, and whether they engage in explanation-seeking behaviour that allows them to resolve those curiosity states. I suspect that, once explanation is divided into its parts, it will appear less odd to suggest that nonhuman animals seek explanations, even in the domain of the social.

By understanding FP functionally, and by focusing on the explanatory function of FP, we see that the class of explainers and explanations might be much larger than has been assumed by those who limit explanations to language-users. But we also see that simple explanation-seeking behaviour can involve a narrative structure, even when the explanation-seekers lack language. For Velleman, a narrative explanation begins with a phenomenological state of emotional upheaval, and ends with the resolution of that emotional state and a subsequent replacement of it by some other state (Velleman, 2003). This emphasis on the coming to be and resolution of an emotional cadence fits nicely with my account of FP explanation. Hutto also accepts this emotional requirement for narrative when he agrees with Sugiyama that narrative involves 'conflict and resolution' (cited in Hutto, this volume). Of course, all these authors also discuss narrative as linguistic behaviour, and the latter two explicitly claim that a narrative is only possible when there is a foundation of linguistic competence. But if we take the conflict and resolution as central to narrative, and leave aside the commitment to a linguistic requirement, then we open the door to the possibility that people can generate a narrative explanation before they can use language. Competent language users certainly *can* tell stories without words, as anyone who has seen a Balinese dance or a Road Runner cartoon can attest. The question that remains is whether pre-linguistic infants can do so.

Children who seek explanations for themselves sometimes manipulate the object of interest. If it is a puzzle box, the child will handle the box in order to discover its causal structure. If the object of interest is a person, the child might re-enact the behaviour of the target, either by moving her body to align herself with the target's gaze, or by imitating a series of behaviours that led up to the behaviour in question. Such re-enactments and repositioning of the body to seek explanations is part of the process of explaining behaviour, and this process fits the conflict and resolution model quite well.

For example, a child who sees someone gathering a pile of leaves and then jumping into it might experience some conflict, if this behaviour is unfamiliar to her. To resolve that conflict, a child may re-enact the behaviour in order to discover why the other acted in this way. After jumping into the leaves herself, the child discovers that the behaviour is enjoyable, and understands the other better. This re-enactment demonstrates the child's understanding of a sequence of events. Once the child has discovered the pleasures of leaf-pile jumping, she has a schema of the series of behaviours that will allow her to understand future similar such behaviours. Unless one denies that nonverbal narratives are possible, the child's construction of the schema that can be used to make sense of similar acts in the future looks a lot like the construction by the child of a narrative. And if a Balinese dance can be a behavioural presentation of a narrative, the same can be said of the child's re-enactment of the leaf-raking and jumping behaviour. Thus, the existence of pre-linguistic children as FP explainers is at least prima facie compatible with the claim that FP explanations take the formal structure of a narrative, if we allow for the possibility of narratives without language, as it seems we should.

If I am right to suggest that individuals who are not competent manipulators and attributors of the propositional attitudes may still seek and even provide explanations for behaviour, then the focus on the linguistic aspect of FP is a red herring. Instead, we can focus on the explanatory nature of FP and, from that starting point, examine how behaviour is explained by different populations, both among humans and other species. The important dividing line here isn't between language users and non-language users, but between explanation seekers and those who do not seek explanations. Before we ever developed the ability to offer reason explanations, we first developed the curiosity that caused us to look for answers. How those answers are formulated might differ among species and cultures, but what unites them is their function, rather than the form of their construction. Once it is accepted that those without language seek explanations, we can do the metaphysics to determine how to understand those explanations — as nonconceptual content, or as biosemantics, or some other system altogether. But before we can take on that task, we must observe behaviour.

References

Allen, C. (1999), 'Animal Concepts Revisited: The Use of Self-Monitoring as an Empirical Approach', *Erkenntnis*, **51**(1), pp. 33–40.

Andrews, K. (2003), 'Knowing Mental States: The asymmetry of psychological prediction and explanation', in Q. Smith & A. Jokic (ed.), *Consciousness: New Philosophical Perspectives* (Oxford: Oxford University Press), pp. 201–19.

Andrews, K. (2008a), 'It's in your Nature: A pluralistic folk psychology', *Synthese*, **165** (1), pp. 13–29.

Andrews, K. (2008b), 'Animal Cognition', in E.N. Zalta (ed.) *The Stanford Encyclopedia of Philosophy* (Winter 2008 Edition), <http://plato.stanford.edu/archives/win2008/entries/cognition-animal/>.

Andrews, K. (2009a), 'Politics or Metaphysics? On attributing mental properties to animals', *Biology and Philosophy*, **24** (1), pp. 51–63.

Andrews, K. (2009b), 'Telling tales', *Philosophical Psychology*, **22**(2), pp. 227–35.

Andrews, K. (In preparation), *Person Reading: Understanding folk psychologies.*

Armstrong, D. (1973), *Belief, Truth and Knowledge* (Cambridge: Cambridge University Press).

Bartsch, K. & Wellman, H. (1995), *Children Talk About the Mind* (Oxford, UK: Oxford University Press).

Berlyne, D. (1954), 'A Theory of Human Curiosity', *British Journal of Psychology*, **45**, pp. 180–91.

Bloom, L., Lahey, M., Hood, L., Lifter, K. & Fiess, L. (1980), 'Complex Sentences: Acquisition of syntactic connectives and the semantic relations they encode', *Journal of Child Language,* **7**, pp. 225–61.

Bretherton, I. & Beeghley, M. (1982), 'Talking about Internal States', *Developmental Psychology*, **18**, pp. 906–21.

Callanan, M.A. & Oakes, L.M. (1992), 'Preschoolers' Questions and Parents' Explanations: Causal thinking in everyday activity', *Cognitive Development*, **7**, pp. 213–33.

Cartwright, N. (1979), 'Causal laws and effective strategies', *Nous*, **13** (4), pp. 419–37.

Cartwright, N. (1983), *How the Laws of Physics Lie* (Oxford: Oxford University Press).

Chak, A. (2007), 'Teachers' and Parents' Conceptions of Children's Curiosity and Exploration', *International Journal of Early Years Education*, **15** (2), pp. 141–59.

Chouinard, M.M. (2007), 'Children's Questions: A mechanism for cognitive development', *Monographs of the Society for Research in Child Development* (Boston, MA: Blackwell).

Churchland, P. (1981), 'Eliminative Materialism and the Propositional Attitudes', *Journal of Philosophy*, **78**, pp. 67–90.

Clancy, P.M. (1989), 'Form and Function in the Acquisition of Korean Why-questions', *Journal of Child Language*, **16**, pp. 323–47.

Dennett, D.C. (1995), 'Do Animals Have Beliefs?', in H. Roitblat & J. Meyer (ed.), *Comparative Approaches to Cognitive Science* (Cambridge, MA: MIT Press).

Dunbar, R. (1996), *Grooming, Gossip, and the Evolution of Language* (Cambridge, MA: Harvard University Press).

Dunn, J. (1988), *The Beginnings of Social Understanding* (Cambridge, MA: Harvard University Press).

Dunn, J. & Brown, J.R. (1993), 'Early Conversations About Causality: Content, pragmatics, and developmental change', *British Journal of Developmental Psychology*, **11** (2), pp.107–23.

Giere, R. (1996), 'The Scientist as Adult', *Philosophy of Science*, **634**, pp. 538–41.

Glennan, S. (2005), 'The Modeler in the Crib', *Philosophical Explorations*, **8** (3), pp. 217–28.

Glennan, S. (2002), 'Rethinking Mechanistic Explanation', *Philosophy of Science*, **69** (3 supplement), pp. S342–53.

Godfrey-Smith, P. (2005), 'Folk Psychology as a Model', *Philosophers' Imprint*, **5**, pp.1–16.

Gopnick, A. & Schulz, L. (ed, 2007), *Causal Learning: Psychology, philosophy, and computation* (New York: Oxford University Press).

Gopnik, A. (2000), 'Explanation as Orgasm and the Drive for Causal Knowledge: The function, evolution, and phenomenology of the theory formation system', in F. Keil & R. Wilson (Ed.), *Explanation and Cognition* (Cambridge, MA: MIT Press), pp. 299–323 .

Heider, F. (1958), *The Psychology of Interpersonal Relations* (New York: Wiley).

Hempel, C.G. & Oppenheim, P. (1948), 'Studies in the Logic of Explanation', *Philosophy of Science*, **15**, pp.135–75.

Hempel C. (1965), 'Aspects of Scientific Explanation', in C. Hempel, *Aspects of Scientific Explanation and Other Essays in the Philosophy of Science* (New York: Free Press), pp. 331–496.

Hickling, A.K. & Wellman, H.M. (2001), 'The Emergence of Children's Causal Explanations and Theories: Evidence from everyday conversation', *Developmental Psychology*, **37** (5), pp. 668–83.

Hood, L., Bloom, L. & Brainerd, C.J. (1979), 'What, When, How and Why: A longitudinal study of early expressions of causality', *Monographs of the Society for Research in Child Development*, **44** (6), pp. 1–47.

Hutto, D.D. (2008), *Folk Psychological Narratives: The sociocultural basis of understanding reasons* (Cambridge, MA: MIT Press).

Hutto, D.D. (2009), 'Folk Psychology as Narrative Practice', *Journal of Consciousness Studies*, **16** (6–8), pp. 9–39 [this volume].

Lewis, D. (1972), 'Psychophysical and Theoretical Identifications', *Australasian Journal of Philosophy*, **50**, pp. 249–58.

Maibom, H.L. (2003), 'The Mindreader and the Scientist', *Mind and Language*, **18**, pp. 296–315.

McCabe, A. & Peterson, C. (1988), 'A Comparison of Adults' Versus Children's Spontaneous Use of Because and So', *Journal of Genetic Psychology*, **149** (2), pp. 257–68.

Malle, B.F. (2004), *How the Mind Explains Behavior: Folk explanations, meaning and social interaction* (Cambridge, MA: MIT Press).

Moll, H. & Tomasello, M. (2004), '12- and 18-month-olds Follow Gaze to Spaces Behind Barriers', *Developmental Science*, **7**, pp. F1–9.

Piaget, J. (1936/1952), *The Origins of Intelligence in Children* (New York: Basic Books).

Piaget, J. (1951), *Psychology of Intelligence* (London: Routledge).

Salmon, W.C. (1994), 'Causality without Counterfactuals', *Philosophy of Science*, **61**, pp. 297–312.

Salmon, W.C. (1984), *Scientific Explanation and the Causal Structure of the World* (Princeton: Princeton University Press).

Schwitzgebel, E. (1999), 'Gradual Belief Change in Children', *Human Development*, **42**, pp. 283–96.

Smith, P. (1982), 'On Animal Beliefs', *Southern Journal of Philosophy*, **20**, pp. 503–12.

Spirtes, P., Glymour, C. & Scheines, R. (1983), *Causation, Prediction, and Search* (New York: Springer).

Van Fraassen, B. (1980), *The Scientific Image* (Oxford: Oxford University Press).

Velleman, J.D. (2003), 'Narrative Explanation', *The Philosophical Review*, **112** (1), pp. 1–25.

Walden, T.A. & Ogan, T.A. (1988), 'The Development of Social Referencing', *Child Development*, **59**, pp. 1230–40.

Wellman, H. & Phillips, A.T. (2001), 'Developing Intentional Understandings' in B. Malle, L. Moses & D. Baldwin (ed.), *Intentions and Intentionality: Foundations of Social Cognition* (Cambridge MA: MIT Press), pp. 125–48.

Woodward, J. (2003), *Making Things Happen: A theory of causal explanation* (New York: Oxford University Press).

Zawidzki T. (2008), 'The Function of Folk Psychology: Mind reading or mind shaping?', *Philosophical Explorations*, **11**, pp.193–210.

Shaun Gallagher

Two Problems of Intersubjectivity

Abstract: I propose a distinction between two closely related problems: the problem of social cognition and the problem of participatory sense-making. One problem focuses on how we understand others; the other problem focuses on how, with others, we make sense out of the world. Both understanding others and making sense out of the world involve social interaction. The importance of participatory sense-making is highlighted by reviewing some recent accounts of perception that are philosophically autistic — i.e., accounts that ignore the involvement of others in our perception of the world.

Key terms: Intersubjectivity, social cognition, participatory sense-making, perception, philosophical autism.

The problem of social cognition goes by a variety of names in a variety of disciplines — the problem of other minds (in traditional philosophy of mind), intersubjectivity (in phenomenological philosophy), theory of mind (in psychology, recent philosophy of mind, and the cognitive sciences). There are at least two questions involved in this problem: How do we recognize others as conscious or minded agents/persons, *and* how do we understand their specific behaviours, actions, intentions, and mental states? Most recent work, especially in the cognitive neurosciences, focuses on the second question, and for purposes of this paper I'll do the same. In this form the problem of social cognition has been the focus of numerous empirical and theoretical studies across the disciplines, and there continue to be ongoing debates about best approaches to this problem. Rather than rehearse these debates in any detail, in this paper I will provide a brief outline of current thinking on social cognition in order to distinguish this problem from a second problem of intersubjectivity, which, following De Jaegher and Di Paolo (2007), I'll call the problem of participatory sense making. I'll also suggest that although these two problems are closely related, they should not be conflated. So my primary task here is to make the distinction between these two problems as clear as I can, and to show why the problem of participatory sense making is an important problem that needs more attention.

Standard and Alternative Approaches to Social Cognition

The familiar story about social cognition is that there are two main contenders to be considered as possible solutions. Indeed, debates about these two approaches dominate the literature and seemingly leave little room for alternative theories. The two standard approaches are 'theory theory' (TT) and simulation theory (ST). According to TT, we use a theory about how people behave (folk psychology) to infer or 'mindread' (or mentalize) the beliefs, desires, intentions of others. This practice is sometimes considered to be explicit, a matter of conscious introspection, or implicit, something that we do so often that it becomes habitual. Theory theorists also disagree about whether our ability to mindread is acquired by means of experience (e.g., Gopnik & Meltzoff, 1997) or is the result of a modular development that comes online sometime around the age of four years when, as traditionally thought, children are able to pass false belief tasks. In contrast to TT, ST suggests that we have no need of a theory to understand others; rather, we have the capacity to put ourselves in the shoes of others and to employ our own mind as a model, with which we simulate — create 'as if' or pretend beliefs, desires, intentional states — and then project these mental states into the mind of the other person to explain or predict their behaviour. Again, simulation theorists can disagree about how much this is a conscious process, and how much it may be implicit. Most recently ST received a boost from the research on mirror neurons. It is now a common claim that the mirror resonance system constitutes an implicit simulation when we observe the actions of others by activating our own motor system in a way that matches the observed action (see e.g., Gallese, 2007; Goldman, 2006).[1]

---

[1] I've argued against the ST interpretation of the mirror system and in favour of an interpretation in terms of an enactive social perception (Gallagher, 2007a; 2008d). Sinigaglia (2009 — this issue) outlines a similar approach. To clarify one important issue in this discussion, the idea that motor expertise (the subject's own motor ability developed through

Perhaps the most significant development in recent years is how these two different approaches have been brought together in hybrid versions that combine theory and simulation approaches. Goldman, for example, who has been a strong proponent of ST, integrating both explicit and implicit (neural) versions, also makes room for theory (2006).

TT and ST, and their interpretations of the science, are based on three basic suppositions.

1. Both of these approaches frame the problem in terms of the lack of access that we have to the other person's mental states. Since we cannot directly perceive the other's thoughts, feelings or intentions, we need some extra cognitive process (theorizing or simulating) that will allow us to infer what they are. This supposition defines the problem.
2. Our normal everyday stance toward the other person is a third-person observational stance. According to most of the descriptions given in this literature, we observe the other person's behaviour as a starting point for mindreading (via theoretical inference or simulation), with the aim of explaining or predicting further behaviour.
3. These mentalizing processes constitute our primary and pervasive way of understanding others.

In support of the latter supposition, for example, on the TT side, the psychologist Bertram Malle states: 'Theory of mind arguably underlies all conscious and unconscious cognition of human behaviour, thus resembling a system of Kantian categories of social perception — i.e., the concepts by which people grasp social reality' (2002, p. 267). And on the ST side, Alvin Goldman suggests that 'The strongest form of ST would say that all cases of (third-person) mentalization employ simulation. A moderate version would say, for example, that simulation is the *default* method of mentalization ... I am attracted to the moderate version. ... Simulation is the primitive, root form of interpersonal mentalization' (2002, pp. 7–8).

Among several alternatives to TT and ST, I have argued for what I call interaction theory (IT) (Gallagher, 2001; 2004; 2005; 2008a;

---

prior experience) can enhance the mirror resonance process is often cited by simulation theorists as evidence that mirror resonance is indeed a simulation process. But the role of motor expertise can easily be interpreted in terms of a more specific set of sensory-motor capabilities informing enactive social perception. It's what makes the social perception enactive, rather than simulative. As Sinigaglia might want to say, mirror in action is mirror enaction.

2008b; 2008c; Gallagher & Zahavi, 2008). That IT is a genuine alternative to the standard approaches can be seen in the fact that it challenges the three basic assumptions just mentioned.

1. IT rejects the Cartesian idea that other minds are hidden away and inaccessible, and it cites evidence, from phenomenology and developmental psychology, that we directly perceive the other person's intentions, emotions, and dispositions in their embodied behaviour. In most cases of everyday interaction no inference is necessary.
2. Our normal everyday stance toward the other person is not third-person, detached observation; it is second-person interaction. We are not primarily spectators or observers of other people's actions; for the most part we are interacting with them on some project, or in some pre-defined relation.
3. Our primary and pervasive way of understanding others does not involve mentalizing or mindreading; in fact, these are rare and specialized abilities that we develop only on the basis of a more embodied approach.

To be able to see clearly the distinction between the two problems of intersubjectivity that I am going to outline, it's necessary to summarize some of the more relevant aspects of IT. There are three components to IT, and I'll focus on the first two. Following termininology originating with Colwyn Trevarthen (1979; Trevarthen & Hubley, 1978) in his developmental studies, I'll refer to these as *primary* and *secondary intersubjectivity*. Primary intersubjectivity (which makes its appearance early in infancy, starting at birth) includes some basic sensory-motor capacities that motivate a complex interaction between the child and others. Secondary intersubjectivity (which begins to develop around 1 year of age) is based on the development of joint attention, and motivates contextual engagement, and acting with others. The third component of IT is narrative competency (which begins to develop around 2–4 years), and involves narrative practices that capture intersubjective interactions, motives, and reasons.

Primary intersubjectivity is expressed in an initial form in the phenomenon of neonate imitation (Meltzoff & Moore, 1977; also see Gallagher & Meltzoff, 1996). A newborn infant can pick out a human face from the crowd of objects in its environment, with sufficient detail that it can imitate the gesture it sees on that face. The infant's ability to track another person's eye direction (Baron-Cohen, 1995; Csibra & Gergely, 2006; Johnson et al., 1998; Senju et al., 2008) is an important capacity for understanding where they are looking and what they might take as significant. In addition, infants are capable of discerning emotions and intentions in the postures, movements, facial expressions, gestures, vocal intonations, and actions of others (Hobson, 2005). Infants automatically attune to smiles and other facial gestures with an enactive, mimetic, response (Schilbach *et al.*, 2008). Human infants show a wide range of facial expressions, complex emotional, gestural, prosodic, and tactile face-to-face interaction patterns, absent or rare in non-human primates (Falk, 2004; Herrmann *et al.*, 2007). At 9–11 mos. they are able to see bodily movement as expressive of emotion, and as goal-directed intentional movement, and to perceive other persons as agents (Walker, 1982; Hobson, 1993; 2005; Senju *et al.*, 2006; Baldwin & Baird, 2001; Baird & Baldwin, 2001; Baldwin *et al.*, 2001).

Infants, however, are not taking an observational stance; they are *interacting* with others. For example, infants vocalize and gesture in ways that are affectively and temporally 'tuned' to the vocalizations and gestures of the other person (Gopnik & Meltzoff, 1997, p. 131). The child smiles, the adult responds with a related expression, drawing forth a continued response from the child. The reciprocity in such mutual behaviour leads Reddy (2008) to call this a 'proto-conversation'. Such behaviour involves temporal synchronizations and desynchronizations. By the second month of life infants are sensitive to such reciprocity (the timing and turn-taking) while interacting with others and it provides a sense of shared experience or intersubjectivity (Rochat, 2001).

Importantly, primary intersubjectivity is not something that we leave behind as we mature. We continue to rely on our perceptual access to the other's affective expressions, the intonation of her voice, the posture and style of movement involved in her action, her gestures, and so on, to pick up information about what the other is feeling and what she intends. This has frequently been pointed out by phenomenologists such as Scheler (1954) and Merleau-Ponty (1962), but also by Wittgenstein.

> Look into someone else's face, and see the consciousness in it, and a particular shade of consciousness. You see on it, in it, joy, indifference, interest, excitement, torpor, and so on. ... Do you look into yourself in order to recognize the fury in *his* face? (Wittgenstein, 1967, §229).

> In general I do not surmise fear in him — I *see* it. I do not feel that I am deducing the probable existence of something inside from something outside; rather it is as if the human face were in a way translucent and that I were seeing it not in reflected light but rather in its own (Wittgenstein, 1980, §170).

On average, around the age of one year, the advent of joint attention and the ability to share pragmatic and social contexts transitions into what Trevarthen calls secondary intersubjectivity. Of course movements, gestures, actions, and so forth, are never suspended in thin air — they are embodied; now, however, they come to be seen as embedded in the world. In secondary intersubjectivity the world begins to do some of the work as we try to understand others. The pragmatic and social situations within which we encounter others help us to make sense out of the other person. The things around us set the stage for carrying out certain actions. Children at 18 months are capable of recognizing uncompleted intentions of others because they know from the setting and the instruments at hand what the person is trying to accomplish (Meltzoff, 1995; Schilbach *et al.*, 2008; Woodward & Sommerville, 2000). Children also start to learn the significance of social roles as they are tied to specific environments (Schutz, 1967; Ratcliffe, 2007), and this helps them to make sense out of the other person's behaviour.

Secondary intersubjectivity gives us access to the others' intentions as they develop in the immediate environment, here and now. Around the age of two, and certainly as the child develops through the third and fourth years, they start to understand more complex actions and interactions as they are stretched out over longer time periods. Language acquisition and participation in communicative practices assists this extension of secondary intersubjective understanding, and helps to inform the development of narrative competency. Starting in a preliminary way around two years, and fostered by the stories that we read to children, narrative builds and expands on secondary intersubjectivity and starts to provide more subtle and sophisticated ways of framing the meaning of the other's intentions and actions (Gallagher & Hutto, 2008).

Here I'll mention two hypotheses in regard to narrative competency. The *implicit framing hypothesis* states that gaining narrative competency means that we start to implicitly make sense of our own and others' actions in narrative frameworks. Our perception and understanding of the behaviours of others come to be pre-reflectively shaped by narrative (Gallagher, 2006). The *narrative practice hypothesis* (Hutto, 2008a,b) states that narrative provides the concepts that are basic to folk psychological practice. If in fact we are capable of taking a mindreading stance — that is, if we come to require an explanation of the other's behaviour in terms of her mental states — something that may happen in relatively rare or puzzling cases, or in circumstances where we may be inclined or forced to take a third-person perspective on others[2] — this is possible in part because we gain conceptual and generalizable knowledge of others through narrative practices. Our narratives can become, reflectively, folk-psychological narratives.

Much more can be said, and has been said by numerous researchers, about primary intersubjectivity, secondary intersubjectivity, and narrative competence. Philosophers who are trying to work out a theory of social cognition clearly have to pay attention to the extraordinary work of the developmental psychologists, and owe them a great debt for the wealth of empirical data that they have provided. TT, ST and IT, however, all make some appeal to developmental studies, and it seems that the data are open to multiple interpretations, so that even the developmental psychologists have not found a consensus on this front.

Participatory Sense Making

As may be expected, a number of criticisms of the IT alternative have been raised from the perspectives of TT and ST (see, e.g., Currie, 2008; Herschbach, 2008a; 2008b; also Goldman, 2007; Stitch, 2008). IT has also come under more friendly fire, however, specifically in commentary by Hanne De Jaegher and Ezequiel Di Paolo (2007; 2008; De Jaegher, 2009), and it is this criticism that I would like to discuss here.

De Jaegher & Di Paolo raise three objections to IT as I have outlined it. The first objection is that what IT says about interaction and the direct perception of the others' embodied emotions and intentions can too easily be appropriated by TT and ST. This is especially tied to the way that I characterize direct perception in the context of social cognition (Gallagher, 2008b). Much of what I say strikes De Jaegher (2009) as similar to what I criticize TT and ST for with respect to taking an observational stance. One could take my description of social perception as a description of observing others only if other aspects of my analysis, and specifically my criticism of the observational stance, were ignored. In the context of interaction theory, however, it should be clear that perceptual access to the other's movements, gestures,

---

[2] This is often the case in traditional false-belief tasks where the subject is explicitly requested to take an observational stance toward a third person (i.e., toward a person other than the subject herself or the experimenter, with whom the subject is in a second-person relation). It can also happen in cases where we suspect that others may not be telling the truth or may be hiding something from us. We may come to this suspicion, however, only on the basis of the capacities described under the headings of primary and secondary intersubjectivity, or, of course, on the basis of other relevant narratives.

facial expressions, etc., is in the context of and in the service of ongoing interaction. Social perception is enactive, or as Reddy puts it, perception 'is not merely observation. All perception is embedded in
living and doing' (2008, p. 29).

I have no doubt, however, that such descriptions could be appropriated by TT or ST. Indeed, holding to a certain theory frequently determines the way that data is interpreted. Thus, despite the fact that much
of the data that Meltzoff explicates in his developmental work can be
cited as supporting certain ST approaches, or more clearly, I think, IT,
Meltzoff himself argues for a TT interpretation (Gopnik & Meltzoff,
1998). Similarly, the ToM emphasis on mindreading leads Baron-
Cohen (1995) to regard much of the developmental data about eye-
tracking, intentionality detection, and shared attention as evidence of
mere precurors to the main show of mindreading as demonstrated in
false-belief tasks (also see Malle, 2002). Many of the defenders of TT
and ST explicitly suggest that it's possible to appropriate various
aspects of IT. Thus, for example, Currie (2008) suggests that the kinds
of claims that IT makes about primary intersubjectivity would not be
denied by the ST/TT folk. 'Indeed, all the one's I know about have
insisted that there is a whole lot of stuff going on well before children
acquire belief-desire psychology and which quite clearly counts as
facilitating competent interaction with other people, and they have
speculated on what the precursor states might be that underpin early
intersubjective understanding, and make way for the development of
later theorizing or simulation' (p. 212; similar claims are made by
Goldman, 2007; and Stitch, 2008). I have to accept, then, that despite
the clear differences in what I have identified as three basic suppositions (as outlined above and in other places, e.g., Gallagher, 2008a),
TT and ST may nonetheless try to appropriate much of what is said by
IT. Given this strategy, a defender of IT may be motivated, at the very
least, to play the Trojan Horse option and hope that the appropriation
will lead more to accommodation than assimilation.

A second objection raised by De Jaegher and Di Paolo is based on
their more radical notion of interaction. That is, if IT champions interaction, it does not go far enough in its concept of interaction. The
more radical notion turns out to be an emphasis on the detailed timing
involved in interaction, and the idea that what emerges from interaction is not reducible to the individuals involved. Interaction has a certain autonomy that is not reducible to the capabilities of any one person.
I certainly accept that this is the case, and if IT has not emphasized this
sufficiently, it can certainly accept it as a friendly criticism.

I am much more interested in the third objection, however. This may be best summarized by stating that IT has missed the significance of 'participatory sense making'. When De Jaegher and Di Paolo talk about participatory sense making, they refer to the fact that enactive '[e]xchanges with the world are inherently significant *for the cognizer and this is the definitional property of a cognitive system:* the creation and appreciation of meaning or *sense-making in short'* (Di Paolo, Rohde & De Jaegher, in press). As De Jaegher (2009) puts it, 'Sense-making is the active engagement of a cogniser with her environment'. Importantly, however, sense making happens not merely by means of an enactive, embodied movement, but also through coordinated interaction with others, and precisely this is participatory sense making (PSM).

De Jaegher & Di Paolo suggest that the concept of PSM is simply missing in the IT account of social cognition, and the account could be improved if it were reoriented to PSM. Their idea, then, is 'to reframe the problem of social cognition as that of how meaning is generated and transformed in the interplay between the unfolding interaction process and the individuals engaged in it' (2007, p. 485).

My response to this particular point is that PSM is a closely related, but different problem from the problem of social cognition, at least as the latter is understood in TT, ST and IT. That is, as De Jaegher & Di Paolo develop the concept of PSM, it is clear that they understand it to address the issue of how intersubjectivity enters into meaning constitution, and most generally the co-constitution of the world. The question that PSM addresses is: How do we, together, in a social process, constitute the meaning of the world? In contrast, the problem of social cognition is centered on the following question: How do we understand another person? Now I believe that these two problems are closely related. For example, one might think that the problem of PSM is the more general problem which includes social cognition since if we are trying to make sense out of the world, certainly we find other persons in the world, so making sense out of others must be part of PSM. Thus, De Jaegher and Di Paolo (2007) are interested in how aspects of the interaction affect the way interactors understand each other, e.g., in dialogue how emotional attributions are influenced by the temporal delay and are reciprocally constructed (pp. 497–8) — and they think of this as an example of PSM. But I think that in a more primary sense it goes the other way, that is, that our understanding of the world is shaped by our interactions with, and in our understanding of, other people. This latter sense is definitely emphasized by De

Jaegher and Di Paolo, and in some sense is the central meaning of the term 'participatory'.

Despite the close relationship between these two problems, I want to also insist on their difference. The difference is summarized in terms of their respective targets: in one case, the world (most generally), and in the other case, other agents or persons. I want to defend the idea that understanding another person is quite different from understanding a tool or an object, and indeed, that even perceiving another person is different from perceiving a tool or an object (Gallagher, 2008b). Making sense of the world together (in a social process) is not the same thing as making sense of another person within our interactive relationship, even if that interactive relationship is one of participatory sense making. One process may contribute to the other; but they are different processes. De Jaegher and Di Paolo characterize the process of PSM as involving interaction with others — specifically, the meaning of the world emerges through our interaction with others. In some sense, to the extent that intersubjective interaction is involved in both social cognition and PSM, we have two different questions that have a common core to their answer.

In most of what De Jaegher and Di Paolo say about PSM, the difference between these problems remains implicit, but there is a certain ordering, in the sense that participatory sense making for the most part seems to presuppose that I am capable of making sense of the other person in our interaction (this is clearest in De Jaegher & Di Paolo, 2007). Perhaps the closeness of these problems comes out in the conception of secondary intersubjectivity where our abilities to see and interact with others in our everyday dealings with the world — as we use objects, navigate situations, etc. — help us to understand their intentions, feelings, attitudes, dispositions and so on. We can think of the capacities gained in secondary intersubjectivity as contributing to how we can make sense of the world together.

Philosophical Autism

I think I can make the distinction between the problems of social cognition and PSM clearer by considering what happens if theorists ignore the phenomenon of PSM. At the same time this will point to the importance of this concept. To do this I'll focus on some recent accounts of perception that ignore the problem of PSM. I suggest that precisely because they do ignore PSM, these accounts remain philosophically autistic (for some of this analysis see Gallagher, 2008c). An account of perception or cognition is philosophically autistic if it ignores the effects social interaction has on perception or cognition. I'll focus on two recently published works.

The first is a book by Samuel Todes entitled *Body and World* (2001). Todes argues, influenced by the phenomenological tradition, that it is not possible to provide an account of our cognitive experience of the world without an account of the body's role in that experience. He sets out to show how we perceive objects, and how that experience is shaped by the body's capacity for movement through the physical environment. His descriptions are enriched with examples from sports, dance and ordinary motor responses like turning. His primary aim is to provide a phenomenological account of object-perception — and he explicitly sets aside questions about social cognition, or person-perception, which, he admits, is likely a different kind of experience: 'the way I know *persons* differs from the way I know *objects*' (p. 2).

> All issues in the social philosophy of the human body, all issues concerning our body's role in our knowledge of persons, are carefully avoided. ... for the purposes of this study of the human body as the *material* subject of the world, our experience is simplified by disregarding our experience of other human beings. ... Throughout this book I assume that this question is answerable, without giving the answer or claiming to do so (2001, p. 2).

One might think that's 'fair enough'. But Todes goes further: he assumes that object-perception can be analysed without introducing any considerations about our interaction with others. On Todes' strategy, we would come to understand the fullness and complexity of human experience by first understanding how an isolated body, moving alone in the world, perceives non-living objects, and then adding to this an analysis of how others enter into the picture. The phenomenal dimension of social interaction that characterizes human existence at least from birth, on his view, has nothing to do with the way we perceive objects.

The problem here is not the bracketing of the problem of social cognition — which may indeed be fair enough since an analysis of object-perception may not require an account of social cognition; rather, the problem is the bracketing of participatory sense making — and by bracketing this latter problem I suggest that Todes' account of object-perception is philosophically autistic. The concept of PSM actually provides a good definition of philosophical autism. An account of how we perceive or interpret the world is philosophically autistic if it ignores the contribution of PSM.

Accounts of action can also be philosophically autistic if they ignore PSM. In this regard we can note in brief that Hubert Dreyfus was influenced by Todes, as he explains in his introduction to *Body and World*, and we can see a similar philosophical autism in Dreyfus' influential analysis of expert action. For Dreyfus (Dreyfus & Dreyfus, 1986), expertise is an instance of embodied human performance — on a continuum with basic lifeworld practices. But in his account of expertise, social and cultural contexts play no part. Selinger and Crease (2002) summarize:

> From Dreyfus's perspective, one develops the affective comportment and intuitive capacity of an expert solely by immersion into a practice; the skill-acquiring body is assumed to be able, in principle at least, to become the locus of intuition without influence by [social] forces external to the practice in which one is apprenticed (Selinger & Crease, 2002, pp. 260–1).

This kind of account, which leaves out relevant social factors that involve biography, gender, race or age, however, simply doesn't hold up (Collins, 2004; Gallagher, 2007b; more generally see Young, 1990; Sheets-Johnstone, 2000). Although Dreyfus's account of acquiring expertise does mention apprenticeship, he fails to provide any details about how we learn from others. It almost seems that we are on our own when it comes to learning, and there is no mention of those social processes that we normally would consider important to learning — imitation, communication, working together, narratives, etc.

In the present context, perhaps the most interesting and relevant case of philosophical autism can be found in Alva Noë's (2004) detailed account of enactive perception. This is interesting and relevant precisely because De Jaegher and Di Paolo frame their account of PSM as an enactive account of social cognition. At least on this one issue we can see some important differences in enactive theories.

Noë offers detailed discussions of vision, causation, content, consciousness and qualia, perceptual perspective, constancy and presence, as well as critiques of computational theories of cognition and sense-data theories. He presents an excellent account of the embodied dimension of enactive perception. And yet the world in which we act and perceive, although full of *things*, seems, in his account, underpopulated by other people. There is a lot of the first-person embodied perspective engaged in a variety of pragmatic and epistemic pursuits — but no second-person perspective. Thus, throughout Noë's analysis, we find elements like central nervous systems, sensory organs, skin, muscles, limbs, movements, actions, physical and pragmatic situations to deal with — his account is entirely embodied, emphatically embedded, and exhaustively enactive. The point, however, is not that he fails to offer an account of social cognition — like Todes this is simply not his project. Rather, the point is that there is no consideration given to the role that others (and our social or intersubjective interactions with them) may play in the shaping of perceptual processes.

For Noë, 'the key to [the enactive theory] is the idea that perception depends on the possession and exercise of a certain kind of practical knowledge' (2004, p. 33). The mind is 'shaped by a complicated hierarchy of practical skills' (p. 31). If we ask, *how do we get this practical know-how*, his answer is not unlike the answer provided by Todes and Dreyfus — embodied practice and action. Consider, however, that we might actually get it from others — imitating their actions, interacting with them, communicating with them, entering into intercorporeal resonance processes — and doing this even before we know what we are doing — from birth onwards. For Todes, Dreyfus and Noë, fully embodied individual perceivers and practitioners seemingly move about the world without meeting up with others, and nothing about others seems to significantly count in their analyses of embodied, enactive perceptions and expert actions.

The Importance of Participatory Sense Making

Both phenomenology and empirical science suggest something different. Perhaps Jean-Paul Sartre offers the most dramatic description of the significance of others for the constitution of world meaning. He gives a nice example of sitting alone in an empty park, enjoying the ambiance, when someone else walks into the park.

> Suddenly an object has appeared which has stolen the world from me. Everything [remains] in place; everything still exists for me; but everything is traversed by an invisible flight and fixed in the direction of a new object. The appearance of the Other in the world corresponds therefore to a fixed sliding of the whole universe, to a decentralization of the world which undermines the centralization which I am simultaneously effecting (Sartre, 1969, p. 255).

This may be a little too dramatic, but Sartre is trying to capture the ontological significance of the presence of others. This is not Sartre's famous 'peeping Tom' example, where someone is caught looking through a keyhole and as a result is objectified and experiences shame. The latter is clearly a case of social cognition and emphasizes the importance of the gaze of the other. As Rochat (2004, p. 259) puts it, 'infants develop in a world inhabited by the gazes of others staring at them'. The park example is not this; rather it's the problem of participatory sense making in perhaps its most basic form.

Sartre's intuition here is confirmed by recent science which shows that our attention to objects changes when others are present — even if it is not explicitly guided by others. The way that others look at objects, for example, or the way that we encounter objects in joint attention, influences the perception of objects in regard to motor action, significance and emotional salience (see Becchio *et al.*, 2008 for a good review of this literature). Let me point to three instances of such phenomena which lend support to the idea that PSM plays an important role in how we attend and react to the world: action priming; object evaluation; and an intersubjective Simon effect. I'll conclude with a brief word about shared attention.

Action priming. It's a familiar fact now, from the mirror neuron literature, that when we see someone reach for an object our own motor system is activated. But it is also the case that if we simply see them gaze at an object, motor-related areas of the brain — dorsal premotor cortex, the inferior frontal gyrus, the inferior parietal cortex, the superior temporal sulcus — are activated. Others prime our system for action with objects (Friesen *et al.*, 2005; Pierno *et al.*, 2006; 2008).

Object evaluation. Subjects presented with a face looking towards (or away from) an object evaluate the object as more (or less) likeable than those objects that don't receive attention from others. When an emotional expression is added to the face one get's a stronger effect (Bayliss *et al.*, 2006; 2007). Social referencing, where the effect of this kind of emotional communication is clear, occurs early in infancy (Klinnert *et al.*, 1983). Infants have a propensity to glance at their care-givers when faced with an ambiguous situation and to respond behaviourally toward a perceived object or event on the basis of emotional signals. This suggests that our perception of objects is shaped not simply by pragmatic or enactive possibilities, but also by a certain intersubjective saliency that derives from the behaviour and emotional attitude of others toward such objects. It is also the case that if we see another person act with ease (or with difficulty) toward an object, this will also influence our feelings about the object (Hayes *et al.*, 2007).

Intersubjective Simon effect. In a traditional stimulus-response task, participants respond to different colours, pressing the button with their left hand when they see the colour blue flashed in front of them, and pressing a different button with their right hand when they see red. They are asked to ignore the location of the colour (which might be flashed on the right or the left of their visual field). It turns out that incongruence between the location (L or R) and response mode (L hand or R hand), results in increases in reaction times (Simon, 1969). In other words, it will take you slightly longer to press the button with your right hand if you see the relevant colour on the left side of your visual field.

As you might expect, when a subject is asked to respond to just one colour with one hand, there is no conflict and no effect on reaction times regardless of where the colour is flashed. When, however, the subject is given exactly the same task (one colour, one hand) but is seated next to another person responding in a similar manner to a different colour — each acting as if one of the fingers in Simon's experiment — reaction times increased (Sebanz et al., 2006).

These three examples suggest at least that the presence of others calls forth a basic and implicit interaction that shapes the way that we regard the world around us. But this should be no surprise if we think of how the phenomenon of joint attention shapes the way attention works. Evidence from developmental studies of joint attention show that we gain access to a meaningful world through our interactions with others. The other person's gaze, alternating between infant and the world, guides the infant's attention. Even an infant at 8 months follows the direction of gaze behind a barrier — it understands that the agent is seeing something that it does not see (Csibra & Volein, 2008; Frischen et al., 2007). We learn to see things, and to see them as significant in practices of shared attention. In addition, our perception of things often involves an emotional dimension which can derive from a shared feeling as we interact with others and share their attention to specific objects.

Shared attention, as it characterizes secondary intersubjectivity, is that process where interacting with others becomes an interaction with the world — where understanding others throws light upon the world in participatory sense making, and understanding the world throws light upon others as we see them act and as we interact with them in that world. This is where answers to the two problems come together in a mutual process. These two problems, however, should not be conflated, even if they are closely related in just this way.

One might ask how far back we can push PSM? Might PSM also be involved in primary intersubjective processes, and might we say that PSM already characterizes the infant's relations with others from the very beginning? No doubt more research is necessary to answer this question. What we can say, however, is that the emergence of joint attention and secondary intersubjectivity plays an essential role in participatory sense making.

Going forward, we can also say that participatory sense making is obviously not limited to the perceptual and immediate interactive processes described here. More nuanced social and communicative practices enrich the social and pragmatic contexts of secondary intersubjectivity. As we mature, narrative practices clearly enhance PSM.[3] In narratives, the world around us takes on meanings that are not reducible to purely physical environments or merely instrumental settings. Indeed, through narratives and in many cases through specific technologies, we are able to live in socially constituted multiple realities (Schutz, 1974) — think here about literary and theatrical productions, but also film, television, video games and virtual simulations — and we extend our cognitive accomplishments into cultural institutions, some of which liberate us, and some of which enslave us (Gallagher & Crisafi, 2009). For the most part, to the extent that these remain participatory (and here this term can take on a political significance) there is both good and bad to be found in such productions. In contrast, when sense making ceases to be participatory, as in the extremes of autism or delusional experience (Gallagher, 2009), we often categorize it in medical terms by calling it pathological. Such categorizations, of course, are themselves instances of participatory sense making, as are all theoretical and scientific practices.

Acknowledgments

Earlier versions of this paper were presented at philosophy colloquia at Emory University and McGill University, and as a keynote lecture at *The Body, the Mind, The Embodied Mind: Second Annual University of South Florida Graduate Student Conference*. My thanks to all of the helpful comments I received at each of these venues. Thanks also to Ezequiel Di Paolo and Corrado Sinigaglia for their constructive comments as journal reviewers. This work was supported by a National Science Foundation grant (# 0639037) as part of the European Science Foundation Eurocore project, Consciousness in the Natural and Cultural Context (CNCC) and the BASIC research group

---

[3] This is certainly not a novel idea (see Bruner, 1990; Fiske, 1993). In some discussions of sense making the term 'social cognition' is taken to have a wider meaning than the idea of understanding others (theory of mind, or intersubjective interaction). It means something more like a socially constructed cognition, and in that sense it includes participatory sense making as we use that phrase here. Likewise, the term simulation might mean different things outside of ST. Thus, for example, Fiske, in her review article, 'Social cognition and social perception' writes about 'using stories and simulations to make meaning' (pp. 170 ff.). What she means, in the terminology employed in the present paper, is 'using true and fictional narratives in sense making'.

(http://www.esf.org/activities/eurocores/ programmes/cncc/pro-jects/list-of-projects.html).

References

Baird, J.A. & Baldwin, D.A. (2001),'Making Sense of Human Behavior: Action parsing and intentional inference', in B.F. Malle, L.J. Moses & D.A. Baldwin (ed.), *Intentions and intentionality: Foundations of social cognition* (Cambridge, MA: MIT Press), pp. 193–206.

Baldwin, D.A. & Baird, J.A. (2001), 'Discerning Intentions in Dynamic Human Action', *Trends in Cognitive Science*, **5** (4), pp. 171–8.

Baldwin, D.A., Baird, J.A., Saylor, M.M. & Clark, M.A. (2001), Infants Parse Dynamic Action', *Child Development*, **72**, pp. 708–17.

Baron-Cohen, S. (1995), *Mindblindness: An essay on autism and theory of mind* (Cambridge, MA: MIT Press).

Bayliss, A.P., Paul, M.A., Cannon, P.R. & Tipper, S.P. (2006), 'Gaze Cueing and Affective Judgments of Objects: I like what you look at', *Psychonomic Bulletin & Review*, **13**, pp. 1061–6.

Bayliss, A.P., Frischen, A., Fenske, M.J. & Tipper, S.P. (2007), 'Affective Evaluations of Objects are Influenced by Observed Gaze Direction and Emotional Expression', *Cognition*, **104**, pp. 644–53.

Becchio, C., Bertone, C. & Castiello, U. (2008), 'How the Gaze of Others Influences Object Processing', *Trends in Cognitive Sciences*, **12** (7), pp. 254–8.

Bruner, J. (1990), *Acts of Meaning* (Cambridge, MA: Harvard University Press).

Collins, H.M. (2004), 'Interactional Expertise as a Third Kind of Knowledge', *Phenomenology and the Cognitive Sciences*, **3** (2), pp. 125–43.

Csibra, G. & Gergely, G. (2006), 'Social Learning and Social Cogniton: The case for pedagogy', in Y. Munakata & M.H. Johnson (ed.), *Processes of Change in Brain and Cognitive Development. Attention and Performance XXI* (Oxford: Oxford University Press), pp. 249–74.

Csibra, G. & Volein, A. (2008), 'Infants can Infer the Presence of Hidden Objects from Referential Gaze Information', *British Journal of Developmental Psychology*, **26**, pp. 1–11.

Currie, G. (2008), 'Some ways to Understand People', Philosophical Explorations, **11** (3), pp. 211–8.

De Jaegher, H. (2009), 'Social Understanding through Direct Perception? Yes, by Interacting', *Consciousness and Cognition*, **18** (2), pp. 535–42.

De Jaegher, H. & Di Paolo, E. (2007), 'Participatory Sense-making: An enactive approach to social cognition', *Phenomenology and the Cognitive Sciences*, **6** (4), pp. 485–507.

De Jaegher, H. & Di Paolo, E. (2008), 'Making Sense in Participation. An enactive approach to social cognition', in F. Morganti, A. Carassa & G. Riva (ed.), *Enacting Intersubjectivity: A Cognitive and Social Perspective to the Study of Interactions* (Amsterdam: IOS Press), pp. 33–48.

Di Paolo, E.A., Rohde, M. & De Jaegher, H. (in press), 'Horizons for the Enactive Mind: Values, social interaction, and play', in J. Stewart, O. Gapenne & E. Di Paolo (ed.), *Enaction: Towards a New Paradigm for Cognitive Science* (Cambridge, MA: MIT Press).

Dreyfus, H.L. & Dreyfus, S. (1986), *Mind over Machine: The Power of Human Intuition and Expertise in the Era of the Computer* (New York: Free Press).

Falk, D. (2004), 'Prelinguistic Evolution in Early Hominids: Whence motherese?' *Behavioral and Brain Sciences*, **27** (4), pp. 491–503.

Fiske, S.T. (1993), 'Social Cognition and Social Perception', *Annual Review of Psychology*, **44**, pp. 155–94.

Friesen, C.K., Moore, C. & Kingstone, A. (2005), 'Does Gaze Direction really Trigger a Reflexive Shift of Spatial Attention?', *Brain and cognition*, **57**, pp. 66–9.

Frischen, A., Bayliss, A.P. & Tipper, S.P. (2007), 'Gaze Cueing of Attention: Visual attention, social cognition, and individual differences', *Psychological Bulletin*, **133**, pp. 694–724.

Gallagher, S. (2001), 'The Practice of Mind: Theory, simulation or primary interaction?', *Journal of Consciousness Studies*, **8** (5–7), pp. 83–108.

Gallagher, S. (2004), 'Understanding Interpersonal Problems in Autism: Interaction theory as an alternative to theory of mind', *Philosophy, Psychiatry, and Psychology*, **11** (3), pp. 199–217.

Gallagher, S. (2005), *How the Body Shapes the Mind* (Oxford: Oxford University Press/Clarendon Press).

Gallagher, S. (2006), 'The Narrative Alternative to Theory of Mind', in R. Menary (ed.), *Radical Enactivism: Intentionality, Phenomenology, and Narrative* (Amsterdam: John Benjamins), pp. 223–9.

Gallagher, S. (2007a), 'Simulation Trouble', *Social Neuroscience*, **2** (3–4), pp. 353–65.

Gallagher, S. (2007b), 'Moral Agency, Self-consciousness, and Practical Wisdom', *Journal of Consciousness Studies*, **14** (5–6), pp. 199–223.

Gallagher, S. (2008a), 'Inference or Interaction: Social cognition without precursors', *Philosophical Explorations*, **11** (3), pp. 163–74.

Gallagher, S. (2008b), 'Direct Perception in the Intersubjective Context', *Consciousness and Cognition*, **17**, pp. 535–43.

Gallagher, S. (2008c), 'Intersubjectivity in Perception', *Continental Philosophy Review*, **41** (2), pp. 163–78.

Gallagher, S. (2008d), 'Neural Simulation and Social Cognition', in J.A. Pineda (ed.), *Mirror Neuron Systems: The Role of Mirroring Processes in Social Cognition* (Totowa, NJ: Humana Press), pp. 355–71.

Gallagher, S. (2009), 'Delusional Realities', in L. Bortolotti & M. Broome (ed.), *Psychiatry as Cognitive Science* (Oxford: Oxford University Press), pp. 245–66.

Gallagher, S. & Crisafi, A. (2009), 'Mental Institutions', *Topoi*, **28** (1), pp. 45–51.

Gallagher, S. & Hutto, D. (2008), 'Primary Interaction and Narrative Practice', in J. Zlatev, T. Racine, C. Sinha & E. Itkonen (ed.), *The Shared Mind: Perspectives on Intersubjectivity* (Amsterdam: John Benjamins), pp. 17–38.

Gallagher, S. & Meltzoff, A.N. (1996), 'The Earliest Sense of Self and Others', *Philosophical Psychology*, **9**, pp. 213–36.

Gallagher, S. & Zahavi, D. (2008), *The Phenomenological Mind* (London: Routledge).

Gallese, V. (2007), 'Before and Below "Theory of Mind": Embodied simulation and the neural correlates of social cognition', Philosophical Transactions of the Royal Society, *B—Biological Sciences*, **362** (1480), pp. 659–69.

Goldman, A.I. (2002), 'Simulation Theory and Mental Concepts', in J. Dokic & J. Proust (ed.), *Simulation and Knowledge of Action* (Amsterdam: John Benjamins), pp. 1–19.

Goldman, A. (2006), *Simulating Minds: The Philosophy, Psychology and Neuroscience of Mindreading* (Oxford: Oxford University Press).

Goldman, A. (2007), Simulation-theory: Hybrid vs interaction-narrative practice. Paper presented at conference on Narrative Alternatives to Theory of Mind. University of Hertfordshire (July, 2007).

Gopnik, A. & Meltzoff, A.N. (1997), *Words, Thoughts, and Theories* (Cambridge, MA: MIT Press).

Hayes, A.E., Paul, M.A., Beuger, B. & Tipper S.P. (2007), 'Self Produced and Observed Actions Influence Emotion: The roles of action fluency and eye gaze', *Psychological research*, **72**, pp. 461–72.

Herrmann, E., Call, J., Hare, B. & Tomasello, M. (2007), 'Humans Evolved Specialized Skills of Social Cognition: The cultural intelligence hypothesis', *Science*, **317** (5843), pp. 1360–6.

Herschbach, M. (2008a), 'False-belief Understanding and the Phenomenological Critique of Folk Psychology', *Journal of Consciousness Studies*, **15** (12), pp. 33–56.

Herschbach, M. (2008b), 'Folk Psychological and Phenomenological accounts of Social Perception', *Philosophical Explorations*, **11** (3), pp. 223–35.

Hobson, P. (1993), 'The Emotional Origins of Social Understanding', *Philosophical Psychology*, **6**, pp. 227–49.

Hobson, P. (2005), *The Cradle of Thought* (Oxford: Oxford University Press).

Hutto, D.D. (2008a), *Folk psychological narratives: The sociocultural basis of understanding reasons* (Cambridge, MA: MIT Press).

Hutto, D. (2008b), 'The Narrative Practice Hypothesis: Clarifications and implications', *Philosophical Explorations*, **11** (3), pp. 175–92.

Johnson, S., Slaughter V. & Carey, S. (1998), 'Whose Gaze will Infants Follow? The elicitation of gaze-following in 12-month-old infants', *Developmental Science*, **1**, pp. 233–8.

Klinnert, M.D., Campos, J.J., Sorce, J.F., Emde, R.N. & Svejda, M. (1983), 'Emotions as behavior regulators: Social referencing in infancy', in R. Plutchick & H. Kellerman (ed.), *Emotions in Early Development, Vol. 2., The Emotions* (New York: Academic Press), pp. 57–86.

Malle, B.F. (2002), 'The Relation between Language and Theory of Mind in Development and Evolution', in T. Givón & B.F. Malle (ed.), *The Evolution of Language out of Pre-Language* (Amsterdam: John Benjamins), pp. 265–84.

Meltzoff, A.N. (1995), 'Understanding the Intentions of Others: Re-enactment of intended acts by 18-month-old children', *Developmental Psychology*, **31**, pp. 838–50.

Meltzoff, A. & Moore, M.K. (1977), 'Imitation of Facial and Manual Gestures by Human Neonates', *Science*, **198**, pp. 75–8.

Merleau-Ponty, M. (1962), *Phenomenology of Perception*, Trans. C. Smith (London: Routledge & Kegan Paul).

Noë, A. (2004), *Action in Perception* (Cambridge, MA: MIT Press).

Pierno, A.C., Becchio, C., Wall, M.B., Smith, A.T., Turella, L. & Castiello, U. (2006), 'When Gaze turns into Grasp', *Journal of Cognitive Neuroscience,* **18**, pp. 2130–7.

Pierno, A.C., Becchio, C., Tubaldia, F., Turella, L. & Castiello, U. (2008), 'Motor ontology in Representing Gaze-object Relations', *Neuroscience Letters*, **430**, pp. 246–51.

Ratcliffe, M.J. (2007), *Rethinking Commonsense Psychology: A Critique of Folk Psychology, Theory of Mind and Simulation* (Basingstoke: Palgrave Macmillan).

Reddy, V. (2008), *How Infants Know Minds* (Cambridge, MA: Harvard University Press).

Rochat, P. (2001), *The Infant's World* (Cambridge: Harvard University Press).

Rochat, P. (2004), 'Emerging co-awareness', in G. Bremner & A. Slater (ed.), *Theories of Infant Development* (New York: Wiley-Blackwell), pp. 258–82.

Sartre, J.-P. (1969), *Being and Nothingness: An Essay on Phenomenological Ontology*, trans. H.E. Barnes (London: Routledge).

Scheler, M. (1954), *The nature of sympathy* (London: Routledge and Kegan Paul).

Schutz, A. (1967), *The Phenomenology of the Social World*, Trans. G. Walsh & F. Lehnert (Evanston: Northwestern University Press).

Schutz, A. (1974), *Collected Papers Vol. 1. The Problem of Social Reality* (Dordrect: Springer).

Schilbach, L., Eickhoff, S.B., Mojzisch, A. & Vogeley, K. (2008), 'What's in a Smile? Neural correlates of facial embodiment during social interaction', *Social Neuroscience*, **3** (1), pp. 37–50.

Sebanz, N., Bekkering, H. & Knoblich, G. (2006), 'Joint Action: Bodies and minds moving together', *Trends in Cognitive Sciences*, **10** (2), pp. 70–6.

Selinger, E.M. & Crease, R.P. (2002), 'Dreyfus on Expertise: The limits of phenomenological analysis', *Continental Philosophy Review*, **35**, pp. 245–79.

Senju, A., Csibra, G. & Johnson, M.H. (2008), 'Understanding the Referential Nature of Looking: Infants' preference for object-directed gaze', *Cognition*, **108**, pp. 303–19.

Senju, A., Johnson, M.H. & Csibra, G. (2006), 'The Development and Neural Basis of Referential Gaze Perception', *Social Neuroscience*, **1** (3–4), pp. 220–34.

Sheets-Johnstone, M. (2000), 'Kinetic Tactile-kinesthetic Bodies: Ontogenetical foundations of apprenticeship learning', *Human Studies*, **23**, pp. 343–70.

Simon, H. (1969), 'Reactions Towards the Source of the Stimulation', *Journal of Experimental Psychology*, **81** (1), pp. 174–6.

Sinigaglia, C. (2009), 'Mirror in Action', *Journal of Consciousness Studies* (this issue).

Stitch, S. (2008), 'Social Cognition, Folk Psychology and Theory-theory', Paper presented at the NSF Collegium on Social Cognition and Social Narrative, San Marino University (July, 2008).

Todes, S. (2001), *Body and World* (Cambridge MA: MIT Press).

Trevarthen, C.B. (1979), 'Communication and Cooperation in Early Infancy: A description of primary intersubjectivity', in M. Bullowa (ed.), *Before Speech* (Cambridge: Cambridge University Press), pp. 321–47.

Trevarthen, C. & Hubley, P. (1978), 'Secondary Intersubjectivity: Confidence, confiding and acts of meaning in the first year', in A. Lock (ed.), *Action, Gesture and Symbol: The Emergence of Language* (London: Academic Press), pp. 183–29.

Walker, A.S. (1982), 'Intermodal Perception of Expressive Behaviors by Human Infants', *Journal of Experimental Child Psychology*, **33**, pp. 514–35.

Wittgenstein, L. (1967), *Zettel*, G.E.M. Anscombe & G.H. von Wright (ed.), trans. G.E.M. Anscombe (Berkeley: University of California Press).

Wittgenstein, L. (1980), *Remarks on the philosophy of psychology* (Vol. II), G.H. von Wright & H. Nyman (ed.), trans. C.G. Luckhardt & M.A.E. Aue (Oxford: Blackwell).

Woodward, A.L. & Sommerville, J.A. (2000), 'Twelve-month-old Infants Interpret Action in Context', *Psychological Science*, **11**, pp. 73–7.

Young, I. (1990), *Throwing Like a Girl and Other Essays* (Bloomington: Indiana University Press).

Corrado Sinigaglia

Mirror in Action

Abstract: *Several authors have recently pointed out the hyper-mentalism of the standard mindreading models, arguing for the need of an embodied and enactive approach to social cognition. Various attempts to provide an account of the primary ways of interacting with others, however, have fallen short of allowing for both what kind of intentional engagement is crucial in the basic forms of social navigation and also what neural mechanisms can be thought to underpin them. The aim of the paper is to counter this fault by showing that most of the primary ways of making sense of others are motor in nature and rooted in a specific brain mechanism: the mirror mechanism. I shall argue that the mirror-based making sense of others not only can be construed within the enactive approach to social cognition, but also allows us to refine it, supplying a plausible and unitary account of the early forms of social interaction.*

1. Introduction

Over the last few years, several philosophers and psychologists have questioned more and more the two-party system that for a long time has ruled the social cognition debate, turning it into the fight between those who hold that such a cognition depends on a mindreading ability based on a more or less explicit use of a folk psychological theory (Theory-Theory party, TT) and those who appeal to our capacity to imagine ourselves in others' shoes, pretending their beliefs and desires (Simulation-Theory party, ST). Shaun Gallagher and Daniel D. Hutto (among others) have frequently and at length argued that, inspite of the differences between the advocates of the two parties, TT and ST would share the same paradoxical fate, both overstating the role and scope of mindreading in social cognition and also oversimplifying the folk psychological skills that have to be acquired in order to make sense of the behaviour of others (see, for example, Gallagher, 2001; 2006; 2008; Gallagher & Hutto, 2008; Hutto, 2004; 2006; 2007; 2008a; b; see also Hutto & Ratcliffe, 2007; Hobson, 2004; Ratcliffe, 2007; and Sloors, 2007).

With regard to the first point, both parties would share the supposition that 'whenever we encounter others (or at least in most encounters) we attempt to explain or predict their behaviour by divining their mental states' — and this is tantamount to saying that 'our normal everyday stance toward the other person is an observational stance' and that 'mentalizing processes (theorizing and simulating) constitute our primary and pervasive way of understanding others' (Gallagher, 2008, p. 164). However, phenomenology and developmental psychology demonstrate that most of our everyday commerce with others does not rely on an observational stance toward them, but rather tends to be interactive and engaged, involving 'neither predictions nor explanations *per se*' but instead embodied practices and expectations that are 'not only quicker but also more powerful and reliable ways of relating to others and navigating social dynamics' (Hutto, 2007, p. 44). In other words, they demonstrate that 'mentalizing or mindreading are, at the best, specialized abilities that are relatively rarely employed', depending on 'more embodied and situated ways of perceiving and understanding others' (Gallagher, 2008, p. 164).

With regard to the second point, both TT and ST would presuppose 'some kind of commerce with the principles of intentional psychology, whether this is imagined to take the form of a tacit or explicit theoretical understanding or a practical capacity to manipulate one's own mental states in accord with them', but 'presupposing the existence of such abilities is not the same as adequately *explaining* how they first came to be in place' (Hutto, 2008a, p. 24). By highlighting the 'logical distinction' between attributing beliefs and desires and understanding reasons, Hutto has pointed out that, 'contrary to their advertisements', the advocates of the two rival parties do not provide any 'deep understanding' of what it really takes to be a folk-psychologist, leaving unanswered the critical question as to how we get to master the folk psychological 'principles governing the interaction of the [propositional] attitudes, both with one another and with other key psychological players (such as perception and emotion)' and to apply them to particular cases requiring to take into account variables such as circumstances and individual histories (Hutto, 2007, p. 48). This is the reason why Hutto has launched his Narrative Practice Hypothesis (NPH), claiming that children normally acquire the mastery of psychological principles and the ability to apply them 'by engaging in story-telling practice, with the support of others. The stories about those who act for reasons — i.e. folk psychological narratives — are the foci of this practice. Stories of this special kind provide the crucial training needed for understanding reasons. They do this by serving as exemplars, having precisely the right features to foster an understanding of the *forms* and *norms* of folk psychology' (Hutto, 2007, p. 53).

It is not my intention to discuss in this paper whether and to what extent NPH really breaks the two-party system providing a theoretically progressive and empirically sound alternative to both TT and ST for the ways of developing folk psychological competencies and making sense of others as those who act for reasons. Nor do I intend to discuss whether folk psychological narratives actually prevent people to turn to theory of mind or simulation practice or rather end up presupposing theoretical reasoning on and/or imaginative pretending of others' beliefs and desires. These subjects will be dealt with by other authors.

The aim of my paper is to deal with what is at the core of the first above-mentioned point, that is, the nature and scope of the most primary and pervasive ways of perceiving and understanding others. Two reasons motivate my focussing on the basic ways of social cognition. The first is that it is true that Gallagher and Hutto have repetitively emphasized that 'before we are in position to theorize, simulate, explain or predict mental states in others, we are already in position to interact with and to understand others in terms of their expressions, gestures, intentions, and emotions' (Gallagher & Hutto, 2008, p. 20). But it is equally true that many advocates of the TT and ST parties would not have difficulty in acknowledging that *before* and *below*[1] mindreading 'there is much going on which underpins competent interaction with other people' (Currie, 2008, p. 212; see also Goldman, 2006).[2] There is now wide agreement among developmental psychologists that infants display sophisticated social cognitive skills

[1] I have borrowed this expression *verbatim* from Gallese (2007).

[2] 'I am inclined to accept something which Gallagher has called the *supposition of universality*: "Our reliance on theory (or our reliance on simulation or some combination of theory and simulation) is close to universal. That is, this folk-psychological way of understanding and interacting with others is pervasive in our everyday life" (Gallagher, 2004, p. 200). But holding this principle is consistent with thinking that, while the use of some method — simulation, theory, or both — of finding out beliefs and desires is close to universal, it regularly goes along with, and indeed depends on, the use of more primitive

well before they develop full-blown meta-representational abilities. In particular, there is mounting evidence that infants become able to detect others' action goals and intentions during the first year of life and that this ability does not involve any kind of mentalizing (see, for example, Csibra & Gergely, 2007; Sommerville & Woodward, 2005; see also Gallese *et al.*, 2009 for a review). However, in spite of such a consensus on what these basic ways of interacting with others *are not* (they *do not* involve mentalizing, they do not require mastering mental state concepts such as belief, desire, and so on), what they really *are in nature* and what relevance they have for social cognition from both a psychological and philosophical point of view are still an object of controversy. Although I do not think that what occurs before and below mentalizing necessarily forces the choice between the two or three main parties (TT, ST and NPH), the elucidation of primary ways of intersubjective engagement can supply basic constraints that have to be met by mindreading models.

The second reason is that, differently from full-blown mindreading abilities, most of the primary ways of interacting with others seem to be rooted in, or can at least be referred to specific neural mechanisms. Indeed, the discovery of a mirror mechanism in monkey and human brains helps to shed new light on the various and strictly intertwined processes at the basis of our making sense of others. Again, I am not posing a one-to-one relationship between the personal and sub-personal level; on the contrary, I agree with Susan Hurley when she remarks that, even without assuming a simple isomorphism between the two levels, sub-personal processes can provide information that enables personal level processes (Hurley, 2006), thus facilitating a more accurate account of our everyday engagement with others.

There are three sections to come. Section 2 briefly illustrates the key mirror neuron properties and discusses the mirror mechanism and its core function in understanding others' behaviour. For the sake of brevity (and convenience) I shall only take into account the mirror system for action as most of the mirror neuron debate has been centred on this domain. This of course does not mean to say that I am not appreciating the significance of other kinds of mirroring, starting with the emotional one, and their role in social navigation. Section 3 deals with the originality of mirror-based action understanding, arguing that the latter not only can be construed within the enactive approach to social cognition, but also allows us to refine it. Section 4 explores

modes of intersubjective understanding, which includes, for all I know, the perceptual methods suggested by Gallagher and Hutto' (Currie, 2008, p. 213).

what the mirror mechanism can tell us about the primary ways of interacting with others and the development of intentional understanding.

2. The Mirror Mechanism

Mirror neurons are a specific class of neurons that discharge when an individual performs a given motor act and when s/he observes a similar motor act performed by another. They were originally discovered in the ventral premotor cortex (area F5) of macaque monkeys (Rizzolatti *et al.*, 1996; Gallese *et al.*, 1996). Further single cell studies (Gallese *et al.*, 2002; Fogassi *et al.*, 2005) recorded motor neurons with mirror properties in sectors of the inferior parietal lobule (IPL) that are reciprocally connected with the ventral premotor cortex (Rizzolatti & Luppino, 2001).

Neurophysiological and brain imaging studies have also provided evidence for the existence of a mirror system for action in the human brain. Indeed, it has been shown that action observation activates the lower part of the precentral gyrus plus the posterior part of the inferior frontal gyrus and the rostral part of the inferior parietal lobule, the brain regions that are considered to form the 'core' of the human mirror system (see Rizzolatti & Craighero, 2004 for a review; see also Fabbri-Destro & Rizzolatti, 2008). Although the monkey and human mirror system present homologue localizations, they differ in other aspects: while mirror neurons in the monkey respond to the observation of transitive and some communicative motor acts only, the human mirror system is sensitive to a larger range of intransitive motor acts as well as to mimicked actions too (see Rizzolatti & Sinigaglia, 2008a, for more details). In addition, the human mirror system seems to be more tuned to the timing of observed motor acts than the monkey mirror system, and this might explain its role in imitation and learning (see Miall, 2003).

The relevance of the mirror neuron discovery stems from identifying an immediate coupling between (sensory) perception and (motor) execution of a given action. It has been hypothesized that such a coupling has to be construed in terms of a direct matching mechanism (see Rizzolatti *et al.*, 1996; and Gallese *et al.*, 1996). According to this hypothesis (the Direct Matching Hypothesis, DMH), the observation of an action performed by others evokes, in the observer's brain, a motor activation that is akin to that which spontaneously occurs during the planning and effective execution of that action. The difference is that while in the latter case the motor activation becomes an *overt* motor act, in the former it remains at the stage of a *potential* motor act.

The sensory information concerning the perceived act would be directly matched with such potential motor act, thus enabling the observer to immediately understand the witnessed behaviour of others. DMH does not exclude that other more complex mechanisms, such as those that are supposed to be at the basis of many inferential or meta-representational processes, may be at work and play a role in this function. It simply maintains the originality of a direct matching between the observation and the execution of an action, pointing out that the observer's ability to understand the actions of others primarily capitalizes on her/his own motor ability to act (Rizzolatti *et al.*, 2001; Rizzolatti & Sinigaglia, 2007).

To get more insight into the nature and reach of mirror mechanism (what is actually *matched*? What does the *directedness* of matching really imply?), and to better elucidate its hypothesized function in action understanding (is action mirroring really construable as action understanding? If this is the case, what kind of understanding does mirror mechanism enable?), a brief review of the *motor properties* mirror neurons share with most of other F5 and IPL motor neurons is appropriate. Single cell recordings showed that most F5 and IPL motor neurons code goal-related motor acts (such as grasping, holding, manipulating, etc.) rather than simple movements. Indeed, many F5 and IPL motor neurons discharge when the monkey performs a motor act such as grasping a piece of food, irrespective of whether it uses its right or left paw or even its mouth. Other motor neurons are more selective, discharging only for specific effectors or grip. However even in these cases the motor responses cannot be interpreted in terms of single movements: neurons discharging during certain movements (the flexing of a finger, for example) performed with a specific motor goal, such as grasping an object, discharge weakly or not at all during the execution of similar movements that compose a different motor act such as scratching (Rizzolatti *et al.*, 1988; Rizzolatti *et al.*, 2000). Recently, hand-related F5 motor neurons have been recorded in monkeys trained to grasp objects using two different types of pliers: 'normal pliers', which require the sequential movement of opening and then closing the fingers, and 'reverse pliers', which require movements in the opposite sequence, that is, closing and then opening the fingers (Umiltà *et al.*, 2008). All recorded F5 neurons were sensitive to the goal-related movements of the pliers, preserving the same relation to the different phases of grasping in both conditions, regardless of the fact that diametrically opposite hand movements were required to achieve the motor goal.

These findings clearly suggest that (i) most of F5 and IPL motor neurons code movements in terms of their own motor goal-relatedness and that (ii) such motor goal-relatedness can be coded with different degrees of generality. However, goal coding appears to be a distinctive functional feature upon which the cortical motor system is organized not only in action execution but also in action perception. I have already mentioned that defining the functional characteristic of mirror neurons is that they become active both when an agent performs a given motor act and when s/he watches it being performed by someone else. In this regard, it is worth noting that there are at least two types of congruence that characterize mirror responses. In some cases, this congruence can be extremely strict: the executed motor act and the observed motor act turns out to be one and the same. In most cases, however, the congruence is broader. Though not identical, executed and observed actions are clearly connected: for instance, mirror neurons that become active during hand grasping actions can be activated by the observation of mouth-grasping actions (Rizzolatti *et al.*, 2001).

I have argued elsewhere that there is no reason to account for the different types of congruence in terms of different kinds of neural mechanism (Sinigaglia, forthcoming). In particular, there is no reason to assume that the directedness of matching limits the mirror mechanism to the strictly congruent mirror neurons, especially when these neurons are supposed to work at a mere kinematic level (see, for instance, Csibra, 2007). The fact that in the observer's brain, the sight of a motor act performed by someone else recruits the same neurons that would become active if s/he were planning and effectively executing that act, means that mirror neurons code the motor goal-relatedness that identifies that particular motor act, independently of whether it is executed by the agent him/herself or simply observed while being carried out by someone else. What is directly matched is the motor-goal relatedness that characterizes both the effective observed and the effective executed motor acts: in the light of their motor properties, it comes as no surprise that mirror neurons may code observed motor acts with different degrees of generality. On the contrary: the directedness of matching does not imply a one-to-one mapping, and even when this is the case, as for the strictly congruent mirror neurons, the mirror mechanism does not run at the level of mere kinematics, but captures the motor goal-relatedness of the observed act. Indeed, both strictly and broadly congruent mirror neurons are sensitive to the goal-relatedness of the observed movements, even if they code it in a different way, the former being more detailed and the latter more general. As a result, what is matched, and how it is matched, depends on the degree of generality that characterizes the motor responses of a given (set of) mirror neuron(s) as well as on its degree of congruence (Sinigaglia, 2008a; Rizzolatti & Sinigaglia, 2008b).

This explains why mirror neuron activation is not strictly bound to the completeness of the sensory information or to only one sensory modality. Indeed, mirror neurons have been shown to respond to partially seen motor acts (Umiltà *et al.*, 2001) as well as to sound-producing motor acts (e.g. ripping paper), independently of whether they were seen, heard or both seen and heard (Kohler *et al.*, 2002). This also explains why mirror neuron activation is related not only to single motor goals, but also to motor intentions displaying specific motor goal hierarchies. Indeed, this broadening of the range of mirror mechanism can be fully highlighted starting from the motor properties of mirror neurons.

By recording single IPL neurons during eating and placing actions, Fogassi *et al.* (2005) found that most of the tested hand-grasping neurons are 'action constrained', forming pre-wired motor chains and discharging differentially depending on whether the executed grasping was a grasping for eating or a grasping for placing. The sensitivity of the cortical motor system to the motor intention with which a single motor act may have been carried out facilitates the fluidity of acting that is typical of intentional behaviour, since the motor intention is displayed in the motor sub-goals that lead to its achievement from the start: from the first launch of hand movements, grasping a piece of food is grasping *for* eating and not *for* placing, and *viceversa*. But what is even more important, this sensitivity to the motor goal architecture that characterizes a whole motor action as such broadens the range of the mirror mechanism without altering its nature. In fact, Fogassi *et al.* (2005) showed that most of the recorded IPL 'action constrained' motor neurons had mirror properties and discharged differentially depending on the motor intention with which the single observed act of grasping appeared to be carried out (e.g. grasping *for* eating or grasping *for* placing). These data suggest that the sight of a hand-grasping motor act evokes in the observer far more than a single potential motor act; it evokes an entire chain of potential motor acts, which actually prefigures the motor intention that may underlie the observed movements. This in no way denies the role of object semantics and context in the elicitation of a given motor chain (grasping for eating vs. grasping for placing); on the contrary, it shows that the observed scene is directly mapped onto motor neurons forming pre-wired motor chains, and that it is in virtue of this mapping that the mirror activation turns out to be selective not only to single motor goals but also to motor intentions.

This has been demonstrated as holding true also for the human mirror system for action. In an fMRI study conducted by Iacoboni *et al.* (2005), participants were presented with three types of videos showing grasping actions without context, the context only, and hand actions embedded in contexts facilitating intention recognition. Compared with the other two conditions, hand actions embedded in contexts yielded a significant signal increase in the caudal part of the inferior frontal gyrus, i.e. in a region of the frontal node of the human mirror system. This suggests that the human mirror system also is able to code the motor intention with which single motor acts may be performed. More recently, Cattaneo *et al.* (2007) have shown, albeit indirectly, that such motor intention coding in humans is based on a motor chain organization similar to that found in a monkey. In one condition of their EMG experiment participants (who were all children) were instructed to either grasp a piece of food to eat it or to place it into a container while in another condition they were required simply to observe an experimenter performing these actions. The recording of the mouth-opening mylohyoid (MH) muscle activity during the execution and observation of both actions showed that both the execution and observation of eating produced a marked increase of MH muscle activity in children as early as the reaching phase in grasping for eating, while no MH activity was found in the execution and observation of placing actions.

These findings are even more interesting in the light of what is being done with children with autism. Indeed, in the same EMG experiment Cattaneo *et al.* (2007) asked children with autism to execute and observe eating and placing actions. They found that, as for typically developing children, there was no MH activity in children with autism during the execution and the observation of placing; however, MH activation during the execution of eating occurred in children with autism much later than in typically developed children, and there was no activation at all when the eating was observed being performed by someone else. This means that the motor system of children with autism could plan an action just as a simple sequence of unrelated single motor acts (e.g. reaching, grasping, and bringing to the mouth), preventing them from disentangling the sensory information regarding the observed action, i.e. from mapping the motor intention with which those motor acts are carried out. Object semantics and contextual information are *per se* not enough; as the comparison between typically developed children and children with autism shows, they can facilitate action mirroring only if the observed motor acts can be mapped onto the observer's motor repertoire not just as single motor goals but as part of specific motor hierarchies; in other words, only if the motor intention processing can be rooted in the observer's capacity to act.[3]

3. The Mirror-Based Making Sense of Others

So much for the mirror mechanism in itself: but what about its function? According to the DMH, the mirror neuron mechanism, by directly matching the motor goal-relatedness of witnessed and executable motor acts, enables the observer to immediately understand the behaviour of others (Rizzolatti *et al.*, 2001; Rizzolatti & Sinigaglia, 2007). Construing action mirroring in terms of action understanding is obviously not tantamount to claiming that the mirror mechanism covers every way (or every layer) of understanding actions done by others. Nor does the DMH involve the assumption that every way of action understanding depends on (is related to) mirror activation. This assumption is not only empirically groundless, but also ends up completely failing to grasp the originality of mirror-based action understanding. Indeed, what mirror neuron properties suggest is that the nature and scope of such an understanding are strictly tied to the nature and scope of the motor goal-relatedness that characterizes a set of movements as being part of a given motor act (or a given chain of motor acts), independently of whether such an act is executed by an individual or simply observed while being carried out by another. It is in virtue of this motor goal-relatedness that the same movement may be executed and perceived as different, due to its being embedded in different motor acts, characterized by different motor goals, and different, even diametrically opposite movements may be executed and perceived as similar, as being part of the same motor act, sharing the same motor goal-relatedness.

There is no doubt that the meaning of an action cannot be reduced to its own motor goal-relatedness, even in the case of basic motor acts like grasping, holding, etc. I can pick up the small glass in front of me because I believe that it contains my favourite whiskey and I wish to taste it again. But I can grasp the glass because I am dehydrated and I want to assuage my thirst, or I can do it as being completely absorbed in something else, e.g. in writing a paper. However, although the

---

[3] A discussion of the relation between mirroring and autism is beyond of this paper. For the role of motor chain impairment in autism see also Fabbri-Destro *et al.*, 2009; Rizzolatti *et al.*, 2009; and Gallese *et al*, 2009.

reasons behind my acting are different, the movements of my hand display a motor goal-relatedness that makes them something more than mere bodily movements; it makes them part of a specific motor act (or a specific chain of motor acts), directed toward a certain object (with a certain shape, a certain size, etc.) in a given way (grasping). Quite apart from being the outcome of whatever prior belief and desire I had, my act of grasping, like every other basic motor act, is defined by its own motor goal-relatedness that makes the coherent composition of the various movements to be executed possible, enabling me to control them. It is such motor goal-relatedness that allows someone else to immediately understand *what* I am doing (and maybe *why* I am doing it), i.e. to immediately recognize that the movements of my hand are something more than mere bodily movements, that is, that they are part of a specific motor act (or a specific chain of motor acts), directed toward a certain object (with a certain shape, a certain size, etc.) in a given way (grasping).

That action mirroring does not involve the belief-desire machinery alleged to be at the core of mind-reading ability does not imply that the mirror mechanism underpins at most a mere behaviour reading, providing us with 'an extremely limited picture of intentional attribution', characterized by a 'lure of behaviorism', which cognitive science should resist (Borg, 2007, pp. 8 & 14). Rather, by running at the motor goal and intention level, mirror mechanism helps us shed new light on the primary ways of making sense of others' behaviour, showing that action understanding can be rooted in one's own ability to act even before our mindreading capability comes into play (Sinigaglia, 2008b). Indeed, as this ability to act develops, diversifies, and becomes increasingly sophisticated, mirror-based action understanding develops, diversifies, and also becomes increasingly sophisticated.

There are a number of studies that point out that the more the motor goal-relatedness is fine-grained in action execution, the greater is the sensitivity of mirror mechanism to the observed actions. I have already mentioned Umiltà *et al.* (2008) experiment on reverse pliers: it is worth noting here that some of recorded F5 neurons showed mirror properties, discharging when trained monkeys were watching the experimenter grasping a piece of food either with a precision grip or a normal or a reverse pliers. But the motor roots of action mirroring are even more evident in the production and observation of skilled actions such as dancing, piano playing or basketball: in these cases mirror activation appears to be strongly modulated by the observer's motor ability (Calvo Merino *et al.*, 2005; Calvo Merino *et al.*, 2006; Haslinger *et al.*, 2006; Aglioti *et al.*, 2008).

This is in line with phenomenology: my way of experiencing an action performed by someone else depends on my motor expertise, and may therefore differ accordingly. Imagine that I am watching a Beethoven piano concerto live: if I have no knowledge of actually piano playing, I will not be able to perceive and appreciate the pianist's finger movements as being goal-related, i.e. as executing a given chord or a given sequence of chords. Of course, I know that what is going on in front of me is a piano concert; perhaps I know the pianist too; maybe I have heard that Beethoven piano concerto already or have seen it played before ... But this kind of knowledge *per se* would not enable me to perceive the pianist's hand movements as being part of a goal-related motor act, i.e. to understand the *kinetic melody* that characterizes them, anticipating the appropriate sequences of finger patterns and distinguishing them from those hand movements that can be equally well controlled, but have nothing to do with piano playing. This holds true also for dancing, playing basketball or football, as well as for any other skilled motor action: what the phenomenology of these actions tells us is that the richer our motor repertoire is the sharper our sensitivity to others' motor goals and motor intentions, so that our ability to act shapes our experiencing and making sense of others' behaviour to the extent that the latter can be construed as a modality of the former, at least at the basic level.

Is all that enough to claim that mirror-based making sense of others' actions can be characterized as an enactive way of understanding? It would appear not. Indeed, two objections have been raised against such a claim, the first denying that action mirroring is *enactive* in nature, the second disputing the interpretation of its function as *understanding*. Let me begin with the first.

By highlighting the role of coordination and interaction processes in characterizing social understanding as a participatory sense-making action De Jaegher and Di Paolo have recently questioned the relevance of the mirror mechanism for an enactive approach to social cognition, claiming that it remains

> within the framework of a detached individual trying to figure out the other [...] The problem of such a figuring out participates in and is itself shaped by coordination dynamics remains untouched. Appropriate correlations in social activity are what we are trying to explain. Transferring their cause to a neural correlation is simply to re-describe the problem. Explanations based on mirror neuron provide no more than a snapshot view of how recognition of intentional action could work. The

problem is that the same recognition could equally be part of a coordinated or un-coordinated period in an interaction, and the difference
between the two could not therefore be explained by its mechanism. It is
this difference that, we argue, plays a crucial role in how the interaction
unfolds (De Jaegher & Di Paolo, 2007, p. 495).

Now, it is true that as of yet there are still no mirror studies on the coordinated play of move and countermove that characterizes most of our
daily social interactions. But this does not imply that mirror-based
making sense of others could be reduced either to 'a detached individual trying to figure out the other' or to a mere 'snapshot view of how
recognition of intentional action could work'. First of all, the experimental setting typical of mirror research has not to be confused with
the function of mirror mechanism. The fact that mirror investigation
usually attempts to decouple the acting and perceiving phases,
because this is the only way that the motor responses to the observation of others' actions can be convincingly labelled as 'mirror', does
not signify that mirror-based making sense of others is detached, disengaged, i.e. purely spectatorial in nature. Quite the opposite: what
the mirror mechanism really suggests is that our making sense of others can be enactive in nature even when we are just observing others'
actions. In other terms, what it really suggests is that even the *pure*
perception of others' actions can be considered as a *limit case* of an
actual interaction.

Far from simply re-describing the problem of social cognition, the
mirror mechanism allows us to delve into the multilayered 'structured
and structuring process' (De Jaegher & Di Paolo, 2007, p. 495) of
social interaction, showing that our making sense of others could be
based on both a virtual and actual coordination, where the latter differs from the former only in the degree of engagement but not in
nature. De Jaegher and Di Paolo are right when they claim the need to
assume the 'interaction process' as a 'point of departure', without
making 'the error of considering only the interaction and ignoring the
individual elements in it' (De Jaegher & Di Paolo, 2007, p. 494).
However, such a claim is absolutely compatible with the mirror-based
making sense of others. Indeed, why should others' motor goals and
intentions be mapped on our own *motor* repertoire unless it is to
enable us to interact with each other? Because it is embedded in our
own capacity to act, mirror-based making sense of others not only
helps us to appropriately respond to others' actions in either a cooperative or competitive way, thus driving the interaction to be actual, but
is also shaped by the concrete dynamics of interaction, where we
experience the mutual influence of our and others' motor goals and

intentions. Of course, this does not mean that every kind of 'participatory making sense' has to be reduced to the action mirroring; rather, it suggests that the same mechanism may underpin both actual and potential interactions. This is not a limitation, as De Jaegher & Di Paolo (2007) seem to believe, but an advantage: it is because it functions even in absence of a real interaction or a real intention to interact that the mirror-based making sense of others can contribute to the emergence of a social cognition, disclosing a shared ground of motor acts and motor intentions which at the same time shape and are shaped by our engaged and enactive ways of interacting with each other. Again: as our ability to act and to interact develops, diversifies and becomes increasingly sophisticated, our making sense of others also develops, diversifies and also becomes increasingly sophisticated; and as the latter develops, diversifies and also become increasingly sophisticated, so does the former. This mutual dynamic relation is at the core of basic social engagements and has its roots in the mirror mechanism as well as in the making sense of others that the latter underpins.

The second kind of objection has mostly been raised by Dan Hutto. Speaking in the name of radical enactivism he has recently challenged that mirror-based making sense of others functions as action understanding, and not just its enactive character (Hutto, 2008a, ch. 3 & 6).[4] In his view, it is due to its enactive character that mirror-based making sense of others can not be interpreted in terms of action understanding. Indeed, as he restates in this volume:

> it remains unclear exactly how to ground such talk of 'understanding' (or precisely what it implies) if one is not also prepared, not only to assume that contentful mental representations exist, but to provide a

---

[4] It is worth noting that Hutto's objections are radically different from Csibra's (2007) and Jacob's (2009) criticisms to the mirror mechanism and its function. While Hutto questions the construal of the mirror-based making sense of others in terms of action understanding because of its 'incautious' use of a representationalist language, Csibra and Jacob maintain that interpreting the mirror mechanism in terms of a direct matching mechanism must inevitably be in conflict with the interpretation of its function as critical for action understanding. In Csibra's words: '[Most findings] reflect a tensione between two conflicting claims implied by the direct matching hypothesis: the claim that action mirroring reflects low-level resonance mechanism, and the claim that it reflects high-level action understanding. The tension arises from the fact that it seems that the more mirroring is nothing else but faithful duplication of observed actions, the less evidence it provides for action understanding; and more mirroring represents high-level interpretation of the observed actions, the less evidence it provides that this interpretation is generated by low-level motor duplication' (Csibra, 2007, p. 446). In Sinigaglia (2008a) and Sinigaglia (forthcoming) I tried to reply to Csibra's and Jacob's criticisms, showing how they are mainly due to both a partial reading of mirror properties and also to a biased construal of both action and action understanding.

workable theory of content that can explain and delineate their properties.

A more cautious strategy, which I recommend, would be to reserve attributions of 'understanding' exclusively for those language-based (and more specifically narrative-based) forms of intersubjective engagement that have their own special properties and complexities. And the truth is that we have other, more perspicuous ways of making sense of primary forms of intersubjective interplay (Hutto, 2009, p. 18).

I completely agree with Hutto that 'our fundamental ways of engaging with others' are, 'at root, non representational and unprincipled in character, taking the form of expressive and embodied interactions', so that 'postulating special-purpose modules, theory-of-mind devices and related paraphernalia is unnecessary and indeed deeply mistaken if, in fact, primary intersubjective engagements are based on a direct responsiveness to the psychological situation of others, perceived in and through their expressions' (Hutto, 2008b, p. 423). I also agree with Hutto's radical enactive approach to intentionality, in particular with his distinction between intentional and propositional attitudes, where the former exhibit intentional directedness without being directed to propositions (Hutto, 2008a, p. 45). However, I do not believe that these arguments can be fruitfully used against the construal of mirror-based making sense of others as action understanding. Of course, I appreciate the reasons motivating Hutto's caution, and I am empathizing with his aversion to any intellectualistic and hypermentalistic account of our primary contacts with the others. Nonetheless, I still think that the mirror-based making sense of others, or, to borrow Hutto's own term, the mirror-based 'responsiveness' to others' motor goals and intentions can be construed in terms of action understanding without therefore falling into of the morass of an unwarranted cognitivism and abstract mentalism.[5]

The issue here is not terminological. Not every kind of motor mirroring involves a direct matching between observed and executable motor acts and/or motor actions. There are many motor resonance processes (such as, for instance, motor contagion or purely motor mimicry) that run at a lower level than that of action mirroring (Rizzolatti *et al.*, 1999). Thus talking of action understanding allows us to distinguish the different kinds of mirroring and to acknowledge that there is a higher-level mirroring tuned to motor goals and motor

---

[5] My perspective here is not so different from that proposed by Gallagher when he speaks of mirror-based action understanding in terms of 'social direct perception'. On the other hand, I think that Gallaghers' view, contrary to what he states (Gallagher, 2007), is not incompatible with the model of embodied simulation advanced by Gallese (2003; 2005). On this point see Gallese, Caruana & Sinigaglia (in preparation).

intentions that contributes to our primary making sense of others' behaviour. And talking of mirror-based making sense of others or mirror-based action understanding allow us to highlight this contribution, that is, to account for how our 'primary intersubjective engagements [could be] based on a direct responsiveness to the psychological situation of others, perceived *in* and *through* their expressions' (Hutto, 2008b, p. 423; my italics). This kind of understanding has nothing to do with the classical picture of mindreading, nor can it be interpreted in terms of a propositional attitude attribution, that is, as making sense of a person's reason for performing a given action. Hutto is right when claiming that 'a social agent's growing interactive repertoire should not be explained in terms of the maturation of "theories of mind" or simulative abilities per se. The great bulk of sophisticated social interactions can be understood without supposing that participants are making any contentful attributions of (or inferences about) mental states. Our basic ways of engaging with others are not inferentially mediated' (Hutto, 2008b, p. 423). However, appealing to 'an organism's having intentionally-directed *responsiveness* to the intentional attitudes of others' (Hutto, 2009, p. 18) ends up being nearly as abstract as the much deprecated contentful explanation, because it leaves what is at the root of such a responsiveness and what are its range and nature unexplained. What the mirror mechanism tells us is that this responsiveness is 'intentionally-directed' because of it being rooted in the organism's own capacity to act, so that the range of its directedness is strictly bound to the range of this capacity to act. Last, but not least, what the mirror mechanism tells us is that this responsiveness can take the form of an enactive and embodied action understanding, because of its directedness to others' motor goals and motor intentions: this explains why it might directly guide both our actual and potential interactions with others, thus shaping and at the same time being shaped by our social engagements.

In sum, although I can easily accept as true that mirror responses 'are not content involving in the way the intellectualistic tradition seeks to understand them' (Hutto, 2008a, p. 57), since they do not presuppose any abstract cognitive mediation, being characterized by a direct matching of perceived and executable actions, nonetheless I do believe that one should avoid hypostatizing the notion of action understanding, reserving it only for narrative based forms of intersubjective engagements. Of course, mirror-based action understanding differs greatly both in character and scope from narrative-based action understanding, and this difference has to be accounted for by highlighting the originality and specificity of mirror-based making sense of others. In this regard, however, the notion of responsiveness, even understood in terms of 'indexically inspired action coordination routines' (Hutto, 2008a, p. 51), seems to be not enough. The difference between the sensitivity to others' movements or others' body parts and the sensitivity to others' actions is not just a matter of complexity, of more or less 'baroque tracking strategies' (Hutto, 2008a, p. 51); rather, it pertains to diverse ways of being-sensitive-to differing both in neural mechanism and phenomenology: only mirror responsiveness can grasp others' motor goals and intentions, what makes others' bodily movements something more than mere movements or mere body parts in movement, and grasping goal and intentions, even at the motor level and in motor terms, is nothing else but *understanding*.

4. Primary Intersubjective Interactions

Mirror-based making sense of others meets one of the most critical assumptions being at the basis of an enactive approach to social cognition: our primary ways of interacting with others not only are not replaced by the most advanced ones, but also 'mature and become more sophisticated in adulthood' (Gallagher, 2008, p. 167). I have already mentioned the role of mirror mechanism and motor expertise in shaping our primary ways of making sense of others *below* any kind of mindreading. But what happens *before* full-blown mindreading abilities develop? What does the mirror mechanism tell us about developmentally primary ways of intersubjective dealings?

During their first year of life infants are generally thought to be able to recognize bodily movements performed by someone else as goal-related motor acts without attributing propositional attitudes such as beliefs, desires or reasons to others (Baird & Baldwin, 2001; Tommasello & Haberl, 2003; Hamlin *et al.*, 2007). There is a wide agreement that this ability makes a critical contribution to the full development of primary intersubjectivity (Meltzoff & Brooks, 2007), and several studies have suggested that it might be rooted in infants' motor expertise, in the capacity to act that they develop during their first year of life. Indeed, a series of looking-time experiments have shown that infants of 5/6 months of age — the age by which they master the ability to perform smooth and efficient reaching and grasping movements (Bertenthal & Clifton, 1998) — are in a position to distinguish between the goal-relatedness of some basic hand motor acts and their kinematics: they looked longer at the hand grasping a new object but following the same trajectory as that of the habituation test (new goal/old path), than at a hand grasping the same object as in the habituation test but following a different trajectory (old goal/new path). This did not occur when the observed scene involved objects (e.g. a claw) or, even more interestingly, bodily movements that were incoherent with respect to a given motor goal (e.g. the back of the hand was approached to the object in order to grasp it) (Woodward, 1998; 1999). Infants are shown to be sensitive to the goal-relatedness of observed movements even at 3 months of age, but only when facilitated by previous motor experience. In fact, 3 month-old pre-reaching infants were given a reaching intervention either prior to or following the habituation test used to assess their ability to recognize a simple reaching motor act. Only those infants who received the reaching intervention prior to the test recognized the observed movements as reaching movements (Sommerville *et al.*, 2005).

Motor expertise shapes infants' action understanding not only of simple motor acts, like reaching for a toy, but also of tool-use action as well as of complex motor actions, displaying specific motor goal hierarchies. Sommerville *et al.* (2008) investigated the impact of active versus observational experience on infants' understanding of a tool-use action such as retrieving an out-of-reach object with a cane by submitting 10 month-old infants who either had previously been actively trained in using the cane or had simply watched someone else using the cane in a habituation task. The results showed that only the actively trained infants were sensitive to the goal-directedness of the cane-pulling sequence, as their sensitivity was related to the extent to which they could successfully use the cane to reach the out-of-reach objects. With regard to motor intention understanding, it has been shown that by 12 months of age infants are not only able to plan specific motor goal hierarchies but also to detect the hierarchical goal structure of a sequence of motor acts performed by someone else (Woodward & Sommerville, 2000); the importance of this finding is enhanced by data from the recent study of 10-month-old infant looking times which has demonstrated that only those infants who were themselves able to organize determined sequences of hierarchically organized motor acts were able to recognize the same sequences performed by others (Sommerville & Woodward, 2005). Finally, 12 month-old infants have been shown to produce proactive goal-directed eye movements when observing a goal-directed placing action only to the extent they can perform it (Falck-Ytter *et al.*, 2006).

These data suggest that an action observation and execution matching mechanism such as the mirror mechanism probably undergoes critical developments within infancy, thus accounting for infants' growing sensibility to others' motor goals and motor intentions

(Lapage & Théoret, 2007). By using a high density EEG net Nyström (2008) recently recorded brain activity in 6 month-old infants and adults while they watched both goal-related and non goal-related movements. The results showed a significantly higher ERP activation in both the 6 month-olds and the adults in the goal-directed movement condition only, providing evidence for the presence of a mirror mechanism in infants as young as 6 months. Of course, this does not imply that infants make sense of others' behaviour only in virtue of their own motor ability to act. Many studies have pointed out that infants may take advantage of very different cues in order to grasp the goal-relatedness of others' movements. It has been suggested, for instance, that they may exploit the self-propelledness of observed movements (Baron Cohen, 1995; Premack, 1990), the regularities exhibited from watched behaviours (Povinelli, 2001; Baird & Baldwin, 2001) or the efficiency and equifinal variation of the ongoing streams of action (Gergely et al., 1995; Király et al., 2003). However, though it is likely that 'infants capitalize on a variety of mechanisms and information sources to support their action understanding' (Sommerville et al., 2008, p. 1254), the mirror mechanism seems not only to provide a convincing and more parsimonious explanation of most infants' ways to understand others' actions (see Sinigaglia, 2008a; and Gallese et al., 2009, for more details on this point), but also allows to construe the various and ever-growing body of findings of developmental psychology research within a theoretically unitary and neurophysiologically sound framework, starting from the evidence concerning the infants' primary ways of interacting with others that occur even in the first days or hours of their life.

In the latter regard, neonatal imitation represents one of the most striking primary social interactions. More than 30 years ago, Meltzoff and Moore (1977) reported that 12- to 21 day-old infants matched specific human facial gestures by differentially responding to observed mouth openings, tongue and lip protrusions by opening their own mouth, protruding their own tongue and lips. Even more strikingly, Meltzoff and Moore (1983; 1989) showed that 36 hour-old newborns imitate facial gestures. These results have been replicated and partially corroborated by several other studies (see Meltzoff & Moore, 1997, for a review), suggesting that imitation might be construed as 'a marker of innate intersubjectivity in action' (Meltzoff & Brooks, 2007). But how can newborns imitate others' facial gestures, given that usually there are no mirrors in the cots that would allow them to see their own faces? And what such an imitation should be for? Meltzoff and Moore (1977; 1997) proposed that early facial imitation is based on active intermodal mapping (AIM) that would enable infants to compare their own gestures against the seen targets and at the same time to correct their own responses and to home in on the target acts. However, such a mapping might be accounted for by primarily referring to a mirror-based motor resonance mechanism rather than to a mere proprioceptive feedback loop. Indeed, the mirror-based direct matching not only seems to provide both early and mature imitation with a common mechanism (Gallese, 2003; see also Ferrari & Gallese, 2007), but also allows better highlighting of the *function* of neonatal imitation and its relationship with more developed forms of intersubjective engagement such as infants' sensitivity to others' motor goals and intentions.

Indeed, imitation has been generally considered as a powerful 'means of making contact in the absence of any common language', as 'a psychological door through which one is immediately led into a world of intentional relations with another person' (Reddy, 2008, p. 45). In the case of neonatal imitation, making contact takes the form of a sort of dyadic conversation: newborns seem to replicate the observed movement in an attempt to correspond their mothers' attempts to communicate with them (Kugiumutzakis, 1999). This would explain both the specific timing of neonatal imitation and the eliciting effect of a face-to-face engagement as well as the fact that the imitated gestures (lip and tongue protrusion, mouth opening) are at first glance as much odd as deeply entrenched in the infants' motor behaviour, being endowed with a specific affiliate meaning. It is worth noting here that the same holds true also for neonatal imitation in nonhuman primates. Myowa-Yamakoshi *et al.* (2004) reported that facial imitation in chimpanzees occurs very early after birth, suggesting that this is the way newborns orient to the conspecifics' face. Using the same methodology adopted by Meltzoff & Moore (1977), Ferrari *et al.* (2006) investigated the imitative responses of 1- to 14-day-old macaque monkeys to human facial and hand gestures. They found that at the age of 3 days infant macaques are able to imitate human adults smacking their lips or protruding their tongue, that is, two gestures that play a crucial role in dyadic communicative exchanges because of their affiliative relevance. More recently Ferrari *et al.* (in press) demonstrated that interindividual differences in neonatal imitation in macaque monkeys reflect specific cognitive components of a broader developmental pattern because of their association with differences of specific hand- and mouth motor chains (such as reaching-for-grasping) whose production recruits the parietal and frontal areas that are known to be endowed with mirror properties.

I have already mentioned the difference between mirror-based motor resonance and mirror-based action understanding, where the latter, but not the former, has to deal with the motor goals and intentions of others. The mirror mechanism enables both human and non-human primate infants to 'resonate' with the others, facilitating 'the most appropriate motor responses for tuning their behaviors to individuals who show affiliative behaviors toward them' (Ferrari *et al.*, 2006, p. 1506). In other words, mirror-based motor resonance would allow both the infant and mother (caregiver) to make contact, thus achieving the parity condition that is prerequisite of any forms of social engagement and communication (Rizzolatti *et al.*, 1999). This kind of mirror responsiveness does not pertain to the motor goal-relatedness of transitive acts such as grasping or manipulating, nor should it be confused with the action mirroring that may be at the basis of more mature forms of intentional communication. Being rooted in the infant's motor repertoire, it cannot but capitalize on the deepest entrenched motor responses such as lip smacking and tongue protrusion, facilitating their execution. However, once the infants' motor repertoire develops and refines, including goal-related motor acts such as grasping or goal-related motor chains such as reaching-for-grasping (or even more complex such as reaching-for-grasping-for-bringing-to-the-mouth or reaching-for-grasping-for-placing), the mirror mechanism diversifies its functioning, enabling infants to make sense of others in terms of their own (potential) motor goals and motor intentions.

Concluding Remarks

In this paper I have argued that most of our pervasive and primary ways of interaction with each other are based on the mirror mechanism, a neural mechanism that enables us to immediately understand the actions and intentions of others without involving any form of mentalizing. By directly mapping others' motor behaviour onto our own motor repertoire, this mechanism highlights how our social engagement has its roots in our own motor system and in its capability to be attuned with others. This attunement may occur at the level of mere motor resonance, as in the case of neonatal imitation; however, it may also take the form of a mirroring of others' motor goals and intentions that does not flow into an overt replication of observed motor behaviour but remains at the stage of a potential action, thus shaping our perception of others' movements as being something more than simple bodily movements, i.e. as being part of a given motor act characterized by a specific motor goal-relatedness or a specific motor goal hierarchy.

At both levels the mirror-based social engagement appears to be enactive in nature, regardless of whether it takes the form of actual interaction with others or of a mere perception of others' behaviour. Of course, this is not to say that every form of primary intersubjective engagement should be strictly reduced to the mirror mechanism, nor does it mean that this mechanism alone might account for the 'participatory' making sense of surrounding things that distinguishes our experience of the world as a shared world (De Jaegher & Di Paolo, 2007). It has to be recognized instead that the mirror mechanism allows an intersubjective space of action to emerge without being constrained to explicitly intersubjective actions. In other terms, it renders our expressions and gestures immediately shareable and socially relevant without being the need of any communicative intention, thus feeding the 'hunger for social engagement' that characterizes our life from the first few days after birth (Hobson, 2004, p. 43).

Acknowledgements

I would like to thank Vittorio Gallese, Daniel D. Hutto, Jean-Michel Roy, and one anonymous reviewer for their very helpful comments on this paper. This study was supported by the Italian Ministero dell'Università e della Ricerca, Cofin 2007.

References

Aglioti, S.M., Cesari, P., Romani, M. & Urgesi C. (2008), 'Action Anticipation and Motor Resonance in Basketball Players', *Nature Neuroscience*, **11** (9), pp. 1109–16.

Baird, J. & Baldwin D.A. (2001), 'Making Sense of Human Behavior: Action parsing and intentional inference', in B.F. Malle, L.J. Moses & D.A. Baldwin (ed.), *Intentions and intentionality. Foundations of social cognition* (Cambridge, MA: MIT Press), pp. 193–206.

Baron-Cohen, S. (1995), *Mindblindness: An essay on autism and theory of mind* (Cambridge, MA: MIT Press).

Bertenthal, B. & Clifton, R.K. (1998), 'Perception and Action', in W. Damon, D. Kuhn & R. Siegler (ed.), *Handbook of child psychology: Vol. 2. Cognition, perception, and language* (New York: Wiley), pp. 51–102.

Borg, E. (2007), 'If Mirror Neurons are the Answer, what was the Question?', *Journal of Consciousness Studies*, **14** (8), pp. 5–19.

Calvo-Merino, B., Glaser, D.E., Grezes, J., Passingham, R.E. & Haggard, P. (2005), 'Action Observation and Acquired Motor Skills: An FMRI study with expert dancers', *Cerebral Cortex,* **15**, pp. 1243–9.

Calvo-Merino, B., Grezes, J., Glaser, D.E., Passingham, R.E. & Haggard P. (2006), 'Seeing or Doing? Influence of visual and motor familiarity in action observation', *Current Biology,* **16** (19), pp. 1905–10.

Cattaneo, L., Fabbi-Destro, M., Boria, S., Pieraccini, C., Monti, A., Cossu, G. & Rizzolatti, G. (2007), 'Impairment of Actions Chains in Autism and its Possible role in Intention Understanding', *Proceedings of The National Academy of Sciences*, **104** (45), pp. 17825–30.

Csibra, G. (2007), 'Action Mirroring and Action Understanding: An alternative account', in P. Haggard, Y. Rosetti & M. Kawato (ed.), *Sensorimotor foundations of higher cognition. Attention and performance XII* (Oxford: Oxford University Press), pp. 453–9.

Csibra, G. & Gergely, G. (2007), '"Obsessed with Goals": Functions and mechanisms of teleological interpretation of actions in humans', *Acta Psychologia (Amsterdam)*, **124** (1), pp. 60–78.

Currie, G. (2008), 'Some ways to Understand People', *Philosophical Explorations*, **11** (3), pp. 211–8.

De Jaegher, H. & Di Paolo, E. (2007), 'Participatory Sense-making. An enactive approach to social cognition', *Phenomenology and the Cognitive Sciences*, **6**, pp. 485–507.

Fabbri-Destro , M. & Rizzolatti, G. (2008), 'Mirror neurons and mirror systems in monkeys and humans', *Physiology* (Bethesda), **23**, pp. 171–79.

Fabbri-Destro, M., Cattaneo, L., Boria, S. & Rizzolatti, G. (2009), 'Planning Actions in Autism', *Experimental Brain Research*, **192**, pp. 521–5.

Falck-Ytter, T., Gredeback, G. & von Hofsten, C. (2006), 'Infant Predict other People's Action Goals', *Nature Neuroscience,* **9** (7), pp. 878–9.

Ferrari, P.F., Visalberghi, E., Paukner, A., Fogassi, L., Ruggiero, A. & Suomi S. (2006), 'Neonatal Imitation in Rhesus Monkey', *PLoS Biology*, **4** (9), pp. 1501–8.

Ferrari, P.F. & Gallese, G. (2007), 'Mirror Neurons and Intersubjectivity', in Braten, S. (ed.), *On being moved. From mirror neurons to empathy* (Amsterdam/Philadelphia: John Benjamins Publishing Company), pp. 73–89.

Ferrari, P.F., Paukner, A., Ruggiero, A., Darcey, L., Unbehagen, S. & Suomi S.J. (in press), 'Interindividual Differences in Neonatal Imitation and the Development of Action Chains in Rhesus Macaques', *Child Development*.

Fogassi, L., Ferrari, P.F., Gesierich, B., Rozzi, S., Chersi, F. & Rizzolatti, G. (2005), 'Parietal Lobe: From action organization to intention understanding', *Science,* **302**, pp. 662–7.

Gallagher, S. (2001), 'The Practice of Mind: Theory, simulation or primary interaction?', *Journal of Consciousness Studies*, **8** (5–7), pp. 83–108.

Gallagher, S, (2004), 'Understanding interpersonal problems in autism: Interaction theory as an alternative to theory of mind', *Philosophy, Psychiatry, & Psychology*, **11**, pp. 199–217.

Gallagher, S. (2006), 'The Narrative Alternative to Theory of Mind', in R. Menary (ed.), *Radical Enactivism: Focus on the Philosophy of Daniel D. Hutto* (Amsterdam/Philadelphia: John Benjamins).

Gallagher S. (2007), 'Simulation trouble', *Social Neuroscience*, **2** (3–4), pp. 353–65.

Gallagher, S. (2008), 'Inference or Interaction: Social cognition without precursors', *Philosophical Explorations*, **11** (3), pp. 163–74.

Gallagher, S. & Hutto, D.D. (2008), 'Understanding Others through Primary Interaction and Narrative Practice', in Zlatev, J., Racine, T.P., Shina, C. & Itkonen, E. (ed.), *The Shared Mind: Perspectives on Intersubjectivity* (Amsterdam: John Benjamins), pp. 17–38.

Gallese, V., Fadiga, L., Fogassi, L. & Rizzolatti, G. (1996), 'Action Recognition in the Premotor Cortex', *Brain,* **119**, pp. 593–609.

Gallese, V., Fogassi, L., Fadiga, L. & Rizzolatti, G. (2002), 'Action Representation and the Inferior Parietal Lobule', in Prinz, W. & Hommel, B. (ed.), *Attention and Performance XIX* (Oxford: Oxford University Press), pp. 247–66.

Gallese, V. (2003), 'The Manifold Nature of Interpersonal Relations: The quest for a common mechanism', *Philosophical Transactions of The Royal Society of London, Series B Biological Science*, **358**, pp. 517–28.

Gallese, V. (2005), 'Embodied Simulation: From neurons to phenomenal experience', *Phenomenology and the Cognitive Sciences*, **4**, pp. 23–48.

Gallese, V. (2007), 'Before and Below Theory of Mind: Embodied simulation and neural correlates of social cognition', *Philosophical Transactions of the Royal Society of London, Series B Biological Science*, **362**, pp. 659–69.

Gallese, V., Rochat, M., Cossu, G. & Sinigaglia, C. (2009), 'Motor Cognition and its Role in the Phylogeny and Ontogeny of Action Understanding', *Developmental Psychology*, **45**, pp. 103–13.

Gallese, V., Caruana, F. & Sinigaglia, C. (in preparation) 'What is so Special with Embodied Simulation'.

Gergely, G., Nàdasdy, Z., Csibra, G. & Bìrò, S. (1995), 'Taking the Intentional Stance at 12 months of age', *Cognition*, **56**, pp. 165–93.

Goldman, A. (2006), *Simulating Minds: The Philosophy, Psychology and Neuroscience of Mindreading* (Oxford: Oxford University Press).

Hamlin, J.K., Wynn, K. & Bloom, P. (2007), 'Social Evaluation by Preverbal Infants', *Nature*, **450** (7169), pp. 557–9.

Haslinger, B., Erhard, P., Altenmuller, E., Schroeder, U., Boecker, H. & Ceballos-Baumann, A.O. (2006), 'Transmodal Sensorimotor Networks during Action Observation in Professional Pianists', *Journal of Cognitive Neuroscience*, **17**, pp. 282–93.

Hobson, P. (2004), *The Cradle of Thought. Exploring the Origins of Thinking* (Oxford: Oxford University Press).

Hurley, S. (2006), 'Active Perception and Perceiving Action: The shared circuit model', in T. Gendler & J. Hawthorne (ed.), *Perceptual Experience* (New York: Oxford University Press), pp. 205–59.

Hutto, D.D. (2004), 'The Limits of Spectatorial Folk Psychology', *Mind and Language*, **19**, pp. 548–73.

Hutto, D.D. (2006), 'Unprincipled Engagements: Emotional experience, expression and response', in R. Menary (ed.), *Radical Enactivism: Focus on the Philosophy of Daniel D. Hutto* (Amsterdam/Philadelphia: John Benjamins), pp. 13–38.

Hutto, D.D. (2007), 'The Narrative Practice Hypothesis: Origins and applications to folk psychology', in D. Hutto (ed.), *Narrative and Understanding Persons*, Royal Institute Philosophy Supplement, **60**, pp. 43–68.

Hutto, D.D. (2008a), *Folk Psychological Narratives: The Sociocultural Basis of Understanding Reasons* (Cambridge MA: MIT Press).

Hutto, D.D. (2008b), 'Limited Engagements and Narrative Extensions', *International Journal of Philosophical Studies*, **16** (3), pp. 419–44.

Hutto, D.D. (2009), 'Folk Psychology as Narrative Practice', *Journal of Consciousness Studies*, **16** (6–8), pp. 9–39. [This volume]

Hutto, D.D. & Ratcliffe, M. (ed, 2007), *Folk Psychology Re-assessed* (Dordrecht: Springer).

Iacoboni, M., Molnar-Szakacs, I., Gallese, V., Buccino, G., Mazziotta, J. & Rizzolatti, G. (2005), 'Grasping the Intentions of Others with one's Owns Mirror Neuron System', *PLoS Biology*, **3**, pp. 529–35.

Jacob, P. (2009), 'The Tuning-fork Model of Human Social Cognition: A critique', *Consciousness and Cognition*, **18**, pp. 229–43.

Király, I., Jovanovic, B., Prinz, W., Ascherleben, G. & Gergely, G. (2003) 'The Early Origins of Goal Attribution in Infancy', *Consciousness and Cognition,* **12**, pp. 752–69.

Kohler, E., Keysers, C., Umiltà, M.A., Fogassi, L., Gallese, V. & Rizzolatti, G. (2002), 'Hearing Sounds, Understanding Actions: Action representation in mirror neurons', *Science,* **297**, pp. 846–8.

Kugiumutzakis, G. (1999), 'Genesis and Development of Mimesis in Early Imitation of Early Facial and Vocal Models', in J. Nadel & G. Butterworth (ed.), *Imitation in Infancy* (Cambridge: Cambridge University Press), pp. 36–59.

Lepage, J.F. & Théoret, H. (2007), 'The Mirror Neuron System: Grasping other's actions from birth?', *Developmental Science,* **10** (5), pp. 513–29.

Meltzoff, A.N. & Moore, M.K. (1977), 'Imitation of Facial and Manual Gestures by Human Neonates', *Science,* **198**, pp. 75–8.

Meltzoff, A.N. & Moore, M.K. (1983), 'Newborn Infants Imitate Adult Facial Gestures', *Child Development,* **54**, pp. 702–9.

Meltzoff, A.N. & Moore, M.K. (1989), 'Imitation in Newborn Infants: Exploring the range of gestures imitated and the underlying mechanism', *Developmental Psychology,* **25**, pp. 954–62.

Meltzoff, A.N. & Moore, M.K. (1997), 'Explaining Facial Imitation: A theoretical model', *Early Development and Parenting,* **6**, pp. 179–92.

Meltzoff, A.N. & Brooks, R. (2007), 'Intersubjectivity Before Language: Three windows on preverbal sharing, in Braten, S. (ed.), *On being moved. From mirror neurons to empathy* (Amsterdam/Philadelphia: John Benjamins Publishing Company), pp. 149–74.

Miall, R.C. (2003), 'Connecting Mirror Neurons and Forward Models', *Neuroreport,* **14** (17), pp. 2135–7.

Myowa-Yamakoshi, M., Tomonaga, M., Tanaka, M. & Matsuzawa, T. (2004), 'Imitation in Neonatal Chimpanzees', *Developmental Science,* 7, pp. 437–42.

Nyström, P. (2008), 'The Infant Mirror Neuron System studied by High Density EEG', *Social Neuroscience,* **3** (3), pp. 334–47.

Povinelli, D. (2001), 'On the Possibility of Detecting Intentions Prior to Understanding them', in B.F. Malle, L.J. Moses & D.A. Baldwin (ed.), *Intentions and intentionality. Foundations of social cognition* (Cambridge, MA: MIT Press), pp. 225–48.

Premack, D. (1990), 'The Infant's Theory of Self-propelled Objects', *Cognition,* **36** (1), pp. 1–16.

Ratcliffe, M.J. (2007), *Rethinking Commonsense Psychology: A Critique of Folk Psychology, Theory of Mind and Simulation* (Basingstoke, UK: Palgrave MacMillan).

Reddy, V. (2008), *How Infants Know Minds* (Cambridge MA: Harvard University Press).

Rizzolatti, G., Camarda, R., Fogassi, M., Gentilucci, M., Luppino, G. & Matelli, M. (1988), 'Functional Organization of inferior area 6 in the Macaque Monkey: II. Area F5 and the control of distal movements', *Experimental Brain Research,* **71**, pp. 491–507.

Rizzolatti, G., Fadiga, L., Gallese, V. & Fogassi, L. (1996), 'Premotor Cortex and the Recognition of Motor Actions', *Cognitive Brain Research,* 3, pp. 131–41.

Rizzolatti, G., Fadiga, L., Fogassi, L. & Gallese, V. (1999), 'Resonance Behaviors and Mirror Neurons', *Archives Italiennes de Biologie,* **137**, pp. 85–100.

Rizzolatti, G., Fogassi, L. & Gallese, V. (2000), 'Cortical Mechanisms Subserving Object Grasping and Action Recognition: A new view on the cortical motor functions', in Gazzaniga, M.S. (ed.), *The Cognitive Neurosciences,* 2nd Edition (Cambridge, MA: MIT Press), pp. 539–52.

Rizzolatti, G. & Lupino, G. (2001), 'The Cortical Motor System', *Neuron*, **31** (6), pp. 889–901.

Rizzolatti, G., Fogassi, L. & Gallese, V. (2001), 'Neurophysiological Mechanisms underlying the Understanding and Imitation of Action', *Nature Reviews Neuro-science*, **2**, pp. 661–70.

Rizzolatti G. & Craighero L. (2004), 'The Mirror Neuron System', *Annual Review of Neuroscience,* **27**, pp. 169–92.

Rizzolatti, G. & Sinigaglia, C. (2007), 'Mirror Neurons and Motor Intentionality', *Functional Neurology*, **22** (4), pp. 205–10.

Rizzolatti, G. & Sinigaglia, C. (2008a), *Mirrors in the Brain. How our Minds Share Actions and Emotions* (Oxford: Oxford University Press).

Rizzolatti, G. & Sinigaglia, C. (2008b), 'Further Reflections on how we Interpret the Actions of Others', *Nature*, **455**, p. 589.

Rizzolatti, G., Fabbri-Destro, M., Cattaneo, L. (2009), 'Mirror Neurons and their Clinical Relevance', *Nature Clinical Practice. Neurology*, **5**, pp. 24–34.

Sinigaglia, C. (2008a), 'Enactive Understanding and Motor Intentionality', in Morganti, F., Carassa, A. & Riva, G. (ed.), *Enacting Intersubjectivity: A Cogni-tive and Social Perspective to Study of Interactions* (Amsterdam: IOS Press, pp. 17–32.

Sinigaglia, C. (2008b), 'Mirror Neurons: This is the question', *Journal of Con-sciousness Studies*, **15** (10–11), pp. 70–9.

Sinigaglia, C. (forthcoming), 'Mirroring and Understanding Action'.

Slors, M. (2007), 'Intentional Systems Theory, Mental Causation and Empathic Resonance', *Erkenntnis*, **67**, pp. 321–36.

Sommerville, J.A. & Woodward, A.L. (2005), 'Pulling out the Intentional Struc-ture of Action: The relation between action processing and action production in infancy', *Cognition*, **95** (1), pp. 1–30.

Sommerville, J.A., Woodward, A.L. & Needham, A. (2005), 'Action Experience Alters 3-month-old Perception of Other's Actions', *Cognition*, **96** (1), pp. 1–11.

Sommerville, J.A., Hildebrand, E.A. & Crane, C.C. (2008), 'Experience Matter: The impact of doing versus watching on infants subsequent perception of tool-use event', *Developmental Psychology*, **44** (5), pp. 1249–56.

Tomasello M. & Haberl K. (2003), 'Understanding Attention: 12- and 18-month-olds know what is new for other persons, *Developmental Psychology*, **39** (5), pp. 906–12.

Umiltà, M.A., Kohler, E., Gallese, V., Fogassi, L., Fadiga, L., Keysers, C. & Rizzolatti, G. (2001), '"I know what you are doing": a neurophysiological study', *Neuron*, **32**, pp. 91–101.

Umiltà, M.A., Escola, L., Intskirveli, I., Grammont, F., Rochat, M., Caruana, F., Jezzini, A., Gallese, V. & Rizzolatti, G. (2008), 'How Pliers Become Fingers in the Monkey Motor System', *Proceeding of the National Academic of Sciences of the United States of America*, **105** (6), pp. 2209–13.

Woodward, A.L. (1998), 'Infants Selectively Encode the Goal Object of an Actor's Reach', *Cognition,* **69**, pp. 1–34.

Woodward, A.L. (1999), 'Infant's Ability to Distinguish Between Purposeful and Non-purposeful Behaviors', *Infant Behavior & Development,* **22** (2), pp. 145–60.

Woodward, A.L. & Sommerville, J.A. (2000), 'Twelve-month-old Infants Inter-pret Actions in Context', *Psychological Science*, **11**, pp. 73–7.

Marc Slors

The Narrative Practice Hypothesis and Externalist Theory Theory

For Compatibility, Against Collapse[1]

Abstract: *What defence does the Narrative Practice Hypothesis (NPH) have against the charge that it is a covert form of externalist theory theory (TT)? I discuss and reject Dan Hutto's own strategies and argue that the NPH remains vulnerable to a threat of collapse into externalist TT as long as narrative folk-psychological explanation is differentiated from simple belief-desire explanation merely by a degree of complexity, subtlety and/or context-sensitivity. It is entirely plausible, however, that there is a more principled distinction between these two types of explanation of human behaviour. I defend such a distinction and show how it eliminates the threat of collapse into TT entirely.*

According to Dan Hutto's narrative practice hypothesis (NPH) (Hutto, 2004; 2007; 2008a; 2008b) folk-psychology (FP) is fundamentally a narrative competence. This hypothesis is explicitly intended to replace the notion of FP as a folk-*theory* of mind (ToM). Given the variety of notions of 'theory' in this domain, though, it may not be entirely clear whether and to what extent the NPH is really incompatible with everyone's understanding of FP as a theory. In this paper, I will argue that the NPH, as presented and defended by Hutto,

---

[1]   Thanks to Leon de Bruin, Dan Hutto, Derek Strijbos and two anonymous referees for very useful comments.

faces a threat of collapse into some version of what is known as the 'externalist' variety of the so-called theory theory of folk-psychology (ETT). However, I will also argue that this threat can be avoided by accepting a principled distinction between simple belief-desire explanations of actions and full-blown narrative reason-explanations.

The paper is set-up as follows: in Section 1 I shall outline the NPH and its superficial resemblance to externalist TT. I shall also identify two arguments employed by Hutto against externalist TT, of which I will claim only one can serve as Hutto's main defence against a possible collapse of the NPH into a form of TT: the rejection of mental holism. In section 2, I shall argue that this rejection of mental holism is incompatible with the ontological commitments of the NPH. Moreover, I shall argue that this rejection does not, as Hutto takes it, follow from the empirical facts. This renders the threat of collapse into TT all too real for the NPH. In Section 3, however, I will explain why the NPH does not collapse into TT. I shall argue that the narrative element in folk-psychological reason explanations is an addition to belief-desire psychology rather than an extension of it. While externalist TT may explain belief-desire psychology, this additional narrative element is out of its reach. Hence, the possible compatibility of externalist TT with the NPH does not amount to a collapse of the NPH into a form of TT. Moreover the claim of the NPH that TT does not fully capture real-life folk-psychological explanations remains intact.

1. The Narrative Practice Hypothesis and Externalist Theory Theory

Let me start by outlining the NPH, its possible compatibility with externalist TT and Hutto's principled reason to reject this compatibility.

1.1 The NPH

The NPH is a theory about the nature and acquisition of folk-psychological (FP) competence that differs considerably from either of the only two options available up until recently: the theory theory (TT) and the simulation theory (ST). It has managed to carve out a theoretical niche for itself by subtly, and plausibly, changing the subject of the debate on FP. FP, according to Hutto, is not a spectator sport. It doesn't serve the purpose of predicting or explaining behaviour from a disengaged third-personal standpoint. Rather, it serves the purpose of facilitating social interaction, which requires, most of the time, an engaged second-person perspective. Thus, what needs to be explained is primarily our ability to render actions intelligible in a socially acceptable fashion in order to facilitate our daily dealings with each other. This is done by giving *reasons* for actions. Reason-giving according to the NPH is storytelling, not theorizing.

The idea that reason-giving *is* theorizing is propounded by all versions of the TT. But also by the dominant version of ST (e.g. Goldman, 2006). For 'if simulation plays a vital role in the process of understanding others, it does so by feeding the outcomes of operations involving recreative/enactment imagination or co-cognition into theorizing activity that brings ToM [Theory of Mind] principles into play' (Hutto, 2008b, p. 177). When it comes to explaining our acquisition of FP competence, TT and dominant versions of ST commit us to innate or acquired ToM abilities; extreme cases of such a commitment are ToM modules (Leslie, 1992; 1994) or child-as-scientist hypothesis (Gopnik, 1996; Gopnik & Wellman, 1992).

Hutto forcefully argues against both (Hutto, 2008a, pp. 143–77). There is no need to buy into the strong cognitivism that infuses the traditional ToM views on FP acquisition. The basis from which we can explain the acquisition of FP competence, rather, is what Hutto labels 'unprincipled bodily engagements'. These are our non-conceptual, embodied, primitive, but at times remarkably intelligent interactive capacities. Hutto explains how the use of language allows us to transform those engagements into the FP interactions of our daily lives (Hutto, 2008a, pp. 87–100; 129–42). In this explanation, typical folk-psychological concepts such as 'belief' and 'desire' are normally acquired in the course of our early development (see next section), but start to acquire their full use only when children develop the capacity to understand and create narratives. Hutto: '(…) children come into possession of all the pieces needed for playing the understanding-action-in-terms-of-reasons game before they can actually play it. What they are missing in their early years is not the necessary components, but knowledge of the basic rules' (2008a, p. 27). But in fact, 'rules' still sounds too theoretical as the term designating the FP 'principles' that interrelate beliefs and desires. The point is that '[a]ccording to the NPH these "principles" are revealed to children not as a series of rules but by showing them in action, through narratives, in their normal context of operation' (2008a, p. 29).

Thus — and that is one of its aims — the NPH explains the nature and acquisition of our ability to understand and explain actions in terms of beliefs, desires and reasons within an enactivist, embodied, non-representationalist view of 'the mental'.

1.2 Externalist TT

In their (1994), Stich and Ravenscroft distinguish between what they call 'internalist' and 'externalist' conceptions of FP. Since I will be interested in the theory theory of FP only in this section, the relevant distinction to make is between internalist TT (ITT) and externalist TT (ETT). ITT is the prototypical sort of TT that the NPH argues against; it is the theory according to which our FP capacities are grounded in an innate or acquired theory of human psychology that is represented in our minds/brains. The NPH is incompatible with ITT. Those who suspect that the NPH may be compatible with TT must have a version of ETT in mind.

Stich and Ravenscroft introduce the externalist reading of FP and in effect ETT as follows:

> We might equally well elect to use the term 'folk psychology' in a way that is more akin to Lewis' usage — as a label for the collection of folk psychological 'platitudes' that people in our culture readily recognize and assent to. Or, since the collection of 'platitudes' is likely to be large and ungainly, we might reserve the label 'folk psychology' for a set of more abstract generalizations — a 'theory' if you will — that systematizes the platitudes in a perspicuous way and that (perhaps in conjunction with some other commonly known information) entails them. That systematization might well invoke terms and concepts that are quite unfamiliar to ordinary folk, in the same way that an attempt to systematize our linguistic intuitions probably would (Stich and Ravenscroft, 1994, p. 460).

According to ETT, FP-as-a-theory is present, not necessarily in our minds/brains, but in our FP practices. That is, our actual practice of understanding and explaining actions in terms of beliefs, desires and reasons, is supposed to be structured by a system of principles or rules. We need not be aware of this system, just like we are not aware of the rules of the grammar of the language we speak. But just like our actual speech and writing displays systematicity on closer inspection, so does our FP practice.

Is ETT ruled out by the NPH? It depends. Of course, the presence of FP-as-a-theory in our practices might be explained in terms of our possessing an internal theory of mind, that is, in terms of a theory represented in our brains (i.e. ETT and ITT are not necessarily mutually exclusive). Since the NPH is hostile to ITT, such a version of ETT will be incompatible with it. But to the extent that ETT does not invoke ITT, some version of it may well fit in with the enactivist anti-representationalism of the NPH. Why would it not be the case that even though we acquire FP competences through exposure to narratives, what we in fact learn through such exposure is how to use and apply the implicit rules of an (external) FP theory?

It is this possibility that I would like to investigate in this paper. Although I shall indicate in the third section why I think the NPH is not a covert version of ETT, I will first argue that Hutto's own arguments against the compatibility of ETT with the NPH are not convincing. In order to do that, I will have to be more precise about which variety of ETT is most likely to be compatible with the NPH.

For even versions of ETT that shun an explanation of the alleged theoretical nature of our FP practices in terms of an internal FP-theory had by the practitioners might be incompatible with the NPH. ETT might construe FP such that 'the folk' conceive of beliefs and desires as theoretical postulates 'similar to electrons, atoms, or gravity' (Hutto, 2008a, p. 32). And such a view of the propositional attitudes is exactly what the NPH seeks to avoid and replace. To explain an action in terms of its reasons is *not*, according to the NPH, to hypothesize an explanans of that action in the form of private, internal beliefs and desires that are hidden from view. Rather, it is to situate that action in what Hutto calls a FP narrative. In FP explanations, according to Hutto, beliefs and desires operate as parts of narrative descriptions of actions; they are not theoretical postulates.

But there is a different class of theoretical postulates than electrons and atoms that Hutto seems to be overlooking. Consider Mendel's postulate of *genes* at the time when he formulated his laws of genetics. Before the discovery that genes are in fact DNA (or are realized by DNA), genes are defined not as determinate entities, but rather as the causal roles played by *some* entity. As e.g. David Lewis (1966; 1972) noted, mental states such as beliefs and desires can be defined similarly, in terms of the causal role they play. 'A mental state M (say, an experience)' according to Lewis 'is definable as the occupant of a certain causal role R — that is, as the state, of whatever sort, that is causally connected in specified ways to sensory stimuli, motor responses, and other mental states' (Lewis, 1972, pp. 249–50). Accordingly, Lewis conceived of FP as a term-introducing theory that fixes the various causal roles mental state types are said to play relative to each other according to the users of FP. This is a form of ETT: Lewis says nothing about internal theories of mind (see also e.g. Jackson, 1998; Braddon-Mitchell & Jackson, 2007).

Some variant of this form of ETT may seem like a contender for being compatible with the NPH. But refinements are in order still. For, on the one hand it may be argued that electrons and atoms can also, on closer inspection, be defined in terms of their causal or theoretical roles. On the other hand, genes turn out to be identical with DNA, a complex molecule, i.e. something with a status similar to atoms and electrons. In order to circumvent this problem and to keep the distinction between the types of theoretical postulate I wish to employ intact (in the present context this is the role-realiser distinction, but I will broaden the distinction later on), we may note that mental states as causal role states are multiply realisable: the same causal role state can be realised at different times or in different individuals by different neural structures.[2] Mental states are thus not type-identical with neural states, and explanations of actions in terms of beliefs and desires cannot be reduced to explanations in terms of neural causes. Hence, mental states as causal role states have a status that is different from genes as a causal roles concept in that type-identification with some definite objective physical item is not feasible. Mental states as causal role states may be the postulates of a term-introducing theory, but that certainly doesn't mean they are like electrons, atoms or gravity.

To be sure, the claim here is not that the NPH or Hutto's position in general is compatible with Lewis's views on FP or psychophysical identification in terms of a role-realiser relation. The claim is that a version of ETT that depicts FP as a term-introducing theory that defines mental states in terms of multiply realisable causal role states seems compatible with the NPH. Such a version of TT does not postulate an internal theory of mind and neither does it portray FP as a theory that postulates entities similar to electrons and atoms.

The crucial move here is to distinguish between theoretical postulates that are obviously incompatible with the enactivist anti-representationalism of the NPH and those that are not. The distinction between roles and realisers helps, in this respect, but other distinctions may help too. Daniel Dennett, for instance, doesn't conceive of beliefs and desires as causal role states. But he does conceive them as theoretical postulates that are different from electrons, atoms and gravity, i.e. different from what Reichenbach called *illata*. Beliefs and desires, according to Dennett, are *abstracta* — theoretical postulates like centres of gravity or vectors — that capture and predict our behavioural regularities, perhaps not accurately to the last detail but certainly fast, practical and effective. On his view, there is no need to postulate any neural realisation as concretely isomorphic to them as occupiers of causal roles:

---

[2] Two remarks. First: I diverge from Lewis's 1972 proposal here. Lewis is interested in psycho-physical identification and hence in unique realisation. Second, the idea of multiple realisation is familiar from Fodor (1974). But it is worth emphasizing that it does not imply or favour Fodor's own ITT (e.g. Fodor, 1975).

> Jacques shoots his uncle dead in Trafalgar square and is apprehended on the spot by Sherlock; Tom reads about it in the Guardian and Boris learns of it in *Pravda*. Now Jacques, Sherlock, Tom and Boris have had remarkably different experiences (…) but there is one thing they share: they all believe that a Frenchman has committed murder in Trafalgar square. (…) Ordinary folk-psychologists have no difficulty imputing such useful but elusive commonalities to people. If they insist that in doing so, they are postulating a similarly structured object in each head, this is a gratuitous bit of misplaced concreteness (Dennett, 1987, pp. 54–5).

Folk-psychologists may be depicted as theorists, in Dennett's scheme, but only in a particular sense. FP is not a theory that refers to concrete entities in order to explain and predict behaviour, regardless of what either philosophers or FP users think (Dennett, 1995). But the *abstracta* invoked by FP are, according to Dennett, structured into what may be described as a theory about 'the performance specifications of believers' (Dennett, 1987, p. 59). Here too, the claim is not that Dennett's position is entirely compatible with the NPH. The claim is merely that ETT might be conceived roughly along Dennettian lines, and that such a version of TT appears prima facie compatible with the NPH.

The ways in which Dennett and Lewis set apart causal role states and *abstracta* from the kind of theoretical postulate that is incompatible with the NPH requires reference to a form of mental holism. It is through defining beliefs and desires in terms of their holistic interrelation with each other and with contextualised behaviour that it becomes possible to conceive of them as something other than the concrete theoretical postulates — the *illata* — that the NPH denies to be at play in FP. Thus, Dennett explicitly claims that mental states are defined holistically within FP while Lewis conceives of FP as a huge theoretical sentence in which mentalistic terms such as 'belief' or 'desire' can be replaced by variables that play specific causal roles as defined by the Ramsey sentence of FP as a whole. Mental holism is a non-accidental aspect of the kind of ETT that may, as I argued, appear compatible with the NPH. This is important for what is to follow.

1.3 Hutto's arguments against ETT

Hutto's attacks on TT focus primarily on ITT and there is little attention for ETT. As far as I can see Hutto offers two arguments against the kind of ETT that I claimed to be prima facie compatible with the NPH in the previous subsection. One partly implicit strategy, to be found throughout Hutto's (2008a), is his claim that the mental holism that is crucial for the kind of ETT that may be compatible with the NPH is in fact refuted by facts from developmental psychology. Another strategy is Hutto's later argument (2008b) that the Lewis-style version of ETT that might appear compatible with the NPH cannot be considered a proper theory. I take this argument to be applicable as well to a Dennett-style ETT. In this subsection I shall outline both arguments. I will start with the second one and argue that it fails, leaving the first argument as Hutto's main buffer against the claim that the NPH may turn out to be another form of TT.

The basic idea behind the second argument is that when ETT conceives of FP as a theory that is implicitly present in our daily practices (rather than in our heads), then '(...) "theory" is surely the wrong word since the second T in TT would not denote a "theory" in any interesting or substantive sense. (...) [It] would not be an articulation of the "principles" *used by* folk psychological practitioners in making their everyday attributions, predictions or explanations. [They] would not be (...) *used by* the folk in their daily routines any more than Newtonian laws are used by planets in order to conduct their business' (2008b, p. 180).

I am not convinced that this is a good argument. Consider a parallel example: Suppose we reject a Chomskian view of natural language according to which all language users possess some internally (i.e. neurally) stored generative grammar; language is grammatical, to be sure, but the grammar is present in our linguistic practices, so to speak, not in our heads. We gain knowledge of our grammar, on such a view, by carefully observing and analysing the principles at play in our linguistic practices. But does this view imply that if we gain such knowledge, 'it would not be an articulation of the "principles" *used by* [linguistic] practitioners'? There surely is a strong tendency to speak of principles *used* by people here. So if there is not a similar tendency to describe the planets as *using* Newtonian laws we must explain the difference. Hutto's argument assumes that we can't explain the difference. I think we can. I will stick to FP while explaining it.

Crucially, planets are objects and folk-psychologists are agents. That is, unlike planets, folk-psychologists initiate their own actions, in this case the acts of interpretation of each other's behaviour. In that sense, planets are governed by Newtonian laws (at least for the sake of this argument) while folk-psychologists are not in a similar way *governed* by the principles of externalist FP. Folk-psychologists may, in Dennett's terminology, choose to apply the intentional strategy (i.e. apply FP), but they may also opt for a design strategy or a physical strategy. Or they may apply a faulty or idiosyncratic version of FP.

Precisely because there are options and precisely because the folk-psychologist herself decides on one of these options while initiating the act of FP interpretation, it is natural to express this by saying that she *uses* the FP strategy (*rather than* some other strategy) to interpret someone's actions.

The fact that the folk-psychologist is likely not to be able to state explicitly the principles of the strategy she is using does not block this conclusion. Many language users are unable to formulate the grammatical principles at play in their speech. To demand that folk-psychologists be able to state the principles of FP in order to count as using FP-as-a-theory would be to discount almost all forms of TT. For the huge majority of TT-ists claim that FP-as-a-theory is used implicitly.

Hutto's later argument against ETT, then, fails to convince. What remains is the strategy applied against ETT in his 2008 book: the rejection of mental holism. Here Hutto reasons as follows: The ability of children to understand moderately complex narratives (of the kind Hutto claims are involved in the acquisition of FP competence) develops after children acquire the concepts of desires and beliefs. For this reason, Hutto emphasizes at different occasions that these narratives

> are *not* responsible for introducing an understanding of mental concepts, such as desire and belief for the first time, rather (...) they put on show how these attitudes can integrate with one another (...). The NPH assumes that kids already have a practical grasp on what it is to have a desire or belief before learning how to integrate their discrete understanding of these concepts in making sense of actions in terms of reasons. FP narratives enable this by showing how these core attitudes and other mental states behave *in situ* (Hutto, 2008b, p. 178).

Conveniently, this separation of (the grasp of) FP concepts (e.g. beliefs and desires) from (the grasp of) the 'principles' interrelating them in FP explanations of actions allows Hutto to distance himself from the kind of mental holism involved in the kind of ETT that I argued to be possibly compatible with the NPH. Hutto:

> (...) the claim that the meaning of mental predicates depends wholly on their lawful relations is apparently undermined by the fact that children develop a practical understanding of the different propositional attitudes at distinct stages in their careers. Thus they have a grasp of the concept of desire, quite independently of and prior to having an understanding of the roles they play in making sense of a person's reason for action. And an understanding of both of these attitudes appears to precede an understanding of the roles they play in making sense of a person's action (Hutto, 2008a, p. 31).

This, then, is the principled ground on which Hutto is able to claim that the NPH is *not* a covert version of ETT.

2. Belief-Desire Interaction and the Threat of Collapse

So, in (my reconstruction of) Hutto's view, in order to safeguard the NPH from collapsing into a form of TT, it is crucial to claim that 'children come into the possession of all the pieces needed for playing the understanding-actions-in-terms-of-reasons game before they can actually play it' (Hutto, 2008a, p. 27). In this section I will argue that this principled distinction between 'the pieces' and 'the game' or 'the FP components' (propositional attitudes and other psychological states) and the 'principles' interrelating them, cannot be upheld. I will argue that the distinction is hard to square with Hutto's anti-internalistic, interpretationist view of the mind, and that the developmental psychological data Hutto invokes to argue for this distinction do not in fact show what he takes them to show. Finally, I will trace the NPH's threat of collapse into TT back to what I take to be its root: the assumption that narrative reason explanation is continuous with simple belief-desire psychology on a scale of increasing complexity. Rejecting that assumption, I will argue, should be the strategy for avoiding a collapse.

2.1 Mental holism in view of Hutto's interpretationism

One of the features (and according to many, including myself, attractions) of the NPH is that it offers a complete account of human action and interaction without drawing on a traditional notion of 'mind' as involving internal representations (such as in the mental realist positions that gave rise to ITT), or even a notion of mental states that calls for a theoretical account of tractable neural implementation (such as offered e.g. by Lewis). On the one hand, the unprincipled engagements from which our narratively guided FP practices grow involve intentional but not propositional attitudes. To apply the notion of mental *content* at this level would be to miss the point (Hutto, 2008a, ch. 3). On the other hand, the high-level reason talk of FP gets its explanation at the socio-cultural rather than the neuro-psychological level. At this level there are mental contents, but these cannot be traced back or reduced to the neural structures of the people to whom the relevant mental states are ascribed.

What, ontologically speaking, is it to ascribe a belief or a desire to someone on this picture? I think the answer here should be that the position Hutto advocates is some form of interpretationism, probably of a more Davidsonian than Dennettian kind. Just like Hutto argues that to have a concept of 'belief' is to have certain social abilities (2008a, p. 129–31), I take it that on his account to ascribe a belief is to interpret someone's behaviour so as to allow or express the possibility of specific interactions. FP in Hutto's conception is, as Dennett (1995) puts it, 'a craft', not a description or theory (it should be said, though, that Hutto's interpretationism is not as permissive as Dennett's; see 2008a, pp. 42–3).

The point I wish to make in this section is that interpretationism is usually taken to involve a degree of mental holism that appears to contradict the assumption that it is possible to possess the components of FP, i.e. be able to apply the concepts of 'belief' and 'desire', in abstraction from knowing how these components interact (cf. Malpas, 1992, ch. 3). This is best illustrated by cases in which the FP interpretation is underdetermined by the action at issue. An example may help to convey the idea. Suppose I am at a birthday party and I see my 11 year old nephew reach for a glass of beer that is on the table. Since I do not believe he desires beer, I will attribute to him the belief that there is, say, apple juice in the glass, because I know that's what he likes. Then I realize that it is common these days for young children to boast about drinking alcohol. Maybe he is impressed by stories of classmates and doesn't want to stay behind. In that case I should attribute to him the desire to drink beer and the belief that there is beer in the glass. What a simple example such as this shows is that the ascription of beliefs and desires are linked. I cannot, when altering my interpretation of my nephew, merely alter, say, the desire I ascribe to him and leave the belief intact; there's no point in reaching for a glass of apple juice when you want a beer. Typically, it is the assumption of rationality that interpretationists refer to when explaining why we ascribe beliefs and desires in pairs, and not atomistically.

But are beliefs and desires *always* invoked in tandem? Take another example:

> The boy's sign says 'LEMONADE — 12 cents a glass.' I hand him a quarter, he gives me a glass of lemonade and then a dime and a penny change. He's made a mistake. Now what can we *expect* from him when we point out his error to him? That he will exhibit surprise, blush, smite his forehead, apologize, and give me two cents. Why do we expect him to exhibit surprise? Because we attribute to him the belief that he's given me the right change — he'll be surprised to learn that he hasn't (…). Why do we expect him to blush? Because we attribute to him the desire not to cheat (or be seen to cheat) his customers (Dennett, 1987, p. 84).

M. SLORS

Here it seems that the surprise is explained by the boy's belief that he has given the right change. The blushing on the other had is explained by his desire not to cheat. At first glance there is no belief-desire *inter-action*. And since this example is from an uncontaminated interpretationist source, it may seem to show that interpretationism does allow for the possibility to ascribe beliefs and desires without being aware of how these interrelate. If that were the case, Hutto can have his cake and eat it; he can stick to an interpretationist ontology of the propositional attitudes and accept (at least in some cases) the kind of mental atomism that is required by his separation of FP components from FP 'principles'.

But on closer inspection it is not true that there is no belief-desire interaction in examples such as these. Why would the boy blush if he didn't believe he might be seen as having cheated? Or look at the bracketed phrase in the last sentence of the quote. It matters whether the boy doesn't want to cheat or whether he does want to cheat but doesn't want to be seen cheating. In the former case the expression of surprise is explained by his belief to have given the right change. In the latter case, the expression is explained by his attempt to hide his real intentions and his wish to make it look like he believed he had given the right change whereas he didn't in fact believe that. The point of this second example is that if one were to claim of a given situation that it can best be viewed as a situation in which someone understands the behaviour of someone else merely through the attribution of a single belief or desire, one needs to take great care to show that no implicit background beliefs or desires are overlooked.

The relation between holism and interpretationism is a strong one. If the point of attributing beliefs and desires is not to refer to an independent mental reality but instead to make sense of the behaviour of others, as Hutto has it,[3] and if, as the examples above show, this requires ascription of specific *sets* of interrelated beliefs and desires then it is hard to imagine how one can be an interpretationist without accepting mental holism. Having said that, though, the purpose of this brief subsection is not to present a knock-down argument to the effect that Hutto's ontological commitments force him to abandon the components-principles distinction. There are various forms of interpretationism and it does not seem a priori impossible that on some loose version of it some form of mental atomism is feasible. But if

---

[3] Chris Sinha (2009) interprets Hutto in line with the phenomenological, hermeneutic and Wittgensteinian approaches to mind, action and language of the *verstehen* tradition. Obviously, I agree.

atomism and interpretationism are held to be compatible, that compatibility certainly needs to be argued for.

2.2 Do empirical facts indicate a distinction between FP components and FP 'principles'?

Hutto *does* argue, in some sense at least, for the fact that young children acquire the concepts of 'belief' and 'desire' as full blown propositional attitudes prior to knowing how to interrelate them by rehearsing and interpreting some empirical evidence from developmental psychology. In Chapter 7 of his (2008a) he sketches the emergence of these concepts in children from what I take to be a largely interpretationist point of view. In some detail he shows how linguistic competence extends the abilities involved in having a primitive grasp of desires and beliefs as 'mere' intentional attitudes into abilities that can be understood as having a grasp of beliefs and desires as propositional attitudes. In his account, Hutto takes care to emphasise the extent to which the acquisition of full-blown concepts of 'desires' and 'beliefs' are independent: 'Desires come first in our linguistically scaffolded mentalistic understanding of things: children are capable of attributing these long before they can make competent belief ascriptions' (Hutto, 2008a, pp. 135–6). In this subsection I want to argue that it is not at all clear that this does indeed show that the concepts of 'belief' and 'desire' are indeed acquired before children grasp the principles that interrelate them. Instead, I will argue, there is much to be said for the opposite.

First, a preliminary observation. Though it is well documented that the 'linguistically scaffolded' concept of 'desire' precedes the 'linguistically scaffolded' concept of 'belief' by some six months, this does not mean that the development of these concepts can be separated entirely. For both concepts build on earlier acquired non-linguistic abilities that are often (in my view overconfidently and somewhat misleadingly) referred to as the 'nonverbal' grasp of 'beliefs' and 'desires'. The first occurrences of these abilities are not easily or uncontroversially separated temporarily. At any rate, both abilities (I deliberately avoid 'concepts' which I shall reserve for linguistically scaffolded abilities) occur long before their linguistic counterparts do. Thus, though controversial, it is claimed that 18-month olds already have some understanding of the desire of others:

> (…) [C]hildren were shown two bowls, one of goldfish crackers and one containing broccoli. The experimenter would look cheerfully at the broccoli and say 'Yum!' and make a disgusted face toward the crackers

and say 'Yuck!' Then the experimenter would hold out her hand and ask, 'Can you give me some?' (...) 18-month-olds succeed in giving the experimenter the one that she showed a preference for, broccoli, even though it is not their own choice (Bloom, 2004, pp. 18–9).

Similarly, (and also controversially) Onishi and Baillargeon (2005) have claimed that 15 month-olds have some grasp of the false beliefs of others, using a violation-of-expectation version of the false belief task. Southgate *et al.* (2007) criticise this study for being ambiguous: the results can also be explained by the assumption that children attribute ignorance instead of false beliefs. But they themselves present a disambiguated version of the non-verbal false belief task, showing that 25-month olds appear to pass it. It is far from clear how we should interpret these data (see e.g. Herschbach, 2008). But it does seem clear that long before children acquire a linguistic concept of 'desire', which is six months prior to acquiring the concept of 'belief', they have been able to make non-linguistic 'attributions' that are at least in some sense predecessors of *both* the concepts of belief and desire.

So, when children develop the linguistic concept of 'desire' (around 3.5 years of age) it is not entirely true that this concept exists in isolation. Still, it is a well established fact that 3.5-year olds are able to attribute desires linguistically while not being able to attribute beliefs in that way. The first point I'd like to make is that, also in view of the previous remark about non-linguistic predecessors, there does not seem to be a clear demarcation of when a child can be said to have acquired a full-blown concept of a specific propositional attitude — it all depends on what one calls 'a concept'. And given this, one begs the question against the mental holist when it is said that the concept of 'desire' is acquired before knowing how to interrelate it with e.g. the concept of 'belief'. It makes perfectly good sense, from the point of view of the holist, to say that a child hasn't acquired the full blown concept of 'desire' *until* she knows how it interacts with beliefs. *If* it is the case that a 3.5-year old does not know how a desire and a belief interrelate (the possibility of a linguistic concept of 'desire' interacting with a non-linguistic context in which there is a primitive grasp of beliefs, remains open), then she has acquired a *proto*-version of the concept of 'a desire' but not the real thing yet. The case for isolated desire concepts is inconclusive to say the least.

As for beliefs, Hutto's case is even less strong, for the simple reason that by the time children are said to acquire that concept (by the age of 4), the linguistic ability to attribute desires is already in place. There may certainly seem to be instances in which children explain actions in terms of isolated belief attribution. But here we need to ask whether the lesson of the second example of the previous section is sufficiently heeded: are we sure there are no implicit desire attributions that play a role in the background? Consider what may seem to be a paradigmatic example of action explanation/prediction based on the attribution of a single belief: Baron-Cohen, Leslie and Frith's (1985) version of the false belief task, the so-called Sally-Ann test. Here's the standard picture that is used to illustrate the test:

Figure 1
The standard picture illustrating the Sally-Ann test

The semi-final sentence makes the background-desire, in co-operation with which the false belief is supposed to explain Sally's looking in the basket, entirely explicit. And even if we were to erase that sentence, the transition from 'now Sally comes back' to 'where will Sally look for the ball' obviously presupposes that Sally *wants* her ball. It would be absurd to claim that children do not understand the belief-desire interaction going on here. It is overwhelmingly likely that they do. And the possibility that they co-determine each other's role and meaning is entirely open.

Hutto does not deny this. He gives a wonderful three-page description of how the concept of 'belief' develops out of the cognitive friction that is certain to emerge in the conversational interplay that children in between 3 and 4 years are capable of. It is almost unthinkable (though Hutto is silent on this) that this interplay at all times avoids what we would characterise as belief-desire interactions e.g. of the kind illustrated by the first example in the previous section. Indeed Hutto writes that 'children are more or less simultaneously learning what beliefs are while also becoming familiar with the specific role they play in folk-psychology. For it is during the period of 3 to 4 years of age that they start having the relevant kinds of conversational interplay with caregivers as well as being introduced to people narratives' (Hutto, 2008a, p. 138). This statement is, at least at first glance, at odds with the separation of FP components and FP principles. The consistency of Hutto's position might appear to be saved by emphasizing that narratives are introduced as an item that is logically distinct from the acquisition of beliefs. But the same cannot be claimed of conversational interchange: Hutto *does* describe the emergence of the concept of belief as requiring interchange and hence in all likelihood as being a product of having witnessed many belief-desire interactions.

Thus, even to some extent by Hutto's own standards, it is very plausible that children know how beliefs and desires interact from the moment they have the full concept of 'a belief'; the separation of FP components and FP principles cannot be illustrated by means of referring to the developmental psychological facts. And the kind of interaction that children seem to be aware of is exactly the kind mental holists refer to. Indeed it is of the kind presupposed by externalist TT.

2.3 The threat of collapse and a different strategy to avoid it

The fact that Hutto says that children start being exposed to (folk-psychological) narratives in between the ages of 3 and 4 does not mean that his claim is that by the age of 4 children have a rudimentary grasp of FP. On the contrary, while TT-ists claim that when children can pass the false belief test by the age of 4 (see, however, Carpendale & Lewis, 2004) this marks their ability to wield a primitive version of FP, Hutto argues that it is precisely the fact that children are only able to understand reason explanations at later ages — approximately from the age of 5 onwards — that illustrates the fact that passing the test is not enough for FP. The continued exposure to narratives, apparently, is needed, according to Hutto, for true FP competence.

What, then, is the relation between the knowledge of simple belief-desire interactions that children possess by the age of 4 (see previous section) and full blown FP competence? Precisely because Hutto does not admit *that* children by the age of 4 have at least some understanding of FP principles, he does not answer this question. But from his book and his many articles an answer can be distilled: complexity and subtlety. Full FP competence differs from the simple belief-desire psychology I claim children of 4 years acquire knowledge of, by being infinitely more complex (e.g. in plotting the interrelations of the attitudes with all sorts of other mental states such as emotions and perceptions as well as with items such as character traits and moods) and subtle (e.g. in charting how circumstances and a range of other variables might be relevant).

If this is indeed the relation between the simple belief-desire psychology of the 4-year old and the full blooded FP of adults, then it seems Hutto has no argument against the external TT-ist who claims that the narrative structure of FP does not exclude the idea that FP *implicitly* is still a term-introducing theory. Once it is recognized that the simple belief-desire psychology of, say, the false belief test is precisely the sort of psychology that proponents of ETT wish to draw on when devising their notion of FP as a term-introducing theory ('*this* is how the notion of a belief functions: if you want x, believe that y-ing will get you x, you will y, *ceteris paribus*'), complexity and subtlety introduced through narratives will not help to make full-blown FP non-theoretical. It will only serve to make full-blown FP a complex and subtle theory.

Here, the way out for the NPH might seem to be to argue that the simple belief-desire psychology of the 4-year old is already narrative by nature. Indeed in the passage I quoted at the end of the previous subsection, that is what Hutto appears to do. And indeed, the Sally-Ann example is an example of a *story*! But this move does not help. If simple belief-desire psychology is called 'narrative', this very much undermines the informativeness of the notion of 'a narrative'. The NPH depends, as a theory distinct from TT, on the contrast between the notion of 'a story' and the notion of 'a theory'. This contrast disappears (especially given the absence of a *definition* of 'narrative' that sets it apart from 'theory') when one of the prime examples of the belief-desire interactions that serves to illustrate the idea of a term-introducing theory is called a narrative. Calling simple belief-desire interactions narratives will only encourage those who suspect that the NPH is a variety of implicit ETT.

But note that this threat of collapse of the NPH into a form of TT hinges on the idea that full-blown FP reason explanation is continuous with simple belief-desire psychology. By rejecting the idea that full-blown FP explanation is just a more complex form of the same type of belief-desire psychology that ETT accounts for, (i) the apparent compatibility of the NPH with ETT as outlined in section 1, and (ii) the failure of Hutto's anti-holism strategy against ETT can be shown *not* to amount to the collapse of the NPH into ETT. Compatibility does not amount to a collapse when full-blown FP explanation is discontinuous with simple belief-desire psychology in the sense that the narrative element in FP explanation that is stressed by the NPH is a further addition to belief-desire psychology that is beyond the reach of ETT. I will argue for such discontinuity, and hence against the collapse of the NPH into TT, in the next section.

3. The Division of Labour between Belief-Desire Interaction and Narrativity

In this section I will argue that the idea of a discontinuity between simple belief-desire psychology and full blown FP reason explanation is, despite being unorthodox, indeed highly plausible. Narrative FP explanations do involve belief-desire structures. But the contribution of narratives to the explanation of actions cannot, I claim, be understood as an extension in the direction of complexity, context-dependence and subtlety of belief-desire schemata.

3.1 Some examples and their analysis

In order to distinguish the roles of belief-desire interaction on the one hand and narratives on the other in full-blown FP explanations of actions, it will be helpful to consider some examples of such explanations. Oddly enough, there are not that many examples of full-blown narrative explanations of actions to be found in Hutto's book. A striking one, though, is to be found in the beginning of the book. It is about the explanation of some initially incomprehensible behaviour by Hutto's wife. Hutto writes:

> On the morning of my flight [my wife] agreed to drive me to Heathrow after I had first dropped off my car at the garage. So, we set off in our separate cars and she took the lead (...). As we came to the relevant intersection, she stopped at a set of red traffic lights, but uncharacteristically failed to signal. (...) To my amazement when the lights changed she did not turn, began driving towards the town center, straight past the garage at which she herself made the booking. (...) At this point, I was

faced with a rather tricky interpretive problem. Given that my wife is very competent and reliable, lacking any malicious streak or any known reason to treat me badly, I was at an utter loss to make sense of her actions (Hutto, 2008a, pp. 18–9).

Afterwards, Hutto's wife's explained her behaviour in narrative form:

(...) After the incident she explained that although it was true that she had phoned the garage to make the appointment herself, and she had used the number I had given her, she believed it was the number of our old garage, which is located in the next village (Hutto, 2008a, pp. 19–20).

This example typically shows what Hutto takes to be the point of narrative FP explanations: 'Folk psychological narratives are used to make sense of (...) seemingly aberrant actions. Typically — or at least when they work — they help us to understand why someone has acted in a way that has strayed from our normal expectations (on the assumption that they have acted for a reason nonetheless' (Hutto, 2008a, p. 37). This idea about the function of narrative explanation is shared by Alisdair Macintyre (MacIntyre, 1981). Consider the following example:

I am standing waiting for a bus and the young man standing next to me suddenly says: 'The name of the common wild duck is *Histrionicus histrionicus histrionicus.*' There's no problem as to the meaning of the sentence he uttered: the problem is, how to answer the question, what was he doing in uttering it? Suppose he just uttered such sentences at random intervals; this would be one possible form of madness. We would render his action of utterence intelligible if one of the following turned out to be true. He has mistaken me for someone who had yesterday approached him in the library and asked: 'Do you by any chance know the Latin name of the common wild duck?' *Or* he has just come from a session with his psychotherapist who has urged him to break down his shyness by talking to strangers. 'But what shall I say?' 'Oh, anything at all.' *Or* he is a Soviet spy waiting at a prearranged rendez-vous and uttering the ill-chosen code sentence which will identify him to his contact. In each case the act of utterance becomes intelligible by identifying its place in a narrative (Macintyre, 1981, p. 210).[4]

---

[4] Macintyre also seems to agree with Hutto (or, given the fact that Macintyre's book appeared in 1981, Hutto with Macintyre) on the genesis of our narrative FP capabilities: 'It is through hearing stories about wicked stepmothers, lost children, good but misguided kings, wolves that suckle twin boys, youngest sons who receive no inheritance but must make their own way in the world and eldest sons who waste their inheritance on riotous living and go into exile to live with the swine, that children learn or mis-learn both what a child and what a parent is, what the cast of characters may be in the drama into which they have been born and what the ways of the world are. Deprive children of stories and you

These are helpful examples. But what do they show? Do they show that there are highly complex schemes of beliefs and desires at play in narrative explanations in which these beliefs and desires *interact* with other psychological states, situations, character traits, etc. They might. But I think there is a much more elegant and clear analysis.

Take Hutto's own example. Behind the story, a fairly simple belief-desire structure is visible. Hutto's wife:

> *wants* to drive him to the airport after having dropped his car off at the garage.

She also

> *believes* that the phone number Hutto gave her was the number of their old garage, so that the appointment she had made was an appointment with that old garage in another village.

There are, of course numerous background beliefs (about traffic lights, traffic rules about when to signal, etc.) and desires (wanting to abide by the rules when driving, etc.) at play. But that is also the case in the most simple belief-desire explanations (think about Sally's background belief that balls do not change place by themselves and usually stay where they are put). So these background beliefs and desires are *not* at play because of any narrative involvement; which is exactly why Hutto omits them too in his recounting of this particular narrative explanation. Where, then, does narrativity enter in this example?

Well, look at the individual belief and the individual desire cited above. The belief that 'the phone number Hutto gave his wife was the number of their old garage, so that the appointment she had made was an appointment with that old garage in another village' *itself* contains a narrative. And similarly for the desire 'to drive Hutto to the airport after having dropped his car off at the garage'. That is what the narrative element does in this particular example: it *fills in* the individual belief and desire of an otherwise simple explanatory belief-desire scheme, rendering the belief and the desire *themselves* very complex. But not by breaking them down into further beliefs and desires. Even if that were a possibility, it would be cognitively much more labourious than the narrative procedure of inserting a compressed sequence of events relevant to the action to be explained, leaving all the attitudes that might have been involved aside (note that the narrative contents of the above belief and desire do not contain further

---

leave them unscripted, anxious stutterers in their actions as in their words' (Macintyre, 1981, p. 216)

attitudes). Compare this with the same simple belief-desire scheme in the Sally-Ann case: Sally *wants* her ball and *believes* it is in the basket. That's it. The difference with Hutto's example, the difference that narrativity makes, is in the complexity, not of the belief-desire *scheme*, but in the belief and the desire *themselves*.

The outcome of an explanation in which the beliefs and the desires themselves have a narrative form is that the action that is explained is made intelligible not merely as the logical result of attitudes immediately preceding the action, but as a part of a longer story, i.e. as coherently fitting into the agents *auto*biography. This diachronic element in the explanation is not a part of the belief-desire interaction that 4 year-olds are to some extent capable of understanding, it is a part of the narrative contents of the belief and the desire themselves that 4 year olds are not yet capable to entertain. The work that is done by narrativity in Hutto's example is different from the work that is being done by the 'formal' belief-desire interaction. The simple belief-desire structure in Hutto's narrative explanation is the skeleton of the explanation. The real work in the explanation is done by the narratives that have the *form* of a belief and a desire. To use a different metaphor, the belief-desire structure is the canvas on which the actual narrative explanation is painted.

What about Macintyre's example? In the first reading of the example, the person standing next to Macintyre (or the 'I' in the example) at the bus stop *believes* that he has met Macintyre in the library yesterday when Macintyre (or the 'I') asked him what the Latin name of the common duck is while he failed to provide the answer he now has ready at hand. He *desires* to help Macintyre (or the 'I') by providing him with the answer, even if it is one day late. Again, there is a simple belief-desire structure (again with a huge background of other beliefs and desires not relevant to the narrativity at play) which provides the skeleton of the explanation. And again the individual belief and desire are filled-in by the narratives. The same analysis applies to the other two readings, but I take it that the point is clear.

What is the role of narratives relative to the belief-desire structure of an explanation? I would say it is the chunking — in the psychologist's sense of 'compressing' — of large amounts of diachronically ordered information relevant to the explanation of the action. The narratives that 'fill' the beliefs and desires of full-blown FP explanations do not merely summarise more beliefs and desires, they do something more. They introduce a diachronic 'logic' to the events that are either believed or desired. On the one hand this diachronic logic makes a large amount of information highly tractable by highlighting only

M. SLORS

relevant events, where 'relevant' means 'relevant to the story'. On the other hand this diachronic logic makes it possible to make an action intelligible by letting it fit into this logic from the point of view of the agent.

So, this is the hypothesis: children by the age of 4 have mastered simple belief-desire interaction (to some extent at least), but they have *not* yet acquired the ability to chunk large amounts of diachronically ordered information in the specific way that is relevant to mature FP explanations. For that they need to acquire narrative competency. And they start to acquire that, roughly, from the age of 5 onwards. In this respect it is interesting to note (as Hutto does in a footnote, 2008a, p. 254) that

> whereas pre-school-aged children tend to connect events in a linear fashion, 5-year olds begin to use complex syntax to impose a causal temporal hierarchy that contrasts important events with background information (Capps *et al.*, 2000, p. 201).

That, I hypothesize, is precisely what narratives do: compress diachronically ordered and structured information, highlighting the relevant bits. That information, thus compressed, gets fed into the belief-desire structures children already are familiar with.

3.2 Persons

But there is more that narratives do than *just* compress information. They structure diachronically related events in a specific *format* (the MP3 of FP), i.e. along the axes of embodied *persons* as diachronically existing unified characters. The point I want to make in this short subsection is that the acquisition of narrative abilities by children after they have acquired some insight into belief-desire interaction can be characterized by the development of the notion of 'a person' or 'a self' as a diachronically coherent agent.

Unlike Hutto, Macintyre makes a point of highlighting the fact that the notion of an agent, person or self as a diachronically unified being on the one hand and the notion of a narrative, story or history on the other require each other. For Macintyre it is even impossible for us to construe the idea of personal identity without our narrative capabilities:

> Empiricists (...) tried to give an account of personal identity solely in terms of psychological states or events. Analytical philosophers, in so many ways their heirs as well as their critics, have wrestled with the connection between those states and events a strict identity (...). Both have failed to see that a background has been omitted, the lack of which

makes the problems insoluble. That background is provided by the concept of a story and the kind of unity of character which a story requires (Macintyre, 1981, p. 217).

We need not go as far as Macintyre does with respect to the problem of personal identity in order to appreciate the relevance of this to our present discussion: persons-as-diachronically-unified-selves *are* an inalienable part of the FP narratives Hutto's NPH is about. So, if narrative competence starts to emerge around the age of 5, that is when children start to grasp the idea of people as psychologically diachronically unified agents. Of course smaller children also have a grasp of, say, their parents as diachronically continuous beings. But just like the abilities underlying what Hutto calls 'unprincipled bodily engagements' get transformed through the use of language into belief-desire psychology (Hutto, 2008a, ch. 5–7), there is a *further* transformation marked by the acquisition of narrative capacities: the primitive embodied notion of 'person' becomes a diachronically unified psychological entity, a self. Note again that we need not go as far as Macintyre does: it may be the case that narratives *constitute* selves, so that the ability to grasp narratives allows for the emergence of the FP notion of 'a person'. But it may just as well be that by the age of 5 children start to acquire the capacity to grasp the idea of the diachronic unity of psychological beings as such. And that may parallel the emergence of narrative capacities, or even explain it. It is even more likely, to my mind, that there really is no fact of the matter here about which side is right. Keeping the quote by Capps *et al.* at the end of the previous subsection in mind, I would say that it is most likely that *both* narrative capacities and the concept of persons or selves arise from developments in the syntactical abilities of 5-year olds as two sides of the same coin. Thus, the idea is that just as unprincipled bodily engagements get transformed through language into belief-desire psychology by the age of 4, a further development of linguistic abilities allows for the introduction of the notion of persons by the age of 5; not so much as a term that is used as frequently as 'believes that' or 'wants to', but as the characteristic 'compression format' of narrativity.

3.3 Conclusion

The functions of narrativity in FP explanations — compressing information, introducing a diachronic logic to events from the viewpoint of the agent, introducing the notion of a diachronically coherent person in reason explanations, etc. — cannot be reduced to the functions of belief-desire interaction. That, at least, was the point of this section. Since ETT is merely about the interaction of propositional attitudes — however sophisticated and complex — it follows that mature FP explanations fall outside the scope of ETT to the extent that they involve narrativity. The compatibility of the NPH with ETT (Section 1) and the improbability of the anti-holism attack on ETT (Section 2), then, do not and cannot amount to a collapse of the NPH into ETT. Moreover, Hutto's claim that TT doesn't explain real-life FP (or FP *stricto sensu*) remains intact. Not, however, because all versions of it are crucially wrong, but because all versions of it leave something crucial out.

References

Baron-Cohen, S., Leslie, A.M. & Frith, U. (1985), 'Does the Autistic Child have a "Theory of Mind"?', *Cognition*, **21**, pp. 37–46.

Bloom, P. (2004), *Descartes Baby: How child development explains what makes us human* (London: Arrow Books).

Bradon-Mitchell, D. & Jackson, F. (2007), *Philosophy of Mind and Cognition* (Oxford: Blackwell).

Capps, L, Losh, M. & Thurber, C. (2000), 'The Frog Ate the Bug and made his Mouth Sad: Narrative competence in children with autism', *Journal of Abnormal Child Psychology*, **28**, pp. 193–204.

Carpendale, J.L.M. & Lewis, C. (2004), 'Constructing an Understanding of the Mind: The development of children's social understanding within social interaction', *Behavioral and Brain Sciences*, pp. 79–151.

Dennett, D.C. (1987), *The Intentional Stance* (Cambridge MA: MIT Press).

Dennett, D.C. (1995), 'Two Contrasts: Folk craft versus folk science, and belief versus opinion', in *Brainchildren: Essays on designing minds* (London: Penguin), pp. 81–94.

Fodor, J. (1974), 'Special Sciences', *Synthese*, **28**, pp. 97–115.

Fodor, J. (1975), *The Language of Thought* (Cambridge MA: Harvard University Press).

Goldman, A.I. (2006), *Simulating Minds: The Philosophy, Psychology and Neuroscience of Mindreading* (New York: Oxford University Press).

Gopnik, A. (1996), 'Theories and Modules; Creation Myths, Developmental Realities, and Neurath's Boat', in P. Carruthers & P.K. Smith (ed.), *Theories of Theories of Mind* (Cambridge: Cambridge University Press).

Gopnik, A. & Wellman, H.M. (1992), 'Why the Child's Theory of Mind Really *is* a Theory', *Mind and Language*, 7 (1–2), pp. 145–71.

Herschbach, M. (2008), 'False-belief Understanding and the Phenomenological Critics of Folk-Psychology', *Journal of Consciousness Studies*, **15** (12), pp. 33–56.

Hutto, D.D. (2004), 'The Limits of Spectatorial Folk-Psychology', *Mind and Language*, **19**, pp. 548–73.

Hutto, D.D. (2007), 'The Narrative Practice Hypothesis: Origins and applications of folk-psychology', D.D. Hutto (ed.), *Narrative and Understanding Persons*, Royal Institute of Philosophy Supplement, (Cambridge: Cambridge University Press).

Hutto, D.D. (2008a), *Folk Psychological Narratives: The Sociocultural Basis of Understanding Reasons* (Cambridge, MA: MIT Press).

Hutto, D.D. (2008b), 'The Narrative Practice Hypothesis: Clarifications and implications', *Philosophical Explorations,* **11** (3), pp. 175–92.

Jackson, F. (1998), *From Metaphysics to Ethics* (Oxford: Clarendon Press).

Leslie, A. (1992), 'Autism and the "Theory of Mind" module', *Current Directions in Psychological Science,* **1**, pp. 18–21.

Leslie, A. (1994), 'Pretending and Believing: Issues in the theory of ToM', *Cognition,* **50**, pp. 211–38.

Lewis, D. (1966), 'An Argument for the Identity Theory', *Journal of Philosophy,* **63**, pp. 17–25.

Lewis, D. (1972), 'Psychophysical and Theoretical Identifications', *Australasian Journal of Philosophy,* **50**, pp. 249–58.

Macintyre, A. (1981), *After Virtue: A Study in Moral Theory* (London: Duckworth).

Malpas, J. (1992), *Donald Davidson and the Mirror of Meaning* (Cambridge: Cambridge University Press).

Onishi, K.H. & Baillargeon, R. (2005), 'Do 15-month-old Infants Understand False Beliefs?', *Science,* **308** (5719), pp. 255–8.

Sinha, C. (2009), Review of Daniel D. Hutto Folk Psychological Narratives: The sociocultural basis of understanding reasons, *Language and Cognition,* **1** (1), pp. 137–43.

Southgate, V., Senju, A. & Csibra, G. (2007), 'Action Anticipation through Attribution of False Belief by two-year-olds', *Psychological Science*, **18** (7), pp. 587–92.

Stich, S. & Ravenscroft, I. (1994), 'What is Folk Psychology?', *Cognition,* **50**, pp. 447–68.

Heidi Maibom

In Defence of (Model) Theory Theory

Abstract: *In this paper, I present a version of theory theory, so-called model theory, according to which theories are families of models, which represent real-world phenomena when combined with relevant hypotheses, best interpreted in terms of know-how. This form of theory theory has a number of advantages over traditional forms, and is not subject to some recent charges coming from narrativity theory. Most importantly, practice is central to model theory. Practice matters because folk psychological knowledge is knowledge of the (empirical) world only if it is combined with knowledge of how to apply it. By combining the general and the particular in this way, model theory gives a deep and explanatorily satisfactory account of the centrality of practice. Model theory accounts not just as well as, but better than, narrativity theory for the fact that our folk psychological explanations appear to contain, or form part of, narratives.*

The question of what underlies our ability to ascribe beliefs, thoughts, feelings, and intentions to people continues to attract attention. Recent years have seen a variety of attempts to update, even overturn, older proposals, in particular the theory theory and the simulation theory. One line of attack is headed by the suggestion that narrativity is more central to folk psychological competence than previously thought. Weak versions of this proposal constitute an important amendment, or addition, to traditional accounts, particularly ontogenetic ones. Strong versions, however, reject important presuppositions of older theories. Usually they embody a duality of claims: on the one hand, they reject the idea that the ability to simulate or theorize about others' mental states is sufficient for folk psychological competence, and on the other they argue that narration is essential to it. Without language and narration there is no 'true' folk psychological competence. 'True', or 'full-blown', folk psychological competence involves, according to Daniel Hutto (2008b), ascriptions to people of reasons in the form of propositional attitudes. Folk psychology has traditionally been understood as enabling social interaction of a somewhat sophisticated nature. It is becoming increasingly clear, however, that it does not, in many cases, require the ability to ascribe reasons to people (e.g. Maibom, 2007; Morton, 2003; Povinelli, 2001; Tomasello *et al.*, 2003). Narrativity theory, therefore, limits itself to a subset of abilities involved in structuring human social interaction.

In this paper, I defend theory theory against the charges of narrativity theory. The version of theory theory that I favour is so-called model theory. According to model theory, theories are families of models, which represent real-world phenomena when combined with relevant hypotheses (Giere, 1988). This form of theory theory has a number of advantages over traditional forms. Among them is that the importance of practice falls out of it. Practice is not just important for the obvious reasons that if you can't use something it does you little good; this is as true of knowledge as it is of skipping ropes. It is important because folk psychological knowledge is knowledge of the (empirical) world only if it is combined with knowledge of how to apply it. By combining the general and the particular in this way, model theory gives a deep and explanatorily satisfactory account of the centrality of practice. In addition, model theory accounts not just as well as, but better than, narrativity theory for the fact that our folk psychological explanations appear to contain, or form part of, narratives. This is partly due to the fact that practice is central to this version of theory theory, not because practice essentially involves the consumption of linguistic narratives. According to this theory, theoretical knowledge is only knowledge of real-world phenomena to the extent that we *know how to apply it.*[1] For reasons, which I explain later, linguistic narratives do play an important role in folk psychological knowledge on such a picture. But they are not fundamental to it.

---

[1]   This should not be confused for a competence-performance distinction. The model theory does not simply point out that folk psychological knowledge must include knowledge of how to apply representations of real-world phenomena to the world. The claim of model theory is that theories do not represent anything empirical except when combined with relevant hypotheses.

The main trouble with narrativity theory, as I see it, is that it is, at one and the same time, too chauvinist — in its insistence that all narratives are linguistic — and too liberal — in its vague characterization of what a narrative is, making pretty much *all* linguistic productions narratives. But if all, or nearly all, linguistic productions are narratives, what distinguishes folk psychological ascriptions from any of our other language-involving practices? By contrast, model theory provides an account of *why* narratives play such an important role in folk psychological ascriptions. It does so by referencing structures — theoretical models — that are not simply common to all linguistic productions. For reasons, such as these, it will not surprise the reader to learn that I suggest that model theory should be considered very seriously by those who are attracted to different ways of looking at folk psychology that give more room to its character as a *practice*.

1. The Lure of Narrativity

Let us begin by considering some of the attractions of narrativity theory. In part, this line of thought springs from a discontent with traditional construals of folk psychology, in particular the theory theory. The main focus are classical versions of the theory theory, such as those proposed by Paul Churchland (1981) and Jerry Fodor (1987). Much recent work has been done on theory theory that, to my mind at least, does much to improve on earlier versions (e.g. Godfrey-Smith, 2004; 2005; Maibom, 2003; 2007; Stich & Nichols, 2004). I therefore disagree with a number of the criticisms raised against theory theory. However, I want to focus on one of the virtues of the narrativity thesis, namely its emphasis on the *practice*. I first say something brief about the development of folk psychological competence in children before moving on to what will be the main focus of the paper, namely how to understand adult competence.

One of the things that narrativity theorists like to point out is that instruction and practice are central to acquiring competence with folk psychological explanations (Hutto, 2008b). Children do not normally take up a detached scientific attitude towards things and other people. They do not experiment with people or sit around systematically working through different explanatory hypotheses concerning human behaviour. Nor should we assume that folk psychological competence is simply innate. No, children *learn* to explain action in terms of beliefs and desires by example. Not only are they exposed to explanations, self-reports, and gossip, but parents also tend to invest in a lot of costly instruction, inducing the child to interpret herself, by doing it for her, or presenting her with a couple of different options. And it turns out that, as a matter of fact, narratives are the perfect vehicles of instruction. What makes them particularly useful is that:

> [i]n such stories, the core mentalistic framework — the rules for the interaction of the various attitudes — remains constant. However, other important features vary. Thus, children learn the important differences that the contents of the attitudes make to understanding action, as well as the contributions made by a person's character, history, and larger projects (Hutto, 2009, p. 14).

This allows children to grasp the 'subtleties and nuances needed for making sense of intentional actions in terms of a person's reasons' (Hutto, 2009, p. 14). Narratives show a person's reasons *in situ* 'against appropriate backdrops and settings' (Hutto, 2008a, p. 427).

Now, stories tend to play a pivotal role in human culture. Myths are at the one extreme and just ordinary gossip at the other of the range of human narratives. Usually either serves well to impart information about human motivation. But the fact that a certain ability is nourished in our society by engaging in certain practices does not, of course, mean that it can *only* be acquired this way. It could simply be an idio-syncratic feature of our culture. It is worth noting that, by and large, children acquire similar skills and abilities at roughly the same age — talking, walking, pretend-playing, etc. — whatever the effort of their parents. Only severe deprivation and abuse are proven to halt the natural process of physical and cognitive development (Harris, 1998; Pinker, 2002). We cannot, therefore, simply conclude that because our childhood was full of stories, fairy tales, and other narratives, that without those sorts of narratives we would not have acquired folk psychological competence. But whereas it is an open empirical question whether narratives *per se* are required for the acquisition of folk psychology, it is an undisputed fact that children cannot acquire the relevant competence without learning how to apply psychological categories on the ground, as it were. And stories and gossip are certainly excellent practice tools.

Since the main aim of narrativity theory is to revise our ideas about adult capacities, I want to set aside the issue of development here, and focus on the constitutive tools of folk psychological competence. Narrativity theorists press traditional accounts on the issues of the appropriate *application* of psychological properties and the specificity of the practice. I here ignore how it touches on simulation theory, and shall focus just on theory theory. Early forms of theory theory lent themselves to the objection from application by their almost exclusive focus on knowledge contents: counterfactual supporting generalizations featuring psychological concepts. Such an oversight can be remedied. However, there are a number of reasons to prefer a different theory theory; one that deploys an account of scientific theories, according to which application is central to their representational powers. The second complaint is more serious for the theory theory. For it is meant to strike at the very heart of what is central to this idea: that folk psychological knowledge is constituted, in part, by systematizations of behaviour. This knowledge has to have a broad scope, showing generalities that cut across different situations and agents. However, narrativity theorists propose that folk psychological explanations — certainly those in terms of reasons — are, as a matter of fact, often: i. contextualized; ii. specific to a particular individual; and iii. particular. This stands in apparent contrast to scientific explanations. I shall present a version of the theory theory that is immune to these objections. Granted, I argue that folk psychological explanations are only particular and specific in a certain sense. That sense, however, is the only one that is compatible with the generality that we require for explanations to be *good* explanations. I argue that this version of theory theory is preferable to more traditional versions and accounts for the importance and centrality of practice and narratives better than narrativity theory does.

2. Model Theory

Model theory differs from traditional theory theory accounts on a number of dimensions. According to model theory, knowledge of, and ability to apply, theoretical models account for (all or parts of) our folk psychological ascriptions (Godfrey-Smith, 2004; 2005; Maibom, 2003; 2007). Whereas traditional theory theories construe folk psychological knowledge in terms of knowledge of laws or counterfactual supporting generalizations, model theory conceives of such knowledge as composed of knowledge of families of models and knowledge of theoretical hypotheses.

Theoretical models are sets of objects with relations, properties and functions defined over them (Suppes, 1960; Suppe, 1989; Giere, 1988). My favourite example of a theoretical model from the sciences is a two-particle Newtonian system with an inverse square force (Giere, 1988). In such a model, the two particles are related in terms of the force they exert on one another.[2] Theoretical models are abstract

---

[2]   I.e. $F = Gm_1 m_2/d_2$.

objects. Taken on their own, without additional hypotheses that specify how (in what respects) and the degree to which they fit real-world systems, they do not represent anything. If we look at the Earth and Moon in isolation, we see that, as a system, they approximate a two-particle Newtonian system with an inverse square force. Obviously, the shapes, sizes, masses and centres of masses of the objects differ. For instance, the centre of mass of the Moon is 2 km off its geometric centre, whereas the centre of mass of a Newtonian particle is point mass. Nevertheless, the bodies in the model fit the Moon and Earth to a high degree of approximation with respect to their position, relation, and velocities. Theoretical hypotheses, therefore, are highly significant in determining what, exactly, a model represents. According to Giere, students of physics acquire theoretical hypotheses by being exposed to examples of applications in textbooks and classroom settings. They acquire facility with applying the models through practice.

It may be useful here to think of another example of a model. Let us consider the tit-for-tat model of iterated forms of the prisoner's dilemma from decision theory. The model consists of two rational agents interacting under certain constraints (those set out by the dilemma). It presents their various options and the optimal (from the perspective of the model) way of interacting. But without attendant theoretical hypotheses, it does not yet represent real-world human interactions. Typically, the tit-for-tat approach is used to model human cooperative situations. Cooperation often involves one person benefiting another with some action of hers, with the other person acting to benefit the first one at a later time. Either person is faced with a dilemma of sorts: should I act so as to benefit the other? Here the model fits to the extent to which the potential interaction partners are assumed to be (practically) rational, they have no interfering bonds of affection, their options fit that of cooperation or defection to a reasonable degree of approximation, they possess no other relevant information about the other person's history of cooperation and defection, the prospects for future interaction are significant, and so on. The tit-for-tat approach is, as a matter of fact, a model that forms part of some people's folk psychological theory.[3] It fits the practice of buying rounds in pubs. If someone buys you a drink, you buy her a drink, and so on and so forth. If she does not reciprocate, you refrain from buying

---

[3]   Even though, as I argue in Maibom (2007), it need not represent psychological properties *as such*.

her another round.[4] But more illustrative of a specifically folk psychological model is what I call the intentional action model.

It is often said that one of the generalizations of folk psychology is 'people intend to do what they do'. The many exceptions to this generalization make it obvious that it must be attended by a thick *ceteris paribus* clause. The trouble is, of course, that it is unclear that the generalization is even true *ceteris paribus*. Do you always intend to say what you say, for example? Do you intend to scratch your itch or to interpret events so as to maintain a positive self-image (Taylor & Brown, 1988)? This does not seem plausible. Model theory avoids such difficulties (Maibom, 2003).[5] An intentional action model represents action as the result of an intention. In fact, an appropriate description of the intention matches an appropriate description of the action. If there is a lack of fit between the two, questions are raised about the degree to which the action is intentional, or about the correctness of the individuation of either the action or the intention. Famously, in order for someone to *murder* someone else, he must have the appropriate intention to kill the person in question. Otherwise the action is not appropriately described as murder. An intentional action model portrays intentions as relatively unspecified internal states of agents that produce action under certain circumstances. Other models may represent the nature of such intentional states. What makes the intentional action model useful is knowledge of the relevant theoretical hypotheses.

The intentional action model fits what people do under many circumstances, but certainly not all. Accidents are a case in point. There is a reason that we never describe anyone's falling over as 'he threw himself to the ground'. Someone only throws herself to the ground if she intends to do so. However, there are many cases where the situation is considerably more complex. Take this passage from Hercule Poirot's last case:

> For you see, Hastings, *you* killed Barbara Franklin.
>
> *Mais oui*, you did!
>
> [...]

---

[4]   This is a good example of the fact that we need not suppose folk psychological theories to be only interpretive and not productive. If we know where we figure in a social structure, we know what is expected of us because we represent how the system works. I explain this in more detail in section 4 and Maibom (2007).

[5]   One might argue that *ceteris paribus* laws combined with a competence-performance distinction will do the trick. I have argued against this suggestion in detail in Maibom (2003), pp. 304–6.

Mrs Franklin asks you all up to her room. She makes coffee with much fuss and display. As you tell me, her own coffee is beside her, her husband's on the other side of the bookcase-table.

And then there are the shooting stars and everyone goes out and only you, my friend, are left, you and your crossword puzzle and your memories — and to hide emotion you swing round the bookcase to find a quotation in Shakespeare.

And so they come back and Mrs Franklin drinks the coffee full of the calabar bean alkaloids that were meant for dear scientific John, and John Franklin drinks the nice plain cup of coffee that was meant for clever Mrs Franklin (Christie, 1975, pp. 179–82).

In one sense Hastings did, in fact, kill Barbara Franklin. For his action was the immediate cause of her drinking the poisoned coffee. And we are often in the habit of thinking of actions in this way. I might only succeed in pushing someone over who is already unbalanced; nevertheless, it seems right to say that I pushed him over. In another sense, of course, Hastings did very much not kill Mrs. Franklin. He did not intend to kill Mrs. Franklin. As a matter of fact, he was unable to conceive of his action in a way that would have to be true for him to have the relevant intention since he was ignorant of the presence of the alkaloid. Hastings only intended to move the bookcase around to check a quote in Shakespeare. This peculiar situation is one in which it is a real open question whether one should apply the intentional action model. Similarly, when we consider one of the famous trolley cases, for example, we are faced with this dilemma. Does the fact that someone will die as a result of one's actions being a merely foreseen, but not intended, consequence make it the case that the intentional action model applies poorly to the action in question? Or is the foreseeing itself sufficient to make the action intentional? It is certainly not unreasonable to apply the model. The question is what advantage there is to regarding the situation in terms of the model *given* the degree of the fit. An answer to that question presumably has to do with moral permissibility and moral blameworthiness (cf. Kamm, 1998). The relevance of this choice — to apply or not to apply the intentional action model — is highlighted by Joshua Knobe's (2003) interesting studies on intentional action judgments. He demonstrates that people are much more likely to judge someone who does not care about the morally unacceptable outcomes of his actions as having intentionally brought about negative results, than they are to judge someone who does not care about the morally desirable outcomes of his actions as having intentionally brought about a positive outcome.

The thing to note about models — and this is why I provided so many examples of them — is that theoretical hypotheses are central to their applicability to the world. Furthermore, whether one applies one model or another to the world is not entirely straightforward, and one agent may apply a model where another would refrain from doing so. So model theory also explains the many individual differences that are observed between people in their attitudes towards others' mental lives. Some people might think the intentional action has a decent fit in a situation where another would deny that this is the case. This no doubt has to do with a variety of different factors, not least of which is the particular experiences of the subject. I do not want to focus on individual differences here, just note that its ability to account for such differences is an additional virtue of the account. What I want to talk more about is theoretical hypotheses since they are the link to the topic here: the importance of narratives to folk psychological knowledge and competence.

3. Hypothesis, Application and Experience

In an earlier paper, I suggest that theoretical hypotheses are best regarded as constituted by procedural knowledge or know-how (to-apply), not as explicitly represented information (Maibom, 2007). The idea is implicit in model theory, as I understand it. It is not simply that training teaches the scientist to apply models to real-world systems by enumerating the sorts of real-world systems that fit the model. Rather, training gives the scientist an open-ended ability that allows her to apply her models to systems and objects that she was not exposed to in the learning situation.

Someone like Giere puts an enormous stress on the learning situation. It is the physics textbook that, as it were, forms the basis of his model theory. But the physics textbook has a limited range of examples. A theoretical hypothesis links two individual systems by means of a circumscribed analogy. Now what makes a theoretical model the powerful tool that it is, is its scope of application. For instance, a two-particle Newtonian system has the power to represent a great variety of different real-world systems. But each theoretical hypothesis, when considered on its own, links this system to just one real-world system. An expert has knowledge of a great number of theoretical hypotheses in addition to theoretical models. It is this knowledge, which makes her the expert. But we do not expect an expert to be proficient *only* with what she has had previous experience of. Training in an area isn't supposed to give you experience only with the particulars in that area. We expect someone's expertise to give her the ability to extrapolate from her experience, to come up with new suggestions and solutions, and so on. In other words, we expect her knowledge to generalize and be productive. Compare this to learners of a language. We do not expect them only to be able to apply their knowledge of grammar to sentences that they have already been exposed to. We train them to gain an open-ended facility with a particular language. For this, we rely on pre-existing learning structures to do their job. We feed them exemplars, and they do the rest.

Experts' ability to identify new real-world systems as fitting theoretical models that they know may be due to the fact that theoretical hypotheses typically link theoretical models with *kinds* of objects or systems, not particulars (as the Earth-Moon system example might suggest). A potentially infinite number of planet-satellite systems are like a two-particle Newtonian system with an inverse square force in certain respects and to a certain degree. Likewise, a potential infinity of grandfather clocks is like simple pendulums — a harmonic oscillator — in certain respects and to a certain degree (Giere, 1988). Thus, if you know your theoretical model fits one system of a particular kind, you tentatively infer that it also fits other systems of the same kind. What helps delimit the number of systems that are usefully regarded to be like, say, a two-particle Newtonian system is, at least partly, the respects and degrees of fit specified in the theoretical hypothesis, as well as other available theoretical models. In choosing a model, we choose the one that fits the system *best*. Jupiter and Europa, for example, are not usefully modelled as a two-particle system because of the presence of other moons, such as Ganymede and Io, exerting their own gravitational pull on them. Note, however, that it is not the mere presence of other satellites that is at issue, but their mass. Earth has recently acquired a new moon, Cruithne.[6] However, Cruithne is so small — it is a mere 5 km. wide — that it does not affect the fit between the Earth-Moon system and a two-particle Newtonian system much.

What training does is a complex issue. On the one hand, it often exploits pre-existing capacities, like categorical judgments. We learn, for example, to apply the model of a harmonic oscillator to a grandfather clock. On the other hand, it sometimes forms the basis for classification in the first place. People can be trained to make very difficult

---

[6] Cruithne will most likely orbit the Earth for the next 5,000 years. By comparison, the Moon will continue orbiting Earth for much longer, although it, too, is moving away from us.

discriminations, as is evident in chicken sexing.[7] At any rate, extensive training is required in order to learn how to apply theoretical models. Being able to apply Newtonian theory to the Earth and the Moon alone won't get you very far. But coming to be able to see a wide variety of different systems as Newtonian systems requires familiarity with a range of real-world systems, the similarity between which one comes to see, in part, because of the model(s). Training with real-world phenomena is therefore of crucial importance to the scientist. Whereas I doubt that any theorist of science would deny that training scientists to apply their knowledge to real-world phenomena is crucial, the model approach is particularly sensitive to this feature of scientific knowledge. You cannot create a scientist without training. Without knowing her theoretical hypotheses, the scientist's knowledge is hollow: it is only knowledge of abstract systems.

As I have already suggested, knowledge of theoretical hypotheses is not well regarded as explicit knowledge of particular propositions. Certainly not all of it is. A scientist might start out with knowledge of such propositions, but as her ability expands, it will come to consist, at least in part if not fully, of knowledge-how to apply her theoretical models. A proficient scientist knows, roughly, when her models are applicable, but such knowledge is, in part, the fruit of training and experience.

4. Training the Folk Psychologist

How does the above explication of theoretical hypotheses relate to folk psychology? Well, model theory uses scientific knowledge as a model of everyday knowledge. In effect, the expertise of the ordinary person in folk psychological ascriptions is modelled on the expertise of the scientist.[8] Just like scientific knowledge combines knowledge of models with knowledge of how to apply them (theoretical hypotheses), folk psychological knowledge requires experience in application. And such experience usually takes training. Over the last decades, there has been tremendous focus on the development of folk psychological skills in children. But to truly master folk psychology, one must continue to learn throughout life. Compared to the evidence from child psychology, however, there is relatively little data on adult learning and expertise.

---

[7]   To the naked eye, male chicks and female chicks are indistinguishable. Over hundreds of trials, however, people can eventually learn to tell them apart (Horsey, 2002).

[8]   It should be noted, however, that Godfrey-Smith and I differ on how representative of scientific knowledge we think knowledge of models is (cf. Godfrey-Smith, 2005).

By contrast to a scientist's training, children's introduction to psychological explanation and understanding is relatively informal and unstructured. Nevertheless, children are explicitly taught much folk psychology, and much of it by verbal means. Parents talk to each other about themselves and others; siblings do too. Children are told and tell each other stories. Almost all stories are about agents. Children play games with their parents and each other. Many of those games involve pretence. Pretend-play is particularly useful for the acquisition of knowledge about what persons who have particular roles do, for example, what doctors, grocers, and teachers do.[9] Just like play prepares other animals for adult life, pretend-play prepares children for the extreme sociality of human life. Compare this to the training of students who, in a way, play at being scientists in the physics lab. Self-reports are presumably also central to learning. People *tell* children what they think and feel, and why. For instance, they instruct their children not to hit them because it hurts; to do something for them because it will make them happy; etc. Children ask their parents questions about what they think and feel too. All of this forms an important basis for their acquisition of folk psychological models and hypotheses. And one should not forget that parents induce their children to think of others as agents with thoughts, feelings, wants etc. by interpreting people to them.

This is about as far as my learning theory goes. It should be noted that people probably never stop learning new things about human psychology. The acquisition of folk psychology is a lifelong enterprise. And we learn by listening to what others say, gossiping, and so on. We learn not only how to apply our models, but acquire knowledge of new models also. Nevertheless, knowing-how to apply folk psychological models is essential to folk psychological knowledge if it is to be knowledge of real-world phenomena.[10]

I have stressed the application here to try to remedy the fact that this aspect of theoretical knowledge is often overlooked or ignored. Such a stress, however, should not overshadow the fact that theoretical models are the organizing force behind our knowledge. They subsume real-world states of affairs; they make sense of diverse phenomena in terms of certain structures, relations, and properties. Models figure essentially in (the background of) folk psychological explanations, as

---

[9] Elsewhere, I call these models social models (Maibom, 2007).

[10] This is not to say, of course, that a model theory presupposes realism about mental states; Godfrey-Smith likes model theory, in part, because it has no such presumptions (Godfrey-Smith, 2004).

these attempt to see an individual situation as an example of something more general. It presents individual processes as exemplifying a particular causal order (to a certain degree and in certain respects).

So far, I have mainly availed myself of traditional examples of folk psychological knowledge, transposed to model-form. It gives the impression of model theory as a relatively uniform structure. I don't believe that it is. Contrary to Hutto, I don't think it is useful to think of folk psychological explanation exclusively in terms of reason explanations. Indeed, I wonder whether such a conceptualization is even compatible with the broad construal of narratives that Hutto avails himself of. What gives the most complete explanation of our ability to think of others in terms of psychological properties, what allows us to predict their behaviour, and understand them better, is a more heterogeneous account. Elsewhere I have argued that folk psychological theory consists of at least three broad families of models, only one of which features the traditional concepts of folk psychological explanation and prediction. The other families feature models of goal-directed behaviour and models of social roles and organizations (Maibom, 2007).

Models of behaviour feature goal-directed behaviours in an environment, where these behaviours may be seen as responses to the exigencies of the environment and leading to changes in it. The possession of knowledge of such models does not require possession of such concepts as intention, but merely a teleological notion of goal. Having a goal in this sense is standing in a relation to an object in, or feature of, the environment; it is an extensional, not an intentional, notion (Maibom, 2007; Bermúdez, 2003). Thus, models of behaviour represent behaviour as goal-directed, but not as intentional. Models such as these can be applied to animal behaviour generally, including human behaviour, with excellent results. Predictions, explanations, and understanding flow easily from applications of such models. Knowledge of such models also helps explain a lot of relatively sophisticated behaviour on the part of nonhuman animals and small children, as it does not presuppose linguistic competence. Part of folk psychological competence, at least, is essentially unrelated to *linguistic* narratives. Other families of models may require linguistic competence to be mastered. But this is due to their involving structures the representation of which requires such competence. It is not essentially related to folk psychological competence (see Maibom, 2007; Bermúdez, 2003).

Social models are models of individuals in social structures and institutions. Individuals occupy roles, which determine how they interact with others depending on their roles. Although one might be able to understand these individuals' actions as having a certain purpose or goal, a full understanding of them includes the purpose of the structure or institution itself. In such models, social structures and institutions usually do not act, even though they have purposes. What acts on these purposes, however, are the individuals within the structure. In a way, the logic of social models is the inverse of that of folk psychological models. In the latter, the main actor, the agent, acts as a function of his beliefs and desires (etc.). In social models, the main actors act as a function of the larger structure of which they form part (Maibom, 2007). Knowledge of social models help explain why it is we usually know how to interact with people — even if at a relatively superficial level — once we know their, and our own, role in a social structure. Knowing what to do once you have identified someone as a waiter and yourself as a customer is relatively straightforward. Nothing about the private states of the waiter needs to be considered.

Families of social models help highlight a feature of theory theory that is often not considered; it can be productive. It does not simply allow you to interpret others or predict their behaviour; it gives you information about what to do. Social models outline the role of individuals in social structures and, as such, do not merely help you interpret what others are doing or anticipate their actions; they tell you what to do given the particular role that you are occupying. Social models have a distinct normative element, although it may not be represented as such. Thus, a common assumption about theory theory — that it is merely interpretative, and cannot be used, in any direct way, to decide what to do — is false (e.g. Heal, 1994). In fact, I think it is false of *all* families of folk psychological models. As sociologists are well aware, most people have an intense desire to conform. Most people also know that it is often useful to look to others to discover what the best course of action is to reach one's goals. Knowing what people tend to do when they desire certain things and entertain certain beliefs is therefore often very useful indeed when it comes to deciding what to do. This is not to say that we are prone to use *all* our models in decision-making. We quite likely represent quite a lot of models of how people tend to react under certain circumstances that play no role in our own reactions. After all, many of the things people tend to do, do not constitute the best courses of action. But, I want to suggest, if we do not already think that a particular course of action is unwise because of its negative consequences, knowing that people are prone to undertake it under certain circumstances can certainly motivate us to do the same.

Model theory assumes that practice is central. You can have knowledge of models alone, but it won't do you much good since, on its own, it concerns only idealized and abstracted relations and properties. Only by means of theoretical hypotheses does it become knowledge of real-world phenomena. This does *not* mean that folk psychology is all in the practice. And, furthermore, it is not an essentially narrative practice. It is a practice of deploying and consuming models, which, as it so happens, tends to deploy narratives.

5. The Model Theory Advantage

So theory theory, in the form of model theory, can account for why practice is needed and why folk psychological predictions, explanations, and interpretations are so intricately intertwined with narratives. But why should we prefer it to narrativity theory? Indeed, why prefer it to classical theory theory, which may work just fine with a couple of adjustments? Model theory has at least four advantages over traditional theory theory. First, it explains why people are not good at enunciating their knowledge in terms of universal or counterfactual supporting generalizations without us having to posit *tacit* knowledge, which is itself problematic (Maibom, 2003; Goldman, 2006). Second, it explains how there can be such divergent interpretations of what structures we impute to others when we think of them in terms of beliefs, desires, etc. (Godfrey-Smith, 2004). Third, it stresses the rather important fact that the ability to apply psychological models is central to folk psychological competence. This helps explain why simply programming a computer with the requisite psychological algorithms is not sufficient to make it respond the right way. There is a lived quality to most of our knowledge that is hard to explain in terms of certain accounts of theoretical and scientific knowledge. Model theory, with its focus on the ability to *apply* models, as described above, avoids such difficulties. And fourth, it provides a good account of individual differences in folk psychological attribution without giving up on the idea that we all share quite a bit of knowledge.

The advantages model theory has over narrativity theory are a little different. Theory theories generally are frameworks of understanding knowledge that are systematic, detailed, and widely applicable. They construe ordinary knowledge on the model of scientific knowledge, because it is better understood. What is central to this picture is that it provides a good account of *how* knowledge generalizes, of how we manage to systematize an extraordinary range of phenomena and understand them as different manifestations of the same general principles. By contrast, narrativity theory is rather vague on this point. Someone like Hutto acknowledges that the core structure of intentional explanations stays constant, although it is not entirely clear how to conceptualize this core, other than that it is linguistic, but not theoretical. So how do the two theories account for the role of narrativity in folk psychology, specifically in folk psychological explanations?

Consider a canonical narrative, the fairy tale of Little Red Riding Hood. We can extract this folk psychological explanation from the story: Little Red Riding Hood went into the forest because she wanted to visit her grandmother, and she lived in the forest. Now, this is an instance of singular causal explanation. There is no explicit reference to laws, counterfactual supporting generalizations, models, or anything of that sort. Indeed, narrativity theorists are likely to argue that the explanation is contextualized, specific and particular to Little Red Riding Hood.[11] So what is explanatory about the explanation? It is not entirely clear. On the one hand, Hutto insists that it is in virtue of its specificity and particularity that narrative reason explanations explain so well. The specific and particular provides a fuller, or richer, explanation than the general (Hutto, 2008b, p. 8). On the other hand, Hutto acknowledges that the core of folk psychology, which he thinks of as information about causal relations between beliefs, desires, and action, stays constant across explanations. But it is unclear to what extent explanations rely on this structure or on something else.

By contrast to narrativity theory, model theory has a very specific proposal about why the Little Red Riding Hood scenario is explanatory. The explanation makes implicit reference to a relevant model, concerned with typical action production. We might say that the relevant model occupies the background of the explanatory context. Without it, what Little Red Riding Hood believes and wants would not explain her actions, or, at any rate, would not explain them *well*. The context of the story, however, is far from irrelevant. In effect, the consumer of the explanation needs to be able to see this instance as one in which the model applies. And the fact that the scenario bears a similarity to other scenarios that instantiate the model is important. Recall that both knowledge of a model and knowledge of its application are central to folk psychological competence and, therefore, explanation. Referencing Little Red Riding Hood's beliefs and desires is explanatory because they fit a model in certain respects and to a certain

---

[11] To be fair, Hutto does not claim that all folk psychological explanations are contextualized, specific, and particular. I am assuming that if they often have these characteristics, then a canonical example of such an explanation has a good chance of having these characteristics.

degree. So the model theory not only has a place for, but, in a sense, requires contextualization and reference to, the specific and particular. However, what does the explanatorily heavy lifting are not the specific or particular aspects of the situation.

A particular belief and a particular desire may make the difference in bringing about an action. But it is not in virtue of the particular that they do so. These particular beliefs and desires have features or properties that have certain causal powers. An account of the action that references this belief and desire does not constitute a good explanation merely in virtue of referencing them as causes. It relies on a background of knowledge of *what beliefs and desires do*, generally speaking; i.e. the explanatory element is not unique, but an instance of a general phenomenon, at least in principle.[12] Peter Lipton (2004, p. 14) maintains that the idea of control is central to the notion of cause as that which makes the difference between a phenomenon occurring and not occurring. Of course control presupposes repeatability. However, if we are to think of an event and its causes in terms of their particularity and specificity, it is unclear how we could conceive of it as repeatable. Knowledge of the singular and particular gives you no predictive handle on things; no possibility of being able to manipulate, influence, or affect the structure of the world. It is against the background of generalities — models in this instance — that referencing these causes explain.

Would narrativity theorists agree with the above idea? If they do not, I challenge them to produce a better account of explanation. If they do agree, it nevertheless remains true that the model theory provides a better account of the phenomena that we observe, including the narrative aspect of folk psychology. Our explanations contain the contextual, particular, and specific because the practice is what makes the model represent features of real-world agents. This aspect falls out of the model theory directly. The model theory also explains why certain kinds of linguistic productions play a privileged role in folk psychological explanations. They do so because they bring out how objects, properties, and relations fit a model and the respects of the fit. It is not just that narratives are tools for learning how to apply models. They demonstrate the correctness of the use of the model. Little Red Riding Hood desires to visit her grandmother. Her grandmother is ill, her mother gives her bread and wine to help nurse her back to health, and makes Little Red Riding Hood promise to bring this to the

---

[12] There is, of course, an interesting question of how to conceive of God and God's actions if you are a monotheist. I leave that issue aside for the moment.

grandmother. It is almost over-determined that she should desire to visit her grandmother. Agent-centred stories give reality, as it were, to the rather abstract relations holding between objects and properties in a model. By comparison to narrativity theory, model theory makes very clear the role of particular kinds of narratives in folk psychological explanations. Model theory, I argue, provides a better account of the folk psychological practice — including the importance of narratives.

Acknowledgements

Thanks to Gabriele Contessa, Daniel Hutto, and anonymous reviewers of this issue for helpful criticisms and comments. This paper was written while supported by a grant from the Social Sciences and Humanities Research Council of Canada.

References

Bermúdez, J. (2003), *Thinking Without Words* (Oxford: Oxford University Press).

Christie, A. (1975), *Curtain: Hercule Poirot's Last Case* (London: William Collins Son & Co Ltd.).

Churchland, P. (1981), 'Eliminative Materialism and the Propositional Attitudes', *Journal of Philosophy*, **78**, pp. 67–90.

Fodor, J. (1987), *Psychosemantics* (Cambridge, MA: MIT Press).

Giere, R. (1988), *Explaining Science* (Chicago, IL: University of Chicago Press).

Godfrey-Smith, P. (2004), 'On Folk Psychology and Mental Representation', in H. Clapin, P. Staines & P. Slezak (ed.), *Representation in Mind: New Approaches to Mental Representation* (Amsterdam: Elsevier Publishers), pp. 147–62.

Godfrey-Smith, P. (2005), 'Folk Psychology as a Model', *Philosophers' Imprint*, **5** (6).

Goldman, A. (2006), *Simulating Minds* (New York: Oxford University Press).

Harris, J. (1998), *The Nurture Assumption: Why Children Turn Out the Way They Do* (New York: Free Press).

Heal, J. (1994), 'Simulation vs. Theory Theory: What is at issue?', in C. Peacocke (ed.), *Proceedings of the British Academy 83: Objectivity, Simulation and the Unity of Consciousness: Current Issues in the Philosophy of Mind* (Oxford: Oxford University Press), pp. 129–44.

Horsey, R. (2002), 'The Art of Chicken Sexing', *UCL Working Papers in Linguistics*, **14**.

Hutto, D. (2008a), 'Limited Engagements and Narrative Extensions', *International Journal of Philosophical Studies*, **16**, pp. 419–44.

Hutto, D. (2008b), *Folk Psychological Narratives* (Cambridge, MA: MIT Press).

Hutto, D. (2009), 'Lessons from Wittgenstein: Elucidating folk psychology', *New Ideas in Psychology*, 27, pp. 197–212.

Kamm, F. (1998), *Morality, Mortality: Volume One: Death and Whom to Save from It* (New York: Oxford University Press).

Knobe, J. (2003), 'Intentional Action in Folk Psychology: An experimental investigation', *Philosophical Psychology*, **16**, pp. 309–24.

Lipton, P. (2004), 'What Good is an Explanation?', in J. Cornwell (ed.), *Explanations* (Oxford: Oxford University Press), pp. 1–22.

Maibom, H. (2003), 'The Mindreader & the Scientist', *Mind & Language*, **18**, pp. 296–315.
Maibom, H. (2007), 'Social Systems', *Philosophical Psychology*, **20**, pp. 557–78.
Morton, A. (2003), *The Importance of Being Understood: Folk Psychology as Ethics* (London: Routledge).
Pinker, S. (2002), *The Blank Slate: The Modern Denial of Human Nature* (New York: Viking).
Povinelli, D. (2001), 'On the Possibilities of Detecting Intentions Prior to Understanding them', in B. Malle, L. Moses & D. Baldwin (ed.), *Intentions and Intentionality: Foundations of Social Cognition* (Cambridge, MA: MIT Press), pp. 225–48.
Stich, S. & Nichols, S. (2004), *Mindreading: An Integrated Account of Pretence, Self-Awareness, and Understanding Other Minds* (New York: Oxford University Press).
Suppe, F. (1989), *The Semantic Conception of Scientific Theory and Scientific Realism* (Chicago, IL: University of Illinois Press).
Suppes, P. (1960), 'A Comparison of the Meaning and Uses of Models in Mathematics and Empirical Sciences', *Synthese*, **12**.
Taylor, S. & Brown, J. (1988), 'Illusion and Wellbeing', *Psychological Bulletin*, **103**, pp. 193–210.
Tomasello, M., Call, J. & Hare, B. (2003), 'Chimpanzees Understand Psychological States — The question is which ones and to what extent', *Trends in Cognitive Science*, **7**, pp. 153–6.

Matthew Ratcliffe

There Are No Folk Psychological Narratives

Abstract: *I argue that the task of describing our so-called 'folk psychology' requires difficult philosophical work. Consequently, any statement of the folk view is actually a debatable philosophical position, rather than an uncontroversial description of pre-philosophical commonsense. The problem with the current folk psychology debate, I suggest, is that the relevant philosophical work has not been done. Consequently, the orthodox account of folk psychology is an uninformative caricature of an understanding that is implicit in everyday discourse and social interaction, and also in literary narratives. I conclude by considering two recent departures from it, so-called 'experimental philosophy' and Daniel Hutto's 'narrative practice hypothesis'. Both, I claim, take steps in the right direction but retain unhelpful assumptions that they inherit from the orthodox view.*

Introduction

It is commonplace in philosophy of mind and cognitive science to maintain that interpersonal understanding is enabled by a 'folk psychology', central to which is an ability to attribute propositional attitudes, principally beliefs and desires, in order to predict and explain behaviour. For example, if you know that Bernard believes there to be a banana in the fruit bowl and that Bernard desires to eat a banana, you can predict that — all things being equal — Bernard will eat the banana. This conception of folk psychology is often regarded as beyond rational dispute. For example, Botterill and Carruthers (1999) state that 'we cannot help but think of each other in such terms'

(p. 10); 'common-sense psychology the world over recognises the difference between these two broad categories of intentional state [belief and desire]' (p. 35). Hence the current folk psychology debate is concerned with which abilities facilitate the attribution of propositional attitudes, rather than with whether 'using belief-desire psychology to predict and explain behaviour' is an adequate characterisation of something that we do. The two accounts on offer are 'theory' and 'simulation' theories. According to 'theory theories', belief-desire psychology depends upon employment of a largely tacit, systematically organised conceptual framework, whereas simulation theories claim that we use our own cognitive apparatus in order to model what other people are thinking and experiencing. Both theories come in many different guises, and the current consensus is that an adequate account of folk psychological ability will incorporate some combination of the two.[1]

I will not be addressing theory or simulation theories here but instead the competence that they both presuppose and seek to explain: folk psychology, construed as the ability to attribute beliefs and desires in order to predict and explain behaviour. It is important to distinguish this from a looser conception of folk psychology as 'whatever interpersonal understanding consists of'. My criticisms here will be directed exclusively at the former (hereafter, FP). I will argue that, although perhaps superficially intuitive (especially to those who have been indoctrinated into belief-desire psychology by formal philosophical training), FP is an inadequate account of what is central to interpersonal understanding, and it is deserving of rejection. This conclusion implies that the theory theory is false. If we reject the claim that people employ FP, we reject by implication the claim that they do so by using a FP theory. Likewise, the claim that FP is enabled by simulation needs to go. However, this does not rule out the possibility that some of the abilities referred to by the term 'simulation' contribute to social understanding. What is rejected is the more specific claim that we rely upon simulation to accomplish FP (Ratcliffe, 2007, ch. 7). Similarly, interpersonal understanding is no doubt aided by theories on occasion. However, we do not employ the kind of theory postulated by the 'theory theory', as we do not do what this theory assumes we do.

---

[1] For collections of classic articles on folk psychology, theory of mind and simulation, see Davies and Stone (1995a; 1995b). For a more recent simulation-theory hybrid account, see, for example, Nichols and Stich (2003). For a survey of the folk psychology debate, see Ratcliffe (2007, ch. 1).

A Strawsonian Critique of Folk Psychology

What is meant by the claim that FP is a 'folk' or 'commonsense' psychology? Proponents of FP emphasise the concepts 'belief' and 'desire'. So we can assume that FP involves a conceptual understanding or, most likely, a combination of conceptual and non-conceptual abilities, rather than non-conceptual skills alone. It is also important to emphasise that FP is an account of how people *actually* understand each other's behaviour, rather than an account of how they think that they think in interpersonal scenarios. People may not have a clear idea about what is central to their thinking about others, and so FP needs to be distinguished from what we might call a 'folk folk psychology'. The latter is what you get when you ask people what they think, whereas the former is an account of how they actually think.

Investigating which concepts are fundamental to our thinking about people and about the world more generally is not an easy task. The fruits of such an enquiry need to be distinguished from superficial and possibly widespread intuitions. Consider Peter Strawson's (1959) work on 'descriptive metaphysics', the project of charting the structure of our actual conceptual scheme. One of the conclusions drawn by Strawson is that a distinction between minds and bodies is not fundamental to our thinking. Rather, the concept of 'person' is primitive and remains presupposed by such distinctions. This is reflected in everyday language, where 'I' am a being that has both thoughts and legs. This is contrary to the view of the substance dualist, for instance, who would maintain that 'I' have thoughts and feelings but am only contingently associated with a pair of legs or, alternatively (and counter-intuitively), that 'I' has different referents in the cases of thoughts and legs. So people are not, deep down, 'folk dualists'. Strawson adds that even a distinction between mental and non-mental characteristics *of persons* fails to respect our actual conceptual scheme. In place of 'mental' and 'physical' predicates, he refers to M- and P- predicates, where the former apply to material things including persons, whereas the latter apply only to persons. So 'is thinking' would be a P-predicate, whereas 'weighs 90 kilograms' would be an M-predicate. However, P-predicates are not simply 'psychological'. We talk of persons but not of other entities (except perhaps some non-human animals) 'going for a walk', 'smiling' and so on (Strawson, 1959, p. 90). Predicates like these do not fall neatly on one side or the other of the psychological/non-psychological boundary.

Is Strawson right about the primacy of 'persons' over 'minds' and 'bodies' in our conceptual scheme? I think so, and it is worth noting

that many philosophers and psychologists, working in different traditions, have come to similar conclusions (see, for example, Husserl,
1989; Hobson, 2002; Lowe, 1996; Macmurray, 1957; Ratcliffe,
2007). But regardless of whether or not one agrees with Strawson, the
point to note is that what he offers is a debatable philosophical position that took considerable philosophical work to formulate, rather
than a casual, uncontroversial statement of what the 'folk' think. Yet
his subject matter here is indistinguishable from that of FP: the
fundamental structure of our thinking about people.

Strawson's view is not necessarily incompatible with FP. It could be
maintained that we attribute beliefs and desires to persons, and that
they are a sub-class of P-predicates which play a crucial role in predicting and explaining behaviour. It is all very well to say that someone is smiling or going for a walk but, if we want to predict or explain
these behaviours, we do so by appealing to the relevant beliefs and
desires: P is smiling because P desires money and believes that she has
won the lottery. The lesson I want to draw is just that (a) it takes philosophical work to formulate a credible philosophical position and (b)
an account of what is fundamental to interpersonal understanding, in
contrast to an account of 'what some people think that they think', will
be a philosophical position. The problem with FP is that the kind of
philosophical work that is required has not been done.

FP did not originate in philosophical reflection upon what people
actually think. Instead, it arose through the imposition of a set of
pre-formulated philosophical assumptions upon the 'folk'. It owes
much to Wilfrid Sellars (1956/1963) and David Lewis (e.g. 1972/
1980), both of whom suggested that everyday psychological understanding relies upon a theory. As Lewis puts it, 'think of commonsense psychology as a term-introducing scientific theory, although
one invented long before there was such institution as a professional
science' (1980, p. 213). More than anything else, FP is inspired by the
kind of functionalism advocated by Lewis (e.g. 1972/1980) and others. If mental state types are defined by their causal roles, then understanding mental states and how they relate to behaviour will surely be
a matter of understanding, by means of a theory perhaps, the relevant
causal roles. Central to this understanding, it is assumed, is a distinction between those states that inform us (beliefs) and those that motivate us (desires).[2] Then, when simulation theory arrived in 1986, it
inherited the same account of FP, whilst rejecting the view that people

[2] See also Heal (1995) for a discussion of the relationship between functionalism and the
theory theory.

are tacit functionalists who rely upon a theory of mental states and their causal roles.[3] A lot of empirical research has of course been done in the context of the theory of mind debate, but most of it simply pre-supposes FP as a conceptual framework through which to devise experiments and interpret results. It is concerned with discovering which mechanisms support FP, how they develop and how they might have evolved. For example, as several critics have pointed out, the much-discussed False Belief Task tends to be interpreted in FP terms from the outset (Gallagher, 2001; Costall & Leudar, 2004; Ratcliffe, 2007, ch. 2; Hutto, 2009). FP's origin does not in itself make it false. It could be that the relevant philosophical theories do indeed correspond fairly well with 'what the folk think', or that its proponents just got lucky. However, in what follows, I will suggest otherwise.

Whereas Strawson emphasises how deeply engrained the concept 'person' is within our conceptual scheme, much of the FP literature fails to acknowledge that there is anything distinctive about respond-ing to someone as a person. The theory theory treats interpersonal understanding as a complicated instance of mechanistic understand-ing. The interpreter posits internal machinery in order to predict and explain outward behaviour, just as she might if presented with a com-plicated artefact. There is a distinctive kind of internal machinery involved, but FP is nonetheless construed as a species of mechanistic thinking. As Heal (1995, p. 45) notes, for the theory theorist, 'people are just complex objects in our environment whose behaviour we wish to anticipate but whose causal innards we cannot perceive'. In con-trast, some versions of the simulation theory acknowledge that emo-tional engagement with the interpreted person can play an important role in understanding. Hence Gordon (1996, p. 11) distinguishes 'hot' from 'cold' methodologies, where the former but not the latter rely upon the interpreter's own emotional and motivational capacities. However, even in the case of simulation theory, the standpoint that is assumed for the interpreter is often curiously disengaged. Whereas much if not most interpersonal understanding takes place in contexts of interaction between people, both theory and simulation accounts of FP tend to emphasise the perspective of a detached spectator.

A number of authors have recently argued that second-person inter-action, where both parties encounter each other as 'you', is a better place to look if we want to understand everyday social understanding, and that doing so reveals the shortcomings of FP. Rather than

---

[3] See Ratcliffe (2007, ch. 2) for a more detailed account of the origins of FP. See also Leudar and Costall (2004) for a discussion of how current thinking regarding folk psychology and theory of mind originated in questionable philosophical assumptions.

attributing internal mental states to an observed third-party, we understand each other *through* structured interaction. In addition, we are often able to *perceive* the meanings of expressions, actions and gestures, without having to infer the presence of underlying, internal mental states. Interactions usually take place within a framework of shared norms, which also play a significant role in interpretation. If you know what various artefacts are for, what the norms of conduct are in a situation and which behaviours are associated with which social roles, you can predict and explain a great deal of what people do without having to fall back on an ability to assign mental states. Thus, when we consider interpersonal interaction embedded in shared social situations, it seems that reliance upon a belief-desire psychology is often not required (see, for example, Gallagher, 2001; 2005; McGeer, 2001; Hobson, 2002; Hutto, 2004; 2008a; Ratcliffe 2005a; 2007).[4]

However, the contrast between second-person interaction and third-person observation does not serve to distinguish *personal* from *impersonal* understanding. As Goldie (2000) observes, there is a difference between a third-person and an objective perspective. In adopting the former, we still regard the object of study as a person, rather than an impersonal object. What is missing from the disengaged and often seemingly impersonal stance of FP is nicely conveyed by Strawson, who contrasts the attitude of detached enquiry with what he calls a *reactive attitude*, and argues that engaging with someone as a person involves the latter. A reactive attitude is a stance of 'involvement or participation in a human relationship', which makes possible such relations as gratitude, forgiveness and mutual love (2008, p. 7).[5] This kind of attitude incorporates a vulnerability to others, a potential to be affected by them in a range of ways. It is not that we perceive another person, proceed to simulate her and then feel like her, but that we are open to her from the start in a way that comprises of our appreciation of her as a person.[6] Strawson's 'objective attitude' is not wholly impersonal. One could adopt this attitude to someone whilst still recognising that she *is* a person, but what one does not do here is respond to her *as* a person. Unlike entering into a human relationship, an objective attitude involves understanding someone as 'an object of social policy; as a subject for what, in a wide range of sense, might be called treatment' (2008, p. 9). We might, Strawson says, adopt such a detached attitude to someone suffering from psychiatric illness. And

---

[4] See also the essays collected in Hutto and Ratcliffe (ed, 2007).

[5] This essay, 'Freedom and Resentment', was originally published in 1962.

[6] See Scheler (1954) for a similar view.

sometimes we retreat from a personal relationship in order to escape the discomfort and effort that interpersonal relatedness can involve. In such cases, we concentrate on 'understanding "how he works" with a view to determining our policy accordingly or to finding in that very understanding a relief from the strains of involvement' (2008, p. 13).

The detached predictive-explanatory stance of FP resembles the objective attitude more so than it does the reactive attitude. Indeed, Strawson himself comments on the tendency amongst philosophers to neglect reactive attitudes and inadvertently impose their own detached, contemplative stance upon their object of study. There is, he says:

> ... something it is easy to forget when we are engaged in philosophy, especially in our cool, contemporary style, viz. what it is actually like to be involved in ordinary inter-personal relationships, ranging from the most intimate to the most casual (2008, p. 7).

Proponents of FP have, I suggest, focused upon a standpoint that is best characterised as a partial withdrawal from the personal. The contrast between third-person observation and second-person interaction, as employed by several recent critics of FP, does not quite capture this complaint (although the second-person stance is indeed likely to be more typical of reactive engagement). One can explicitly address someone as a 'you' whilst refraining to some extent from a reactive attitude and regarding her instead as something to be dealt with or managed. And third-person observation can involve a reactive attitude, a sense of relatedness that incorporates the potential to be affected in various ways by the observed person's activities.

If we combine Strawson's account of persons with his discussion of how we respond to others as persons through reactive attitudes, we get a philosophical position rather than an uncontroversial statement of commonsense. But, given that this position is the product of both philosophical work and attentiveness to the relevant phenomena, it has, I suggest, better credentials than FP as an account of our 'folk view'. However, a Strawsonian view does not require the complete rejection of FP. An emphasis upon the importance of persons and reactive attitudes, in place of the detached, impersonal stance that typifies discussions of FP, remains consistent with the view that we employ a belief-desire psychology. For example, Dennett (1978) argues that a 'personal stance', involving the reactive attitudes, is something that we can only adopt once we have already adopted an 'intentional stance' that allows us to attribute beliefs and desires. Of course, Strawson's work is equally compatible with the view of Gallagher

(2001) and others that belief-desire psychology is much more limited in scope than generally supposed. One option is to accept that an understanding of reactive attitudes requires the possession of belief-desire psychology and is therefore similarly limited. Another is to maintain that some or all reactive attitudes do not depend upon belief-desire psychology. Indeed, perhaps some of them are largely or wholly comprised of perceptual, affective, bodily responses to the psychological predicaments of others.

In the remainder of this paper, rather than merely restricting the scope of FP and reconceptualising it by embedding it in a personal stance, I will argue for the stronger claim that people do not employ a belief-desire psychology at all. Outrageous as this might at first sound, my admittedly eliminativist position is not, contrary to Hutto's (2008b) assessment of Ratcliffe (2007), an extreme or 'radical' form of eliminativism. I deny that we employ a belief-desire psychology, but this is not synonymous with the implausible claim that people do not understand each other in terms of beliefs and desires. My claim is that the terms 'belief' and 'desire' — as they feature both in everyday discourse and also in examples offered on behalf of FP — refer to a heterogeneous range of psychological phenomena that everyday conversations and narratives distinguish with ease. Interpersonal interpretation typically relies upon much more nuanced conceptions of people's psychological predicaments than those offered on behalf of FP. Statements of the form 'x believes that p and desires that q, and so — all things being equal — x will do r' are seldom helpful. FP is not simply 'false' but, all the same, it is so abstract and uninformative that it warrants rejection rather than revision.

It is most likely the case that reference to belief-desire pairs is a useful convention when addressing certain kinds of philosophical problem, and I do not wish to criticise this practice. What I reject is the view that it reflects, in any *illuminating* way, the structure of everyday interpersonal understanding. So I am not recommending that philosophers stop this kind of talk altogether. Rather, what I want to suggest is that, once the gulf between FP and everyday interpersonal understanding is made clear, it becomes apparent that FP is not psychologically informative. If a philosophical use could be found for FP that was non-committal with respect to the structure of interpersonal understanding, I would have no objection to it (although 'FP' would be a misleading name for this use of belief-desire psychology). What I object to is the claim that this is a fruitful description of what people actually get up to, which can serve as a focus for productive research in philosophical psychology and other disciplines.

Beliefs and Desires

Strawson remarks that the term 'folk psychology' is employed, 'with apparently pejorative intent', to refer to:

> ... the ordinary explanatory terms employed by diarists, novelists, biographers, historians, journalists, and gossips, when they deliver their accounts of human behavior and human experience — the terms employed by such simple folk as Shakespeare, Tolstoy, Proust and Henry James (1985, p. 56).

FP is generally taken to be a conceptual understanding that is implicit in everyday social life, rather than an understanding that is evident in the works of great writers. Even so, there is surely some overlap between the two. In addition, enculturation into certain styles of literary narrative could well feed into how we understand and interact with people (Hutto, 2008a). At the very least, I think it is fair to treat the kinds of psychological discriminations that people are sensitive to when constructing and interpreting literary narratives as indicative, to some extent at least, of our 'folk psychological' abilities more generally. There are no grounds for suggesting that the psychological understanding we employ when writing and interpreting literature is wholly or mostly absent from our interpretations of people. It is also worth noting that literary interpretation likewise involves and may even require a kind of reactive attitude, rather than detached intellectual contemplation. For example, Jenefer Robinson argues that 'our emotional responses to novels, plays, and movies help us to *understand* them, to understand characters, and grasp the significance of events in the plot' (2005, p. 105). It is through our emotional engagement with the text, she suggests, our ability to be affected by it, that we discover 'subtleties in character and plot' that would be unavailable to the detached reader.[7]

As Strawson indicates, the term 'folk' does look rather out of place when applied to the construction and interpretation of great literature. So do predecessor terms such as the 'plain man' (Sellars, 1963, p. 135). Such terms give the impression of a conceptual understanding that is separate from that of the epistemically privileged enquirer, an understanding that is quaint and primitive, which we can look down upon and survey impartially. But what we find when we turn to literary narratives is a rich, nuanced understanding that has not yet yielded to systematic analysis. Interpretation is a difficult, skilful, open-ended

---

[7] I do not discount the possibility that some kind of 'simulation' plays a role here. However, even if one does talk of simulation in this context, it need not be simulation in the service of FP.

task, and the psychology of literary characters can seldom be summarised by a simple FP-type formula.[8] Exactly the same goes, I think, for how we understand people more generally. We cannot describe a folk psychology from the stance of a neutral spectator with God-like access to the fundamentals of social life. Instead, we must engage in philosophical reflection and, in the process, try to make explicit and interpret — to the best of our abilities — an understanding that we ourselves continue to share in. As illustrated by the fact that descriptive metaphysics is difficult, there is no easily accessible conceptual scheme of the 'folk', of the 'plain' person.

Our proponent of FP might respond by insisting that it really is obvious that people understand each other by attributing beliefs and desires, and that this ability is pretty fundamental to social life. Not everything in our conceptual repertoire is difficult to explicate and FP is a case in point. However, despite routine reference in philosophy and cognitive science to how 'the belief that p' and 'the desire that q' explain 'action r', it is not wholly clear what a belief, a desire or even a propositional attitude actually is. It seems fair to assume that FP use of the term 'belief' departs from at least some everyday uses such as 'I don't believe you' or 'I believe in God'. FP 'belief' is about accepting propositions, rather than about trust or religious commitment. In believing something, we assent to some proposition, such as 'the cat is on the mat', 'the Eiffel Tower is in Paris', 'I am a human being' or 'the world exists'. But what is it to assent to a proposition? It does not always involve taking a sentence that describes a state of affairs to be true. When I see my young son crawling towards me, my belief that 'Thomas is in front of me' does not first of all take the form of recognising that the sentence 'Thomas is in front of me' is true. Rather, I take it *to be the case* that Thomas is in front of me. Regardless of whether and to what extent the formation of this conviction requires linguistic ability, the object of the conviction is not first and foremost a sentence. If FP were to restrict the term 'propositional attitude' to 'sentential attitudes' (cases where a sentence is taken to be true), then

---

[8] Robinson (2005, p. 139) distinguishes 'folk psychological understanding' from the kind of sophisticated, nuanced, conceptually untidy understanding that we find in good literature, apparently on the basis that 'folk psychology' refers to explicit categorisations made by ordinary language speakers, whereas much of what good literature communicates is not couched in terms of explicit folk psychological categories. However, what she refers to is a 'folk folk psychology', what we think that we think, rather than a 'folk psychology' in the deeper sense of what we actually think. FP is meant to capture what is fundamental to social understanding rather than what people might think is fundamental. So it should indeed be committed to accommodating the understanding that we find in literature and elsewhere.

FP would only encompass a tiny minority of our beliefs about other people. Sentential attitudes have even more limited application in the case of desire, where what one desires is almost always a state of affairs rather than the truth of a sentence. So let us understand the 'propositional attitude' of belief in a more general way to mean the attitude of taking something to be the case. The problem now is that there are many different ways of taking something to be the case.

The FP literature is riddled with beguilingly simple examples of belief-desire explanation, involving people running after departing trains, going to the fridge to get a beer, stopping at traffic lights and so on, all of which — we are told — are easily explained in belief-desire terms. But such explanations fail to distinguish between a range of different ways in which things are taken to be the case, from habitual acceptance to explicit contemplation to emotionally charged experience. The term 'belief' is a placeholder that does not differentiate them and consequently fails to provide an adequate explanation of behaviour. The point applies even more clearly to desire. A desire for an ice cream is clearly a very different kind of attitude from a desire for world peace, sex, love, friendship, emotional security or cocaine. There are many different kinds of 'desire'.

Consider the oft-cited example of why someone is carrying an umbrella. For example:

> Suppose we want to explain why Janis took her umbrella with her to work. Identifying her mental states seems to do the job admirably. For instance, if we say she believed it was going to rain and that she had a desire to keep dry, these claims about her appear to satisfy our need for an explanation (Campbell, 2005, p. 138).

Does this explanation really satisfy? Suppose I turn to you on a rainy day and ask, with a look of genuine curiosity, why Bernard is holding an umbrella. Rather than treating this as a sensible question, you are more likely to respond with a look of bemusement and ask for further clarification as to why I am even asking. The response 'he believes it will rain and he wants to stay dry' would most likely be used only in a sarcastic way, to indicate that it is a stupid question. Why is this? Interpersonal interpretation usually works under the assumption that interpreter and interpreted share a common world and are receptive to many of the same norms. It is not a case of simulating the other person or imaginatively projecting oneself into his position. Rather, one starts off by taking it as given that *we* are responsive to many of the same things in the same way. For example, an umbrella is not understood as 'to prevent me from getting wet' and then also 'to prevent you from getting wet' but, rather, as having the function of preventing people from getting wet, regardless of who they are. If one already knows what an umbrella is, what the shared norms associated with umbrella use are and that it is raining, it is quite obvious why Bernard carries an umbrella; one does not need to think about his psychological states.[9] In contrast, if it's a nice day but not so sunny as to warrant a sunshade and we see Bernard walking along with his umbrella open, we may well wonder what he is up to. But clearly 'he believes it will rain and he wants to stay dry' will not suffice as an explanation here either, as what we want to know is why someone would believe, under such circumstances, that it is likely to rain. No simple statement of belief or desire will do the trick. What is required is an appreciation of how or why Bernard has come to believe and desire what he does. Perhaps his belief is understandable in the light of established norms plus certain circumstances — someone lied to Bernard about the weather. Or it might be that Bernard is eccentric in some way and prone to beliefs and desires that do not conform to shared norms of reasoning and conduct.[10]

The general point applies not only to social norms and artefact functions but also to the norms of reasoning (although it is far from clear what the shared norms of reasoning actually are). Much of the time, we take it for granted that people will follow certain established patterns of reasoning, that they will do *what one ought to do*. So we often do not need to think about their psychological processes in order to work out what they are likely to do (Ratcliffe, 2007, ch. 7). Of course, our advocate of FP might respond that, in such cases, we continue to *presuppose* that the person has beliefs and desires with appropriate contents, even though these states need not be explanatorily relevant. But suppose they were relevant. When we try to understand why a particular person acted in a particular way, a wide range of subtly different psychological states might be invoked. These do not fall neatly into two principal categories — belief and desire — and it is important to further discriminate the kinds of psychological state that we attribute to people. Let us return to the example of believing that it is wet and wanting to stay dry. Even if a belief-desire explanation were

---

[9]   See McGeer (2001) for a detailed discussion of how shared social norms serve to simplify the task of understanding what other people do.

[10] As Goldie (2000; 2007) observes, references to personality and character can do a lot of explanatory work. Hence an account of Bernard's idiosyncratic traits might explain his behaviour better than an account of his beliefs and desires. Goldie (2007, p. 104) also stresses that everyday explanations are generally 'much more revealing, much more far-reaching, and much more varied than belief-desire explanations'.

relevant here, it would still be inadequate. Consider the following brief narratives concerning Bernard's umbrella:

1. Bernard left the house and unthinkingly picked up his umbrella, as he did every day other than during the summer.
2. Bernard left the house, looked up at the dark sky, thought 'rain' and went back to get his umbrella.
3. Bernard put on his nice new suit and suddenly felt worried about how it could be ruined if it got soaked. So he took his umbrella out just in case.
4. Bernard heard the weather forecast and so made a note that he needed to take his umbrella out.

Any of these could be related as 'Bernard carried his umbrella because he thought it might rain and did not want to get wet', where 'thought' and 'want' can be substituted for 'believed' and 'desire'. However, the psychological states involved in each case are different, and even simple everyday narratives and interpretations are sensitive to these differences. In the first case, we have a habitual behaviour that does not involve explicitly entertaining the possibility of rain. In the second, we have an experience of a dark sky which is either closely associated with or even inextricable from the conviction that it might rain. Perhaps this conviction is dispassionate, perhaps not. The third case clearly involves a *feeling* of concern relating to the possibility of rain. The fourth case, in contrast, is fairly dispassionate and consists of the routine acceptance of information that one hears, followed by appropriate action. All involve 'taking it to be the case' that it might rain, but referring to them as the same kind of propositional attitude is not sufficient. An appreciation of why Bernard does what he does — regardless of whether that appreciation is explicitly voiced or implicitly taken for granted — is usually more nuanced than that, and is embedded in a context of shared practice.[11]

Cases where belief incorporates feeling are, I think, especially problematic for the simple 'platitudes' of FP. Take a case where someone receives good or bad news and says 'I just can't quite believe it yet'. What is going on here? Does she believe that p or believe that not p? One can put a tick next to a sentence and assert that it is true but, at the same time, not fully *accept* the state of affairs in question. Genuine conviction, in some cases at least, requires feeling. Consider the belief that one will die. In Tolstoy's novel *The Death of Ivan Ilych*, for

---

[11] Various others have noted the heterogeneity of belief and a tendency amongst philosophers to treat the concept rather simplistically (see e.g. Needham, 1972; Morton, 2007).

example, there is an appreciation of the gulf between being convinced by assertions such as 'all men are mortal; I am a man; and I am therefore mortal' and a genuine realisation of one's mortality, of the fact that it is oneself who will die rather than just any old token of the type Homo sapiens. One might sincerely think that one dispassionately accepts the inevitability of one's own death, but on those occasions when it fleetingly 'sinks in', it can seem suddenly unfathomable, unbearable. Both in unfeeling assent and in feeling realisation, one 'believes that p'. But the two kinds of attitude are very different indeed.

Realisation of one's own mortality, like a range of other 'beliefs', is not a purely 'informational' belief state, separate from 'motivational' desires. It is unavoidably self-affecting, significant. Lack of a clear-cut informational/motivational distinction applies to a wide range of other psychological states too, including various different kinds of emotion that we attribute to each other. Take the experience of being afraid of a fast-approaching and dangerous animal. One's experiences and thoughts cannot here be separated into disinterested information about what is approaching, accompanied by relevant motivations, which then combine so as to produce action. Instead, the entity is perceived as mattering in a certain way, as dangerous. It is not at any point perceived or thought about in a manner that is extricated from its significance. One might retort that we don't know enough about what emotions consist of to accept this claim, as exemplified by the wide range of conflicting philosophical accounts of the nature of emotion. So the informational/motivational distinction is safe, for the time being at least.[12] However, if I am right, we are on even shakier ground when it comes to belief, as philosophical debate regarding the nature of belief is just as pressing but less developed.

In fact, construing interpersonal understanding as revolving around an 'emotion psychology' is arguably just as legitimate, if not more so, than invoking a 'belief-desire psychology'. Of course, a combination of emotions is neither necessary nor sufficient to account for a particular behaviour. But the same goes for a combination of beliefs and desires. Someone who doesn't want to get wet and believes that it is about to rain might get in the car and drive to work, rather than taking an umbrella. We understand people as acting out of hope, fear, desperation, anger, love, hate, grief, jealousy, excitement, boredom and a vast range of other emotional states, which often interact with each

---

[12] See, for example, the essays in Solomon (ed, 2004) for several different accounts of the nature of emotion.

other in complicated ways. Like the various kinds of belief, many of them incorporate the recognition that something is the case. For example, one is usually angry or sad about something that has *actually* happened. Other emotions are directed at non-actual or unknown states of affairs, as in the case of hoping, yearning, dreading, fearing and so on. The latter motivate us in a range of ways, and the former inform as well as motivate.[13] It cannot simply be taken for granted from the outset that the informational aspect had by some emotions takes the form of a 'belief' that interacts with a separate motivational component.

The inseparability of information and motivation not only applies to emotions. We routinely experience things as significant in one way or another in the absence of any discernable emotional response. In some cases, there is no motivation involved. For example, one can see that a cup is for drinking from, regardless of whether or not one is thirsty. But, in other cases, perception incorporates a disposition to respond; the thing calls out to us in some way. This aspect of perception is famously described by J.J. Gibson (1979) in terms of 'affordances', what the environment offers an organism. But we also find sophisticated phenomenological accounts of it in the works of Husserl (e.g. 1973), Merleau-Ponty (e.g. 1962) and numerous others. For example, Husserl refers to the perception of certain possibilities as enticing, as exerting a kind of affective pull upon us. If we allow that some instances of 'taking something to be the case' are perceptual/experiential beliefs, motivational neutrality is implausible. We experience many things in terms of their practical meanings, their significance for us, and we interpret others as doing so too.

If we restrict 'belief' to attitudes that are inferred from experience, rather than allowing for 'experiential beliefs', we limit its scope considerably and so fail to accommodate all those convictions that are not the product of inference. Of course, this is not to accept that inferential beliefs are separable from motivation either. When thinking about something, is it always the case that what we think about can be cleanly separated from, for instance, a feeling of urgency, curiosity, excitement or dread that surrounds it? Or do some thoughts *have* feeling built into them? And there are numerous other examples that could be employed to call into question the information/motivation distinction, such as moral beliefs, for example, where a belief about what is right can surely motivate. Of course, 'moral belief' is not a homogeneous category either and people who hold the same propositional

---

[13] Gordon (1987) makes the helpful distinction between 'factive emotions', which are directed at actual states of affairs, and 'epistemic emotions', which are directed at non-actual states of affairs or unknown outcomes.

attitude 'p is wrong' may act in a range of ways. Again, more nuanced descriptions of people's convictions are required in order to understand why they do what they do.

Existential Feelings

Many psychological states that feature in literary narratives and everyday conversations do not fit into any of the familiar categories employed by philosophers and psychologists (such as 'belief', 'desire', 'intention', 'emotion', 'perception' and so on), even if it is acknowledged that some such categories inadvertently accommodate a lot more than is commonly supposed. Much of our 'folk psychology' has gone unnoticed, uncategorised. To illustrate this, I will focus on one aspect of experience and thought that often crops up in everyday conversation and literature but is not recognised by FP. Consider the famous lines:

> I have of late — but wherefore I know not — lost all my mirth, forgone all custom of exercises; and indeed it goes so heavily with my disposition that this goodly frame, the earth, seems to me a sterile promontory, this most excellent canopy, the air, look you, this brave o'erhanging firmament, this majestical roof fretted with golden fire, why, it appears no other thing to me than a foul and pestilent congregation of vapors (*Hamlet*, Act 2, Scene 2).

Amongst other things, this communicates, I think, something that I call 'existential feeling' (Ratcliffe, 2005; 2008). An existential feeling is not an intentional state directed at a particular state of affairs. It is a 'way of finding oneself in the world', which constitutes a sense of belonging and reality. Although Hamlet refers specifically to how certain things seem to him, what he expresses is more encompassing that that. It is a way of experiencing himself, the world and the relationship between them that shapes all his perceptions and thoughts.

People attempt to communicate a wide range of existential feelings, and in many different ways. For example, there are references to feelings of unfamiliarity, not being with it, feeling dislodged or out of place, and to everything seeming somehow strange, not quite right, not real. People sometimes talk of feeling cut off from the world, or of everything seeming oddly significant or insignificant, uncanny or perhaps surreal. There are also references to feeling part of things, at home in a place, at one with nature, with other people or with the world. The term 'mood' might capture some of these but not all. Many are too fleeting to count as moods, and most of them are described as 'feelings' rather than 'moods'. So an emphasis on the usual inventory

of moods distracts from the wide range of existential feelings that people express. In addition, it seems likely that at least some of the psychological states that we call 'moods' are intentional states directed
towards a wide range of things, whereas existential feelings are
'pre-intentional'. By this, I mean that an existential feeling is not an
attitude such as taking something to be the case, hoping for something
or dreading it. Instead, it is an experiential background that
determines the kinds of intentional state that are possible.

My interpretation of these feelings (Ratcliffe, 2008; 2009) draws on
the phenomenological writings of Husserl, Heidegger, Merleau-
Ponty, Sartre and others, and is as follows: We experience things as
significant to us in a range of different ways; they offer up various different kinds of salient possibility. For example, some things appear as
practically significant, a category within which there are numerous
subcategories, such as 'significant only to me' or 'significant to people in general', 'easy to use', 'useful but inaccessible', 'useable but
not required', 'urgent', 'enticing' and so on. There are also many ways
in which potential happenings can be significant: they might be threat-
ening, comforting, exciting and so on. An existential feeling is not a
way in which any particular thing or even a range of things appear significant. Rather, it is a shift in the *kinds* of significance that experience
incorporates. In order to be able to experience a particular thing as, for
instance, 'practically significant', experience has to incorporate the
possibility of things appearing as practically significant. In the
absence of that possibility, one could not even encounter something as
'insignificant', as doing so involves appreciating that it could be otherwise. The same point applies to other kinds of possibility, such as
pleasure, threat, emotional communion with other people, tangibility
and so on. Hamlet is not disenchanted by a contingent assortment of
perceived objects. He has lost 'all' his mirth. The possibility of mirth
at anything has gone. And the world that used to offer up a range of
enticing possibilities now appears as a 'sterile promontory', a place
where enticing possibilities (for him at least) are absent. Many people
suffering from severe depression report a similar transformation of
experience, where the possibilities of pleasure, practical significance
and emotional communion with other people are removed from
experience (Ratcliffe, 2009).

A loss of certain kinds of possibility from experience can also
amount to a loss, diminution or alteration of the sense of reality. In
order to take a certain entity to be real or, more specifically, to be present, one must have a sense of the differences between present and not
present, and real and unreal. In other words, one must have a sense of

reality. And this sense of reality is changeable in all sorts of ways. For example, in a world where the possibility of tangibility is absent, things would look strangely distant, not quite there. A different kind of shift would occur in a world that no longer offered possibilities for others and thus appeared strangely self-centred, perhaps even dream-like. And a world where things no longer appear practically signifi-cant would be a place bereft of the usual habitual familiarity, a place from which one felt disconnected (Ratcliffe, 2008, ch. 4 and 7). Such changes are shifts in the kinds of conviction that are possible. If a sense of reality is changed or eroded, one cannot take things to be the case in quite the same way anymore, however much one might assert 'I believe that p is so'. Hence people sometimes say that nothing feels quite real, that everything looks strangely distant, as though one were watching a television screen, and a wide range of other things. More subtle alterations in existential feeling are commonplace. They are difficult to express concisely because what is involved is not a change in the way particular things appear, which takes place within the con-text of a shared world. Rather, it is a shift in the background sense of belonging to a world, in the shape of all experience, in the kinds of possibility that the world has to offer.

It is also important to appreciate that existential shifts are bound up with changes in the feeling body. Hamlet's 'heavy' disposition is, quite literally I think, a bodily sluggishness and conspicuousness. Not all bodily feelings are experiences that have the body or part of the body as their primary object. Some such feelings are also ways in which things other than the body are perceived. Consider the sense of balance. An experience of bodily disorientation is at the same time a way of perceiving — or perhaps failing to perceive — one's surround-ings. Several phenomenologists have stressed the inextricability of bodily feeling and the experience of worldly possibilities (see, for example, Husserl, 1973; 1989; Merleau-Ponty, 1962; Sartre, 1989). Sartre's account of 'shame', for instance, recognises something that is both a change in bodily feeling and a loss of one's possibilities.[14] The conspicuous, awkward, vulnerable body that feels the gaze of the other is a body that loses its habitual, comfortable dwelling in the world. The shift in existential feeling is both a change in how one's body is experienced and in the space of possibilities that one inhabits.

---

[14] See Ratcliffe (2008, Chapters 4 to 7) for a detailed discussion of Husserl, Merleau-Ponty, Sartre and others on the relationship between bodily feeling and the experience of possi-bility. See Ratcliffe and Broome (forthcoming) for a discussion of Sartre on interpersonal relations, bodily feelings and the 'death' of possibilities.

Descriptions of what I call 'existential feeling' frequently crop up in literature. Consider the following:

> He doesn't like the word 'homesick', doesn't feel it does justice to what it's supposed to describe. He prefers the long, pulling, mournful vowels of the German word, *Heimweh*. For him, it's not just a mild case of nausea — he feels flattened, steamrollered, horrified, miserable, disjointed, desperate. It's as if he's the wrong species for this place: there's not enough sun, the air doesn't have the right ratios of gases, everything is too spread out, too sprawling, and he can barely understand what people are saying to him. He never realised how much he thought in Cantonese. Maybe it's because he's never been to Britain before, but he's never felt so cut off, so far away from Hong Kong and everything he knows and everything he likes and everything that makes up his life and him (O'Farrell, 2004, p. 56).

The passage communicates a lot more than just existential feeling. But it does include an overall shift in how the character finds himself in the world, a sense of being dislodged, estranged, alienated and not at home in the world, which structures all his experiences and thoughts. This aspect of experience is not neatly conceptualised, ready-made for philosophers to analyse. Nonetheless, it is something that people often try to express and is surely part of our so-called 'folk psychology', given that everyday discourse and narratives include at least some degree of conceptual understanding of it. Consider the following quotation:

> 'I feel disconnected, as though I'm watching this happen to someone else, in a film, perhaps, or a play. I suppose it's a defence mechanism. Of course it could just be alcohol'.

> 'That natural anaesthetic. Yes, I feel the same' (Duigan, 2001, p. 72).

Here we have both an expression of existential feeling and an acknowledgement of understanding. In addition there is theorising as to possible causes.[15] The kind of understanding involved is very different from an understanding of intentional states. It is not about kinds of attitude but about a space of possibilities that determines the kinds of attitude that are possible. It sometimes involves a shift in the *form* of belief. The world might seem bereft of a sense of reality, leaving one uttering propositions without being able to kindle any genuine conviction regarding their truth. Conversely, things might seem

---

[15] This kind of experience is referred to by psychiatrists as 'depersonalisation'. It accompanies a range of psychiatric conditions and can also crop up in non-psychiatric contexts, such as in illness, jetlag or a bad hangover. When it persists for a long period without accompanying complaints it is regarded as a psychiatric illness in its own right. See Ratcliffe (2008, ch. 6) for further discussion of depersonalisation.

intensely real, vivid or profoundly significant, in ways that are often hard to express. For example:

> I experienced a moment of piercing metaphysical excitement. It seemed suddenly intoxicating that each life could be defined by its endless per-mutations — tragic, comic, mundane — all causes and effects of each other, and of other lives, and yet all in their essence unknowable and unpredictable (Duigan, 2001, p. 287).[16]

All of this adds further complexity to the 'folk' appreciation of 'be-lief'. Of course, talk of existential feelings, the space of possibilities and the sense of reality is not a 'folk' view, something that has been explicitly formulated in the context of everyday life. It is a philosophi-cal position (or, rather, a brief sketch of a philosophical position that I develop more fully elsewhere). It is an attempt to explicitly analyse an aspect of experience that we already have some vague pre-theoretical understanding of. But, as illustrated by my discussion of Strawson, the same applies to any philosophical account of 'what the folk think'. Even if one rejects my analysis and dismisses the concept of 'existen-tial feeling', it remains the case that there is a vast range of nuanced 'feelings' that people try to express, many of which are closely associ-ated with changes in the experience of reality, belonging and signifi-cance. Analyse this aspect of our psychology however you like but it does not fit into orthodox conceptions of FP.

Hence FP is not 'folk psychology' but an abstract over-simplifica-tion of certain features of interpersonal understanding, which is obliv-ious to other features, including what I call 'existential feeling'. The everyday 'folk', amongst whom we should include philosophers, sci-entists and everyone else (there isn't a sub-category of 'non-folk'), are a lot more complicated and difficult to interpret than is often assumed. However, we also have a lot more to assist us in interpreting each other than FP explicitly acknowledges. Rather than surveying others from afar, we tend to understand them through interaction and dia-logue in the context of shared social situations and norms, participat-ing in a range of different kinds of relationship with them. And, as for prediction, it is important to recognise that social life relies upon mutual regulation more so than standoffish attempts to predict. We work together to make ourselves predictable, and also understand-able, to each other (Morton, 2003).

---

[16] Thanks to my wife Beth for pointing out these three passages, after I asked her to look for existential feelings in the novels she was reading.

Steps in the Right Direction

I will conclude by discussing two recent developments, both of which take important steps away from the orthodox picture of FP but neither of which, in my view, go far enough. First of all, there is 'experimental philosophy', which seeks to empirically investigate people's intuitions and concepts. Although trying to find out what people think, rather than imposing a philosophical view upon them from the start, amounts to progress, it is also important to appreciate that empirical enquiry of this kind must have a self-reflective aspect to it. By this, I mean that, in addition to employing empirical studies to investigate whether people think p or q, one should keep in mind the possibility that the conceptual distinctions through which one interprets them are symptomatic of a questionable philosophical outlook. By analogy, the question 'are you in favour of the war on terror or are you for terror?' involves a refusal to acknowledge other alternatives. Likewise, I think that a tendency to interpret experimental results through an overly restrictive set of philosophical assumptions is sometimes at work in experimental philosophy, just as it is in orthodox FP.

Take, for example, some recent work by Knobe and Prinz (2008). They rightly acknowledge that orthodox FP is based upon a '*grand vision* of the nature of folk psychology' according to which prediction and explanation are central, rather than upon a more philosophically open investigation of what people actually think (2008, p. 78). So they set out to investigate what people really think about certain things. However, they also make the war on terror mistake, assuming from the beginning that 'when people are trying to determine whether an entity is capable of having certain kinds of mental states, they can think of it either from a *functional* standpoint or from a *physical* standpoint' (2008, p. 67). Consequently, their experimental set-up and interpretation of results are shaped by the premise that we do one or the other. They offer evidence for the view that people are unwilling to grant 'phenomenal consciousness' to entities such as corporations, regardless of their functional constitution. Thus our willingness to attribute certain kinds of mental states, specifically those involving phenomenal consciousness, is sensitive to non-functional attributes. For example, when people are presented with the following two statements, the second is generally judged to be more palatable than the first: 'Acme Corp. is feeling regret'; 'Acme Corp. regrets its recent decision' (2008, p. 77). Of course, such findings can be challenged. For instance, the first claim may look less intuitive because the regret lacks an object. Suppose we instead have 'Acme Corp. feels genuine regret over its recent decision' and 'Acme Corp. has regret'. I bet that most people would prefer the first. So a lot depends on how the alternatives are phrased. To further complicate things, there is no guarantee that experimenter and subject share the same understanding of relevant claims and terms. In fact, it is debatable whether the experimental philosopher herself has a clear enough grasp of certain concepts to test the conditions under which other people are willing to apply them. For example, Knobe and Prinz assume that the 'folk' have a concept of 'phenomenal consciousness', but consciousness is a notoriously troublesome topic in philosophy and the term is used in a wide range of ways. It is rather incautious to assume that philosophers and the 'folk' more generally all share a conception of this kind of consciousness. Terms such as 'feeling' are used in many ways too. So associating feeling with phenomenal consciousness is also questionable.

Most problematic though is the assumption we are restricted to either a functional or a physical standpoint when interpreting others' mental states. What about the alternative possibility that our willingness to attribute certain mental states is contingent on whether or not we adopt a personal standpoint towards the entity in question? Granted, there is much philosophical work still to be done in clarifying what it is to experience someone as a person but to not even entertain the possibility is surely symptomatic of a philosophy imposing itself upon the 'folk'. It can be very informative indeed to know when one is dealing with a person. For instance, it means that one can enter into distinctive kinds of relation with her that one cannot enter into with an impersonal entity, regardless of whether that entity is physically or functionally construed. Thus, although experimental philosophy is a potentially positive move, there is the risk that the experimenter's own explicit conceptual scheme will be imposed upon the implicit scheme of the 'folk'.

A more substantial departure from orthodox FP is Daniel Hutto's recently proposed 'narrative practice hypothesis'. Hutto accepts that many instances of interpersonal interaction do not involve the exercise of FP at all. Instead, we rely upon a shared appreciation of social situations and upon a bodily, perceptual, affective responsiveness to the purposes and goals of others. However, he retains FP in a significantly reduced role, rather than rejecting it altogether. For Hutto, FP is not the cornerstone of all social life but something we sometimes resort to in order to make sense of seemingly anomalous actions in terms of reasons. On occasion, we need the 'exercise of a skilled understanding of attitudes, importantly beliefs and desires, and how they interrelate' (2008b, p. 424). Hutto refers to this as FP *strictu sensu* and distinguishes it from a less committal conception of our folk psychology as *however the everyday folk understand each other*. He acknowledges that 'nothing concrete' answers to a looser conception of folk psychology, as people understand each other in different contexts by relying upon a heterogeneous bundle of abilities without a single, unifying core (2008a, p. 3).

Contrary to the orthodox view, Hutto also maintains that FP itself is not something that all psychologically healthy people reliably acquire without any effort. Belief-desire psychology has a narrative structure and FP narratives are 'skilled productions' by those who have 'mastered a certain technique' (2008b, p. 426). Hence FP depends upon a specialist training, which Hutto admits may be absent from certain cultures. It is therefore no more 'folkish' than an understanding of football games, the internet or driving. For Hutto, then, the term 'FP' remains only as a matter of convention. Philosophers have long referred to belief-desire psychology in this way and so he conforms to the tradition, even though the usual connotations do not apply anymore. In fact, Hutto (2009) does confess to using the term with some hesitation.

Hutto further argues that simulation and theory are not required for FP. At most, they are 'supplementary methods', which do not usually play a role in the practice of reason-giving (2008a, p. 5). In their place, he champions the 'narrative practice hypothesis' of FP development, the hypothesis that we develop FP ability by 'engaging with stories about people who act for reasons'. The emphasis is on structured interaction between children and caregivers, focused around progressively sophisticated shared engagement with certain kinds of narratives, on 'active participation in a particular kind of sociocultural practice in which certain kinds of narratives play a pivotal role' (2008b, p. 427). Hutto claims that fairy stories such as *Little Red Riding Hood* are the 'best means of revealing how propositional attitudes work together' (2008a, p. 30). He also acknowledges that the relevant narrative structures can be found in a wide range of contexts, including many conversations. A familiarity with these narratives does not merely teach children to attribute propositional attitudes. It also allows them to place actions within contexts of intelligibility and to appreciate how propositional attitudes and their contents are affected by other aspects of our psychology, such as moods and character traits:

> … in such stories a person's responses are shown in situ, against appropriate backdrops and settings. For example, children learn how

character, history, current circumstances and commitments to larger projects make a difference to what we do and why (2008b, p. 427).

Hutto inherits philosophical talk of a 'framework incorporating the central propositional attitudes of belief and desire' and continues to refer to this as a 'core mentalistic framework' (2008a, p. xii). However, given his position, it is not clear why this should be a 'core' framework. He does not even insist that all reason-giving narratives appeal to beliefs and desires. All he says is that reference to beliefs and desires is 'sometimes' needed in order to explain why someone acted for a reason (2008b, p. 426); 'at least some of our actions are performed for reasons in the restricted sense (understood as belief/ desire pairings)' (2008a, p. 2). So, most of the time, we do not use belief-desire psychology at all and, even in the kinds of situation where it might be used, it is not always needed. Hutto does not take a FP narrative to be any reason-giving narrative. He restricts the category 'FP narrative' to narratives that explicitly or implicitly appeal to beliefs and desires. There is a 'sub-type of narrative' about people 'who act for reasons of the kind that minimally implicates beliefs and desires' (2008c, p. 177). But what makes this a genuine sub-type, rather than a sub-type that is identified only because Hutto has already decided that there is a distinctive practice of 'belief-desire psychology'? Things start to look circular here: Why does a belief-desire pattern stand out above all the other kinds of reason that we give? Answer: because there is a distinctive kind of narrative. But what makes this kind of narrative distinctive? Answer: because it contains a belief-desire pattern. Once FP is given such a minimal role and then complicated by the inclusion of other kinds of reason, why individuate it as a distinctive practice at all? Through force of philosophical habit perhaps, Hutto still sees a belief-desire garden through the weeds that he has rightly let grow over FP.

Hutto regards propositional attitudes as essentially linguistic in nature. This is not to say that they are sentential attitudes though. An attitude can have a linguistic structure without being directed at a linguistic object. So Hutto's propositional attitudes presumably encompass 'taking things to be the case', rather than just 'taking sentences to be true'. If so, there is the concern raised earlier that they are quite heterogeneous and that narrative understanding implicitly or explicitly involves much more nuanced interpretations. Hutto also defines a broader class of 'intentional attitudes', which involve purposive bodily responsiveness to things and people, without the mediation of language or any kind of representation (2008a, p. xii). He is not wholly clear on the scope of 'belief'. In Hutto (2008a), he takes beliefs to be propositional attitudes but elsewhere he refers to 'belief' and 'desire' as two broad kinds of 'intentional attitude' (2008b, p. 432). A belief is one's 'take' on the world and a desire motivates (2008b, p. 434). Now, if 'belief' and 'desire' are understood in the more general sense, they encompass a wide range of psychological phenomena. And, if they are understood in the narrower sense, they are still likely to encompass several different phenomena and, at the same time, they will be too restrictive to accommodate many reasons for action that people refer to as 'beliefs'. A reason often involves a habitual pattern of activity rather than an explicit mental state: 'I thought that you would be in Room A because that is where we always meet'. There is also the issue of whether literary and other narratives respect a distinction between propositional and intentional attitudes. So far as I can tell, terms such as 'believe' and 'think' are used without any indication that there is a distinctive subclass of beliefs and desires that comprise a belief-desire psychology. We do not find a circumscribed FP or an intentional/propositional distinction if we look at the surface structure of narratives. And, if we look deeper, we embark upon a difficult interpretive task. Things rapidly get very complicated and FP gives way to a more nuanced understanding. Hutto acknowledges that:

> ... a full and properly nuanced awareness of what is involved in acting for a reason requires acquaintance with narratives of a much more sophisticated kind than those that figure in preschool dialogues and simple fairy tales (2008a, p. 36).

But where do you draw the line between a belief-desire narrative and a more nuanced narrative? What you can't legitimately do is start off with the intention of finding a narrative upon which to impose belief-desire psychology, proceed to ignore the more nuanced narratives, then disregard others that are too simple, irrelevant or don't fit the mould (so goodbye to *The Very Hungry Caterpillar* and to *War and Peace*), and then finally read it into *Little Red Riding Hood*. The fact that one might discern the pattern in such stories does not mean that it is actually there in any illuminating sense. The same goes for the fact that we can easily prompt people to respond in ways that fit the belief-desire schema. If you ask someone whether or not a person who went to get an ice cream believed that there was an ice cream van there and desired an ice cream, then of course you will get a 'yes'. But this would be to make the war on terror mistake — if you restrict the alternatives, it is easy to get the reply you want.

Adam Morton suggests that folk psychology is 'as real as a constellation. The Great and Little bears, for example, are patterns in the sky that strike us as salient' (2007, p. 220). I think this is a helpful analogy. Due to enculturation into a set of intellectual practices, certain philosophers and cognitive scientists see a belief-desire psychology in social life. But just as the night sky is not really organised by whatever constellations we might see in it, interpersonal understanding is not organised by the belief-desire psychology of the philosophers. Whereas Dennett (1991) takes belief-desire psychology to be a 'real pattern', it is better regarded as an 'unreal pattern'; there is no discrete practice of 'belief-desire psychology'. So, where Hutto sees 'a highly nuanced and skilled practice — albeit one that makes use of the core mentalistic framework' (2008a, p. 39), I see only the highly nuanced and skilled practice. However, we are in broad agreement over the shortcomings of FP and, aside from the fact that Hutto tries to salvage what is left of FP, our positions are very close to each other. In the end, the difference between us may come down to a pragmatic disagreement over whether it remains useful to continue talking of a belief-desire psychology or 'FP' once we have retreated so far from orthodox accounts of it.

Once we admit that most human interactions do not require FP, that interpersonal understanding includes much that does not fit into FP, that even reason explanations do not always require FP, that explanations and narratives are frequently more nuanced than FP and that 'belief' and 'desire' are not as tidy as is often assumed, we get to the point where we might as well give up on talk of a 'belief-desire psychology' altogether. In order to explore the structure of interpersonal understanding, we can draw on a vast archive of literary sources, in addition to work in developmental psychology and cognitive science, ordinary language philosophy, phenomenology, psychopathology, discourse analysis and a lot more. But there is no need to impose the FP framework upon any of this. Instead, we can embark upon a philosophical enquiry that appreciates the complexity of interpersonal relations and is sensitive to its own presuppositions.

Acknowledgements

I am grateful to Peter Goldie, Mitchell Herschbach, Daniel Hutto and Victoria McGeer for very helpful comments on an earlier version of this paper. Thanks also to my wife Beth for supplying me with quotations from novels.

References

Botterill, G. & Carruthers, P. (1999), *The Philosophy of Psychology* (Cambridge: Cambridge University Press).

Campbell, N. (2005), *A Brief Introduction to the Philosophy of Mind* (Peterborough, Ontario: Broadview Press).

Costall, A. & Leudar, I. (2004), 'Where is the "Theory" in Theory of Mind?', *Theory and Psychology,* **14**, pp. 623–46.

Davies, M. & Stone, T. (ed, 1995a), *Mental Simulation: Evaluations and Applications* (Oxford: Blackwell).

Davies, M. & Stone, T. (ed, 1995b), *Folk Psychology: The Theory of Mind Debate* (Oxford: Blackwell).

Dennett, D.C. (1978), 'Mechanism and Responsibility', in Dennett, D.C. (ed.), *Brainstorms* (Montgomery, VT: Bradford Books), pp. 233–55.

Dennett, D.C. (1991), 'Real Patterns', *Journal of Philosophy,* LXXXVIII, pp. 27–51.

Duigan, V. (2001), *Days like These* (London: Vintage).

Gallagher, S. (2001), 'The Practice of Mind: Theory, Simulation, or Interaction?', *Journal of Consciousness Studies,* **8** (5–7), pp. 83–107.

Gallagher, S. (2005), *How the Body shapes the Mind* (Oxford: Oxford University Press).

Gibson. J.J. (1979), *The Ecological Approach to Visual Perception* (Hillsdale, New Jersey: Lawrence Erlbaum Associates).

Goldie, P. (2000), *The Emotions: A Philosophical Exploration* (Oxford: Clarendon Press).

Goldie, P. (2007), 'There are Reasons and Reasons', in Hutto, D.D. & Ratcliffe, M. (ed.), *Folk Psychology Reassessed* (Dordrecht: Springer), pp. 103–14.

Gordon, R. (1987), *The Structure of Emotions* (Cambridge: Cambridge University Press).

Gordon, R. (1996), '"Radical" Simulation', in Carruthers, P. & Smith, P.K. (ed.), *Theories of Theories of Mind* (Cambridge: Cambridge University Press), pp. 11–21.

Heal, J. (1995), 'Replication and Functionalism', in Davies, M. & Stone, T. (ed.), *Folk Psychology: The Theory of Mind Debate* (Oxford: Blackwell), pp. 45–59.

Hobson, P. (2002), *The Cradle of Thought* (London: Macmillan).

Husserl, E. (1973), *Experience and Judgment*, Trans. Churchill, J.S. & Ameriks, K (London: Routledge).

Husserl, E. (1989), *Ideas Pertaining to a Pure Phenomenology and to a Phenomenological Philosophy: Second Book*, Trans. Rojcewicz, R. & Schuwer, A (Dordrecht: Kluwer).

Hutto, D.D. (2004), 'The Limits of Spectatorial Folk Psychology', *Mind and Language,* **19**, pp. 548–73.

Hutto, D.D. (2008a), *Folk Psychological Narratives* (Cambridge Mass.: MIT Press).

Hutto, D.D. (2008b), 'Limited Engagements and Narrative Extensions', *International Journal of Philosophical Studies,* **16**, pp. 419–44.

Hutto, D.D. (2008c), 'The Narrative Practice Hypothesis: Clarifications and Implications', *Philosophical Explorations,* **11**, pp. 175–91.

Hutto, D.D. (2009), 'Lessons from Wittgenstein: Elucidating Folk Psychology', *New Ideas in Psychology,* **27**, pp, 197–212.

Hutto, D.D. & Ratcliffe, M. (ed. 2007), *Folk Psychology Reassessed* (Springer).

Knobe, J. & Prinz, J. (2008), 'Intuitions about Consciousness: Experimental Studies', *Phenomenology and the Cognitive Sciences,* **7**, pp. 67–83.

Leudar, I. & Costall, A. (2004), 'On the Persistence of the "Problem of Other Minds", in 'Psychology: Chomsky, Grice and Theory of Mind', *Theory and Psychology,* **14**, pp. 601–21.

Lewis, D. (1972/1980), 'Psychophysical and Theoretical Identifications', in Block, N. (ed.), *Readings in Philosophy of Psychology: Volume I* (London: Methuen), pp. 207–15.

Lowe, E.J. (1996), *Subjects of Experience* (Cambridge: Cambridge University Press).

Macmurray, J. (1957), *The Self as Agent* (London: Faber & Faber).

McGeer, V. (2001), 'Psycho-Practice, Psycho-Theory, and the Contrastive Case of Autism: How Practices of Mind become Second nature', *Journal of Consciousness Studies,* **8** (5–7), pp. 109–32.

Merleau-Ponty, M. (1962), *Phenomenology of Perception*, Trans. Smith, C. (London: Routledge).

Morton, A. (2003), *The Importance of being Understood: Folk Psychology as Ethics* (London: Routledge).

Morton, A. (2007), 'Folk Psychology does not Exist', in Hutto, D.D. & Ratcliffe, M. (ed.), *Folk Psychology Reassessed* (Dordrecht: Springer), pp. 211–21.

Needham, R. (1972), *Belief, Language, and Experience* (Oxford: Blackwell).

Nichols, S. & Stich, S. (2003), *Mindreading* (Oxford: Clarendon Press).

O'Farrell, M. (2004), *The Distance between Us* (London: Review).

Ratcliffe, M. (2005), 'The Feeling of Being', *Journal of Consciousness Studies,* **12** (8–10), pp. 43–60.

Ratcliffe, M. (2007), *Rethinking Commonsense Psychology: A Critique of Folk Psychology, Theory of Mind and Simulation* (Basingstoke: Palgrave Macmillan).

Ratcliffe, M. (2008), *Feelings of Being: Phenomenology, Psychiatry and the Sense of Reality* (Oxford: Oxford University Press).

Ratcliffe, M. (2009), 'Understanding Existential Changes in Psychiatric Illness: The Indispensability of Phenomenology', in Broome, M. & Bortolotti, L. (ed.), *Psychiatry as Cognitive Neuroscience* (Oxford: Oxford University Press), pp. 223–44.

Ratcliffe, M. & Broome, M. (forthcoming), 'Existential Phenomenology, Psychiatric Illness and the Death of Possibilities', in Crowell, S. (ed.), *Cambridge Companion to Existentialism* (Cambridge: Cambridge University Press).

Robinson, J. (2005), *Deeper than Reason: Emotion and its Role in Literature, Music, and Art* (Oxford: Clarendon Press).

Sartre, J.P. (1989), *Being and Nothingness*, Trans. Barnes, H.E. (London: Routledge).

Scheler, M. (1954), *The Nature of Sympathy*, Trans. Heath, P. (London: Routledge).

Sellars, W. (1956/1963), 'Empiricism and the Philosophy of Mind', in his *Science, Perception and Reality* (London: Routledge), pp. 127–96.

Solomon, R.C. (ed, 2004), *Thinking about Feeling: Contemporary Philosophers on Emotions* (Oxford: Oxford University Press).

Strawson, P.F. (1959), *Individuals* (London: Methuen).

Strawson, P.F. (1985), *Skepticism and Naturalism* (London: Methuen).

Strawson, P.F. (2008), *Freedom and Resentment and Other Essays* (Abingdon: Routledge).

Tolstoy, L. (1960), *The Death of Ivan Ilych* (New York: Signet).